Written by three prominent scholars of international relations, this textbook offers a clear, engaging, and comprehensive introduction to the most pressing issues of the day. Students will walk away armed with a rich combination of analytical savvy, theoretical foundations, and historical context that will make them truly informed global citizens.

Sarah E. Kreps, *Cornell University, USA*

This second edition sets a new benchmark for textbooks in this area. It provides an almost canonical introduction to our discipline, flavored with core research insights and up-to-date illustrations from international politics, such as Brexit, cyber-attacks, and the Paris agreement. Together with a multimedia companion website for teachers and learners, this book will greatly meet the needs of a new generation of IR students.

Thomas Sommerer, *Stockholm University, Sweden*

Structured around a set of enduring questions, this second edition skillfully connects the dots of history, theory and main issues in world politics. Accessible and comprehensive, it gives students all the tools they need to make sense of current international events.

Thijs Van de Graaf, *Ghent University, Belgium*

Joseph Grieco, G. John Ikenberry and Michael Mastanduno have written a fine second edition of *Introduction to International Relations*. This is a stand-out introductory text in many respects. It is global in scope and comprehensive in terms of history and theory. It is packed full of great highlights. The research insights feature introduces students to cutting-edge research, which will no doubt inspire their curiosity and enhance their research skills. As a whole, the text provides a clear structure (levels of analysis) and an appealing framework (enduring questions) for introducing students to the grammar of International Relations. This is a must have for undergraduate students and for instructors interested in an innovative and stimulating syllabus. Written by authorities in the discipline, *Introduction to International Relations* is sure to become a go-to text for both students and instructors alike.

Keith Smith, *King's College London, UK*

A wonderfully stimulating reading experience, grounded in theoretical classics that cuts a swathe through established historical narratives and the predominance of western thought. A truly international volume for students seeking a 21st century understanding of International Relations and perhaps how they might influence it.

Ian Nelson, *University of Nottingham Ningbo, China*

This elegant text should become the standard for introductory courses in international relations. Through an outstanding fusion of history, theory, and practice, it helps students understand how and why international politics works the way that it does. The framing of "Enduring Questions" provides a theoretical anchor that helps students see the big picture while never losing sight of the details.

Seth Weinberger, *University of Puget Sound, USA*

Three of the big names in the field have got together to produce this outstanding introduction to international relations – what's not to like?! This second edition builds on the excellent work of the first, with the expanded theoretical chapter being especially welcome. The textbook is beautifully written and presented, does not dwell on bygone theoretical debates, and is accessible without sacrificing academic rigour.

Alex Mackenzie, *University of Liverpool, UK*

At a time when there is an increasing demand for university classrooms to directly address the global challenges of today, the second edition of *Introduction to International Relations* is a valuable and necessary contribution. This updated textbook offers students an intelligent and balanced introduction to the study of global politics. Building both on historical cases and contemporary examples, Grieco, Ikenberry, and Mastanduno aptly demonstrate how certain international relations theories and concepts are relevant tools to help us understand, debate and develop solutions to complex, puzzling, and ever-shifting global problems and opportunities. The newly integrated "Research Insight" sections also provide accessible and useful summaries of the latest scholarly debates and findings over some of the most controversial international relations questions.

Nicolas Blarel, *Leiden University, The Netherlands*

This latest edition provides students with an informative, comprehensive and user-friendly format with maps, study questions and other learning aides clearly conveying the objectives of every chapter.

Christopher Kroh, *University of North Georgia, USA*

This is an excellent textbook for students in introductory International Relations courses. Grieco, Ikenberry and Mastanduno clearly and effectively present key theoretical perspectives along with engaging contemporary applications. This book serves as a great introduction to the field.

Andrey Tomashevskiy, *Rutgers University, USA*

This textbook provides an informative, engaging and comprehensive introduction to International Relations by three leading scholars in the field. Its coverage of the key areas of the discipline, including security, political economy and the contemporary challenges of International Relations offers students a fascinating insight into the world they confront today. Its many pedagogical innovations, including its Enduring Questions, Research Insights, Making Connections and Levels of Analysis features in each chapter will be great for stimulating discussion and reflections in the classroom.

Tom Chodor, *Monash University, Australia*

Grieco, Ikenberry and Mastanduno have produced an eminently readable, accessible and engaging guide to the study of contemporary world politics. The book's unique design and companion website also make it a resource-rich teaching and learning tool. I only wish I'd had this smartly designed textbook when I was a student.

Fiona Adamson, *SOAS, University of London, UK*

INTRODUCTION TO
INTERNATIONAL RELATIONS

SECOND EDITION

PERSPECTIVES, CONNECTIONS, AND ENDURING QUESTIONS

JOSEPH
GRIECO

G. JOHN
IKENBERRY

MICHAEL
MASTANDUNO

 macmillan international HIGHER EDUCATION  RED GLOBE PRESS

First edition published 2015
Second edition published 2019 by
RED GLOBE PRESS

Red Globe Press in the UK is an imprint of Springer Nature Limited, registered in England, company number 785998, of 4 Crinan Street, London, N1 9XW.

Red Globe Press® is a registered trademark in the United States, the United Kingdom, Europe and other countries.

ISBN 978–1–352–00422–9

This book is printed on paper suitable for recycling and made from fully managed and sustained forest sources. Logging, pulping and manufacturing processes are expected to conform to the environmental regulations of the country of origin.

A catalogue record for this book is available from the British Library.

A catalog record for this book is available from the Library of Congress.

Contents in Brief

Contents

Contents

Contents

Contents

List of Features

Making Connections, Theory and Practice

Making Connections, Then and Now

Making Connections, Aspiration versus Reality

Differing Perspectives

Differing Theoretical Approaches

Research Insight

List of Illustrative Material

Figures

Maps

Tables

Photos

About the Authors

Joseph Grieco is Professor in the Department of Political Science at Duke University. He is the co-author (with G. John Ikenberry) of *State Power and World Markets: The International Political Economy*, and is the author of *Cooperation among Nations: Europe, America, and Non-Tariff Barriers to Trade* and *Between Dependency and Autonomy: India's Experience with the International Computer Industry*. He is the author or co-author of articles and notes that have appeared in *International Studies Review, American Journal of Political Science, International Organization, Journal of Peace Research, Journal of Conflict Resolution, International Studies Quarterly, British Journal of Politics and International Relations, Korean Journal of International Studies, Security Studies, Review of International Studies, American Political Science Review, Journal of Politics*, and *World Politics*. He has had research fellowships at Princeton, Harvard, and the Social Science Center in Berlin, and his research has been supported by the US National Science Foundation, the John D. and Catherine T. MacArthur Foundation, and the German–Marshall Foundation. As an International Affairs fellow with the Council on Foreign Relations he served at the Office of the US Trade Representative and the International Monetary Fund. He has taught in the International Relations program at the University of Bologna at Forli, and since 1996 he has been a Visiting Professor at the Post-Graduate School of Economics and International Relations at the Catholic University of Milan.

G. John Ikenberry is the Albert G. Milbank Professor of Politics and International Affairs at Princeton University in the Department of Politics and the Woodrow Wilson School of Public and International Affairs. He is also Co-Director of Princeton's Center for International Security Studies and a Global Eminence Scholar at Kyung Hee University in Seoul, Korea. In 2013–14, he was the 72nd Eastman Visiting Professor at Balliol College, Oxford. In 2018–19, he was a Visiting Fellow at All Souls College, Oxford. Professor Ikenberry is the author of many books, including *Liberal Leviathan: The Origins, Crisis,*

and Transformation of the American System. His book *After Victory: Institutions, Strategic Restraint, and the Rebuilding of Order after Major Wars* won the 2002 Jervis–Schroeder Award presented by the American Political Science Association for the best book in international history and politics. He is the co-director of the Princeton Project on National Security. He is a member of the American Academy of Arts and Sciences. Among his many activities, he served as a member of the Policy Planning Staff in 1991–92, as a member of an advisory group at the State Department in 2003–4, and as a member of the Council on Foreign Relations Task Force on US–European relations, the so-called Kissinger-Summers commission. He is also a reviewer of books on political and legal affairs for *Foreign Affairs.*

Michael Mastanduno is the Nelson A. Rockefeller Professor of Government and from 2010 through 2017 was Dean of the Faculty of Arts and Sciences at Dartmouth College in Hanover, NH. He has taught at Dartmouth since 1987, and his areas of research and teaching specialization include international relations theory, US foreign policy, and the politics of the world economy. His current research concerns the rise of China and its implications for international economics and security. His articles have appeared in many journals including *World Politics, International Organization, International Studies Quarterly,* and *International Security.* He is author or editor of numerous books including *Economic Containment, Beyond Westphalia?, International Relations Theory and the Asia-Pacific, Unipolar Politics, US Hegemony and International Organizations,* and *International Relations Theory and the Consequences of Unipolarity.* Professor Mastanduno lectures frequently in Europe and Asia and has been a guest faculty member at the London School of Economics, University of Tokyo, the Graduate School of Economics and International Relations at Milan, and the Geneva Center for Security Policy. He has been awarded fellowships from the Brookings Institution, the Salzburg Seminar, the Council on Foreign Relations, and the East–West Center. He served during sabbatical from Dartmouth as an assistant in the Office of the US Trade Representative, and he is a member of the Council on Foreign Relations.

Preface to the Second Edition

Why does our field need yet another introductory textbook? We three authors have arrived at an answer through a long series of conversations based on our three decades of experience teaching International Relations to interested and always interesting undergraduates. We recognize that students new to the discipline seek to understand what is happening *now* in a complex world that excites them intellectually but is difficult to fully comprehend. The problem is that courses which place too much emphasis on current events may engage for the moment, but leave students short of the tools needed for sound analysis when, inevitably, the headlines change. On the other hand, courses that focus too heavily on disciplinary or scholastic debates risk leaving new students feeling like outsiders, lacking the context and background to appreciate what is at stake. Professional scholars make sense of the complexity of the world through international relations theories; their natural inclination is to impart knowledge of those theories and their specialized jargon at ever increasing levels of nuance and specificity to initiate even our newest students. Yet, we know that dosage matters: too much theory leaves a new student of international relations overwhelmed and wondering how these debates and typologies matter for the real world, while too little leaves a student unprepared to navigate a complicated and confusing substantive terrain.

We take a different approach to these dilemmas. We begin with the premise that the essentials of international relations are animated less by the news of the day or by the latest twist in theoretical paradigms, and more by a set of long-standing questions that have engaged and challenged generations of international relations scholars and students. We call these *enduring questions* and we motivate each chapter around one of them. Instructors using our book will immediately recognize a familiar organizational structure built around theories and approaches, security studies, international political economy, and contemporary challenges and the future of the international system. But students will be invited to engage with the material in a different way. Once students appreciate that international relations is about grappling with large, challenging questions that have stood the test of time, we believe they will demand the tools necessary to make their own attempt to answer them. Our text provides those tools and offers a variety of approaches and answers to these questions, reflecting differences in the scholarly field of international relations and, in some cases, among ourselves.

We have tried to convey the material of our field in language that is clear and intuitive to undergraduates. We believe it is possible, indeed necessary, to be both comprehensive in coverage and accessible in style. Our intention has not been to make the material artificially easy, but to employ a direct style of writing so that our text welcomes new participants into the enduring conversations of our field, rather than treat them as visitors who need passports and phrase books as they tour a foreign land with exotic customs and language. We aim to inspire students, who are also citizens, to join and remain engaged in those conversations. By developing an appreciation of the enduring questions of our field, and the political, economic, and social dynamics that underlie those questions, student-citizens will be more capable not only of understanding today's headlines but also those international issues and problems that arise long after they have completed their introductory course.

Thematic Framework

We believe the best way for students to attain a firm understanding of international relations is to be able to recognize *enduring questions* in the unfolding of international relations; to grasp the analytical utility of the *levels of analysis*; to understand the interplay of *theory and history*; to *make connections* between the past and present, theory and practice, and political aspirations and practical realities; and to view the world from *different perspectives*.

Enduring Questions

Each chapter following the introduction is organized around an enduring question of international relations. Such questions about relations among countries recur throughout history, have important consequences, and are the subject of considerable policy and scholarly debate. For example, consider the question 'In what ways does participation in the world economy help or hinder the development of poorer countries?' America's founding fathers debated that question in the late eighteenth century, the leaders of a newly unified Germany debated it at the end of the nineteenth century, and politicians in China, Brazil, and India struggle with it today. Political scientists and economists have joined that debate over the centuries, often putting forward radically differing answers. Those answers are profoundly consequential for countries seeking to free millions of people from the grip of poverty, and for ambitious leaders seeking to promote national economic strength in order to compete more effectively in the international arena.

As we progress through the chapters that follow, each focusing on an important area of international relations, we begin with a broad, enduring question of international relations to frame the substance of each chapter and to help students recognize that, notwithstanding the presumed novelty of today's fast-paced world, many of the critical issues of contemporary international politics have recurred in one form or another across time. The enduring questions that we address on a chapter-by-chapter basis are summarized in Box 1.1 in Chapter 1. We weave enduring questions throughout the chapters, and at the end of each we revisit that chapter's enduring question and its significance.

Levels of Analysis

The levels-of-analysis framework is a long-standing and battle-tested device for categorizing theories, arguments, and insights about international relations. It is valuable both to instructors seeking to organize and teach our field and to students making their initial attempts to understand it. We employ and systematically highlight the individual, state, and international system levels of analysis. For example, our discussion of why the Cold War ended invites students to debate the relative explanatory weight of the role of great leaders and social movements, the calculations of state interest on the part of the United States and Soviet Union, and the shifting balance of economic and technological power between these two superpowers. Our chapters on international political economy go beyond the standard 'trade, money, and investment' format and encourage students to view economic interactions and outcomes from the perspective of the world economy as a whole as well as through the ambitions and strategies of nation-states at different stages of development.

Our goal is for students to move easily across the different levels, yet to be aware of the analytical and theoretical implications of making those moves. At the end of each major section in a chapter, we offer a boxed summary feature prompting students to reflect on the substantive material just presented at one or more relevant levels of analysis. These boxes use icons to represent the different levels of analysis so that instructors and students have an easily identifiable point of reference.

Theory and History

Theoretical frameworks are vital in the study of international relations; they allow us to make sense of the past and anticipate possible patterns in the future. Most new students, however, have minimal knowledge of the history of the international system and that constrains their capacity to appreciate either the context in which international relations theories developed or the reason why theories are so important. Our text addresses this problem by providing a comprehensive chapter on the history of international relations and placing it *before* introducing students to the theoretical frameworks and traditions of the field. Scholars have often put forward theories of international relations as a reaction to developments in the world; one must have some baseline knowledge of that world in order to appreciate what has motivated theoretical debates and is at stake within them. We also emphasize that theory and history interact at different levels of analysis, for example by following the chapter on broad theoretical traditions with one on the analysis of state-level foreign policies.

Making Connections

The ability of students to identify and discuss connections across ideas, themes, and issues is an important skill in the development of critical thinking. In the study of international relations, it is obviously critical to appreciate the links between domestic and international politics and between international politics and economics. Other types of important connections may be less obvious to students, so in each chapter we have provided special boxed features that enable students to make connections between theory and practice, between then and now, and between aspirations and reality. This second edition also contains a new feature called 'Research Insight.'

- *Making Connections, Theory and Practice:* By highlighting this connection we help students appreciate both the value and the limits of the standard theories of international relations as devices for organizing and explaining international events. In Chapter 3, for example, we include a box that explores 'Realism and State Rationality: The Issue of State Self-Defeatism.' We observe that realism views states as rational actors making sober calculations of power and interests. In reality, however, states sometimes embark on ideological crusades or other types of self-defeating behavior that works to the detriment of their security. To unravel this puzzle, we encourage students to look to the domestic level of analysis and note that certain types of societal coalitions can have strong influences on a state's foreign policy and drive it in a self-destructive direction.

- *Making Connections, Then and Now:* The boxes that focus on these connections help students to gain insight by uncovering the historical sources of contemporary international initiatives. In Chapter 2, for example, we provide a box on 'The Persistence of the Munich-Appeasement Analogy,' showing how that pre-World World II episode shaped the thinking of President Lyndon Johnson about the Vietnam War in 1965 and the calculations of President George W. Bush on the eve of the Iraq War of 2003. We ask students to consider why this type of analogy is so appealing to policy makers, and also to explore whether the logic of the Munich analogy would be persuasive in the event a future American president contemplated military conflict with Iran or North Korea.

- *Making Connections, Aspiration versus Reality:* The boxes that make explicit connections between aspiration and reality remind students of the often profound differences between how the world is and how students, teachers, and national leaders might like it to be. For example, in Chapter 13 we provide a feature entitled 'Compliance with the Kyoto Protocol.' We show students that among the countries that committed to a treaty to reduce greenhouse gas emissions, some countries met their stated targets while others did not. Why are governments often unable to follow through on commitments they make to improve the global environment? Students may use this feature to debate the role of domestic politics in international behavior, and even to consider the fairness of treaties that hold different countries to different standards in pursuit of a common objective.

- *Research Insight:* This feature, new to the second edition, applies findings in academic research to contested or puzzling national and international policy topics. The purpose is to remind students, in each chapter, of the important contributions scholars make to understanding international relations, In Chapter 5, for example, we take up the question of why powerful states, strong enough to go to war on their own, nevertheless seek authorization to do so from the United Nations Security Council. We review recent research that suggests state leaders, by working through the UN system, gain valuable information about the likely support of or resistance to their initiative. We cite other research which shows that the greater the international support for military initiative, the more likely it will garner domestic support as well.

Differing Perspectives and Differing Theoretical Approaches

We display two other boxed features chapter by chapter to emphasize to students the importance of viewing the world, and international relations theories about it, from multiple perspectives. First, we use a box labeled Differing Perspectives to help students appreciate that how an individual, group, or indeed a political community views a particular international relations issue depends significantly on, among other factors, whether the actor in question is weak or powerful, secure or insecure, or wealthy or poor. For example, countries that already possess nuclear weapons tend to think differently about the dangers of the further spread of nuclear weapons than do countries that do not have those weapons and perceive threats from their neighbors. Our emphasis on multiple perspectives will help students grasp the variety and complexity of the motivations, interests, and goals among the many actors on the international stage. In Chapter 11, we feature Fernando Henrique Cardoso on the benefits of international economic integration, 1970s versus the 1990s and early 2000s. As a Latin American scholar writing in the 1970s, Cardoso counseled developing countries to minimize their links to the world economy. Later, as president of Brazil during the 1990s, he fully embraced his country's global economic integration. Did Cardoso simply change his mind, did Brazil change its economic position, or did the world economy itself change? We encourage students to consider, discuss, and debate how differing perspectives affect the nature of international relations, and how developments in international politics, in turn, change the perspectives of actors.

Second, and beginning in Chapter 3, we include a box labeled Differing Theoretical Approaches. These boxes each pick a particular outcome or decision of relevance to the chapter and describe, in a simple and intuitive way, how scholars working from the perspective of different theoretical traditions (such as liberalism, constructivism, realism, Marxism, and feminism) might explain that outcome or decision. For example, in Chapter 4, which focuses on explanations of foreign policy and foreign policy change, we discuss how constructivists, realists, and Marxists might account for why the United Kingdom and the United States long supported South Africa's *apartheid* regime, yet in the mid-1980s shifted to a strategy of economic sanctions designed to isolate the regime and pressure it to make domestic changes.

Organization of the Book: Integrating Theory, History, and Contemporary International Relations

Chapter 1 serves as our introduction to the study of global politics. We describe how and why international relations are part of the everyday lives of people around the world, including the students reading this book and probably taking their first class in international relations. We provide some basic terms and concepts, elaborate upon the thematic framework of the book, and provide a rationale for our emphasis on recognizing enduring questions, utilizing levels of analysis, making connections, and viewing international relations from differing perspectives.

Beyond the introductory chapter, the book is divided into four parts:

- Part I: Foundations of International Relations (Chapters 2, 3, 4, and 5).
- Part II: War and Peace: An Introduction to Security Studies (Chapters 6, 7, and 8).
- Part III: Wealth and Power: An Introduction to International Political Economy (Chapters 9, 10, and 11).
- Part IV: Contemporary Challenges and the Future of International Relations (Chapters 12, 13, and 14).

Part I: Foundations of International Relations

Part I provides the analytical tools that are integral to the study of international relations. We begin by tracing the evolution of the international system. World politics did not begin in 1945, much less in 1990. Thus, Chapter 2 examines – in broad thematic strokes – global history between 1500 and 2012, covering both the non-Western and the Western origins of the international system. In this chapter we introduce students to key moments in the development of states and the international system up to 1900; then we examine the origins, conduct, and consequences during the twentieth century of World War I and World War II, as well as the origins and ending of the Cold War. In this second edition, we have devoted greater attention to defining features of the contemporary international system, including the return of great power politics, globalization, and the populist backlash against it, evidenced by the United Kingdom's decision to exit the European Union and the US election of President Donald Trump, and the rise of global terrorism and the response to it.

In Chapter 3, we offer a comprehensive introduction to the primary theoretical frameworks of international relations. We explain why it is important to think theoretically about international relations, and we explore in detail the theoretical traditions of liberalism, realism, constructivism, Marxism, and feminism. Chapter 4 moves from the level of the international system to that of the individual country and provides an overview of foreign policy analysis. Interests and strategies are core concepts in the study of international relations; we examine their internal and external sources, and discuss how and why interests and strategies change over time.

This second edition includes a new chapter on international law and organizations. We view law and organizations as part of the basic infrastructure or architecture of international relations, and thus we include the chapter in the 'Foundations' section of the book. This chapter, Chapter 5, analyzes the different types of international law and how international law differs from domestic law; reviews the roles played by international laws and organizations in key areas of international political and economic activity; explains why laws and organizations emerge, with sensitivity to different explanations provided by liberal, realist, Marxist, and constructivist thinkers; and discusses why sovereign states may comply with international laws, even those which appear to constrain their behavior.

Part II: War and Peace: An Introduction to Security Studies

Part II of the book introduces the subfield of security studies. In Chapter 6 we examine the pathways and mechanisms that sometimes lead states to war. We describe the main characteristics and frequency of international wars and explore the types of issues over which states sometimes fight wars. We also examine wars within states, or civil wars, which are intrinsically important and can have a variety of weighty implications for international relations. In Chapter 7 we explore the parallel issue of the pathways leading states to peace. We examine the importance that leaders and especially ordinary people have assigned to peace, and identify various mechanisms that governments and citizens have used to promote peace. Peace-building efforts are lodged at different levels of analysis, and thus we explore international mechanisms (for example, international law and institutions, and hegemony), transnational mechanisms (for example, peace movements and economic interdependence) and state-level mechanisms (for example, diplomacy and power balancing) to provide students with a comprehensive understanding.

We turn in Chapter 8 to the issues and problems pertaining to weapons of mass destruction (WMD), as well as their effects on international relations. Our goal is for students to appreciate the relationships between technology and the use of force in general and in particular the profound effects that WMD and, most importantly, nuclear weapons have had on war-making and peace-making in international relations. This chapter describes the unprecedented destructive capacity of nuclear weapons, explains the peculiar logic of nuclear deterrence, examines the problem of nuclear proliferation and the dangers posed by the possession and spread of chemical and biological weapons, and discusses the dangerous liaisons that may be bringing together non-state actors, terrorism, and weapons of mass destruction. This second edition also takes up the possible impact of new technologies, drones, and cyber-warfare, on international politics.

Part III: Wealth and Power: An Introduction to International Political Economy

Part III introduces students to the subfield of international political economy, or IPE. We seek to highlight and identify connections between wealth and power by shifting our focus back and forth between international relationships and the foreign policies of states. Chapter 9 begins with the premise that students new to International Relations need to be familiar with the basic concepts of international economics (for example, comparative advantage, or the movement of exchange rates) to appreciate how international politics and economics interact. We focus in Chapter 9 on trade, money, and investment. We draw upon both economics and political science to analyze the reasons for and consequences of trade, and explain why some states nevertheless choose strategies of protection. We also introduce the types and dynamics of international financial transactions, including the role of exchange rates and the activities of multinational corporations. We explore the institutionalized mechanisms through which states manage their economic relationships, and we concentrate on how states have learned to promote and manage economic globalization in part through forming and working through such international institutions as the World Trade Organization (WTO) and the International Monetary Fund (IMF).

Once students have a basic grasp of economic concepts and of the substance and workings of the world economy, we move in Chapter 10 to the state level and examine how states seek to shape the global economy to promote their influence, defend their national interests, and maintain when possible their national economic autonomy. We explore the major perspectives on the relationships between states and markets as they inform the economic choices of states in a competitive geopolitical world; the relationships among state-building, war, and markets; the role of powerful states in the creation of open markets; the relationship between economic interdependence and interstate conflict; and the use of economic relations as political tools. Chapter 11 focuses in particular on developing and emerging economies. We provide perspectives on the meaning of economic development and review the economic experiences over recent decades of different groups of developing countries. We also introduce students to the structural challenges that past linkages to the global economy pose for poorer countries as they have sought to achieve economic development, and explore opportunities and problems that contemporary globalization in trade and finance may present to developing countries. We devote a section of this chapter to the particular opportunities and challenges facing prominent emerging economies such as Brazil, China, India, Russia, and South Africa.

Part IV: Contemporary Challenges and the Future of International Relations

Part IV focuses on contemporary versions of recurring challenges to the international system. Chapter 12 analyzes the reasons for and the consequences of weak and failing states in the international system. Failed states enable the operation of terrorists, pirates, drug gangs, and warlords. We also probe the issue of human rights, and in particular whether the international community has a responsibility to protect individuals in failed states who are being harmed by their home governments, even if doing so violates the sovereignty of those states. Chapter 13 takes up the international environment and natural resources as international political issues. We describe key global environmental and resource issues involving the atmosphere, the oceans, and the land, and we investigate why such problems arise, how governments try to address them, and what helps or hinders those efforts. We also explore links between environmental and resource problems on the one hand and civil and international conflict on the other.

Chapter 14 serves as the conclusion to the textbook. Here we invite students to draw on the enduring questions, connections, and perspectives they have absorbed throughout the course to think systematically about the future. We assist that effort by laying out several visions of the future of world politics. We draw contrasts between those who believe that the distribution of global power will be important in shaping the future of world politics and those who do not, and in particular we explore the implications of international systems characterized by one or multiple great powers. We juxtapose the ideas of globalization optimists, who focus on the beneficent effects on world politics of the global spread of the democratic peace, with the views of globalization pessimists, who worry about the clash of civilizations and the renewed significance of religion. We also engage with the possibility that the international system might be moving toward a period of global fracture, that is, an uneasy world of interacting pre-modern, modern, and post-modern zones of world politics.

Distinguishing Emphases and Components of the Book

In summary, instructors and students will find the following distinguishing features in our text:

- Each chapter begins with an enduring question that frames the substance of the chapter and helps students recognize key issues in the field of international relations.
- Each chapter begins with a clear specification of learning objectives and ends with a list of further reading and suggested study questions.
- Each chapter utilizes the levels-of-analysis framework and connects it to our enduring question using boxed features and easy-to-recognize icons.
- Each chapter contains six text boxes to help students make the critical connections between theory and practice, between then and now, between aspiration and reality, to highlight differing perspectives, both in general and in terms of international relations theories, and to appreciate the findings and insights of current academic research.
- A chapter (Chapter 2) that analyzes the key themes in the formation and evolution of the international system from 1500 to the present.
- A separate chapter (Chapter 4) that is devoted to the concepts needed to analyze the foreign policies of particular states and that allows instructors and students to move back and forth across the international and national levels of analysis.
- Sustained attention to both economic and security issues, and to their interaction in the past and current international systems.
- Systematic treatment of important issues in contemporary international relations, such as the rise of non-state and transnational actors, the role of the environment in world politics, the problem of failed states, and the populist backlash against globalization found in the advanced industrial world following the financial crisis of 2008–10.
- A chapter (Chapter 8) dedicated to the special problems posed by nuclear and other weapons of mass destruction.
- An extended discussion of rising powers – China, Brazil, India, Russia, and South Africa – in the current international system.
- An innovative concluding chapter that draws upon enduring questions and multiple perspectives to encourage students to think creatively yet systematically about alternative futures for world politics.

A Note to Students

Your world appears to be in a constant state of rapid change. Things that seemed important ten or even five years ago – especially if they involve technology, mobile phones, or social networking – today seem out of date. You will find that change is also a salient feature of international relations; this book will help you to recognize the profound transformations that have taken place over the space of several decades and even several centuries.

Yet there is some truth to the nineteenth-century French proverb (and the twenty-first-century popular song) that 'the more things change, the more they stay the same.' It is critical, especially when change appears to be the normal state of affairs, to grasp the enduring continuities that help define and shape international relations. This book will enable you to appreciate both continuity and change in the fascinating international landscape, and to recognize that not everyone sees the international landscape in the same way. We invite you to use this book as a starting point to explore the terrain of international relations yourself, with your fellow students and friends, and over the course of your life.

Acknowledgements

First and foremost, we thank our undergraduate students at Dartmouth, Duke, and Princeton; from them we have gained inspiration and learned that the enduring questions in international relations can be addressed most effectively by way of reasoned and respectful debate. We also wish to thank the many anonymous reviewers who provided thoughtful criticisms and helpful reactions to the first edition and to our draft chapters for this second edition. We offer a special thank you to Henry Frost, Dartmouth class of 2015, Pirzada Ahmad, Dartmouth class of 2018, and Charles Chen, Dartmouth class of 2021, who prepared the materials for this book's accompanying website thoughtfully and creatively. Finally, we wish to acknowledge the contributions and assistance of our colleagues at Red Globe Press, and especially Nikini Arulanandam and Andrew Malvern, who guided us through the development of this second edition with expertise and enthusiasm.

JOSEPH GRIECO
G. JOHN IKENBERRY
MICHAEL MASTANDUNO

The authors and publishers are grateful to the very many instructors who acted as an external review panel, assessing draft material and made many useful comments and suggestions for this edition, including:

Mervyn Bain, University of Aberdeen, UK
Leslie Baker, Mississippi State University, USA
Tabitha Benney, University of Utah, USA
Adam Bower, University of St Andrews, UK
Shannon L. Bridgmon, Northeastern State University, USA
Benito Cao, University of Adelaide, Australia
Eunbin Chung, University of Utah, USA
Kerry Crawford, James Madison University, Virginia, USA
Michele L. Crumley, East Tennessee State University, USA
Gigi Gokcek, Dominican University of California, USA
Darren Hawkins, Brigham Young University, USA
Mark Hibben, Saint Joseph's College of Maine, USA

Hanna Samir Kassab, Northern Michigan University, USA
Kathryn LaFever, Miami University, USA
Lavina Lee, Macquarie University, Australia
Jakob Lempp, Rhein-Waal University of Applied Sciences, Germany
Michael Mayo, St. Petersburg College, USA
Charles Miller, Australian National University, Australia
Lawrence Morton, University of North Georgia, USA
Ian Nelson, University of Nottingham Ningbo, China
Svetoslav Nenov, Coventry University, UK
Marc Simon, Bowling Green State University, USA
Cigdem V. Sirin, University of Texas at El Paso, USA
Keith Smith, King's College London, UK
Krista Tuomi, American University - Kogod School of Business, USA
Thijs Van de Graaf, Ghent University, Belgium
M. Joel Voss, University of Toledo, USA
Joseph L. Warner, Florida State College, USA

Tour of the Book

Enduring Questions
Give shape and focus to each chapter and help you address contemporary issues in a broader context.

Chapter Contents
Break down the major sections in each chapter to guide your learning.

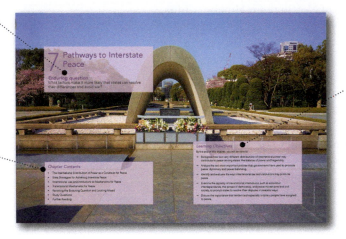

Learning Objectives Keep specific educational goals in mind as you work through the chapter.

Key Terms
Highlight important terminology as it arises with a complete glossary at the back of the book.

Simulations Step into the shoes of policy makers as they make decisions and then consider the consequences, positive or negative, of your actions!

Study Questions
Reflect on the material covered and develop your own position on contested issues and problems.

Levels-of-analysis framework Consider the different levels (e.g., the individual, the state, or the international system as a whole) when confronting a problem or puzzle in international relations.

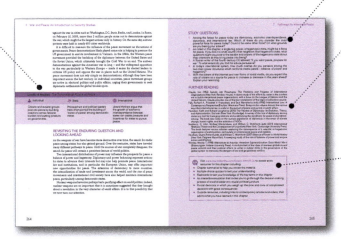

Further Reading
Guides those of you interested in pursuing the material of the chapter more deeply.

Companion website
Remember to go online to access further useful learning and teaching tools!

Making Connections, *Theory and Practice*
Recognize that theoretical frameworks are essential tools to make sense of a complicated world, and yet do not always adequately explain the real-life behavior of states and decision makers.

2.1 MAKING CONNECTIONS
Theory and Practice

Religious Identity and the Franco-Ottoman Military Alliance

Theory: States with Common Identities Should Find Cooperation Easier than States with Conflicting Identities

In Chapter 3, we will explore different theories of international relations, including constructivist theory, which suggests that belief systems influence the foreign policy decisions and actions of national leaders. We might expect then that state leaders sharing similar worldviews, including religious beliefs, find it easier to cooperate with each other than leaders with radically different worldviews.

Practice: The Alliance between Catholic France and the Muslim Ottoman Empire

After France lost several battles against Habsburg military forces, and Francis I, the French King, was taken prisoner for a time after a major defeat at the hands of the Habsburgs in 1525, the French King attained a military alliance with

2.2 MAKING CONNECTIONS
Then and Now

The Persistence of the Munich Analogy

Then: President Lyndon Johnson Argues for Escalation in Vietnam, August 1965

… If we are driven from the field in Vietnam, then no nation can ever again have the same confidence in American promise or in American protection…. Nor would surrender in Vietnam bring peace, because we learned from Hitler at Munich that success only feeds the appetite of aggression. The battle would be renewed in one country and then another country, bringing with it perhaps even larger and crueler conflict, as we have learned from the lessons of history.
Source: Johnson (1965): 262.

Now: President George H. Bush's War Ultimatum to Iraq, March 2003

We are now acting because the risks of inaction would be far greater…. The cause of peace requires all free nations to recognize new and undeniable

Making Connections, *Then and Now* Appreciate how intellectual and policy problems recur over time, and are addressed by scholars and policy makers in different historical and cultural contexts.

Making Connections, *Aspiration vs Reality*
Remember that the best intentions of states and their leaders are sometimes frustrated. Leaders often compromise one set of objectives to achieve others.

2.3 MAKING CONNECTIONS
Aspiration versus Reality

The United States and Support for Democracy during the Cold War

Aspiration

The Truman Doctrine in 1947 promised to help 'free peoples' to oppose 'totalitarian regimes.' President John Kennedy in 1961 promised that the United States would 'pay any price, bear any burden, meet any hardship, support any friend, and oppose any foe in order to assure the survival and the success of liberty.' The Reagan Doctrine of 1985 declared that America's mission was 'to nourish and defend freedom and democracy.'

Reality

American policy makers worried that leftist governments could easily be captured by anti-US communist elements, and thus preferred to support right-wing authoritarian (and non-democratic) regimes that took a pro-US and anti-communist position. President Franklin Roosevelt captured this sentiment when

2.4 DIFFERING PERSPECTIVES

The Cuban Missile Crisis of October 1962

Background
In October 1962, the United States discovered that the Soviet Union was placing nuclear missiles on the island of Cuba. The ensuing crisis lasted two weeks and brought the superpowers closer to nuclear war than at any other time during the Cold War.

The Soviet Perspective: Why Take Such a Risky Step?
The Soviet leaders may have placed missiles in Cuba to gain leverage over the United States in Berlin. Also, the Soviet Union faced a leadership challenge from Mao Zedong, who believed China was more faithful to the Communist ideal of spreading global revolution; Soviet leaders may have believed that this bold step would reinvigorate their position as leader of the world Communist movement.

The American Perspective: Why a Naval Blockade?
American leaders debated various options and eventually decided to impose a naval blockade of Cuba. The blockade was intended to send a double message: the United States was willing to risk war, but was also allowing time (it would take Soviet ships several days to reach the blockade) for a possible diplomatic solution to be worked out.

The Cuban Perspective: Will We Be Defended?
The problem for Cuba was possible American aggression. The United States clearly opposed the Communist regime of Fidel Castro, which gained power in Cuba in 1959. The Kennedy administration tried and failed to overthrow Castro in the ill-fated Bay of Pigs invasion of April 1961.

Differing Perspectives Be sensitive to different viewpoints depending on history, culture, economic and social status, and an array of other factors.

Differing Theoretical Approaches
Explore different understandings and assumptions made by scholars on what matters most in explaining behavior.

3.6 DIFFERING THEORETICAL APPROACHES

Sources of Change in International Relations

Realism

War is a major source of change in world politics. In every historical era, war – particularly among major states – has dramatically changed the geopolitical landscape. In the wake of war, powerful rising states have emerged to dominate the system, while defeated states have gone into decline. War has forced states to mobilize their economies and societies, leading to innovations and changes in government capacities. World War I is a good example of how a major war transformed politics, economics, and world affairs. It led to the destruction of vast empires, brought the United States to the center of world politics, and fueled changes in European politics that played out over the next half century.

Liberalism

Liberals argue that change in world politics comes from ongoing trade, exchange, innovation, and learning that occurs within and between countries.

5.2 RESEARCH INSIGHT

Why Seek Authorization for War from the UN Security Council?

The Problem

International relations is sometimes called a 'self-help' system. States are responsible for defending their own territories and have the option to go to war if they so desire. If a government is strong enough to initiate war unilaterally or with a coalition of partners, why bother seeking authorization from the UN Security Council? The Council has 15 members with diverse viewpoints, five of whom can single-handedly veto any resolution. Why take this time-consuming and politically risky step?

The Research Insight

Recent academic research addresses this question with emphasis on the *information-conveying* qualities of international organizations. Even if a country has the capacity to 'go it alone', it has much to gain by engaging the Security Council. Voeten (2005) finds that Security Council deliberation provides

Research Insight Examine findings from empirical research so that you can separate political opinion from conclusions drawn from evidence-based research.

Online Teaching and Learning Resources

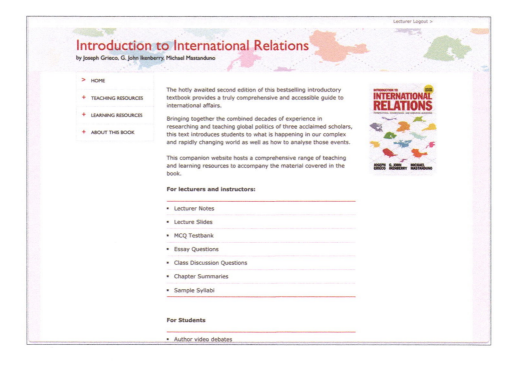

www.macmillanihe.com/Grieco-IntroIR-2e is a freely accessible website containing an array of comprehensive and innovative resources for both instructors and students.

Author Video Debates

The website offers eight videos in which the authors engage in lively debate. These videos demonstrate different viewpoints in international relations and are intended to inspire students to engage in further debate.

There are two videos relating to each part in the book; these can be viewed at the start of each new part as an introduction to what topics will be covered. The questions debated have been chosen both to expand upon the issues raised in the book and to highlight key questions in world politics.

- Part I: Foundations of International Relations
  Q1: Why do we have so many theories of international relations?
  Q2: Do international laws and international organizations promote peace, prosperity, and justice?

- Part II: War and Peace: An Introduction to Security Studies
  Q1: How important are diplomacy and military force in today's world?
  Q2: Are China and Russia 'revisionist states'?

- Part III: Wealth and Power: An Introduction to International Political Economy
  Q1: What does globalization mean today, and what are its effects and challenges?
  Q2: How does the global economy help (or hinder) poorer countries?

- Part IV: Contemporary Challenges and the Future of International Relations
  Q1: What are the main global challenges facing the international community?
  Q2: What might the future hold for international relations?

Resources for Students

The website also offers a range of useful resources for students to aid revision and critical thinking.

- **A comprehensive study guide** for each chapter including:
  Chapter summaries
  Multiple choice and discussion questions
  Flashcards of key terms in international relations
  Timelines of key historical events
- **Pivotal decisions.** In these interactive games, students must consider the pros and cons of a complicated decision with grave consequences. Some of these decisions are genuine historical dilemmas that world leaders have faced. Others are possible dilemmas that the student can grapple with using the tools they have acquired by studying this book.
- **Interactive simulations.** In these exercises, students again play the part of a world leader at a crucial political juncture. However, instead of considering the pros and cons of a particular decision, they must simulate the entire decision-making process. Each decision they make leads to new circumstances and decisions. A box in each chapter invites students to take up the simulation that applies to that chapter's material.
- **Outside resources,** including links to contemporary articles, videos, and games, which have been selected to illustrate the continuing relevance of the enduring question in each chapter.

Resources for Instructors

A selection of resources has been provided to help instructors plan and deliver their courses.

- **A testbank** containing a total of over 500 multiple choice questions organized by chapter
- **Essay questions** for each chapter
- **Lecture slides** to aid teaching
- **Class discussion questions**
- **Lecture notes** that outline the key points in every chapter
- **A sample syllabus**

The World

1 Netherlands	7 Slovenia	13 Serbia
2 Belgium	8 Croatia	14 Albania
3 Luxembourg	9 Slovakia	15 Macedonia
4 Switzerland	10 Hungary	16 Moldova
5 Czech Republic	11 Bosnia & Herzegovina	17 Armenia
6 Austria	12 Montenegro	18 Azerbaijan
		19 Kosovo

Iceland

Sweden
Finland
Norway
Denmark
Estonia
Latvia
Lithuania
United Kingdom
Rep. of Ireland
Germany
Poland
Belarus
France
Ukraine
Portugal
Spain
Italy
Romania
Bulgaria
Greece
Georgia
Turkey
Kazakhstan
Russian Federation
Mongolia
Uzbekistan
Kyrgyzstan
Turkmenistan
Tajikistan
Cyprus
Syria
Lebanon
Israel
Jordan
Iraq
Iran
Kuwait
Qatar
Afghanistan
Pakistan
N. Korea
S. Korea
Japan
China
Bhutan
Bangladesh
Nepal
India
Thailand
Laos
Cambodia
Vietnam
Myanmar (Burma)
Taiwan (Formosa)
Tunisia
Morocco
Algeria
Libya
Egypt
Saudi Arabia
U.A.E
Oman
Yemen
Western Sahara
Mauritania
Mali
Niger
Chad
Sudan
Eritrea
Djibouti
Ethiopia
Somalia
Senegal
Burkina
Guinea
Cote D'ivoire
Ghana
Nigeria
Cameroon
Central African Rep.
South Sudan
Togo
Benin
Eq. Guinea
Gabon
Congo
Democratic Republic of the Congo (Zaire)
Uganda
Kenya
Rwanda
Burundi
Liberia
Sierra Leone
Guinea-Bissau
The Gambia
Tanzania
Malawi
Angola
Zambia
Zimbabwe
Mozambique
Madagascar
Namibia
Botswana
Eswatini
Lesotho
Republic of South Africa
Philippines
Brunei
Malaysia
Singapore
Indonesia
Papua New Guinea
Sri Lanka
Australia

INDIAN OCEAN

Europe

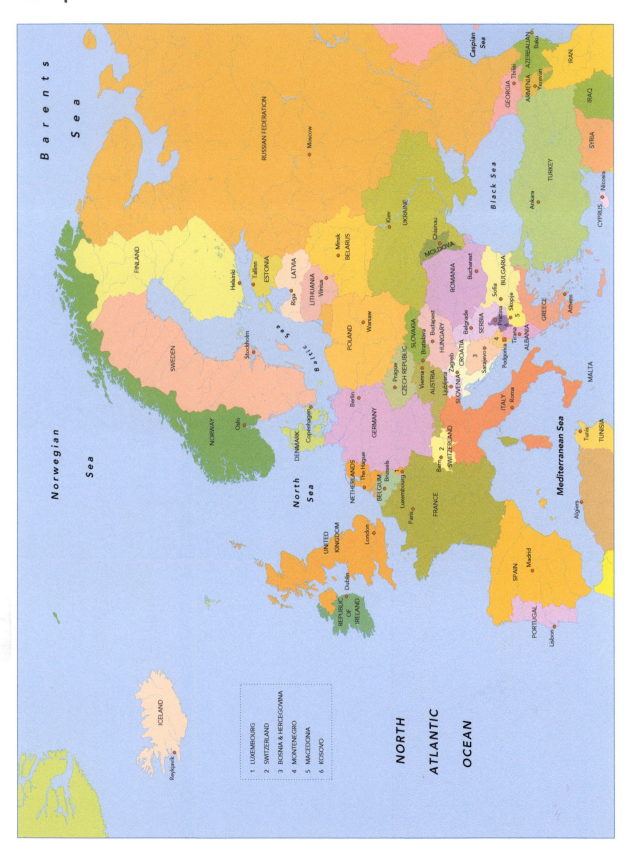

Middle East

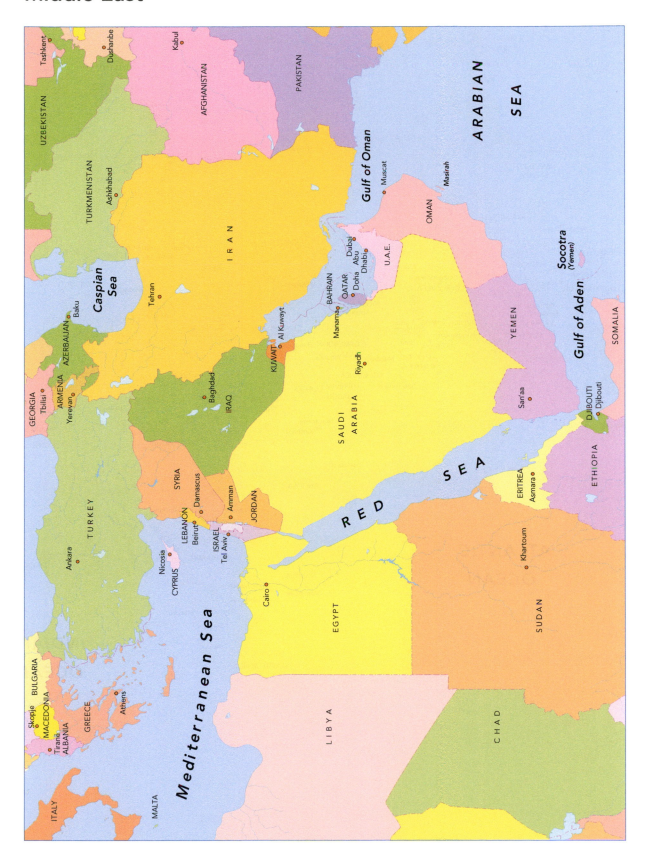

Africa

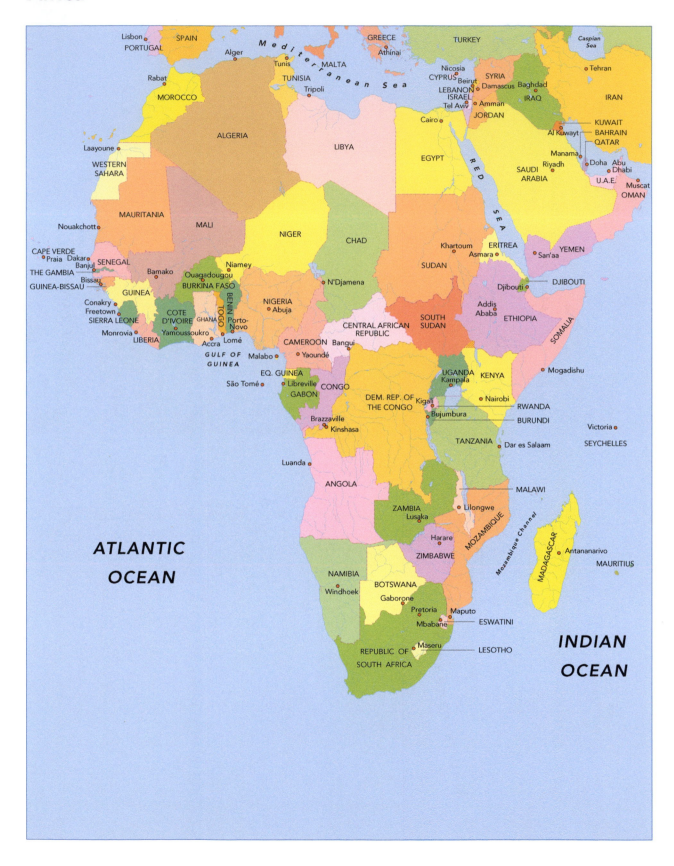

South America

Central America

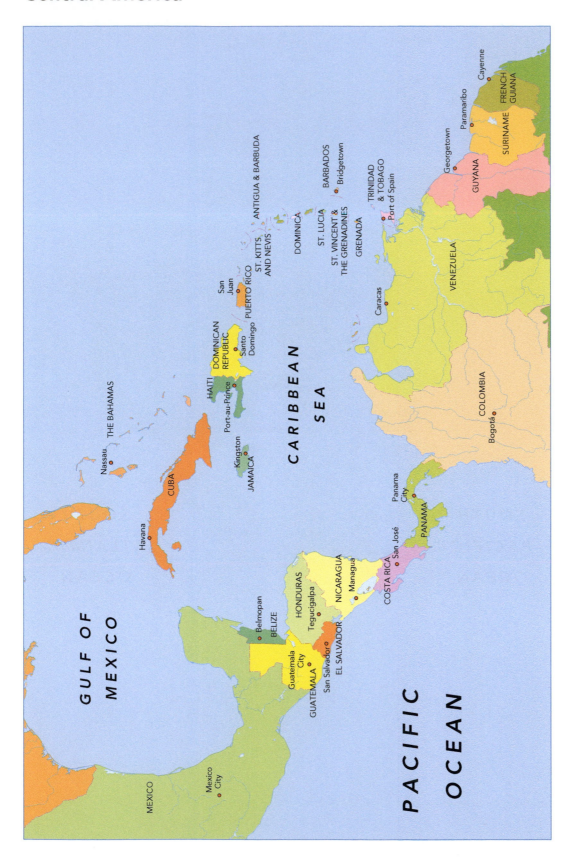

North America

Asia

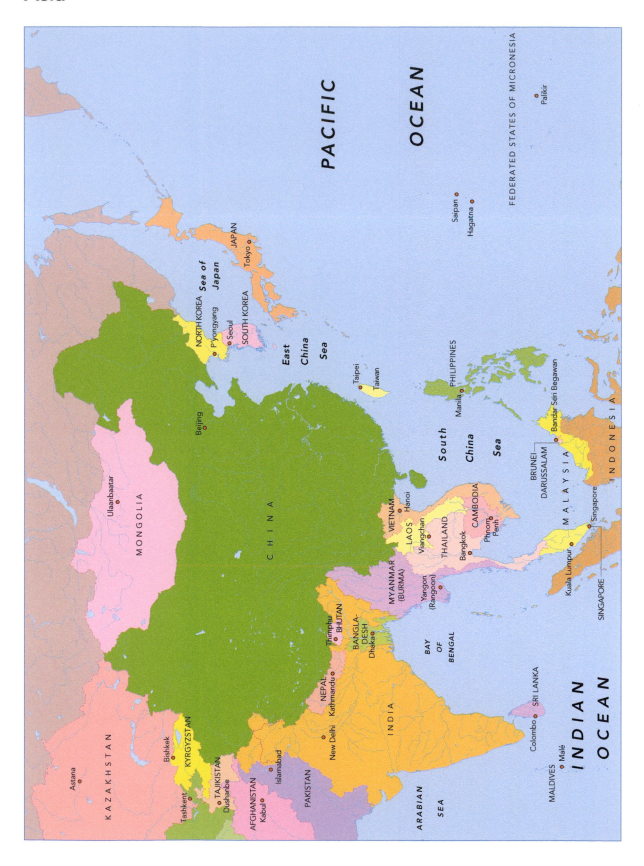

PACIFIC

OCEAN

FEDERATED STATES OF MICRONESIA

Palikir

Saipan
Hagåtña

JAPAN
Tokyo

Sea of Japan

NORTH KOREA
P'yongyang
Seoul
SOUTH KOREA

East China Sea

KAZAKHSTAN

Astana

MONGOLIA
Ulaanbaatar

CHINA

Beijing

Taipei
Taiwan

PHILIPPINES

Manila

South China Sea

Bandar Seri Begawan

BRUNEI
DARUSSALAM

INDONESIA

MALAYSIA

Bishkek
KYRGYZSTAN

Tashkent

TAJIKISTAN
Dushanbe

AFGHANISTAN
Kabul

PAKISTAN
Islamabad

NEPAL
Kathmandu

New Delhi

BHUTAN
Thimphu

BANGLA-
DESH
Dhaka

MYANMAR
(BURMA)
Yangon
(Rangoon)

VIETNAM
Hanoi

LAOS
Viangchan

THAILAND
Bangkok

CAMBODIA
Phnom
Penh

Kuala Lumpur

Singapore

SINGAPORE

INDIA

BAY
OF
BENGAL

SRI LANKA
Colombo

Malé

MALDIVES

ARABIAN
SEA

INDIAN

OCEAN

Australasia

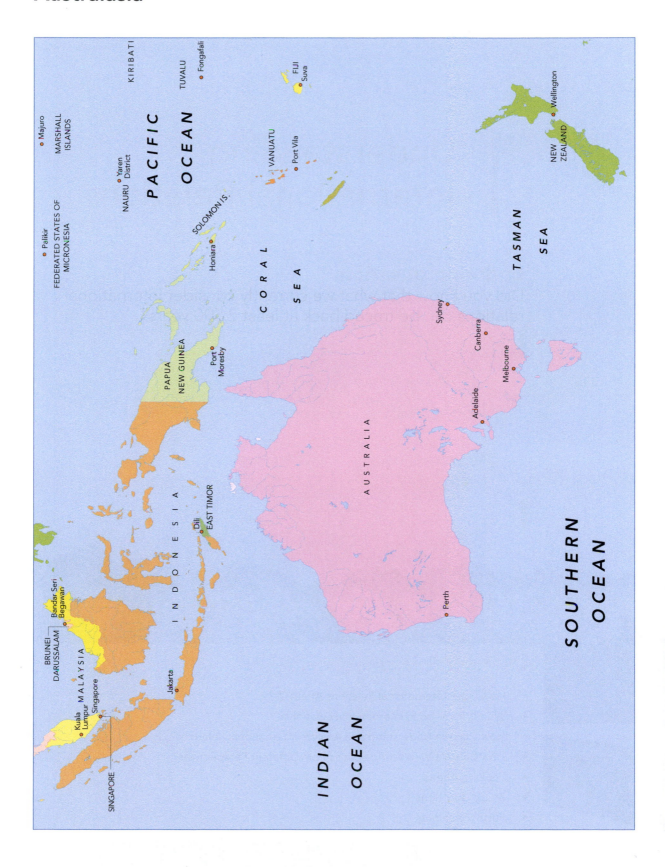

1 Understanding International Relations

Enduring question
Did you know that what we currently consider international relations can be traced back at least 2,500 years?

Chapter Contents

Learning Objectives

By the end of this chapter you will be able to:

→ Understand why international relations matter.

→ Apply a basic vocabulary and the levels-of-analysis device to international relations and foreign policy.

→ Analyze the use of enduring questions in international relations.

→ Recognize the need to make connections between international relations theory and practice, the past and present, and aspirations and reality to develop a better understanding of international relations.

→ Evaluate the significance of viewing world politics from multiple perspectives.

Photo by Sérgio Rola on Unsplash

3

During the fifth century BCE, the relevant political groups were Greek city-states (e.g. Athens or Sparta) rather than modern nation-states. International relations in that period in some ways looks similar to what it is today (city-states traded with each other, participated in cross-border sports competitions, practiced diplomacy, formed alliances, and fought wars against each other as enemies and as allies against the Persian Empire), but, of course, the modern international system also looks very different.

We define international relations as the political, economic, social, and cultural relations between two countries or among many countries. In this, we also include relations countries have with other important actors such as global corporations or international organizations. Today's nation-states operate in a global system of interaction. Goods, technology, and money change hands with the click of a mouse rather than with the launch of a sailing ship. States still fight wars, but the destructive capacity of modern weapons, especially nuclear weapons, introduces a strong element of caution into how states resolve conflicts with each other. Non-state actors, such as global corporations, environmental advocacy groups, and criminal and terrorist networks cross borders and share the stage with countries and their governments.

This book introduces you to the fascinating and complex world of international relations. The best way to begin to acquire a solid knowledge of this field is to master some basic terms and concepts that are used to describe international relations and foreign policy and to learn how to employ the levels-of-analysis framework for organizing and understanding arguments and ideas about international relations. Second and most importantly, we believe you can begin to master the complexity of international relations by exploring what we call enduring questions. These are questions which have engaged and challenged generations of international relations scholars and students – large, challenging questions that have stood the test of time. Finally, we believe it is critically important that you are able to make connections about international relations that relate the past to the present, theory to practice, and aspiration to reality. You should also be comfortable viewing world politics from multiple perspectives. We will explain what we mean by each of these defining features of our book as we introduce you in this chapter to the field of international relations.

HOW DOES INTERNATIONAL RELATIONS AFFECT US?

If you happen to be one of the many people to own an iPhone (as of 2016, over one billion had been sold worldwide), you are probably familiar with Apple, the famous American computer company. Although the iPhone was designed and marketed by Apple in California, its components are produced all over the world. A South Korean company, Samsung, and a Chinese company, Sunwoda Electric, manufacture the battery. The camera and flash memory come from Japan. The touchscreen is made by a US company, Broadcom, with factories in one dozen locations including Israel, the United Kingdom, India, and Brazil. The various components are sent to Taiwan, where companies named Foxconn and Pegatron assemble and ship phones to customers around the globe (Costello 2017; Xing and Detert 2010). As a consumer, you benefit directly from this global network of trade: the mobile phone you buy and the service you receive are more affordable than if your phone had been built and serviced all in one country. Some East Asian, European, and American workers share in the benefits of this trade as well, since the more phones that are sold, the more US-, European-, and East Asian-based jobs are created to produce and service them.

The stakes in international relations sometimes involve conflict and war rather than, or alongside, trade and mutual economic benefit. One watershed moment occurred on September 11, 2001, when members of the Al Qaeda transnational terrorist organization hijacked a number of airliners and crashed two of them into the Twin Towers of the World Trade Center in New York City, a third into the Pentagon (the headquarters of the US Department of Defense) in the nation's capital, and a fourth headed toward another Washington target (before being stopped by a passenger uprising that resulted in the plane crashing in Pennsylvania). In total, over 3,000 people died during the September 11 attacks, including several hundred police and fire workers who tried to save the initial victims in the Twin Towers. These attacks prompted a US-led invasion of Afghanistan, whose Taliban government had been giving refuge to Al Qaeda, and served as one justification for a second and far more controversial US-led war, against Iraq, in 2003. It also prompted US special-forces and spy operations against Al Qaeda in numerous countries, including one in Pakistan in May 2011 in which its leader, Osama bin Laden, was killed.

The events of September 11 gave rise to a longer-term war against terrorism, that has been a prominent part of America's recent engagement with international relations. But taking a longer view, we should recognize that in relative terms Americans have been among the peoples of the world least affected by foreign wars. In the Vietnam War, one of the longest and costliest wars fought by the United States, 58,000 Americans were killed and about 300,000 were wounded. However, in 1995, the Vietnamese government estimated that 2 million civilians in the North and another 2 million in the South also died during the war. Vietnamese casualties represented a shocking 13 percent of the total population of that country.

The citizens of France and Germany treated each other as adversaries for almost 100 years. These two countries fought a major war against each other in 1870 and were the principal combatants in two devastating World Wars, between 1914 and 1918 and again between 1939 and 1945. It is not surprising that, for many decades, the French and German people regarded each other with suspicion and resentment and considered each other mortal enemies. But, since 1945, the French and German governments have cooperated with each other politically and economically in what is today called the **European Union** (EU) – a group of 28 European countries (27 if the United Kingdom leaves as planned in 2019) that abide by common laws and practices – and militarily in an alliance called the **North Atlantic Treaty Organization (NATO)**, which requires the United States and its European partners to come to the defense of each other in the event of a military attack against one of them. Today, war between France and Germany is almost unthinkable, and in 2012 the European Union was awarded the Nobel Peace Prize in recognition of its historical accomplishments. French and German citizens freely cross each other's borders and work in each other's factories and offices. The Germans and French even gave up their long-standing national currencies, the Deutschmark and the French franc in 2002; they now share, along with 17 other European Union members, a common currency called the **euro**. Today, members of the European Union worry very little about war with each other and very much about economic instability as they struggle to recover from a financial crisis that has threatened their own prosperity and that of the global economy.

International relations involve not just war and the movement of goods and money across borders, but also the ability of people themselves to move across those borders. If you are not a citizen, national governments require you to have special permission (for example, in Australia an employer-sponsored 457 visa, or in the

European Union
A group of 28 European countries that abide by common laws and practices.

North Atlantic Treaty Organization (NATO)
A defense pact formed in 1949 between the US, the UK, and several other western European states. It has since expanded and is still very active today.

Euro
The common currency of the eurozone.

United States, an identification document commonly known as a green card) before you may legally work in their country. Even visiting different countries simply as a tourist often requires you to request permission in the form of a visa from the respective governments of those countries. The citizens of some countries have an easier time crossing borders than do the citizens of others; in 2012, for example, citizens of Sweden and Finland could enter 168 other countries without needing a visa, while Chinese citizens could only enter 41 countries and Pakistani citizens only 32 countries visa-free (Visato.com 2012). But even these opportunities would have been a luxury compared to what international relations imposed on people living in Eastern Europe between the late 1940s and late 1980s. During that time an **Iron Curtain**, a term coined by British leader Winston Churchill to capture the profound political and human divisions, separated the western and eastern parts of Europe. The communist governments of Eastern European countries tried to prevent their citizens from traveling to the West because they feared people would find freedom so attractive that they would not return home. The eastern and western parts of today's German capital city, Berlin, were divided by the **Berlin Wall**. East Berliners trying to escape across the wall to West Berlin were routinely shot by East German guards.

International relations powerfully affect our everyday lives. There are 196 countries in the world today (that includes Taiwan, which operates as a country but which is also claimed by the People's Republic of China as a part of its own country) and they interact with each other over a wide variety of political, economic, social, cultural, and scientific issues. They also interact with an array of **international governmental organizations (IGOs)** – organizations that states join to further their political or economic interests – such as the United Nations (UN), International Monetary Fund (IMF), World Health Organization (WHO), World Trade Organization (WTO), and Organization of Petroleum Exporting Countries (OPEC). Countries also deal regularly

Iron Curtain
A term coined by British leader Winston Churchill to capture the profound political and human divisions separating the western and eastern parts of Europe.

Berlin Wall
The wall that divided Soviet East Berlin from American, French, and British West Berlin during the Cold War, until its fall in 1989.

International governmental organizations (IGOs)
Organizations that states join to further their political or economic interests.

Photo 1.1 The Fall of the Berlin Wall, 1989
Germans from East and West standing on the Berlin Wall in front of the Brandenburg Gate, November 10, 1989, one day after the wall opened.

Source: Engler/ullstein bild via Getty Images.

with private actors whose work crosses borders, such as the US-based conglomerate General Electric, the Chinese-based computer company Lenovo, the international health crisis response team Médecins Sans Frontières (Doctors Without Borders), and transnational political and social movements such as the Muslim Brotherhood and the World Social Forum. Your task is to gain an understanding of those relationships, and so we begin by laying some of the necessary foundations.

WHO IS INVOLVED IN INTERNATIONAL RELATIONS?

The initial step is to identify the fundamental actors in international relations. While the question of which actors in international relations are most important is controversial and will be taken up in many of the chapters that follow, for now we can identify at least three important classes of key actors in international relations.

First, we are interested in individual **national leaders**. These are individuals, like the President of the United States, the Prime Minister of Pakistan, or the Chancellor of Germany, who hold executive offices as a result of which they are entitled to make foreign policy and military decisions on behalf of their countries. We also include those individuals, such as the Russian Defense Minister or the Brazilian Minister of Agriculture, who as a result of the offices they hold give counsel to and implement the decisions of their respective core executive leaders, like the Russian or Brazilian President.

Second, we are interested in **states**. In international relations we often say 'India' has this or that foreign policy interest, or that 'China' has this or that strategy toward 'Russia,' or that 'Venezuela' is making use of this or that foreign policy instrument to attain some goal. India, China, Russia, and Venezuela are among the 196 states in the current international system. But what, in general, is a state? It is a political entity with two key features: a piece of territory with reasonably well-defined borders, and political authorities who enjoy **sovereignty**, that is, they have an effective and recognized capacity to govern residents within the territory and an ability to establish relationships with governments that control other states.

The state should be distinguished from another key international relations actor, the nation. States are political units, while **nations** are collections of people who share a common culture, history, or language. The term **nation-state** refers to a political unit inhabited by people sharing common culture, history, or language. Although nation-state is used frequently in international relations literature, often as a synonym for country, pure nation-states are rare: possible examples might include Albania, where over 95 percent of the population consists of ethnic Albanians, or Iceland, which has a language and culture found only on that island. Nations often transcend the boundary of any single state; members of the Chinese nation, for example, are found in mainland China and in Taiwan, but also in Singapore, Malaysia, and other parts of Southeast Asia.

Similarly, states often contain more than one nation. The former Soviet Union included not only Russians but Armenians, Ukrainians, Georgians, Latvians, and Lithuanians, among others. Many African countries were created from former colonies whose borders were not drawn along national lines. Kenya, for example, contains numerous ethnic groups, including the Kikuyu and Luo, with their own languages, cultures, and traditions. Scotland is a distinctive nation that is part of the United Kingdom (Great Britain), and Catalonia is a distinctive nation that is part of Spain. Both Scotland and Catalonia, with their own cultures and languages and long histories of political autonomy, have recently contemplated breaking away from their multinational states and creating their own independent nation-states. It is not

National leaders
Individuals who hold executive offices as a result of which they are entitled to make foreign policy and military decisions on behalf of their countries.

State
A political entity with two key features: a piece of territory with reasonably well-defined borders, and political authorities who enjoy sovereignty.

Sovereignty
The effective and recognized capacity to govern residents within a given territory and an ability to establish relationships with governments that control other states.

Nation
Collections of people who share a common culture, history, or language.

Nation-state
A political unit inhabited by people sharing common culture, history, or language.

Photo 1.2 Protests in Catalonia, 2017

In October 2017, the parliament of Catalonia, a region of Spain with some political autonomy, held a referendum on independence which the central government in Madrid declared illegal.

Source: Angel Garcia/Bloomberg via Getty Images.

Non-state actors
Actors other than states that operate within or across state borders with important consequences for international relations.

surprising that one of the fiercest rivalries in global sports is between the football clubs FC Barcelona (based in Catalonia) and Real Madrid (based in the capital of Spain).

Third, to understand international relations we need to analyze **non-state actors**. These are actors others than states that operate within or across state borders with important consequences for international relations. Multinational enterprises such as the US-based soft drink company Coca Cola, the Netherlands-based electronics firm Philips, and the Japan-based conglomerate Mitsubishi are non-state actors with important business operations across the globe. The Catholic Church and the Muslim Brotherhood are active regionally and globally and are thus important non-state actors; and, with radically different aims and methods, several criminal groups, such as mafias and drug cartels, and terrorist organizations such as ETA (a Basque group that has used violence to pursue Catalonia's separation from Spain) and Boko Haram (a Nigerian group that forbids Muslims from participating in Western-style social or educational activities) are consequential non-state actors. ISIS (the Islamic State of Iraq and Syria), a terrorist group that grew out of Al Qaeda, gained global attention in 2014 when it captured large swaths of territory in Iraq and Syria and claimed to create a transnational Islamic State, or caliphate. By 2017 ISIS lost much of its claimed territory, including its stronghold of Mosul, Iraq, yet remained a formidable non-state actor.

Civil society
Collections of non-state actors that operate outside the sphere of government or business control.

Finally, the term **civil society** refers broadly to a collection of non-state actors that organize and operate in a so-called third sphere, outside the control of government or business. Examples might include charities, groups of citizens demonstrating for political change, and volunteer organizations working to assist victims of natural disasters. To the extent they operate across borders, members of civil society may have a meaningful impact on foreign policy and international relations.

How Do These Actors Get What They Want in International Relations?

What do these actors want and how do they get what they want in international relations? Here it is useful to distinguish interests, strategies, objectives (or goals), and policy instruments.

When we say that a state (or nation-state) has an **interest**, we mean that the state's wish either to maintain or attain some condition of the world is sufficiently important to it that it is willing to pay meaningful costs. For example, in recent years, the Chinese government has revealed that it has an interest in attaining sovereignty over the South China Sea, perhaps because that area may be rich in oil and natural gas. In making that claim it has come into conflict with numerous neighboring states such as Indonesia, Malaysia, the Philippines, and Vietnam, who also claim sovereignty over parts of that sea space (see Map 1.1). Not surprisingly, the South China Sea has become a potential focal point for conflict in world politics.

How do states promote or defend an interest? They do so by the development and implementation of a strategy. A **strategy** essentially connects means to an end. If China's ultimate **objective** or goal is to attain sovereignty over the South China Sea, part of its strategy might be to induce such countries as Vietnam and the Philippines to renounce their own claims over the South China Sea, and to recognize Chinese sovereignty over the area. China will rely on policy instruments to help it obtain that goal. **Policy instruments** can take a variety of forms, which we will examine in detail in Chapter 4. In the South China Sea case, China thus far has used multiple policy instruments including diplomacy, propaganda, economic incentives, and low levels of military force to persuade or coerce other states to recognize its claim. The term **statecraft** is often used to refer to the use of policy instruments by state leaders to achieve foreign policy objectives.

HOW CAN WE UNDERSTAND AND ANALYZE INTERNATIONAL RELATIONS?

We now have a basic language for the description of the actions and interactions of states, which we will build on with additional terms over the course of the book. You will also encounter many different arguments, ideas, and theories about international relations. To help you break down and grasp such a multitude of ideas, this book employs several features to aid your learning. It is grounded in *theory*, exploring several different intellectual traditions; it uses *levels of analysis* as a framework for organizing different theories, and it uses *enduring questions* to encourage you to think more holistically about important issues. A thorough understanding of international relations also includes the exploration of national, regional, and global contexts, common and differing interests among actors, and causal relationships that can affect outcomes. This kind of critical thinking requires that you make three types of connections in your study of the issues: between *theory and practice, then and now*, and *aspiration and reality*; these are presented in every chapter through the Making Connections features.

Theoretical Foundations

Theories help us understand *why* something occurred in international relations, and the likelihood that it will happen again. As you will see in subsequent chapters, there are many such theories, and debates over how useful or valid theories are. How do we keep track of these different arguments, ideas, and theories? How do we compare

Interest
Some condition of the world sufficiently important that a state is willing to pay meaningful costs to attain or maintain it.

Strategy
The overarching connection of means to an end for a state. A strategy aims at a policy objective, and outlines what policy instruments will be used to attain that objective.

Objective
A state's goal in international relations, generally the attainment or maintenance of some interest.

Policy instrument
A tool used by a state's government to attain its interests. Policy instruments come in many forms, divided into persuasive and coercive forms.

Statecraft
The use of policy instruments, including military force, economic sanctions or incentives, or diplomacy to achieve foreign policy objectives.

Theory
A group of ideas intended to explain some empirical phenomenon.

Map 1.1 A National Interest: China and Its Claims to the South China Sea
This map shows why the South China Sea is an area of geopolitical dispute in the current international system. The region is potentially rich in energy resources and several countries, including China, Malaysia, Vietnam, Indonesia, and the Philippines, claim that the territory falls within their jurisdiction. In recent years China has employed a variety of diplomatic and coercive tactics to try to convince other countries that they should recognize China's claim.

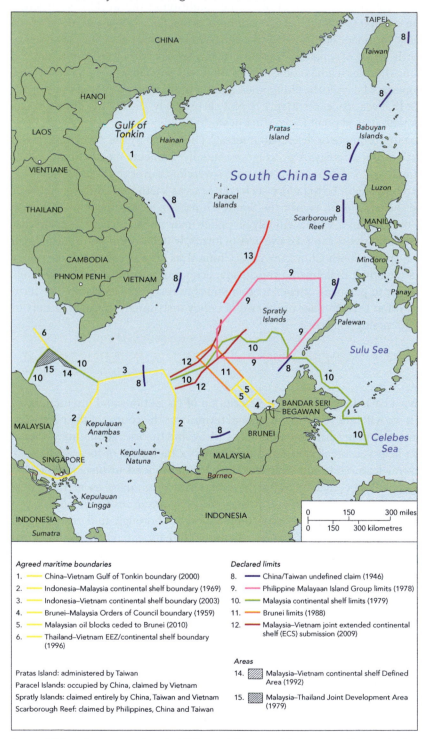

Agreed maritime boundaries

1. —— China–Vietnam Gulf of Tonkin boundary (2000)
2. —— Indonesia–Malaysia continental shelf boundary (1969)
3. —— Indonesia–Vietnam continental shelf boundary (2003)
4. —— Brunei–Malaysia Orders of Council boundary (1959)
5. —— Malaysian oil blocks ceded to Brunei (2010)
6. —— Thailand–Vietnam EEZ/continental shelf boundary (1996)

Pratas Island: administered by Taiwan
Paracel Islands: occupied by China, claimed by Vietnam
Spratly Islands: claimed entirely by China, Taiwan and Vietnam
Scarborough Reef: claimed by Philippines, China and Taiwan

Declared limits

8. —— China/Taiwan undefined claim (1946)
9. —— Philippine Malayaan Island Group limits (1978)
10. —— Malaysia continental shelf limits (1979)
11. —— Brunei limits (1988)
12. —— Malaysia–Vietnam joint extended continental shelf (ECS) submission (2009)

Areas

14. ▨ Malaysia–Vietnam continental shelf Defined Area (1992)
15. ▨ Malaysia–Thailand Joint Development Area (1979)

Source: US State Department. See also US Energy Information Administration, 'Country Analysis Brief: South China Sea', February 2013.

them to each other so that we can get a better sense of each and assess their relative strengths and weaknesses?

Theories help us to describe and explain the world. They are analytical devices that make assumptions, put forward causal arguments, and offer predictions about the workings of the international arena. Theories are usually not completely right or wrong but may be more or less useful. Any particular theory might be useful for some time, until it is challenged by new evidence or overtaken by a better theory that someone develops. In the sixteenth century, the Polish-born scientist Copernicus gave us a new and (after some of his supporters had the misfortune of being burned at the stake) better theory of astronomy. Using observations and mathematical calculations, he theorized that the sun was the center of the universe and the earth moved around it, challenging the long-standing geocentric theory that placed the earth and, by implication, human beings at the center of the universe. The creation and testing of theories is an important part of any scientific enterprise, and in this book, we use two different features to enable you to understand the differences between several theories and interrogate their usefulness.

Appreciating Differing Theoretical Approaches

As will be discussed in detail in Chapter 3, theories designed to explain international relations are usually grouped within broad schools of thought such as realism, liberalism, Marxism, and constructivism. Proponents within each school make a set of assumptions about what is important, or what matters most, in international relations. Realists, for example, tend to emphasize that states use their power to pursue interests within a context of **anarchy**, in which no authoritative world government resolves disputes or compels the redistribution of resources from rich to poor states. Nation-states are ultimately on their own. Liberal thinkers see certain types of states as more conflict-prone than others and emphasize that economic interdependence brings states together and encourages peace and cooperation. Marxist thinkers view a state's economic system as the ultimate engine of its foreign relations, believing that the behavior of a capitalist state in the world arena is driven by the needs of its economic actors for markets and resources. Unlike liberals, Marxists also see international economic relations as exploitative – some states and groups within states benefit at the expense of others. Constructivist thinkers stress that ideas about how the world works – for example, whether or not slavery is seen as an acceptable social practice – shape or 'construct' international politics as much as money or armies do.

Anarchy
The fact that in international relations there is no centralized authority, no government of the whole world to adjudicate disputes among states and protect weak ones from strong ones.

None of these approaches or the theories associated with them is a clear winner in explaining the complicated world of international relations. Each approach has its strengths and weaknesses, and its scholarly proponents and detractors. Although the realist approach became dominant after World War II, today many scholars find its assumptions and theories unsatisfying. Scholars of international relations approach their field from a wide variety of perspectives (Lebow and Risse-Kappen 1995). Part of the excitement of studying international relations is to participate in this ongoing contest of arguments and theories as we try to make sense of the world around us. As a student, you should be intellectually open to, but critical of, all theories, including those seemingly favored by your text book authors (who in their professional writings frequently disagree with each other!). Beginning in Chapter 3, in each chapter a boxed feature called Differing Theoretical Approaches showcases the ongoing conversation among different theoretical traditions in international relations.

Making Connections between Theory and Practice

All students of international relations need to appreciate the links between theory and practice. One nice example of an international relations theory is Vladimir Lenin's theory of imperialism and war. We wouldn't normally consider Lenin a political scientist; he was the revolutionary leader of the Bolshevik movement that brought communists to power in Russia in 1917, beginning its transformation to the multinational empire of the Soviet Union. But Lenin analyzed international relations systematically, as a political scientist. He wrote a short book, *Imperialism: The Highest Stage of Capitalism*, that contains an elegant theory of international relations.

Imperialism
A state strategy in which one country conquers foreign lands to turn them into colonies.

Lenin was trying to understand **imperialism** – the political domination of weaker countries by stronger ones. He argued that large banks and corporations in Europe and America at the end of the nineteenth century needed new markets to maintain their economic profits. After a while, profits declined at home so they had to look abroad, where capital was scarce and investments were more profitable. To capture new markets in places like Africa, the capitalists in Germany prodded the German government to conquer some African territories, giving them exclusive colonial control over the people and resources in these territories. The British banks and corporations got their government to take similar steps, and so did the American, French, and other capitalist powers. Lenin thereby explains the **scramble for Africa**,

Scramble for Africa
The carving up of Africa by colonial powers after 1870.

Map 1.2 Imperialism and Colonialism in Africa on the Eve of World War I
During the latter part of the nineteenth century, European great powers engaged in a 'scramble for Africa.' Their motives were political, strategic, and economic; Lenin emphasized the economic motive in crafting his theory of imperialism.

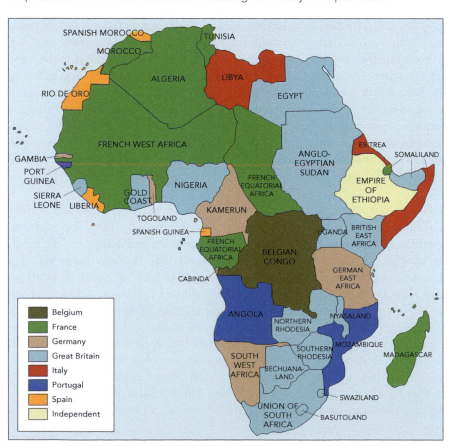

Map 1.3 Africa Today
Today's Africa is composed of sovereign states – there are no longer any colonial powers formally in charge of African territories, as there were in 1914. The impact of colonialism remains, however, in the location of borders, politics and administration, and patterns of economic dependence between African and more powerful countries in Europe and North America.

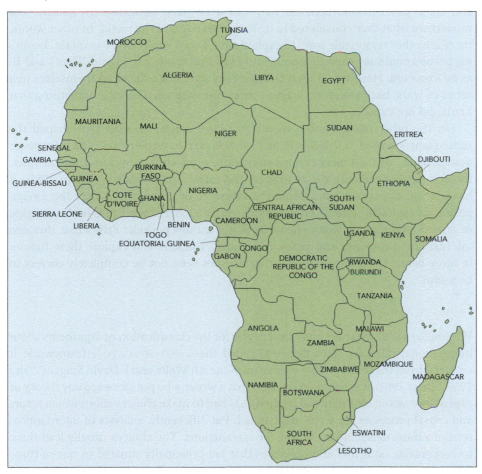

or the carving up of that continent by colonial powers after 1870, as a function of the simultaneous need of various capitalist countries to expand. When all the existing territory was taken, capitalist countries had no choice but to fight each other in order to redistribute the territory. This is how Lenin explained World War I, which was being fought when the Bolshevik revolution was carried out. Lenin also argued that capitalist countries would keep fighting each other until they exhausted themselves, allowing nation-states with economies that were less profit-driven (that is, socialist states) to take over.

Lenin's theory is important because it tries to make sense of two big outcomes in international relations: imperialism and great-power war. Theories are most useful when they are connected to practice, or when they help us understand otherwise puzzling things about the world we observe. In this text, we will not ask you to learn and debate theories for their own sake, even though some political scientists may do that. We are interested in theories in so far as they illuminate the complex world of international relations.

So, how useful is Lenin's theory? Evidence accumulated over time suggests strengths and weaknesses. Many of the overseas investments of the capitalist powers during his era were directed to other capitalist powers, rather than to capital-scarce areas like Africa. This is puzzling for a theory that emphasizes the economic incentives of conquest. Also, historians have come up with a variety of non-economic reasons for late nineteenth-century imperialism, including the propositions that colonies were a source of prestige in a great-power competition and some governments believed they had a civilized obligation to control and modernize what they considered to be backward parts of the world. In other words, there are other reasonable ways to explain what Lenin was trying to explain. Lenin's supporters could say capitalist powers did fight each other in World Wars I and II, as he expected. However, at least thus far they have not exhausted themselves in a series of wars, but have found ways to cooperate with each other – something that Lenin did not expect.

On the other hand, Lenin's theory provided crucial insights that shaped the subsequent study of our field. It has led scholars to explore the 'law of uneven development,' or the tendency for countries to grow their power at different rates, thereby putting pressure for change on the international system (Gilpin 1981). It has sparked ongoing debates about the influence of corporations over the foreign policies of capitalist states. And it reminds us that global capitalism is both an engine of growth and its own worst enemy in that it creates periodic crises that threaten international prosperity and peace. Subsequent chapters will explore these themes in more detail; the point for now is that theories need not be completely correct to be useful.

Levels of Analysis

Levels of analysis
Different ways of looking for answers to questions in international relations, generally grouped into the individual, state, and international levels.

We employ a well-regarded analytical device for the classification of arguments about international relations. This device is called the **levels-of-analysis** framework. It emerged from the writings of two scholars, Kenneth Waltz and J. David Singer (Waltz 1959; Singer 1961). It is based on the view that a writer who puts forward any theory or explanation about international relations has had to make choices about which actors and causal processes are to be emphasized. Put differently, analysts of international relations must decide *where to look* for explanations. The choices usually lead them to concentrate on actors and processes that are principally situated in one of three different categories, or levels of analysis.

Individual Level of Analysis

Many explanations and arguments in international relations focus on actors and processes that are situated at the individual level of analysis; this involves looking at the impact of individual decision makers (like presidents and their main advisors) on international relations and foreign policy. It also involves examining the impact of individual citizens (such as Raphael Lemkin, a lawyer who defined the crime of genocide, as discussed in Chapter 5), who might have a significant influence on international relations. There are several classes of individual-level theories about foreign policy and the causes of war, which we will discuss in detail in Chapters 3, 4, and 6. Some scholars believe, for example, that to understand the causes of World War II requires you to focus on the personal experiences and ambitions of Adolf Hitler, the dictator who led Germany into war.

Other studies at the individual level of analysis have focused on the psychological capacity of state leaders and on how limitations on how human beings process information, especially in moments of stress and crisis, can lead to errors in judgment.

When national leaders make these types of errors, it could lead to diplomatic crises and even war. We will also see that most feminist theories of international relations are cast at the individual level of analysis: these works, we will see in Chapters 3 and 6, propose that the upbringing of males often leads them to be more prone to risk taking and violence, including the choosing of military solutions rather than diplomacy to resolve conflicts of interest.

State Level of Analysis

The state level of analysis comprises arguments that focus on the political or economic characteristics of countries or states. A good example of a state level-of-analysis argument is **democratic peace theory**, a set of ideas developed by many international relations scholars including Michael Doyle and Bruce Russett (Doyle 1997; Russett 1993). That argument suggests that what states do abroad, including whether they get into conflict with one another, is heavily influenced by the domestic political institutions of the country. States with democratic governments, the theory suggests, are very unlikely to fight wars with one another, for reasons we will explore in Chapters 3 and 6. Another state level-of-analysis theory we will examine later in this chapter concerns economic systems: a long-standing argument by critics of capitalism is that states with capitalist economic systems at home are more likely to fight wars with one another than would be true if those same states were organized according to different principles. We will also encounter other types of argument about economic policy at the state level of analysis. The governments of countries in which multinational businesses exert a lot of influence, for example, might pursue strategies of open trade and investment because those policies support the financial interests of powerful companies.

International Level of Analysis

Finally, many arguments about world politics emphasize the international level of analysis. Countries do not exist in isolation; they interact with each other. Taken collectively, states and non-state actors coexisting and interacting at any point in history form an **international system**. That system has its own features and characteristics which themselves might strongly influence how countries behave. For example, many political scientists emphasize anarchy, or the fact that in international relations there is no centralized authority, no government of the whole world to adjudicate disputes among states and protect weak ones from strong ones. Scholars working at this level of analysis emphasize that international relations is a 'self-help' system – states in the final analysis must rely on themselves to defend their territory or political autonomy in the face of more powerful or aggressive actors. As we will

Photo 1.3 Adolf Hitler

Adolf Hitler, the head of Germany's Nazi Party, was appointed Chancellor of Germany in 1933 and quickly transformed Germany's Weimar Republic into a dictatorship. Hitler felt Germany had been humiliated by the victorious Western powers after World War I, and he believed the German people were a superior breed that required 'living space' through territorial conquest. Many view his aggressive foreign policy as the key cause of World War II.

Source: PA Images.

Democratic peace theory
The theory that democracies are unusually peaceful toward each other. Democracies, or republics, are understood as states that have elected governments, a free press, private property, and the rule of law.

International system
States and non-state actors, taken collectively, coexisting and interacting at some point in history.

discuss in Chapter 5, the United Nations might be seen as an imperfect attempt to take on some of the functions of the non-existent world government.

Here is a simple way to remember the differences across levels of analysis. Ask yourself this fundamental question about international relations: what causes war? Scholars working at the individual level might answer that war is caused by overly aggressive or ambitious leaders. Some analysts place the blame (or give credit) for the 2003 Iraq War on the personal calculations of US President George W. Bush, who may have perceived an opportunity to topple a dictator, Saddam Hussein, who tried to assassinate Bush's father, George H.W. Bush, after the Persian Gulf War of 1991. Scholars who place their 'analytical bets' at the second level provide a different answer; they argue that wars are caused by certain types of states, or by powerful groups within states (like oil companies), regardless of the particular personal ambitions or characteristics of their leaders. Scholars working at the international system level might say that it doesn't matter whether leaders are good or bad, whether states are democratic or non-democratic, or whether big companies are politically powerful or not. What matters for these scholars is the international situation in which states find themselves. Lacking any centralized governing authority, any state at any time could start a war because it feels threatened by other states, needs more resources or territory than it already has, or has some other reason to use force against some other state in the system.

None of these arguments or theories is necessarily right or wrong. Each would need to be tested logically and against the evidence that the past and present of international relations offers to us. The important first step, aided by the levels of analysis, is to categorize arguments and understand the assumptions they make about what matters most in international relations. For that reason, in each chapter that follows we employ special features to remind you to think about arguments, theories, and ideas with the aid of the levels-of-analysis framework. After every major section of each chapter, we use a box to summarize the material you have just learned from the perspective of different levels. We use simple icons in these boxes to represent the different levels visually. In some cases these boxes will display information at each of the three levels; in other cases, depending on the nature of the material covered, we will display information only with regard to one or two of the levels.

It is also important to recognize that the levels of analysis are not isolated from each other. Often a good explanation will combine or integrate ideas from different levels. For example, why do the United States and European Union have such close economic ties to each other? Part of the answer might be found at the international level: the transatlantic partners are military allies, and close military cooperation encourages and reinforces close economic cooperation. Part of the explanation may be found at the state level as well: the United States and countries of the European Union are capitalist democracies with relatively similar political systems and strong business sectors that operate across borders and thus have a mutual interest in open trade and investment.

Although in this text we focus on three basic levels of analysis, scholars sometimes make finer distinctions that incorporate additional levels. Some, for example, highlight a regional level situated analytically between the state level and the international level (Tow 2009). Regional characteristics – for example, the existence or absence of well-established regional institutions like the EU, or historical legacies, like the colonial past in Southern Africa or the memories of World War II in East Asia – might help us to understand why some parts of the world are more prone to conflict than are others.

International relations are complicated, and what happens within them often blurs or cross-cuts the neat dividing lines between different levels. The levels-of-analysis framework can never fully capture the complexity of activity on the world stage. However, it is a useful analytical tool and a starting point for helping us to make sense of that complexity.

Making Connections: Aspiration versus Reality

In trying to understand the causal motivations that drive actors at different levels we must recognize that there is a profound difference between how the world is and how we might like it to be. It is natural to approach world politics with a particular set of values or aspirations. Different people have different values, and it would be difficult to identify a set of universal values upon which everyone across time, place, and culture would agree. Nonetheless, it is probably fair to assume that most people prefer peace to war and would welcome the eradication of global poverty. Many people believe in some notion of equality for the world's population. Some people believe that countries, especially wealthy or powerful ones, have an obligation not only to their own citizens, but to people living beyond their borders as well.

These values and others are often frustrated in world politics. War and poverty are all too common. International relationships are characterized by great inequalities in power and wealth. Some people have excellent life opportunities, while others are virtually imprisoned by the difficulty of their circumstances, depending on the country or region they inhabit. The governments of wealthy countries express good intentions to share wealth and combat oppression outside their borders, and they sometimes follow through. But all too often, as we will see in Chapter 11, they fail to meet their commitments on foreign aid to poorer countries. They also often look the other way in the face of human suffering in foreign countries, as evidenced by the world's slow reaction to the humanitarian tragedies in Bosnia and Rwanda during the 1990s, in the Darfur area of Sudan during the early 2000s, and in Syria beginning in 2013.

International relations must, in the first instance, entail the study of the world not as it should be but as it is – keeping in mind that scholars and observers may not always agree on what constitutes the world 'as it is.' Our primary concern must be to describe how states actually behave and explain why they behave as they do, even if we find that behavior repulsive from our own political or moral vantage point. Explanation and prescription are separate tasks and should be treated that way. But they are also connected; understanding why states behave the way they do is a necessary first step for anyone seeking ways to change that behavior. Consider, for example, various explanations for the problem of war. If international relations research shows that democratic states are less likely than non-democratic states to fight wars in general and with each other, then the transformation of non-democratic states into democracies is a worthwhile though potentially difficult strategy in pursuit of peace. But if wars are more likely caused by other factors, such as excessive nationalism, resource scarcities, overpopulation, or competing territorial claims, then different prescriptions are in order. In each chapter below, we use a boxed feature to help you recognize the connections between aspiration and reality.

Recognizing Enduring Questions

It is natural to associate the study of international relations with current events. Daily and weekly news outlets bombard us all with reports on whether Israelis and Palestinians will be able to make peace, whether the North Korean nuclear crisis will destabilize Northeast Asia, how the European Union will negotiate the United Kingdom's exit, whether the United States and China will maintain harmonious relations, whether sub-Saharan African countries will prosper or face food shortages, and numerous other issues. This textbook will help you make sense of current international events. But international relations, and the effort to understand them, range far beyond analyses of the politics of the moment.

The *modern* international system dates from the creation of nation-states and the Peace of Westphalia of 1648, which we will discuss in greater detail in Chapter 2. But we can trace the systematic attempt to study international politics back considerably further, at least to the writings of a classic Greek thinker named Thucydides. Thucydides wrote a detailed account of the great Peloponnesian War, a conflict between two powerful Greek city-states, Athens and Sparta, and their respective allies, between 431 and 404 BCE. In writing this analysis, he said, 'My work is not a piece of writing designed to meet the taste of an immediate public, but was done to last forever' (Thucydides 1954: 48). Although the term was not used commonly back then, Thucydides was in fact acting as a political scientist. He was interested not just in reporting on the war of his day, but in understanding more generally the problem of warfare, or why humans organize themselves into groups and engage in armed conflicts. Thucydides used the experience of the Greek city-states to ponder the ethical issue of whether 'might makes right,' or whether the more powerful groups in human society have the right to govern the weaker. He drew upon Athens' failed expedition to Sicily near the end of the war to question why powerful states make foolish errors in international relations, overextending themselves in ways that ultimately lead to the collapse of their own position of power. Thucydides wrote about a set of events at a particular time, but his larger goal was to illuminate what he considered to be the core problems of international relations.

Our book proceeds in a similar spirit. We believe that the best way to unravel the complexity of international relations is to focus on what we call **enduring questions**. Enduring questions in international relations are those questions that share the common characteristics of being recurring, unresolved, and consequential. Take, for example, the question we noted earlier, 'what causes war?' That question is *recurring*: it was as relevant in the city-state politics of ancient Greece, the dynastic struggles of early modern Europe, and the colonial wars of nineteenth-century Africa as it is in the politics of the contemporary global system. It is also an *unresolved* question. Some scholars believe wars occur because human beings are inherently evil. Some think war results because there are not enough scarce resources (like oil) to satisfy everyone's desires. Others argue that certain kinds of states are more war-prone than others. There are many other reasonable answers, and, as you will find in Chapters 3 and 6, scholars have made good progress addressing this enduring question. But have not resolved it to everyone's satisfaction. Finally, enduring questions are *consequential*. They matter greatly to people, states, and the international system. Solving the problem of why war occurs would potentially affect the lives of tens of millions of people.

Enduring questions allow us to separate what is significant and foundational in the study of global politics from what is trendy or simply the 'news of the day.' The insights you gain in an international relations class should remain relevant over long periods of time, rather than expiring when the issues that were hot topics when you took the class are no longer in the news. By now you are aware that there are dozens or even hundreds of particular events unfolding in the international arena at any given time. The enduring question approach offers a navigational strategy, a series of well-worn paths to help you make your way through the maze of information and events.

Enduring questions
Questions which have engaged and challenged generations of international relations scholars and students – large, challenging questions that have stood the test of time. This book is organized around these questions.

There is no set number of enduring questions and no standard list on which everyone might agree. Different scholars would likely vary to some degree in the questions they consider to be the most enduring in the study of international relations. We have already mentioned what we consider to be one enduring question, the question of why states fight wars. Here are several other examples of enduring questions you will encounter in the chapters that follow. Box 1.1 provides a list of the enduring questions that we use to organize and motivate the study of international relations chapter by chapter.

1.1   ENDURING QUESTIONS IN INTERNATIONAL RELATIONS

Chapter 2	How did a fragmented world become a global, integrated system of states for which order is an ongoing problem?
Chapter 3	How do theoretical traditions in international relations differ on how to understand actors and their behavior on the global stage?
Chapter 4	What motivates and influences the behavior of states toward one another?
Chapter 5	How important are international laws and organizations in a world of sovereign states?
Chapter 6	Why is war a persistent feature of international relations?
Chapter 7	What factors make it more likely that states can resolve their differences and avoid war?
Chapter 8	How have weapons of mass destruction, and in particular nuclear weapons, changed the practice of international relations?
Chapter 9	How does international politics shape the global economy?
Chapter 10	How do governments manage international economic relations to further national political objectives?
Chapter 11	Does participation in the world economy help or hinder the economic development of poorer countries?
Chapter 12	Can the state continue to overcome challenges to its authority?
Chapter 13	How does the natural environment influence international relations?
Chapter 14	Will the international system undergo fundamental change in the future?

Making Connections: Then and Now

Why should you care about history? Why seek connections between the past and the present? An understanding of the past affects how people, including policy makers in different countries, think about and act in world politics. International relations in Africa, for example, are shaped by the continent's colonial legacy and the arbitrary way European governments constructed territorial boundaries. In 2002, Nigeria and Cameroon each claimed the oil-rich Bekassi Peninsula as part of its respective territory. In defending its claim before the International Court of Justice, neither country cited a cultural attachment to the land or the preferences of the local inhabitants. Instead, each produced a map from a 1913 border agreement between Germany, which had colonized present-day Cameroon, and the United Kingdom, which had colonized present-day Nigeria. The Court found Cameroon's claim (and presumably its map) more persuasive, and on that basis Nigeria agreed to cede the peninsula to its neighbor (Fisher 2012).

In 1930 the United States passed a piece of international trade legislation popularly known as the Smoot-Hawley Tariff Act (after its sponsors, Senator Reed Smoot and

Representative Willis Hawley). The act raised US tariffs, or taxes, on about 20,000 goods coming into the United States from other countries. This legislation outraged other governments, many of which responded by increasing their own tariff levels. This all happened on the eve of the Great Depression, and many economists believe that the Smoot-Hawley tariff was an important reason why the depression of the 1930s was so deep and catastrophic for the global economy (Irwin 2011).

After World War II, policy makers in the United States and Western Europe learned the lesson of Smoot-Hawley. They sought freer trade, or lower taxes on goods coming into their countries from abroad. As we shall see in Chapter 9, in difficult economic times countries are often tempted to raise barriers to imported goods in order to protect jobs at home. In the United States and elsewhere, even today, the specter of Smoot-Hawley and the Great Depression is raised in political debates as a warning to resist that temptation because in a global economy, any effort by a country to protect its markets usually leads to efforts by other countries to protect theirs, leaving all countries worse off than when they began. In short, understanding the past experience of trade policy, and how it has been interpreted by leaders over the decades, helps give us the proper context for understanding contemporary debates about foreign economic policy and global trade.

Different people may draw different lessons from major historical experiences. For some Europeans, the key lesson of fascism's rise during the 1930s was that dictators like Germany's Hitler or Italy's Mussolini needed to be confronted with military force rather than appeased though diplomacy. For other Europeans, the lesson is that economic distress leads to political extremism. Far-left and far-right political movements take power when economic cooperation breaks down and jobs vanish. For some Americans, the lesson of September 11 may be 'better safe than sorry' – it is better to preemptively attack a potential enemy now than wait and risk a costlier conflict in the future. This kind of thinking influenced American policy makers who argued in 2002 that the United States should invade Iraq and overthrow Saddam Hussein before he developed a nuclear weapons capability. For other Americans, the lesson of September 11 might be 'come home America' – the idea that the United States is overextended, and its global military presence is creating a target for terrorists worldwide. The point is not to debate the correct lesson, but to appreciate that different understandings of the experiences of the past give us insights into why states behave as they do in the present.

History gives us perspective not only on any country's behavior, but on the nature and evolution of the international system as a whole. An understanding of the past helps reveal which features of the present international order are truly novel. However, an appreciation of the past may also reveal remarkable continuities in the practice of international relations alongside large-scale changes. Consider the following news account provided by a contemporary observer of events:

> The Athenians also made an expedition against the island of Melos ... The Melians are a colony from Sparta. They had refused to join the Athenian empire like the other islanders, and at first had remained neutral without helping either side ... Now [the Athenians], encamped with force in Melian territory and, before doing any harm to the land, first of all sent representatives to negotiate.

> *Athenians*:   We do not want any trouble in bringing you into our empire and we want you to be spared for the good both of yourselves and of ourselves.
>
> *Melians*:   And how could it be just as good for us to be the slaves as for you to be the masters?

Athenians: You, by giving in, would save yourselves from disaster; we, by not destroying you, would be able to profit from you.

The Melians, left to themselves, reached a conclusion … 'We are not prepared to give up in a short moment the liberty which our city has enjoyed from its foundations for 700 years.' … The Athenian representatives then went back to the army and the Athenian generals, finding that the Melians would not submit, immediately commenced hostilities … Siege operations were carried on vigorously, and the Melians surrendered unconditionally to the Athenians, who put to death all the men of military age whom they took, and sold the women and children as slaves. Melos itself they took over for themselves …

The observer, of course, was Thucydides, and the events took place around 416 BCE (Thucydides 1954: 400–8). By today's standards, the diplomacy in this famous 'Melian dialogue' is brutally frank and the resolution – separating the men from women and children, then killing all the men and enslaving the women and children – is a form of barbarism that we associate with the distant past in human civilization. No one came to help the Melians, and Thucydides leads us to believe that what happened over Melos was not out of the ordinary.

Map 1.4 Greece in the Era of the Peloponnesian War
Four hundred years before Christ, Greek city-states interacted with each other as members of a local international system. Sparta was a powerful city-state on land, and Athens was a sea-faring city-state. The Greek city-states also interacted and battled with outsiders, most importantly the Persian Empire, which was organized on the eastern side of the Aegean Sea.

21

Today, colonialism is a thing of the past, and slavery and genocide are outlawed by international agreements. As we will see in Chapter 5, a large body of international laws and agreements has arisen to protect human rights and prosecute leaders and other individuals who commit crimes against humanity. In the current international system, we would expect that other states would react to the kind of raw aggression exhibited by the Athenians with outrage, and victims could reasonably count on members of the international community to try to deter the aggressor and come to the aid of victims if aggression took place.

But, before celebrating our modernity and moral superiority too hastily, consider this second news account:

> Bosnian Serb forces had laid siege to the Srebrenica enclave, where tens of thousands of civilians had taken refuge from earlier Serb offensives in north-eastern Bosnia ... They were under the protection of about 600 lightly armed Dutch infantry forces. Fuel was running out and no fresh food had been brought into the enclave since May.

> Serb forces began shelling Srebrenica ... The Bosnian Serb commander Ratko Mladic entered Srebrenica... accompanied by Serb camera crews. In the evening, General Mladic delivered an ultimatum that the Muslims must hand over their weapons to guarantee their lives ...
> Buses arrived to take women and children to Muslim territory, while the Serbs began separating out all men from age 12 to 77 for 'interrogation for suspected war crimes.' It is estimated that 23,000 women and children were deported in the next 30 hours ...

> Hundreds of men were held in trucks and warehouses. In the five days after Bosnian Serb forces overran Srebrenica, more than 7,000 Muslim men are thought to have been killed. (BBC News 2013; Rohde 1997)

The tragic events of Srebrenica took place not in ancient times but in 1995, during the Bosnian war that followed the collapse of the former multinational state of Yugoslavia. Neither the United Nations forces on the ground, the United States, nor members of the European Union came to the aid of the Bosnian Muslims, who were separated and slaughtered in much the same way that the Athenians dealt with the Melians more than 2,000 years earlier. Unlike their Athenian counterparts, the Serbian aggressors were put on trial and convicted of various war crimes, including genocide, at the International Criminal Tribunal for the Former Yugoslavia. On March 30, 2010, the Serbian parliament adopted a resolution that condemned and apologized for the war crimes that took place at Srebrenica, and subsequently the President of the Republic of Serbia wrote a public apology as well (Tadec 2010). The norms of the current international system certainly differ from those of the ancient Greek system; what was considered 'normal' practice back then is viewed as reprehensible and even criminal today. Nonetheless, and apology notwithstanding, the exercise of power by political actors in pursuit of their interests was tragically similar in Melos and Srebrenica.

Research Insight

Enduring questions help us connect the past to the present. We also focus on enduring questions because they help us more effectively understand the development and current status of the study of international relations. Focusing on the core problems in the field reveals what we know and do not know about international relations. In Chapter 3, we introduce the major schools of thought in the study of international relations. Each of these theoretical schools, or paradigms, is based on different assumptions about how the world works and offers different interpretations and explanations of the knottiest problems in international politics. In subsequent chapters, we explore what international relations research across different intellectual traditions has discovered in attempting to answer these questions.

We also include in each chapter a feature called 'Research Insight' that reviews what academic researchers have found on a puzzling or controversial international relations question. In Chapter 5, for example, we explore why powerful states consult the UN Security Council before going to war – even though they could certainly use military force without such authorization. In Chapter 10, we consider what political science and economics research finds about the relationship between globalization – the process of closer economic integration among countries – and inequality, both within and across countries.

In this section, we have highlighted three organizing frameworks: theories, levels of analysis, and enduring questions and three types of connections: between theory and practice, past and present, and aspirations and reality. This book will prompt you to make other connections as well; you will encounter two others regularly in the chapters ahead. One is the connection between international politics and international economics. Although economics is a separate academic discipline from political science, an understanding of international relations requires a familiarity with the basic concepts of economics and the substance of international economic issues. We highlight the interplay of politics and economics in our examination of the history, theory, and practice of international relations.

Another important connection is between domestic and international politics. The external or foreign policies of states are significantly affected by the internal or domestic politics of states. Domestic politics, in turn, are influenced by what happens in the international arena. Any successful student of international relations must also be a student of domestic politics. In Chapter 4, we explore the connections between domestic and international politics by focusing on the determinants and consequences of foreign policy behavior.

Understanding theories, using levels of analysis, recognizing enduring questions, and making connections are critical analytical tools to help guide you through the maze of international relations. In the next section we discuss something equally valuable – the ability to view world politics from multiple perspectives.

HOW CAN WE VIEW WORLD POLITICS FROM DIFFERENT PERSPECTIVES?

Do we believe the current international order is desirable, or would we like to see it changed? The answer to that question depends critically on who 'we' are. If we are the governing authority and citizens of a rich and powerful country like the United States, we might consider the contemporary international order – where we perceive our own country as near or at the top of the international hierarchy – as desirable and perhaps even just. But from the perspective of countries that lack resources or desire more influence, the international order probably looks much less attractive, and also less fair. You also must be able to identify and appreciate how different leaders, governments, and perhaps even whole nations can have differing perspectives on the same question.

Perspectives vary across nation-states and within them as well. Many observers consider what is loosely termed 'the West,' or the countries of North American and Western Europe, as the most privileged actors in world politics. But some countries in the West, for example Greece, which has been forced to endure painful economic austerity as a result of recent financial crises, may perceive themselves as far less privileged than other Western countries, for example Germany. Similarly, some groups within prosperous Western countries – think here of working-class white or minority populations within Western Europe or the United States – may not consider themselves particularly privileged even though they are citizens of countries that are on the whole wealthy and powerful. The West is neither monolithic nor homogeneous, and the same is true of other regions of the world. Africa is a diverse continent comprised of 54 countries from A to Z (Algeria to Zimbabwe) whose populations speak close to 2,000 languages. The perspective of a citizen in politically stable Botswana, where annual per capita (per person) income averages about $15,000, is likely to differ from that of a citizen of the Central African Republic, where political violence is commonplace and per capita income is only about $600 annually (Legatum Institute 2016).

It is critical to consider world politics from multiple perspectives. The study of international relations seeks to understand the behavior of states and people across borders, and that behavior is influenced by how people – and collections of people within nation-states – view the international arena and their place within it. Some years ago, the political scientist Graham Allison captured this reality with an important phrase, 'where you stand depends on where you sit' (Allison 1971). Allison was referring to relations between different parts of the US government, but his aphorism applies more widely. In other words, how you think about an issue in world politics is likely affected by the particulars of your own situation: whether you are an American, Russian, Egyptian, or Indonesian; rich or poor; male or female; and a member of the majority in a country or a racial or ethnic minority.

The same holds true for nation-states. The *national perspective* of a country is affected by a variety of factors, including historical experience. A former great power will view the world differently from a former colony of a great power. The Chinese, who for centuries enjoyed the position of political and cultural leader of Asia, have a different worldview than their neighbors, the Vietnamese, who were occupied by and resisted occupations by the Chinese, French, and Americans. The national perspective will also be shaped by racial, ethnic, and religious characteristics; a nation-state like Japan that is relatively homogeneous ethnically will likely have a different perspective on immigration, for example, than a multiethnic Indonesia or a nation-state with strongly entrenched religious factions (Christian and Muslim) like Lebanon. Size and relative power shapes perspective; the larger a nation-state is and the more power it enjoys, the more likely it is to try to shape or alter its international environment, instead of simply reacting to it. Geographic position matters as well. Whether a country views the international system as benign or threatening depends at least in part on whether it is landlocked and surrounded by larger states or situated securely behind natural barriers like oceans or mountain ranges.

In the chapters that follow we will continually remind you of the importance of viewing world politics from multiple perspectives. We begin that process here by drawing your attention to two important features of international relations.

Recognizing Great-Power Centrism

Sensitivity to multiple perspectives will help you guard against the tendency – a natural one if you happen to live in a wealthy nation such as, for example, the United States or Germany or the United Kingdom today – to view international relations solely or largely from the perspective of the relatively powerful and prosperous. Historically, the so-called great powers received a lot of attention in the study of international relations because they wielded disproportionate influence on the global stage.

Photo 1.4 Remembering the Vietnam War
On April 30, 1975, the capital of South Vietnam, then named Saigon and today called
Ho Chi Minh City, was captured by North Vietnamese forces, effectively ending the
Vietnam War. The memorial in the picture was part of celebrations in Ho Chi Minh
City marking the 40th anniversary of the end of the war.

Source: HOANG DINH NAM/AFP/Getty Images.

What is wrong with viewing international relations from the perspective of the
powerful? Nothing – if it is recognized as such and juxtaposed to other perspectives.
Americans, for example, just as citizens of any powerful and wealthy country, must
recognize that most of the people in today's world are not American and that the
United States is only one of 196 countries in the global system. The rich variation
in history, geography, identity, culture, and aspiration that characterizes the global
landscape affects international relations. If we proceed from the explicit or even
implicit assumption that one country's values, ideals, and institutions are universal,
or that the rest of the world is simply an imperfect replica of that country, then we
are going to miss the critical insights that the study of international relations offers.

This point was driven home – painfully to Americans – in the aftermath of
September 11, 2001. One immediate reaction of many ordinary US citizens to these
tragic events was to ask 'who are these people, and why do they hate us?' Understanding
the answer requires an appreciation of the differences between organized, non-state
terrorist entities like Al Qaeda, the much larger group of Muslims living in the Middle
East and Southwest Asia who may both admire and resent the United States, but
are not drawn to violence to express their sentiment or advance their interests, and
non-democratic regimes, like that in Saudi Arabia, who have cooperative relations
with the United States but do not command the support of large segments of their
own populations. Americans have also come to understand that the United States
is resented by some simply because it is so powerful; by others because it represents
an all-pervasive, modern consumer culture; or also due to the fact that US foreign
policies have traditionally supported repressive governments in the region and have
favored the interests of one party in a conflict in the Middle East, Israel, over the
interests of other parties, such as the Palestinians.

One of the great students of international relations, Hans Morgenthau, proposed
after World War II his four fundamental rules of diplomacy. One rule directed every
nation-state to 'look at the political scene from the point of view of other nations'

(Morgenthau 1985). His advice may be tempting to ignore if you happen to live in stable, influential, prosperous, and secure countries. But most people do not, and thus it is vital for students of international politics to recognize and analyze the subject from multiple vantage points.

Recognizing Cleavages within the International System

Sensitivity to multiple perspectives will also allow you to recognize that there are always key divisions, or cleavages, within any international system. In the current international system, for example, there persists a division between rich and poor, or **developed** and **developing countries**, particularly on international economic issues. In developed states, where standards of living are higher, people worry that jobs are and will continue to be lost in international trade to developing states, where labor is much cheaper. American workers worry about competition from China and Mexico, while German and French workers worry about competition from labor in Greece or Turkey. Developed countries also feel that developing ones should do their part to advance international economic cooperation by opening their markets to the products of the North. The view from the developing world is different. Developing states point out that it is difficult to develop in a world economy dominated by established, rich states. Developing economies want special exceptions in international trade and they want access to developed-country markets, like agriculture, even if the developed countries do not have symmetrical access to their markets. These debates, discussed in Chapter 11, are played out in various international forums, such as the United Nations and the World Trade Organization.

There are, of course, different perspectives within developed and developing countries as well. In the United States, people tend to believe the government should play a more modest role in influencing the international or domestic economy than is typically expected in European countries and Japan. In the less developed world, countries that are primarily agriculture exporters (like Ghana, which exports cocoa) view the world economy differently than oil producers and exporters (like Venezuela or Kuwait). Exporters of manufactured goods, like South Korea or Taiwan, will have a different perspective on trade negotiations as well.

There are also developed-developing country divisions on environmental issues. The United States refused to ratify a global agreement on carbon emissions, the Kyoto Protocol, because it felt the burden of reducing emissions was not shared equally among all countries, including big developing countries like China. In 2017, the United States announced its intention to withdraw from a subsequent agreement, the Paris Climate Accord. Developing countries argue that the existing rich countries developed without worrying about the natural environment, and now expect today's poorer countries to inhibit their own development due to environmental problems (which poorer countries see as caused by the advanced industrial

Developed countries Wealthy countries with advanced economies.

Developing countries Poor countries with small economies whose residents have not, on average, attained the living standards typically enjoyed by residents of wealthy countries.

Photo 1.5 Producing Cocoa in Ghana
A farmer in Ghana inspects drying cocoa seeds that are laid out on wooden beds within a cocoa plantation.

Source: Pixabay/dghchocolatier.

part of the world). Developing countries like India and China also demand aid and technology from advanced industrial countries to assist them in limiting emissions and adapting to the impact of climate change. These debates will be discussed in detail in Chapter 13.

The divisions between developed and developing countries have been exacerbated by **globalization**, the process by which countries of the world are becoming more tightly connected to each other economically and even culturally. Globalization has enabled developing countries such as China to grow rapidly and pull hundreds of millions of people out of poverty. But it has also increased inequality in the developed world, as better educated workers have enjoyed sharp increases in income and wealth while the less educated have faced intense job competition from around the world and have seen their wages stagnate. As we explore in Chapter 2, a backlash against globalization helped pave the way for **Brexit**, the decision by the United Kingdom following a popular referendum to withdraw from the European Union. Concerns about the impact of globalization also contributed to the 2016 election of Donald Trump, a political outsider who promised to build a wall between the United States and Mexico and to renegotiate or abandon trade agreements that from his perspective advantaged foreign workers over American ones.

There *used* to be an important cleavage in international relations between East and West. During the Cold War (1945–89), the world was divided between communist and non-communist countries. The Western countries viewed themselves as defending the rights of the individual and political and economic freedoms. The communist countries, generally located in the eastern part of Europe but also in Asia and Central America, viewed capitalism as exploitative and saw themselves defending social values, such as full employment and a more equitable distribution of income and wealth. As Chapter 2 explores, each side in this conflict viewed the other as a threat and tried to enlist the support of neutral countries to its cause. The East–West division in world politics ended in 1991, with the collapse of the Soviet Union, the leader of the Eastern side.

The existence of cleavages or divisions among states within any international system leads us to what historically has been a vexing problem in international politics, that of **dissatisfied states**. Dissatisfied states are those who feel an existing international system threatens their values, compromises their interests, or blocks their aspirations. These states may remain frustrated, patiently build their power, or become aggressive to advance their relative positions. Germany, Japan, and Italy after World War I are classic cases of dissatisfied states. Italy desired colonial possessions befitting its self-image as a great power. Germany sought respect and influence after what it considered the humiliation of the settlement that ended World War I. Japan, a vulnerable island economy, desired economic security, which its leaders believed could be best achieved by occupying its resource-rich neighbors. The dissatisfaction of these states and their determination to rectify it was an important cause of World War II.

A dissatisfied state is potentially dangerous, but it is not always easy to recognize. States may act aggressively because they are dissatisfied and intent on undermining the international system, or because they feel threatened and insecure. During the Cold War, policy makers and analysts in the Western countries continually debated whether the Soviet Union was a dissatisfied state intent on world domination, or a troubled and insecure great power that needed to control its immediate neighborhood because it felt threatened by a more technologically advanced set of Western countries. The debate was important. If the Soviet Union was primarily aggressive, it needed to be contained; if it was primarily insecure, then reassurance and cooperation might be the more appropriate foreign policy. The failure to contain an aggressive country

Globalization
The ongoing process of international economic and technological integration, made possible by advances in transportation and communication.

Brexit
The 'British exit,' or decision made by British citizens in a popular referendum to have the United Kingdom leave the European Union.

Dissatisfied states
States who feel that their influence, status, and material benefits should be higher than what they are actually achieving.

could lead to trouble if that country believed itself free to dominate others. But an aggressive response to an insecure country could be provocative, reinforcing fear and insecurity and leading to a conflict that perhaps neither side wanted. International relations scholars refer to this general problem of how states interpret and react to the intentions of others as the **security dilemma**. Although it is not always easy to distinguish dissatisfied states from defensive states, it is important to do so because the stakes are very high. In today's international system, many analysts are debating the extent to which China is (or will become) a dissatisfied state that will eventually disrupt international order regionally or globally, a defensive state mainly seeking to resolve its internal problems and command a degree of international respect, or a satisfied state content to accept the current rules of the international order. Analysts who view China as dissatisfied point to its assertive pursuit of territorial claims in the East and South China Seas and to the nationalist rhetoric of its leader, Xi Jinping. Analysts who view China as a satisfied state point to its integration into the Western-dominated world economy and its willingness to participate in international organizations.

Security dilemma
A situation in which a state takes actions to become more secure yet ends up becoming less secure due to the reaction it provokes in other states.

In the current international system, it is also plausible to consider Russia a dissatisfied state. Russia ruled the Soviet Union as one of only two superpowers at the top of the international hierarchy during the Cold War. When the Cold War ended and the Soviet empire collapsed, Russia experienced economic deprivation and a sharp loss in international prestige and influence. Vladimir Putin, Russia's leader since 2000, has sought to centralize his authority at home, reinvigorate a sense of Russian patriotism, and restore Russia's influence abroad. In 2014 Putin annexed Crimea, a region of Ukraine (now an independent country that was part of the former Soviet Union), of strategic, historical, and cultural significance to Russia. Putin sent Russian forces, the so-called little green men, without official uniforms and insignia, into other parts of Ukraine, and also intervened militarily, on the side of dictator Basharal-Assad, in Syria. Russia is widely suspected of using cyber-attacks to meddle in democratic elections abroad, including in the 2016 US presidential election.

A similar debate is taking place at a regional level, concerning the intentions and aspirations of Iran in the Middle East and North Korea in East Asia. To some, Iran is a disruptive force seeking weapons of mass destruction to threaten Israel and Sunni-controlled regimes (Iran is controlled by Shiites) in the Gulf region. To others, Iran is an insecure middle power that feels threatened by the world's dominant power, the United States, and its powerful regional ally, Israel. The United States today is closely associated politically and militarily with Iran's traditional enemy, Iraq. Iran and Iraq fought a costly and bloody war throughout the 1980s. The appropriate foreign policy depends, to some extent, on whether one has a clear understanding of the perspective of the country in question.

The same point applies to North Korea, an isolated Communist country ruled since 2011 by a boisterous young dictator, Kim Jong-un. In defiance of United Nations resolutions and sanctions, North Korea has developed and tested nuclear weapons and has launched ballistic missiles over the territory of neighboring Japan. The United States, Japan, and South Korea view North Korean behavior as aggressive and provocative and as the greatest source of possible conflict in East Asia. For their part, North Korea perceives these capitalist democracies, and especially the United States, as posing an existential threat to the survival of their political system. North Korea believes the possession of a nuclear arsenal will help to deter these hostile and more powerful adversaries.

In the subsequent chapters, we will remind you continually to view world politics from different perspectives, recognize great-power centrism, and appreciate cleavages within the past and present international system. These insights, along with our emphasis on different theoretical perspectives, the levels of analysis framework, and the enduring questions approach provide you with critical tools to understand international relations.

LOOKING AHEAD

This textbook is divided into four sections. In Part I, Chapter 2, we provide the historical background necessary to appreciate enduring questions and give context to contemporary international politics. In Chapter 3 we introduce the basic theories and concepts in the study of international relations. Chapter 4 moves to the state level of analysis to explore statecraft and explain the foreign policy strategies adopted by different countries. Chapter 5 is focused at the international level and introduces international laws and organizations as key features of the international system. Taken together, these discussions provide a 'toolbox' that will help you make sense of the practice of international politics described and analyzed in subsequent chapters.

Part II is devoted to an introduction to the issues of war and peace, or what is known in international relations as the subfield of security studies. In Chapters 6 and 7, we discuss the causes of war, and the mechanisms in the international system that lead states to resolve disputes peacefully. In Chapter 8, we analyze the special problem of weapons of mass destruction, and their impact on the theory and practice of international relations.

Part III turns to the relationship between international politics and economics. In Chapter 9, we provide the basic building blocks of the world economy, focusing on trade and money and the global institutions of the world economy. This basic background is critical for you, as a student of international relations, to grasp before diving more deeply into how politics and economics interact. In Chapter 10, we examine foreign economic policy, and how governments use international economic relations to further their political objectives. Chapter 11 investigates the special problems and opportunities developing countries encounter as they seek to associate with, but not be overwhelmed by, the global economy.

Part IV looks at emerging challenges to the international system and world of nation-states. In Chapter 12, we examine the role of non-state actors, such as terrorists, warlords, and drug dealers, who have *privatized* political violence and, in some cases, challenged the authority of sovereign states. We also explore the obligation of the members of the international community to protect people whose human rights are threatened by their own governments, or who are the victims of war or natural disaster. We then turn in Chapter 13 to international environmental problems and the response of states, individually and collectively. In conclusion, Chapter 14 challenges you to draw on what you have learned and think creatively about the future of international relations. We provide summary observations and explore six alternate visions of the future world order.

Each chapter also pays particular attention to the major frameworks introduced above – the enduring question, the levels of analysis, making connections, and viewing world politics from multiple perspectives. We also constantly challenge you with discussion questions, which we hope will help you structure your thinking about the material we cover in the text. As you explore the enduring problems and contemporary texture of international relations, we invite you at each step to engage the material with a critical eye. We ask you to challenge yourself by drawing your own conclusions about the problems of war and conflict in international relations, as well as the opportunities for cooperation and the attainment of international peace in this, your twenty-first century.

STUDY QUESTIONS

1. In what ways do you think international relations affect your life?
2. What do you most want to learn about as you read this book and take what is likely to be your first and hopefully not only course in international relations?
3. From your viewpoint, which of the enduring questions about international relations discussed in this chapter, and pursued throughout this book, are the most interesting and important? Why?
4. What perspective do you think you are bringing to this course and the study of international relations? That is, when you think about international relations, do you do so from the viewpoint of a citizen of a particular country, as a young person, or as a male or female? What are the stakes and interests you bring to your study of international relations? How might that perspective be influencing the way you approach the field?

FURTHER READING

Axelrod, Robert (2006) *The Evolution of Cooperation*, rev. edn (New York: Basic Books). This is a classic social science study that has direct implications for international relations. Axelrod examines how cooperation emerges among self-interested actors – and how they resist the temptation to cheat each other – even when there is no central authority to police their behavior.

Drezner, Daniel (2011) *Theories of International Politics and Zombies* (Princeton: Princeton University Press). This is an unusual and irreverent introduction to international relations theories. Drezner goes through a variety of the leading theoretical traditions in international politics and shows how each might help us explain and react to the threat of a zombie invasion. An easy way to digest theory!

Jervis, Robert (1976) *Perception and Misperception in World Politics* (Princeton: Princeton University Press). In this classic study of foreign policy and international relations, Jervis explains when and why the perceptions of world leaders diverge from reality. The consequences of misperception may be conflict and sometimes inadvertent war.

Keck, Margaret and Kathryn Sikkink (eds) (1998) *Activists Beyond Borders: Advocacy Networks in International Politics* (Ithaca: Cornell University Press). This book nicely illustrates the importance of non-state actors in international relations. Keck and Sikkink and their contributors show how and why coalitions form across borders to address problems such as slavery, women's suffrage, human rights, and environmental degradation.

Kupchan, Charles (2012) *No One's World: The West, the Rising Rest, and the Coming Global Turn* (Oxford: Oxford University Press). Kupchan sees the Western-dominated international order coming to an end as other rising states follow their own political and economic paths. No country or countries will dominate the world as the West did – the future international order will be 'no one's' world.

Mahbubani, Kishore (2004) *Can Asians Think?* (Singapore: Marshall Cavendish). This book of essays is a nice application of the need to view the world from multiple perspectives. Mahbubani is critical of the idea that the values of Western civilization are universal, and argues that other civilizations make important though at times underappreciated contributions to the human endeavor.

 Visit **www.macmillanihe.com/Grieco-IntroIR-2e** to access extra resources for this chapter, including:
- Chapter summaries to help you review the material
- Multiple choice quizzes to test your understanding
- Flashcards to test your knowledge of the key terms in this chapter
- Outside resources, including links to contemporary articles and videos, that add to what you have learned in this chapter

Part I

Foundations of International Relations

Author Debates

 Visit **www.macmillanihe.com/Grieco-IntroIR-2e** to watch the authors debating key issues discussed in this Part.

Video 1: Why do we have so many theories of international relations?

Video 2: Do international laws and international organizations promote peace, prosperity, and justice?

2

The Emergence of a Global System of States, 1500–Today

Enduring question

How did a fragmented world become a global, integrated system of states for which order is an ongoing problem?

Chapter Contents

Learning Objectives

By the end of this chapter, you will be able to:

→   Understand why history matters to international relations.

→   Describe how a system of states emerged in Europe and how those states came to control much of the world.

→   Know and assess the causes and global political effects of World Wars I and II, which ended Europe's rule over much of the world.

→   Recognize why the Cold War emerged after 1945, understand its impact on international relations, and appreciate why it ended unexpectedly between 1988 and 1991.

→   Understand the perspective of developing countries seeking to prosper economically and exercise political autonomy after World War II.

→   Have a grasp of the key features of the contemporary global system.

Today's international system is a product of historical change. Some changes have been recent: while 51 independent states formed the United Nations in 1945, 193 states were members in 2017. Other changes have taken place over centuries: China was perhaps the most advanced state on earth in 1500, it then experienced decline and even subjugation by Japan and Western states during the 1900s, and during the past three decades it has once more become a global powerhouse.

How did we come to live in a system of states? We address this important question in this chapter. We will also highlight in this chapter the historical issue of international order, that is, a period of sustained peace and cooperation among states. We will see below that international order can be fragile and that war, while rare, is an ever-present threat to international order. Why, we ask below, do peace and order often share the stage of history with violence and disorder?

To address these questions thoroughly we need to explore different theories of international relations as well as contemporary international affairs. This we will do in the chapters to follow. But to address these questions we need in the first instance to know the essential features of international history.

There are three more specific reasons we need to understand international history. First, we are still living with its consequences, whether they are, for example, poverty and civil strife in sub-Saharan Africa, Palestinian–Israeli violence, or American debates about US activism in global affairs. Second, scholars often use historical materials to test theories of international relations, and if we know the basics of international history then we will be in a much stronger position to assess those tests. Third, as we discussed in Chapter 1, leaders, officials, and media commentators often invoke historical analogies in support of their policy positions; only if we know international history can we assess the utility of such analogies that draw from the past in dealing with issues in the present.

Humans began to live together in territorial entities as early as the 6th millennium BCE in what is today's China, in numerous kingdoms in ancient Mesopotamia (today's Iraq and Syria) by the middle of the 4th millennium BCE, and in ancient Egypt during the first half of the 3rd millennium BCE. Those territorial entities engaged in commerce and exchanges of people and ideas but also often formed offensive and defensive alliances directed against each other, and they sometimes conquered one another or their neighbors. As we discussed in Chapter 1, Greek city-states formed a vibrant international system during the 5th century BCE. Where, then, should we begin a discussion of the historical roots of today's international relations? We suggest – knowing that any choice is likely to cause us to overlook important events – that a helpful point at which to begin our brief discussion of world history is approximately the year 1500 CE. At that time, European political entities began to undergo a political process both domestically and internationally that, over a period of four centuries, produced our modern system of states.

The chapter is divided into sections, looking at periods of historical development and charting a course from 1500 to the present day. The first provides a snapshot-view of the main political entities in 1500 in different parts of the world, including those in Asia, Africa, the Near East, the Americas, and Europe. Second, we examine the process, from 1500 to 1900, by which European states emerged, formed a regional state system, and by their actions and interactions with other parts of the world also laid the foundations for today's global international system. The next stage focuses on the years from 1900 to 1945, which began with Europe at the pinnacle of its power and ended, after two world wars, with the diminution of European global influence, the rise of the United States and the Soviet Union, and the birth of scores of new states and the creation of today's truly global system of states. The fourth section examines how the struggle between the Soviet Union and the United States emerged and shaped world politics between 1945 and 1990 in a period known as the Cold War. We then consider the postwar world from the perspective of new and developing countries in the international system, and finally describe the end of the Cold War and key features of today's contemporary global system.

STARTING POINT: THE WORLD IN 1500

Consider the world in the year 1500. As can be seen in Map 2.1, except for a nascent system of states in Europe, much of the eastern hemisphere consisted not of states, but of **empires**. An empire is a political entity that contains a substantial geographical space, often many different peoples, and over which a single powerful ruler governs. For example:

Empires
Political entities that contain a substantial geographical space, often many different peoples, and over which a single powerful ruler governs.

- **China** in 1500 possessed a population of about 300 million, and the largest and most advanced economy on earth (Maddison 2006: 261, 263). It had a relatively coherent empire by 1500 and had been ruled for some time by a succession of imperial dynasties (Roberts and Westad 2013: 437–57), that is, an order in which members of a given extended family and their associates, over a number of generations, maintain power within an empire.
- **Japan** in 1500 had a population of about 15 million and, while it had an emperor, the country was fragmented into small political entities, led by local military leaders (Maddison 2006: 241, 263). This changed in the early 1600s: a warlord, Tokugawa Ieyasu, attained control over most of Japan, and the resulting family-based ruling dynasty, the Tokugawa Shogunate, governed Japan until 1868 (Roberts and Westad 2013: 465–68).

Map 2.1 The Eastern Hemisphere in 1500
In 1500, much of the Eastern hemisphere, such as in China as well as in Africa, consisted of large empires; in Western Europe a nascent system of independent states was forming.

Source: Inspired by Thomas Lessman, Talessman's Atlas of World History. Maps are available for free at www.WorldHistoryMaps.info.

Photo 2.1 Remnants of the Aztec Empire
Detail of Aztec crocodile heads on the Temple of Quetzalcoatl at Teotihuacan, near Mexico City, Mexico.

Source: Harvey Meston/Getty Images.

- **India** in 1500 was home to a culturally and economically advanced population of about 110 million. During the first half of the 1500s, successive members of the Mughal dynasty, Muslim descendants of the Mongol conqueror Genghis Khan, conquered and politically unified most of India, and continued to rule much of the Indian subcontinent until the early 1700s (Roberts and Westad 2013: 537–44; Maddison 2006: 241, 263).
- **The Ottoman Empire** began when Muslim Turkish tribes entered Asia Minor (modern-day Turkey) in the eleventh century; by the mid-1400s, they conquered Asia Minor and, in 1453, the capital city of the Byzantine Empire, Constantinople (Crowley 2005). By the 1600s, the Ottoman Empire included all of Asia Minor, the Balkans region, a good part of central Europe, the Middle East, and North Africa (Roberts and Westad 2013: 397–405).
- **Sub-Saharan Africa** in 1500 was home to perhaps 38 million people (Maddison 2006: 239). Sub-Saharan Africa and northern Africa at that time enjoyed substantial economic activity. To the west, the Mali Empire was the largest African political community during the 1300s and the 1400s; it was replaced by the Songhai Empire during the 1500s.
- **Europe** in 1500 consisted of perhaps 82 million people in Western Europe, Eastern Europe, and what is today western Russia. Dynastic families, such as the Valois in France, the Tudors in England, and the Habsburgs in a territory from Austria to Belgium and even Spain, governed these early European states, which we call **dynastic states**. Dynastic states, it should be noted, did not develop in all the main parts of Western Europe during this period. Italian city-states remained independent of one another, and some 300 independent political entities, such as duchies (an area occupied by a duke or duchess) populated German-speaking lands in central Europe.
- **The Americas** in 1500 (see Map 2.2) was most populated in today's Mexico (perhaps 7.5 million), Peru (4 million), and Brazil (1 million); another 2 million people lived in what are now the United States and Canada, with additional populations on the Caribbean islands (Maddison 2006: 233, 243, 263). Two main empires were in existence around 1500 in the Americas: the Aztec Empire, in the central part of today's Mexico, and the Incan Empire, stretching some 2,500 miles along the Andes mountain range in the western part of South America (Roberts and Westad 2013: 475–81).

Dynastic states
States ruled by 'imperial dynasties' or 'dynastic families,' in which members of a given extended family, over a number of generations, maintain power within a state or empire.

The world of 1500 was fragmented into relatively discrete regions characterized by empires or, in Europe, a complex tapestry of dynastic states, city-states, or small duchies. Within these discrete regions there were important inter-entity interactions, and in some cases highly limited contacts with one another, such as trade between Europeans and Chinese merchants. Yet, today we live in a world of states with

Map 2.2 Inca, Mayas, and Aztec Empires in the Western Hemisphere in 1500
In the year 1500, there were two important empires in the Western hemisphere: those of the Inca and the Aztecs, and remnants of a third, the Maya.

extensive international relationships. What brought those states into existence? How did they encounter one another and form the more coherent network of international relationships that we see today? Those are the questions we take up in the next section.

Levels of Analysis *The World of 1500*		
👤 Individual	👥 State	🌐 International
Most individuals in 1500 played little or no role in the governance of the entities in which they lived.	Large regions of the eastern and western hemispheres in the 1500s consisted of empires.	By 1500 a nascent system of dynastically ruled states came into existence in Europe.
	Dynastic states, city-states, and other small entities such as duchies governed Europe in the 1500s.	
	China was a consolidated state in 1500.	

THE FORMATION OF THE INTERNATIONAL POLITICAL SYSTEM, 1500–1900

European states set the world in motion toward the system of states in which we all still live today. To understand this process, we need to examine how a system of states emerged in Europe between 1500 and 1815. We also need to see how and why these

European states came to control the Americas, sub-Saharan Africa, and the Indian subcontinent, and how they made similar inroads in China and the Ottoman Empire, but not Japan.

A State System Emerges in Western Europe

From the 1400s to the 1600s, a state system, or a group of competing states, gradually came into being in Europe (Dehio 1962; Tilly 1975; Tilly 1990; Kaiser 2000). It emerged from two sources. The first was European **feudalism,** which is a system in which individuals acted as 'vassals' and received land in exchange for swearing loyalty to specific high-ranking leaders (e.g., counts, dukes) and, at the apex of the system, the king. Second, in German-speaking areas in Central Europe, a loose and largely symbolic association termed the Holy Roman Empire was controlled by the Habsburg dynasty by the early 1500s.

The formation of the European state system was the unintended consequence of a succession of failed efforts over 300 years by powerful European leaders to use war to establish control and create an imperial order over the European continent. Those leaders with imperial ambitions catalyzed the historical process by which independent, interacting, and often competing states were created in Europe. The resulting states, and the state system they formed, became entrenched, producing the nucleus for today's global system of states.

The imperial efforts were made by the Habsburg Emperor Charles V between 1519 and 1556; his son Philip II during the late 1500s; the Austrian and Spanish Habsburgs during the Thirty Years War of 1618–48; France's King Louis XIV between 1667 and 1715; and France again between 1789 and 1815, most spectacularly after General Napoleon Bonaparte seized power in 1799 in a military coup and made himself emperor in 1804. The last bid was made by Germany under Adolph Hitler between 1933 and 1945, which we will cover later in this chapter. Leaders of other European states formed alliances and a **balance of power** to counter these efforts, and these balancing alliances ultimately defeated each bid for empire.

One such example of a network of alliances took place from the 1520s to the 1550s, with France at its core. To prevent the Habsburgs from attaining military and political hegemony in Europe, France allied on the one hand with a host of small German principalities, and on the other hand with the Ottoman Turks. This network of alliances raises interesting questions about the importance of identity – in this instance, religious identity – in foreign policy, and we pursue this issue in detail in Box 2.1. For the moment, consider this: for almost seven centuries – from the Muslim conquest of Spain in the eighth century, through the Christian crusades in the Levant in the eleventh, twelfth, and thirteenth centuries, through the subsequent rise of the Ottomans – Muslim states and rulers posed a fundamental challenge to Europe and its states and monarchs. Yet, notwithstanding that common challenge from the Muslim world, Catholic France, determined not to be dominated politically by Habsburg co-religionists, during the first half of the 1500s crafted a formal military alliance with the Muslim Ottoman Turks, and worked with that country against their mutual enemy, the Habsburgs. In the same vein, fearful that Emperor Charles V would bring Europe under Habsburg control, Catholic France supported Protestant German princes in their initial rebellion against the Habsburgs in the first half of the 1500s. Later, during the Thirty Years War of 1618–48, Catholic France again intervened on behalf of the Protestants against the Austrian and Spanish Habsburgs, at first providing subsidies to the Dutch Republic and Sweden, and later going directly to war against the Habsburgs. Thus, French monarchs demonstrated repeatedly over

Feudalism
A system in which individuals act as 'vassals' and receive land in exchange for swearing loyalty to specific high-ranking leaders (e.g., counts, dukes) and, at the apex of the system, the king.

Balance of power
Process by which a state or coalition of states increase their capabilities to prevent the dominance of an opposing state or group of states.

a period of 150 years that they were willing and able to put aside differences with two communities with which they had the most fundamental of differences in identity – Muslim Ottomans and Protestant Germans – to prevent the establishment of a Habsburg empire in Europe.

The Thirty Years War was concluded in 1648 by a series of agreements that have come to be known as the **Peace of Westphalia**. Each signatory to the treaties, including the Germanic states that previously had at least a nominal duty to defer to the Habsburg Holy Roman Emperor, was now a free agent, including on such important matters as the establishment of Catholicism or Protestantism within their jurisdictions as the state-sponsored religion, and the crafting of alliances and other agreements with other states. We live in a system of sovereign states over which there is no higher political authority, and to describe this system scholars of international relations often say that we live in a **Westphalian state system**. Sovereignty, as we discussed in Chapter 1, implies that each state has political authority within its territory and each can establish its own foreign policy toward other states. The inclusion of these two provisions in the Peace of Westphalia recognized and formalized the existence of what in fact was already an interstate system in Europe. That system of states, we will see below, gradually expanded to include the entire globe.

Peace of Westphalia
Treaties that ended the Thirty Years War and divided Europe into sovereign states independent of higher authorities.

Westphalian state system
The modern state system in which each state is sovereign, with no higher authority (such as a church or empire).

2.1   MAKING CONNECTIONS
Theory and Practice

Religious Identity and the Franco-Ottoman Military Alliance

Theory: States with Common Identities Should Find Cooperation Easier than States with Conflicting Identities

In Chapter 3, we will explore different theories of international relations, including constructivist theory, which suggests that belief systems influence the foreign policy decisions and actions of national leaders. We might expect then that state leaders sharing similar worldviews, including religious beliefs, find it easier to cooperate with each other than leaders with radically different worldviews.

Practice: The Alliance between Catholic France and the Muslim Ottoman Empire

After France lost several battles against Habsburg military forces, and Francis I, the French King, was taken prisoner for a time after a major defeat at the hands of the Habsburgs in 1525, the French King attained a military alliance with Suleiman the Magnificent, leader of the Ottoman Turkish Empire. In 1531, King Francis explained to the Venetian ambassador why he had aligned France with the Ottoman Turks. He said that 'I cannot deny that I wish to see the Turk all-powerful and ready for war, not for himself – for he is an infidel and we are all Christians – but to weaken the power of the emperor, to compel him to make major expenses, and to reassure all the other governments who are opposed to such a formidable enemy.' That is, notwithstanding the fact that they were both largely Catholic, the drive by the Habsburgs for European domination combined with the rejection by France of such domination caused bitter enmity between the two, to the extent that even though they came from mutually hostile religious traditions, France worked with the Ottoman Empire against the Habsburgs.

Source: the quotation is from Crowley (2008): 66.

Students should be careful not to conclude that the European state system was launched *in full* by the Peace of Westphalia in 1648. The nascent interstate system arguably came into being as early as 1555, with the Peace of Augsburg. At that time, German princes who had been fighting the Holy Roman Emperor Charles V compelled the latter in the Augsburg settlement to allow the princes, and not the Emperor, to decide the religion of their subjects within their respective principalities. The princes claimed and to some degree attained an essential element of domestic sovereignty (de Carvalho, Leira, and Hobson 2011).

The Peace of Westphalia may have been a turning point in establishing the idea of sovereign states, but it did not end the quest by particular European states to establish an empire in that part of the world. In 1672, 1681, and in 1700, France's King Louis XIV launched or became involved in large European wars as a part of his strategy to establish French hegemony over the continent. In each case, Holland played a key role in organizing a counter-coalition against France, and among other allies the Dutch were successful in recruiting and working with two of their former enemies, the Austrians and, perhaps most remarkably, their former masters (and deeply hated because of that) the Spanish. France, financially exhausted by its European wars and for its support of the Americans in their revolution against Great Britain between 1776 and 1783, itself succumbed to revolution in 1789. French revolutionary governments, and then France under Napoleon Bonaparte, waged a sequence of wars against European states – the former known as the French Revolutionary Wars of 1792–1802, the latter the Napoleonic Wars of 1803–15 – because of which France came very close to establishing hegemony over much of Europe. However, Napoleon was defeated in 1814 and 1815 as a result of an alliance of a democratizing England and an autocratic Prussia, Russia, and Austria.

Concert of Europe
An agreement among the great powers, beginning in the early nineteenth century, to maintain order collectively within Europe.

In pointed reaction to the French Revolutionary and Napoleonic wars, the allies Britain, Prussia, Austria, and Russia agreed in 1814–15 to establish a **Concert of Europe** (Albrecht-Carrie 1968; Ikenberry 2001; Lascurettes 2017). The Concert of Europe consisted of an agreement among these great powers to meet in what were called congresses, to discuss possible threats to the European status quo and, where feasible, to act in concert to maintain peace and order within Europe. That is, they sought to create an international order; a period of sustained peace and cooperation among the great powers (although not necessarily between great and lesser powers).

The Concert had several initial successes. At a congress in 1818 that met in Aix-la-Chapelle (today's Aachen, Germany), these great powers agreed to a withdrawal of foreign military forces from France and recognized France, by then firmly under a reinstalled monarchical rule, as a full-fledged member of the community of European great powers. In addition, in 1820, Austria, Russia, and Prussia (Britain and France sent only official observers) met as a congress in Troppau (then controlled by Austria, now in the Czech Republic) and accepted an Austrian plan to use military force to suppress a liberal (and thus antimonarchical) rebellion in Naples. At a congress in Verona in 1822, all the major powers except Britain agreed not to support a Greek independence movement as well as to authorize a French military campaign in Spain, which took place in 1823, again to suppress an antimonarchical insurrection.

The congresses at Troppau in 1820 and Verona in 1822 underscored the point that the Concert had become by then in substantial measure a diplomatic instrument by which the states most committed to the retention of absolutist monarchies within Europe, that is, Austria, Prussia, and Russia, could coordinate their efforts toward that end. Britain and ultimately France became alienated from and less active in the Concert. In addition, the Concert system failed to resolve a profound diplomatic dispute between France and Britain on the one hand and Russia on the other, involving Russia's movement against a progressively weaker Ottoman Empire. The dispute ended in the Crimean War of 1854–56 between Russia and a coalition consisting of Britain, France, the Ottomans, and the Kingdom of Sardinia-Piedmont. Moreover, the Concert played no role in managing the outbreak or suppression of attempted liberal rebellions in 1848 in France, Germany, Hungary, and numerous Austrian-controlled parts of Italy. It was also absent in the European diplomacy and ultimately the wars that led to the emergence in the 1860s and early 1870s of a unified Italy and a unified Germany. Germany under Chancellor Otto Von Bismarck gestured toward the idea of a continuing Concert of Europe when he organized the Congress of Berlin in 1878, discussed below, to bring to a conclusion a war between Russia and the Ottoman Empire. Yet, the congress system and the Concert faded into irrelevance by the turn of the century and played no discernible role managing subsequent diplomatic tensions in Europe that ended in 1914 with the onset of World War I. Despite the Concert's limitations, however, the idea had been laid that an association of states, led by the great powers, might steer international relations in a more peaceful direction. We will see this concept reappear with the ill-fated League of Nations and, in our own times, the United Nations.

European Pursuit of Foreign Empire

From the mid-1500s to the late 1800s, Europeans conquered the Americas, South Asia, and sub-Saharan Africa, largely subjugated China and the Ottoman Turks, and tried but failed to colonize Japan (Roberts and Westad 2013: 633–60, 791–845). Europeans sought foreign colonies because many state leaders believed in the doctrine of **mercantilism**. According to this doctrine, military power is the central goal of states; such power rests on financial wealth; and world financial wealth is a fixed quantity. One's own state could become wealthier (and thus more powerful) only at the expense of the wealth (and power) of other states. The best way to attain wealth and power, according to the doctrine, came to be that of imperialism, a state strategy by which one country conquers foreign lands to turn them into **colonies**, or areas over which they have political and economic control, so the conquering country can exploit the colonized lands and the peoples inhabiting them either through trade or by settling the conquered territories.

Mercantilism
A doctrine that states that military power is the central goal of states; such power rests on financial wealth, and the financial wealth of the world is a fixed quantity.

Colonies
Areas and people conquered and exploited by a colonizing power over which the colonizer has political and economic control.

European Subjugation of the Americas, Sub-Saharan Africa, and India

During the 1300s and 1400s, Chinese ships moved spices and manufactured goods to India; Muslim ships then moved these goods to Middle Eastern ports; and Venetian traders took the cargoes to Europe. By the early 1500s, Portugal broke into this lucrative business by sailing down the African coast, then north to India and the islands of today's Indonesia, as well as to China and Japan. By 1500, Portugal also discovered and began to colonize Brazil. Spain, seeking a new path to East Asia by supporting Columbus's expedition, reached the Americas instead, conquered the Aztec Empire in 1519, the Inca Empire in 1531, and soon thereafter found in those regions gold and especially silver in abundance (Kamen 2004). The Dutch, by the early 1700s, supplanted the Portuguese in much of East Asia and the East Indies (today's Indonesia), and the French established small colonies in North America and the Caribbean.

The British established the largest overseas empire (Ferguson 2004). By 1700, they had founded colonies along the Atlantic seaboard, as well as on numerous islands in the Caribbean. British trading posts were operating in the Indian ports of Bombay, Madras, and Calcutta (modern-day Mumbai, Chennai, and Kolkata). Britain's victory over France in wars during the first half of the 1700s left it in possession of all of Canada and in a preeminent position in much of India. America's successful War of Independence against Britain between 1775 and 1783 sharply constrained Britain's position in and control over the Americas. It also led to overspending by France in support of the American rebels as a way of competing with the British; the consequence was instead a profound weakening of the French monarchy and, indirectly at least, the coming of the French Revolution of 1789. Britain's victory over Napoleon in 1815 gave it possession of the Cape of Good Hope, all of India, Malta, and a number of additional sugar-rich islands in the Caribbean. By the early 1900s, as can be seen in Map 2.3, a popular saying at the time was that 'the sun never sets on the British Empire.'

During the nineteenth and early twentieth centuries, the major European imperial powers, joined by the United States, Germany, Japan, Belgium, and Italy, fortified their existing colonial holdings and extended their empires to new regions. The United States seized Texas, California, and the American Southwest by defeating Mexico in a war from 1846 to 1848; it formally annexed Hawaii in 1898; and that same year, by defeating Spain, it seized Cuba, Puerto Rico, Guam, and the Philippines. Britain undertook direct rule in India in 1857 after an attempted rebellion by Indian army units, and in 1882 took control of Egypt, which had been in the process of breaking away from the Ottoman Turkish Empire. At the same time, France seized Algeria

Map 2.3 The British Empire, Early 1900s
Britain by 1900 possessed an empire that spanned the globe from Canada through Egypt and India and all the way to New Zealand.

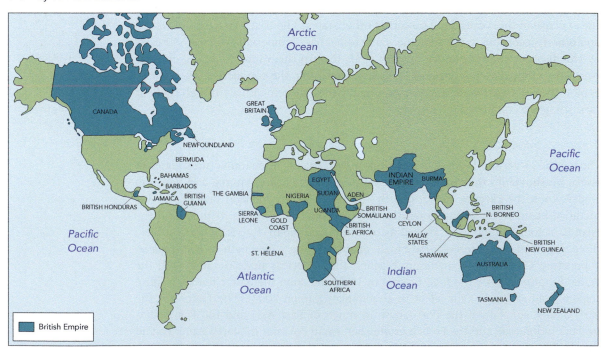

and Tunisia, and made inroads into Morocco. By 1900, Belgium was in control of the Congo region, Portugal expanded into Angola and Mozambique, and Italy seized Libya during 1911 and 1912. Germany by 1900 gained territories in eastern, western, and southwestern Africa, and the Netherlands consolidated its control over the East Indies.

The consequences of European imperialism for the conquered peoples were catastrophic. We see this most graphically in the form of slavery. During the seventeenth and eighteenth centuries there developed what historians call the Atlantic Basin **'rum triangle'** trade, which is depicted in Map 2.4. British traders transported British manufactured goods, such as clothing, to western African ports, and traded those goods for Africans who had been kidnapped by professional slavers or captured by other Africans during intertribal wars. The traders would then transport the Africans by ship under barbarous conditions to Caribbean plantations. There, the traders exchanged the Africans for sugar or rum, which they then sold in England. The Africans, isolated from their families and tribes, malnourished, and terrorized, were worked to death on slave plantations. A very similar trading triangle linked New England rum makers, West African slavers, and Caribbean sugar plantation owners.

Rum triangle
A transatlantic trading triangle active in the seventeenth and eighteenth centuries between Europe, West Africa, and the Americas.

Map 2.4 Atlantic Basin Triangle Trade in the Seventeenth and Eighteenth Centuries
During the seventeenth and eighteenth centuries, the rum triangle represented both the highest levels of economic integration and the most extreme human misery.

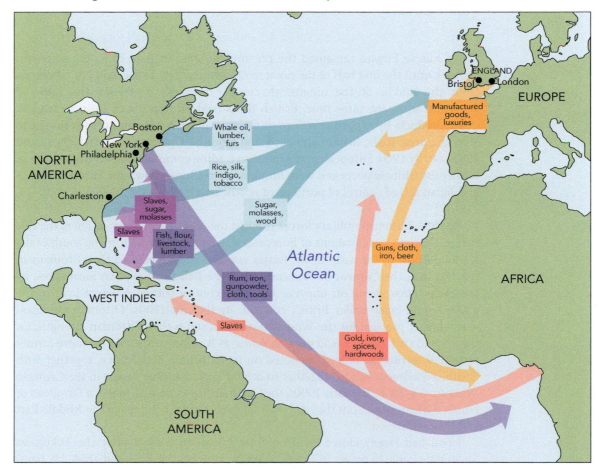

Photo 2.2 Slaves in Inhumane Shipping
African slaves were placed in crowded, inhumane conditions on the voyage to the Americas, during which many perished.

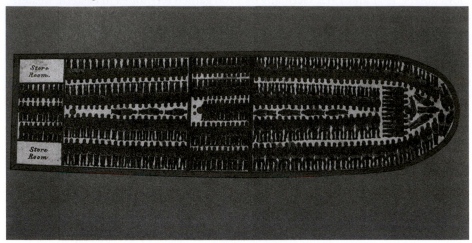

Source: Bettmann.

Kidnapped slaves were also transported through this system to the British colonies in North America, where they were forced to labor in the cultivation of tobacco and cotton.

China and the Ottomans are Subdued and Japan Successfully Resists

The Chinese Empire remained the preeminent state in Asia from the sixteenth century until the first half of the nineteenth century. Yet, a succession of rebellions from the middle of the nineteenth century seriously weakened the Imperial government. At the same time, British firms paid for imports of Chinese tea and other products by exporting opium to China; when Chinese authorities sought to stop the drug trade, Britain launched and won the Opium Wars of 1839–42 and 1856–60. By 1900, European and American trading communities were operating in numerous Chinese ports and were immune from Chinese law, and European states and Japan seized control of portions of northeastern China (McNeill 1965: 710–11, 714–17).

By 1683, Ottoman military forces reached the outskirts of Vienna. Then, the tide turned. Various combinations of European states pushed the Ottomans south of the Danube River. By the early 1830s, Russia expelled and supplanted the Ottomans in the Ukraine, the Crimea, the Caucasus, and the Balkans. Egyptian local elites, by the early 1800s, shook off imperial Ottoman control (although Egypt later in the 1800s would come under British control). By the mid-1800s, Ottoman weakness was a bigger problem for the Western European states than Ottoman strength, for they feared that Russia would grow in power as it came to control ever more former Ottoman territories. Indeed, as noted on p. 41, Britain and France, together with Sardinia-Piedmont banded together to defend Turkey against Russia in the Crimean War of 1853–56. By the early 1900s, the Ottoman Turks were no longer a European or North African power, but they did maintain substantial holdings in the Middle East and the Gulf region.

Japan had largely closed itself off from European contact after the Tokugawa Shogunate came to power in the early 1600s. However, in 1853 and 1854, US naval ships entered Tokyo Bay, and their commander, Commodore Matthew Perry, compelled the Japanese government to sign treaties to open itself to trade on terms highly favorable to the United States. Russia, Britain, and France soon compelled Japan to grant them comparable access. It appeared that Japan might soon suffer the same fate as China. Yet, when the traditional Shogunate governing elite failed to resist these pressures from the United States and other Western powers, a wing of the Japanese nobility seized power in 1867 and tilted the balance of influence at the pinnacle of Japanese society away from the Shogun in favor of Emperor Meiji, who ascended his throne in 1868. The new government set Japan on a course of selective adaptation of Western science, education, and industrial technology for the purposes of fostering a strong Japanese economy and, more pointedly, a strong Japanese military able to resist Western encroachments. These leaders of the modernizing element of the Japanese nobility came to be known as the **Meiji Restoration**. Japan soon showed that, rather than becoming a target of imperialism, it could become a successful imperialist itself. It defeated China in a war of 1894–95, and seized control of Formosa, and defeated Russia in an even bigger war in 1904–05, and occupied parts of northern China and Korea.

Meiji Restoration Beginning with the rise of Emperor Meiji in 1868, leaders who set Japan on a course of selective adaptation of Western science, education, and industrial technology for the purposes of strengthening Japan economically and militarily.

Why Were European States Successful Imperialists?

Four factors contributed to the success of the European imperialists (Diamond 1999; Jones 2003; Acemoglu and Robinson 2012). First, the European states, and later the United States, enjoyed technically superior weapons. For example, by the early 1500s, the Portuguese used large ships with multiple masts, which gave them a decisive edge in terms of the numbers of guns they could deploy. In a key naval battle in 1509 against Muslim ships, Portugal won and thereby gained control of the Arabian Sea (McNeill 1965: 571). Second, the West enjoyed stronger economic bases: by 1913, the average economic output per person in Western Europe was about $3,500; in China it was about $550, and in India it was a bit higher than $670 (Maddison 2006: 262). Third, because Europeans for decades had been caught up in a competitive, war-prone states system, they were induced to mobilize resources and find ways to foster economic growth and technological advances, which made them more formidable foes against non-Westerners.

Finally, Western Europeans benefited from a climate, geography, and history of disease that made it easier for them to emerge as powerful forces in world history. A temperate climate enhanced Europe's ability to develop agriculture, and relatively easy transportation across Europe and further east permitted Western Europeans to develop commerce and learn of technological advances from one another and distant communities. In addition, European populations suffered from such diseases as smallpox, influenza, measles, and typhus for centuries. When the Spanish and later the Dutch and English went to the Americas, they brought those diseases with them. The result for indigenous peoples was catastrophic: for example, perhaps 75 percent of the peoples of the Aztec and Incan empires died from Western-transmitted diseases, making their conquest by European invaders all the more easy (Maddison 2006: 37; McNeill 1965: 571–2; Diamond 1999).

European states in 1900 controlled much of the world's landmass and peoples. Yet, by the mid-1940s, by their own actions, most European states were in ruins; the United States and the Soviet Union had come to command the stage of world history; and Europe's collapse at least indirectly helped set the scene for the single greatest development of our times, the rise of China (Ferguson 2006). We examine how Europe's self-destruction occurred in the next section, which explores the sources, conduct, and aftermath of World War I and World War II.

👤 Individual	👥 State	🌐 International
From the 1500s to the early 1800s, leaders of major states in Europe – successive Habsburgs, Louis XIV, and Napoleon Bonaparte – tried but failed to establish control over the European continent.	European states attained sovereignty and projected power overseas from the 1500s to the early 1800s.	The European system of sovereign states was formalized by the Peace of Westphalia in 1648.
		No state achieved hegemony in Europe because of balancing by threatened states.
		The imbalance in power between European states and empires in the Americas and Asia led to the European conquest of the latter.

WORLD WAR I AND WORLD WAR II, 1900–45

We can see most vividly the problems of order and peace in the international system when we study the first half of the twentieth century, a period of two world wars and the collapse of European hegemony over the world (Keylor 2011). We begin our examination of this deadly epoch with a discussion of World War I. We then focus on the failed efforts by European states to re-establish a global order after that war, and finally, we study the onset and conduct of World War II.

World War I

Causes of World War I

World War I had many causes (Lieber 2007), but four in particular command our attention: European leaders perceived changes in relative balances of capabilities that made war seem to be necessary and potentially useful as a way of solving fundamental interstate conflicts of interest; those leaders established alliances that instilled mutual fear and suspicion; they harbored false beliefs about the ease of winning a war; and they lost control of a regional crisis (Clark 2012; Joll and Martel 2007; Miller *et al.* 1991).

First, at the outset of the 1900s leaders of many important European states believed that changes in relative capabilities made conflict inevitable and caused them to believe that, if war had to come, it might be better to fight it in the near term rather than wait for a future in which military success seemed highly unlikely. So, for example, British and French leaders, and influential commentators as well, believed that Germany was simply becoming militarily, industrially, and even culturally hegemonic. This movement toward German hegemony, if unstopped, would make impossible France's re-capture of Alsace and Lorraine, lost as noted above to the new German Empire in 1871, and would make inevitable Germany's success in challenging Britain's position in Europe but also its supremacy on the high seas. At the same time, German leaders believed that, yes, they had attained a position of power that had yet to be acknowledged by France and especially Britain, but lingering in German thinking was a specter, the rising industrial and military power of Russia. Germany also saw that Austria-Hungary was failing as a multicultural empire, and thus had to be propped up, and that Italy was more a burden than an asset. Hence, if a crisis with Britain, France, and Russia came, it might be better to act sooner rather than wait until a time when Germany might be in a less favorable position to fight. Austria-Hungary knew that its position as a great power was in serious doubt, and thus when challenged by a new upstart, Serbia, it believed it needed to act firmly and quickly. These perceptions did not cause the European states to choose war in 1914, but they did create an atmosphere in which the avoidance of war today might seem to be less intelligent than a decision for it.

Second, consider the role of alliances. In 1870–71, the Prussian chief minister, Otto von Bismarck, led Prussia to a decisive military victory over France. In the afterglow of that victory, Bismarck pressed formerly independent German states into a new, Prussian-dominated German Empire. Also by virtue of the Prussian victory the new German Empire annexed two French areas, Alsace and Lorraine. As the first Chancellor for this new, enlarged Germany, Bismarck sought to isolate France with alliances and to stabilize Europe to reinforce what had become a favorable European situation for Germany. For example, Bismarck in 1878 sponsored the Congress of Berlin under the auspices of the old Concert of Europe and helped craft a peace treaty between Russia and the Ottoman Empire that brought to a conclusion the war they had been fighting since the previous year and that brought about independence for numerous new pro-Russian states in the Balkans. To isolate France, Bismarck in 1879 signed a military alliance with Austria-Hungary; Italy joined this accord in 1882, and thus was founded the **Triple Alliance**. Bismarck also signed a secret agreement with Russia in 1887, the Reinsurance Treaty, in which Germany and Russia each promised they would not be dragged into a war with one another by their respective allies, Austria and France.

In 1888, a new German Emperor, William II, came to power. He dismissed Bismarck in 1890, and decided not to renew the Reinsurance Treaty. France and Russia soon began talks that led in 1894 to a formal military alliance. In addition, William II decided in 1898 to build a world-class navy. This struck fear in Britain, which had become accustomed to dominating the seas. After failing to reach a diplomatic accommodation with Germany, Britain's leaders turned to France in 1904 and settled a number of outstanding differences and did the same with Russia in 1907. Thus, by 1907, two blocs faced off in Europe: the Triple Alliance of Germany, Austria-Hungary, and Italy; and the **Triple Entente** of France, Britain, and Russia.

The third step to major war was prompted by an illusion. In the early 1900s, many European leaders, as well as important members of European society, looked back at recent European wars – Prussia had initiated quick and successful wars against Denmark in 1864, Austria in 1866, and, as noted above, France in 1870–71 – and thought that future wars would be similarly fast and profitable. German military leaders believed they had a blueprint for quick victory, the **Schlieffen Plan**, named after its author, General Alfred von Schlieffen. The plan called for German forces to stand on the defense against Russian forces, to undertake a massive sweep through Belgium and France (see Map 2.5, panel 1), and, after outflanking and destroying French forces, to then turn east and destroy the Russian army.

Fourth, and finally, in 1914 the leaders of the major European states lost control of what started as a local, limited crisis in the Balkans. They had avoided clashing with each other when states in the Balkans went to war in 1912 and 1913, but 1914 was a different matter (as reported in Table 2.1).

Triple Alliance
A military alliance finalized in 1882 between Germany, Austria-Hungary, and Italy sought and signed by Germany to isolate France.

Triple Entente
A military alliance finalized in 1907 between France, Britain, and Russia, forming the other pole (countering the Triple Alliance) that divided early twentieth-century Europe.

Schlieffen Plan
A German military plan believed by the Germans to be foolproof in which German forces undertake a massive sweep through Belgium and France and, after outflanking and destroying French forces, then turn east and destroy the Russian army.

Table 2.1 Timeline: The Summer Crisis of 1914 and the Onset of World War I

June 28	A Bosnian terrorist with possible ties to the Serbian government assassinates the heir to the Austro-Hungarian Habsburg throne, the Archduke Franz Ferdinand.
July 6	Germany gives Austria-Hungary unconditional backing, what historians call a 'blank check', which may have emboldened the Austro-Hungarians.
July 23	Austria-Hungary presents a severe ultimatum to the Serbian government.
July 25	Serbia rejects elements of the Austro-Hungarian ultimatum.
July 28	Austria-Hungary declares war on Serbia and begins military operations.
July 30	Although the British, German, and Italian governments recommend negotiations, Russia undertakes general mobilization of its army.
July 31	Germany demands that Russia stop its general mobilization and that France promise neutrality if Germany fights Russia. Both demands are rejected.
August 1	Germany declares war against Russia.
August 3	Germany declares war against France.
August 3	Italy declares its neutrality (would join the UK and France against Germany and Austria-Hungary in 1915).
August 4	The UK declares war on Germany.
October 28	Turkey enters the war on the side of Germany and Austria-Hungary.

The Course of World War I

Germany defeated Russia in the East by early 1917. Russia in turn experienced during that year a sequence of two revolutions that resulted in the abdication of the Russian Tsar as well as the coming to power of the Bolshevik party under Vladimir Lenin, Russia's withdrawal from the war in 1918, and the onset of a civil war in Russia that ended with the total victory of the Bolsheviks and the creation of the Soviet Union in 1922. In the West, German forces overran Belgium rapidly in August 1914 and moved deeply into France by early September, but they failed to implement the Schlieffen Plan and outflank the British and French armies. By the end of 1914, the British and French had pushed German forces back from Paris and established a front line that ran through southern Belgium and northern France. A Western Front came into being (see Map 2.5, panel 2): French, British, and, from the fall of 1917, American forces faced off against German forces along a deadly trench line that ran from the English Channel to the Swiss border. The major battles of World War I would be fought on the Western Front, although important and highly lethal military campaigns also took place along the Austrian-Italian border, over control of the Dardanelles in Ottoman Turkey, and in the Middle East.

The United States, after German submarine attacks, declared war on Germany in April 1917. Fresh American divisions allowed the allies to defeat the last German

Map 2.5 The Schlieffen Plan of 1905 and the Western Front in Late 1914
While the Schlieffen Plan aimed for a fast knock-out, Germany actually experienced military stalemate and, ultimately, defeat on the Western Front.

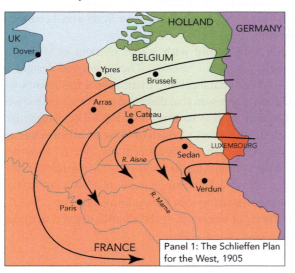

Panel 1: The Schlieffen Plan for the West, 1905

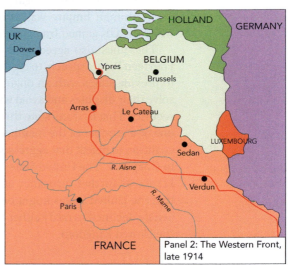

Panel 2: The Western Front, late 1914

offensives in the West in 1918. In November, Kaiser William II abdicated and escaped to the Netherlands; Austria-Hungary surrendered, and the last Habsburg Emperor, Charles II, also abdicated. German representatives requested an armistice; it went into effect on November 11. Some 8.5 million troops and sailors had been killed in combat; another 21 million had been wounded.

The Aftermath of World War 1: The Versailles Treaty and the League of Nations

France, the United Kingdom, and the United States essentially dictated peace terms to the Central Powers (Germany, Austria-Hungary, and the Ottoman Empire). US President Woodrow Wilson had held out the prospect for a relatively gentle peace for Germany with his Fourteen Points speech of January 1918, and when German authorities sued for peace in October 1918 they indicated that they hoped it would be on the basis of the Fourteen Points. In the end, however, Wilson failed to persuade the United Kingdom and especially France to choose that path, and instead the allies crafted a particularly harsh peace treaty for Germany, signed at Versailles, France, on June 18, 1919. By virtue of the treaty, Germany returned Alsace and Lorraine to France. Germany also lost all its overseas colonies, mostly to France and the United Kingdom (UK). Germany was forbidden to have an air force or an army that exceeded 100,000 troops, and it had to accept occupation by Allied forces of the Rhineland, the part of Germany on either bank of the Rhine River. It was also required to pay reparations to the European victors, later set at a staggeringly high $35 billion (the equivalent, in today's dollars, of over $500 billion). Finally, Germany was required to accept responsibility for starting the war.

The Versailles settlement dismantled the empires of Germany, Russia, Austria-Hungary, and the Ottomans. This had been anticipated by Wilson in his Fourteen Points speech, in which he called for national self-determination, that is, members of a clearly identifiable ethnic-linguistic community or nation should as a matter of right and prudence have their own independent state, and not be oppressed within an empire. All told, the settlement brought into being seven new states. Out of Russian territories came into being Finland in the far north, and Estonia, Latvia, and

Lithuania in the Baltic region; and Poland, Czechoslovakia, and Yugoslavia emerged from formerly Russian and Austro-Hungarian lands in Eastern and Southeastern Europe. Austria and Hungary were separated and made small independent states. The Ottoman Empire was also disassembled: France received Syria and Lebanon, while the UK gained Iraq and Palestine.

The allies also agreed at Versailles, in accord with a core element of Wilson's Fourteen Points speech, to establish the **League of Nations**. The League was designed to provide states with an ongoing international legal and institutional framework to solve their disputes and avoid war. The League was also designed to provide collective security. That is, if any state threatened or actually used military force illegally against one or a number of the members, all the members pledged to form an overwhelming coalition to defeat that aggressor. We will return to this concept of collective security in Chapter 7. The United States and the United Kingdom signed a defense treaty with France as further insurance against renewed German aggression. However, fearful that the United States might become obligated to join future European wars, the US Senate declined to ratify either the Treaty of Versailles or the alliance with France and the United Kingdom.

The Interwar Period: Failed Global Reconstruction, 1919–39

After grave turbulence in the immediate aftermath of World War I, the great powers began to work together effectively and, combined with renewed global prosperity, there seemed between 1924 and 1928 to be a chance that the world might enjoy a new age of international cooperation. However, between 1929 and 1933, the global economy collapsed in the face of the Great Depression, and German Nazism and Japanese imperialism emerged and created new challenges to Western democracy (Steiner 2005). Against these pressures, the Versailles settlement and the League of Nations proved ineffective in maintaining global peace and stability and, eventually, the world entered a Second World War, which was even more deadly and consequential than the first (Taylor 1996/2005; Bell 2007; Overy 2008; Iriye 1987; Sagan 1988).

Versailles, Locarno, Kellogg-Briand, and the New Europe

In July 1919, democratically elected German delegates met at Weimar and established a democratic constitution and what came to be called the **Weimar Republic**. France, however, still feared Germany, and insisted on a strict implementation of the Versailles Treaty, including reparations that were crippling the German economy. When Germany failed in 1923 to meet its reparations payments, France instigated the **Ruhr Crisis**: it tried to compel German reparation payments by occupying Germany's highly industrialized Ruhr valley. Germans replied with work stoppages; the German government took the decision to pay workers simply by printing money and the economy experienced hyperinflation, or a vast explosion of prices. Faced with an imminent German economic collapse that could spill over into the world economy, the United States in 1924 mediated an international agreement, the Dawes Plan, named for its author Charles Dawes, whereby France left the Ruhr, Germany's reparation obligations were reduced, and private international banks lent Germany money to be used for reparations payments.

Further progress toward European political reconciliation came in 1925, with the **Locarno Accords**. Under the terms of those agreements, Germany accepted its borders with France and Belgium, the United Kingdom and Italy promised to guarantee Germany's compliance with those commitments, and Germany agreed

---

League of Nations
An international body established by the Treaty of Versailles at the end of World War I and designed to provide states with an ongoing international legal and institutional framework to solve their disputes and avoid war.

Weimar Republic
Republic formed by democratically elected German delegates in the aftermath of World War I to replace the old imperial system.

Ruhr Crisis
When Germany failed to meet its reparations payments in 1923, France occupied Germany's Ruhr valley. The Germans replied with work stoppages; the German government paid its workers simply by printing more paper money, and hyperinflation ensued.

Locarno Accords
An agreement in which Germany accepted its borders with France and Belgium, and promised to resolve border disputes with Poland and Czechoslovakia via arbitration rather than force.

to resolve its border disputes with Poland and Czechoslovakia through arbitration, not military force. In 1926, Germany was admitted to the League of Nations. In 1928, the **Kellogg-Briand Pact** (named after its authors, US Secretary of State Frank Kellogg and French Foreign Minister Aristide Briand) outlawed war, calling instead for the peaceful settlement of disputes. Ultimately, 62 countries signed the Pact, including Germany, Italy, and Japan and, as we will see below, it ultimately failed to constrain the use of force. Global trade also enjoyed revitalization during this period and was as large relative to total world output as was the case in 1913, prior to the start of World War I (Maddison 2006: 363).

Causes of World War II

As with World War I, there were many causes of World War II. We can for the sake of economy of space emphasize two main pathways: the collapse of the global economy and the rise of dictatorships in Europe during the 1930s; and the failure of the Western democracies to act in concert with one another or to deter aggression by the dictators early rather than, as was necessary, to fight them after they had become formidable foes. The Western democracies also failed to find allies among the dictatorships and the Soviet Union, and thus in the end they had to stand alone against a very dangerous Nazi Germany and Imperial Japan.

The Great Depression and Rise of the Dictators, 1929–39

At the end of the 1920s, Europe appeared to be on the road to economic recovery and international reconciliation: in other words, the nations seemed close to establishing a reasonably peaceful order among themselves. But the road soon ended in disaster. In October 1929, the US stock market crashed, many banks failed, and economic activity collapsed – it was the start of the **Great Depression**. Many countries turned to **beggar-thy-neighbor policies**, through which a national government tried to shift onto neighbors the deleterious consequences (especially unemployment) of the global contraction in economic activity. As discussed in Chapter 1, the United States Congress in 1930 passed, and President Herbert Hoover signed, the **Smoot-Hawley Tariff**, which raised average US tariff rates above 40 percent. Other countries naturally retaliated. Global commerce and finance collapsed, and these policies worsened the Great Depression (Frieden 2006: 127–228).

Democracy held firm during these hard years in the United States, the United Kingdom, France, and several other countries, but it failed in Germany, as the Weimar Republic collapsed. Adolf Hitler became Chancellor in January 1933 and was soon the unquestioned ruler of Germany. For different reasons but with similar results, even before the Great Depression, in 1922, Benito Mussolini and his Fascists had seized power in Italy; in Japan, a militaristic faction had seized control by the

Photo 2.3 Emergency Aid in New York City during the Great Depression
In this 1932 file photo, jobless and homeless men wait outside to get free dinner at New York's municipal lodging house during the Great Depression.

Source: Transcendental Graphics/Getty Images.

Kellogg-Briand Pact
A 1928 international pact outlawing war, authored by US Secretary of State Frank Kellogg and French Foreign Minister Aristide Briand.

Great Depression
An international economic disaster precipitated by the 1929 crash of the US stock market. The disaster promptly blocked Europe's path to economic recovery and political reconciliation.

Beggar-thy-neighbor policies
Policies designed to shift the negative consequences of the global economic downturn onto a state's neighbors, pursued by many countries during the Great Depression.

Smoot-Hawley Tariff
A 1930 US law that raised tariffs to high levels to protect the US economy. The act had disastrous consequences and contributed to the Great Depression in the United States.

late 1920s; and in the Soviet Union, Joseph Stalin had attained complete control by the early 1930s (Mazower 1998).

The League of Nations could not provide security to its members. In 1931, Japan attacked and occupied the northern part of China, with no effective response from the League. In 1935, Italy attacked Ethiopia (then called Abyssinia): the League ruled the attack illegal, but because the United Kingdom and France were hoping to attract Italy or at least not propel it toward Germany, they made sure that the League imposed only modest sanctions. The Anglo-French attempt to retain Italy failed: in 1936, Italy and Germany intervened in the Spanish civil war to support the rebel, and fellow fascist, General Francisco Franco. The League called for non-intervention, but the Soviet Union supported the government in Madrid. The United Kingdom, France, and the United States (which due to Congress's opposition was not a member of the League, despite President Wilson's promotion of it) did nothing. Franco took over the country in 1939.

While these developments were alarming, the main threat to world peace in the 1930s emanated from Germany. Hitler pulled Germany out of the League of Nations in October 1933. In March 1935, he announced that Germany would no longer be bound by the armament restrictions in the Treaty of Versailles. France, the UK, and Italy reached an agreement in April 1935 to resist German expansionism and, in May 1935, France signed a security accord with the Soviet Union. Yet, these countries had no unified strategy toward Germany. In June 1935, the UK announced that it had reached a bilateral agreement with Germany to limit their respective navies, which surprised and angered the French. In 1936, Italy – alienated from the UK and France over Ethiopia – collaborated with Germany in Spain.

Hitler continued to extend his gains. In March 1936, in clear violation of the Versailles settlement, Hitler ordered German troops to reoccupy the Rhineland. In the ensuing **Rhineland Crisis**, the United Kingdom and France consulted, but ultimately decided to do nothing. In March 1938, Hitler sent troops into Austria and brought about the forced unification of the two countries. Neither France nor the UK resisted, and Italy, which had resisted German moves toward unification in 1934, now accepted it.

In these years, British and French leaders followed a strategy of **appeasement**, that is, an effort by one state to reduce conflict with another by accommodating the demands of the latter (Lobell 2007; Ripsman and Levy 2008). In this instance, the UK and France sought to appease Nazi Germany. The British and French pursued appeasement to its logical conclusion in 1938, regarding the Czechoslovakia crisis. That country was a democracy, a member of the League of Nations, and a military ally of France. In the summer of 1938, Hitler claimed that 3.5 million ethnic Germans living in the western part of Czechoslovakia, called the Sudetenland, were being persecuted by the Czechoslovak government, and a German invasion seemed imminent. To avoid that, the UK's Prime Minister Neville Chamberlain and France's Prime Minister Edouard Daladier met with Hitler and Mussolini in Munich on September 29 and 30, where they agreed that the Sudetenland would be transferred to Germany. The Czechoslovaks were not invited to the conference and were informed of its outcome only after the meeting.

This arrangement, known as the Munich Agreement, represented the last effort by the Western democracies to avert war through appeasement. As we will see in a moment, that effort failed. **Munich** has since become a powerful historical **analogy** that is used in policy debates about how to deal with potential aggressors, as can be observed in Making Connections Box 2.2.

Rhineland Crisis
In March 1936, in clear violation of the Versailles settlement, Hitler ordered troops to reoccupy the Rhineland. The United Kingdom and France did not respond forcefully, allowing Hitler to continue to bully Europe.

Appeasement
An effort by one state to reduce conflict with another by accommodating the demands of the latter.

Munich analogy
A reference, sometimes invoked by political leaders, to the 1938 transfer of a part of Czechoslovakia to Nazi Germany by Western European democratic leaders. It is generally invoked as a criticism of policy or strategy that resembles appeasement.

2.2   MAKING CONNECTIONS
Then and Now

The Persistence of the Munich Analogy

Then: **President Lyndon Johnson Argues for Escalation in Vietnam, August 1965**

… If we are driven from the field in Vietnam, then no nation can ever again have the same confidence in American promise or in American protection…. Nor would surrender in Vietnam bring peace, because we learned from Hitler at Munich that success only feeds the appetite of aggression. The battle would be renewed in one country and then another country, bringing with it perhaps even larger and crueller conflict, as we have learned from the lessons of history.

Source: Johnson (1965): 262.

Now: **President George H. Bush's War Ultimatum to Iraq, March 2003**

We are now acting because the risks of inaction would be far greater…. The cause of peace requires all free nations to recognize new and undeniable realities. In the twentieth century, some chose to appease murderous dictators whose threats were allowed to grow into genocide and global war.

Source: Bush (2003a).

The Munich-appeasement historical analogy influenced the rhetoric and possibly the decision for war of two US presidents separated by almost four decades, suggesting that the Munich analogy has a very powerful hold on the US understanding of world politics, and highlighting how important it is for students, observers, and practitioners to know whether such analogies are valid or not.

War Comes Again to Europe and the World, 1939–45

Hitler told Chamberlain at the Munich meetings that he had no more territorial ambitions in Europe. This seemed to signify the success of appeasement and possible fortification of peace in Europe. But the strategy had not worked. In March 1939, Hitler invaded the last independent part of the Czechoslovakian state, Bohemia-Moravia, which was not German in ethnic composition. On March 20, he also made territorial demands against Poland. At this point, the UK changed course: on March 31, the British cabinet promised to defend Poland, and the UK and Poland signed a military alliance on April 6.

During the spring and summer of 1939, the UK and France sought to enlist the Soviet Union as an ally against Germany. Hitler offered Stalin more than had the UK and France: in August 1939, Nazi Germany and the Soviet Union signed the **Nazi–Soviet Non-Aggression Pact**. While the Nazis and Soviets promised not to attack each other, they also arranged for an attack on and partition of Poland. Germany attacked Poland from the west on September 1, and the Soviet Union did so from the east on September 17. The UK and France declared war on Germany on September 3. Once more the fundamental, enduring problems of peace and order had come to the forefront of the Continent.

Attacked from two sides, Poland collapsed within a month, and was divided between Germany and the Soviet Union. In the west, France's border fortifications, the Maginot Line, named after one of its early backers, Minister of War André Maginot, at first seemed to deter a German attack. However, in April and May 1940, Germany attacked westward, using a new strategy, *Blitzkrieg*, or lightning war, in which rapidly moving German armored columns pushed through weak spots in

Nazi–Soviet Non-Aggression Pact
A pact signed between Nazi Germany and Soviet Russia in 1939 in which the two countries agreed not to attack each other and to jointly attack Poland, dividing the country between them.

enemy lines and enveloped enemy forces. By early June, Germany occupied Norway, Denmark, the Netherlands, and Luxembourg. German forces then defeated both the French army and the British expeditionary force in Belgium and France, forcing the French to surrender and the British to retreat from the port of Dunkirk (a retreat dramatically depicted in the 2017 film by the same name).

The UK, led from May 1940 by Winston Churchill, stood alone against Nazi Germany. Hitler tried to compel the UK's surrender by launching air attacks in what came to be known as the Battle of Britain. British air defenses held. Hitler, in one of the most mysterious decisions taken during the war – but perhaps believing that the UK would not capitulate unless it had no hope of attracting allies – turned east and launched in June 1941 a massive surprise attack against the Soviet Union. By late 1941, the United States was providing the UK with food, fuel, and weapons, and naval escorts to protect shipping of those supplies across the Atlantic. Japan, allied with Germany and Italy since September 1940, then launched a surprise air strike against the US naval base in Pearl Harbor on December 7, 1941. America declared war on Japan on December 8; and Hitler and Mussolini declared war on the United States, opening the Pacific Theater of World War II. We present the major developments in bringing the war to an end in both theaters in Tables 2.2 and 2.3.

Table 2.2 Timeline: The End of World War II, European Theater

Battle of Stalingrad
A battle between September 1942 and February 1943 in which Soviet forces destroyed a massive German army. It was a major turning point of World War II's European Theater.

Fall 1942–Winter 1943	**Battle of Stalingrad**, during which Soviet Union (now part of the Allied powers) destroy a massive German army and turn the tide against the Axis powers.
1943	American and British forces defeat German and Italian forces in northern Africa, invade Sicily and then Italy, and induce Italian surrender and shift to Allies.
June 1944	American, British, and Canadian forces land at Normandy and liberate France by the end of the year.
Winter–Spring 1945	Soviet forces thrust into eastern Germany; Anglo-American-Canadian forces also move into Germany.
April 1945	Soviet forces attack Berlin; Hitler commits suicide on April 30.
May 7, 1945	German military commanders surrender unconditionally.

Table 2.3 Timeline: The End of World War II, Pacific Theater

June 1942	United States inflicts a major blow against Japan's naval forces at the Battle of Midway.
1942–45	US forces slowly made their way across the Pacific toward the Japanese homeland.
August 6 and 9, 1945	United States drops an atomic bomb on Japanese cities of Hiroshima and Nagasaki, respectively.
August 8	The Soviet Union declares war on Japan.
August 15	Emperor Hirohito announces Japan's surrender to the United States.
September 2, 1945	Japan and allies sign a formal instrument of surrender aboard the American battleship *Missouri* in Tokyo Bay.

Competing states that fail at peace often turn to violence: World War II showed what that could mean. Sixty million people died as a result of hostilities during that war (Ferguson 2006: 649). The Germans alone killed almost 6 million Jews, and tens of millions of Poles and Russians. The Soviets for their part killed hundreds of thousands of their own people, as well as tens of thousands of Poles (Snyder 2010). Europe, Japan, and Russia lay in ruins. The United Kingdom was bankrupt. One international order had died. A new world, which we take up in the next section, would come into being.

Our review of international politics during the first half of the twentieth century has shown numerous examples of the instability and fragility of international order and offers a multiplicity of possible answers as to why such instability and fragility are enduring features of world politics. These include the uneven growth of nation-state power; the inability of great powers to manage regional conflicts diplomatically; the rise of dissatisfied states with expansionist ideologies; economic deprivation; and the failure of international organizations to respond to aggression. These are all important causes of conflict to which we will return in later chapters. Their persistence helps us to appreciate why international order is critical yet fragile.

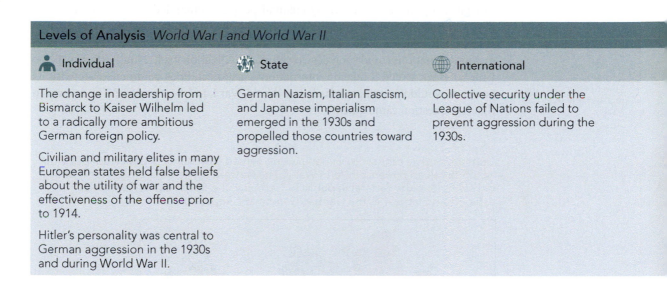

Levels of Analysis *World War I and World War II*		
👤 Individual	**👥 State**	**🌐 International**
The change in leadership from Bismarck to Kaiser Wilhelm led to a radically more ambitious German foreign policy.	German Nazism, Italian Fascism, and Japanese imperialism emerged in the 1930s and propelled those countries toward aggression.	Collective security under the League of Nations failed to prevent aggression during the 1930s.
Civilian and military elites in many European states held false beliefs about the utility of war and the effectiveness of the offense prior to 1914.		
Hitler's personality was central to German aggression in the 1930s and during World War II.		

THE GLOBAL STRUGGLE OF THE COLD WAR, 1945–89

At the close of World War II, the collaboration between the United States and the Soviet Union began to break down, and a bitter rivalry developed between the two states though a full-fledged military confrontation was avoided. This lead several observers, including the British writer George Orwell, the American businessperson Bernard Baruch, and the American writer Walter Lippmann, to suggest that a new era had dawned, one of Soviet–American 'Cold War.' The **Cold War**, which was in place from the mid-1940s to the late 1980s, was a time of high tension and ever-present risk of war between the United States and the Soviet Union (Gaddis 2006; LaFeber 2006; Dunbabin 2008). In this section we explore the political conditions that existed after World War II, the reasons the Cold War began, and the characteristics of the Cold War as a type of international order.

Cold War
Period from the mid-1940s to the late 1980s in which there was high tension and risk of war between the United States and the Soviet Union.

The World in 1945

United Nations (UN)
An international organization, that today includes virtually all countries, founded in 1945 to increase political and economic cooperation among its members.

Relief and optimism in 1945 coexisted with fear and exhaustion. On the one hand, the United Kingdom, the United States, and the Soviet Union had defeated Hitler's Germany. Moreover, in the fall of 1944, these three main allies agreed at Dumbarton Oaks, in Washington, DC, to create the **United Nations (UN)**: the hope was that an ongoing association of major powers (the big three plus France and China), institutionalized through the UN, would establish and maintain the postwar peace. As we discuss in Chapter 5, these five powers would each enjoy a veto over major decisions by the UN, thus rendering it more flexible and credible than the interwar League of Nations, which lost its political credibility when the great powers proved unwilling to abide by their formal League commitments and intervene on behalf of victims of aggression during the 1930s.

Self-determination
The idea that every people should determine and manage their own political systems. Self-determination was a popular idea among colonized people fighting for independence and decolonization.

On the other hand, much of the prewar international order lay in ruins. Germany had lost its sovereignty and was divided by the victors into four occupation zones, one each for the Soviet Union, the United States, the United Kingdom, and France (see Map 2.6). The Soviet Union had suffered the loss of almost 24 million citizens and soldiers. The United Kingdom and France had suffered extensive loss of life and economic damage. The European powers lost both their capacity to rule colonies, and any claim to legitimacy for doing so. Many colonial peoples demanded **self-determination**, that is, the ability to determine and manage their own political systems, as we explore later in this chapter. New military technologies, and particularly nuclear weapons, meant that nations could soon destroy human civilization itself. Finally, there was the United States: would it take on international responsibilities commensurate with its power or would it return, as it had after World War I, to **isolationism**? The answer to that last question came quickly.

Isolationism
The practice by the United States, before World War II, of avoiding alliances and engaging only sporadically in European balance-of-power politics and the management of global affairs.

Map 2.6 Postwar Occupation Zones for Germany
Germany and its capital city of Berlin were divided into four occupation zones by the victorious allied powers of World War II. The western zones were brought together in 1949 to form the Federal Republic of Germany; the Soviet eastern zone was established that year as the German Democratic Republic.

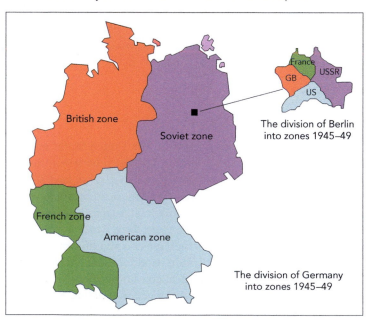

Explaining the Origins of the Cold War

Why did the Cold War begin? In engaging the debate on this question, we will recognize the importance, as emphasized in Chapter 1, of viewing the world from different perspectives.

Responsibility of the Soviet Union

One view is that the Cold War started because of the aggression of the Soviet leader, Joseph Stalin, and US responses to that aggression (Schlesinger 1967; Feis 1970; Jervis 2001). As Soviet military forces pushed Nazi forces westward, Stalin began to install pro-Soviet, communist governments in countries throughout Eastern and Central Europe. For example, in February 1945, at a conference in Yalta, Stalin made clear that in postwar Poland, the Soviets would only tolerate a friendly government controlled by Communists rather than one organized democratically. When the war in Europe ended in 1945, Stalin joined the US effort in the Pacific – just long enough to claim the Northern Territories as spoils from the war with Japan. At home, Stalin intensified repression, crushing any significant dissent from the Communist Party and his personal control of it.

The US at first seemed uncertain of the correct response to the Soviet Union's expansion. Then, in February 1946, US diplomat George Kennan penned his famous Long Telegram from the US embassy in Moscow (published the following year under the pseudonym of 'X') and argued that the Soviet Union could not be treated as a cooperative partner. The US soon articulated toward the USSR, in part under Kennan's influence, a strategy of **containment**, that is, the deployment by one state of diplomacy, economic assistance, and military power to counter and check what it believes are efforts by an adversary state to extend its global sphere of influence. In response to perceived Soviet designs on Greece and Turkey, President Harry Truman in February 1947 pledged that US assistance would be given to 'free peoples everywhere facing external aggression or internal subversion.' This became known as the **Truman Doctrine**. In 1948, a coup in Czechoslovakia meant that the nations of Eastern Europe, except for Yugoslavia, were indeed under the control of the USSR. The United States responded with the **Marshall Plan** – named for Secretary of State George Marshall – to rebuild Western European countries economically so they might withstand Soviet pressures, and in 1949 the United States, the United Kingdom, and several Western European states formed a defense pact, the North Atlantic Treaty Organization (NATO), which we noted in Chapter 1. At the same time, the Communist Party led by Mao Zedong took over mainland China and allied with the Soviet Union. China and the Soviet Union supported Communist North Korea in attacking non-Communist South Korea in 1950; the United States organized an international coalition to defend the South. The Cold War, which in this narrative was mostly a US–European reaction to Soviet aggression, was in full swing.

Responsibility of the United States

Some historians and political scientists believe the United States was responsible for the onset of the Cold War. Supporters of this view argue that the United States and other capitalist states were hostile to the Soviet Union from its inception, and this hostility included an armed intervention by the United States, the United Kingdom, and Japan between 1918 and 1920 to try to prevent the Bolsheviks from consolidating their control over Russia. Because of its vulnerable situation after 1945 and especially

Containment
a strategy by which one state employs diplomacy, economic assistance, and military power to counter and check what it believes are efforts by an adversary state to extend its global sphere of influence.

Truman Doctrine
The declaration by Harry Truman that US assistance would be given to 'free peoples everywhere facing external aggression or internal subversion.' Truman declared this pledge in response to perceived Soviet designs on Greece and Turkey.

Marshall Plan
A US plan to counteract Soviet influence in Europe by providing economic aid to help European nations rebuild after World War II.

its continuing fear of Germany, the Soviet Union's core postwar foreign policy objectives were to keep a formidable historical enemy weak and divided and maintain a 'buffer zone' of friendly states – states that shared the Soviet political and economic system – in Eastern Europe. The Soviet Union simply wanted, as a matter of prudence, a **sphere of influence** in Eastern and Central Europe, that is, a geographic-political space, consisting of one or more countries, whose foreign and domestic policies and political institutions are greatly influenced by an external power. The United States refused to accept this Soviet requirement for a sphere of influence in Eastern and Central Europe. It did so even though the United States reserved the right to install friendly democratic governments in Japan, Italy, and the western part of Germany, not to mention to continue to maintain a sphere of influence in Latin America. In sum, according to this narrative, the United States sought to make the whole world safe for US democracy and private capitalism. Worried about its security, the natural response of the Soviet Union was to strengthen control at home, consolidate its hold over Eastern and Central Europe, look for new allies, and maintain and strengthen its military capacity.

Sphere of influence
A geographic-political space, consisting of one or more countries, whose foreign and domestic policies and political institutions are greatly influenced by an external power.

Tragic Mistake or Inevitable Clash?

A third perspective suggests that the Cold War was tragic and avoidable (Halle 1991). Each side assumed the worst of the other and interpreted the behavior of the other as ominous and threatening rather than prudent and defensive. In other words, the onset of the Cold War was due to a security dilemma: each state's attempt to become more secure ended up, by the reaction it provoked, making it less secure.

For example, Stalin stressed in a speech in early 1946 that, even though the war was over, the Soviet Union still faced many enemies and had to maintain its vigilance. Western leaders read the speech as a signal of aggressive Soviet intentions abroad, but it could be that Stalin attempted to paint for the Soviet people a frightening picture emanating from abroad to justify continued central control rather than relaxation at home. At the same time, the Truman Doctrine and Marshall Plan reflected US anxiety that Communist movements might exploit postwar instability in Europe. It was probably not intended to signal a global US crusade, but the Soviet Union feared otherwise.

Bipolarity
In an international system, the characteristic of being driven by the existence of and competition between two especially powerful states.

Finally, according to a fourth view, the Cold War was an inevitable collision between two continental powers (Brzezinski 1986). The logic of **bipolarity**, or an international system driven by the existence of and competition between two especially powerful states, or superpowers, created incentives for each country to try to accumulate allies to join its side, and isolate the other great power in the hope that its global influence and ability to threaten might be contained. From this perspective, regardless of which particular states rose to the top of the international hierarchy, a cold war or similar conflict would have emerged as long as only two great powers defined the structure, which is indeed the situation that was left at the end of World War II.

The onset of the Cold War reminds us once more that peace and order are difficult to attain in world politics. The different levels of analysis can help provide an explanation. As we discuss in Chapter 4, claims that communist systems or capitalist systems may be prone to aggressive or expansionist foreign policies direct our attention to the state level of analysis and the relationship between domestic political systems and foreign policies. The argument about the structural causes of the Cold War, and in particular the security-dilemma thesis, directs us to the international system level. So too, the fact that leadership perception or misperception of a potential adversary can lead to a spiral of conflict that perhaps neither side intends underscores the importance of the individual level of analysis.

2.3 MAKING CONNECTIONS
Aspiration versus Reality

The United States and Support for Democracy during the Cold War

Aspiration

The Truman Doctrine in 1947 promised to help 'free peoples' to oppose 'totalitarian regimes.' President John Kennedy in 1961 promised that the United States would 'pay any price, bear any burden, meet any hardship, support any friend, and oppose any foe in order to assure the survival and the success of liberty.' The Reagan Doctrine of 1985 declared that America's mission was 'to nourish and defend freedom and democracy.'

Reality

American policy makers worried that leftist governments could easily be captured by anti-US communist elements, and thus preferred to support right-wing authoritarian (and non-democratic) regimes that took a pro-US and anti-communist position. President Franklin Roosevelt captured this sentiment when he said of the dictator of the Dominican Republic, Rafael Trujillo: 'He may be a son of a bitch, but he is our son of a bitch.'

For example, in 1953, the CIA helped overthrow Iran's elected government and the installation of the authoritarian Shah; in 1954, the CIA helped organize a coup against the elected government of Guatemala, and its replacement by a military regime; at different times the United States supported authoritarian rulers in the Philippines, Cuba, Nicaragua, Vietnam, and Chile (after helping overthrow the elected government), among others.

The Cold War as an International Order

The Cold War international order had two distinctive features. First, it was characterized by enduring alliances. Each superpower had a set of long-standing alliance relationships with important middle-level powers. NATO and the **Warsaw Pact**, which was the multilateral alliance the Soviet Union established in 1955 between itself and the Eastern and Central European states under Soviet control, faced off against each other across the European dividing line that Winston Churchill famously called the Iron Curtain. The United States and the Soviet Union each worried that if one or two countries 'fell' to the other side, it could lead other countries to join the side of the superpower that seemed to be winning. Thus, the United States worked diligently to maintain solidarity in what political scientists called the First World, which consisted of itself, the advanced industrial democracies of Western Europe, Canada, and Japan, while in turn the Soviet Union sought to maintain strict obedience to its rule in the communist Second World, which consisted of itself, the Eastern and Central European states, as well as China and North Korea. This led each superpower to compete for influence in the so-called Third World of non-aligned and often newly independent countries in Asia, Africa, and Latin America

Warsaw Pact
An alliance between the Soviet Union and several mid-level powers in Europe. The Warsaw Pact formed a Soviet sphere of influence in much the same way that NATO formed an American one.

(Westad 2005). In the United States, the image of 'falling dominos' was a powerful one that helped justify US intervention in Vietnam. It also helped justify US support for undemocratic governments that were anti-communist, as we note in Box 2.3, including those of Ferdinand Marcos in the Philippines and that of the Shah of Iran.

Second, the Cold War was characterized by a balance of terror that prevented direct war between the two superpowers. By the 1970s, the United States and Soviet Union each possessed over 30,000 nuclear warheads and a diverse array of systems from land, sea, and air to deliver them. Once the United States and Soviet Union had sufficient weapons to destroy each other's population and territory – even after being struck first – they were essentially in a situation of mutual assured destruction, or MAD. Mutual assured destruction made the United States and Soviet Union cautious, not only about initiating nuclear war, but about fighting *any* war with each other. As will be discussed in Chapter 8, it also led to arms control negotiations, in which the United States and Soviet Union sought first to stabilize and later to reduce their nuclear arsenals.

Proxy wars
Military conflicts of the Cold War in which the US and USSR never directly engaged each other, but instead backed opposing sides of smaller conflicts to gain influence throughout the world.

Although characterized by the absence of great-power war, the Cold War was not an era of peace. The United States and Soviet Union fought each other repeatedly in **proxy wars**. The United States and its allies fought against Chinese, but not Soviet, troops during the Korean War. The Soviet Union assisted North Vietnam in its war with the United States. Later, the United States supported rebel forces that defeated the Soviet Union in Afghanistan. Both superpowers supplied arms and financial assistance to their respective client states in the Middle East during the Arab–Israeli Wars of 1967 and 1973, and to rival sides during the Angolan civil war. The major military casualties of the Cold War were borne by populations in Asia, Africa, and the Middle East. The closest the two superpowers came to direct military conflict was during the Cuban Missile Crisis of 1962; as Box 2.4 explains, they managed to resolve that conflict without escalating militarily.

Photo 2.4 Soviet Military Parade, 1971
During the Cold War, the Soviet Union amassed a formidable military arsenal of sophisticated weapons.

Source: Rolls Press/Popperfoto/Getty Images.

2.4   DIFFERING PERSPECTIVES

The Cuban Missile Crisis of October 1962

Background

In October 1962, the United States discovered that the Soviet Union was placing nuclear missiles on the island of Cuba. The ensuing crisis lasted two weeks and brought the superpowers closer to nuclear war than at any other time during the Cold War.

The Soviet Perspective: Why Take Such a Risky Step?

The Soviet leaders may have placed missiles in Cuba to gain leverage over the United States in Berlin. Also, the Soviet Union faced a leadership challenge from Mao Zedong, who believed China was more faithful to the Communist ideal of spreading global revolution; Soviet leaders may have believed that this bold step would reinvigorate their position as leader of the world Communist movement.

The American Perspective: Why a Naval Blockade?

American leaders debated various options and eventually decided to impose a naval blockade of Cuba. The blockade was intended to send a double message: the United States was willing to risk war, but was also allowing time (it would take Soviet ships several days to reach the blockade) for a possible diplomatic solution to be worked out.

The Cuban Perspective: Will We Be Defended?

The problem for Cuba was possible American aggression. The United States clearly opposed the Communist regime of Fidel Castro, which gained power in Cuba in 1959. The Kennedy administration tried and failed to overthrow Castro in the ill-fated Bay of Pigs invasion of April 1961. Cuba's Communist leaders wanted assurances from their Communist partner and great power patron that they would be protected. The missiles were a tangible sign of Soviet willingness to protect Cuba.

The NATO Perspective: Will We Be Sold Out?

America's allies clearly wished to avoid nuclear war, but the US commitment to defend them from the Soviet Union included a US pledge to fight a nuclear war, if necessary, to stop a Soviet attack of Europe. NATO governments worried about the credibility of this US commitment. In a crisis, if the United States truly faced the prospect of a nuclear war that would destroy its own territory and population, would American leaders really follow through on their pledge? The Cuban crisis could not provide a definitive answer but might offer clues to help answer this difficult question.

The UN Perspective: Can War Be Avoided?

Preventive diplomacy was the priority of Secretary General U. Thant. He made himself available to both superpowers and acted as a diplomatic intermediary. For example, he gained assurances from each side during the naval blockade that it would do whatever possible to avoid a direct military confrontation at sea, and he conveyed that understanding to the other.

   The Cuban Missile Crisis underscores how different leaders may view the same issue from completely different perspectives, and how those differences in perspectives can propel them to the brink of war with one another. In this instance, peace was maintained. Soviet ships did not challenge the blockade, and US President John Kennedy and Soviet leader Nikita Khrushchev crafted a mutual face-saving solution. The Soviets promised to remove their missiles from Cuba. The United States pledged not to invade Cuba. The United States also indicated it would remove its own missiles from the territory of its ally close to the border of the Soviet Union, Turkey.

The End of the Cold War and the Collapse of the Soviet Union

Two beliefs dominated scholarly thinking during the Cold War. The first was that the bipolar system of the United States and Soviet Union would last indefinitely, and the second was that if the Cold War did end, it would likely end in conflict. Both beliefs proved to be wrong. Largely due to nonviolent political resistance, Hungary, Poland, Romania, Bulgaria, and Czechoslovakia broke free of Soviet control by the end of 1989, and the Warsaw Pact collapsed between 1989 and early 1991. The Berlin Wall was torn down at the end of 1989, and the following year East Germany joined the Federal Republic of Germany, that is, West Germany, with Berlin as the capital of the newly reunified Germany. The Soviet Union ceased to exist at the end of 1991, and broke apart into 15 constituent nation-states, including Russia (see Map 2.7). Leaders of the United States and the Soviet Union/Russia concluded arms control agreements that called for deep cuts in their nuclear arsenals and conventional forces in Europe.

Why did the Cold War end peacefully and on favorable terms for the West? As with the origins of the Cold War, scholars provide different answers to this question.

Soviet Economic Reform and Its Unintended Political Consequences

According to this first view, the peaceful end of the Cold War resulted from multiple political processes unleashed by Soviet economic failure. By the early 1980s, Soviet economic growth had almost ceased, and innovation was almost non-existent. High energy prices during the 1970s had hidden Soviet economic weakness, because the Soviet Union was a big oil and gas producer, but the collapse of those prices in the early 1980s made it plain that the Soviet economy had to be reformed. In 1985, Mikhail Gorbachev rose to the top of the Soviet political hierarchy with a firm conviction that the system required a fundamental shake up if the Soviet Union expected to retain its position as a superpower over the long term.

Map 2.7 The Territory of the Former Soviet Union after Its Collapse into 15 Sovereign States
The collapse of the Soviet Union led to the formation of many new states, which have since taken different paths. Lithuania, Latvia and Estonia have become 'Western' in orientation and joined the European Union and NATO. Others, such as Belarus, have maintained close ties with the core political entity of the former Soviet Union, Russia. Others have come into direct conflict with Russia – Russia invaded and occupied Georgia in 2008 and annexed Crimea, part of Ukraine, in 2014.

Gorbachev built his program of reform around *perestroika*, an economic restructuring, and *glasnost*, or a political opening, that could take place in both the Soviet Union and its Eastern and Central European allies. Once it was unleashed, economic reform and political openness spread more rapidly and deeply across Eastern Europe than Gorbachev anticipated. For example, in Poland, the Solidarity labor movement and the Catholic Church pressed the Communist government in 1989 to allow free elections, which led to an overwhelming victory for Solidarity. The Hungarian parliament followed by authorizing the formation of opposition parties and, by 1990, an anti-Communist majority asked the Soviet Union to remove its military forces from Hungarian territory. In the past, these political provocations would have been suppressed by Soviet tanks, as was the case in Hungary in 1956 and Czechoslovakia in 1968. Gorbachev seems to have believed that such repression would derail his reforms at home and that Eastern Europe, the beneficiary of Soviet aid and energy subsidies, had become more of an economic liability than a political asset. Once it became clear that Soviet repression was not forthcoming in Eastern and Central Europe, one Communist leader after another was toppled, executed, or forced to flee.

The final element in this volatile mix was nationalist discontent in the Soviet Union itself. The political opening allowed the 'Western' peoples of Latvia, Lithuania, and Estonia, the Muslims of Central Asia, the Christians of Armenia, and the nationalists of Ukraine to express their resentment at being repressed by the Russian elite. In late 1988, Estonia boldly declared itself a sovereign state within the Soviet Union, with the right to issue passports and fly its own flag. Lithuania and Latvia followed by declaring outright secession, that is, their intent to leave the Soviet Union. Gorbachev tried to suppress these movements with the threat of military force. His political position was vulnerable to a larger struggle between the advocates of a return to the old order and those favoring even bolder reform. The forces of radical reform prevailed long enough for the constituent republics of the Soviet Union, including the Russian republic itself led by reformer Boris Yeltsin, to declare their independence, leading in late 1991 to the demise of the Soviet Union.

In short, the end of the Soviet Union and the Cold War were the unanticipated consequences of a bold experiment undertaken by Gorbachev in what turned out to be a remarkably fragile political environment.

Reagan Made Them Do It

A second interpretation emphasizes the role of the United States in facilitating the Soviet collapse. President Ronald Reagan in 1983 characterized the Soviet Union as the 'evil empire.' The Reagan team also pursued a $1.6 trillion defense program over five years, including an anti-missile defense system, the Strategic Defense Initiative (SDI), or what critics called 'Star Wars.' Most scientists were skeptical that such a project could ever succeed. But the very boldness of the United States' project highlighted the vast technological superiority the West enjoyed over the Soviet Union.

The Reagan administration pressured the Soviet Union in other ways. It abandoned arms control efforts and sent aid to rebel forces in countries where Soviet influence held sway but not decisively – Angola, Cambodia, Nicaragua, and most importantly Afghanistan, where Soviet forces quickly became bogged down in a Vietnam-like quagmire of their own making.

These aggressive moves forced Soviet leaders to face the weakness of their own system and their geopolitical position. It would be hard enough, with the economy shrinking, to satisfy the multiple demands of defense, consumption, and empire.

The United States made it even harder by exposing the bankruptcy of the system and raising the costs of defense and empire, forcing the elite of the Soviet Union to undertake the risky reform steps that ultimately led to its demise.

The Power of the People, Not the Leaders

According to this last perspective, while such leaders as Gorbachev and Reagan played a key role in ending the Cold War, the fundamental sources of radical international change lay not among the leaders but within the societies of the United States, Europe, and the Soviet Union. In this view, Gorbachev and Reagan were only vehicles through which social change was carried out.

During the 1970s, economic interdependence began to develop between East and West. During this period of **détente**, or relaxation of tensions, Western businesses and farmers made profits selling factory equipment, consumer goods, and grain to the Soviet Union and Eastern Europe. The peoples of the Communist world came to appreciate the benefits of Western consumerism and began to question the popular notion in their political cultures that the West was seeking to conquer and occupy their homelands.

By the early 1980s, as the US–Soviet conflict intensified, anxiety over a possible nuclear war spread globally. A massive peace movement emerged in Western Europe, fearful that the Reagan administration, by abandoning arms control and emphasizing rearmament, might drag Europe into an inadvertent nuclear war. In the United States, the nuclear freeze movement developed almost simultaneously, calling on the American and Soviet governments to stop building nuclear weapons of any kind. The largest demonstration ever held in New York's Central Park took place in 1982, when 500,000 people supported the nuclear freeze. The antinuclear movement mobilized doctors (for example, Physicians for Social Responsibility) on both sides of the East–West divide, scientists who anticipated an extended nuclear winter in the event of war, and clergy who urged governments and citizens to confront the religious and moral implications of pointing weapons of mass destruction at the innocent civilians of another country.

These social forces found a receptive hearing in the Reagan–Gorbachev partnership. These two leaders unexpectedly developed a personal rapport and agreed that they shared responsibility to minimize the risk of nuclear war. They responded to the demands of ordinary citizens in a way that led to a questioning of Cold War wisdom and, eventually, an end to the conflict.

The peaceful end of the Cold War was a remarkable international event, and it has ushered in a new international order with distinctive features. We discuss that order later in this chapter.

Détente
A relaxing of tension in the middle of the Cold War in which economic interdependence began to develop between East and West.

Levels of Analysis *The Global Struggle of the Cold War*

Individual	State	🌐 International
Stalin's personal aggressiveness may have contributed to Western fears at the end of World War II.	The United States and the Soviet Union each believed that states in their respective spheres of influence required domestic institutions complementary to their own: democratic and capitalist in the West, authoritarian and socialist in the East.	The two world wars destroyed the European balance-of-power system that had formed the basis of international order for 300 years.
Leaders, especially Mikhail Gorbachev but also Ronald Reagan, played key roles in bringing the Cold War to a peaceful conclusion.		The collapse of the Soviet Union ended the bipolar structure of the international system.

THE VIEW FROM THE SOUTH: DECOLONIZATION, THE NON-ALIGNED MOVEMENT, AND THE QUEST FOR A NEW INTERNATIONAL ECONOMIC ORDER

During the Cold War most states were a part neither of the First World nor the Second World, but instead constituted the Third World, that is, the non-aligned countries in most of Latin America, Africa, Asia, and the Middle East. The South moved through important transformations during the Cold War and, in the process, changed the international system as well.

Decolonization

One key development after 1945 was the creation of new states through the process of **decolonization**, or the achievement of independence by states formerly controlled by a colonial power (Spruyt 2005). Decolonization began long before World War II. In 1776, the original 13 American colonies asserted their independence from Great Britain; during the early part of the nineteenth century, Brazil broke away from Portuguese control, and Argentina, Chile, Ecuador, Peru, and Bolivia achieved independence from Spain. Decolonization revived after World War I when the international community, under the auspices of the League of Nations, began a process of preparing former colonial territories for eventual self-government.

Decolonization
The process by which imperial powers relinquished their overseas holdings leading to an increase in the number of independent nations around the world.

The process accelerated significantly during and after World War II. For example, Lebanon gained independence from France in 1941 and Korea from Japan in 1945. The United States granted independence to the Philippines in 1946. Soon after the war, Jordan, India, Pakistan, Burma, and Sri Lanka achieved independence from what had been the British Empire.

The dismantling of the French Empire proved especially tumultuous. France fought for eight years and then finally abandoned its struggle to retain control over Vietnam in 1954. The United States, having supported France with money and advisors, would soon be deeply involved in a subsequent civil and international war regarding Vietnam. Between 1954 and 1962, France fought an even more bloody and divisive war over Algeria, which gained independence in 1962. The United Kingdom and France each granted independence to numerous African countries during the 1950s and 1960s. The white-minority government of Rhodesia (now Zimbabwe) declared its independence against the wishes of the United Kingdom in 1965. The UN imposed economic sanctions against Rhodesia, and some members of the black majority population formed a guerrilla movement that fought and eventually overthrew the white-minority government in 1979. In 1975, Portugal finally succumbed to local and international pressure; its former colonies of Angola and Mozambique broke free. Decolonization was occasionally a peaceful process, but often it was a violent one involving interstate and civil war.

Decolonization had many causes. **Nationalism**, an intense sense of national community by a particular people in a geographically defined space, increased significantly over the two world wars, and led many people in the South to question the legitimacy of an international order in which some states were ruled formally by other states. As noted above, the idea of self-determination complemented that appeal of nationalism. By 1945, both colonizing and colonized states also came to question the economic benefits of their political enmeshment. European powers also faced the mounting administrative and military costs of maintaining colonial control over populations increasingly willing to resist them.

Nationalism
A term that describes an intense political identity a people share, or a sense of collective fate as a political community.

Decolonization transformed the international system. In 1880 a handful of European great powers exercised control over much of the rest of the world. By 1980,

Map 2.8 Patterns of Decolonization
Colonial empires were established over centuries but collapsed relatively quickly in the aftermath of World War II.

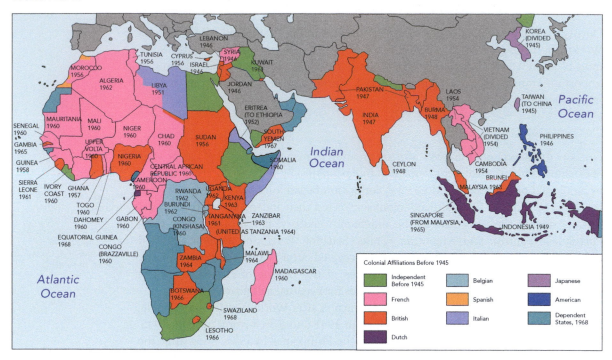

world politics consisted of two superpowers, an array of European and Asian middle powers, and some 100 new states that struggled simultaneously to determine their national identities and to craft a role on the international stage.

The Non-Aligned Movement and Pressure for a New International Economic Order

Non-Aligned Movement
A movement founded in 1955 to create a pathway by which member states could remain aloof from the confrontations of the Cold War. The NAM now includes over 100 countries, representing over one-half of the world's population.

For some leaders of the Third World, the role of new countries was obvious: southern states needed to be non-aligned, that is, not tied to either the Eastern or Western bloc but constituting a political entity of their own. In 1955, the leaders of India, Egypt, Yugoslavia, Ghana, and Indonesia hosted a summit meeting at which 29 countries announced their formation of the **Non-Aligned Movement (NAM)**. Its goal was to provide a pathway to avoid the confrontations of the Cold War. The first NAM summit took place in 1961 in Belgrade, Yugoslavia, and summit meetings have been held approximately every three years since then, with the latest hosted by Iran in 2012. The NAM now includes over 100 countries, representing nearly two-thirds of the members of the United Nations and over half of the world's population. The attempt to forge southern political unity was reinforced by collective efforts in the economic arena, an effort that met with limited success, as we will discuss in more detail in Chapter 11.

Southern states after the Cold War have been characterized more by political and economic heterogeneity than by unity. The term 'Third World' no longer meaningfully applies. Some states, such as China, India, Brazil, and South Korea, have powerful emerging economies that have moved from primary commodity production to manufacturing and even technology-intensive activity. Others, such as Somalia and Chad, are in such bad shape in terms of domestic political and economic distress that they are termed failed states, or states in which governments are so weak and divided they cannot provide law and order for their home population. Advanced industrial countries find themselves paying attention to both the powerful emerging economies, because they are sources of markets and imports, and failed states, for humanitarian reasons and because they are a breeding ground for anti-Western resentment and, in some cases, terrorism.

The idea of a 'third world' as a prize to be captured by democracy or communism was an artifact of the Cold War. When the Cold War ended, the international system became more meaningfully a global one, which we turn to next.

Levels of Analysis *Decolonization, the NAM, and the 'Third World'*		
👤 Individual	🧍 State	🌐 International
Leaders of a few key developing countries played a prominent role in organizing the South's Non-Aligned Movement.	The achievement of independence by states formerly controlled by a colonial power is known as decolonization.	The international system was transformed after 1945 as the 'Third World' sought self-determination and brought about a vast expansion in the number of states in the system.

THE CONTEMPORARY INTERNATIONAL ORDER, 1989–PRESENT

We live today in a global system of states and non-state actors. That system is characterized by both conflict and cooperation, and the perennial problems of conflict management and the maintenance of international order remain with us. Three features of the current international order stand out: the return of great-power politics, the challenge of globalization, and the prevalence of international terrorism.

From the Unipolar Era to the Return of Great-Power Politics

Some analysts speculated that the demise of the Soviet Union created unipolarity, or a distribution of relative capabilities such that there is only one extraordinary global power and all other states are of markedly lesser capabilities and political influence (Montiero 2014; Ikenberry, Mastanduno, and Wohlforth 2011). From this perspective, the United States was after 1991 the world's single superpower and the only state that enjoyed truly global influence. The United States took advantage of its position at the top of the international hierarchy in the two decades after the end of the Cold War to further aspects of the international order that reflected its interests and values. These included the promotion of democracy, the expansion of NATO to include former Warsaw Pact countries and even parts of the former Soviet Union, and the global spread of America's version of free market capitalism. The United States took on the role of 'global policeman' when, in 1991, it responded to Iraq's occupation of its neighbor Kuwait by launching the First Persian Gulf War. US officials organized and led a broad international coalition that was formally authorized by the UN Security Council and included the support of Russia, a traditional ally of Iraq, to drive Iraq out and restore the sovereignty of Kuwait.

The states of Europe, during the 1990s, were engaged through the European Union (EU) in an ambitious effort to join peacefully into a political and economic union that pools to a great degree their individual sovereignty. The EU both broadened its participation and deepened its members' integration. Twenty-eight countries belong, including members of the Warsaw Pact (Bulgaria, the Czech Republic, Slovakia, Hungary, Poland, and Romania), states that emerged from the breakup of the Soviet Union (Estonia, Latvia, and Lithuania), and states that had been part of the former

Yugoslavia (Croatia and Slovenia). Nineteen EU members gave up their national currencies in favor of a common European currency, the euro. The international attractiveness of the United States, the powerful democracy that won the Cold War, and the European Union, a widely recognized zone of democratic peace and prosperity, led many analysts to proclaim the triumph of Western values (Fukuyama 1992), and to conclude that 'the West' as a collective entity possessed soft power, or the ability to influence other countries and world politics by the appeal of its culture and values (Nye 2004).

The decade of the 2000s proved more turbulent than that of the 1990s. The terrorist attacks of September 11, 2001, described in Chapter 1, shocked the United States and it responded by invading Afghanistan, the sanctuary of Al Qaeda leader Osama bin Laden, and by launching a Second Persian Gulf War to remove Saddam Hussein from power in Iraq. The Second Gulf War proved far more controversial than the first, with many states, including two of America's closest allies, France and Germany, objecting to what they considered to be the dangerous and unilateral exercise of American military power. The United States came to be perceived less as a benign global leader and more as an imperial power. As the wars in Afghanistan and Iraq wore on inconclusively, however, even the United States came to question the utility of its military strategy. President Barack Obama, elected in 2008, sought to scale back America's commitments in the Middle East and Persian Gulf, though not altogether successfully.

America's calculations in the Middle East have been complicated by the emergence of Iran as a regional power that is influencing events in Iraq, Lebanon, Syria, and elsewhere. Iran's rise was facilitated by the elimination of two of its regional adversaries, ironically, at the hands of the United States: the Taliban regime in Afghanistan, and Saddam Hussein's regime in Iraq. As discussed in Chapter 8, the world's major powers (the United States, Russia, China, the United Kingdom, France, and Germany) signed an agreement with Iran in 2015, lifting economic sanctions in exchange for limits on Iran's nuclear weapons program. The agreement temporarily ended US efforts to isolate Iran and offered tacit recognition to its role as a regional power.

Simulations: What would you do? Visit the companion website to take on the role of the US President in 2021 and play along as a crisis heats up between Iran and Israel!

In two other key regions, the second decade of the twenty-first century has been characterized by the return of great-power politics. As the Cold War ended, governments in the United States and Europe hoped that Russia would be integrated as a cooperative partner into the Western-centered international order. Russia subsequently joined international economic organizations such as the International Monetary Fund (IMF) and World Trade Organization (WTO). The Group of 7 (G-7), a club of Western industrialized nations that collectively managed the global economy, was expanded to include Russia and became the G-8. By 2010, however, Russia and the West were mutually disillusioned. Russia's leaders felt that the economic benefits anticipated from integration into the world economy never materialized, and they resented that NATO expanded to the east, through the former Warsaw Pact area and in effect to Russia's doorstep.

Russia under Vladimir Putin has sought to restore its influence. In 2008, Russia intervened militarily in the neighboring state of Georgia to support forces in two Georgian provinces, South Ossetia and Abkhazia, looking to separate from Georgia. After five days of fighting the Georgian military was forced out of these two provinces and Russia recognized their independence. Most other countries did not, viewing these provinces instead as parts of Georgia under Russian occupation.

In 2014, Putin, responding to what he considered Western efforts to draw Ukraine away from Russia and into the West, invaded the Crimean Peninsula of Ukraine, a territory heavily populated by ethnic Russians, and reclaimed it as part of Russia. Russia also intervened in eastern Ukraine in support of pro-Russian rebel forces seeking to break away from the control of the Ukrainian government. The United States and European Union responded with diplomatic efforts to halt the fighting and economic sanctions to punish Russia for its incursions. As of 2018, the conflict in Ukraine wore on and efforts to reset relations between Russia and the West were generally unsuccessful. NATO countries, in particular the new Baltic members and Poland, urged the United States to bolster alliance defense and deter any further Russian aggression. Although it would be premature to proclaim a new Cold War, it became clear that Russia was not willing to be a subordinate player to the West and that Russian–Western relations were characterized more by conflict than by cooperation.

Since the end of the Cold War, China has pursued a strategy of rapid integration into the world economy and the economies of China and the West have become more deeply interdependent. But security tensions heightened in East Asia as China increased its military spending and expanded its regional influence. As noted in Chapter 1, China asserted its territorial claims in the South China Sea, going as far as to construct new islands there and claim sovereignty over the surrounding sea and air space. China similarly pushed its claims in the East China Sea, declaring that uninhabited islands (called Senkaku by the Japanese and Diaoyu by the Chinese), claimed by both countries but currently administered by Japan, are part of China's core national interest. The United States responded by reasserting its right to navigate freely in the South and East China Seas. It also strengthened ties with traditional regional allies such as Japan and Australia while exploring deeper relationships with other key regional players such as India and Vietnam. While the United States viewed these steps as a prudent means to reassure allies and deter regional aggression, China feared that the United States was seeking to contain China and advance its own regional influence at China's expense.

As discussed in Chapter 8, East Asian tensions increased further due to North Korea's pursuit of a nuclear weapon and ballistic missile program in defiance of international protests and UN sanctions. Regional diplomatic efforts undertaken over two decades to resolve the North Korean nuclear question proved unsuccessful. As of 2018, the United States feared that North Korea might develop the capacity to reach the US mainland with a nuclear-armed ballistic missile. The United States urged China to pressure its North Korean ally, but there are limits to how far China is willing to push, since it fears the instability of a possible North Korean regime collapse more than North Korean nuclear weapons.

Some 25 years after the end of the Cold War, the United States remains the world's dominant military and economic power. But its international status and influence are increasingly challenged by other states pursuing their own interests and agendas including Russia in Europe, China and North Korea in East Asia, and Iran in the Middle East. In the First Persian Gulf War, the United States found that it could intervene militarily and achieve its objectives either with the support of, or without serious opposition from, other major powers around the world. Today, the ability of the United States to project its power is more complicated. Regional players in pursuit of influence have re-emerged and the great game of international politics, after a brief hiatus, has resumed.

Globalization and Its Discontents

A second distinctive feature of the contemporary international order is globalization, the process by which national economies have become more closely integrated regionally and globally. Today goods, services, technology, money, and ideas move more rapidly across borders than ever before. In 1994, 123 countries signed an agreement to create the WTO, which liberalized trade across goods and services, facilitated investment and the protection of intellectual property, and created a new mechanism to enable countries to settle disputes. The two Communist giants of the Cold War signed on: China joined the WTO in 2001 and Russia, after 19 years of negotiations, in 2012. The forward movement of globalization was further reflected in the 1990s by the Washington Consensus, a set of policy recommendations put forth by the IMF, World Bank, and US Treasury (each based in Washington, DC) that promoted free markets and the reduction of government involvement in the economies of developing countries around the world. By the end of the century it appeared to many that globalization was an irresistible and inevitable force that would bring prosperity to both richer and poorer countries (Friedman 2005). Globalization's poster child was China, where hundreds of millions of people were brought above the poverty line due to that country's integration into the world economy and subsequent rapid growth over several decades.

The terrorist attacks of the 2000s (described below) suggested that at least some international actors viewed globalization, and with it the spread of Western liberal culture and values, as more of a threat than an opportunity. But the real challenge to globalization emerged from within the borders of its core proponents in the West. In 2008, the global financial crisis began and was widely acknowledged as the most significant international economic crisis since the Great Depression of the 1930s. The crisis emerged in the United States with the collapse of America's inflated real-estate market and spread rapidly around the world (Kirshner 2014). It involved sharp declines in economic growth and stock values, and the collapse, and subsequent government rescue, of well-known major banks and investment firms including Merrill Lynch, American International Group, and the Royal Bank of Scotland. The economy of Iceland nearly collapsed as all its major commercial banks, which had invested heavily in mortgage-backed securities, defaulted.

Governments and central banks around the world moved quickly to inject money into national economies and prevent a second Great Depression. Although this effort was successful, ten years later, the consequences of the crisis were still felt in the form of sluggish growth worldwide, and a reappraisal within many countries of the desirability of globalization and deep integration in the liberal world economy.

Much of the political backlash against globalization has been associated with **populism**, or political movements that promise to support the rights and interests of common people as opposed to the interests of a privileged elite. From the populist perspective, globalization has enabled the rich to get richer while poor and working-class groups in industrial societies have experienced job losses or stagnant wages due to competition from countries in which wages and living standards are lower. The financial crisis only reinforced this view; ordinary people lost their jobs and homes while economic elites (e.g., bankers and investors) were rescued by government intervention. Populism comes in many varieties from the far-left version in Latin America (for example, Hugo Chavez in Venezuela) to the far-right, anti-immigration movements in Europe (for example, the Fidesz Party in Hungary or Alternative für Deutschland in Germany). Common themes among populists are distrust of elites

Populism
A political idea or movement that proposes to support the interests of common people rather than those of a privileged elite.

and 'experts,' suspicion of free trade and open borders, and a longing for a real or imagined past characterized by cultural or racial homogeneity. The influential weekly, *The Economist*, characterized the debate over globalization as one pitting nationalist advocates of 'drawbridges up' against internationalists who believe all countries are better off with 'drawbridges down.'

Two recent developments at the forefront of national and international politics have dramatized the debate over globalization. In 2016, by a vote margin of roughly 52 percent to 48 percent, citizens of the United Kingdom voted for Brexit, or the United Kingdom's exit from the European Union. The vote, which shocked both the United Kingdom and the world, was a blow to both European integration and globalization. The supporters of Brexit, reflecting populist sentiment, defied the opinions of experts and elites who argued that exiting would be politically and economically harmful to the United Kingdom. Instead, anti-immigration sentiment (membership in the EU requires the UK to maintain borders open to all EU countries), suspicion of the EU governing bureaucracy in Brussels, and a belief that the UK contributed more to the EU budget than it received in benefits carried the day. If the Brexit negotiations proceed as planned, the United Kingdom would separate from the EU in 2019 and thereby abandon some 750 agreements regulating its policies across trade, transportation, agriculture, and a host of other issues.

Also, in 2016, the United States unexpectedly elected as President a political outsider, Donald Trump, who promised to 'made America great again' by restricting immigration, renegotiating trade liberalization deals, forcing allies to shoulder more of the burden of common defense, and extricating the United States from what he viewed as burdensome international environmental agreements. Trump, notwithstanding his personal status as a billionaire, claimed to speak for the common person left behind by globalization. Postwar US presidents have typically embraced America's alliances, its participation in the liberal world economy, and its leadership role in addressing international political and security problems. Trump, in rhetoric and worldview, is a major exception.

The Prevalence of International Terrorism

International terrorism has emerged as a third defining feature of the contemporary international order. Terrorism, or the use of violence (often against civilians) in pursuit of political objectives, is a type of asymmetrical warfare practiced by weaker international actors against more powerful ones. Since the early 1990s, the non-state actor Al Qaeda has objected to America's military presence in the Middle East. Its operatives bombed the World Trade Center in New York in 1993 and carried out attacks against US embassies in Kenya and Tanzania in 1998 before launching the massive attacks in New York and Washington on September 11, 2001. Other non-state actors similarly have employed the terrorist weapon for political purposes. In 1996 Hezbollah, working in coordination with Iran and against US and Israeli policies in the Middle East, bombed the US military base in Khobar, Saudi Arabia. Earlier, in 1983, Hezbollah carried out a truck bombing at a US Marine barracks in Beirut, Lebanon as part of an (ultimately successful) effort to force the United States to withdraw its peacekeeping force from that country.

Many prominent acts of international terrorism since the end of the Cold War have targeted the territory or political and military personnel of the United States. This is not surprising in that the United States emerged as the most powerful state in the international system, deployed military forces in the Middle East and Persian

Photo 2.5 Khobar Towers, Saudi Arabia
The 1996 explosion at Khobar Towers, a US military base in Saudi Arabia, was carried out by the non-state actor Hezbollah in coordination with Iran. Nineteen US military personnel were killed in the attack.

Source: Getty Images.

Gulf, and closely supported Israel which is viewed by many in that region as an imperial oppressor of the Palestinian people. But other Western states have been targeted as well. In March 2004 an Al Qaeda terrorist cell carried out bombings in Madrid, Spain, killing 192 people. The presumed motive was to influence the upcoming Spanish elections by getting voters to punish the ruling government which had supported the Second Persian Gulf War in Iraq. In July 2005, four terrorists carried out coordinated suicide attacks in the London underground rail system, killing 52 people. In videotaped statements, the bombers paid homage to Osama bin Laden, pledged obedience to God, and accused democratically elected Western governments of committing atrocities against Muslim people. Terrorist attacks continued to plague Europe over the subsequent decade, with incidents as recently as 2016 and 2017 in cities including Berlin, Paris, London, Brussels, and Istanbul. Although the motives of terrorists, particularly in the Middle East, are widely assumed to be based in religion, Box 2.5 describes academic research that finds that terrorists are driven more by political and strategic calculations than by ideological or religious fervor.

The United States, with the support of numerous allies and partners, responded to the attacks of September 11, 2001 with a so-called global war on terrorism. After a long struggle it weakened and, with the key role played by Iraqi Sunni tribes in the 'Sunni awakening' in 2007, eventually defeated Al Qaeda in Iraq. As described in Chapter 1, American forces located and killed Osama bin Laden in Pakistan in 2011. With the demise of Al Qaeda, however, came the rise of a more extreme terrorist entity, ISIS (Islamic State in Syria and Iraq, or simply Islamic State). ISIS is notorious for its extreme brutality including public beheadings, mass murders, the execution of gay men, and the treatment of groups of (Yazidi) women as sex slaves. Unlike Al

2.5 RESEARCH INSIGHT

What Motivates Suicide Terrorism?

Terrorism is a salient problem of twenty-first century international politics. But what motivates terrorists, particularly those whose terrorist acts are simultaneously suicide missions?

A popular line of argument, frequently reinforced in the press, is that suicide terrorists are inspired by religious fervor. Not so, say two political scientists who have studied cases of suicide terrorism in considerable detail. Robert Pape, in *Dying to Win: The Strategic Logic of Suicide Terrorism*, examined over 400 cases of suicide terrorism since 1980 (Pape 2006). He found that what terrorist attackers have in common is not religious or ideological commitments but a specific strategic goal – to compel powerful states to withdraw their military forces from territories the terrorists value greatly. Al Qaeda, for example, used terrorism first to drive the Soviet Union out of Afghanistan, and later to drive the United States out of Saudi Arabia and the Middle East more generally.

In *Dying to Kill: The Allure of Suicide Terror*, Mia Bloom similarly downplays religious motivations. She emphasizes instead strategic and organizational goals (Bloom 2005). Suicide terrorist attacks are intended to inspire local civilian populations to join or at least support the terrorist organization that carried them out. If terrorist groups are competing, they might use suicide attacks in an effort to dominate their rivals or outbid them for popular support. Bloom also highlights the role of female suicide bombers; they enjoy the tactical advantage of surprise since most people expect males to play this role. Female attackers, Bloom finds, are typically motivated not by religious belief but by the sense that they, too, have a responsibility to sacrifice for the larger political cause. Female attackers are also often motivated by revenge at the loss of husbands, brothers, or sons.

Does this mean religion is irrelevant to suicide terrorism? No. According to Pape and Bloom, religion may be important as a recruiting tool, and as a means for suicide terrorists to rationalize killing innocent people. It may also help suicide attackers overcome the natural fear involved in taking their own lives. Religion, however, is neither the primary motive of terrorists nor the primary explanation for terrorist behavior.

The French scholar Olivier Roy agrees that religion is not the primary motive but provides an alternative explanation for suicide terrorism in *Jihad and Death: The Global Appeal of Islamic State* (Roy 2017). For Roy, the jihadist slogan, 'we love death like you love life' carries significant weight and he emphasizes not strategic calculations but the inherent appeal of nihilism and death to many of the young terrorist recruits of the Islamic state.

Qaeda, which moved from place to place, ISIS seized large pieces of territory in Iraq and Syria in 2014 and declared the establishment of a **caliphate**, or state governed in accordance with Islamic law run by a caliph or God's deputy on earth. ISIS, in other words, sought to transform itself from a non-state actor into a state with control over territory and population. At the peak of its power in 2014–15 ISIS controlled about one-third of Iraq and large parts of Syria, a combined land mass roughly the size of the United Kingdom. The Iraqi government, with the support of US air power, drove

Caliphate
A state governed in accordance with Islamic law.

ISIS back and in 2017 retook the key city of Mosul. ISIS was driven back from Syria as well. Although greatly weakened and unable to maintain its caliphate, ISIS continues to sponsor and carry out terrorist attacks in Europe and elsewhere.

Al Qaeda also has been weakened but not eliminated. Al Qaeda has dispersed into territories in the Middle East, Arabian Peninsula, Africa, and on the Indian subcontinent. It has repositioned itself as a more moderate jihadist alternative to ISIS. Al Qaeda's post-bin Laden leaders view themselves in a long struggle, and believe that their ultimate objective, a caliphate, can only endure once the West is exhausted and removes its forces from the Middle East. Once the West is out of the picture, local governments supported by the West can be overthrown and the caliphate established.

Levels of Analysis *The Contemporary International Order*		
Individual	**State**	**International**
Some individuals gain from globalization through economic exchange and travel.	Europe, in the form of the European Union, is more than a collection of sovereign states, but not quite a unified sovereign state itself.	Non-state actors use asymmetrical methods such as international terrorism to pursue their objectives in relations with powerful nation-states.
Globalization may be threatening to other individuals by challenging traditional cultural mores and creating greater economic competition.	The United Kingdom, formally associated with European integration since 1973, decided in 2016 to exit the European Union.	As in previous historical periods, the interstate system seems impervious to control by a single power.

REVISITING THE ENDURING QUESTION AND LOOKING AHEAD

We began this chapter with a twofold enduring question: how did the interstate system come into being, and why is the maintenance of peace and order in that system a persistent problem? In response to the first element of the question, we showed you how European states emerged in the centuries after 1500, and why, because competition among themselves and conquest of others, Europe acted as the catalyzing agent for the formation of the international system we inhabit today. In response to the second element of the question, we explained how the inability of European states to manage international tensions led to wars and depression, and eventually a world dominated by two continental superpowers. That world did not experience world war, but it was marked by tensions and crises. It was short-lived by historical standards, and today we have entered an international environment that is in some ways more peaceful than in previous decades, yet in some ways it is more uncertain and is still fraught with the risk of conflict due to the return of great-power politics, the stresses of populism and nationalism, and the prominence of international terrorism.

A sense of history is critical to any student seeking to understand the logic and dynamics of international politics. Armed with that background knowledge, we may now move ahead to examine how scholars have sought to make sense of the complexity of international politics. In the next two chapters we examine theories of international relations and foreign policy decision-making. Chapter 3 takes you through various ways international relations scholars have tried to comprehend a complicated world. We explore five different perspectives or major frameworks for thinking about international relations – liberalism, realism, constructivism, feminism, and Marxism-Leninism.

STUDY QUESTIONS

1. What are the key benefits of having a solid knowledge of the past when thinking about international relations today? Are there any risks in framing our ideas about the present international situation in terms of the past?
2. China was very powerful in Asia, extending its reach as far as today's Middle East, during the fifteenth century, but by the nineteenth century it had become a target of predation by Japan and Western powers such as the United Kingdom. Today the United States is remarkably powerful, but if history is any guide, will America eventually be surpassed by other states, such as newly powerful China?
3. What do you see as the key lessons of the interwar period (1919–39) for international order?
4. What kind of 'order' was established after World War II? Do you think it was a fair and just order? Who gained the most and who lost the most from the terms and conditions of the post-World War II order?
5. Are you surprised that the Cold War ended without a major Soviet–American war? Why did it end without major bloodshed?
6. If you were the leader of a developing country, would you prefer the bipolar world of the Cold War or the current era of globalization?
7. Can you imagine an end to the war on terrorism? How might that conflict be resolved?

FURTHER READING

Black, Jeremy (2005) *World History Atlas*, 2nd edn (London: Dorling Kindersley). A good historical atlas, almost always available at a university or public library, greatly facilitates the attainment of a strong grasp of history. This atlas has superb maps, a logical presentation of them, and informative accompanying commentary.

Clark, Christopher (2012) *The Sleepwalkers: How Europe Went to War in 1914* (New York: Harper Collins). Clark shows that the onset of war in August 1914 was due both to immediate failures of diplomacy to manage the crisis that erupted after the assassination of Archduke Ferdinand, and the buildup of domestic and international tensions in Europe from at least the 1870s.

Kennedy, Paul (1987) *The Rise and Decline of the Great Powers: Economic Change and Military Conflict from 1500 to 2000* (New York: Random House). For more than two decades Kennedy's book has provided scholars and students of international relations with one of the best one-volume historical treatments of both the internal and external relations of the major European powers, as well as the Soviet Union, Japan, and the United States.

Taylor, A.J.P. (1996/2005) *The Origins of the Second World War* (New York: Athenium). This is the most widely read (and controversial) analysis of the onset of World War II in Europe. Taylor's thesis is that the Western European democracies (and, he suggests in a preface for the American reader, at least indirectly, the United States) were as responsible for the onset of the war as Adolf Hitler.

Tuchman, Barbara (1962/2004) *The Guns of August* (New York: Ballantine Books). This is the historical work on the origins of World War I that has probably had the greatest impact on the field of international relations.

 Visit www.macmillanihe.com/Grieco-IntroIR-2e to access extra resources for this chapter, including:

- Chapter summaries to help you review the material
- Multiple choice quizzes to test your understanding
- Flashcards to test your knowledge of the key terms in this chapter
- An interactive simulation that invites you to go through the decision-making process of a world leader at a crucial political juncture
- Pivotal decisions in which you weigh up the pros and cons of complicated decisions with grave consequences
- Outside resources, including links to contemporary articles and videos, that add to what you have learned in this chapter

3 Theories of International Relations

Enduring question

How do theoretical traditions in international relations differ on how to understand actors and their behavior on the global stage?

Chapter Contents

Learning Objectives

By the end of this chapter, you will be able to:

→ Recognize why the struggle for national power and security in a world of anarchy characterizes the realist tradition.

→ Analyze the interests and impulses of democratic and market-oriented states, which inform the liberal tradition.

→ Appreciate the importance of the industrial revolution and class conflict to the Marxist tradition.

→ Evaluate the effects of ideas and belief systems on individuals, groups, and states; this perspective describes the constructivist tradition.

→ Understand the role of gender as an influence on foreign policy and international relations in the feminist tradition.

Scholars have tried to understand the root causes of conflict and cooperation for more than two thousand years. Over the centuries, they have watched the great dramas of international relations unfold – the emergence of empires and nation-states, war and rivalry among great powers, the boom and bust of global commerce, the building of alliances and political communities, the clash of cultures, religions, and ideologies – and tried to make sense of it. They have asked simple yet fundamental questions: What explains war? Why do states trade with each other? Why do states cooperate or quarrel? Do democratic states act differently than autocratic states in the conduct of foreign policy? How does the global capitalist system impact relations among states? Are countries around the world trapped in a global system of violence and insecurity or can they cooperate to build peace? Scholars have debated these and other enduring questions for centuries and continue to debate them today.

We noted in Chapter 1 that, with so much happening across places and time, international relations may appear hopelessly complex. How do we make sense of it all? As part of their ongoing effort to understand and explain international relations, scholars have developed a set of tools called theories. A theory, we noted in Chapter 1, is a simplified picture that helps us understand *why* something happened in international relations and the likelihood it will happen again. Theories are analytical devices that make assumptions and offer causal arguments. Rarely are theories completely right or wrong; it is helpful instead to think of them as more or less useful.

Individual theories may be very specific, but in the study of international relations they tend to be grouped within broader categories that we may call theoretical frameworks or traditions. Theoretical traditions (sometimes called paradigms, perspectives, or worldviews) are ways of thinking about international relations, and different theoretical traditions place different weight on what matters most in understanding international relations. Each makes a series of assumptions and then directs you to a different set of driving forces to make sense of the complexity of world politics. Realists, constructivists, liberals, feminists, and Marxists look out at the same world, but they each urge you to focus on very different features or, more precisely, causal mechanisms to understand that world. In this chapter, we explore these five theoretical traditions, highlighting the assumptions, concepts, and patterns of behavior that each school of thought finds most important.

THE REALIST TRADITION

From ancient times to the present, people have puzzled over the pervasiveness of conflict and violence among human groups, such as tribes, city-states, kingdoms, empires, and nation-states. Some of the earliest insights about conflict between political groups reflect what we call the *realist tradition* of thinking about international relations. Realism sees international relations as a struggle for power and security among competing nation-states in a dangerous world. According to the realist perspective, in a world of anarchy, by which we mean the absence of a higher authority (such as a world government), in which nation-states must provide their own security, competition and conflict are inevitable. In international politics, the resolution of conflicts between states will be shaped by the distribution of power between them. We identify the core ideas of this tradition by beginning with realism's assumptions, and then turn to its main propositions about how the world works and its predictions for the future.

Realist Assumptions

Realism is a simple vision that sees competition for power among groups or states as the central and enduring feature of international relations. It is built on five assumptions.

First, realists start with the observation that groups – currently states – exist in an anarchical world in which no higher authority can enforce rules or order. Anarchy does not mean chaos; instead, states take measures of their own accord to protect themselves. In such a world, power is the coin of the realm, or the currency with which states do business in international relations. States achieve security or realize their interests to the extent of their power. As realists argue, in a world of anarchy the powerful prevail and the weak submit. The archetypical statement in this respect is Thucydides' famous observation about the Greek conquest of Melios that 'the strong do what they wish while the weak suffer what they must' (Thucydides 1954). When realists look at the long history of international relations, they see competition and the struggle for power, and sometimes even war, as the central drama. States and diplomats come and go across the global stage, but a struggle for security and power has been the recurring theme in relations among states. For realism, this *sameness* or enduring pattern of international politics across time is due not to the character of peoples or governments, but the result of international anarchy. With no higher governing authority to protect them, states tend to be fearful of other states, and seek to increase their power to protect themselves and get what they want from the international system.

The second assumption for realists is that states are the main actors in international relations. Because anarchy creates insecurity, people divide themselves into conflict groups. Today, the most common form these conflict groups take is the state. Governments offer their people protection from the ravages of an insecure international system. They tax, spend, and deploy power. Citizens are tied to the state and rely on it for their wellbeing. Other actors in international relations, such as international organizations, religious institutions, and private corporations, may flourish. But they are decidedly secondary in the ways and means of world politics. States command center stage as the political units that harness power and compete with other states.

Third, realists assume that states are reasonably rational actors that can recognize the international circumstances in which they find themselves and risks and opportunities in the international domain. When states undertake actions, they can perceive the prospective benefits and losses and can adjust their behavior when the costs of actions exceed their benefits. Assuming that states in general act rationally is not the same as saying that every state always acts this way. As we note in Box 3.1, states sometimes persist over long periods of time in behaving in ways in which the costs vastly exceed the gains. One of the challenges for the realist theoretical framework is to explain such seemingly irrational behavior.

Fourth, security is the central problem of international politics. This follows from the reality of anarchy. States operate in an international system where war and violence always lurk. Foreign policy is first and foremost an exercise in national security. Leaders must constantly scan the horizon looking for threats and dangers. States may want to spread lofty values around the world and create open trading systems, but, in the final analysis, states must worry about being exploited or attacked by other states. In certain eras of world history – as during the world wars of the twentieth century – all pretense of civility is stripped away and states struggle for survival. In these times, the bare essentials of international relations are revealed, and the bare essentials are about power and survival.

3.1 MAKING CONNECTIONS
Theory and Practice

Realism and State Rationality: The Issue of State Self-Defeatism
Theory: Realist Theory and the Rationality of States

Realist theory argues that states are serious and sober calculators of costs and benefits. It is generally not in a state's interest to engage in ideological crusades to remake the world or pursue self-defeating acts motivated by pride or arrogance. Leaders will want to take steps to increase the power of the state through its economic and military capabilities. But leaders will be careful not to go to war when they are certain to be defeated or expend the wealth of the nation on fruitless military campaigns. Rationality as understood by realist theorists dictates the prudent matching up of ends to means.

Practice: Germany and Japan in the 1930s Threatened Others and Triggered Coalitions that Brought Their Complete Defeat

In Jack Snyder's 1991 *Myths of Empire*, he describes the way in which Nazi Germany and Imperial Japan built domestic military-industrial coalitions and pursued aggression within their regions, triggering the formation of overwhelming counter-coalitions that brought the states to utter and complete defeat.

> Great powers in the industrial age have shown a striking proclivity for self-inflicted wounds. Highly advanced societies with a great deal to lose have sacrificed their blood and treasure, sometimes risking the survival of their states, as a consequence of their overly aggressive foreign policies. Germany and Japan proved so self-destructive in the first half of this century that they ended up in receivership [i.e. defeated and occupied by other major powers].

In theory, states are depicted as rational decision makers. In practice, they can be loose and dysfunctional coalitions of societal interests who together pursue self-destructive foreign policy.

Source: Snyder (1991): 1.

Finally, realists argue that the search for security is a competitive endeavor, so they expect competition and conflict to be inherent in world politics. There are winners and losers. Power has a relational quality. If one state grows stronger, others necessarily grow weaker. Some states are richer than others, and since power and wealth go hand in hand, to be richer is to be more secure and prosperous. Because of this logic, realists expect competition to be a natural and enduring feature of the international system. Conflict is inherent in relations among states. Peace and cooperation can be achieved at least temporarily and in specific ways, but it is not a permanent condition. States are always looking out for themselves, so they aim to exploit opportunities to gain an advantage on other states.

Realist Propositions

Building on these assumptions about the nation-state, anarchy, and security competition, realists advance a variety of key propositions or concepts. In this discussion, we focus on the main propositions, such as those involving power balancing, alliances, security dilemmas, relative gains, power transitions, and nationalism.

For realists, a core proposition is that the balance of power is a basic dynamic that states have pursued across the centuries. As we discussed in Chapter 2, the balance of power is a strategy that states employ to protect themselves in a world of anarchy and danger. Faced with rising power and threats from other states, a state can attempt to protect itself by generating countervailing power. For example, if one state amasses military power by manufacturing tanks and fighter aircraft that threaten a neighboring state, that neighboring state can respond by amassing its own military power to defend itself. If the threatened state generates enough military capabilities, the threatening state is less likely to attack. In effect, power is used to neutralize or balance power.

The threatened state can also neutralize or balance power by forming a coalition of states with enough collective military power to counterbalance the threatening state. Indeed, one of the oldest tendencies in international relations is for the rise of a powerful state to trigger the formation of a coalition of states that seek to protect themselves as a counterbalancing group. For example, as discussed in Chapter 2, the military growth and expansion of Napoleonic France in the late eighteenth century resulted in a coalition of other European countries, led eventually by the United Kingdom, with sufficient aggregated military power to defeat France and push it back into its borders. Likewise, during the Cold War, the United States and the Soviet Union each sought to aggregate enough power through internal military mobilization and partnerships with other states to keep the other in check. Power was used to balance power.

The fact that states exist in anarchy means they can never be sure of each other's intentions. This has the potential to lead to a process we noted in Chapter 1, the security dilemma. A security dilemma exists between states when one state seeks to ensure its survivability in the international system by acquiring military power but, in doing so, triggers insecurity in another state, leading it to try to protect itself by acquiring military power – thus making both states less secure than when they started (Herz 1950; Jervis 1978). This situation can lead to a reciprocal dynamic of insecurity and an arms race. Defensive mustering of power triggers a counter-reaction which, in turn, triggers a counter-counter-reaction. It is important to note that this is a dynamic driven by *defensive* steps undertaken by both states. Each simply wants to protect itself, but what looks like protection or defense to one state may appear to be the means for aggression or offense in the eyes of its neighbor. Security dilemmas, then, are the result of the interplay of differences in the perspectives of states' motives, actions, and the absence of a centralized international government to which states can appeal for protection. For an example of how such differences in perspectives and understandings of states can lead to arms races and regional tension, see Box 3.2.

A companion proposition to the balance of power is that states will respond to threatening situations by forming **alliances**. Alliances, we saw in Chapter 2, are coalitions of states formed for mutual protection. The most famous and long-lasting alliance in the world is the North Atlantic Treaty Organization (NATO), which ties together the United States and its European partners. Originally established in 1949 at the beginning of the Cold War as an organization of joint protection against the Soviet Union, it has survived the end of the Cold War and remains an organization that combines American and European military capabilities to be used for various conflicts in and around Europe. For realists, alliances are the main form of cooperation among states. They are temporary associations that pool military power to guard against or deter a common foe. **Deterrence**, or the use of power resources to discourage an adversary from taking aggressive action, is for realists an important mechanism for keeping the peace in an anarchical setting.

Alliances
Coalitions of states formed for mutual protection.

Deterrence
The use of power resources to discourage a state from acting aggressively.

Photo 3.1 Secretary of State Dean Acheson Signs the NATO Alliance Pact
The United States, from the time of its founding, had sought, in the words of
President George Washington, to 'avoid entangling alliances' in its relations with
other countries. US participation in the NATO alliance, which became a permanent
peacetime alliance, signaled a significant shift in US foreign policy. This photo shows
Secretary of State Dean Acheson signing the North Atlantic Treaty in 1949.

Source: NATO.

 Simulations: What would you do? Visit the companion website to participate in a scenario as the
Federal Minister of Foreign Affairs for Germany facing pressure from key NATO allies to deploy
nuclear force.

Relative gains
As opposed to absolute
gains, which are simply
the total materials gains
made by a state, relative
gains focus on the
gains one state makes
compared to a rival.
Realists emphasize the
importance of relative
gains.

The basic predicament of states operating in a world of anarchy leads realists to
another important proposition: states care deeply about **relative gains** or relative
position. As noted above, realists believe that it is a state's material power capacities
that give it the ability to pursue its interests and protect itself in a dangerous world.
The stronger a state is, the more likely it is to realize its goals and guard itself against
enemies. But the critical point is that power is relative; for one state to get more of it
necessarily means that other states will have less. Realists argue that states are in an
ongoing and unending competitive game to enhance their power. In an anarchic world,
states must be continuously making decisions on whether their actions increase power
or not. That is, states care more about *relative* gains than absolute gains. Absolute
gains would be the total of benefits that a particular agreement or action yields. Free
trade, for example, may produce very large absolute gains for the system of states. But
power considerations lead states to evaluate the benefits in relative terms. If free trade
generates great absolute gains but leaves other potentially threatening states relatively
better off, then realists believe a state will be reluctant to engage in free trade.

This question of absolute versus relative gains is very important in current debates about US policy toward China (see discussion in Box 3.2). Realists worry more than proponents of other theoretical traditions that by increasing trade with China, the United States is helping to increase China's *relative* power, and that may weigh against the national security of the United States in the future, even though the United States, in absolute terms, is gaining as well. In general, the realist worry for a state is that other states will *gain* more, and, over time, this will give them power advantages. Thus, realists argue that states will exhibit a tendency to make choices based on the relative benefits that accrue to the various parties.

3.2 DIFFERING PERSPECTIVES

China, Southeast Asia, and the Security Dilemma

China's Perspective

Many people view China today as a powerful state rising to great power status. But Chinese leaders have reason to see the world differently. They view the United States as the most powerful state in international relations, and one that may be looking to diminish China's regional influence. The United States is allied with Japan, a neighbor of China that is technologically more advanced, and one with which China shares a history of animosity. America also has close military relationships with some Southeast Asian states, for example Singapore and Thailand, and it has a long-standing alliance relationship with Australia. For China, continuing to modernize its military capability is a prudent defensive step given the uncertainty of its region and the potential hostility of neighboring states and their great power ally.

Southeast Asian States' Perspective

States in Southeast Asia such as Singapore, Malaysia, Thailand, Vietnam, and Indonesia see it differently. They view China as a large and powerful neighbor, upon whom they are economically dependent, and who appears to have a strong interest in exercising regional influence even at the expense of smaller states. Rapid increases in Chinese defense spending, fueled by rapid economic growth, and China's claims to disputed territories in the South China Sea make the leaders of Southeast Asian states nervous. A natural and prudent response is to increase their military spending. In the last two decades, for example, Singapore and Malaysia more than doubled their defense spending. Smaller countries in the region have also enlisted the support of the United States, which has strengthened its defense relationships with Singapore, Thailand, and Vietnam and has announced plans to station more troops and ships in Australia and elsewhere in the region. These moves only reinforce China's anxieties, leading it to continue to grow its own defense spending and thereby perpetuating the action–reaction dynamic of insecurity that characterizes the security dilemma.

Realists also focus on the problem of **power transitions**. One of the great dramas of international relations is the long-term historical dynamics of the rise and decline of states. Germany rose up in the late nineteenth century to challenge Great Britain; in the current era, China is rising to challenge the Western great powers. International change results when technological innovations and uneven

Power transitions
When the relative power of two (or more) states changes, often due to technological innovations and uneven economic growth.

economic growth lead to shifts in the relative power positions of states. The realist proposition is that power transition moments – when a rising state comes to equal or surpass an older powerful state – are fraught with danger. E.H. Carr, a British scholar, has called this the problem of **peaceful change**, or the problem of how the international system copes with the transition of order based on the domination of one state over another state (Carr 1939). Conflict is possible at these moments because as the rising state grows more powerful, it will become dissatisfied with the existing international order presided over by a dominant but declining state. It has more power and wants the international system to accommodate its interests and accord it the status and rights due to a rising state. On the other hand, the older and declining state will be threatened by the rising state and seek to preserve its declining dominance.

Peaceful change
The problem of how the international system copes with the transition of order based on the domination of one state over other states.

Power transitions do not inevitably end in war. Germany did rise to challenge British dominance of the nineteenth-century international system. But the United States also grew more powerful than Britain during these decades; driven by industrialization, it became the world's leading economy and a soon-to-be unrivaled global power. Yet while the British–German power transition generated conflict and war, the British–American transition was peaceful. In British eyes, Germany's military power was a more direct threat, including its efforts to challenge British maritime dominance. The United States was a more remote rising power, across the ocean, and it embraced many British aspirations for an open world economy. Realists argue that power transitions are moments of danger. Whether war and security competition tear the global order apart depends on how rising and declining states define their interests and the ways they decide to defend, overturn, or accommodate themselves to the existing international order.

Finally, realists offer the proposition that nationalism is a dynamic force that motivates states on the international stage. Nationalism is a term that describes the political identity a people share, or a sense of collective fate as a political community. To be part of a nation is to be part of a people with a common history and identity. Nationalism is a feeling people have that they are bound together as part of a natural political entity. The nation is a community of people who live in a world of many peoples, each with their own sense of shared identity. This sense of common identity, or a shared community of fate, gives special meaning to the nation-state. It is also what the state can rely on when it asks for sacrifices by the people on behalf of the nation, such as taxes, obedience to law, and service in the military. Realists emphasize that it is nationalism and loyalty to the nation-state which provide the foundation for dominance of the nation-state and the competitive states system. Nationalism is a potential source of conflict in that it encourages groups of people to emphasize the differences between themselves and other groups.

Within the realist tradition there are a variety of specific arguments and theories, some of which contradict each other. For example, realists agree that anarchy is important, but some realists think that anarchy tends to make states bold and aggressive, while other realists believe that anarchy tends to encourage states to be cautious and defensive. Despite these differences, however, what realists agree on is that when they look out into the world, they see international relations as a struggle for power and security among nation-states. Law, idealism, and morality are human aspirations that make an appearance in the relations among states. But realists argue that power and the search for security are more fundamental, and they will not yield or disappear despite the best efforts of enlightened leaders.

The English School of International Relations

A rich body of international relations theory which shares realist assumptions, but also connects to the liberal and constructivist traditions discussed below, is called the English School. Emerging in the United Kingdom in the postwar era, this tradition emphasizes the realist view that states operate within anarchy, form balances of power, and frequently resort to war. But scholars in the English School go on to emphasize that states have organized themselves into what is called a 'society' of states. In effect, states are more 'social' than realists tend to admit. They have developed rules, norms, and institutions to manage the state system and soften the consequences of its anarchical character. This characterization of international relations as a society of states has led English School scholars to explore the historical dynamics of the modern states system – its origins, spread, and evolving political relationships.

The classic statement of the English School vision is Hedley Bull's *The Anarchical Society* (Bull 1977). Bull begins with the realist view that states are independent and competitive actors in a world of power politics. But he goes on to argue that states have shared interests in managing their anarchical circumstances. States are self-interested, but they share an interest in a predictable and rule-based environment. Bull claims that states share an interest in establishing rules of the game in three areas – restraints on the use of force, sanctity of international agreements, and the security of property rights. These interests mean that states have incentives to build relations with each other, to work together to establish mutual expectations about the terms of their interaction. It is in this way that Bull sees the rise of what he calls 'international society' within the context of the modern states system. International society refers to the wide array of norms, rules, and institutions that reflect and guide relations among states. International law and organizations, discussed in Chapter 5, are important features of international society. As Bull and Watson argue, an international society exists when 'a group of states (or, more generally, a group of independent political communities) which not merely form a system, in the sense that the behavior of each is a necessary factor in the calculations of the others, but also have established by dialogue and consent common rules and institutions for the conduct of their relations, and recognize their common interest in maintaining these arrangements' (Bull and Watson 1985: 1). International society does not allow states to escape from anarchy, but to manage it more effectively.

The focus on the rise and operation of a society of states leads English School theorists to emphasize the importance of diplomacy and dialogue in international relations. What scholars illuminate are the manifold ways in which statesmen over the centuries have worked to establish rules and understandings to manage power politics. Some scholars have focused on the rise of international law as a core institution of international society. Others have focused on the accumulation of rules and norms that regulate the states system – rules and norms relating to sovereignty, self-determination, non-discrimination, and the use of force. Others have focused on the expansion of the nation-state and the states system from Europe to the wider world. In all these areas, scholars offer accounts of the ways states have built the rules and institutions of order and established common norms and expectations about power, property, and rights. The result is a portrait of the modern international system, illuminating the remarkable spread of the system of states and the deepening of its shared norms and rules (Dunne 1998; Buzan 2004).

English School scholars do differ on how 'social' the system of states is. Some scholars emphasize the 'pluralistic' character of international society, where realist dynamics of power and competition remain central, while others emphasize the 'solidaristic' character of international society, arguing that shared rules and norms have progressively weakened the role of power and coercion in world politics, or at least made it less legitimate and tolerable by states. In these various ways, the English School tradition blends realist assumptions and ideas with insights from other international relations traditions, particularly liberalism and constructivism, which we turn to next.

Levels of Analysis *The Realist Tradition*		
👤 Individual	🧑‍🤝‍🧑 State	🌐 International
In realist theory, state leaders are the most important decision makers, pursuing the national interest and maneuvering in a world of competing states.	States – large and small, powerful and weak – are all competing for survival and advantage.	Nationalism is a dynamic force which reinforces the centrality of the nation-state.

THE LIBERAL TRADITION

War and conflict have been pervasive features of international relations. But so too has been the tendency of states to trade, settle disputes, and build cooperative relationships. The liberal tradition offers a variety of ideas about how and why such cooperation takes place in the global system. Liberalism, like realism, is a body of thought that reaches back into the distant past with assumptions and arguments about international relations. While realism sees anarchy and the struggle for power as the defining features of international relations, liberalism sees the internal character of states, particularly the interests and impulses of democratic and market-oriented states, as the most important feature of international relations.

Liberal international theory has three intellectual branches. The first focuses on trade and its impact on international relations. Liberals believe that the spread of capitalism and market relations creates economic interdependence, joint gains, shared interests, and incentives for international cooperation. A second branch focuses on democratic states and their interaction. Here, the view is that democratic polities tend to seek affiliation with other democracies and build peaceful relations. The third branch focuses on the pacifying effects of law and institutions. Liberals view international law and institutions as outgrowths of liberal societies as they seek to establish rule-based relations between them (Doyle 1997). Wielding these ideas, liberal international theory foresees the spread and development of democracy and market relations that transform and soften, even if they do not fully eliminate, the anarchic struggle for power of importance to realism.

Liberal Assumptions

Modernization
The idea that humankind is constantly inventing, innovating, improving, and creating.

Liberal theory is based on a series of five important assumptions. First is the view that the world is in an ongoing process of **modernization**. That is, humankind is constantly inventing, innovating, improving, and creating. Out of this constant process, people and groups advance – they modernize. The process of modernization is pushed forward by the forces of science and technology, which people are constantly using to enhance human capabilities. For example, innovations and discoveries in the last two centuries in telegraph, telephone, and computer technologies have transformed the way people in distant places can communicate and cooperate, and new commercial possibilities and political relationships have followed as well. This vision of human development can be contrasted with realist thinking. Realists tend to view history in cyclical terms, seeing humans making the same mistakes repeatedly. Liberals are more inclined to see progress in which political, economic, and social circumstances of people improve over time. Realists stress the reoccurrence of war; liberals try to find ways to transcend it.

Second, liberals believe that individuals and groups, not states, are the basic actors in international relations. Individuals, societal groups, firms, associations, and other types of groups operate in and across nation-states. Depending on their interests and inclinations, they can also be found building communities and political orders above and below the level of the nation-state. The specific size and character of human communities evolve and change over the eras. For example, liberals are not surprised to see the rise of the European Union in the decades after World War II – a project to build a political community within Europe that transcends the nationalism and sovereignty of the old European states (see Table 3.1).

Table 3.1 European Union Member States
As you can see from this table, the EU currently consists of 28 members (though the United Kingdom is due to exit in 2019). The European Union demonstrates the principles of liberal theorists, as the EU is a political community that attempts to transcend the nationalism and sovereignty of the old European states. The EU still faces issues of coordination, but the organization has learned from these past internal conflicts.

Member Country	Year of EU Entry	Member Country	Year of EU Entry
Austria	1995	Italy	1952 (Founding Member)
Belgium	1952 (Founding Member)	Latvia	2004
Bulgaria	2007	Lithuania	2004
Croatia	2013	Luxembourg	1952 (Founding Member)
Cyprus	2004	Malta	2004
Czech Republic	2004	Netherlands	1952 (Founding Member)
Denmark	1973	Poland	2004
Estonia	2004	Portugal	1986
Finland	1995	Romania	2007
France	1952 (Founding Member)	Slovakia	2004
Germany	1952 (Founding Member)	Slovenia	2004
Greece	1981	Spain	1986
Hungary	2004	Sweden	1995
Ireland	1973	United Kingdom	1973

Importantly, while liberals see individuals and groups as the building blocks of their theories, they also see nation-states and the states system as important. Individuals and groups build larger political groups – such as nation-states – and these larger political groups matter as well. The rise of modern liberal democracies that are based on popular sovereignty and the rule of law, which began in the late eighteenth century, is an important historical breakthrough for liberal theory. The rise and spread of liberal democracy allowed individuals and groups to go beyond old forms of nationalism and empire to strengthen the rule of law and cooperation among nation-states. Individuals and groups are important to liberals because they have the potential ability to transcend old forms of war and hostility between peoples to establish more peaceful and cooperative forms of world politics.

A third liberal assumption is that individuals have incentives and impulses embedded in the deep structures of society to trade, bargain, negotiate, and seek cooperation for joint gain. Liberals argue that individuals can move beyond 'relative gains' thinking and seize possibilities for 'joint gains' based on trade, exchange, and cooperation. Relations among states are not inherently peaceful. But, there is always ample room for individuals and groups to look for ways to advance their interests through cooperation with others within their society and across the global system.

A fourth assumption that liberals make is that modernization and advancement tend to take societies down a common path toward democracy and market society. Modernization across societies and cultures tends to produce similar sorts of challenges and responses; the most general movement is toward loosely convergent sorts of political-economic institutions. That is, liberals see the movement of history as more or less linear, with a pathway that takes developing and advanced societies in the direction of liberal democracy and capitalism. The advanced capitalist societies are at the vanguard of this movement. Through trade, exchange, innovation, and learning, all societies will tend to move in this direction (see Box 3.3).

Finally, out of all these modernizing changes, liberals assume that there is such a thing as progress. The human condition can and will get better. Liberals believe that individuals and groups do indeed learn. They respond to incentives to make their world better. They are sensitive to human rights and the moral correctness of the rule of law. As we have noted, liberals ground their theory of politics in the individual, and individuals possess rights and are worthy of respect. This puts liberals in a position to see progress within and between societies based on mutual recognition of rights and conduct based on the rule of law. Liberals look out at the international system and see that progress has, in fact, occurred; slavery has been abolished, genocide is now a crime against humanity, and despotic rule is seen as deeply illegitimate.

Photo 3.2 The Trials of Ratko Mladić
The ex-Bosnian Serb army leader, Ratko Mladić, makes his first appearance at the International Criminal Tribunal on June 3, 2011 in The Hague, Netherlands. Mladić was charged with atrocities committed during the Bosnian war.

Source: Serge Ligtenberg/Getty Images.

Liberal Propositions

Based on these assumptions, liberals advance a variety of concepts or propositions about how individuals and groups operate within and between states to shape international relations. These propositions involve commercial liberalism, democratic peace, liberal institutionalism, transnationalism, and cosmopolitanism.

3.3 MAKING CONNECTIONS
Then and Now

Changing Character of Economic Doctrines

Then: Diversity of Economic Systems in the 1930s

In the first half of the twentieth century, the industrial and developing states exhibited a wide diversity of types of economic systems. As the Great Depression took hold and the world economy collapsed, countries went their own way. Germany under the Nazis became an authoritarian industrial state, the United Kingdom and France experimented with various sorts of social democracy, the United States remained more market oriented, and the Soviet Union under Stalin consolidated its state socialism system. No consensus existed on economic doctrine or the best model of economic development.

Now: The Washington Consensus of the 1990s

By the 1990s, there was a widespread consensus among capitalist countries, particularly in the West and the developing world, that decontrol, deregulation, and open markets were the best way to promote growth and development. Here is Harvard University scholar Dani Rodrik's description of this consensus:

'Stabilize, privatize, and liberalize' became the mantra of a generation of technocrats who cut their teeth in the developing world and of the political leaders they counseled … [T]his advice inspired a wave of reforms in Latin America and sub-Saharan Africa that fundamentally transformed the policy landscape in these developing areas. With the fall of the Berlin Wall and the collapse of the Soviet Union, former socialist countries similarly made a bold leap toward markets. There was more privatization, deregulation, and trade liberalization in Latin America and Eastern Europe than probably anywhere else at any point in economic history. In Sub-Saharan Africa, governments moved with less conviction and speed, but there too a substantial portion of the new policy agenda was adopted: state marketing boards were dismantled, inflation reduced, trade opened up, and significant amounts of privatization undertaken.

Source: Rodrik (2006): 973–4.

The financial crisis that began in 2008, however, has called the Washington Consensus into question. The crisis began in the United States, the epicenter of the Consensus, and quickly spread around the world. To many observers and participants, the crisis resulted at least in part from the policies of deregulation and liberalization championed by the proponents of the Washington Consensus. As will be discussed in Chapter 9, by 2018, there was much less of a global consensus on the ideas and policies of the Washington Consensus.

The first proposition concerns **commercial liberalism**, which dates to the writings of Adam Smith, an eighteenth-century Scottish social philosopher and pioneer of political economy. Liberals argue that market society and economic interdependence tend to have a *pacifying* impact on relations among states. As the economic relations between two states increase, the interests of these states in

Commercial liberalism
The idea that market society and economic interdependence tend to have a pacifying impact on relations among states. As the economic relations between two states increase, the interests of these states in stable and continuous relations grow.

stable and continuous relations grow. This is because each country depends on the ongoing trade and exchange with the other for its own economic wellbeing. War and destabilizing political conflict between these commercial partners jeopardize profits and employment at home. As a result, liberals argue that as economic relations between nation-states intensify, *vested interests* will emerge in these countries that advocate continued open and cooperative relations.

More generally, Adam Smith argued that the pursuit of wealth could contribute to moral perfection. A free market system could lead the consumer 'by an invisible hand to promote an end which was no part of his intention' (Smith 1937). In so doing, Smith and other liberals hold that a market society will eliminate some of the causes of war by causing states to abandon colonization and tariff barriers as policy tools. With democracy and capitalism, citizens become more rational and materialistic, and more resistant to belligerent nationalism. Liberals have developed these insights, arguing that the evolving character of economic interdependence between states will shape the foreign and security policies they adopt toward each other. Economic prosperity fueled by growing interdependence will make security competition and war less likely because the costs of conflict, particularly to domestic interest groups, will be unacceptably high.

The second and related liberal proposition is that democracies tend not to fight each other. This argument about the democratic peace, which as we noted in Chapter 1 is a leading example of a theory in the contemporary field of international relations, was first proposed by Immanuel Kant in an essay entitled 'Perpetual Peace' in 1795. The argument is that democracies, or what Kant called 'republics,' are unusually peaceful toward each other. Republics, or democracies, are understood as states that have elected governments, a free press, private property, and the rule of law. Kant's expectation was that as democracy spread around the world, so too would peace and stability. He foresaw a widening realm of peaceful relations among democracies, a sort of democratic federation or union of like-minded states that band together and cooperate to create a zone of peace. In this view, democracies are not necessarily more peaceful in their relations with non-democracies, but relations between democracies are special, and peace is to be expected.

Liberal scholars have proposed a variety of reasons why democracies do not fight each other. We will explore their reasoning in detail in Chapter 6, but here we highlight the main elements of their perspective. One reason is that democracies share common preferences; they have similar aspirations about how international relations should be organized. They all want open systems built around stable rules and institutions. In this way, democracies acknowledge each other as legitimate and worthy states whose interests and security must be honored and respected. It is hard for a democracy to declare war on another democracy when they have such strong bonds of shared values and interests. Another reason democracies do not fight each other is because in democracies, citizens bear the costs of war – the costly expenditures of blood and treasure – and they also choose their leaders. Leaders in democracies are held to account for their actions. Citizens are able to avoid the costs of war by voting for leaders who uphold the peace. Another reason for the democratic peace is that democracies tend to have transparent and accountable governments, and this makes it easier for these states to trust each other and cooperate (Russett 1993; Lipson 2003). In all these ways, liberals argue that democratic states have characteristics that allow them to transcend the insecurities of anarchy and build cooperative and integrated zones of peace.

Figure 3.1 World Trends in Governance, 1800–2010
This graph shows the number of democratic, anocratic, and autocratic countries in the world from 1800 to 2010. Notice that since the end of the Cold War, there has been an explosion in the number of democracies in the world, while the number of autocratic states has greatly decreased.

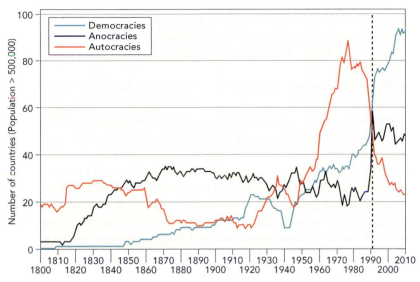

Source: Centre for Systemic Peace, Polity IV Project, www.systemicpeace.org.

A third liberal proposition is that states will build international relations around international law and institutions. We explore the logic and impact of such laws and institutions in Chapter 5 and explore their contribution to peace in Chapter 7. In general, liberals argue that international rules and institutions can play an important role in shaping the operation of relations among states. This view dates to seventeenth-century philosophers such as John Locke and early modern theorists of international law. Political thinking emerged in this era that argued in favor of legal and constitutional rights of individuals within Western polities. The power of the state – and autocratic and monarchical rule – must yield to the rule of law and the sovereignty of individuals. Rights of individuals were seen to be anchored in the appreciation of the fact that all people were equal members of the human community. It was but a small step to recognize that the laws that informed and constrained the exercise of power within liberal societies were also of some significance in relations among liberal democracies. Individuals in other states were also rights-bearing members of humanity, and so leaders of liberal states must also respect the laws that protected these individuals within their own countries.

Liberals have also developed more pragmatic arguments about why and how rules and institutions matter in international relations. In some circumstances, states simply have different interests, so institutions will not help foster cooperation. But in other circumstances, states do not cooperate because they do not trust each other. States do not cooperate because they worry the other states will not hold up their side of the bargain. They are not sure the other state will be a reliable partner. Under these circumstances, when the interests of two states do not inherently conflict with each other, international institutions may serve the important function of reconciling those interests by increasing the flow of information, transparency, and trust. This is **functionalism**; institutions are tools that allow states to overcome barriers of distrust and develop more efficient and durable forms of cooperation (Keohane 1984).

Functionalism
The liberal idea that institutions are tools that allow states to develop more efficient and durable forms of cooperation.

When states agree to abide by a set of rules and institutions, they are agreeing to limit their freedom of action. Liberals argue that states agree to bind themselves to institutional agreements when doing so creates incentives and obligations of other states to do the same. These reciprocal agreements to operate according to rules and institutions create a predictable and functional environment in which all states can pursue their interests. Even powerful states may find a commitment to operate within mutually agreeable rules and institutions is a way to protect their global interests and make their international leadership role acceptable to other states (Ikenberry 2001).

A fourth liberal proposition is that transnational relations provide important connections between states. **Transnationalism** refers to the tendency of groups within countries to build cooperative associations with groups in other countries. An extraordinary array of transnational groups operates across state borders. While realists argue that state-to-state interactions are most important, liberals stress that society-to-society interactions – that is, the interaction of individuals and groups across societies – can also shape patterns of cooperation and conflict within the global system. Transnational groups can come in many varieties, such as environmental groups, human rights organizations, religious sects, and scientific associations. In recent years, the world has also become aware of dangerous transnational groups, such as terrorist organizations, drug traffickers, and organized crime groups. Transnational groups can impact international relations in various ways. In some cases, the goal of these transnational organizations is to act as pressure groups seeking to alter state policies. Environmental groups such as Greenpeace and human rights organizations such as Amnesty International are of this sort. In other cases, transnational groups are associations of experts wielding scientific or other technical knowledge and have an impact in informing the way in which states think about their interests. Some transnational business associations act as *private* governance institutions, facilitating cooperation between corporations on matters such as research and development, technical and regulatory standards, and so forth.

Finally, liberal theory stresses the importance of **cosmopolitanism**. Cosmopolitanism refers to the tendency of peoples in different countries to embrace each other as fellow global citizens. Cosmopolitanism can be contrasted with nationalism. If nationalism entails a shared identity of a group expressed as an allegiance to others within that nation, cosmopolitanism involves the ability of people to identify with others in different lands and cultures. In emphasizing the cosmopolitan tendencies of humankind, liberals are suggesting that people are not trapped in their national identity. They can break out, seek people from other places, and build community between them.

Overall, liberal international theory offers a set of assumptions and propositions that stress the distinctive possibilities for cooperation among modern and advanced market democracies. The general claim is that these societies have incentives and capacities to build complex, stable, and mutually acceptable political relations. Liberal order is distinguished from other types of order, such as balance of power and imperial varieties, because of the way that state power is restrained and channeled. The problems of anarchy are reduced to such an extent that the distribution of power itself does not lead to balancing or coercive domination. Bargains, exchanges, reciprocity, specialization, and security cooperation are aspects of international relations that are captured by liberal theory. In Box 3.4, we compare what academic realists and liberals conclude, based on the assumptions of their respective research traditions, on the likely impact of China's rise on international order.

Transnationalism
The tendency of groups within countries to build cooperative associations with groups in other countries.

Cosmopolitanism
The tendency of peoples in different countries to embrace each other as fellow global citizens. Cosmopolitanism can be contrasted with nationalism.

3.4   RESEARCH INSIGHT

Is a Rising China Likely to Support or Undermine the Existing International Order?

The rise of China – its rapid growth in power and wealth – is one of the most dramatic developments in world politics. A question that scholars and policy makers are debating is how a more powerful China will make choices about its relationship to the existing international order. Will it integrate into and seek a greater voice within the governance institutions of the current international order, or will it oppose and seek to undermine this order?

One view – drawing on a version of realist theory – is that a more powerful China will increasingly seek to reorganize the rules and institutions to accord with its interests and values, and this will bring China into greater direct conflict with the United States. This argument is made by John Mearsheimer in *The Tragedy of Great Power Politics* (Mearsheimer 2003). Mearsheimer develops an 'offensive theory' of great-power politics, looking back at the conflicts that have ensued over the centuries as major states have risen and fallen in power. As a state, such as China, grows in power, its interests become more expansive, and it gains capacities that allow it to challenge the old arrangements. Simultaneously, the older and declining lead state, such as the United States, increasingly sees this rising state as a threat and seeks to block its pathway to global dominance. China, which does not share the West's embrace of liberal democracy and political freedoms, will increasingly try to subvert and replace the existing system, particularly its Western liberal internationalist features.

In *Liberal Leviathan: The Origins, Crisis, and Transformation of the American World Order* (Ikenberry 2011), G. John Ikenberry argues that China has a great deal to gain from participating in the existing international order. After all, China's decades of rapid economic growth have been made possible by its expanding trade and investment with the Western-oriented world economy. Ikenberry argues that the existing order is 'easy to join and hard to overturn.' China is already a leading state in existing global governance institutions – starting with the UN Security Council and the Bretton Woods institutions – and its voice is increasingly heard in global and regional forums. Moreover, China could not overturn and reorganize the existing international order without the support of other rising states, including countries such as India and Brazil. But it is not obvious that these countries – which are liberal democracies – share China's interests or ideology. Rising states need what the existing international order offers, namely multilateral rules and institutions to keep the world economy open and stable.

Who is right? Only the future will tell us. But it is possible that China's impact on the rules and institutions of the global system will be more gradual and piecemeal. China may support some parts of the existing order, such as multilateral trade and investment rules, while opposing parts of the order that seek to enshrine Western values of political freedom and liberal democracy.

Neo-Liberal Institutionalism

One strand of liberal theory focuses directly on the role of international institutions in facilitating cooperation among states and other actors. As we discuss in more detail in Chapter 5, neo-liberal institutionalism begins with the observation that international institutions are a widespread and growing feature of world politics. The United Nations, the International Monetary Fund (IMF), the World Bank, the Non-Proliferation Treaty, the Shanghai Cooperation Organization, the World Health Organization – these and hundreds of other international organizations can be found in all regions of the world and policy domains. Neo-liberal institutional theory argues that international institutions flourish in the global system because they perform 'functions' for states, facilitating cooperation and solving problems.

Neo-liberal institutionalists agree with realists that the world is composed of autonomous and competing states. But they disagree with the realist pessimism that the anarchic system of states is a fundamental obstacle to cooperation. International institutions are a tool that states can use to overcome problems of mistrust and uncertainty about the intentions of others. In effect, institutions facilitate the flow of information between states, giving actors more confidence that others will be reliable partners and keep their commitments. The key insight of neo-liberal institutionalism is that in the modern world, states have a lot of reasons to cooperate. States are increasingly interdependent with each other across economic, political, security, environmental, and social realms. States are self-interested and worry about their security and wellbeing. But if states can solve the problems of cooperation, overcoming uncertainty and mistrust, they can enjoy mutual benefits and gains. For neo-liberal institutionalists, institutions facilitate the spread of information between states, helping them to overcome barriers of mistrust and strengthen the foundations for cooperation (Keohane 1984; Keohane and Martin 1995).

Stepping back, not all people benefit equally from growing trade and cooperation, as liberal theory proposes. Rising inequality of wealth distribution during the industrial revolution gained support for the Marxist-Leninist theoretical framework, examined next.

Levels of Analysis *The Liberal Tradition*

👤 Individual	👥 State	🌐 International
Individuals and groups are important non-state actors in liberal theory, getting involved domestically to shape foreign policy and working across national borders to engage in exchange and other forms of cooperation.	Liberal democratic states have grown in power and influence through long-term processes of economic and political modernization. Democracies tend not to fight each other, and they cooperate with each other more closely than do other types of states.	The spread of liberal democracy, growth in interdependence, and deepening of institutional cooperation create a more stable, prosperous, and peaceful international system.

THE MARXIST TRADITION

When the European states entered the industrial revolution in the early nineteenth century, observers puzzled over how the rise of capitalism would impact the politics and economics of countries around the world. Traditional economies based on agriculture were rapidly transforming into industrial economies with modern corporations, wage workers, steam engines, and new manufacturing technologies. During the nineteenth century, countries in Europe went from rural societies of farmers and villagers to modern urban societies with bankers, businesspeople, and a growing industrial working class. The countries of Europe grew in prosperity and their relations with the rest of the world changed, but not in the way hoped by liberal economists such as Adam Smith. As we point out in Box 3.5, according to liberal economic theory, all would gain from trade. But, at least in the nineteenth century, too often the rich European countries became the wealthy core of an emerging world economy, while peoples and nations in less advanced areas became the poorer periphery. Within the countries of the industrializing West, economic inequality also increased. Great wealth was created by the industrial revolution but working people and the poor benefited the least.

3.5   MAKING CONNECTIONS
Aspiration versus Reality

Liberal Visions of Shared Benefits of Economic Growth

Aspiration: Adam Smith, *The Wealth of Nations*

Adam Smith argued in his seminal statement of market economics that nations will grow and prosper if their people are free to use their skills and capital to productive ends. Workers and businesses would be most efficient when they specialized at what they did best, creating a division of labor within and between nations. Governments were to protect property rights, enforce laws, and provide public infrastructure such as roads. As Smith argued, the individual's pursuit of his or her self-interest would indirectly and unintentionally promote the wealth and advancement of the general public.

> As every individual, therefore, endeavors as much as he can both to employ his capital in support of domestic industry, and so to direct that industry that its produce may be of the greatest value; every individual necessarily labors to render the annual revenue of the society as great as he can. He generally, indeed, neither intends to promote the public interest, nor knows how much he is promoting it. By preferring the support of domestic to that of foreign industry, he intends only his own security; and by directing that industry in such a manner as its produce may be of the greatest value, he intends only his own gain, and he is on this, as in many other cases, led by an invisible hand to promote an end which was no part of his intention. Nor is it always the worse for the society that it was no part of it. By pursuing his own interest he frequently promotes that of the society more effectively than when he really intends to promote it.

> Source: Adam Smith, *The Wealth of Nations*, 1976 edn, Book IV, Chapter II, paragraph IX.

Reality: Wealth Inequality between States during the Industrial Revolution, and Today

The nineteenth-century industrial revolution that Smith foresaw entailed the growth of great wealth in countries like Great Britain and continued poverty and squalor elsewhere, such as colonial India. A similar dynamic takes place today and informs the debate over the advantages and drawbacks of globalization. Proponents of globalization point to the overall growth in the world economy that has occurred as borders have opened to the flow of goods, services, capital, and technology. Critics of globalization point to the growing disparities in income and wealth within and across states. Inequality, based on the workings of global capitalism, is the core concern of the Marxist tradition.

As scholars puzzled over the implications of the industrial revolution for domestic and international politics, a school of thought pioneered by the political economist, Karl Marx, emerged in the mid-nineteenth century that focused on class and class conflict. Marx sought to understand how the industrial revolution – and the rise of capitalism as an economic system – worked. He sought to identify capitalism's winners and losers and how capitalism and economic change shaped politics and political life. In sum, this Marxist tradition focuses on conflict and revolution thought to be associated with economic change and the rise of rich and poor classes within and across countries.

Marxism is not explicitly a theory about international relations. It is a theory about capitalism – its logic and unfolding dynamics in world history. Marxist theory is premised on the notion of historical materialism. This is the idea that history – and the actors that operate on the global stage across eras and regions – are shaped and motivated by their underlying material or economic basis. As the material basis of society changes, so too does history. In effect, the Marxist claim is that the most fundamental fact about people and societies is their material or economic circumstance. Societies are shaped and reshaped around the need to produce the material requirements of life. In the modern era, capitalism has provided the organizing logic shaping the productive forces within and between societies. This deeply rooted and ever-changing system of capitalism provides the structural setting in which peoples, classes, and states operate. Importantly, in the view of Marxist theory, it is the owners of the productive forces of capitalism who ultimately control politics and society as well. From this perspective, Marxist scholars have managed to say a great deal about the interests and motivations of actors within the global arena.

Marxist Assumptions

Marxist theory about international relations begins with five assumptions. First, political interests and relationships are determined by a person's position within the transforming economic system. Economics – or the material setting in which people are situated – shapes politics. Or to put it in Marxist terms, the economic *base* shapes the political *superstructure*. The **mode of production**, organized in the modern era according to a capitalist logic, shapes the **relations of production**. The relations of production are the social and political relationships that emerge in society – for example, between workers and owners of businesses. The mode of production is the basic organization of the economy. It refers to the deep logic of economic life. In Marx's account, human societies were for centuries organized according to feudal relations of production, where serfs and peasants worked on the land that was owned by nobles or an aristocratic class. It was in the early modern era that capitalism arose as a mode of production, and with it came modern industrial society. Under capitalism, an industrial and commercial class emerged as owners of factories and corporations, and workers emerged as wage laborers. The relations of productions pitted the owners of capital and workers against each other. The world of politics evolved to reflect shifts in the underlying system of production. In other words, in this view, politics is what happens on the surface of societies, and it is shaped by the deep underlying forces of capitalism and industrial development (see Figure 3.2).

Second, the important actors in societies are not individuals or states, but **socioeconomic classes**, or groupings of peoples based on their relationship to the economy. The two most important classes are workers (wage laborers) and capitalists (owners of the banks and businesses that drive the economy). While realists emphasize

Mode of production
The basic organization of the economy – the way in which people relate to one another and to the material world.

Relations of production
The system by which the people in a productive system are related, or the relations between those people. According to Marxism, the relations of production will be characterized by class conflict.

Socioeconomic classes
Groupings of peoples based on their relationship to the economy.

states as the key actors in the global system and liberals focus on individuals and groups, Marxist theory sees classes – within societies and between them – as the actors that directly or indirectly shape politics and international relations.

A third assumption is that the modern state is ultimately organized to serve the interests of the capitalist class – or what is sometimes called the ruling class. This is true even for constitutional democracies that elect their leaders. It is a fundamental claim of Marxist theory that modern states – despite their many differences around the world – have as their goal the protection and advancement of the capitalist class. Protecting and promoting the capitalist class is reflected in narrow instrumental ways when governments intervene to defend the property and profits of the capitalist class. But it is also manifest in a deeper and more structural way as the modern state upholds the rules, institutions, ideas, and privileges of the political order that support the capitalist system. Indeed, the capitalist class rules most effectively when its control over society is least visible.

A fourth Marxist assumption is that **class conflict** will increasingly define the relations among workers and capitalists. As capitalist industrialization unfolds, societies are expected to become increasingly divided between the two classes. The capitalist owners of wealth and industrial production will face off against workers, driven by their antagonistic economic interests. Workers are vulnerable to economic swings of boom and bust. They are exploited by the owners of capital who pay meager wages and keep the profits. For workers, unemployment and poverty always lurk around the corner. Capitalists, on the other hand, are enriched through economic growth. Moreover, these class relations are transnational. Workers share common interests across the industrial countries – a point captured in the old Marxist slogan, 'workers of the world unite!' Capitalists also tend to form transnational alliances, cooperating to protect their wealth, safeguarding international trade and finance, and enforcing the system of private property. Workers try to protect their interests by binding together in trade unions, such as the United Auto Workers, on the assumption that workers have more bargaining power if they act collectively rather than individually.

A final Marxist assumption is that **revolution** is the great source of political change. As class conflict grows more intense in the process of capitalist development, a breakpoint is eventually reached when the workers take control from the capitalist owners. The many overwhelm the few. Workers are expected to seize the ruling institutions of capitalist society – corporations, banks, and the state – and usher in a new political order. Society is to be transformed into a classless system. In Marx's ideal formulation, capitalism is to be turned into communism, a social system in which there is no private property or capitalist state, and workers collectively and harmoniously govern the economy and society. The Soviet Union, though characterized as a communist state, departed significantly from this Marxist ideal in that a small group of Communist Party officials, rather than the working class itself, took control of political power and the authority to allocate resources within society.

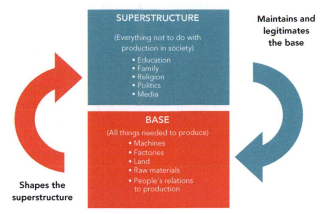

Figure 3.2 Base and Superstructure in Marxism
Marxist theory argues that the deep structure of production (the 'base') shapes and constrains the political and social institutions in which people live and work (the 'superstructure').

Class conflict
Conflict between the capitalist owners of wealth and industrial production and the workers they employ.

Revolution
According to Marxism, in any instance of class conflict a breakpoint is eventually reached when the workers take control from the capitalist owners. Revolution is the dominant mode of political change in the Marxist school.

Photo 3.3 Call to Arms during the Russian Revolution
A poster from the era of the Russian Revolution, showing peasants rising up against the Russian state.

Source: Bettmann.

Marx foresaw a time when the conflicts and contradictions of modern capitalism would lead to revolution and a transformation in the mode of production – a transformation from capitalism to communism. But he also thought that capitalism was an extraordinarily dynamic and efficient system of production. Its powerful forces were transforming the world. Capitalist states would trade, invest, and expand outwards bringing the backward areas of the world into the arms of the capitalist system. Marx was not an opponent of British or European colonialism. He saw it was part of the unfolding logic of capitalism, a process that would need to continue until capitalist societies were mature and ready for revolution.

In the twentieth century, Marxist theory of global capitalism evolved in various ways. As we discussed in Chapter 1, the Russian revolutionary, Lenin, wrote perhaps the most influential Marxist-inspired treatise on the international politics of capitalism in his 1916 booklet, 'Imperialism: The Highest Stage of Capitalism.' Lenin argued that the capitalist class was becoming increasingly centralized in the major industrial countries, led by cartels of wealthy and powerful financial and industrial elites – what he called finance capitalism. To keep their workers peaceful, these elites in the advanced capitalist states were exporting their capital to poor underdeveloped countries to finance resources and cheap labor production. The poor and the backward regions of the world were being brought into the world capitalist system, and this was changing the relationship between capitalist states. This dynamic of finance capitalism allowed Lenin to explain why revolution would not come – as Marx had predicted – in the most advanced countries but rather in the exploited less developed countries (Lenin 1916). With World War I as a backdrop, Lenin argued that the Western great powers, together with their finance capitalist elites, would be increasingly driven to compete to divide up and exploit the undeveloped world. Once they divided the world, they would fight great-power wars to re-divide it. Thus, it was imperialism and war – and not Marx's contradictions with the relations of production – that spelled the doom of advanced capitalism. Other Marxists during Lenin's time and later have continued to debate whether the global capitalist class would ultimately be divided into competing nation-states – reinforced by nationalism and geopolitics – or united in a global coalition to protect their shared interests.

In more recent decades, Marxist-inspired theory on international relations has explored the various ways in which global capitalism operates as a system of power. Some writings focus on the shifting winners and losers that emerge within global capitalism. Trade and open markets do not benefit all people in all places. The spread of capitalism worldwide has mobilized societies and raised many people up out of poverty. But the rich continue to get richer, while the poor – which is the vast majority of the people on earth – remain poor. Many non-Marxist scholars seek to explain these dynamics of inequality (see Stiglitz 2002), but Marxist theory is particularly committed as a theoretical tradition to identifying the divergent interests and outcomes that emerge from the expanding and transforming dynamics of capitalism. Other Marxist-inspired scholars have turned to the exploration of the ideologies and institutions that serve to preserve and protect the global capitalist system. Some scholars offer arguments about **hegemony** to explain the way in which leading

Hegemony
The dominance of one state over other states. Many scholars believe that a hegemonic international system is most prone to peace.

capitalist states – most notably in the current era, the United States – dominate the resources and institutions of world politics (Cox 1981; Cox and Sinclair 1996; Gill 1992). Hegemony for Marxist scholars is a system of power where leading capitalist states exercise domination and control over weaker societies and peoples, often doing so indirectly through the influence of their ideologies and institutions.

Marxist Propositions

From these assumptions, Marxist theory offers a variety of insights about how capitalist states and international relations operate.

One proposition is that states – particularly those states in the advanced industrial countries – will act in ways that protect and advance the interests of capitalism and the capitalist class. This is not to argue that the governments of the leading capitalist countries will always promote the interests of specific businesses or banks. The proposition is that modern states will act to 'keep the world safe' for capitalism. This means that states will uphold property rights and the rules and institutions that support modern capitalism. In this regard, Marxist theory helps illuminate an entire history of state involvement in building, defending, and expanding the world capitalist system. This can be seen in the ways in which Western states over the last two centuries have pursued foreign policies that protect and advance the financial and commercial interests within their countries. The late nineteenth-century scramble for Africa, the partition of China, the 'informal imperialism' pursued by Western capitalist states in Asia and Latin America, and today's version of open market capitalism promoted by the IMF and World Bank are episodes where states and capitalists worked together for economic and geopolitical advantage. While realists also expect to see states acting to advance the economic interests of their countries, they do so for national interest reasons. Marxists see states working on behalf of capitalism.

Marxists differ on precisely how business controls the state and argue that there are *structural* and *instrumental* capitalist influences on foreign policy. Structural influences of capitalism on foreign policy refer to the ways in which states automatically pursue policies that advance and protect the interests of capitalism. This is what Karl Marx himself argued when he said that 'the state is the handmaiden of capital.' Governments, after all, are dependent on a growing economy for taxes. They have an interest in making sure that the national economy is thriving. In this way, governments will protect the interests of capitalism. Governments will certainly not want to scare off businesses by imposing high taxes or expropriating their property. Governments will also seek to support rules and institutions within the global system that are supportive to trade and investment. In these ways, capitalism has a structural impact on what states do.

Marxists also point to instrumental influences of capitalism on foreign policy. In this case, it is the active lobbying of businesses that influences what states do. Capitalists are, in fact, well organized to influence government policy in most countries. Business associations have full-time representatives to lobby parliaments and presidents, and business elites are among the biggest donors to political campaigns (see Table 3.2). If 'money speaks' in politics, business groups use this advantage to influence governments. For example, in the United States, business groups with an interest in China have spoken loudly in favor of Sino-American trade and investment. More generally, the history of American foreign policy is full of episodes when business interests – oil companies or investment groups – pressure the government to intervene in the developing world on their behalf. Scholars continue to debate when and how these instrumental interests matter in international relations.

Table 3.2 Lobbying Washington: The Pharmaceutical Industry
Big business spends large sums of money seeking favourable regulatory, tax, and other policies from the government.

Company	Federal Lobbying Spending	Federal Political Donations
Pharmaceutical Research & Manufacturers of America*	$261,462,800	$2,050,816
Pfizer Inc.	$148,959,918	$14,650,120
Amgen Inc.	$127,145,000	$10,918,097
Eli Lilly & Co.	$99,891,110	$7,177,066
Merck & Co.	$82,307,510	$8,379,548
Novartis AG	$82,183,146	$3,373,050
GlaxoSmithKline	$69,201,000	$8,015,472
Bristol-Meyers Squibb	$55,460,776	$2,259,752
Bayer AG	$55,458,453	$2,043,595
Sonofi-Aventis	$53,120,834	$2,735,767

*PhRMA is a trade organization. The rest are drug manufacturers or wholesalers.
Note: Figures are from the Center for Responsive Politics. Pfizer provided different numbers: $145.9 million for lobbying and $12.2 million for political contributions through its PACs. Its contributions figures, however, do not include donations from company employees.
Source: Reproduced with permission of OpenSecrets.org, Center for Responsive Politics.

Transnational business
Businesses that operate across state lines.

Another proposition is that **transnational business** will be a salient feature of world politics. As capitalism expands, businesses increasingly look outward into the international system for markets. In the nineteenth century and again in the decades after World War II, international trade grew rapidly. So, too, did international investment, where banks and corporations invest their money in foreign businesses. In recent decades, this *internationalization* of business has increased, and individual companies have established production operations in many different countries. These international businesses, or multinational corporations, include companies such as General Electric, Toyota, and Nestlé. Often, these companies become so internationalized that it is difficult to identify their home country; the world is their playing field.

Marxists argue that with the rise of transnational business, capitalists tend to win, and workers tend to lose. That is, capitalists can cooperate to protect their wealth and maintain their privileged positions. International capitalists have options; they can establish operations in various countries and, when conditions are not favorable to their business interests, they can shut down their operations and go elsewhere. National governments, therefore, have incentives to treat international business well, providing tax breaks and favorable deals so they will stay put. Workers, on the other hand, are not as mobile. They cannot move around as readily, and so their bargaining position is weaker. While international capitalists can fly around the world in search of business deals, workers find it difficult to organize across countries. Marxists argue that international relations will bear the marks of this class conflict; national workers will press their governments for protection and international capitalists will lobby for an open world economy.

In sum, while realists see states struggling for power, and liberals see opportunities for states to cooperate, Marxists see politics and international relations as part of a deeper historical process of capitalist development. As the world capitalist system evolves, states and peoples organize and struggle accordingly. While liberals assert that economic interdependence is ultimately beneficial to all people and provides incentives for states to cooperate, Marxists believe that economic relations within and between countries are inherently unequal and exploitive. Economics does not breed peace – it generates conflict. Marxists do think that this conflict will someday be overcome through communist revolution. In the early decades of the twentieth century – before and after the Russian Revolution – some Marxists thought that the long-sought communist revolution had begun. But the Soviet Union ended up not establishing communism, but something very different – a despotic socialist state. Marxists believe that progress is possible, and class conflict can be overcome through revolution, but this dream for progressive change has yet to occur.

Marxism has enduring relevance as an analytic construct in international relations. In certain eras – such as the 'roaring '90s' – Marxism seemed less relevant. Trade and investment expanded and economic growth reached around the world. In those circumstances, Marxist ideas about class and class conflict give way to liberal ideas about mutual gain and the 'lifting of all ships.' But economic crises bring the insights of Marxism back into focus. The 2008 financial crisis highlights the tendency of capitalism to carry the seeds of its own destruction and to concentrate wealth – and by implication power – in the hands of fewer and fewer large actors, such as the large investment firms on Wall Street.

Marxism provides a useful counter-perspective to liberalism. Liberals tend to see globalization as a force for good, linking the world more closely together and generating economic gains for everyone. Marxism is more focused on the winners and losers in the global capitalist system. Globalization has drawn the world together, but it has also led to sharper divisions between haves and have-nots. The United States and other advanced countries have seen their economies 'globalized' in recent decades. But globalization has led to concern in these countries over the hollowing out of their industrial sectors – the high-paying manufacturing jobs – leaving educated elites and those working low-wage service jobs to struggle within an increasingly unequal society.

Levels of Analysis *The Marxist Tradition*

Individual	State	International
Individuals are divided into classes and their interests and political capacities are shaped by their economic circumstances.	Capitalist states are class societies, ruled by powerful economic elites. Capitalist states both exploit and dominate weaker societies and pursue war and foreign quest for economic gain.	The international system is shaped by the imperatives of capitalist growth and the powerful capitalist states that dominate it.

THE CONSTRUCTIVIST TRADITION

In different ways, realists, liberals, and Marxists all make arguments about the impact of power and interests on international relations. Another theoretical perspective focuses on the role of ideas and the ways in which 'what people believe' shapes what individuals, groups, and states do. This constructivist perspective comes in several varieties, but it is unified by the view that ideas and beliefs matter in how actors define and pursue their interests. People do not simply act on self-evident interests or operate in a realist world of anarchy. International relations, according to constructivists, are 'socially constructed.' What people think and believe matters regarding how they act in the world. While constructivism as a tradition in international relations is relatively new, the notion that ideas matter is an old notion reflected in a broader philosophical tradition known as **idealism**.

Idealism
The notion that ideas matter in international relations.

Constructivist Assumptions

Constructivist theory is built around four assumptions. First, the *interests* of individuals, groups, and states are not given or set in stone. Interests are shaped by the *identities* of actors. How people see themselves – for example, as a patriot, scientist, Christian, Muslim, Westerner, African, or citizen of the world – will shape how they think about their interests and what they want to achieve in politics. The realist, liberal, and Marxist theoretical traditions tend to see the interests of individuals as derived from specific social and political structures, such as anarchy, democracy, market society, or class position. In contrast, constructivists see much more diversity in the positions – and identities – of individuals.

Second, identities are molded by a variety of ideational factors – culture, religion, science, and normative beliefs. Constructivists do not fully discount the role of the material setting of individuals in shaping their identities. A steel worker or a bond trader operates within a setting that helps shape his or her thinking. But constructivists argue that identities emerge from the interplay of these real-world settings and the evolving ideas and beliefs inside the heads of people.

Third, elite individuals in both society and the state are the most important actors. The ideas and identities that these elites possess tend to shape the way the groups and states they lead act within the international system. Thus, it is necessary to look closely at what leaders think and believe to explain what they do. Ideas shape the world.

Finally, communication plays an important role in shaping and changing identities. The interactions of elites and the networks they operate within are important in creating and reinforcing ideas and beliefs. Through communication and networking, elites tend to produce collective or shared worldviews that shape how interests are defined and pursued. The focus of constructivists is on critical historical moments when elites communicate and build consensus on who they are as groups and states, and how to think about problems. Interaction, networking, and communication shape the way actors think and behave.

Constructivist Propositions

Four key concepts or propositions follow from this constructivist worldview. First, constructivists argue that 'the world is what you believe it is.' If people can be convinced and come to believe that the world is guided by universal moral standards, they will act that way. In a direct challenge to realism, one leading constructivist has argued: 'anarchy is what states make of it' (Wendt 1999). The world is anarchical, but this does not imply that interstate relations will operate as realist theory predicts. Anarchy is shaped by how people think about it. As state elites learn more about each other, they can change their expectations and come to see each other as friends rather than foes. The United States does not worry about the United Kingdom's vast nuclear arsenal, but it frets that North Korea may have a small number of primitive nuclear bombs.

Indeed, anarchy can be manifest in several different ways. One type of anarchy is the harsh world that realists describe. This is a world in which states regard other states as enemies that deserve no respect, are not necessarily legitimate or sovereign, and can be conquered if circumstances allow. This is anarchy manifest as the law of the jungle. Another type of anarchy is where states view each other as rivals, but not enemies. States are not interested in conquering others simply because they can; instead, they seek to preserve the status quo, respect the rights of others to exist, and use force only for defensive purposes and in the name of stabilizing the system. The role of force is shaped by norms, absolute gains are often preferential to relative gains, and cooperation is possible. Yet another type of anarchy is one where states view other states as friends; states cooperate to maximize collective gains, the use of force is generally viewed as illegitimate, sovereignty is respected, and collective security replaces national security. According to the constructivist view, none of the types of anarchy is more natural or inevitable than the others, and through *learning* and *socialization*, which results from interaction between elites, the world can move toward more cooperative and collective security-oriented anarchy.

A second constructivist proposition is that states operate within a **global civil society**. In this sense, constructivism is compatible with liberalism's emphasis on cosmopolitanism. Civil society is the realm of private activity that lies outside the political system. It is the realm of private associations, where religious, ethnic, and civic groups flourish. Civil society exists within countries but it also operates between countries, often manifest in transnational groups and associations. Global civil society is, in effect, the total of these transnational groups and activities. Constructivists agree with liberal theorists that these transnational networks and exchanges are important mechanisms for spreading norms and ideas, and for building trust and consensus among countries. For constructivists, global civil society facilitates elite learning and socialization, providing the communication networks through which elites develop ideas and identities that shape state policy, and gives shape to the character of anarchy.

A third constructivist proposition is that **normative change** is a major way in which world politics evolved from era to era. Constructivists argue that the learning and socialization that takes place across the global system does tend to move the world in a progressive direction. Norms do change; often, although not always, for the better. The institution of slavery was outlawed by the end of the nineteenth century. The practice of *apartheid* was ended in South Africa in the 1980s. In the postwar era, as discussed in Chapter 5, new norms of humanitarian intervention emerged that give the international community the right and obligation to intervene in the domestic affairs of states to protect individuals from genocide or other forms of collective violence.

A final constructivist proposition is that state elites exist within and are influenced

Global civil society
The realm of private activity that lies outside the political system, where religious, ethnic, and civic groups flourish. Global civil society refers to these transnational groups and activities across borders.

Normative change
The idea that as global learning and international socialization occur, ideas about what is or is not acceptable or 'normal' change. As normative change occurs, it can impact international relations.

Photo 3.4 Cape Town, South Africa, 1952
A scene from the long struggle against *apartheid* in South Africa. Black South Africans challenge white supremacy laws by occupying a 'Europeans Only' train carriage on the way into Cape Town.

Source: Bettmann.

Strategic culture
Refers to assumptions about the nature of the global system – for example, which states are friends and enemies – and strategies of action that are shared by government elites.

by **strategic culture**. As noted earlier, constructivists argue that states have *identities* that help shape how their leaders think about the nation's interests. Building on this view, constructivists go on to also argue that state leaders operate in a strategic culture that shapes foreign policy choices. Strategic culture refers to assumptions about the nature of the global system – for example, which states are friends and enemies – and strategies of action that are shared by government elites. Russia, Japan, the United Kingdom, France, China, and the United States all have different strategic cultures because of differences rooted in specific historical experiences and national security lessons crystallized in ideology and traditions of grand strategy (Johnston 1995). These differences in strategic culture give countries distinctive *personalities* as states, even as they operate in similar global situations. To understand how leading states will make choices, it is necessary to unpack the assumptions and ideational frameworks with which state leaders rank preferences and make grand strategic choices.

Recall our discussion in Chapter 2 of why the Cold War ended. Constructivists place great weight on the role of Gorbachev, and on how he embraced a set of ideas to transform Soviet strategic culture. Gorbachev and his reformers believed war with the West was not inevitable, and there was greater room for cooperation with capitalism than traditional Soviet strategic culture had earlier believed. For constructivists, the world changed not because material power changed, but because ideas changed (Lebow and Risse-Kappen 1995).

In looking at the ways that ideas and identities shape the choices of states, some scholars have focused specifically on the role of gender as a shaping influence. We now turn to this emerging area of scholarship.

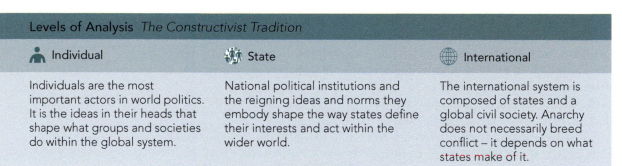

Levels of Analysis *The Constructivist Tradition*

👤 Individual	👥 State	🌐 International
Individuals are the most important actors in world politics. It is the ideas in their heads that shape what groups and societies do within the global system.	National political institutions and the reigning ideas and norms they embody shape the way states define their interests and act within the wider world.	The international system is composed of states and a global civil society. Anarchy does not necessarily breed conflict – it depends on what states make of it.

CRITICAL THEORY AND THE FEMINIST TRADITION

Alongside the theoretical approaches described above, various other schools of thought have emerged that offer critiques of the basic assumptions of traditional theories of international relations. Many of these theories and ideas can be grouped under the banner of 'critical theory,' which step back from the debates over world politics to question and critique the deep foundations of power, society, and ideas, particularly as they are portrayed by realism and liberalism. The aim of critical theory is not to build and test empirical hypotheses about international relations, but to question the intellectual frameworks and systems of power that mainstream scholars simply assume.

Robert Cox, a leading critical theorist, has famously distinguished between two types of theories – 'problem-solving' and 'critical theories.' Problem-solving theory, as Cox sees it, 'takes the world as it finds it, with the prevailing political and social relationships and the institutions in which they are organized, as the given framework for action.' In this way, '[t]he general aim of problem-solving is to make these relationships and institutions work smoothly by dealing effectively with sources of trouble' (Cox 1981: 128–29). Critical theory, Cox argues, 'does not take institutions and social and power relations for granted but calls them into question by concerning itself with their origins and how and whether they might be in the process of changing. … Critical theory is directed to the social and political complex as a whole rather than the separate parts.' (Cox 1981: 129). Similar to constructivism and Marxism, critical theory seeks to expose the ways in which the ideas and institutions that people take for granted – capitalism, liberal democracy, the Western nation-state system – are built around structures of power and domination. The categories and concepts we use in building and evaluating theory – and indeed the 'bodies of knowledge' we use to understand the world – are themselves parts of the prevailing social order. Cox argues that 'theory is always for someone and for some purpose' (Cox 1981: 129). Critical theory, in all its various ways, seeks to illuminate these deep structures of power.

One area of study in international relations that is inspired by the insights of critical theory is the feminist tradition. Feminist scholarship has emerged in recent decades to challenge traditional assumptions and visions of world politics, and it has developed its own distinctive theoretical tradition. Feminist thinking is wide ranging and offers provocative counterpoints to old mainstream theoretical ideas about states, war, and power politics. The focus of feminist theory is on the role of gender in society and world affairs. It seeks to illuminate biases and neglected ways of viewing international relations.

The Feminist Tradition

One of the groundbreaking feminist explorations of international relations is Cynthia Enloe's *Bananas, Beaches, Bases: Making Feminist Sense of International Politics* (Enloe 2014). The book provides a vivid historical account of the way women have been subordinated to men in various industries and institutions within the expanding global system such as tourism, agriculture, and the armed forces. In Enloe's portrait, women play a role in the world economy and geopolitical system primarily as subordinate and undervalued laborers – domestic workers, diplomatic wives, agricultural workers, and prostitutes outside military bases. Women are everywhere in international relations, but the lenses through which we view international relations tend to obscure and hide their presence. The great globalizing forces in world politics – multinational corporations, diplomatic relations, military alliances – are depicted as driven by the grand pursuits of men. In the background and with considerably less power, we find women playing undervalued and often demeaning supporting and subordinate roles. The important insight that Enloe advances – which is at the heart of the feminist critique – is that states and international relations have 'gendered' structures of domination and interaction. Feminism is like Marxism in that each emphasizes the structural inequality in political, economic, and social systems. Capitalism and the system of states is a system of domination, and women tend to be at the lower reaches and on the bottom. Traditional theories of international relations fail to acknowledge or analyze this hidden reality.

Building on this insight, beginning in the 1980s, scholars of international relations considered the implications of gender for how we study world affairs. The focus was not just on the disadvantaged role of women in global affairs, but also the development of a feminist critique of traditional geopolitical and state power theories of world politics that have for the most part been constructed by men – that is, theories that look at the world from the perspective of state leaders, who also tend to be men. Scholar Robert Keohane poses the question that feminist theory asks: 'How have distinctively male values, and social structures in which male values are given priority, affected the concepts developed in international society?' (Keohane 1989). The goal of the feminist tradition in international relations is to expose the gender bias that pervades the traditional theories of states and power politics, and to offer alternative views of world affairs from the standpoint of the weak and powerless.

Two general lines of argument, or sets of propositions, have emerged most clearly and forcefully in the feminist tradition. One is a critique of male-oriented assumptions about world politics, challenging the 'realist' orientation of prevailing theory. The other is the claim that gender bias has diminished the roles and capabilities of women in the actual conduct of international relations.

Feminist Propositions

In critiquing prevailing ideas and theories about international relations, feminist thinkers focus primarily on realist theory and its ideas about states, war, and power politics. Gender assumptions and biases are found at every level of this theoretical tradition. The language is male-oriented, sending the subtle or not-so-subtle message that world politics is a 'man's world.' After all, scholars talk of 'statesmen' and 'mankind.' The classic realist thinker, Hans Morgenthau, defines power as 'man's control over the minds and actions of other men' (Morgenthau 1985). The title of Kenneth Waltz's classic study is *Man, the State, and War* (Waltz 1959). The language of states and power – the 'high politics' of international relations that scholars focus on – suggests that the terrain of world politics is a man's terrain. The hidden assumption is that the rough and tumble 'public sphere' is a man's world, while the 'private sphere' of family and home is a woman's world.

Along these lines, in her influential feminist study, *Women and War*, Jean Bethke Elshtain argues that the great writings on war, by theorists from Thucydides to Machiavelli to modern realists, offer a vision of 'high politics' in which the public sphere is inhabited by men, wielding power and determining the fates of peoples and societies (Elshtain 1987). The scholarly study of international relations, Elshtain argues, has become a professionalized male-dominated world closed off from the wider values of society. 'Encumbered with lifeless jargon, systems and subsystems dominance, spirals of misperception, decision-making analysis, multipolar, intervening variables, dependence, interdependence, cost-effectiveness, IR specialists in the post-Second World War era began to speak exclusively to, or "at," one another or to their counterparts in government service' (Elshtain 1987). The discourse of international relations has become a closed intellectual system with deep assumptions about the masculinity of power and world politics. In making this feminist critique, Elshtain seeks to open both the scholarly and political discussion of war and peace by calling for a more open 'civic' discussion of war and the exercise of power. By breaking down the gendered character of the study of international relations, the issues of war and peace can be seen and debated from more angles. More voices and sensibilities – including the voices and sensibilities of women – can be brought into the public debate over the great decisions of war and peace. The 'high politics' of international relations can become more open to a wider social and international conversation.

Feminist scholarship shares this aim of opening up and breaking down old gender-biased ways of thinking about international relations. If concepts such as state, power, anarchy, and war are masculine ideas, or at least ideas whose primacy in the study of international relations is reinforced by male gender biases, a feminine approach to international relations might emphasize cooperation, mutual gain, interdependence, and societal understanding. As Ann Tickner observes, 'Most feminists are committed to the emancipatory goal of achieving a more just society,' which, for them, includes ending the subordinate position of women (Tickner 1997).

One implication is that if women are given more opportunities to hold power – to lead governments and make decisions about war and peace – they will do so with different priorities and sensibilities. Studies by anthropologists and biologists do give some evidence that males and females have different predispositions toward violence and aggression rooted in differences in their genetic and biological characteristics, such as the presence in males of the hormone testosterone. These biologically driven differences are seen by some experts to generate different social behaviors, including a greater tendency of males to engage in violence and aggressive actions. As we will see in Chapter 6, there are even some experimental studies that test male and female students, finding that males are more likely to be overconfident and attack the enemy in simulated war games (Johnson 2006). Some experts see culture as more important in shaping differences between the genders in social behavior – and there certainly is a lot of variation across history and countries of the world in the role of women in war and as wielders of power (Goldstein 2001).

A second line of feminist argument is that women have been systematically under-represented in both the study and practice of international relations. The basic insight starts with the observation that, although gender relations differ from country to country, they are nonetheless almost always unequal. In this respect, the historian Joan Scott argues that gender has been a way for societies to signify relationships of power. The claim is not that women are different – that they embody different values or sensibilities – but that they are simply under-represented in the scholarly world of international relations and the governmental corridors of power (Scott 2018).

Despite advances in education and the modernization of societies, such as in Western Europe and the United States, there remains deep-rooted inequality of opportunity and representation for women. Within the field of political science, one study indicates that only 26 percent of the 13,000 professors are women, and an even smaller percentage of professors who study international relations are women (Malinak 2008). Women also tend to study and teach different subjects than men. Women are more likely to study transnational actors and international organizations, specialize in developing regions, such as Latin America and sub-Saharan Africa, and focus on the role of ideas and identities in their work. Men are more likely to study American foreign policy and issues of war and peace, specialize in the great powers, and use realist theories of world politics.

In the world of foreign policy and diplomacy, the under-representation of women is also striking. In the United States there has never been a female President, although Secretary of State Hillary Clinton came close to being the first. She also had the distinction of being one of only two female US Secretaries of State since the 1990s. When

Photo 3.5 Leaders in Germany and the United Kingdom
Prime Minister of the United Kingdom Theresa May (R) and German Chancellor Angela Merkel (L) at the German Chancellery in Berlin, Germany on July 20, 2016. Even in the 21st century, most world leaders are still men, but women are beginning to make headway.

Source: Mehmet Kaman/Anadolu Agency/Getty Images.

heads of state travel each September to the United Nations for its annual opening, most of these leaders are men. While there have been female leaders in countries such as India (Indira Gandhi), Israel (Golda Meir), the Philippines (Corazon Aquino), and others, only British Prime Ministers Margaret Thatcher and Theresa May and German Chancellor Angela Merkel have been leaders of one of the great powers. Worldwide, women filled only 22 percent of parliamentary seats in 2017, although this figure is up from 11 percent in 1995 (United Nations data).

Feminists focusing on the problem of inequality and under-representation are not arguing that women would make better leaders or that the world would be more peaceful if women ran the planet. Their argument is not that women are somehow morally superior to men. Rather, these feminist thinkers argue simply that it is a question of justice – and, indeed, that it is a lost opportunity not to draw upon the talents and capacities of fully half of humanity. Some writers do argue that women might be better diplomats and state leaders. Francis Fukuyama argues in a famous essay that women are in fact more sensitive to a wider set of social values and, if in charge, would be more inclined to seek peaceful solutions to the world's problems (Fukuyama 1998). But this view has been challenged by some leading feminist scholars. Ann Tickner argues that in fact this thesis that associates women with peace and moral superiority has the effect of keeping women out of power. 'The association of women with peace can play into unfortunate gender stereotypes that characterize men as active, women as passive; men as agents, women as victims; men as rational, women as emotional,' Tickner notes. 'Not only are these stereotypes damaging to women, particularly to their credibility as actors in matters of international politics and national security, but they are also damaging to peace' (Tickner 1999). The goal of feminist theory is not to seek the advance of women into positions of power because they bring more lofty values and aspirations. It is because their under-representation in positions of power stems from the social injustice and inequities that speak ill of today's economic and political systems.

Considering the five theoretical frameworks, how do the roles of actors and actions in each tradition differ? We offer a brief comparison next.

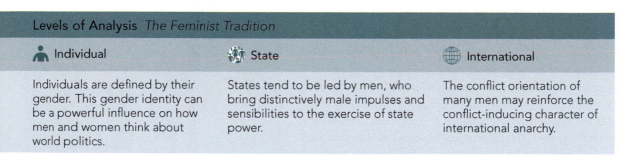

Levels of Analysis *The Feminist Tradition*		
🧍 Individual	👪 State	🌐 International
Individuals are defined by their gender. This gender identity can be a powerful influence on how men and women think about world politics.	States tend to be led by men, who bring distinctively male impulses and sensibilities to the exercise of state power.	The conflict orientation of many men may reinforce the conflict-inducing character of international anarchy.

COMPARING TRADITIONS

These five theoretical traditions provide useful ways to look at international relations. It is not necessary to decide if one is right and the others are wrong. They each provide a window on the world. Each claims to capture the dynamics of world politics. In the chapters ahead, we will make use of these traditions. In doing so, we can make some comparisons between them based on what they think are the important actors and forces at work in the global system.

3.6   DIFFERING THEORETICAL APPROACHES

Sources of Change in International Relations

Realism

War is a major source of change in world politics. In every historical era, war – particularly among major states – has dramatically changed the geopolitical landscape. In the wake of war, powerful rising states have emerged to dominate the system, while defeated states have gone into decline. War has forced states to mobilize their economies and societies, leading to innovations and changes in government capacities. World War I is a good example of how a major war transformed politics, economics, and world affairs. It led to the destruction of vast empires, brought the United States to the center of world politics, and fueled changes in European politics that played out over the next half century.

Liberalism

Liberals argue that change in world politics comes from ongoing trade, exchange, innovation, and learning that occurs within and between countries. Through these processes, societies advance and modernize. World politics changes as the countries themselves become more advanced – liberal, capitalist, and democratic – and as the relations between these countries become more interdependent and cooperative. The post-1945 rise of the European Community – later called the European Union – is a major example of what liberals see as advancement.

Marxism

Marxists argue that change in world politics is generated by political conflict that is rooted in the capitalist system. Economic inequality and the divergent economic interests between classes provide the setting for struggle between peoples, classes, and states. Marx originally argued that these conflicts would result in revolution within capitalist societies, ushering in communism. Later Marxist scholars have focused on a wider array of conflicts, including clashes between wealthy and poor countries.

Constructivism

Constructivists argue that change in world politics emerges from the evolution in norms and worldviews that guide the behavior of people and societies – including the behavior of state leaders. The decline in the acceptability of slavery during the nineteenth century and empire in the twentieth century are examples of major shifts in normative orientations.

Feminism

Like constructivists, feminist theorists argue that dominant ideologies and orientations in world politics are formed over long periods of time. Feminists point to the way gender roles and expectations get established, leading to the marginalization of women in world affairs. For change to occur, societies need to become more aware of these often-hidden or unremarked-upon biases. Change comes when people's ideas about gender change. Women who do rise to prominence in world politics – as foreign ministers or heads of states – can become role models, thereby helping to change ideas and expectations.

Table 3.3 Comparing Theoretical Traditions

	Realism	Liberalism	Marxism	Constructivism	Feminism
Actors in world politics	State leaders speak for the national interest	Diverse range of societal individuals groups, and institutions	Economic classes, particularly business elites and institutions	Government and social elites	Individual leaders and citizens
Behavior of actors	Primarily to advance power and interest of the state, i.e. a struggle for power defined by conflict	Inclined toward cooperation for mutual gain	Workers forced to accept division of labor; capitalists seek to preserve their privileged position	Communication and interaction to share knowledge and build consensus	Redress balance between masculine and feminine values
Influential forces	War	Learning	Revolution	Spread of ideas	Gender
The direction of history	Cyclical	Linear	Working toward revolution	Progressively inclined but not as certain about linear direction as liberals	Peace and justice more likely if women are fully incorporated into leadership

In terms of the actors that dominate world politics, realists argue that state leaders speak for the national interests. Liberals argue that foreign policy reflects the diversity of people and groups within society, as well as the ties they develop across states. Marxists trace the broad patterns of world politics to economic classes, particularly business elites. Constructivism tends to look to government and societal elites who are the carriers of ideas that influence the actions of states. Feminism focuses on the gender of leaders and citizens and the male bias in the way people think about international relations.

The traditions differ regarding the behavior of these actors as well. Realists see states acting primarily to advance the power and interests of the state, and this brings states into conflict with each other. In other words, world politics, according to realists, is a struggle for power defined by conflict between states. Liberals see states as more inclined toward cooperation. Individuals and groups in society are always looking for ways to advance their interests by working with others, a dynamic most consistently seen in relations among liberal democracies. Marxists see economic inequality and class conflict as the fundamental dynamics within and between states. Constructivists focus on the ways in which elites within and across states communicate with each other, interacting in ways that share knowledge and build consensus on important questions of peace, prosperity, stability, and order. Feminist theories seek to expose the biases in how scholars think about international relations, showing how masculine values often get emphasized at the expense of feminine values – and these theories also emphasize how gender inequality exists in the 'man's world' of international affairs.

Realists see world politics shaped and reshaped by war. It is war that ultimately serves to destroy the old relations between states, paving the way for newly powerful states. Liberals, in contrast, see learning as a much more powerful force of change in world politics. States are not doomed to repeat their mistakes. Societies can learn and make advancements in their relationships with others. Marxists see revolution as the master mechanism of change. Economic classes are fundamentally antagonistic. When class relations become so prone to conflict and violence, revolutions can erupt that serve to overturn the old political order and usher in new social relations. Constructivists see the spread of ideas as the most important mechanism of change, a process that is pushed forward by political activist groups, including social groups and international nongovernmental organizations. Feminists stress the pathways by which gender can influence both how leaders act in world affairs and how scholars understand and interpret that action.

Finally, the traditions differ regarding the direction of history. Realists see history as cyclical. States are ultimately caught up in continuous cycles of war and change, rise and fall. Liberals see the direction of history as more linear. Peoples and societies can cooperate and make their lives better. Marxists see class conflict ultimately leading to revolution that ushers in more equal and just social relations. Constructivists tend to see a progressive logic to change in world politics, but are usually less certain than liberals that the world can and will be made better. In this sense, they do not have explicit visions of the advancement of humankind. But they do see elites across the world engaged in dialogue and communication. This dialogue and communication can lead to conflict, of course. But it can also give states opportunities to find common ground and remake world politics. Feminists believe that history is shaped by gender and that the prospects for peace, war, conflict, and cooperation among states will be influenced by gender relations within those states.

Levels of Analysis *Comparing Traditions*

Individual	State	International
Different theoretical perspectives place different weights on the importance of individuals; constructivism and feminism place the individual at the center of analysis; realism places the individual at the margins of its theory.	Realism, constructivism, and feminism downplay the significance of domestic institutions; liberalism and Marxism place them at the heart of their respective analyses, although the former stresses political institutions while Marxism-Leninism focuses on economic institutions.	Realism places its main emphasis on the international system; feminism and constructivism argue that the effects of the international system depend on how actors perceive that system; and liberalism and Marxism argue that the effects of the international system are contingent on the domestic institutions of states.

REVISITING THE ENDURING QUESTION AND LOOKING AHEAD

This chapter has surveyed five competing theoretical traditions in the field of international relations. These traditions each provide assumptions and arguments about the way the world works. Do we need to pick among these five theoretical traditions? Is one of them right and the others wrong? The answer is no. The world is an amazingly large and diverse place. Over the centuries, it has exhibited an extraordinary array of human behavior. No one theoretical tradition can explain everything that puzzles us about international relations. They are all potentially useful as tools of explanation. As we explore the enduring problems of international relations, we have a lot of tools. The arguments of one tradition or another may be more convincing in specific circumstances or historical episodes, but we want to keep all of them ready to be used.

It is useful to think of these theoretical traditions as *lenses* through which we observe international relations. The traditions tell us where to look, even if they cannot always confidently predict what we will find in any given situation. Each theoretical tradition offers a different lens, and each lens highlights different actors and activities in the international system. When we put on the realist lens, we see states and the struggle for power. We see the problems of anarchy everywhere – security dilemmas, power balancing, and nationalism. When we put on the liberal lens, we see individuals and groups engaged in complex activities of cooperation and institution building. We see states organizing open systems of trade and the emergence of communities of democracies. When we put on the Marxist lens, we see class conflict and economic struggle between the rich and poor across the globe. We see an ever-changing system of world capitalism shaping and reshaping conflict and cooperation around the world. When we put on the constructivist lens, we see great movements of ideas and norms. We see elites communicating and learning through international networks, and state identities shaping the way countries make foreign policy and organize the global system. When we put on the feminist lens, we see both the importance of gender differences and the role of gender in the perpetuation of political, social, and economic inequalities within and across states.

Each of these lenses allows us to see different things and raises specific actors and dynamics to the foreground and moves other actors and dynamics to the background. As we explore the history and evolving character of international relations, we want to keep all these lenses at the ready. In looking at international history, as well as foreign policy of states in the present period, we also want to have the analytical tools that students of foreign policy have developed. It is to the examination of that toolbox for the analysis of foreign policy that we next direct our attention.

STUDY QUESTIONS

1. Which theoretical tradition of international relations is most appealing to you? Which is the least appealing? Why?
2. Is it important that we have theories of international relations? Why or why not?
3. Realist theory has been the most central or prominent theory in the past. Do you think it will be as important in the future? Why or why not? Which theory seems to have a more promising future?
4. How do we know if one or another theory of international relations is more helpful to us as we try to understand international relations?
5. Which theoretical tradition of international relations do you wish national leaders in major countries like the United States and China, for example, paid closer attention to as they formulate their foreign policies?

FURTHER READING

Bull, Hedley (1977) *The Anarchical Society: A Study of Order in World Politics*, 3rd edn (Basingstoke, UK: Macmillan). A founding statement of the English School of international relations, emphasizing both the existence of anarchy among states and an international community.

Doyle, Michael (1997) *Ways of War and Peace: Realism, Liberalism, and Socialism* (New York: Norton). A magisterial survey of the leading theoretical traditions in the study of international relations. It includes portraits of the philosophical thinkers whose ideas have informed these traditions.

Keohane, Robert O. and Joseph S. Nye (1977) *Power and Interdependence: World Politics in Transition* (Boston: Little, Brown). Offers a liberal internationalist perspective on world politics, emphasizing the fragmented and decentralized character of power within a complex and evolving modern international system.

Tickner, J. Ann (2014) *A Feminist Voyage Through International Relations* (New York: Oxford University Press, 2014). A compendium of the work of one of the leading feminist theorists of international relations, including her later articles on race, religion, and imperialism.

Waltz, Kenneth (1959) *Man, the State, and War: A Theoretical Analysis* (New York: Columbia University Press). A landmark study of the ideas of classical political theories on questions of war and peace. Waltz famously divides these theories into 'images' or levels of the international system and sources of war – the individual, state, and international structural levels.

Wendt, Alexander (1999) *Social Theory of International Politics* (Cambridge: Cambridge University Press). Wendt offers foundational thinking for the constructivist approach to international relations.

 Visit **www.macmillanihe.com/Grieco-IntroIR-2e** to access extra resources for this chapter, including:
- Chapter summaries to help you review the material
- Multiple choice quizzes to test your understanding
- Flashcards to test your knowledge of the key terms in this chapter
- An interactive simulation that invites you to go through the decision-making process of a world leader at a crucial political juncture
- Pivotal decisions in which you weigh up the pros and cons of complicated decisions with grave consequences
- Outside resources, including links to contemporary articles and videos, that add to what you have learned in this chapter

4 The Analysis of Foreign Policy

Enduring question
What motivates and influences the behavior of states toward one another?

Chapter Contents

Learning Objectives

By the end of this chapter, you will be able to:

→ Compare the study of international relations and the analysis of foreign policy and appreciate how both are necessary to understand international affairs.

→ Identify the two core attributes, interests and strategies, of any country's foreign policy.

→ Analyze the range of policy instruments that a country may utilize in its foreign policy.

→ Apply the levels-of-analysis framework to explore the sources of a country's foreign policy.

→ Utilize the levels-of-analysis framework to identify the conditions under which a country may change its foreign policy.

During the 1950s, China was allied with the Soviet Union and considered the United States its principle geopolitical adversary. China worked closely with the Soviet Union and fought opposite the United States during the Korean War of the 1950s and the Vietnam War of the 1960s. China did not even have diplomatic relations with the United States until the 1970s. By the 1980s, however, China not only established diplomatic relations, but moved closer to its former adversary, the United States, politically and economically. In contrast, by the end of the 1960s, China's leaders came to view the Soviet Union more as an adversary than as an ally. China and the Soviet Union fought a border war in 1969.

Today, China enjoys cordial political relations, and limited economic relations, with Russia. It has close economic relations with the United States; in fact, the two countries are highly dependent on each other commercially and financially. However, China's political relations with the United States are changing again and have become significantly colder. Many believe the two countries are emerging as geopolitical competitors as they compete for influence in the South China Sea and in East Asia more generally.

These twists and turns in China's external relations point to the enduring question addressed in this chapter: what motivates and influences the behavior of states toward one another? We will address this question by breaking it down into more manageable pieces in the sections to follow. First, we will consider the matter of what exactly is a foreign policy. Second, we will utilize the levels-of-analysis framework to investigate the sources of foreign policy or, more precisely, we will investigate the attributes of individuals, states, and the international system that influence the selection of foreign policies by governments. Third, we will seek to identify the conditions under which states change their foreign policies.

The enduring question of what motivates the behavior of states toward one another is unresolved and consequential. Some analysts prefer 'inside-out' explanations; they focus on domestic sources of foreign policy, and debate the extent to which interest groups, public opinion, or the structure of government helps us to understand the behavior of states. 'Outside-in' analysts believe that international or external sources are the key determinants of foreign policy. External sources include how powerful or weak a country is relative to other countries, and the extent to which a country finds itself in a peaceful or threatening neighborhood. Scholarly debates over what accounts for foreign policy are unresolved in that no single factor is a clear analytical winner in explaining the foreign policies of different countries, across different issues, and across time. Understanding foreign policy is critical because the foreign policy choices that states make have profound implications for relations among states. Thus, it is important in an international relations text to devote sustained attention to the determinants of foreign policy.

FOREIGN POLICY ANALYSIS: CONNECTIONS TO INTERNATIONAL RELATIONS

To explore the enduring question of which factors account for the foreign policies of states, we first examine how the analysis of foreign policy differs from and complements the study of international relations.

The Study of International Relations and the Analysis of Foreign Policy

In general, scholars of international relations are interested in interactions between two or more states, and particularly in why some of those interactions are cooperative while others are competitive and may even end in war. The theories we examined in

Chapter 3 fundamentally try to understand interstate interactions, and especially the conditions that cause those interactions to be peaceful or conflictual. In contrast, students of foreign policy, which is the decision by a government to take certain actions toward foreign governments or foreign non-state actors, want to understand why that government has decided to take those actions and why it has crafted particular strategies to promote or defend the interests involved.

The negotiation of the Paris Agreement on Climate Change, reached in December 2015, provides a good opportunity to see the differences between the relative emphases of scholars of international relations and scholars of foreign policy. A scholar of international relations would be interested in the international dynamics that brought the Paris Agreement into being. That scholar might ask whether the agreement was attained because more powerful countries enticed poorer countries to do so, or because the global scientific community and globally active nongovernmental organizations (NGOs) persuaded national leaders that global warming was a real threat and ought to be addressed through an international agreement.

A scholar of foreign policy might also be interested in how the Paris Agreement came about but would focus on the decisions of specific countries on whether to adhere to it. So, for example, that scholar would want to understand why the United States under President Bill Clinton's administration helped negotiate an earlier agreement on climate change – the Kyoto Protocol of 1997 – but never submitted the Protocol to the US Senate for ratification, which the US Constitution requires for any treaty to come into force for the United States. Scholars of foreign policy would also be interested in understanding why President Barack Obama's administration played a key role in negotiating the 2015 Paris Agreement, but less than two years later the successor administration of President Donald Trump took the rare step of withdrawing from the agreement. A foreign policy analyst might also want to know why China and India, industrializing countries that produce significant amounts of greenhouse gases, declined to participate in the Kyoto Protocol but were willing to adhere to the Paris Agreement. The study of foreign policy can focus on one country, such as the United States, India, or China, or the foreign policy pattern of a country toward another country or a region, such as continuity and change in China's foreign policy toward Japan, or it can focus comparatively across the foreign policies of two or more countries.

The theoretical traditions outlined in Chapter 3 and the analysis of foreign policy in this chapter reinforce each other. Foreign policy analysts often draw from and rely upon theories of international relations to understand the foreign policy decisions and actions of states. For example, some analysts, drawing from the realist tradition, argue that external conditions – such as a country's geographic position or its relative power – constrain and shape that state's objectives and actions in the foreign domain. Scholars from the liberal or Marxist tradition may locate the sources of a state's foreign policy in its domestic political and economic structures, respectively. Constructivist and feminist scholars make the important point that the perspectives of national leaders, including views shaped by their interactions and gender, respectively, play an important role in constraining their views on what is desirable and feasible in foreign affairs. Hence, the theories we examined in Chapter 3 are important both as contending and overlapping arguments about international interactions, and about the actions of specific states that, taken together, help to create international relations.

Scholars of international relations and foreign policy specialists appreciate the importance of one another's work. Foreign policy analysts understand that a country's international context matters a great deal when its leaders identify interests and formulate strategies. In turn, students of international relations recognize that the international interactions of governments have firm roots in the foreign policies of the countries involved in those interactions. If you wish to understand international affairs and why countries sometimes work together, sometimes compete, and sometimes even fight each other, then you must understand both sides of the coin in world affairs, international relations and foreign policy.

CORE CONCEPTS OF FOREIGN POLICY

We now fine-tune language we introduced in Chapter 1 for the analysis of foreign policy, with attention paid to the two concepts of interest and strategy.

Foreign Policy Interests

We often say that a government is pursuing a particular foreign policy because it advances some interest (Jentleson 2010; George and Keohane 1980). An interest, as noted in Chapter 1, is a situation in the world that the leaders of a government want to exist, so much so that they are willing to pay costs to bring it about. National leaders often must accept that there is a gap between their hopes to promote a given interest and their capacity to do so, and that there are often trade-offs between interests; the pursuit of one requires giving up the pursuit of another.

For example, many US leaders believe that the extension of democracy and human rights to China is a US interest insofar as they also believe that a democratic China with human rights protections will be a more peaceful country. However, those leaders often find it necessary to curtail their efforts to promote China's internal transformation due to the reality that they must gain the current Chinese government's cooperation in order to advance other US interests, including stabilization and growth of the international economy, finding a solution to global climate change, and management of numerous international security issues, including Iran's nuclear weapons program and North Korea's often provocative behavior toward South Korea. We explore in Box 4.1 this clash between aspirations and realities involving the interest of US leaders in spreading human rights and democracy to present-day China while also working with its current government.

Foreign Policy Strategy

To advance or defend an interest, a government's leaders develop a foreign policy strategy. A foreign policy strategy, recall from Chapter 1, consists of the specification by leaders of objectives (the outcomes that help advance an interest), and policy instruments (the concrete measures the government takes to reach its objectives and thus advance its interest). For the purposes of discussion, we can distinguish between instruments that seek to reach policy objectives through the *persuasion* of a relevant foreign actor (that might be private or governmental in character), and those instruments that seek to reach policy objectives through the *coercion* of a foreign actor.

Instruments of Persuasion

Diplomacy
The process by which representatives of two or more governments meet and discuss matters of common concern.

Governments sometimes seek to achieve foreign policy objectives by trying to persuade foreign actors to act or desist from acting in one manner or another. One key instrument of such persuasion by governments is **diplomacy**. We will discuss diplomacy in more detail as a means toward peace in Chapter 7. However, diplomacy in general terms is the process by which representatives of two or more governments meet and discuss matters of common concern either bilaterally or in a multilateral

4.1   MAKING CONNECTIONS
Aspiration versus Reality

US Foreign Policy toward China, 2009

US policy makers consistently argue that they place high value on the spread of democracy and human rights around the world. But, as this example shows, those concerns are often forced to take a back seat to other pressing issues such as climate change, the economic crisis then gripping the world, and security problems including the spread of nuclear weapons.

Aspiration: Secretary of State Hillary Clinton on Human Rights and China, December 2009

> The United States seeks positive relationships with China and Russia, and that means candid discussions of divergent views. In China, we call for protection of rights of minorities in Tibet and Xinxiang; for the rights to express oneself and worship freely; and for civil society and religious organizations to advocate their positions within a framework of the rule of law. And we believe strongly that those who advocate peacefully for reform within the constitution, such as Charter 2008 signatories, should not be prosecuted. With Russia, we deplore the murders of journalists and activists and support the courageous individuals who advocate at great peril for democracy. With China, Russia, and others, we are engaging on issues of mutual interest while also engaging societal actors in these same countries who are working to advance human rights and democracy. The assumption that we must either pursue human rights or our 'national interests' is wrong. The assumption that only coercion and isolation are effective tools for advancing democratic change is also wrong.
>
> Source: Clinton (2009).

Reality: Secretary of State Hillary Clinton on Human Rights and China, February 2009

In February 2009, Hillary Clinton was about to leave Seoul, South Korea, for Beijing, China, during an inaugural visit to Asia as Secretary of State. She told reporters that while she would raise with her Chinese hosts the controversial issues of human rights, as well as Chinese policy on Tibet and Taiwan, she thought it might be more productive to focus on issues on which real progress was possible, namely, climate change, the global economic crisis, and a range of security issues. According to the report in the *New York Times*, Clinton said 'There is a certain logic to that,' and further, 'That doesn't mean that questions of Taiwan, Tibet, human rights, the whole range of challenges that we often engage on with the Chinese, are not part of the agenda,' she said. 'But we pretty much know what they're going to say.' For that reason, according to Secretary Clinton, 'We have to continue to press them,' yet at the same time, she indicated, 'But our pressing on those issues can't interfere with the global economic crisis, the global climate change crisis and the security crises. We have to have a dialogue that leads to an understanding and cooperation on each of those.'

Source: *New York Times* (2009).

forum. During these meetings, the representatives seek to persuade each other of the merits of their respective positions with a view toward finding a mutually agreeable solution to some problem or to develop a mechanism by which they can achieve individual gains through some form of joint action. These representatives may be ambassadors who are sent from their respective home countries to reside in the capital city of a host country, or they may be ministerial-rank officials, such as the British Foreign Secretary or the Indian Minister of External Affairs, or they may be the heads of state or governments, such as the US President or the Canadian Prime Minister.

 Simulations: What would you do? Visit the companion website and take on the role of the Prime Minister of a central Asian state. The challenge? To weigh up diplomatic options during an official visit of a neighboring Foreign Minister.

For example, diplomatic representatives from the five permanent members (P5) of the UN Security Council (China, France, Russia, the United Kingdom, and the United States) plus Germany negotiated with representatives of the government of Iran for a number of years on the latter's nuclear program. The P5 plus Germany sought to persuade Iran that it should accept limitations on its nuclear activities. The Iranian representatives in turn sought to persuade the P5 plus Germany that its nuclear activities were not directed toward the attainment of nuclear weapons, but instead were necessary for nuclear energy and medical research and were in accord with Iran's rights and obligations as a signatory to the Nuclear Non-Proliferation Treaty (NPT). A deal was struck in July 2015. Iran agreed to significant limitations on its nuclear weapons program and nuclear-related activities. In exchange, its negotiating partners agreed to lift certain economic sanctions, which allowed Iran to increase oil exports and gain access to some $100 billion of its assets that had been frozen in Western banks. This agreement held reasonably well at first but came under severe stress in May 2018 with the decision of the Trump administration to withdraw from the accord, leaving it unclear whether Iran would in turn also exit the agreement and return to nuclear activities that, from the viewpoint of the United States and others, might be precursors to the development of nuclear weapons.

Diplomacy often takes the form of government-to-government negotiations. But governments also use this tool to influence public opinion in other countries. One obvious example is the Voice of America (VOA), an international news source funded by the US government that produces television, radio, and digital content in over 40 languages to distribute around the world. Non-Western states, considering what they view as the dominance of Western-sponsored media (for example, the BBC or CNN), have responded recently with news outlets of their own. Al Jazeera, a state-funded broadcaster from Doha, Qatar, launched an English channel service called Al Jazeera English in 2006 to engage in and offer a different voice in the debates on international affairs. RT (formerly Russia Today) is an international television network launched in 2005 with the goal of improving the image of Russia abroad. Critics in the West view RT less as a news outlet and more as an instrument of Russian propaganda. Russian critics view the VOA in the same way.

Incentives
Rewards of some form offered by one state to another designed to influence the foreign policy of the recipient. Incentives are a form of persuasion.

Economic incentives
Instruments of persuasion in foreign policy. Economic incentives are basically carrots: country A promises some economic gain to B, and delivers it if B does what A wants it to do.

Diplomacy, then, is one instrument of persuasion in foreign policy. **Incentives**, the extension of a benefit by one state to another if the latter acts in accord with the preferences of the incentive-sending state, are another. As the Iran example above underscores, **economic incentives** constitute an important class of incentives. Economic incentives are basically carrots: country A promises some economic gain to B and delivers it if B does what A wants it to do. For example, West Germany extended very substantial economic aid to the Soviet Union to help facilitate Soviet acceptance in 1990 of the absorption of East Germany into West Germany (Newnham 2002). In the same vein, the European Union has provided economic assistance to members such as Greece, Ireland, and Portugal to help those members meet their short-term funding requirements in the midst of the ongoing economic crisis that began in 2008, but on condition that they undertake internal reforms that will make them more competitive and self-supporting in the future. Finally, in the Iran case discussed above, it was the promise to lift previously imposed economic sanctions that served as an incentive to Iran to agree to the 2015 nuclear deal.

Instruments of Coercion

Leaders sometimes find that diplomacy or incentives are not enough to cause another country to change its behavior. In those cases, leaders may turn to another class of foreign policy instruments, those that are designed to coerce a target government to act or stop from acting in some manner. One class of coercive policy instruments consists of **economic sanctions** (Hufbauer *et al.* 2009; Mastanduno 2011).

Economic sanctions involve the restriction of customary trade and investment relations with a target state. They are basically sticks: A threatens B with some form of economic loss if B does something A does not want it to do or fails to do something A wants it to do. Such sanctions can include the imposition of tariffs or quotas on goods imported from a target country, the boycotting of purchases of goods from suppliers from the target country, or the seizure of financial assets owned by target-country residents that are held in the initiating country's banks or other financial institutions. For example, in late 2011 and early 2012, the United States and member countries of the European Union began a boycott of purchases of oil from Iran, and a prohibition of financial transactions with Iran's central bank, to compel that country to negotiate an end to its efforts to build nuclear weapons. These actions appear to have been taken very seriously by the Iranian government, and it threatened to respond by closing the critically important Strait of Hormuz, through which passes approximately one-fifth of the world's oil exports. The United States responded that it would use military force to keep open the Strait of Hormuz – in other words, it would go to war with Iran. The deal the P5 plus Germany and Iran made in 2015 allowed the two sides to scale back tensions. As noted above, it also shows that yesterday's sticks (the initial imposition of economic sanctions) may be turned into today's carrots (the relaxation of those sanctions in exchange for some type of political concession).

Another class of coercive policy instruments involves propaganda and covert operations. **Propaganda** is the selective use of information, and at times misinformation, in order to advance a country's interests. Propaganda is frequently used as a tool to mobilize one's own population or to demoralize other populations in times of conflict or war. Nazi Germany, for example, relied on a Ministry of Public Enlightenment and Propaganda to produce documents and posters glorifying Germany's accomplishments and belittling its adversaries. During the Cold War, the United States used government-sponsored radio stations (Radio Liberty and Radio Free Europe) to influence the communist-controlled populations of the Soviet Union and Eastern Europe. Today, North Korea's autocratic government uses a steady stream of propaganda to keep its adversaries off balance, and to convince its deprived population that the more prosperous South Korea yearns to be 'purified' from capitalist influences and re-united with the communist North. There is a good chance that Russia used propaganda to influence the US presidential election of 2016, and it has possibly used similar actions to influence elections in Europe.

Covert operations are activities that a government directs against the interests of another government or non-state actor in such a way that the foreign targets and others are kept from knowing that the initiating government is responsible for the

Economic sanctions
The restriction of customary trade and investment relations with a target state. An instrument of coercion in foreign policy. Economic sanctions are basically sticks: A threatens B with some form of economic loss if B does something A does not want it to do, or fails to do something A wants it to do.

Propaganda
The selective use of information, and at times misinformation, in order to advance a state's interests.

Covert operations
Activities that a government directs against the interests of another government or non-state actor in such a way that the foreign targets and others are kept from knowing that the initiating government is responsible for the activities.

Photo 4.1 North Korean Propaganda Poster
This billboard, photographed in September 2011 on a street in Pyongyang, North Korea, depicts the heroism of North Korean soldiers.

Source: Eric Lafforgue/Art In All Of Us/Corbis via Getty Images.

activities. For example, in recent years Iran's government has provided covert support to anti-Israeli groups such as Hamas in Gaza and Hezbollah in southern Lebanon and may have been providing logistical support to Shiite groups that had carried out lethal operations against US forces in Iraq. In May 2011, the United States undertook a covert operation against the non-state actor Al Qaeda and killed its leader, Osama bin Laden. The operation took place in Pakistan, and the United States did not inform the Pakistani government until after the actual raid against bin Laden's compound was completed, leading to a serious diplomatic rift between the two countries (Schmitt and Mazzetti 2011).

Map 4.1 Covert Operation: The Killing of Osama bin Laden
As a result of US covert intelligence gathering, including covert on-site surveillance, Osama bin Laden was found to be living in a large compound in the Pakistani city of Abbottabad. The compound was attacked by a US Navy SEAL team early in the morning on May 2, 2011 and resulted in the killing of bin Laden.

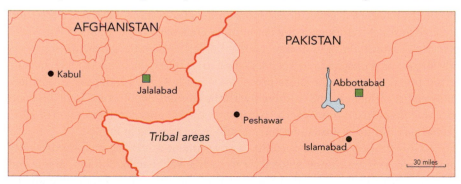

Source: US Department of Defense image. (Use of military imagery does not imply or constitute endorsement of Red Globe Press, its products, or services by the US Department of Defense.)

Similarly, the United States has used covert operations against Iran to try to hamper the development of that country's nuclear program. In 2010 a highly destructive computer virus or 'worm' called Stuxnet was introduced into the computer systems that Iran was using to control important nuclear equipment, destroying much of it in the process. There are also signs that a country that does not want Iran to acquire nuclear weapons – it is probably Israel – has conducted covert operations in Iran that entail the assassination of Iranian nuclear scientists. Four Iranian scientists were killed in car bombings in the two years between January 2010 and January 2012, and Iran may have retaliated with covert bomb operations in February 2012 that sought to kill Israeli diplomats stationed in New Delhi, India, and Tbilisi, Georgia.

The Stuxnet example highlights the importance of **cyber operations,** or the use and manipulation of information on the internet, as a relatively new coercive instrument to advance foreign policy objectives. In 2014, the 'Guardians of Peace' hacked into the files of Sony Pictures and publicized personal information about Sony employees, revealed the salaries of Sony executives, and disseminated copies of yet-to-be-released films. The objective was to force Sony to reconsider launching its film *The Interview,* a comedy about a plot to assassinate North Korean leader Kim Jung-un. Sony did decide to cancel the theater release of the film, and the US government traced this cyber-attack to operatives of the North Korean government. In 2016, Russian operatives were widely suspected of having released information over the internet damaging to US presidential candidate Hillary Clinton. The presumed goal was to favor her opponent, Donald Trump, and more broadly to call into question the integrity of American elections and democracy. Cyber operations are attractive to governments as a foreign policy tool because there is no obvious defense against them, they are not regulated by international law, and they are not sufficiently provocative to justify military retaliation.

Cyber operations
The use or manipulation of information on the internet to advance foreign policy interests.

States may resort to coercive policy instruments involving differing degrees of military force. For example, a state sometimes may turn to **coercive diplomacy** – actions short of the immediate large-scale use of military force such as moving an aircraft carrier closer to the shores of another country to help convince it to rethink some behavior (Art and Cronin 2003). The United States used several such actions during 2018 to signal to North Korea that violence might be around the corner unless the issue of North Korea's nuclear weapons and ballistic missile programs was addressed. These actions included bellicose language from President Trump, backed by flights of US strategic bombers close to the North Korean border and the deployment of US naval forces close to North Korean waters.

Coercive diplomacy
Aggressive actions short of the immediate large-scale use of military force (such as moving an aircraft carrier closer to the shores of another country) designed to convince a country to rethink some behavior.

Finally, the direct use of military force should also be considered a coercive foreign policy instrument. The German strategist Clausewitz famously stated that warfare is just the continuation of diplomacy by other means. After the 2001 terror attacks in New York and Washington, DC, the US government threatened the Taliban leaders in Afghanistan that they had to transfer Osama bin Laden and his aides to US custody, or the US would go to war with the Taliban. The Taliban continued to harbor bin Laden and his Al Qaeda fighters. During 2001 and 2002, the United States used a combination of covert operations, air strikes, and ground forces to help local Afghan factions topple the Taliban authorities, forcing Al Qaeda to retreat to the west of Pakistan. From 2002 until the time of writing, the United States has provided most of the military forces operating in Afghanistan and is trying to keep the Taliban and its Al Qaeda allies from retaking power in that country.

In short, states have many interests, and they can select from a range of strategies to promote or protect them. Where do these interests come from, and why do governments choose particular strategies to pursue them?

Levels of Analysis *The Practice of Foreign Policy*	
Individual	🌐 **International**
National leaders choose which interests to promote in foreign policy and select strategies (goals and instruments) to advance those interests.	Given that they usually need the active cooperation of other states to achieve their interests, most states find it necessary to make some trade-offs with other states in the pursuit of their interests.

THE SOURCES OF FOREIGN POLICY

What are the sources of foreign policy, or more precisely, the sources of foreign policy interests and strategies? The levels-of-analysis framework can be helpful in addressing this question. As we noted in Chapter 1, levels of analysis are used in different ways by scholars. A well-known approach to using levels to illuminate foreign policy was developed by Graham Allison in the early 1970s (Allison and Zelikow 1999).

Allison and Zelikow use three models to understand the origins, conduct, and ending of the Cuban Missile Crisis in 1962. These models focus respectively on a nation-state as a single, cohesive actor, on the operating procedures of government departments, and on political bargaining among top decision makers. The cohesive nation-state model is situated at the international level of analysis; the government department model is situated at the state level of analysis; and the political bargaining model, which emphasizes individuals and their interactions, is situated at the individual level of analysis. Although Allison's models have become a standard way to use the levels of analysis to study foreign policy, his framework does not take into account dynamics that reside within a country's society, such as interest groups and public opinion, that might also influence foreign policy, and they do not examine factors that operate at the level of the personal history or psychology of decision makers. Therefore, in this chapter we take a somewhat different and more comprehensive approach, yet one that still relies on levels of analysis.

Sources of Foreign Policy at the Individual Level of Analysis

National leaders play a disproportionately large role in defining a country's foreign policy (Bueno de Mesquita *et al.* 2003; Chiozza and Goemans 2011). It is useful and important to understand the beliefs of national leaders about foreign policy, for those beliefs are likely to shape how leaders assess threats and opportunities in the international arena (Jervis 2006; Saunders 2009).

Where do national leaders get their beliefs about foreign policy? One possibility is that leaders have well-established personalities before they assume office. For example, as we discuss in more detail in Chapter 3, feminist theorists might argue that, until very recently, most national leaders tended to be male, and a variety of influences on males, including their socialization through late adolescence, make them more inclined to have the belief that international affairs, and indeed all human relationships, involve conflict rather than cooperation (Hudson *et al.* 2008/2009; Hudson *et al.* 2014). Other personality effects aside from those associated with gender might arise from a host of sources, including genetic make-up, childhood socialization, and early adulthood experiences. These personalities in turn may powerfully influence what leaders think about international affairs and foreign policy. For example, some analysts have suggested that Barack Obama's racial identity and early childhood experience living in Indonesia made him America's first 'global' president with sensitivity to multiethnic and multiracial concerns at home and abroad (Sharma 2011). In Box 4.2 we discuss how the personality and experiences of Saddam Hussein may have prompted him to take great risks in deciding to lead Iraq to war in the 1980s and 1990s.

Leaders may also subscribe to certain beliefs because of their having experienced, witnessed, or perhaps learned about some attitude-shaping event in the international domain. Such events might not only influence the ideas of leaders, but perhaps those of many individuals in a particular generation, and even in subsequent generations. In the first Iraq war in 1990–91, President George H.W. Bush behaved in ways that suggested two major past events were influencing his beliefs: Munich and Vietnam. On the one hand, in his arguments for using military force to eject Iraq from Kuwait, he compared Saddam Hussein's aggression against its weaker neighbor to that of Adolph Hitler against Czechoslovakia and the appeasement that fanned Hitler's territorial ambitions. Yet, Bush ended the war abruptly – right after Iraqi forces were expelled from Kuwait but with Saddam still in power in Baghdad – in part because he believed, based on the US experience in Vietnam, that the American public would not support another long and costly war (Record 2002).

The field of political psychology offers rich insights about foreign policy decision-making at the individual level of analysis. Some psychologists argue, for example, that leaders are 'cognitive misers' who, instead of making comprehensive analyses of costs and benefits, rely on simple mental short-cuts when making decisions (Fiske and Taylor 1984). Decision makers become cognitive misers to save time and effort when confronted with large amounts of information or when dealing with a series of issues under conditions of uncertainty. In the above example, President Bush may have been acting as a cognitive miser; his mental short-cut was to assume that the Iraq crisis was similar to other salient international crises and therefore required a certain type of response. Along similar lines, Russell Leng has argued that because India and Pakistan have engaged over time in a series of confrontations and wars with each other, Indian and Pakistani leaders have adopted the mental short-cut of assuming the worst possible motives of the other in subsequent conflicts of interest (Leng 2005). To break the cycle of conflict requires new leaders with different experiences, or existing leaders to avoid this short-cut and make different cognitive assumptions, including the willingness to view new situations from the perspective of their rivals.

Sources of Foreign Policy at the State Level of Analysis

Liberal and Marxist theories of international relations highlight the point that every country's foreign policy is likely to be influenced to some degree by its domestic political, social, and economic institutions and dynamics. In the following discussion, we can place these institutions and dynamics into two general categories: those that are situated largely within the national government of the country under review, and those that are situated largely within its national society. We take up each category in turn, highlighting which dynamics in one or another of the categories spills over and influences dynamics in the other.

Institutions and Politics within National Governments

It is useful initially to draw from the Liberal tradition and to distinguish democratic from non-democratic (that is, authoritarian or autocratic) types of national governments. In general, the foreign policy processes in democratic governments are less centralized and more accessible to society than those processes in non-democratic governments. As Box 4.2 shows, Iraq's decision to go to war against an international coalition in 1990–91 was driven largely by the preferences and calculations of that country's autocratic leader, Saddam Hussein. By comparison, before initiating that war, the democratically elected leaders in the United Kingdom and the United States (Margaret Thatcher and George H.W. Bush respectively) felt it necessary to mobilize the support of their respective legislatures and general publics. They also took the trouble to mobilize an international coalition, in part to convince their domestic populations that there existed a widespread global consensus for military action.

National leaders, both in democratic and autocratic regimes, do not make policy by themselves. Instead, they rely on officials in the executive branch of government, which consists of their immediate advisors, the heads of ministries or departments that are concerned with foreign affairs, and the professional staff of those ministries and departments. Leaders and their subordinates in a country's national government often engage in foreign policy debates, build coalitions, and generally seek to influence each other, and this **bureaucratic politics** can influence that country's interests and strategic choices.

Bureaucratic politics
A possible influence on a country's strategy characterized by national leaders and their subordinates engaging in foreign policy debates, building coalitions, and generally seeking to influence each other.

This foreign policy process will look different across different countries. Compare, for example, the United States and China. In the United States, the parts of the executive branch that are chiefly concerned with foreign policy include the Departments of State and Defense, the Central Intelligence Agency, the Joint Chiefs of Staff on military matters and, on foreign economic matters, the Departments of Commerce and Treasury. To assist them in coordinating this large machinery of government, presidents since the late 1940s have had a National Security Advisor. At moments of major decision, the President, the National Security Advisor, and the heads of the departments most directly concerned meet as the National Security Council (NSC). The National Security Advisor and a staff of experts coordinate the activities of different parts of the government on security and foreign policy matters.

4.2   DIFFERING PERSPECTIVES

Explaining Iraq's Foreign Policy and Decision to Go to War in 1991

In 1990 Iraq occupied its small, oil-rich neighbor Kuwait. An international coalition, led by the United States and the United Kingdom, was formed to oust Iraq from Kuwait, first by imposing economic sanctions, and second by setting a deadline for Saddam Hussein to withdraw from Kuwait or face a devastating military attack. The coalition was far superior militarily and made strong efforts to convince Iraq that it would attack if Iraq did not retreat. Yet, Saddam Hussein refused to back down, ended up in a lopsided war, and suffered a significant military defeat. How might we explain this puzzling Iraqi foreign policy choice? We cannot know for sure, but there are several plausible arguments from different analytical perspectives (Gause 2001).

Saddam's Personality

Leaders always matter in decisions to go to war, particularly so in non-democratic countries where political power is heavily concentrated in the hands of one or a few individuals. Saddam Hussein was ambitious and paranoid, had a proclivity toward violence, and was willing to take risks. Saddam ordered Iraq to invade a more powerful Iran in 1980, hoping to exploit Iran's revolutionary instability and gain advantage over its traditional adversary. That risky war ended as a bloody stalemate eight years later. Saddam also appeared to believe that international actors were continually conspiring against him. He perceived neighbors such as Saudi Arabia and Kuwait as conspiring to squeeze Iraq economically, and others such as Israel and America as conspiring to undermine his power at home.

Misperception and 'Groupthink'

Saddam may have believed that the coalition, and particularly the United States, would not carry through on their threat to attack. Saddam seemed influenced by the US experience in Lebanon in 1983. When a car bomb struck the US embassy and killed over 200 Marines, the Reagan administration pulled its peacekeeping force out of Lebanon. On the eve of the 1991 war, Saddam in effect told US Ambassador April Glaspie that the United States did not have the stomach for war because it was unwilling to suffer large numbers of casualties.

What about other Iraqi leaders, especially the small group of Ba'ath Party officials that advised Saddam Hussein? Some appear to have worried that Iraq was about to suffer a big defeat given the forces arrayed against it. But, they were generally reluctant to disagree with Saddam or share with him views or information contrary to his preferred course of action. Saddam was intolerant of dissent; when he took power in 1979, he summarily executed two dozen Ba'ath Party leaders who had opposed his rise to power. He surrounded himself with like-minded individuals who, even if inclined to disagree, knew better than to do so.

National Economic Distress

The war with Iran in the 1980s exhausted Iraq financially. Iraq demanded 'contributions' from other Gulf states to finance its war effort. When the war ended, and the money stopped flowing, Iraq was in severe economic distress. It needed oil prices to remain high to earn hard currency for economic recovery. Saddam believed Kuwait was overproducing oil and driving down the global price. But by taking over Kuwait he could control Kuwaiti oil supply and keep the global price higher. From this perspective, once Saddam had Kuwait he could not afford to give it up, and therefore he was willing to try to 'ride out' a coalition attack rather than back down.

Geopolitical Opportunism

Iraq under Saddam Hussein fashioned itself as a regional power and the leader of the Arab world. Saddam attacked Iran because its new fundamentalist Shiite regime (Iraq's Ba'ath Party leaders were Sunni Muslims) had aspired to dominate the region. He threatened the Arab world's common enemy, Israel. By taking Kuwait, he hoped to signal to the Arab countries (especially Saudi Arabia) that Iraq was the regional leader and they should accommodate its wishes. By standing up to the United States and international coalition, even if he lost a war, Saddam may have believed that Iraq's prestige would be enhanced on the 'Arab street.'

Students should recognize the operation of the levels of analysis in the differing perspectives described above. Arguments for Iraq's seemingly puzzling decision to go to war range across individual, state, and international levels. Some explanations view Iraq as a rational actor making cost–benefit calculations, while others see non-rational personal characteristics and group dynamics driving the decision.

At each point in this policy process, advisors and subordinates may or may not fully share the beliefs of the President about what the country should do abroad. If they do share those beliefs, they may differ about how best to act to advance US interests, or they may agree about goals but disagree about what their department or agency should do to contribute to the American effort on a given issue. These differences in views occur in part because of the different life experiences officials may bring to their job, or because of differences in the interests of their respective organizations. An often-heard phrase in Washington is, 'Where you stand depends on where you sit.' In other words, if some official sits in the State Department he or she might give special emphasis to good diplomatic relations with other countries; if that same person were to sit in the Defense Department he or she might be more concerned about whether those countries can serve as a base for US forward military operations.

On looking forward to leaving office in 1952, President Harry Truman thought that General Dwight D. Eisenhower, if he were elected President, would incorrectly believe that executing the duties of that office was the same as being a military commander. Truman said of Eisenhower, who had been a brilliant Supreme Commander of Allied Forces during World War II, that if he were to win the presidency, 'He'll sit here [the president's desk] and he'll say, "Do this! Do that!" And nothing will happen. Poor Ike – it won't be a bit like the Army. He'll find it very frustrating' (Neustadt 1976).

The President is the key actor in the US foreign policy process. But the extensive executive bureaucracies of the US government play key roles as well and, sometimes require the President to step in and resolve difficult interagency disputes. Unless the President is skilled in managing institutional and bureaucratic political maneuverings, he or she may inadvertently relinquish foreign policy leadership.

In China, political power over foreign policy is more concentrated. The key decision makers are found in the Politburo Standing Committee, China's top executive ruling body. Recently there have been important power transitions every decade or so, which happen behind closed doors and without voting or input from the mass public. China is a one-party state, but different factions within the Communist Party and especially within the elite Politburo compete for power generally and over China's foreign policy. In recent decades 'reformers,' or top leaders who value closer ties with Western countries and deeper Chinese integration into the world economy, have competed with 'conservatives' who place more emphasis on the state-run part of China's economy and who would prefer to see China act more assertively in East Asia and perhaps even globally. Some scholars make different factional distinctions, between 'generalists' who try to maintain initiative in the Chinese provinces and 'technocrats' seeking to maintain control in Beijing (Shih 2008).

An important political transition took place in China in 2012 (Li 2012). The previous Communist Party Secretary General, Hu Jintao (in charge since 2002) handed power to a new leader, Xi Jinping. Xi is a 'princeling,' or part of a faction of Chinese leaders

Photo 4.2 Leadership of Contemporary China
This photo depicts China's most important governing body, the Standing Committee of the Politburo of the Chinese Communist Party. Notice that, in the middle of the group, is China's most powerful leader, Chinese President Xi Jinping.

Source: WANG ZHAO/AFP/Getty Images.

who come from families of veteran revolutionaries (that is, the communist founding fathers) or other high-ranking officials, and are closely associated with a former Chinese leader Jiang Zemin. Another faction, known as *taunpai* includes leaders who build their careers by rising through the ranks of the Communist Party, usually starting from a young age.

In 2017, at the 19th Communist Party Congress, Xi Jinping consolidated his hold on power. He placed loyal supporters in top party and governmental positions (see Table 4.1). Professional China watchers noted that, rather than favoring the more traditional collective leadership and a balance of power among factions Xi preferred a more personal and autocratic approach to leadership. Chinese Communist leaders traditionally serve two five-year terms and groom their likely successors. At the 2017 Party Congress, Xi revealed no likely successor and did not indicate an intention to step down. In 2018, China's Parliament abolished term limits, making it possible for Xi to rule indefinitely.

Dynamics between Executives and Legislatures

In democracies, liberal theory emphasizes, executive-branch leaders must usually obtain cooperation, approval, or at least consent from the legislative branch for their foreign policies. This is true in parliamentary systems, such as that of the United Kingdom, in which the leader of the executive branch (the Prime Minister) and members of his or her cabinet are drawn directly from the elected legislative branch (the Parliament). It is also true in presidential systems, in which the executive-branch leader – for example, the Chancellor in Germany or the President in the United States – is elected independently of the legislature and appoints his or her own cabinet.

For example, the American political system presents important opportunities for the Congress to constrain the executive branch in foreign policy. The US Constitution stipulates that the President possesses the sole authority to negotiate any treaty with a foreign government, but the constitution also mandates that any such treaty comes into force if and only if the US Senate ratifies the treaty by a two-thirds majority vote.

Table 4.1 China's New Top Leaders: The Politburo Standing Committee, 2017

Name	Age	Confirmed and designated leadership post
Xi Jinping	64	Communist Party General Secretary, Chairman of the Central Military Commission, and President
Li Keqiang	62	Premier of the State Council
Li Zhanshu	67	Chairman of the National People's Congress (NPC)
Wang Zang	62	Executive Vice Premier
Wang Huning	62	Responsible for party propaganda and ideology
Zhao Leji	60	Secretary of the Central Head of the Party's Organization Department
Han Zheng	63	Likely Chairman of the Chinese People's Political Consultative Conference

Source: Information compiled from Chris Buckley, 'These Seven Men Now Run China,' *New York Times*, October 25, 2017.

As we noted in Chapter 2, the significance of the Senate's treaty ratification power was evident in 1919–20 when the Senate refused to ratify the Versailles Treaty, frustrating President Woodrow Wilson's effort to engage the United States fully in the reconstruction of European security after World War I. In the late 1990s President Bill Clinton quietly gave up his efforts to get the Senate to ratify the Comprehensive Test Ban Treaty that his administration signed in 1996. Although different presidents approach Congress differently, it is impossible in the US system to ignore the role of Congress in foreign policy (see examples in Box 4.3).

4.3 MAKING CONNECTIONS
Then and Now

Presidents Woodrow Wilson, Harry Truman, and Barack Obama on Working with Congress on Foreign Policy

Over time, American presidents have gained more and more decision-making power, relative to Congress, in the conduct of foreign policy. However, presidents must still enlist the cooperation of Congress in order to carry out foreign policy effectively. This is as true today as it was 100 years ago. Presidents who choose to ignore or disdain Congress sometimes pay a heavy price, as the experience of Woodrow Wilson demonstrates. Presidents who commit to cooperation with Congress will often reap foreign policy benefits, as the early presidential experience of Harry Truman demonstrated. When presidents and Congress find themselves in confrontation, it is difficult to get very much done in domestic or foreign policy, as Barack Obama found.

Then: President Woodrow Wilson, 1919

In July 1919, President Wilson submitted to the US Senate the Treaty of Versailles and the Covenant for the League of Nations. Several senators who favored ratification wanted to add reservations that would limit US obligations under the Covenant to protect other League members in the event they were attacked.

Asked if he would accept such Senate-imposed reservations on the Covenant, President Wilson said, 'Anyone who opposes me in that, I'll crush.' The Senate ultimately refused to support Wilson's ambitious initiative, leaving him incapable of carrying out the US commitment to the League.

Source: Paterson *et al.* (2006): 208.

Then: President Harry Truman, 1946

In a statement made before White House correspondents in November 1946, President Truman made it clear that he would continue his predecessor's efforts to work with the Congress, including members in the Republican Party, on matters relating to foreign policy.

Truman said at that time: 'I shall cooperate in every proper manner with members of the Congress, and my hope and prayer is that this spirit of cooperation will be reciprocated.' Truman faced a Congress generally reluctant to engage the United States deeply in European affairs after the war. Yet he managed to cultivate sufficient Congressional support for his signature foreign policy initiatives, the NATO alliance and the European Recovery Program (commonly known as the Marshall Plan).

Source: 'Statement by President Truman to White House Correspondents,' November 11, 1946, in Commager (1949): 718.

Now: President Barack Obama, 2013

Obama faced widespread Republican opposition to his legislative agenda during his first term (2009–12) and into his second. He and his congressional adversaries proved unwilling or incapable of finding sufficient common ground to move policies forward. The result was a shutdown of the government due to the failure of the two sides to reach a budget compromise, and a lack of significant legislative achievement except for Obama's controversial health care reform initiative which he forced through Congress only because his party held a majority in both houses during his first two years in office. In foreign policy, congressional opponents sought to stymie Obama whenever possible, for example in his handling of an attack on the US consulate in Benghazi, Libya in 2012, and by opposing his 2013 diplomatic opening to Iran and lobbying for a tightening of economic sanctions against Iran.

On the morning that the US government reopened after having been shut down, Obama expressed his frustration directly to his congressional opponents:

You don't like a particular policy or a particular President? Then argue for your position. Go out and win an election. Don't break what our predecessors spent over two centuries building. That's not being faithful to what this country is about.

Source: Caldwell (2013).

The need for executive leaders to engage politically and gain the support of the legislative branch is true, in varying degrees, across democracies. In 2013, British Prime Minister David Cameron preferred military action in response to claims that the Syrian regime had used chemical weapons against rebel groups and innocent civilians in and around the capital, Damascus. However, the UK Parliament refused and voted against authorizing the United Kingdom's use of force. British Members of Parliament, perhaps reflecting the unease of the British public, felt that the risks of getting involved in another Middle East war outweighed the sense of moral outrage directed at Syria's leader for using chemical weapons (*The Guardian* 2013). The United Kingdom's response to Syria was being coordinated with that of the United States; after the British vote US President Barack Obama decided to step back and request formal approval from the US Congress before committing US military forces. Autocratic leaders, such as Syria's Bashar al-Assad, who was accused of using chemical weapons against the Syrian rebels and civilians, typically do not face similar types of domestic political constraints.

National Politics and Societal Actors

To this point, we have been focusing on political dynamics within governments as a source of foreign policy. Equally if not more important as a source of foreign policy are politics within a country as a whole (Snyder 1991). We explore below three particularly powerful classes of national political dynamics, and societal actors within countries, that influence foreign policy: public opinion and elections, the media, and interest groups.

Public Opinion and Elections

If there is any single thesis about foreign policy and international relations that we can glean from liberal theory, it is that public opinion and elections play an especially important role in shaping foreign policy (Holsti 2004). The case of Syria, discussed above, is instructive. A survey conducted by the German Marshall Fund found that

Photo 4.3 Brexit and Public Opinion
Many elites in government and business preferred the United Kingdom to remain in the EU, but a majority of the public voted otherwise. The cartoon suggests a remorseful conversation between two members of Parliament after the Brexit vote.

'Let's never ask the public for their views ever again'

Source: © Telegraph Media Group Limited 2018.

72 percent of Europeans preferred that the European Union stay completely out of Syria's ongoing civil war. Most Americans – 62 percent – expressed a similar view of the role their government should play. Considering this clear public sentiment, it is not surprising that both European and American governments proved reluctant to intervene. That same survey revealed a more general difference between Europeans and Americans that both reinforces and is reflected in the conduct of their respective approaches to foreign policy: 68 percent of Americans, but only 31 percent of Europeans, agreed with the statement that war is sometimes necessary to obtain justice (German Marshall Fund 2013: 6).

A dramatic illustration of the key role of public opinion in the foreign policy of democratic countries took place in 2016. In a popular referendum, voters in the United Kingdom were asked a simple question: Should the UK leave the European Union (EU) or remain within it? Although many politicians, bankers, business executives, and academics urged a 'Remain' vote, by a margin of 52 percent to 48 percent the public supported 'Leave.' The vote shocked governments and markets worldwide and was arguably the most consequential British foreign policy decision of recent decades. David Cameron, the British Prime Minister who led the Remain campaign, was forced to resign. In the months leading to the vote, Cameron failed to connect well with the public and had trouble articulating the benefits of the UK remaining in the EU. One leader of the Leave movement, Boris Johnson, offered an argument that appealed to many voters, namely that the United Kingdom needed to 'take back control' of its political future. In Box 4.4, we review what recent academic research has concluded on why British voters surprisingly favored Brexit.

Scholars have demonstrated very clearly that US citizens vote on the basis not just of their views on domestic issues, but on foreign policy as well (Hurwitz and Peffley 1987). It is for this reason that, in line with liberal theory, presidential candidates spend significant time on foreign policy, and debate the subject. It should be noted that public opinion may be manipulated by national leaders; according to one line of inquiry, US presidents, by virtue of the vast institutional resources of the White House, can now track and shape the views of the public on most issues, including those relating to foreign policy (Shapiro and Jacobs 2002: 192). Yet, on the whole, there is very strong evidence that the liberal perspective is correct and that US presidents try to accommodate American public opinion on foreign policy issues. One recent study demonstrates that presidents from Lyndon Johnson to Bill Clinton were aware of public opinion on foreign policy matters, and that when it came to that issue area, presidents 'follow[ed] the polls for both governing and electoral purposes' (Sobel 2001: 238–9). It is highly likely that national leaders in other democratic systems, notwithstanding their own capacity to shape in some measure the opinion of their home publics, are similarly constrained in the final analysis by the views of their constituents.

4.4 RESEARCH INSIGHT

Why Did the United Kingdom Decide to Leave the European Union?

The United Kingdom's decision, based on the results of a popular referendum in 2016, to leave the European Union was shocking and unexpected. Following the vote, commentators pointed to an array of possible reasons why the Leave vote prevailed, including popular resentment of bureaucrats in Brussels (the headquarters of the EU), an anti-elite mood among the public, the discontent of those left behind by globalization, and the incompetence of the Remain supporters in making their case. In what ways might academic research illuminate this consequential decision?

In 2017, three academics published a book that analyzed 12 years (2004–16) of public opinion surveys, involving some 150,000 voters, in the United Kingdom (Clarke, Goodwin, and Whiteley 2017). They also had the benefit of surveys carried out immediately before and after the referendum vote. They found, first, that of all the political issues in play, that of immigration resonated most prominently with Leave voters. The leaders of the UK Independence Party, fervent advocates of the Leave campaign, successfully linked migration, a source of anxiety among many voters, with the United Kingdom's participation in the EU. Supporters of Remain managed neither to make the positive case for immigration nor to show that the overall benefits of the EU for the United Kingdom outweighed the costs.

The authors also highlighted the importance of 'baked-in' views, specifically the frequent criticisms of the EU, made over many years, by British politicians including many now in support of Remain. Members of the public who were persuaded by these criticisms presumably had a difficult time believing simultaneously that dire consequences would follow if the United Kingdom left. Finally, evidence showed that 'leader images,' in particular the so-called Boris effect also mattered significantly. Public feelings about Boris Johnson (the former Mayor of London) were particularly strong, and his decision to become a leader of the Leave movement contributed significantly to the Brexit majority.

An important line of research on the matter of public opinion and foreign policy concerns the conditions under which public opinion is likely to turn against a war once hostilities have commenced. A long-standing thesis on this subject is that a democratic public will inexorably turn against a policy action that includes the use of force in direct proportion to the number of casualties (Mueller 1973). The Vietnam War, which the US public initially supported but gradually turned against, appears to support this thesis. A more recent alternative view is that the public does not necessarily turn against a war as casualties mount. Instead, what matters is how that war is going: if the public believes that the country is winning, then it will support military operations notwithstanding battlefield casualties. World War II is a clear example of how the US public continued to support a war effort despite very high US battlefield casualties. It is the persistence of casualties and a loss in confidence that victory is likely, as occurred in Vietnam, which causes public opinion to turn against continuation of the war (Gelpi, Feaver, and Reifler 2009).

The relationship between national leaders and public opinion in the context of war is complex and multidimensional. War and, more generally, external conflicts often boost the popularity of a leader. This phenomenon is often termed the **rally 'round the flag effect**. Fidel Castro of Cuba became a more popular leader at home after the ill-fated Bay of Pigs invasion of 1961 because he was perceived as having stood up for Cuba against external aggression sponsored by the more powerful United States. President George H.W. Bush enjoyed a spike in his approval ratings in 1991 after the United States and its allies expelled Saddam Hussein's forces from Kuwait, although that boost in approval did not carry over to the 1992 presidential election, when Bush was defeated by Bill Clinton in large part because of a lackluster US domestic economy. We noted above that a US covert operation killed Osama bin Laden in early May 2011: in the immediate aftermath President Barack Obama's overall job approval jumped 11 percentage points, from 46 to 57 percent (Dao and Sussman 2011). Not surprisingly, scholars and commentators sometimes suspect that political leaders fabricate or embellish external threats precisely to instigate a rally 'round the flag effect, and to deflect attention from other political problems.

Rally 'round the flag effect
A commonly observed boost in the popularity of a leader due to external conflicts or war.

The News Media and Foreign Policy

The **foreign affairs media** are those individuals and organizations who report or comment on foreign developments in print, on television, over radio, and through the internet. Reporters play a key role in providing information about world events, often at great risk to themselves, and particularly when they operate in war zones. However, the news media not only provides information; scholars have found that news media participants – reporters, commentators, and editors – can indirectly influence national leaders as they grapple with foreign policy problems. The mechanism by which this influence is exercised is termed **framing**, the process by which media participants select or present particular elements of a news story in such a way as to influence the opinions of recipients of the story (Entman 2004). The way the media frames a story can help shape public opinion on foreign policy matters; the choices media participants make about framing a particular issue can affect the degree of freedom political leaders have in positing interests and designing strategies.

Foreign affairs media
Those individuals and organizations who report or comment on foreign developments in print, on television, over radio, and through the internet.

Framing
The process by which media participants select or present particular elements of a news story in such a way as to influence the opinions of recipients of the story.

One helpful study systematically explored the degree to which media framing of a foreign policy matter can influence the recipients of such reporting (Berinsky and Kinder 2006). In an experiment carried out in two phases in the years 2000 and 2002, scholars recruited volunteers, divided them into three groups, and presented each group with slightly different sets of news stories about Serbian forces' brutal attacks in 1999 against civilian residents in the province of Kosovo, which ended with a NATO air strike campaign to stop the Serbian attacks. Volunteers in one group (the *control* group) were given news reports about the Serbia–Kosovo conflict that were, to the extent possible, devoid of a political slant. Individuals in the second group (what the research team termed the *humanitarian* group) were given reports that were largely the same as the straight-news reports but had been slightly adjusted to highlight the atrocities that the Serbs had been committing against the Kosovo residents. Members of the third group (what the team called the *risk-to-America* group) were given reports that highlighted the risks that American air force personnel could encounter in undertaking air attacks against Serbia. The research team found that, compared to the straight-news group and the risk-to-America group, those in the humanitarian group remembered more facts about the Kosovo case that related to Serbian atrocities and, looking back, they were more likely than individuals in the other two groups to say that the US decision to intervene against Serbia was the right thing to do. Even quite small differences across the groups in how the Serbia–Kosovo story was framed led to significant differences in what individuals in the different groups remembered about the issues at stake and how they assessed the wisdom of the air campaign against Serbia.

The media play a larger role in democratic countries than in autocratic countries, where the media typically face restrictions imposed by the central government or are expected to report and frame stories in a manner favorable to the central leaders. Technological changes, however, are making it more challenging even for autocratic governments to control the media. In China, for example, 'online public opinion' has become a new social force that is beginning to influence foreign policy. The Chinese Ministry of Foreign Affairs has become more sensitive to public sentiments because it recognizes how much and what types of international information ordinary Chinese people can obtain over the internet (Junhao 2005; Xin-An 2005). Although Chinese leaders still closely monitor and restrict internet coverage of foreign affairs, the government's monopoly of media control is gradually breaking down. Of course, technological changes also create problems for democracies to the extent that they facilitate the spreading of false news or make it easier for hate groups to spread their messages to large audiences.

Interest Groups

Interest groups are actors of great importance in liberal theories of both domestic and foreign policy. An interest group is a societal or, in some instances, a transnational political body consisting of individuals or organizations that share a common set of political concerns. Examples include the World Wildlife Foundation, the International Chamber of Commerce, Amnesty International, Catholic Charities, and the World Jewish Congress. Individuals band together in such associations, which may be institutionalized, in order to work through that association to persuade leaders and the public to pursue, support, or accept policies that are in accord with the preferences of the association. Interest groups can be found in virtually every country and type of political system. They tend to be most prominent in democracies in which freedom of expression and the right to organize are protected by law. In advanced democratic nations, business, ethnic-religious, humanitarian, and environmentalist groups have long been active in seeking to influence foreign policy (Mearsheimer and Walt 2007).

Interest groups usually organize according to issue; certain groups wish to influence, for instance, their government's trade policies, environmental policies, or overall policies toward a particular country. In France and Japan, politically connected farmers work effectively to influence their country's position in regional and global trade negotiations. In the United States, Jewish and Arab lobby groups try to influence US policy toward Israel and the Middle East. In many cases the preferences of interest groups are sensitive to geographic location. In China, corporations that operate in coastal areas, where factories assemble goods for export, are more supportive of China's integration in the world economy, while state-run enterprises that reside in China's interior and produce (inefficiently) goods for the local market are more skeptical of global integration. In Russia, the largest private energy companies (such as Lukoil) are locked into West European energy markets; despite China's rise, and except for arms exporters, no strong 'Asia lobby' is yet evident in Russian foreign economic policy (Rutland 2006).

Interest groups
Individuals or organizations that share a common set of political concerns and band together in an association to persuade leaders and the public to pursue, support, or accept policies that are in accord with the preferences of the association.

Lobbying
Meeting and speaking
with members of
legislatures and
officials in executive
departments in an
attempt to influence
policy. Interest groups
often engage in lobbying.

Interest groups use a variety of means to try to influence national leaders and the public. In democratic states, interest groups publish or fund the publication of policy papers, purchase advertisements in major newspapers and other media, organize letter-writing campaigns to political representatives, and undertake **lobbying**, or personally meeting and speaking with members of legislatures and officials in executive departments. Interest groups also contribute to political candidates and political parties or organize political fundraisers. Some interest groups – most notably, as we will see in Chapter 13, Greenpeace – organize high-impact publicity events to attract media attention to their concerns.

While we know that interest groups have sought to shape the foreign policies of most countries, foreign policy studies are only beginning to produce systematic research on how much influence such groups have on foreign policy making. One challenge is that while we can observe instances in which interest groups have tried to influence leaders and officials responsible for foreign policy, it is difficult to know if they have been successful even if the government does what the groups have called for. For example, looking at some US policy decisions relating to trade with China or arms sales to Israel, we may know that one or more interest groups pressed for the United States to act in a particular manner on those issues, and we may also know that government leaders took the stance on these issues that matched the position the interest group or groups had been advocating. However, what we do not know is whether the leaders took the stance they did *because* of the interest groups, or if they would have taken the stance even if the groups had not been active. Scholars try to set up research strategies that allow them to isolate the preferences of interest groups and the impact of interest group activity on foreign policy. An example of this type of comparative foreign policy research is described in Box 4.5.

Sources of Foreign Policy at the International Level of Analysis

At least three factors, realist theories emphasize, that are situated at the international level of analysis may shape how a country's leaders define that country's interests and strategies: the country's geography, its relative economic development, and its overall relative capabilities, or power.

Geography

A country's geographic characteristics, combined with its demographics, are likely to influence how its leaders think about interests and strategy. During the nineteenth century the United Kingdom, separated from the great powers of Europe by the English Channel, developed its naval power and expanded its influence overseas while seeking to maintain a balance of power among the European states on the continent. Similarly, from the 1780s to the 1930s, many people in the United States believed that the country could remain free of European entanglements because it was separated from the 'Old World' by the Atlantic Ocean. Mexican and Canadian leaders have also believed that geography matters. One of Mexico's longest-ruling autocratic leaders of the late nineteenth and early twentieth century, Porfirio Diaz, is reported to have said, 'Alas, poor Mexico! So far from God and so close to the United States!' In the same vein, Canada's Prime Minister Pierre Trudeau told an American audience at the National Press Club in Washington that 'Living next to you is in some ways like sleeping with an elephant. No matter how friendly and even-tempered is the beast, if I can call it that, one is affected by every twitch and grunt' (Canadian Broadcasting Company 1969).

4.5   MAKING CONNECTIONS
Theory and Practice

The Influence of Bankers on Foreign Policy across Countries

Theory

Marxists believe banks have significant influence over the decisions of governments to go to war. As we discussed in Chapter 1, Lenin's theory of imperialism, for example, expected big banks, or finance capital, in Western countries to press their governments to adopt aggressive foreign policies to obtain access to new markets. Lenin believed governments would comply to serve the interests of powerful economic actors.

Practice

Recent research suggests this theoretical approach may be off the mark. Jonathan Kirshner shows that bankers do have significant influence on foreign policy, though not always on the critical decision to go to war. More importantly, the preferences of bankers differ from what Marxists expect (Kirshner 2007). In a study of bankers in different countries across different time periods, Kirshner finds that bankers consistently prefer peace to war. Financial actors, whether in France in the 1920s, Japan in the 1930s, America in the 1890s, or the United Kingdom in the 1980s, are interested in economic stability above everything else. A stable economic environment is the best for profit-making, and war is disruptive to economic stability. Kirshner shows, for example, that British bankers failed to support their natural ally, Conservative Prime Minister Margaret Thatcher, during the Falklands crisis of 1981–82 in which Thatcher took the United Kingdom to war against Argentina. During the 1930s, Japanese financial interests opposed the aggressive turn in foreign policy which led Japan to occupy China in 1931 and again in 1937. Japanese bankers preferred a more cautious foreign policy but were overwhelmed by the Japanese military which took control of the state and moved foreign policy in a more belligerent direction.

A country's immediate neighborhood helps to shape its foreign policy. Israel's simultaneously defensive and aggressive foreign policy is influenced by its close proximity to countries it has long seen as adversaries. India borders its traditional rivals, China and Pakistan; much of its foreign policy is preoccupied with managing those relations. Germany's size and prominence in the center of Europe has long been a source of anxiety, and at times opportunity, for smaller neighbors such as Poland. The United States is concerned by North Korea's behavior, but the stakes are arguably larger for China, which borders North Korea and worries that a collapse of that country would lead to large refugee flows into China.

Relative Level of Economic Development

A country's relative economic wealth, and the sources of that wealth, can influence how the country defines its interests and strategies. Historically, countries with the largest and most dynamic economies have had opportunities to translate their wealth into military power and exert considerable influence in global affairs. This was true of Great Britain and eventually Germany in the nineteenth century, and the United States during the twentieth century. The rise of China in the early twenty-first century is a direct function of its rapid economic growth. A country's relative level of wealth and prosperity also affects how it views specific foreign policy issues. For example, many European countries, in possession of mature, developed economies, place a high priority on environmental protection. In sharp contrast, leaders in countries with industries that are only now reaching world-class competitiveness, such as India, Brazil, and especially China, do not believe that their countries are yet able to afford stronger environmental or worker standards, and these leaders have set as an interest the prevention of the imposition of stricter standards.

Relative National Capabilities

A country's relative capabilities are likely to condition both its interests and its selection of goals and policy instruments. A country's relative capabilities determine its international influence, its positive ability to cause others to act in ways it prefers, and its negative ability to resist the efforts of other countries to induce it to do things it would rather not do. A country's relative capabilities are a function of many factors: its demography (including population size but also the balance between young and old, working-age and retired); territorial expanse and such natural resources (if exploited wisely) as arable land, oil, and economically important minerals; overall economic development, as discussed above; literacy as well as scientific and technological sophistication; and the degree to which governing institutions are effective and enable leaders to convert national economic resources into military power and political influence (Waltz 1979; Mearsheimer 2003).

Leaders of especially powerful countries often believe that, in the absence of an effective international government, they have a special responsibility to contribute to the existing international order (Gilpin 1975; Ikenberry 2001). In these circumstances foreign policy may be significantly influenced by a country's relative position in the international system. When war breaks out in central Africa, it is of great concern to Africans. When Serbs and Bosnians fight, it is of great concern to neighboring Europeans. But these situations are also of special interest to far-away powerful states who believe, for better or worse, that they share responsibility for managing regional crises and assuring global order.

We have to this point explored what a foreign policy looks like and from what sources it emerges. We now may turn to the chapter's final question: why do states sometimes *change* their foreign policy?

Levels of Analysis *Sources of Foreign Policy*

Individual	State	International
A national leader's beliefs, which are likely to be shaped by his or her personality, formative political experiences, and motivated biases, play a large role in influencing that leader's approach to foreign policy.	Within a government, institutional and bureaucratic politics, as well as relations between different branches such as the executive and legislative in democratic systems, influence foreign policy.	Several international-level factors can influence both the foreign policy interests and strategies of a country, including its geography, relative economic development, and relative overall power.
Once a leader has made a foreign policy decision, cognitive dynamics may constrain his or her ability to change course in the face of new information.	Within a country, dynamics that largely take place within its society, including elections, public opinion, the news media, and interest groups, substantially shape its foreign policy.	

HOW AND WHY STATES CHANGE THEIR FOREIGN POLICY

We will organize our investigation of the sources of change in foreign policy with the aid of the levels-of-analysis framework, beginning with the individual, then focusing on domestic features of states, and ending with the international level of analysis. Throughout this discussion we will see that different theories of international relations help shed light on why factors operating at the different levels of analysis might bring about change in a state's foreign policy.

Sources of Foreign Policy Change at the Individual Level of Analysis

At least two mechanisms that operate at the individual level of analysis have the capacity to bring about substantial changes in foreign policy. The first mechanism, stressed in constructivist theory, is that of learning by national leaders in such a way that they make significant shifts in foreign policy; the second, emphasized in liberal theory, is the sometimes dramatic impact of changes in leadership on foreign policy.

Leadership Learning and Changes in Foreign Policy

In accord with the expectations of constructivists that we discussed in Chapter 3, national leaders, because of their own foreign policy experiences or those of their predecessors, sometimes change their understanding of world politics or the particular circumstances of their country in the international system. Such learning can bring about significant changes in the way leaders define interests or what they consider to be the best strategies to promote them (Levy 1994).

For example, prior to the Great Depression, government leaders in the United States, Canada, the United Kingdom, Germany, and other industrialized countries mostly subscribed to *laissez-faire* economic ideas; governments should not interfere with market dynamics either at home or in the international sphere. As we saw in Chapter 2, at the outset of the Great Depression, those leaders had few international cooperative mechanisms available to them to deal with the collapse in national demand they were all experiencing, which in turn prompted them to turn to beggar-thy-neighbor prohibitive tariffs on imports or prohibitions on the inflow or outflow of capital. Since the Great Depression, government leaders in the United States, Canada, and Europe have largely believed that government should allow for the free operation of markets at home and overseas, *but* there is room for government intervention both through national monetary and fiscal policies and by way of international governmental coordination (as we will see in Chapter 9, through such entities as the International Monetary Fund and the Group of 20) to mitigate the kind of shocks that we have seen in the world economy during the crisis of 2008–13. The economic beliefs of leaders changed, and major changes in domestic and foreign economic policies were the result (Frieden 2006).

Similarly, an important line of recent research has shown that learning in the face of policy failure adds a key element to our understanding of why the United States switched from neutrality to internationalism at the close of World War II (Legro 2000). President Franklin Roosevelt reflected on President Wilson's failure to obtain America's entry into the League of Nations, and the United States' subsequent shift to a policy of political isolationism during the 1920s and 1930s, and learned that these failures enabled Nazi Germany, Fascist Italy, and Imperial Japan to pursue aggression. That aggression ultimately directly threatened America's security, Roosevelt thought, and that threat could have been averted or halted at lower cost had the United States been more active in world security matters and, in collaboration with other powerful states in a collective security organization, confronted the aggressors. Roosevelt inferred that, to pursue its interest in security, the United States had to shift from a strategy of neutrality to one of **internationalism**, a strategy in which the US would be fully engaged with other states through institutionalized arrangements directed at maintaining world security and promoting global economic prosperity.

Internationalism
A strategy in which a state is fully engaged with other states through institutionalized arrangements directed at maintaining world security and promoting global economic prosperity.

Over time, a given leader may change ideas about his or her country's interests or strategy. For example, Soviet leader Mikhail Gorbachev appears to have fundamentally changed his ideas about Soviet foreign policy from the time he took power in 1985 to the period during which he took steps that decisively ended the Cold War in 1988 (English 2005). At first, Gorbachev appears largely to have accepted the traditional Marxist ideas we discussed in Chapter 3: world politics is basically a continuation of domestic class struggles, the Soviet Union and the United States possessed fundamental conflicts of interest, and core Soviet interests in security could only be advanced by a strategy that included political dominance in Eastern Europe and, as much as possible, military superiority over Western Europe. By 1988, however, Gorbachev radically shifted his foreign policy perspective to what was termed *new thinking* about Soviet foreign policy. Gone from Gorbachev's rhetoric and actions were global class struggle, permanent struggle with the United States, and the need for pro-Soviet regimes in Eastern Europe. He replaced these with an emphasis on shared interests with the West and acceptance of greater freedom of political choice in Eastern Europe.

Leaders' experiences with officials from other countries may change those leaders' beliefs about their own country's situation and strategic options. The experiences of leaders and policy officials in international institutions might also affect their perceptions and values. For example, Gorbachev moved to his *new thinking* stance on Soviet interests and the benefits of cooperation with Western countries as he interacted with decision makers from those countries, especially US Secretary of State George Shultz (Stein 1994). In the same vein, Chinese officials, because of participating in regular talks during the mid-1990s that included several East and Southeast countries, as well as the United States, appear to have moved from skepticism to support for the idea that regional dialogue is an effective mechanism by which China can reassure neighbors of its peaceful intentions (Johnston 2008).

The cases of Roosevelt, Gorbachev, and the recent leaders of China may leave us with the idea that policy makers typically learn what, from the viewpoint of a country's interests, are the *right* lessons from history, and then make the *right* policy adjustments. However, while learning may be a reasonably pervasive feature of foreign policy, the lessons leaders learn may not always yield successful outcomes. For example, while Belgian leaders inferred from World War I that neutrality had left them open to German invasion, the main diplomatic instrument they

Photo 4.4 Leaders and Foreign Policy Change
US President Ronald Reagan and Soviet leader Mikhail Gorbachev developed a close relationship during the latter part of the 1980s, when it became clear to Gorbachev that Reagan was serious about arms control and to Reagan that Gorbachev intended to transform Soviet foreign policy.

Source: Dirck Halstead/The LIFE Images Collection/Getty Images.

subsequently devised, a military alliance with France, did not prevent Germany from defeating and occupying Belgium in 1940. Many factors, not just correct learning, play a role in determining the success or failure of a country's national strategy.

Learning by leaders seems to occur in foreign policy making, and such learning can materially influence how leaders view the interests of their countries and adjust their strategies to promote those interests. What is not guaranteed is that the lessons leaders learn necessarily increase or decrease their chances of success in foreign policy. An important scholarly task then is to identify and understand more fully the conditions under which leaders do or do not learn the right lessons in foreign affairs.

Leadership Turnover

Leaders play a key role in crafting foreign policy, so changes in leadership can bring about changes in foreign policy. Perhaps the most dramatic example of the impact of leadership change on foreign policy during the twentieth century occurred in the former Soviet Union in the 1980s. As we discussed in Chapter 2, Soviet leaders from Joseph Stalin to Leonid Brezhnev maintained iron-fisted control over Eastern Europe, using military force as necessary against Hungary in 1956 and Czechoslovakia in 1968. Mikhail Gorbachev between 1985 and 1988 reversed course on Soviet policy, most notably accepting the loss of Poland, Hungary, and other countries in what had been its empire in Eastern Europe, rather than relying on military force to keep them within the Soviet empire.

Postwar China offers a second example. From the 1950s until well into the 1970s, China was controlled by Mao Zedong, who was committed to making China communist, powerful, and independent through a strategy that combined a high level of state control over the national economy with an almost complete separation from global commerce. The coming to power of Deng Xiaoping in the late 1970s transformed China's economic and foreign policies from an emphasis on communist ideological purity toward to a more pragmatic strategy aimed at economic growth, a strategy that included economic engagement with capitalist countries. Finally, the emergence of Xi Jinping in 2012 has the potential to transform China once again domestically and internationally. Xi set out a plan for China to become a great power and strengthened the Communist Party's control over Chinese society and the economy.

Finally, of course, there is the transition from President Barack Obama to President Donald Trump. The magnitude of the change that Trump is likely to bring into effect not just in relation to the Obama presidency but to postwar US foreign policy remains to be seen. However, whether one considers US relations with Mexico or Australia or the allies in NATO on the one hand, or adversaries such as Iran and North Korea on the other, or whether one considers the trade issue area or that regarding the environment, President Trump has clearly brought a new and disruptive element to US foreign policy.

Sources of Foreign Policy Change at the State Level of Analysis

Two mechanisms that originate and largely operate at the state level of analysis have the capacity to induce substantial change in a country's foreign policy: dramatic changes in a country's domestic political regime, and the political efforts of nongovernmental organizations.

Domestic Regime Change and Shifts in Foreign Policy

Dramatic political changes within a country, such as a change in its political regime, may induce large changes in its foreign policy interests and strategies. Liberal theorists would emphasize that a clear example of such an impact of regime change on foreign policy is Germany in the twentieth century.

At the outset of the 1900s, Germany had a political regime headed by the Kaiser and, as we saw in Chapter 2, his aggression, together with his unchecked control over Germany's foreign and military policies, led Germany to start but ultimately lose World War I. Germany's enemies in the war, the United Kingdom and France, imposed the very harsh Versailles peace treaty on Germany. Germany lost much territory to its east, had Allied occupation forces in its western territories, was forbidden to have strong military forces, and had to pay massive reparations to France, the United Kingdom, and other Allied countries.

In 1919, Germans succeeded temporarily in crafting a democratic constitution. This new Weimer Republic wanted to revise much of the Versailles Treaty. For example, Germany's new leaders wanted foreign forces out of Germany and a reduction in the reparations it owed to the countries it had fought during the war of 1914–18. However, Germany under the Weimar Republic pursued this goal in a cautious, non-confrontational manner, and sought revisions of the Versailles Treaty with the consent of the main European powers, particularly France and the United Kingdom, and in the framework of German integration into the League of Nations. In sharp contrast, when Adolph Hitler's Nazi regime came into power in 1933, it reversed Weimar's policies, overturned the Versailles settlement, and ultimately unleashed a war in Europe that almost perpetrated the destruction of all Jews in Europe. Then again, after World War II and the destruction of the Nazi regime, a new democratic Federal Republic in the western part of Germany turned to a policy of moderation and integration. West Germany aligned itself with the United States and the United Kingdom, became a loyal and important member of such Western institutions as NATO and the European Community (today's European Union), forged a durable peace with its eastern and western neighbors, especially France, and became a key supporter of the state of Israel. The German case drives home a key point: what a state does abroad is likely to be influenced by how it is organized at home.

Nongovernmental Organizations and Changes in Foreign Policy

As we will see in greater detail in Chapter 5, both liberals for many years and, in more recent times, constructivists as well emphasize that nongovernmental organizations (NGOs) and other interest groups have had significant success in influencing the foreign policies of states, as well as the policies of international institutions those states control (Keck and Sikkink 1998). NGOs have sought to exercise this influence by working individually and in networks to persuade the leaders of national governments that they should broaden their definition of interests beyond traditional security or economic concerns, and to include in that definition issues such as human rights and the environment.

Some NGOs, such as Oxfam, Médecins Sans Frontières (Doctors Without Borders), and Catholic Charities, pursue projects in poorer countries relating to health or economic development, and advocate for better foreign aid policies by wealthy donor countries like the United States and key international organizations like the World Bank and the International Monetary Fund. Other NGOs, such as Human Rights Watch and Amnesty International, publicize abuses of human and political rights in countries around the globe through newsletters, reports, and direct contacts with members of the news media. They also press national governments, as well as the European Union and United Nations Human Rights Council, for stronger international protections of such rights. Many environmental NGOs, such as the World Wildlife Fund, the Worldwatch Institute, and the International Union for the Conservation of Nature, use similar strategies to draw public and governmental attention to problems in the environmental realm. Other NGOs use more dramatic strategies: for example, Greenpeace has employed small boats and a helicopter to interfere with what it considers to be illegal and immoral operations of large whaling ships.

There is evidence that internationally active NGOs have sometimes changed the ideas of policy makers and shaped, to some degree, their definition of foreign policy interests or strategies. For example, according to an important constructivist study by Margaret Keck and Kathryn Sikkink, networks linking international and domestic activist groups centered on Amnesty International and Americas Watch, helped move the US government to take more seriously human rights abuses in Latin America particularly in Argentina and Mexico during the 1970s, 1980s, and early 1990s. The study reports similar dynamics involving NGOs influencing important governments in the issue areas of protection of women and the natural environment (Keck and Sikkink 1998).

Photo 4.5 Citizens and Foreign Policy Change
Jody Williams, an American citizen, worked closely with the International Campaign to Ban Landmines to publicize the damage to innocent civilians and force governments to address an important foreign policy issue.

Source: Micheline Pelletier/Sygma via Getty Images.

Moreover, NGO advocacy groups have influenced the policy instruments that national governments employ to protect interests even in the sensitive area of national security. For example, during the 1990s, hundreds of NGOs, coordinated by the International Campaign to Ban Landmines and led by Jody Williams, who would receive a Nobel Peace Prize for her work with the campaign, publicized the way innocent civilians were being killed by anti-personnel landmines. The work of the NGOs helped prompt 122 governments to ban that class of weapons due to a treaty signed in Ottawa, Canada, in 1997 (Price 1998). As we will see in Chapter 13, NGOs have sometimes been effective in influencing global policy regarding the natural environment. Finally, constructivists argue that NGOs played a decisive role in forcing leaders of Western countries to take a strong stand against South Africa's white-minority government during the 1980s (Klotz 1995). As Box 4.6 shows, Marxists, constructivists, and realists rely on different types of explanations for that critical example of foreign policy change.

Sources of Foreign Policy Change at the International Level of Analysis

Finally, factors situated at the international level of analysis, in particular internationally induced shocks and changes in the relative power of a country, can induce changes in its foreign policy.

External Shocks

Constructivist theory would lead us to expect that national communities – leaders, officials, commentators, and politically attentive citizens – may sometimes be jarred out of their ideas about foreign policy by a major external shock. For

4.6 DIFFERING THEORETICAL APPROACHES

Why Did the United States and the European Community Impose Economic Sanctions against South Africa?

Background

South Africa long practiced a political system of institutionalized discrimination known as *apartheid*. A small minority of white South Africans ruled over a large majority of black South Africans. The *apartheid* regime controlled the economy and the political and legal system and determined where black South Africans were allowed to work and live. Beginning in the early 1960s, most members of the United Nations protested *apartheid*, imposed an arms embargo against South Africa, and sought to isolate the *apartheid* regime diplomatically. Several key countries, however, including the United Kingdom and the United States, maintained cordial political and close economic relations with South Africa until the 1980s. Then, in a significant policy shift, the United States and members of the European Community imposed economic sanctions against South Africa in 1986. What explains their initial reluctance to act against *apartheid*, and their subsequent shift to opposing *apartheid* through the use of economic sanctions?

Realism

For realists, foreign policy is designed and executed to serve the core national interests of states. For the United States and its European allies, the central national security issue of the Cold War was the struggle against the Soviet Union and international communism. To Western leaders, South Africa's political regime was morally repugnant, but South Africa was an important ally in the global struggle against communism because it was an unambiguously anti-communist state in the key region of southern Africa. Western powers opted to maintain close ties with South Africa despite their distaste for *apartheid*. Security interests trumped democratic and human rights ideals.

The shift to sanctions in the 1980s is harder for the realist perspective to explain. One possibility is that once Mikhail Gorbachev came to power in the Soviet Union, the Cold War was moving toward its end, and thus support for the anti-communist regime in South Africa was less geopolitically vital. The problem with this explanation is that in 1986 it was difficult for Western leaders to foresee that the Cold War was ending and would do so within five years. A second and perhaps more persuasive realist argument is that the sanctions imposed were more symbolic than instrumental. They allowed Western leaders to take what had become a popular political stand against *apartheid* without doing significant damage to the South African economy. Realists might also point out that in the United States the sanctions were passed by Congress but opposed by President Ronald Reagan. Congress overrode the President's veto and the sanctions legislation became law. The US President, in other words, continued to pursue the national interest of close relations with South Africa; the foreign policy change was driven instead by the legislative branch, reflecting popular sentiment.

Constructivism

Constructivists focus on the importance of norms and ideas in international relations. For constructivists, the sanctions decision was the culmination of a gradual and global mass movement in favor of an anti-*apartheid* norm (Klotz 1995). The idea that *apartheid* was a politically and morally unacceptable regime type for a state in the international community took hold and spread over time. This anti-*apartheid* normative movement was led as much by international organizations (such as the Organization for African Unity) and non-state actors as by the governments of nation-states.

By the 1980s, this anti-*apartheid* norm became too powerful even for major states to ignore; countries such as the United Kingdom and the United States that refused to isolate South Africa began to appear themselves as outliers in the international community. The pressure for foreign policy change in the United States and Western Europe came from below, from domestic political forces, and transnationally, from international and nongovernmental organizations. Western leaders continued to place geopolitical value on the South African connection, but eventually were swept along by the movement and could no longer resist it. Global normative change trumped prior conceptions of national interest.

Constructivists might argue further that even if sanctions had limited economic impact on South Africa, their psychological impact on the South African government was significant. So long as the United Kingdom and the United States supported the regime, South Africa's minority government could continue to feel they were part of an anti-communist coalition rather than a pariah within the international community. The sanctions signaled that even their most loyal international supporters no longer considered *apartheid* tolerable.

Marxism

Marxists could explain the willingness of liberal Western governments to tolerate *apartheid* as a function of the economic interests of private economic actors. South Africa's economy was the largest and most profitable in southern Africa. Western banks, manufacturing firms, and raw material producers long considered South Africa a lucrative host for trade and investment. Government policy in Western countries followed and supported the interests of dominant economic classes.

How then to account for the shift to sanctions? Marxists argue that by the 1980s, South Africa was increasingly less attractive as an economic partner. The well-publicized campaign, led by college students, to convince universities and other large resource holders to divest their portfolios from companies doing business in South Africa forced companies to calculate increasing 'social costs' of their South African activities. At the same time, domestic unrest and uprisings among the black majority population in South Africa (the Soweto uprisings of 1976 were a key turning point) created an atmosphere of economic uncertainty. The *apartheid* regime responded with repression including the declaration of a state of emergency in 1985. Shortly thereafter, Chase Manhattan Bank decided it would not renew its loans to South Africa, and other big banks followed suit. For Marxists, the key variable was that private economic actors reluctantly turned against South Africa for business reasons before Western governments signed on to economic sanctions against the regime. Government actors, in other words, followed rather than led a shift in private economic interests.

example, the Japanese attack in December 1941 against the American naval fleet at Pearl Harbor discredited the isolationist position in American politics and helped pave the way for the United States' more internationalist stance after World War II. In the same vein, the experience of Iran's revolutionary leaders after they attained power in 1979 – an invasion in 1980 by Saddam Hussein's Iraq, the receipt of no outside aid and, in fact, some American aid for Saddam Hussein – has probably scarred those leaders and made them deeply suspicious of the United States and committed to acquiring military power, including if necessary nuclear weapons.

Changes in Relative Power

You will recall from Chapter 2 that US leaders and much of the US political elite during and after World War II came to believe the United States had to do more to support a world order than had been true when the United States occupied a much less important place in the international system. In other words, as realist theory would make the point: as the US relative power position changed, so too did its conceptions of interest and appropriate strategy. These changes do not happen immediately; the United States was already very powerful by the 1930s but did not change its foreign policy significantly. Some analysts see China in a comparable position today – its relative power is rising, but it has not yet adjusted its foreign policy to do more to support international order. This 'lag effect' works in reverse as well. The United Kingdom and France maintained international responsibility typically associated with the strongest states in the system long after their power positions declined in relative terms.

Levels of Analysis *Sources of Foreign Policy Change*		
Individual	State	🌐 International
Foreign policy can take a markedly different course either because new leaders come into office or because current leaders change their beliefs about the country's interests or strategy options.	A change in a country's political regime, or intensive lobbying by non-state actors within the country, can bring about large changes in a country's foreign policy.	External policy shocks as well as changes in a country's relative power may contribute to significant changes in foreign policy.

REVISITING THE ENDURING QUESTION AND LOOKING AHEAD

In this chapter, we have examined the enduring question of what accounts for the foreign policies of states. We reviewed the main elements of foreign policy, namely, interest and strategy, with the latter concept entailing two ideas of goals and policy instruments. We employed the levels-of-analysis framework both to understand why governments, by virtue of the influence of their national leaders, domestic institutions, and societal actors, and international conditions, choose certain interests to advance and devise particular strategies to pursue them.

We used that same levels-of-analysis framework to investigate an important question derived from our central one: why do states' governments sometimes make substantial changes to their foreign policies? In accounting for both foreign policy and foreign policy change, the chapter has showcased the ongoing and unresolved debate among students of international relations and foreign policy. That debate cuts across the levels of analysis and also across the theoretical traditions introduced in Chapter 3. Students who grasp the different types of arguments made by scholars at different levels, and from different theoretical perspectives, will be well equipped to engage the literature on foreign policy analysis, to understand and explain current foreign policy decisions, and eventually to conduct their own research as well.

With this chapter and the previous chapter, we have explored the key language, ideas, and overall approaches that scholars, many media observers, and even some government leaders and officials employ when they think, write, and speak about international relations and foreign policy. In the next chapter, we complete our examination of the foundation of international relations by moving to the level of the international system and studying international laws and organizations. If we think of the international system as a society of states, then international laws and organizations are the formal rules and institutions through which states govern their relations with each other and with non-state actors.

STUDY QUESTIONS

1. Is the formulation of a coherent strategy by a complex government like China, the United States, or the UK possible? Aren't foreign policies the sum of bureaucratic and institutional in-fighting within governments, rather than the result of a rational, systematic assessment by national leaders of what's best for the country?
2. Can you think of how the geographic location of the United States, or Japan, or France has influenced its foreign policy? Has that influence continued or waned over time?
3. Do you think that a country's domestic political institutions influence its understanding of its interests in the foreign domain? Do those institutions play a role in influencing which instruments the country is likely to turn to in advancing its interests?
4. In general, do you think leaders are good 'learners' when it comes to foreign policy?
5. What makes it likely that a leader will learn appropriate lessons from his or her experiences in foreign policy?
6. Do you think NGOs have too much, just about the right amount, or too little influence on the foreign policies of countries in the international system?

FURTHER READING

Allison, Graham and Philip Zelikow (1999) *Essence of Decision: Explaining the Cuban Missile Crisis*, 2nd edition (New York: Longman). This classic work, first published by Allison in 1971, shaped a generation of scholarship on foreign policy by showing that the same set of foreign policy decisions – the Soviet decision to place nuclear weapons in Cuba and the US response – could be understood several different ways. Allison challenged the then conventional rational-actor approach by looking 'inside' the state at the institutional and bureaucratic politics of governments.

Kang, David (2009) *China Rising: Peace, Power, and Order in East Asia* (New York: Columbia University Press). In this foreign policy analysis Kang argues that the states of East Asia are more likely to accommodate China than to balance against it. He draws on constructivist thinking to make the case that historical and cultural norms in East Asian countries lead states to embrace, rather than resist, a hierarchy of authority with China at the top.

Legro, Jeffrey W. (2007) *Rethinking the World: Great Power Strategies and International Order* (Ithaca: Cornell University Press). Legro makes the case that ideas drive foreign policy change. He develops the argument in a broad comparative framework that includes analysis of major foreign policy transitions in Russia, China, Japan, and the United States.

Narizny, Kevin (2007) *The Political Economy of Grand Strategy* (Ithaca: Cornell University Press). Narizny argues that foreign policy strategies are driven by the pattern of interest group coalitions found within a country. He uses this framework to explain the overall foreign policies, or grand strategies, of the United Kingdom and the United States during the nineteenth and twentieth centuries.

Visit **www.macmillanihe.com/Grieco-IntroIR-2e** to access extra resources for this chapter, including:

- Chapter summaries to help you review the material
- Multiple choice quizzes to test your understanding
- Flashcards to test your knowledge of the key terms in this chapter
- An interactive simulation that invites you to go through the decision-making process of a world leader at a crucial political juncture
- Pivotal decisions in which you weigh up the pros and cons of complicated decisions with grave consequences
- Outside resources, including links to contemporary articles and videos, that add to what you have learned in this chapter

5 Framing International Relations: The Role of Laws and Organizations

Enduring question

How important are international laws and organizations in a world of sovereign states?

Chapter Contents

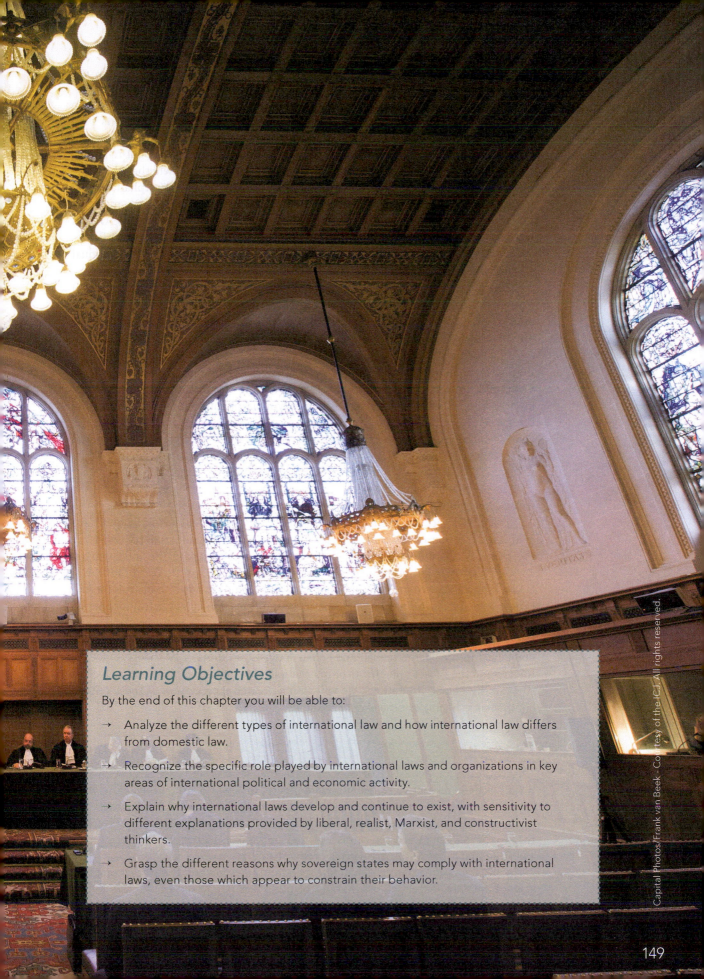

Learning Objectives

By the end of this chapter you will be able to:

→ Analyze the different types of international law and how international law differs from domestic law.

→ Recognize the specific role played by international laws and organizations in key areas of international political and economic activity.

→ Explain why international laws develop and continue to exist, with sensitivity to different explanations provided by liberal, realist, Marxist, and constructivist thinkers.

→ Grasp the different reasons why sovereign states may comply with international laws, even those which appear to constrain their behavior.

It might be surprising to learn that although there is no authoritative 'world government' to regulate international relations, most states, most of the time, recognize and comply with international laws. Also, a significant part of the routine interactions of states takes place through international organizations such as the United Nations and the World Trade Organization. International laws and organizations constitute a critical part of the landscape of international relations. Indeed, in recent years, governments have been grappling with whether there are instances in which state sovereignty – the cornerstone of the Westphalian state system created in the seventeenth century that we described in Chapter 2 – may now need to take a back seat to efforts by international organizations such as the United Nations (UN) as well as private, nongovernmental organizations like Human Rights Watch which promotes respect for and protection of the human rights of individual persons wherever they may live.

This chapter will help you to understand the role and significance of international laws and organizations in contemporary world politics. First, we provide an understanding of the basic concepts related to international law, how international law differs from law in domestic politics, and the important supporting role international organizations play in the development and implementation of international law. International laws and organizations complement and reinforce each other.

Second, to illustrate their key roles, we examine the features of international laws and organizations in several important areas of international life including the launching and fighting of wars, the protection of civilians in harm's way, the defense of human rights, and the use of the world's waterway. International laws and organizations are pervasive in the modern international system, and in later chapters, we will examine how they shape international relations in other important areas, such as the management of global trade and finance (Chapter 9), and the use of the natural environment (Chapter 13).

In the third part of the chapter we explore two fundamental scholarly questions at the intersection of international law, organization, and politics. First, what are the political conditions and processes that produce and sustain the international laws and associated international organizations that we see 'out there' in the world? Second, how effective are international laws and organizations at constraining the behavior of states, and under what political conditions do such constraints operate or fail to operate? Different scholars have addressed these questions by focusing at the individual, state, or interstate level of analysis and by drawing on arguments embedded in the liberal, realist, and constructivist traditions of IR theory. Once we understand the causes and effects of international laws and organizations, as well as their strengths and limitations, we will gain a greater appreciation of these critical components shaping international relations.

BASIC CONCEPTS AND DISTINCTIONS

International law
Explicit rules that stipulate the rights and the obligations that states have with respect to other states or other actors covered by the law.

International law consists of explicit rules that leaders and officials, acting on behalf of their respective states, utilize in greater or lesser degree in deciding what actions they are empowered or constrained to undertake toward other states and other relevant actors in world affairs, including individuals and corporations. Notice that we have emphasized the phrase, greater and lesser degree: it is exploring that variation that is one of the main goals of this chapter.

In any policy area, international law specifies the rights and the obligations that states have with respect to other states or other actors covered by the law. Rights and obligations refer to what a state may legally do when interacting with other states or other relevant actors, and the kinds of behavior it may legally expect others to undertake. These rights and obligations about behavior are usually stated quite clearly in the context of international law in the form of *prescriptions* for actions that the state should or may elect to take, and *proscriptions* for or prohibitions on actions that the state should not take toward other states or relevant actors (Krasner 1982).

For example, today's international law on international trade, discussed more fully in Chapter 9, is set forth in the founding treaty for the World Trade Organization (WTO), which came into force in January 1995. Much of the treaty lays down procedures by which member states come together to negotiate multilateral agreements to reduce different kinds of barriers to trade. By adhering to the treaty, participating in WTO-sponsored negotiations, and signing the resulting trade-liberalizing agreements, member states mutually commit to reducing the trade barriers specified in the agreements. They also have the right to expect others to abide by the agreements. If a member state believes one or more of its partners is not living up to its side of the bargain, the WTO treaty offers detailed rules that prescribe the steps the aggrieved partner can take to seek remedies. A complaining state may not simply impose a unilateral sanction against a partner until and unless the state has followed relevant dispute-settlement procedures outlined in the WTO treaty.

Types of International Law

Most international law that has been established during the past century, and especially in the post-World War II era, takes the form of written treaties that are accepted by signatories through some process of national ratification. There are two general types of law-creating **treaties**. First, there are many treaties that have been constructed and recognized by all or most states in the contemporary international system. These are universal international laws. Second, some treaties may be directed toward the concerns of states in a particular region. This is non-universal international law. Some notable examples of both types of law are listed in Table 5.1.

Treaty
A formal agreement between two or more states designed to settle a dispute or set down guidelines for future action.

Table 5.1 Timeline of Notable Examples of Universal and Non-Universal International Laws

Universal international laws		Non-universal international laws	
1949	Geneva Accords regulating the conduct of war	1949	Origin of North Atlantic Treaty Organization (NATO), today consisting of 29 members across North America and Europe
1968	Treaty on the Non-Proliferation of Nuclear Weapons (NPT accord)	1951–present	Succession of treaties to produce today's 27-member European Union (EU)
1982	Treaty on the Law of the Sea	1967	Treaty that created the Association of Southeast Asian Nations (ASEAN)
2016	The Paris Agreement on climate change	2001	Creation of Shanghai Cooperation Organization (SCO), today includes eight Eurasian countries

Statutory international law
Written laws that are agreed upon and codified by participating states.

Customary international law
Legal norms that, while not written down as formal law, have come to be seen by states as having some capacity to control their behavior.

It is also important to distinguish between **statutory international law** and **customary international law**. Statutory international law consists of written laws that are agreed upon and codified by participating states, such as the Charter of the United Nations (24 pages and initially signed by 50 states) and the WTO treaty (30,000 pages and initially signed by 128 states). Customary international law consists not of a written set of mutually acknowledged rules, but rather a set of unwritten rules whose presence is made apparent by the individual statements and behavior of states. Customary international law arises when one or more states believe consistently over time that some form of behavior is required as a matter of established practice and in accordance with some legal norm. For example, long before the 1982 Law of the Sea Treaty, states asserted the right to control adjacent waters up to three miles from their shoreline. Other examples of customary international law included long-standing injunctions against genocide and slavery. Over time, many important customary international legal norms, including those relating to genocide, slavery, and the law of the sea, have become codified as universal statutory international law.

Much contemporary international law seeks to shape the behavior of states toward other states. For example, the 1949 Geneva Accord lays out rules on how states may fight wars, and the 1968 Treaty on the Non-Proliferation of Nuclear Weapons (NPT) stipulates which states are legally entitled to nuclear weapons (see Chapter 8 for further discussion). However, some international law is not simply 'state to state,' but addresses how states, individuals, multinational corporations, and international institutions should regard one another. International human rights law, for example, seeks to create obligations on how governments should behave toward their national citizens. International investment law creates rules by which multinational corporations and national government resolve disputes arising from the operations of foreign companies within a state's borders.

Types of International Organization

In the discussion above we have made note of bodies such as the UN, the WTO, and the European Union. These are international organizations, and they play an important role in the day-to-day operation of international agreements. They therefore will be a focus of this chapter alongside our discussion of international law.

International organization
A body or association established by two or more states, usually formed to help states implement their obligations under a relevant international law.

In general, an **international organization** is an ongoing association or body with an international membership, scope, and presence. International organizations are often established by a treaty. They both make international laws and are governed by them. Typically, international organizations have states as members and are formed to help states implement their obligations under a relevant international law or agreement, and to monitor compliance of states with the terms of that accord. They also help states resolve disputes within the domain covered by the law or agreement and identify ways by which the original arrangement can be modified to attain improved outcomes for all members.

The European Union is an important example of an international organization. It contains 28 member states (27 if the United Kingdom leaves as planned in 2019). It is based on a series of treaty commitments among its members, including the Treaty of Rome in 1957, which created the initial European Economic Community, the Maastricht Treaty of 1992, which paved the way for the adoption of the euro as a common currency, and the Lisbon Treaty of 2009, which sought to make the EU more democratic by increasing the participation of citizens within the EU's member states. As Figure 5.1 shows, the EU governs the policies of its members and interaction among them across a wide array of domains.

Figure 5.1 Functions of the European Union
The diagram presents the responsibilities and tasks assumed by the EU in three broad areas or 'pillars' covering the common market, foreign and defense policy, and criminal and judicial policy.

The European Union

First pillar: the European Communities	Second pillar: common foreign and security policy	Third pillar: cooperation in justice and home affairs
EC • Custom union and single market • Agricultural policy • Structural policy • Trade policy **New or amended provisions on:** • EU citizenship • Education and culture • Trans-European networks • Consumer protection • Health • Research and environment • Social policy • Asylum policy • External borders • Immigration policy **Euratom** **ECSC**	**Foreign policy** • Cooperation, common positions and measures • Peacekeeping • Human rights • Democracy • Aid to non-member countries **Security policy** • Drawing on the WEU: questions concerning the security of the EU • Disarmament • Financial aspects of defence • Long-term: Europe's security framework	• Cooperation between judicial authorities in civil and criminal law • Police cooperation • Combating racism and xenophobia • Fighting drugs and the arms trade • Fighting organised crime • Fighting terrorism • Criminal acts against children, trafficking in human beings

Source: https://europa.eu © European Union, 1995–2018.

We can distinguish nongovernmental organizations (NGOs), intergovernmental organizations (IGOs), and supranational organizations. Nongovernmental organizations involve private actors rather than states and seek to influence world politics typically in specific issue areas. Human Rights Watch, discussed below, is a good example. Intergovernmental organizations are associations of sovereign states who work on issues of common interest. NATO, in the domain of international security, and the WTO, in the domain of political economy, are current examples. In a supranational organization, member states grant some meaningful degree of authority to the organization in one or more policy areas. The EU, for example, is an intergovernmental organization but also a supranational one: member states no longer exercise independent control over their trade policies, but instead have granted the EU the legal and political authority to negotiate binding trade agreements on their behalf.

We should also distinguish between formal and informal international organizations: the former are founded on the basis of an international treaty while the latter are created as a result of ad hoc, non-binding agreements of participating countries to so work together on some common issue or problem. The UN, the EU, and the WTO are all examples of formal international organizations: they came into being as the result of formal international treaties among states. There are, at the same time, numerous informal international organizations. For example, as we will see in Chapter 9, cooperation among states in the global economic domain has often taken place since the 1970s through two ad hoc associations of nations for which no international law serves as an underpinning, namely, the Group of 7 industrialized countries (which for a time included post-communist Russia, during which the arrangement was called the Group of 8) and a larger Group of 20 countries, which includes both the Group of 7 countries as well as such nations such as Australia, Brazil, China, India, Nigeria, Russia, and South Korea.

Finally, we should differentiate international organizations from international institutions. Some scholars use these terms interchangeably because they overlap significantly. **International institutions** are sets of rules, principles, and expectations that govern interstate interaction. Whereas international organizations tend to be formal and legal, international institutions may be based on either formal rules or informal understandings. The WTO is a specific international organization, while what might be called the 'postwar liberal trading order,' with expectations that states will keep their markets relatively open and will not raise barriers to trade arbitrarily, is an international institution. Two leading scholars of international relations, Beth Simmons and Lisa Martin, have observed that 'in the actual practice of research, the distinction between organizations and institutions is usually of secondary importance, unless the institution under study is especially informal' (Simmons and Martin 2001: 194).

International institutions
Sets of rules, principles, and expectations that govern interstate interaction.

Domestic vs. International Law

Although we may be tempted to consider them as essentially the same, it is important to recognize four key differences between domestic law, or law within states, and international law, law between states. The first and perhaps most fundamental difference relates to how domestic and international laws are applied and enforced. Within nation-states, citizens are subject to the laws of the land; they do not get to pick and choose which ones to observe. At the international level, states are only bound to the laws and treaties they sign. Within most nation-states there is a system for the enforcement of national law that does not include actors who find themselves in a dispute; this system usually includes the ongoing presence and operation of a police force, criminal and civil prosecutors, and judges whose determinations can be enforced by criminal and civil penalties. There is no such centralized governmental authority at the international level to which states can take others when they believe they have been harmed and need to seek legal redress. Instead, for the most part, states are in a self-help legal system: they individually must decide when their legal rights have been violated to the point of suffering some harm, and then they individually need to institute remedies to alleviate or reverse the harm done to them, including on occasion the imposition of sanctions or even the use of military force.

Second, in most national political systems there is a sense of how laws in different areas relate to one another. In many countries, such as the United States, Japan, and Germany, there is a written constitution that stipulates different levels of government and the domains of legal responsibility of those different levels. In other national contexts, such as the United Kingdom, there is not a written constitution, but there is an accumulation of experience, including through a courts system, that produces in political leaders and citizens a set of stable expectations about how law is made and how different laws ultimately are brought into reasonable conformity with one another. The international legal system in contrast is fragmented. Instead of a single, relatively coherent system of civil and criminal law there are islands of international law, such as the law regarding commerce and, quite separately, the laws regarding human rights.

Third, in domestic law, precedents, or how legal decisions of the past impinge on or control legal decisions in the present, are very important. Lawyers and judges who face a case to be argued or adjudicated in the present must consider which case decisions in the past illuminate the legal issues raised by the current case, and as a result which law should be applied. In international legal proceedings – for example, in cases before the Permanent Court of Arbitration (PCA) or the International Court of Justice (ICJ) – advocates and judges may refer to past cases as offering instruction on how to proceed with a current case, but there is no legal requirement or custom that requires or even allows a past case to determine or control how the current case is to be decided. Thus, compared to most domestic legal systems, there is in the international domain much less certainty about what the law is in a given area and how a case ought to be decided.

Finally, there is the matter of jurisdiction. In most domestic legal systems, a person who is being sued in a civil matter or has been charged with an offense to be tried in a criminal proceeding has no right to refuse to be brought to court, although they can ask a judge to move the proceedings to another location if they have a reasonable fear that they cannot have a fair trial where the offense occurred. In international law, there is no automatic requirement that a state respond to another state who seeks redress in an international court. Instead, the respondent state must give its permission to be brought to a particular court. For example, with the International Court of Justice, a state against which a complaint has been brought must agree that the case can be heard before the ICJ, unless it has signed an agreement ahead of time that allows for automatic redress of grievances before the court.

Levels of Analysis   *International Law and Organizations*

👤 Individual	👥 State	🌐 International
International law covers not simply state-to-state interactions, but also, in key areas such as human rights, the relationship between states and individuals.	Law within states is very different from law among states on the dimensions of enforcement, hierarchy among laws, the role of precedents, and the automaticity of jurisdiction.	States find it useful to reach common understandings of acceptable behavior in the international system. They codify those understandings in laws and implement them through institutions.

DOMAINS OF INTERNATIONAL LAW AND ORGANIZATIONS

International law is fragmented: it consists of islands of rules and associated international organizations across several different issue areas. In this section we illustrate several domains of international law. Since the resort to military force is arguably the most important step a sovereign state may take, we begin with international law and organizations that are concerned with the initiation by states of war, and the special role of the UN Security Council. Then, to demonstrate that international laws and organizations reach not only across states but within them, we cover the international law surrounding humanitarian interventions, the holding to account of individuals who violate humanitarian law during wars, and the relatively new concept of the 'Responsibility to Protect' (R2P). We also devote attention to the postwar 'revolution' in human rights law, which stipulates there are civic and political rights common to all individuals regardless of the sovereign state within which they reside. Finally, to illustrate the role of law and organizations in a domain involving the natural environment, we focus on the law of the sea.

These illustrations show that international law provides explicit guidelines on how states may act or refrain from acting in a specific domain. They also demonstrate the complementary role of international laws and organizations. And, we will see that states routinely resort to and abide by international law, although not in every circumstance. To return to our enduring question, international laws and organizations are influential in a world of sovereign states, yet with significant limitations. Most importantly, they depend on the cooperation and participation of states, especially great powers, to be effective.

When May States Launch Wars?

Perhaps the most important issue of international law concerns the circumstances under which a state or group of states possesses a legal right to go to war. We can find an early effort to craft what legal scholars call *jus ad bellum* – or the international law that stipulates the legitimate grounds under which a state may go to war – in the 1919 Covenant of the League of Nations. In modern times the authoritative international rules for war initiation are contained in the Charter of the United Nations, particularly in the work of the UN Security Council and its application of the provisions contained in Chapter VII of the Charter. Tremendous hope was invested in the UN immediately after it was founded in 1945 as the embodiment and creator of a more peaceful and just world (see Photo 5.1), but, as we saw in Chapter 2, East–West competition soon paralyzed the UN Security Council and it remained relatively dormant in security affairs until the end of the Cold War in 1989. Since then the UN Security Council has been markedly more active on the matter of war and peace, and, in the words of international-law expert Christine Gray, 'the UN Charter is the starting point for any discussion of international law on the use of force' (Gray 2014: 619; also see Gray 2008). In Box 5.1, we explore how the United Nations has evolved over time in addressing issues of war and peace.

The UN Charter's general orientation against war is contained in both a prescription and a proscription. This prescription is stated in Chapter I, Article 2, Paragraph 3 of the UN Charter (or, using a convention for citing Charter elements, Article 2.3): 'All Members shall settle their international disputes by peaceful means in such a manner that international peace and security, and justice, are not endangered.' The proscription immediately follows in what is among the most frequently quoted

Jus ad bellum
The international law that stipulates the legitimate grounds under which a state may go to war. In today's world that law is found in Chapter VII of the UN Charter.

Photo 5.1 The United Nations and Moving toward a Better World, 1951
These 1951 UN postage stamps highlight the hope of many at that time that through the UN the international community could break free of the chains of conflict and deprivation of the past and move together toward a better life for all the different peoples of the world.

Source: DeAgostini/Getty Images.

5.1   MAKING CONNECTIONS
Then and Now

The Evolution of the United Nations

Then: Limited Membership and Unmet Expectations

The United Nations (UN) was established at a conference in San Francisco in 1945, with 51 original members. Its founders sought a more durable successor to the League of Nations, which had collapsed during the 1930s when it became clear that most states were unwilling to meet their commitments to aid smaller states (such as Ethiopia during the 'Abyssinia crisis,' described in Chapter 2) that were victims of aggression. The UN was designed to be more flexible; it created a General Assembly comprised of representatives of all member states, and a Security Council that contained five permanent members (the United States, the United Kingdom, France, the Soviet Union, and China) and ten rotating members. Authority to make decisions over war and peace was vested in the Security Council. But to provide flexibility to the great powers, each of the 'perm five' had the ability to veto Security Council initiatives. The result, during the Cold War, was essentially a stalemate, as the Soviet Union and United States lined up on opposite sides of most peace and security issues and one or the other blocked meaningful Security Council initiatives.

Now: Global Membership and Multiple Responsibilities

The membership of the UN has steadily increased and today it has 193 members (at time of writing, South Sudan is the most recent). Many of these new members, from Africa and Asia, were not independent states when the UN was formed, and they are generally smaller and poorer than the original member states. This expansion of membership has altered the activities and orientation of the UN, reducing the influence of the former great powers and giving more voice to smaller nations. The General Assembly is now dominated by the Group of 77, a coalition of developing countries. If the focus on the United Nations in its early years was conflict resolution and the prevention of war between the traditional great powers (as the UN Charter proclaims, to 'save succeeding generations from the scourge of war'), the UN has gradually expanded its focus to challenges of development and 'human security' – eradication of poverty, disease control, aid to refugees, and the promotion of sustainable development, clean energy, and education and social protections. Since the end of the Cold War, the UN has become more active as a forum for advancing global norms and principles of human rights.

The UN Security Council, in contrast, has remained a body composed of the original five major postwar states, with ten additional states joining the permanent five for two-year terms. Many observers view the Security Council structure as 'dated' and in need of reform. But reform is politically difficult. Germany and Japan, for example, would seem plausible candidates for permanent membership due to their relative size and capabilities. But if Germany and Japan gained that status, what about India or large states from Africa and Latin America? Any large-scale reform would require changes to the UN Charter, and those changes could be vetoed by any of the current permanent five members. China, for example, would likely veto any effort to offer a permanent seat to Japan given their long-standing regional rivalry.

Notwithstanding the debate over reform, the Security Council has steadily expanded its role in peacekeeping operations around the world. UN peacekeepers are typically multinational forces that situate themselves between warring parties to prevent or minimize further conflict. As of April 2018, the UN was running 14 peacekeeping operations across the globe, with uniformed personnel from multiple countries participating. For details on specific peacekeeping operations, see Map 5.1 and http://www.un.org/en/peacekeeping/operations/current.shtml.

Map 5.1 UN Peacekeeping Operations, April 2018

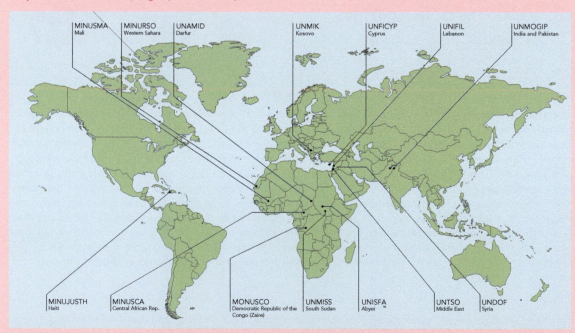

Source: Based on UN map produced by the Geospatial Information Section, April 2018.

language in the UN Charter, namely, Article 2.4: 'All Members shall refrain in their international relations from the threat or use of force against the territorial integrity or political independence of any state, or in any other manner inconsistent with the Purposes of the United Nations.'

Under the terms of the UN Charter, if a state or a group of states believes that military force may need to be used, for example in response to the aggression of other states, the responding states must obtain permission to so use force from the UN Security Council (with one important exception discussed below). The steps for seeking authorization to employ military force are found in a set of interrelated articles entitled, 'Action with respect to Threats to the Peace, Breaches of the Peace, and Acts of Aggression' (Chapter VII of the UN Charter). When you see media reports that one or another state, and especially a powerful one, has gone to the UN Security Council under Chapter VII, you know there is a serious crisis underway and a heightened prospect for war. We provide a summary of the relevant elements of Chapter VII regarding the launching of war, and the special role assigned by the Charter to the UN Security Council, in Figure 5.2.

According to the UN Charter, the UN Security Council is alone empowered to determine when a state has injured another state or group of states to such a degree that may lawfully require the use of military force. The UN Charter does not anticipate that force will be authorized as a first resort against an aggressor, but rather it will be employed only if other means, including economic sanctions, have failed to cause an aggressor to reverse course. For example, in 2017 the UN Security Council authorized the imposition by members of the international community of economic sanctions against North Korea to stop that country from fully developing intercontinental ballistic missiles capable of delivering nuclear weapons against targets across the globe (see Photo 5.2).

Figure 5.2   Elements of Chapter VII of the UN Charter

Article 39 – UN Security Council In Charge: 'The Security Council shall determine the existence of any threat to the peace, breach of the peace, or act of aggression and shall make recommendations, or decide what measures shall be taken in accordance with Articles 41 and 42, to maintain or restore international peace and security.'

Article 40 – Cease and Desist Orders: 'The UN Security Council may … call upon the parties concerned to comply with such provisional measures as it deems necessary or desirable … The Security Council shall duly take account of failure to comply with such provisional measures.'

Article 41 – Sanctions Short of War: 'The Security Council may decide what measures not involving the use of armed force are to be employed to give effect to its decisions, and it may call upon the Members of the United Nations to apply such measures. These may include complete or partial interruption of economic relations and of rail, sea, air, postal, telegraphic, radio, and other means of communication, and the severance of diplomatic relations.'

Article 42 – Lawful War: 'Should the Security Council consider that measures provided for in Article 41 would be inadequate or have proved to be inadequate, it may take such action by air, sea, or land forces as may be necessary to maintain or restore international peace and security. Such action may include demonstrations, blockade, and other operations by air, sea, or land forces of Members of the United Nations.'

Source: UN, Charter of the United Nations, available at http://www.un.org/en/sections/un-charter/chapter-vii/index.html

Photo 5.2 UN Security Council Vote for Economic Sanctions against North Korea, August 5, 2017

In an instance of unanimity, on August 5, 2017, all 15 members of the UN Security Council, acting under Article 41 of Chapter VII of the UN Charter, voted in favor of Security Council Resolution Number 2371, which condemned tests by North Korea of ballistic missiles and its efforts to build nuclear weapons, and imposed additional economic sanctions on that country.

Source: EDUARDO MUNOZ ALVAREZ/AFP/Getty Images.

The legal permission granted by the UN Security Council typically takes the form of a resolution authorizing the use of force. Nine of the 15 Security Council members need to vote in favor of the resolution to authorize force legally. Moreover, the resolution cannot sustain a no-vote by any of the five permanent members of the UN Security Council, under Article 27 of the UN Charter.

The Gulf War of 1990–91 provides an important example of how the legal use of force operates under the supervision of the UN Security Council. Iraq, under the dictatorship of Saddam Hussein, invaded and occupied Kuwait in August 1990. The United States and United Kingdom, acting on behalf of the Security Council, put forward and quickly gained its approval of Resolution 660, which found the Iraqi invasion to be 'a breach of international peace and security' and called for a total withdrawal of Iraqi forces from Kuwait. After a subsequent series of UN Security Council resolutions – some with economic sanctions imposed under Article 41 of Chapter VII – and other diplomatic efforts did not bring about an Iraqi withdrawal, the UN Security Council in November 1990 approved Resolution 678. That resolution gave Iraq one last chance to withdraw from Kuwait, failing which the resolution extended to UN members the legal authority 'to use all necessary means' to expel Iraqi forces from Kuwait. The United States and a coalition of 31 other states then undertook military operations between January and February 1991 that led to the expulsion of Iraqi forces from Kuwait. The ending of the war was formalized with UN Security Council Resolution 687, in April 1991, which terminated hostilities and restored Kuwaiti sovereignty. It also required Iraq to destroy all its biological and chemical weapons, cease all work on nuclear weapons and ballistic missiles, and cooperate with relevant United Nations authorities to verify compliance with these disarmament provisions of the ceasefire.

The Gulf War of 1990–91 demonstrated how states might employ international law and institutions to justify and carry out war against an aggressor state. However, the subsequent Gulf War of 2003 showed that the UN legal system does not reliably constrain national decisions to use military force. By 2002 the United States and United Kingdom believed that Iraq was in violation of UN Security Council Resolution 687 and was moving toward a nuclear weapons capability while also remaining in possession of chemical and biological weapons. In November 2002 the United States and United Kingdom gained passage of Resolution 1441, which found Iraq to be 'in material breach of its obligations' under numerous UN resolutions, including Resolution 687. The Security Council did not authorize war in November 2002 but instead gave Iraq one last chance to cease its Weapons of Mass Destruction (WMD) activities. By March 2003, the United Kingdom and America crafted a resolution specifically authorizing war. However, when it became apparent that a necessary majority of UN Security Council members might not support the resolution, and that Russia and perhaps even France might veto it, the United States, the United Kingdom, and a small coalition of states acted without Security Council authorization and launched a war against Iraq in mid-March 2003. This action proved politically controversial and subjected the lead initiators, the United States and United Kingdom, to considerable international criticism. In Box 5.2, we examine the findings of academic research on why even powerful states request Security Council authorization before going to war.

There is one major exception to the process outlined in Figure 5.2 on the role of the Security Council in determining when military force may be employed. That exception is found in Article 51 of Chapter VII, which states that 'Nothing in the present Charter shall impair the inherent right of individual or collective self-defense if an armed attack occurs against a Member of the United Nations ...'

This language would seem to suggest that so long as a state claims that it is launching the use of military force for reasons of self-defense (which is not defined by the Charter), then it can legally use such force. But Article 51 also offers a significant limitation on the self-defense exception. The sentence that stipulates the right of self-defense presented above is completed by these words: 'until the Security Council has taken measures necessary to maintain international peace and security.' This second clause of the sentence would seem to indeed suggest that a member that is threatened with or experiencing an attack may launch operations of self-defense, but it has a responsibility then to allow the UN Security Council to intervene and manage the crisis. The UN Security Council holds the authority to determine if a claim of self-defense is legitimate or is a pretext for an aggressive, illegitimate undertaking of war.

The United States, following the attacks of September 11, 2001, claimed that Article 51 authorized its war in Afghanistan in pursuit of Osama bin Laden. The United States did convene the Security Council, but rather than request specific Security Council authorization of the use of force, the Bush administration requested and received (Resolution 1368) a condemnation of the September 11 attack and a general call for all states to work together to bring justice to the perpetrators and sponsors of the attacks. In this instance, the United States most likely could have acquired Security Council authorization but chose instead the flexibility to respond unilaterally to the attack on its homeland.

5.2 RESEARCH INSIGHT

Why Seek Authorization for War from the UN Security Council?

The Problem

International relations is sometimes called a 'self-help' system. States are responsible for defending their own territories and have the option to go to war if they so desire. If a government is strong enough to initiate war unilaterally or with a coalition of partners, why bother seeking authorization from the UN Security Council? The Council has 15 members with diverse viewpoints, five of whom can single-handedly veto any resolution. Why take this time-consuming and politically risky step?

The Research Insight

Recent academic research addresses this question with emphasis on the *information-conveying* qualities of international organizations. Even if a country has the capacity to 'go it alone,' it has much to gain by engaging the Security Council. Voeten (2005) finds that Security Council deliberation provides information to a government on what kind of opposition it is likely to face if it proceeds with military action. Will other actors support, grudgingly tolerate, or actively oppose the proposed intervention? Thompson (2006) emphasizes that going to the Security Council conveys information to *other* governments – it signals willingness by the intervening government to take input from others and to build a multilateral coalition in support of its action.

Requesting Security Council approval provides information to a government's domestic audience as well. Chapman and Reiter (2004) find that if a government receives international approval, it is more likely to receive domestic support; having a Security Council resolution magnifies the 'rally round the flag' effect of public support for government leaders facing or initiating military crises. International support reassures publics, especially in democracies, of the soundness of their government's proposal and provides more confidence in the likelihood of success. Grieco *et al.* (2011) similarly finds that Security Council support offers a useful 'second opinion' to publics who might be less inclined to support military action. Recchia (2015) focuses on a different type of domestic audience and finds, especially in cases of humanitarian intervention, that Security Council action can reassure not just the mass public but the military leaders (e.g. in the United States, the Joint Chiefs of Staff) who will be responsible for carrying out the intervention.

Humanitarian Intervention and the 'Responsibility to Protect'

The international law of war initiation regulates when and how it is acceptable for states to initiate the use of force against each other. There are also international laws regulating the way governments may conduct war, which are codified in the Geneva Conventions. But what if the leaders of states, or other political actors, turn the instrument of violence systematically against groups within another state's – or even against their own – *civilian* population? International legal practice has evolved to protect the victims, or at least punish the perpetrators, of atrocities individual state actors have carried out against civilian groups. These individuals, who may have held positions in a government's military, police force, or political leadership, are depicted as war criminals and charged under international law with committing crimes against humanity.

World War II effectively marks the beginning of international humanitarian law. British Prime Minister Winston Churchill, observing Nazi atrocities, stated famously in 1941 that 'we are in the presence of a crime without a name.' A Polish-Jewish lawyer and professor, Raphael Lemkin, gave that crime a name: genocide (Lemkin 1944). **Genocide** refers to violent crimes committed against a national, racial, religious, or ethnic group with the intent of destroying the existence of that group. In 1948 members of the United Nations approved the Convention for the Prevention and Punishment of the Crime of Genocide. As of 2015, 147 states ratified or acceded to the Convention. Participating states commit to treat genocide as an international crime and to take steps to prevent and punish it.

International humanitarian law has evolved in three major phases. **International tribunals** – ad hoc legal proceedings that are less formal than court proceedings and applied to specific international circumstances – were created after World War II and took on new life during the 1990s. Second, in 2002, states regularized humanitarian legal proceedings by creating an International Criminal Court. Third, in 2005 they adopted a new doctrine, the Responsibility to Protect (R2P), which establishes an obligation for states to intervene against governments unwilling or unable to protect their civilian populations. Over time, states have become more invested, through the UN and elsewhere, in the defense of civilians living within the borders of legally sovereign states.

Genocide
Violent crimes committed against a particular national, racial, religious, or ethnic group with the intent of destroying the existence of that group.

International tribunals
Ad hoc legal proceedings that are less formal than court proceedings and applied to specific international situations, such as genocide in Rwanda during the 1990s.

International Tribunals: An Initial Step in Developing Humanitarian Law

International tribunals were created immediately after World War II to bring to justice German and Japanese officials who had committed wartime atrocities. In 1945 the International Military Tribunal (IMT), based in Nuremberg, Germany, tried 22 Nazi leaders instrumental in the mass murder of European Jews. They were charged with 'war crimes, crimes against peace, and crimes against humanity.' Three were acquitted and the rest sentenced either to death or to long prison sentences. The IMT established important principles such as making leaders responsible for atrocities committed by subordinates, and not allowing subordinates to evade justice by claiming to have 'just followed orders.'

The International Military Tribunal for the Far East was created in Tokyo in 1946 by US General Douglas MacArthur, the Supreme Commander of Allied Powers in occupied Japan. Its stated purpose was to try and punish 'Far Eastern war criminals,' and it claimed jurisdiction over crimes carried out by Japanese leaders from the invasion of Manchuria in 1931 to Japan's surrender in 1945. Eleven countries that signed Japan's instrument of surrender provided prosecutorial teams, and

Photo 5.3 The Nuremberg Trials
After World War II, the highly publicized Nuremberg Trials, a list of military tribunals, prosecuted prominent members of the Nazi Party for major war crimes and crimes against humanity.

Source: Historical and Special Collections, Harvard Law School Library.

163

27 senior Japanese military and political leaders were indicted using the same charges and language developed by the IMT. All were found guilty and either executed or sentenced to prison.

Precedents established in the Nuremberg and Tokyo trials were instrumental in launching a second phase of legal development some 50 years later. The triggering events involved brutal civil wars in Rwanda and the former Yugoslavia. During the Bosnian wars of the early 1990s, Bosnian Serb and Croat officials were found to have committed atrocities against Bosnian Muslims, including the 'rape of Srebrenica,' that we described in Chapter 1, and more general attempts at ethnic cleansing, or the elimination or dislocation of Bosnian Muslims from territories claimed by Serbia. In 1993, the UN Security Council set up the International Criminal Tribunal for the Former Yugoslavia (ICTY) at The Hague. This tribunal worked for more than two decades, taking testimony from roughly 5,000 witnesses over some 11,000 trial days (Ristic 2017). As of the end of 2016, 161 officials had been indicted and 83 convicted. The ICTY was the first tribunal to charge an acting head of state, Slobodan Milosevic, of genocide and related crimes. Milosevic died in detention in 2006 before the end of his trial.

In Rwanda, over a three-month period during the spring of 1994, ethnic Hutu extremists sought to wipe out the entire populations of ethnic Tutsis. Hutu soldiers and police set up roadblocks across Rwanda to prevent Tutsis from escaping the slaughter and encouraged ordinary Hutu citizens to participate in the killings. About 800,000 Rwandans died in the conflict while neither the UN, which claimed no mandate in the absence of support from major powers, nor the United States, whose officials carefully avoided the term 'genocide' in referring to the conflict (so as not to trigger an international obligation under the 1948 Geneva Convention), proved willing to intervene (Power 2002).

The International Criminal Tribunal for Rwanda (ICTR) opened in 1995 in Arusha, Tanzania and closed in 2015 after 93 indictments and 62 convictions. It was the first international tribunal to deliver verdicts related to genocide, define rape as an international criminal act, and hold members of the media responsible for encouraging the public to participate in genocide. (Some radio broadcasts referred to Tutsis as 'cockroaches' that must be exterminated.) In 1998, former Rwandan Prime Minister Jean Kambanda pleaded guilty to genocide and was sentenced to life in prison.

Truth and Reconciliation Commissions
Public hearings about humanitarian crimes, such as in South Africa after *apartheid*.

Some states, in seeking to address past abuses, rely not on international tribunals but on a related mechanism: **Truth and Reconciliation Commissions**. These commissions provide opportunities for victims to describe their experiences publicly, and often offer perpetrators amnesty in exchange for public confessions of their abuses. Perhaps the most well-known Commission was established in South Africa between 1995 and 2002, as that newly democratic country sought to come to terms with the legacy of *apartheid*.

The International Criminal Court: Regularizing Humanitarian Law

The international tribunals described above were temporary authorities operating within fixed time frames. In 1998, states gathered in Rome to establish a permanent body to prosecute individuals suspected of international war crimes or genocide. The **International Criminal Court (ICC)** began to function in 2002 with its setting in The Hague. The ICC should be distinguished from the International Court of Justice (ICJ), also located in The Hague, which rules on disputes between governments but lacks the authority to prosecute individuals.

International Criminal Court (ICC)
Permanent body to prosecute individuals suspected of international war crimes or genocide.

The ICC is a 'court of last resort' in that it has jurisdiction only when national governments are unwilling or unable to prosecute suspected war criminals, or when the UN Security Council refers cases to it. In the absence of a Security Council referral, the court may only pursue crimes committed on the territory of or by citizens of a state that has ratified the Rome treaty. This new court has no independent police force; it relies on national governments to bring before it individuals under investigation. By 2017, 124 states were members. The court's first verdict came down in 2012 against a militia leader in the Democratic Republic of Congo who was convicted of war crimes involving the use of children in that country's civil war.

The ICC has faced two significant political challenges in its initial efforts to become established. First, the United States signed the founding treaty (under President Bill Clinton) but has refused to ratify it. US government officials have consistently expressed the concern that under the ICC US military personnel, who operate in numerous countries, might become the target of politically motivated prosecutions. To entice the United States to participate, the Security Council in 2002 voted to exempt US troops from prosecution for a renewable 12-month period. But the Security Council refused to renew the exemption in 2004 as evidence of US forces abusing terror suspects and Iraqi prisoners made its way around the world. Thus, although it engages in intelligence sharing with the ICC, the United States continues to stand outside it. America is not alone – other key players, including Russia, China, and India, refuse either to sign the treaty or to ratify it and become subject to ICC jurisdiction.

Second, the ICC has come under considerable pressure from African leaders who view the court as a product of Western colonialism that is biased against Africa. They point out that nine of the ICC's first ten investigations have targeted black Africans. In 2016, South Africa, Burundi, and Gambia threatened to quit the ICC, and some African officials have proposed a regional African criminal court as an alternative. In Box 5.3, we contrast views of the ICC from Africa, the United States, and the UN. The initial experience of the ICC demonstrates that international laws and organizations rely for their effectiveness on the willingness of states to participate and cooperate.

The Responsibility to Protect: An Emerging Obligation for Sovereign States?

A key feature of the Westphalian tradition is respect for state sovereignty. But what if the leaders of a sovereign state are committing crimes or atrocities against large groups of their own people? In those cases, do other sovereign states have the right, or even the obligation, to intervene? International relations scholars typically offer different answers to this important question; we review several of these perspectives in Box 5.4.

Historically, humanitarian intervention, or intervention by some states to protect the domestic populations of others, has been applied selectively in principle and practice. For example, the 1648 Peace of Westphalia established the general principles of state sovereignty and non-intervention, but also set forth rules governing the kind of control state leaders could apply to the practice of religion and religious minorities on their territories. Stronger states enforced these rules in weaker ones but did not abide by the rules themselves. In nineteenth-century treaties, such as the Berlin Treaty of 1878, great powers agreed that state leaders should tolerate and protect religious and ethnic minorities. But great powers did not enforce this principle when in 1879 Romania declared that no Jew could become a citizen and stood by as the Ottoman government supported a series of massacres against minority Armenians during and after World War I.

Debates over humanitarian intervention resurfaced after World War II and have intensified over the past 25 years in the wake of humanitarian crises in Africa

5.3   DIFFERING PERSPECTIVES

Views of the International Criminal Court from Africa, America, and the UN

The ICC is an important yet controversial international organization. Both the United States and certain African countries view it as an infringement on their sovereignty, though for different reasons. The UN views the ICC as a critical development in international law that prosecutes government officials who carry out crimes against humanity.

President of Uganda, Yoweri Museveni:

I was one of the first to sign the Rome Statute, which established the ICC. I was against impunity when it comes to human rights violations. But many of us African leaders now want to leave the Rome Statute as soon as possible because of this Western arrogance. When we asked the United Nations to suspend the trial [of Kenyan President Uhuru Kenyatta] for a year, which the statutes allow, so that Kenyan elections could be carried out, it was simply rejected…The ICC has lost all credibility. This is our continent, not yours. Who are you to ignore the voice of the Africans?

Source: Spiegel Online (2016).

President of the United States, George W. Bush:

We will take the actions necessary to ensure that our efforts to meet our global security commitments and protect Americans are not impaired by the potential for investigations, inquiry, or prosecution by the International Criminal Court (ICC), whose jurisdiction does not extend to Americans and which we do not accept.

Undersecretary of State for Arms Control and International Security, John Bolton:

[o]ur main concern should not be that the Prosecutor will target for indictment the isolated U.S. soldier … . Instead, our main concern should be for our country's top civilian and military leaders, those responsible for our defense and foreign policy. They are the real potential targets of the ICC's politically unaccountable Prosecutor.

Source: Galbraith (2003): Bush quote at 689, Bolton quote at 691.

Former UN Secretary General, Kofi Annan:

One has to find a way of holding people accountable but not letting justice be an impediment to peace. The emphasis had been on protecting the leaders, but who speaks for the little guy? I remind the Africans that it's wrong for them to say that only African leaders are put into the dock.

Source: Pilling (2016).

Responsibility to Protect (R2P)
Doctrine that in the event of massive humanitarian crises, when host governments are unable or unwilling to respond, other states have an obligation to intervene to relieve the suffering.

and the Balkans. A summit of world leaders in 2005 produced a new doctrine, the **Responsibility to Protect (R2P)**, which holds that in the event of massive humanitarian crises, when host governments are unable or unwilling to respond, other states have an obligation to intervene to relieve the suffering. In other words, R2P suggests conditions under which the Westphalian norm of non-intervention should give way, legitimately, to the obligation of human protection. R2P was adopted in the UN General Assembly as a non-binding resolution rather than as a new law. But over the past decade it has been invoked regularly in UN Security Council resolutions involving international circumstances in which civilians are vulnerable, suggesting to some observers that the idea and obligation might gradually gain traction.

5.4   DIFFERING THEORETICAL APPROACHES

Realist, Liberal, and Constructivist Ideas on Sovereignty and Humanitarian Intervention

In the Westphalian tradition, sovereignty implies the principle of non-intervention. States lacked the legal or legitimate authority to intervene in the domestic affairs of others. When states, typically great powers, did intervene, they sought political justifications, such as the claim that some recognized political authority in the host country had 'invited' them to intervene.

The idea of humanitarian intervention obviously contradicts the principle of non-intervention. How do IR scholars within different theoretical traditions come to terms with this contradiction?

Realism

The contradiction is difficult for realism to resolve (Krasner 1995). Realists see sovereign governments as autonomous domestic actors, constrained by other states externally, yet free to govern affairs internally as they see fit. Humanitarian intervention suggests governments are not autonomous internally; they are constrained by external actors in both their foreign and domestic policies. For realists, the solution to this contradiction lies in the distribution of power. Weaker states have no choice but to tolerate intervention – they are sovereign internally in principle but not in practice. Stronger states may intervene in the domestic affairs of others, but typically can resist any efforts by outsiders to intervene in their domestic societies.

Liberalism

The contradiction is easier to resolve for liberals. They see interdependence and technological change as having eroded sovereignty and blurred the lines between the domestic and international arenas (Rosenau 1995). If realists depict international relations as 'billiard balls' bouncing off one another, liberals see a 'cobweb' model of cross-cutting relationships and overlapping boundaries. The domestic arena is not the sacrosanct preserve of the sovereign state, but is susceptible to influence, penetration, and even intervention by other states, non-state actors, and the international community. Intervention may be legitimate in an era of eroded sovereignty.

Constructivism

For constructivists, changing international norms resolve the contradiction (Finnemore 2008). Neither sovereignty nor any other international principle is immutable; as norms and expectations change, so too do our conceptions of authoritative international principles. As the consensus in favor of humanitarian intervention becomes more robust, the very idea of sovereignty is transformed, and in a way that accommodates the new consensus.

R2P reflects the idea that the system of sovereign states is an international community in which rights and obligations cross borders. But it also raises important questions. At what point is a humanitarian crisis sufficiently serious to justify intervention? Who decides when this responsibility to protect gets exercised – the UN Security Council, the host government, or coalitions of great powers? R2P also raises the concern, voiced by less powerful states, that more powerful states will use the doctrine as a justification to interfere in the domestic affairs of the less powerful. In this debate weaker states have proven to be the more ardent defenders of the Westphalian sovereignty and non-intervention principles.

The record of the recent past, both before and after the formal establishment of R2P, suggests that the idea of protecting vulnerable populations is applied selectively at best. An international coalition led by the United States intervened (at least temporarily) in Somalia's humanitarian crisis in 1993, but not in the far more severe crisis in Rwanda in 1994. An international coalition enforced a 'no fly zone' to protect Kurds in Iraq from the Iraqi government during the 1990s. NATO intervened in Bosnia in 1995 only after hundreds of thousands of Bosnians died, but intervened more quickly (yet without UN Security Council approval, and thus without international legal authority) to protect the people of Kosovo in 1999. The international community failed to achieve through the UN Security Council a consensus that would permit an R2P intervention by external powers during the humanitarian tragedy in the Darfur region of Sudan beginning in the early 2000s. A consensus was achieved to respond to the Libya uprising of 2011, but no consensus emerged to intervene in Syria shortly thereafter and throughout that country's particularly vicious civil war. In Box 5.5, we note the gap between the international community's aspirations and reality regarding the responsibility to protect.

R2P reflects both the development and limits of international law. There is agreement on the importance of a cross-border humanitarian principle, but implementation depends on the interests of and constraints perceived by the more powerful sovereign states.

Simulations: What would you do? Go to the companion website to role play a president dealing with a humanitarian crisis where a neighboring state appears to be on the brink of collapsing into civil war/ethnic conflict.

International Law and the Human Rights Revolution

At the heart of this Westphalian system is the norm of non-interference: states should not intervene in the internal affairs of other states. Yet, as we have seen, increasingly humanitarian principles have been advanced to give the international community the right – and perhaps even an obligation – to intervene and protect people from violence and abuse from their own governments. Although these principles remain contested, particularly by non-Western states, over the last half century broad agreement on the importance of the rights of individual human beings has emerged and spread within the wider system of international law.

The idea of international human rights gained prominence with the American and French revolutions of the late eighteenth century. The American founders and French revolutionaries each identified universal political rights that deserved the moral and constitutional respect of governments. The Declaration on the Rights of Man and the Citizen, passed by the French National Assembly in 1789, proclaimed that all humans were born with universal and equal rights that were understood to be 'natural, unalienable and sacred.' Philosophers such as Thomas Paine, Henry David Thoreau, and John Stuart Mill took up and developed the idea of universal human rights, which eventually inspired political movements around the world.

In the nineteenth century, struggles over human rights were manifest primarily in movements for social reform, including most prominently efforts to outlaw slavery. After passing the British Slave Trade Act of 1807, Great Britain used its considerable power to put pressure on other countries to end the slave trade. The emancipation of American slaves and Russia's freeing of the serfs were important turning points. In later decades, political movements sprang up championing the rights of women, workers, and ethnic minorities. After World War I, the League

5.5   MAKING CONNECTIONS
Aspiration versus Reality

The Responsibility to Protect

Aspiration

The Responsibility to Protect (R2P) doctrine first emerged as an idea in the 1990s, in the wake of the United Nations' perceived failures to prevent mass atrocities in Rwanda and the former Yugoslavia. R2P reflected the aspiration that the international community must do better in protecting helpless civilians caught in the middle of civil wars and other militarized conflicts. In 2005, the UN General Assembly adopted R2P as a non-binding resolution. The premise is that the responsibility to protect one's own people from mass atrocities and gross human rights violations begins with the sovereign state itself, but the international community should be prepared to step in when state leaders are unable or unwilling to meet their obligation. As a last resort, R2P gives the UN Security Council the authority to initiate outside military intervention to prevent or halt mass violence against civilians.

Reality

Two recent cases illustrate the challenge of translating R2P's aspiration into reality. In 2011, the United States and its NATO partners, with the backing of the UN Security Council, invoked the R2P doctrine to justify an air campaign against the forces of Libyan leader Muammar Gaddafi. Gaddafi had made explicit and, to Western states, credible threats to massacre rebels who were secluded in the Libyan city of Benghazi. Yet what began as a mission to protect civilians ended in regime change. Gaddafi was eliminated, and Libya fell into a deep and chaotic civil war. Critics questioned the motives for intervention – was R2P simply a convenient justification to satisfy US and NATO foreign policy interests in deposing an unwanted dictator and perhaps even gaining control of Libya's oil? They also questioned whether the intervention was defensible on humanitarian grounds, given that the proximate outcome was the collapse of state authority with civilians caught in the crossfire between warring factions. US President Barack Obama conceded in 2016 that the Libyan intervention was a significant mistake of his presidency.

A civil war erupted in Syria in 2011, triggered by a popular uprising against the regime of Bashar al-Assad. By 2016, some 300,000 people had been killed and half the Syrian population displaced. Yet, in this case the R2P doctrine was not invoked. Its implementation hinges on agreement among the UN Security Council permanent members. The United States and United Kingdom, despite their distaste for the Assad regime, proved reluctant to intervene. Russia proved willing to intervene – but on the side of its traditional ally, Assad's Syria. China, reflecting the perspective on a developing nation, has been wary of R2P's qualification to the traditional norm of state sovereignty both in general and in the Syrian case. Without major power consensus, intervention is unlikely, even in the face of mass civilian casualties. As Kim Holmes, Assistant Secretary of State under President George W. Bush put it: 'The problem with R2P is that its reality never lives up to its high-sounding principles. If it wanted to, the Security Council could have intervened to stop genocide in Rwanda and elsewhere. The reasons it didn't are the same ones that will likely keep it from doing so elsewhere in the future' (Holmes 2014).

of Nations gave voice in its charter to the promotion of various rights. Generally, however, the advocacy of international human rights in this era was led by religious, reformist, and charitable groups.

The more systematic introduction of human rights into international law began during and after World War II. President Franklin Roosevelt framed America's fight against Nazi Germany in moral as well as national security terms, proclaiming that the United States stood for the international protection of Four Freedoms – of speech and religion and from want and fear. During the war, the State Department drafted a charter for a postwar organization that included an 'International Bill of Human Rights.' The real breakthrough occurred only after the war, as the full extent of the Holocaust became known. In December 1948, the UN General Assembly passed the Convention on the Prevention and Punishment of the Crime of Genocide, responding directly to the searing experience of the Holocaust. This new type of crime – which broke from the more traditional statist logic of laws of war – reframed the linkage between human rights and international law.

The Universal Declaration: Aspiration and Acceptance

On December 10, 1948, the UN General Assembly adopted the Universal Declaration of Human Rights, which sets out basic civic, political, and economic rights that are common to all humankind, a 'common standard of achievement for all peoples and all nations.' The preamble of the Universal Declaration drew directly on Roosevelt's Four Freedoms speech, proclaiming that 'the freedom of speech and belief and freedom from fear and want' are now 'the highest aspiration of the common people.' All human beings, the Declaration affirms, have the right to 'life, liberty, and security,' upheld and protected by the rule of law. It was precisely the disregard for these fundamental human rights, the Declaration argues, that led to the 'barbarous acts' that so 'outraged the conscious of mankind' in World War II. This expression of universal rights, though not legally binding, did establish a platform that would inspire generations of activists promoting human rights conventions and agreements. The challenge for those committed to advancing human rights was how best to give these aspirations force and meaning in the real world.

The Cold War between the United States and the Soviet Union left the UN with little opportunity to build on its founding human rights pronouncements. But even aside from the Cold War stalemate, the world's dominant powers were reluctant to give the United Nations authority to monitor and enforce human rights. The UN Commission on Human Rights was established in 1946, but for its first two decades the Commission pursued a policy of 'absenteeism,' helping states articulate their own positions on human rights but abstaining from investigating or condemning human rights violations. Sovereign states proved unwilling to grant the Commission the power to act against transgressions of human rights.

A turning point came in the 1960s. Decolonization in Asia and Africa brought new member states into the United Nations who began to press for a more active UN role on human rights issues. Provoked in part by the violations of human rights by the *apartheid* government in South Africa, the UN Human Rights Commission adopted a more interventionist policy, allowing itself to conduct investigations and produce reports. By the 1970s the Commission was using geographically focused working groups, allowing experts to specialize their work in regions or countries, and thematic working groups, enabling investigations that focused on particular types of abuses.

The growing activism of newly independent states also resulted in a series of new international human rights covenants. In 1965, led by African and Asian states, the United Nations General Assembly put forward for adoption the International

Commission on the Elimination of All Forms of Racial Discrimination, and in the following year it put forward for ratification the International Covenant on Economic, Social and Cultural Rights as well as the International Covenant on Civil and Political Rights. These three covenants, together with the Universal Declaration, provide the authoritative body of internationally recognized human rights. The actual ratification of these covenants unfolded over the following decades. The covenants provided standards by which states could judge the behavior of other states, but the enforcement of these principles remained at the discretion of national governments.

In the 1970s and 1980s, activists in Western countries prompted new treaties at the UN on discrimination against women, on torture, and on the rights of children. The UN Human Rights Commission became active in tracking human rights developments in troubled countries such as Bolivia, El Salvador, Iran, and Afghanistan. In 1993, the UN General Assembly created a new office – the UN High Commissioner on Human Rights – to coordinate human rights activities across the UN system. Led by an elected official, this administrative body has the capacity to monitor and coordinate responses to human rights violations. In 2006, the UN Human Rights Commission was replaced by a new intergovernmental body, the UN Human Rights Council. The new council is plagued by controversies about its membership since countries that are widely seen as flagrant violators of fundamental human rights are included.

Nevertheless, human rights have remained a salient international concern, and nongovernmental organizations (NGOs) have played a key role in their development. Amnesty International has been prominent in monitoring abuses of human rights and lobbying for stronger international responses to violations. In 1977, it was given the Nobel Peace Prize for its campaign against torture, and later it played an important role in drafting the 1984 Convention Against Torture. Other NGOs, such as Human Rights Watch and Freedom House, are active both globally and within regions with emphasis on both political and social rights. NGOs have an impact

Photo 5.4 Meeting of the UN Human Rights Council
Delegates of the UN Human Rights Council participate, on February 25, 2013, in a discussion which included abuses in North Korea and Mali and the crisis in Syria.

Source: FABRICE COFFRINI/AFP/Getty Images.

primarily in monitoring and publicizing human rights transgressions – documenting abuses, compiling dossiers, conducting eyewitness interviews, and compiling data. The influence of these groups is ultimately based on their reputation as impartial and reliable purveyors of expertise and information.

Western states have taken a particular interest in the promotion of human rights. Germany, in part due to its own troubled past, has proven particularly sensitive. Article 1 of German Basic Law establishes that to respect and protect human dignity 'shall be the duty of all state authority.' More generally, the European Union (EU) has emphasized human rights as a central feature of its nascent foreign policy. EU countries adopted a Charter of Fundamental Rights in 2000 which became binding on all EU members in 2009. In 2012 the EU adopted a strategic framework designed to promote and protect human rights and to make the EU's own policies more effective and consistent (Council of the European Union 2012). Human rights have become increasingly salient in American foreign policy since the administration of President Jimmy Carter (1977–80). The US State Department is now required by law to compile an annual report to Congress on the human rights record of countries around the world. In turn, Congress uses these annual findings as an important criterion for the allocation of foreign aid. Of course, not every US President places the same emphasis on human rights promotion in foreign policy. The Trump administration, for example, has signaled an intention to play down traditional human rights concerns, and the President has expressed his admiration publicly of authoritarian leaders such as Vladimir Putin of Russia, Xi Jinping of China, Recep Tayyip Erdoğan of Turkey, and Rodrigo Duterte of the Philippines.

The emphasis on human rights has not been embraced universally. Some developing countries and particularly states with authoritarian governments have depicted human rights policies as a new version of Western imperialism. This is not surprising considering the dominant international position of Western states, and the fact that ideologically the ideas of individual rights and political freedoms are more easily embraced by Western liberal democracies than by societies and peoples outside the Western world. Some thinkers in the Islamic world have critiqued the 1948 UN Universal Declaration of Human Rights, arguing that it was essentially a secular rendering of the Judeo-Christian tradition and essentially impossible to implement within the cultural and religious context of Islamic countries. This led in 1990 to the adopting by the Organization of Islamic Conference of an alternative Cairo Declaration of Human Rights in Islam, affirming Islamic *sharia* law (law derived from the religious precepts of Islam) as the sole source of human rights. Other Islamic thinkers take a more moderate view, arguing that Western conceptions of human rights and Islam are compatible, but with limits. Certain types of freedom of expression (for example, that which defames religion) and certain types of gender rights (for example, those judged to threaten traditional family structures) are incompatible with Islam (Petersen 2016).

China and Russia have also criticized the existing international human rights regime for the Western-centric values that lurk behind it. They have also charged that Western states have used these human rights norms as legitimating rationales for intervening in weaker countries for self-interested geopolitical or economic motives. China and Russia have also turned around the human rights norms championed by the United States and used them to criticize Washington's human rights record. Showing that it too can be a leader on human rights, China has begun to issue its own assessments of the human rights record of other states, offering its own understanding of core universal rights.

Why do sovereign states, despite their apparent disagreements, care sufficiently about the issue of human rights to develop a framework of international law to regulate it? The most pragmatic motive might be that human rights violations – manifest in systematic government killing of its own citizens or widespread political violence within a country – can spill over into other countries and the wider international system. In the Syrian civil war, for example, the UN has reported that the Assad regime has shown little respect for human rights or international law as it inflicts violence on ethnic minorities and other groups. The result has been over 470,000 deaths, and millions of refugees moving into the wider Middle East and Western Europe. Second, some states might rise to the defense of international human rights as a result of their own ideals and humanitarian concerns. This certainly is a motive for those governments and activist groups who have struggled against a wide range of abuses – genocide, slavery, torture, executions, labor exploitation, and discrimination against women, religious sects, and ethnic minorities. Third, states may care about human rights in other countries because violence and abuses in these states can threaten international peace and security by eroding the moral fabric of the international community. If countries really do embrace the universality of a set of fundamental rights that apply to all people by virtue of their humanity, it is hard for their leaders to simply turn a blind eye to gross violations of these rights, wherever those violations occur.

The World's Oceans and Waterways

About 70 percent of the earth is covered by water, and the world's oceans and waterways are used by numerous states and private actors for multiple purposes including trade, resource extraction, communication, military activities, and tourism. Should waterways be accessible to all, or should coastal states have special authority to control the waters near their shores? International law has long addressed this question in an effort to regulate a key aspect of the global commons.

The current relevant law is contained in the United Nations Convention on the Law of the Sea (LOS treaty). The LOS treaty today has 167 member states that have both signed and ratified the treaty. The United States signed but has not ratified the LOS treaty. Opponents in the US Senate view the LOS treaty as an infringement on US sovereignty with the potential to subject US companies and its military to environmental lawsuits and other types of constraints. However, the United States has consistently affirmed in official statements its willingness to observe the treaty terms as customary law. The LOS treaty of 1982 did put into statutory form a great deal of long-standing customary law. On one key issue discussed below, exclusive economic zones claimed by coastal countries, the LOS treaty of 1982 also essentially ratified the national behavior after 1945 of numerous countries with extensive coastlines, including the United States, Chile, and Peru.

Because several influential states such as Japan, the United Kingdom, the United States, Russia, and China possess both extensive coastlines and make intensive use of distant seas, the LOS treaty seeks to strike a balance between the interests of coastal and sea-using states. It does this by delineating different zones of jurisdiction that may be controlled legally by coastal states; beyond these zones is considered the open seas. The treaty also establishes rules for utilization of economic resources, such as fishing rights or energy extraction, in the zones with national jurisdiction.

The LOS treaty establishes as a coastal state's **Territorial Sea** the area that extends 12 nautical miles from that state's shoreline (1 nautical mile equals 1.15 statute miles or 1.85 kilometers). The coastal state, with only a few exceptions, has nearly complete sovereignty within this 12-mile sea zone off its shore. In addition, the LOS treaty allows each coastal state to claim an **Exclusive Economic Zone (EEZ)** up to 200 nautical miles from its shoreline. For an example of a resulting EEZ claim, that by

Territorial Sea
From customary international law, codified now in the LOS treaty, the area that extends 12 nautical miles from a state's shoreline, and within which the coastal state, with only a few exceptions, has nearly complete sovereignty.

Exclusive Economic Zone (EEZ)
According to the LOS treaty, the area up to 200 nautical miles from a state's shoreline, within which that state's national government has the right to control all sea-related commercial activities by national and foreign agents, for example, fishing or drilling and extracting oil and gas from the seabed below the waters of the EEZ.

High seas
According to the LOS treaty, the area of the seas beyond 200 nautical miles, over which no individual state has exclusive jurisdiction.

Innocent passage
Concept originally in customary international law and now stipulated in the LOS treaty according to which vessels from a sea-faring state may move through a coastal state's territorial waters so long as they do so in an expeditious, non-threatening manner.

Transit passage
Concept originally in customary international law and now stipulated in the LOS treaty according to which vessels from a sea-faring state may move through a strait that connects two bodies of the high seas or two EEZs even if such transit requires movement through the territorial seas of a coastal state.

the United States, see Map 5.2. Approximately 140 states have made such claims of EEZs. Within a coastal state's EEZ that country's national government has the right to control all sea-related commercial activities by national and foreign agents, for example, fishing in the waters or drilling and extraction of oil and gas from the seabed below the waters of the EEZ. Beyond 200 nautical miles, no country has exclusive jurisdiction over the seas, and this area remains the **high seas**. However, if it ever becomes commercially feasible to conduct mining operations in the high seas, that activity will be controlled by an international organization established by the LOS treaty called the International Seabed Authority. This point applies to the Arctic Ocean, which has considerable reserves of oil and natural gas. Map 5.3 shows the EEZs of five states – Norway, Denmark, Russia, Canada, and the United States – with Arctic Ocean coastlines.

Coastal states have almost complete sovereignty over national or foreign activities in their territorial seas, and full control over commercial operations within their respective EEZs. However, the LOS treaty codifies two general rights of navigation that sea-faring states enjoy and that limit the control of coastal states even of their territorial waters. First, the LOS treaty accords to sea-faring states the right of movement within EEZs and even to some extent within the territorial waters of coastal states. Ships from all sea-faring states have the right of '**innocent passage**' through a coastal state's territorial seas. Article 19 of the LOS treaty stipulates that a foreign ship has the right to move through the territorial waters of a coastal state so long as that movement is continuous, expeditious, and 'not prejudicial to the peace, good order or security of the coastal State.' Articles 38 and 39 of the LOS treaty provide sea-faring states with a second right, namely, that of **transit passage**, or the

Map 5.2 US Exclusive Economic Zone under the Terms of the Law of the Sea Treaty
The Law of the Sea Treaty allows states to claim substantial economic sovereignty over the sea up to 200 nautical miles from its coastlines.

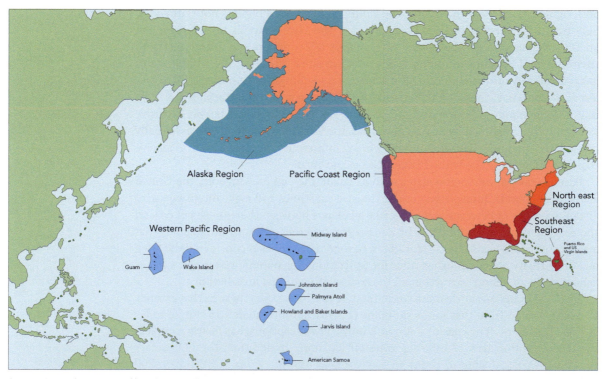

Source: Original map created by US National Ocean and Atmospheric Agency (NOAA).

Map 5.3   Maritime Boundaries in the Arctic Ocean
The Arctic is subject to increasing international attention, due to climate change and the melting of ice, and the potential for natural resource extraction within EEZs and beyond them.

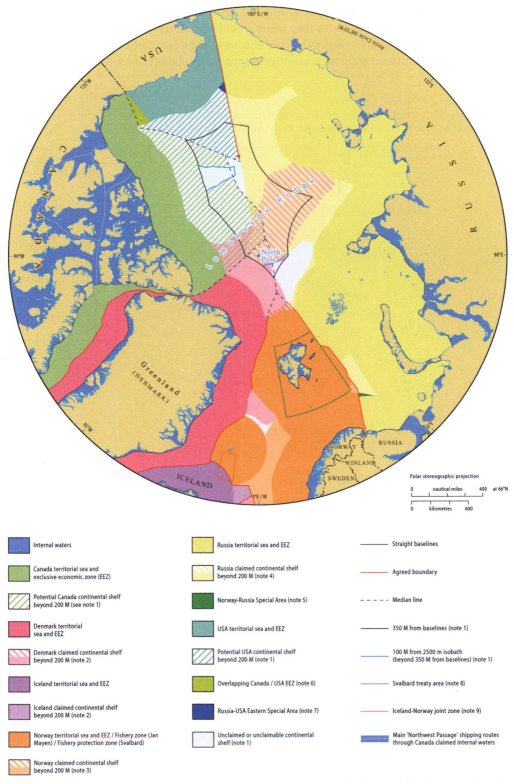

■ Internal waters	■ Russia territorial sea and EEZ	—— Straight baselines
■ Canada territorial sea and exclusive economic zone (EEZ)	▨ Russia claimed continental shelf beyond 200 M (note 4)	—— Agreed boundary
▨ Potential Canada continental shelf beyond 200 M (see note 1)	■ Norway-Russia Special Area (note 5)	– – – Median line
■ Denmark territorial sea and EEZ	■ USA territorial sea and EEZ	—— 350 M from baselines (note 1)
▨ Denmark claimed continental shelf beyond 200 M (note 2)	▨ Potential USA continental shelf beyond 200 M (note 1)	—— 100 M from 2500 m isobath (beyond 350 M from baselines) (note 1)
■ Iceland territorial sea and EEZ	■ Overlapping Canada / USA EEZ (note 6)	—— Svalbard treaty area (note 8)
■ Iceland claimed continental shelf beyond 200 M (note 2)	■ Russia-USA Eastern Special Area (note 7)	—— Iceland-Norway joint zone (note 9)
■ Norway territorial sea and EEZ / Fishery zone (Jan Mayen) / Fishery protection zone (Svalbard)	□ Unclaimed or unclaimable continental shelf (note 1)	▨ Main 'Northwest Passage' shipping routes through Canada claimed internal waters
▨ Norway claimed continental shelf beyond 200 M (note 3)		

Source: Reproduced with permission of IBRU, Durham University, UK. Http://www.durham.ac.uk/ibru/resources/arctic/.

right to pass through any strait that connects two bodies of the high seas or two EEZs even if such transit requires movement through the territorial seas of a coastal state.

The right of transit through straits is particularly vital since many important ocean passageways are so narrow that they substantially fall within the 12-mile territorial seas that states may claim under the treaty. For example, the combined territorial waters of Oman and Iran encompass the Strait of Hormuz, through which passes approximately 30 percent of oil that is transported by sea (see Map 5.4). In

Map 5.4 Maritime Boundaries, Strait of Hormuz
The respective agreed-upon territorial waters of Oman and Iran encompass the Strait of Hormuz, making the right of passage under the LOS treaty extremely important to third-party sea-faring countries.

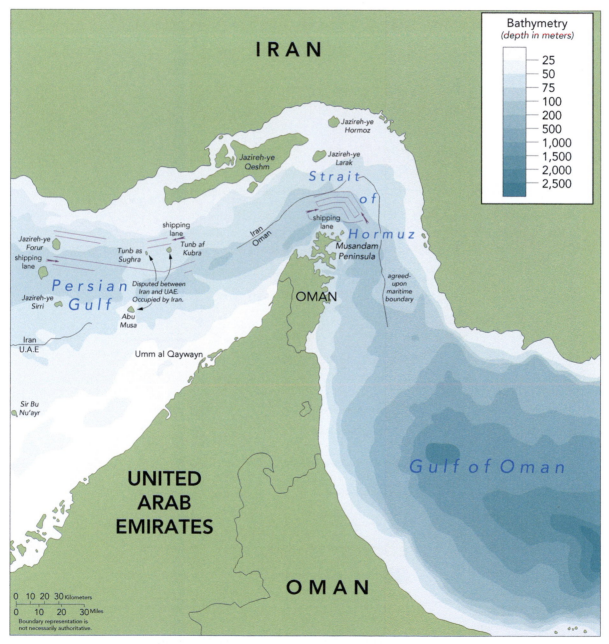

Source: Courtesy of the University of Texas Libraries, The University of Texas at Austin. Available at http://www.lib.utexas.edu/maps/middle_east_and_asia/iran_strait_of_hormuz_2004.jpg.

the absence of the right of transit it is possible that a state like Iran, in a crisis, might claim the right to restrict movement of commercial or naval vessels from the United States or its allies through at least a part of the Strait of Hormuz. The right of transit preempts that possible claim by Iran from the viewpoint of international law.

States generally accept and honor their obligations under the terms of the LOS treaty. However, in recent years a dispute between the Philippines and China in the South China Sea has highlighted some limitations on the effectiveness of international law. China has claimed that, as a matter of long historical record, it possesses sovereignty over the sea space and numerous small islands and other land features in the South China Sea, and that there should be no international arbitration regarding its claims (Ministry of Foreign Affairs 2014). China contends that its territorial seas and EEZ cover some 90 percent of that sea space, including sea space that constitute the EEZs of such countries as Vietnam, Indonesia, Brunei, and the Philippines. As we discussed in Chapter 2, to reinforce its claims the Chinese government has built up land features and fortified them with airstrips. To contest China's claims, the Philippines in 2013 brought a case under the LOS treaty against China in the Permanent Court of Adjudication (PCA), and in July 2016 the PCA found almost wholly in favor of the Philippines and against China (Permanent Court of Arbitration 2016).

Although the verdict was clear, it is not certain that the 2016 PCA ruling will have a substantial influence in the South China Sea. First, China refused completely to participate in the PCA proceeding, arguing in December 2014 that China's sovereignty claims to the South China Sea were indisputable and not a proper subject for judicial proceedings under the LOS treaty. Second, a new president, Rodrigo Duterte, came into office in the Philippines in June 2016. Rather than pursuing the legal victory at the PCA his predecessor had attained, Duterte, in exchange for Chinese economic assistance, proved willing to put aside the PCA ruling and to pursue bilateral diplomacy with China as way of managing their competing claims to the South China Sea.

Our review of international law in the key areas of war initiation, humanitarian intervention and human rights, and oceans and waterways suggests three general observations. First, postwar international law has evolved gradually in the direction of more ambitious and comprehensive agreements. The shift from the General Agreement on Tariffs and Trade (GATT) to WTO, from ad hoc tribunals to the ICC, and from customary arrangements to the Law of the Sea Treaty are illustrative examples. Second, unlike in domestic systems, where law typically emerges from a central legislative process, international law develops from a variety of sources including custom and habit on one hand and international agreements and treaties designed to address a global problem on the other. Third, international law has no central enforcement mechanism. There is no global police force, and no international judicial system widely acknowledged as legitimate and authoritative. Compliance depends on state behavior, which, as we discuss below, can vary over time and depending on political conditions. China resisted the recent PCA decision against it and the Philippines was willing to put it aside even though the PCA ruled in its favor. The United States refuses to abide by the ICC but complies with WTO rulings. Participation in international law is not compulsory – states may pick and choose in which arrangements they participate, and can choose to exit agreements, both recent (the United States' decision in 2017 to exit the Paris Agreement of 2015) or long-standing (the United Kingdom's decision in 2016 to leave the European Union despite formal participation in European regional integration dating back to 1973).

Much of international law concerns the obligations sovereign states have toward each other. But as our discussion of humanitarian intervention indicates, postwar international law has also evolved to address explicitly how states treat groups of people in harm's way. Humanitarian law and the responsibility to protect are part of a larger postwar legal development: the idea that not only states, but also individuals, have rights in international law, even though most individuals are citizens or subjects of the sovereign states that constitute the international system.

Levels of Analysis *Four Key Areas of International Law*		
👤 Individual	State	🌐 International
International law now stipulates that states have a collective 'responsibility to protect' groups of people in situations in which the governing authority is unwilling or unable to offer such protection.	Sovereign states pick and choose which international legal arrangements they enter, participate within, or exit. Compliance with international law depends more on states than on a central enforcement mechanism.	Over time international legal arrangements have become more formal and comprehensive.

THEORETICAL EXPLANATIONS FOR THE EXISTENCE OF INTERNATIONAL LAW AND ORGANIZATIONS

International laws and organizations have developed steadily to cover a range of political, economic, and social issues as the postwar era has progressed. But what accounts for international laws and organizations? Why have they developed in a world of sovereign states?

Below we examine four types of explanations for international law and organizations, which are tied to different theoretical traditions in international relations. Since law and organizations are important components of world politics, it is not surprising that scholars from different intellectual vantage points explain their persistence and weigh their significance differently.

The Liberal Tradition: Law as Functional Problem-Solver

For liberals, international laws and organizations are intrinsically important features of world politics. They help states solve problems by coordinating behavior, resolving collective action dilemmas, and reinforcing the communitarian dimension of state relations. As the Cold War ended and attention to great power rivalries receded, liberal thinkers emphasized the links between international relations and international law. In 2000, a special issue of a leading international relations journal, *International Organization*, was dedicated to how legal obligations and commitments had become increasingly prominent in world politics (Goldstein *et al.* 2000).

International law helps states solve simple yet important coordination problems. In the United States, people are legally required to drive on the right side of the road. In the United Kingdom, they are legally required to drive on the left. Either system works fine if the law exists and is clear; in its absence, chaos would ensue. International law can play a similar functional role in coordinating state behavior. International air traffic control law, for example, regulates when aircraft may enter a country's airspace and at what altitudes planes should fly to avoid collision. The law of the sea performs similar functions in the world's waterways.

Liberals also emphasize the role international law and organization can play in enabling states to achieve mutually beneficial forms of cooperation when to do so they must overcome a serious barrier to cooperation. This cooperation-inhibiting situation exists when states face '**mixed interests**,' a situation in which two states may each benefit from some form of cooperation, but each can do even better by not cooperating. To illuminate how states facing mixed interests have incentives to work together but also encounter a serious obstacle to do so, scholars make use of an analytical device called the **Prisoner's Dilemma**. Liberal scholars argue that international law and organizations can help states overcome the Prisoner's Dilemma and achieve mutually beneficial forms of international cooperation.

The Prisoner's Dilemma highlights a situation in which actors confront 'mixed interests.' Imagine that the police catch two criminals as they are breaking into a liquor store. The police search and find evidence in the getaway car that indicates they have apprehended not just two break-in thieves but possibly two professional contract killers who have killed several people. The police place the two criminals in two separate holding cells at the station. The two prisoners cannot communicate with each other. The local prosecutor arrives and visits each holding cell. She tells each prisoner that if he stays quiet, he will, at the very least, go to prison for five years for the break-in. She also tells each prisoner that if he agrees to testify at trial that both he and his partner are contract killers, and the other does not, then the one who testifies will go free while the other will get 50 years in prison. She also adds this: if both prisoners admit to being contract killers, they will each receive a sentence of 20 years in prison.

The situation the prisoners are facing is depicted in Figure 5.3. Prisoner A's payoffs are listed in the left side of each cell; Prisoner B's payoffs are listed in the right side of each cell. Each year of jail is a bad experience, so for each year a negative 1 is assigned: a jail sentence of 20 years therefore translates into a payoff of negative 20.

Prisoner A may think along the following lines: if I stay quiet (which we call a strategy on the part of A to cooperate with B), and B does the same thing (an outcome of cooperate–cooperate, which is the upper-left cell in Figure 5.3), we both receive five years in jail for the break-in, or a payoff of −5. That is bad, but better than several other outcomes. Still, I am not going to stay quiet, for two reasons. First, I might be able to walk out of here a free man, if I agree to testify about the contract killings and my partner stays quiet. (We will call this a strategy by A to 'defect' from B, which is depicted in the lower-left cell in the Figure 5.3.) Second, if I stay quiet, and he agrees to testify (a strategy of defect by B, which is located at the upper-right cell of the figure), he goes free and I go to jail for 50 years! So, I'll admit to the murders, and if my partner does the same we'll each receive a 20-year sentence (depicted in the lower-right cell of the figure). But there's the chance he'll stay quiet and then I'll walk free, and in any event if I talk I'll avoid 50 years in prison.

Prisoner B thinks exactly along the same lines. The likely result: A and B both admit to being contract killers, and both go to jail for

Mixed interests
In game theory, a situation in which two players may each benefit from some form of cooperation, but each can do even better by successfully cheating on the other, and each is made materially worse off (compared to not cooperating at all) if it is successfully cheated upon by its erstwhile partner.

Prisoner's Dilemma
Analytical device that illustrates both the value of cooperation and the difficulty of obtaining it.

Figure 5.3 The Prisoner's Dilemma
The Prisoner's Dilemma game illustrates how two actors can fail to achieve mutually beneficial cooperation and end in mutually costly non-cooperation. The two actors are confronted with mixed interests that arise from a particular combination of payoffs – they do well by cooperating with each other, but even better by cheating, and they do the worst if they are cheated upon. Because they lack some overarching mechanism to ensure that they faithfully comply with an agreement, they end up doing a lot worse than if they cooperated with each other. International law and organizations can offer a mechanism whereby states can overcome the Prisoner's Dilemma and achieve mutually beneficial forms of international cooperation.

		Prisoner B	
		Cooperate	Defect
Prisoner A	Cooperate	–5, –5	–50, 0
	Defect	0, –50	–20, –20

20 years. Each loses a chance to serve no more than five years in prison, but each has avoided the worst possible outcome, namely, a 50-year sentence.

In situations captured by the Prisoner's Dilemma, each actor or player faces mixed interests. Each is better off (compared to mutual non-cooperation) if he cooperates with the other. Yet, at the same time, each player experiences a strong incentive to cheat, both because of greed and because of fear. Greed operates insofar as each player sees a chance to do much better if it successfully breaks its promise to cooperate; and each player is seized by fear that the other will try to cheat and thus inflict on the player that stays with cooperation a terribly worse outcome.

In these circumstances, and when *there is no outside power that can compel each faithfully to keep to its cooperative commitment*, each player has a powerful incentive to cheat and thus to push both into mutual non-cooperation, making each worse off than if both had cooperated. International relations, with its lack of a centralized government, is precisely such a context in which mixed interests cause states to forego many opportunities to achieve mutually beneficial cooperation.

And yet, there is a possible solution to the Prisoner's Dilemma even without an effective authority that compels mutual adherence to promises. If players believe that they will be interacting with each other repeatedly, then cheating becomes less rational. If player A successfully cheats on player B in the first round of a Prisoner's Dilemma game, it does very well in that round. But how will A do in the second round, the third, the fourth, or the fortieth? With the memory of being cheated in the first round, B will probably retaliate, putting both it and A in mutual non-cooperation, which leaves A (and B) less well off. For A and B, in the face of repeated, iterated plays with each other and with other players, the way to attain the highest long-term cumulative score is a strategy of **conditional cooperation** (also called a strategy of tit-for-tat) that is, each cooperates so long as the partner cooperates. Each retaliates immediately against cheating with cheating, and each returns to cooperation if the partner does so.

Anything that creates a belief on the part of players facing mixed interests that they are in an iterated, repeated-play environment with others causes those players to be less inclined immediately to turn to cheating and instead to experiment with conditional cooperation. This is where liberal internationalists emphasize the potentially cooperation-enabling properties of international law and organizations. They emphasize that international law and organizations turn single-play Prisoner's Dilemmas into iterated plays wherein conditional cooperation is rational and sustainable. In the trade field, for example, two states may believe that if an agreement will be made only once and not be open to renegotiation, each may be tempted to cheat by signing the agreement but not actually reducing barriers to its economy, in the hope that its industry will enjoy greater exports while its national industries will not need to face greater competition from the partner. However, if the country knows that it will be facing the same partner in future trade negotiations, and that partner will decline to reduce trade barriers further unless compliance occurs with the current agreement, and other countries are observing whether the country complies with its current commitments, then that country is likely to conclude that it will do better *over the long term* if it adheres to today's agreement. Moreover, to the extent that the country knows there are mechanisms in place whereby its cheating on trade would be broadcast not only to the target government but to watching third parties, then the chances of successfully cheating even on the current promises goes down dramatically. Current cheating is less likely to succeed, and even if it were successful for a time the country would find itself shunned in the future by its current partner and by other potential partners.

Conditional cooperation
A strategy (also called tit-for-tat) in game theory capable of resolving the Prisoner's Dilemma wherein each player cooperates so long as the partner cooperates; each retaliates immediately against cheating with cheating; and each returns to cooperation if the partner does so.

For scholars in the liberal international tradition, which we discussed in Chapter 3, international law and organizations increase the incentives for compliance within international commitments. A group of states might agree that it is worth the economic sacrifice to impose economic sanctions against a state behaving aggressively (such as Iraq under Saddam Hussein). Each, however, may fear that if it holds back trade, another state may take advantage and reap the economic benefits. The UN Security Council, by institutionalizing the sanctions effort, can provide reassurances that the sanctions will be observed collectively, thereby increasing the incentives for cooperation. States may still cheat, but the costs will be higher once they have committed publicly to participate in the institutionalized effort (Martin 1992).

Liberal scholars also emphasize that legal and institutional arrangements created for one purpose can take on a life of their own, becoming stronger over time and taking on new functional tasks (Keohane 1984). NATO, created to contain the Soviet Union, provides a good illustration. Rather than disband when the Soviet Union collapsed, NATO reinvented itself and played a key role expanding into central and eastern Europe to lock in new democratic institutions and operating 'out of area' to achieve member state objectives in the former Yugoslavia and Afghanistan.

Liberal international relations theory emphasizes the potential for states to cooperate across borders. Law and institutions play key roles in fostering that cooperation and strengthening the 'international community' of sovereign states. Law and institutions embody community-wide values such as the movement of goods, ideas, and people across borders, respect for the dignity of individuals, and protection of the global commons. Liberal theorists believe in the importance of liberal domestic political structures (e.g., a strong legislative body and an apolitical judicial system) and values (e.g., the protection of individual rights), and envision an international community that, on a larger scale, replicates those structures and echoes those values (Slaughter 1995). The development of international law and supporting institutions are central to that vision.

The Realist Tradition: Law as Derivative of State Power and Interests

For realists, international law and organization are of secondary importance in understanding international relations. State behavior and interaction are a function of power and interests, and law and organization, in turn, are shaped by the distribution of power and state interests that flow from it. More specifically, international laws and organizations are created by powerful states to serve their interests and reflect their values. One of the main benefits of being a great power is the ability to determine the 'rules of the game' of international relations. As E.H. Carr notes in his classic realist assessment, 'the law is the weapon of the stronger' (Carr 1964: 176). Hegemonic struggles among great powers are struggles to make the rules; international law is the formal expression of those rules, and international organizations are the institutional embodiment of them.

Laws and organizations help to legitimize state power and make it more acceptable. For example, the United States prefers that other countries embrace its economic model and accept market solutions to financial problems. As we show in Chapter 9, the United States was instrumental in creating the International Monetary Fund (IMF) to advance that interest. It controls the IMF through its voting and veto power, and the IMF in turn imposes guidelines on other states that reflect the US perspective. As we discuss in Chapter 8, the Non-Proliferation Treaty of 1968 is a second example – the great powers, led by the Soviet Union and the United States, pushed forward an international treaty that allowed them to remain nuclear powers while discouraging others from joining the club.

Strong states use law and organizations to institutionalize their values and interests, so that those preferences persist even when those states become relatively less powerful (Ikenberry 2001). By embedding their preferences within general laws and institutions, dominant states establish the presumption that their values are broader community values. Realists interpret along these lines the efforts of Western states to develop international laws to protect individual human rights while depicting their conception of human rights as 'universal.'

For realists, weaker states also have incentives to develop international laws that reflect their own power position and interests. Weaker states try to use law to constrain the behavior of more powerful states. As discussed in Chapter 4, the Paris Agreement, for example, offers weaker states an opportunity to rein in the global warming activities of two of the world's dominant economies, the United States and China. Realists do not find it surprising, either that weaker countries seek to use law and organizations to tie down the strong, or that stronger states opt out of legal arrangements that they fear might inhibit their use of power.

Are international laws and organizations consequential? The above discussion suggests that realists divide on that question. Some argue that international institutions do not matter in the sense of having independent impact on international outcomes (Mearsheimer 1994). The League of Nations, in the classic realist example, was only as strong as the willingness of powerful states to enforce its principles. Other realists believe institutions do matter – to the extent states can use them effectively as instruments or tools to advance their interests. In addition, international law and organization bring order and predictability to world politics. Great powers, due to their privileged position, have a vested interest in international order. Weaker states that live in the shadow of great powers have an interest in order as well, particularly if it is embedded in laws and organizations that protect their sovereignty and territorial integrity.

The Marxist Tradition: Law Reinforces the Economic Divide

The Marxist tradition is similar to the realist in that it views law and institutions as weapons some actors use to influence or dominate others. For Marxists, law is not some type of absolute representation of justice or fairness; it is a relative reflection of the interests of a dominant party in a particular political and economic context. Recall from Chapter 3 that economic class was the central analytical category for Marx, and the exploitation of labor by capital was the core political struggle. Lenin extended this framework to international relations and focused on unequal relations between rich and poor states in the world economy. He shared Marx's view of law, viewing it as 'the registration of power relations,' and 'an expression of the will of the ruling class' (Lenin 1916; Carr 1964: 176).

From this perspective, modern international law developed in the context of Western capitalism and thus serves the interests of the dominant, 'core' capitalist states – who compete economically and even militarily with each other – at the expense of the weaker states on the 'periphery' of world economy. International law legalizes and legitimizes the enrichment of the affluent states. Lenin viewed the League of Nations, for example, as a 'sheer fraud,' an 'alliance of robbers, each trying to snatch something from the others' (Knox 2016: 314). Law and institutions also give license to those states to intervene in the affairs of the less powerful. Whereas liberals might view comprehensive economic sanctions mandated by the UN Security Council as an expression of the will of the international community, Marxists would view those sanctions as a legally sanctioned intervention by Western capitalist states to the detriment of workers and the poor in less developed states. Sanctions advance the political agenda of the Western states but their detrimental effects fall disproportionately on the people of countries like Haiti and Iraq rather than on the objectionable leaders of those countries (Mueller and Mueller 1999).

Marxists view international laws and organizations as playing different yet consistently reinforcing roles as capitalism has progressed through different phases (Chimni 1993; Knox 2016: 322–24). In the early Westphalian period international law offered sovereign protection to advanced capitalist states while allowing them to acquire and exploit colonies. In the era of decolonization, former colonies that were now themselves sovereign states could still be exploited under the cover of a legal framework of free trade and open investment by multinational corporations. Neocolonialism suggested that states on the periphery of the world economy might now be politically independent, yet they remained economically dependent as part of the global division of labor. In the contemporary era of globalization, the capitalist class has become transnational, moving freely across borders, while the working class remains national. International organizations such as the WTO and the IMF, by enforcing the rules and norms of openness and deregulation, facilitate the ability of the Western capitalist states to carry out their project on a global scale.

The Constructivist Tradition: Law Embodies the Norms of World Politics

Constructivist thinkers are closer to liberals than to realists or Marxists in their conception of international law. However, they go further than the liberal emphasis on law and organization as providing functional solutions to collective action problems. For constructivists, international law and world politics are tightly interconnected rather than being separate domains. Law is the institutional expression of politics in an historical context. World political conditions inform international law, and law in turn shapes the behavior of states and other political actors (Reus-Smit 2004).

Recall from Chapter 3 that in the constructivist framework, norms – patterns of social behavior expected of a group – and ideas matter as much as power and material interests in driving world politics. Norms shape how states define their identities and understand their interests. The norm of racial equality, for example, was gradually embraced by states as the postwar era progressed to the point that adherence to that norm became a defining feature for membership in the international community. South Africa's system of racial separation and inequality (*apartheid*) led other states to remove it from international organizations and even led close allies of South Africa to turn against it by the 1990s (Klotz 1995). The effort to isolate South Africa became embedded in a variety of institutional and legal frameworks including the UN, the British Commonwealth (an informal grouping of the United Kingdom and its former colonies), and the Organization of African Unity. Those institutional bodies, in turn, imposed obligations and shaped the behavior of their member states.

Constructivists highlight the role of norm entrepreneurs – a person or group who takes the lead in establishing or changing social norms – in creating political conditions that find their way into laws and organizations (Finnemore and Sikkink 1998). States may initiate normative change, but it may come also from international organizations, nongovernmental organizations (NGOs), or even individuals. In

1999, the Ottawa Treaty, or Mine Ban Treaty, became binding international law and as of 2017 had roughly 160 participating member states. The treaty bans the use, production, and stockpiling of anti-personnel landmines and seeks to eliminate them worldwide. The key players in moving this agreement forward were an NGO, the International Campaign to Ban Landmines, and an American citizen, Jody Williams, who helped to coordinate the effort among citizens and politicians across the world. In recognition of their efforts the two shared the Nobel Peace Prize in 1997. Although not yet fully embraced as customary international law, the Mine Ban Treaty has begun to shape state behavior (Price 2004). Some key international players including the United States, Russia, and China have neither signed nor ratified the treaty.

Since constructivists view politics, law, and organizations as entangled within a specific historical context, they are especially interested in the particular attributes of the current international era. Liberal politics has conditioned modern international law, and together they have become increasingly cosmopolitan. In both world politics and international law states are no longer the sole subjects, individual rights are receiving greater emphasis, and the traditional boundary between the internal politics of sovereign states and the external arena has become more blurred. Humanitarian norms reflect this changing political context, and the laws and organizations embedding them, in turn, affect how states understand themselves and behave. Migrant rights activists have used human rights laws to convince even traditionally homogeneous states such as Japan to accept immigrants (Gurowitz 2004). NATO reshaped its target set in the war against Kosovo in 1999 in deference to humanitarian norms, as 'even the world's most powerful military alliance recognized the need to justify its actions before the court of domestic and world public opinion' (Wheeler 2004: 213).

Liberals, realists, Marxists, and constructivists explain the development and assess the significance of international law and organization in different ways. Together they help us understand both the importance and the limitations of these key international institutions. In the next section, we take up the questions of compliance: to what extent and for what reasons do states comply with international law?

Levels of Analysis *Explanations for International Law*

👤 Individual	👥 State	🌐 International
Norm entrepreneurs may contribute significantly to the development of international law.	Realists see international law as derived from the interest and power of states, rather than as an independent political force. For Marxists, international laws and organizations reflect the interests of dominant economic actors.	Liberals and constructivists view international law and organizations both as consequential and, in different ways, closely connected to international politics.

THEORETICAL EXPLANATIONS FOR THE EFFECTIVENESS OF INTERNATIONAL LAW AND ORGANIZATIONS

To what extent do international laws and organizations constrain the behavior of states? A good deal of liberal, realist, and constructivist scholarship in international affairs centers on this question. Liberals, realists, and constructivists each put forward arguments about the conditions under which international law and organization can influence state behavior. It is not necessary to accept the arguments from one or another of the schools to appreciate that international law and organizations may matter in world politics, but it requires close political analysis to identify when and under what circumstances they can exercise their influence.

The Liberal Tradition

Liberals offer a clear argument about the capacity of international law and organizations to shape state behavior. They begin with an apparent short-coming of democratic foreign policy making compared to authoritarian states – democratic leaders usually cannot speedily announce and implement an important new policy, such as adhering to a WTO trade liberalization treaty or a new human rights agreement. Instead, leaders of the executive branch of democratic governments almost always must go through a process of attaining the consent of other political bodies within the central government, especially that of the legislative branch. In addition, both the executive and the legislature, in assessing a new treaty, are likely to consult with affected interest groups in the broader society to make sure that they concur with the obligations and rights that will emanate from the treaty. Authoritarian leaders will of course be mindful of domestic constituencies as they consider entering into international commitments. However, compared to leaders in democracies, authoritarian leaders are unlikely to face an independent legislature with a reliable recourse to a veto power over the authoritarian leader, and the latter is likely to have an option, physical coercion, that is not as readily available to democratic leaders in pushing through a proposed treaty. In short, authoritarian leaders typically do not face the same range of effective '**veto players**' (Tsebelis 2002), that is, a person or organization within a political system whose consent is required for some policy to be accepted and implemented.

Veto player
A person or organization within a political system whose consent is required for some policy to be accepted and implemented. There are typically more veto players in democracies than in non-democracies.

One effect of the higher density of veto players in democracies compared to non-democracies is that foreign policy is often a slower, more laborious (and perhaps even frustrating!) process. However, precisely because there are many veto players in democratic states, when they do commit to an international treaty that brings into effect a new international law and associated organizational arrangement, that democracy will have done so only with the consent not just of veto players within the government but of its broader society. Thus, there will be a high level of commitment by that democracy to the faithful implementation of the treaty, and the treaty is likely to act as a constraining factor in the relevant policy making not just of the leaders but of other political actors as well. Democracies are more capable of cooperating within institutional arrangements, whether they be military alliances or economic agreements. This heightened degree of domestic political 'lock-in' may also help account for the empirical finding that democratic states are more likely than are authoritarian regimes to comply with their obligations under international human rights treaties.

There are, of course, important exceptions to the general rule that democratic states may be especially capable of making long-term international legal commitments. From time to time an election in a democratic state can produce a turnover in its leadership so different in policy orientation and even personal temperament that the country lurches in its foreign policy, including in matters relating to international law and organizations. As we observe in Box 5.6, this has clearly occurred in respect to the Paris Agreement on Climate Change with the coming into the US presidency of Donald Trump after the administration of Barack Obama.

5.6 MAKING CONNECTIONS
Theory and Practice

Obama, Trump, and the Paris Agreement on Climate Change

Theory: The Democratic 'Lock-In' Argument in Liberal International Theory

Liberal theorists argue that democracies are more likely than authoritarian states to abide by international commitments. Democratic states typically must gain the consent of multiple political and societal actors to make a significant commitment, and thus adherence to that commitment is likely to be more consistent and enduring.

Practice: Different Administrations, Different Foreign Policy Priorities

Domestic political considerations and divergent ideological positions, especially in democracies, can sometimes override the durability of an international commitment. President Barack Obama placed high priority on addressing the problem of climate change through multilateral, collective action. The following President, Donald Trump, reflected a very different domestic constituency and one skeptical of both multilateral agreements and the threat posed by climate change. Trump reversed Obama's foreign policy commitment. Here are representative statements from the two leaders:

President Obama on the Paris Agreement, December 2015:

… A few hours ago, we succeeded. We came together around the strong agreement the world needed. We met the moment.

… Today, the American people can be proud – because this historic agreement is a tribute to American leadership. Over the past seven years, we've transformed the United States into the global leader in fighting climate change.

… So I believe this moment can be a turning point for the world. We've shown that the world has both the will and the ability to take on this challenge. It won't be easy. Progress won't always come quick. We cannot be complacent.

… Today, thanks to strong, principled, American leadership, that's the world that we'll leave to our children – a world that is safer and more secure, more prosperous, and more free. And that is our most important mission in our short time here on this Earth.

Source: US White House (2015).

President Trump on the Paris Agreement, June 2017:

… As President, I can put no other consideration before the wellbeing of American citizens. The Paris Climate Accord is simply the latest example of Washington entering into an agreement that disadvantages the United States to the exclusive benefit of other countries, leaving American workers – who I love – and taxpayers to absorb the cost in terms of lost jobs, lower wages, shuttered factories, and vastly diminished economic production.

Thus, as of today, the United States will cease all implementation of the non-binding Paris Agreement and the draconian financial and economic burdens the agreement imposes on our country.

… under the agreement, China will be able to increase these emissions by a staggering number of years – 13. They can do whatever they want for 13 years. Not us. India makes its participation contingent on receiving billions and billions and billions of dollars in foreign aid from developed countries. There are many other examples. But the bottom line is that the Paris Agreement is very unfair, at the highest level, to the United States.

… The Paris Agreement handicaps the United States economy in order to win praise from the very foreign capitals and global activists that have long sought to gain wealth at our country's expense. They don't put America first. I do, and I always will.

… I was elected to represent the citizens of Pittsburgh, not Paris.

Source: US White House (2017).

Liberal theorists have also identified circumstances under which international law and organizations are likely to constrain state behavior. For example, to the degree that states believe that the international organization within which they are implementing a treaty provides for repeated interactions with one another and thus many opportunities to monitor one another's compliance with the treaty, then the more likely they will pursue conditional cooperation within the organization and thereby resolve Prisoner's Dilemma constraints on cooperation described above.

The Realist Tradition

Realist scholars have identified two conditions that promote compliance by states with international legal obligations and cooperation among them through international organizations. First, realists anticipate that states will be highly likely to work together with the aid of international agreements and organizations when doing so helps them confront some common enemy. States that face a common security threat are likely not just to form but to abide by their commitments under the terms of an alliance of common defense (Walt 1984). The United States, Canada, and the nations of Western Europe, for example, after World War II faced a serious threat from the Soviet Union, and the result was the Atlantic Treaty of 1949 and the formation and efficacious operation of an institutionalized embodiment of that treaty, NATO. NATO appears even to be experiencing a renaissance in recent years, including in terms of closer coordination of NATO military forces (see Photo 5.5), which seems to be due to the Russian takeover of Crimea from Ukraine in 2014. NATO's renewed vigilance is consistent with realist arguments that an increase in external threats can serve as the basis for greater internal cohesion and solidarity within a military alliance.

Realists, however, also argue that the presence of a common external threat may not be sufficient to bring about effective adherence to international legal and organizational commitments. A second condition may be necessary, namely, the presence of a particularly powerful state – a **hegemonic leader** – that is both able and willing to help facilitate such cooperation. That hegemon might pay the disproportionate costs that are needed to maintain an open global economic legal order by keeping its markets open even during times of economic stress and by providing emergency short-term loans to countries that are facing temporary shortages of currency to buy needed imports (Kindleberger 1973/1986; Gilpin 1975). That hegemon might also play a key role in alleviating potential fears that partners may have of one another, fears that otherwise might hinder their compliance with collaborate rules and organizations. For example, during the 1950s and 1960s one reason the countries of Western Europe were able to work closely with one another through the European Economic Community was that the United States, through NATO, provided security to all the main European countries, and thus those countries did not have to worry that economic cooperation among them in the present would produce imbalanced gains and a potentially more powerful and threatening neighbor in the future (Waltz 1979: 71).

Finally, realists would agree with an analysis by Downs, Rocke, and Barsoom (1996) of the central role of national interests in prompting compliance by states with their international legal obligations. These authors put forward an alternative explanation for widespread state compliance with international law: states negotiate the content

Hegemonic leader
A particularly powerful state whose presence, according to realist theory, may be necessary to help facilitate cooperation between and among less powerful partner-states.

Photo 5.5 NATO Training Exercise in Poland, April 2017
In April 2017, these US troops plus soldiers from Poland, the United Kingdom, and Romania, with Croatian forces soon to follow, assembled in Poland to form a new NATO multinational combat battalion, one element of NATO's strategy of buttressing its eastern defenses.

Source: Getty Images Poland/Karol Serewis.

of international laws, and will agree to include in those laws only those rights and obligations regarding their behavior that they wanted to undertake in the first place. Hence, when we see states comply quite faithfully with commitments to reduce trade barriers under the WTO, or to follow the Geneva Conventions regarding the treatment of prisoners of war, it is not because the relevant laws require them to do so, but because their interests are served with those forms of behavior. International laws then do not have their greatest effect *after* they are negotiated, but rather, beforehand, when they play a useful role in serving as a screening device whereby states can ascertain whether, in their relationships with one another, there is some form of behavior that all wish to follow (Von Stein 2005).

The Constructivist Tradition

Constructivists emphasize how international laws and organizations reflect norms that are shared between countries. Just as such shared norms influence the formation of international law and supporting organizations, so too do shared norms condition whether or not international laws and organizations then have an impact on state behavior.

State elites across countries – broadly encompassing national political leaders but also important opinion-leaders such as newspaper editors and columnists and business executives – together with members of the wider public, may converge on a set of common values and beliefs about how international relations should take place, and this may enhance the efficacy of the international laws and organizations. For example, after World War II elite and public opinion in the main industrial democracies – the United States, Germany, Japan, and the United Kingdom – favored a 'mixed economy' policy in which governments would promote freer markets but with policy interventions when necessary to promote employment. This general policy orientation underpinned the basic mission of the GATT to promote trade liberalization but to accept temporary government restraints on the pace of liberalization when and if local industries came under sudden external pressure (Ruggie 1982).

Commonly shared norms about appropriate behavior help underpin the legitimacy and efficacy of international laws and organizations built upon those shared norms. In addition, widely shared norms against particular forms of state behavior give added weight to international laws that are directed toward the limitation or elimination of those behaviors. For example, there is evidence that a **taboo** – a strong widely held normative condemnation against some form of behavior – against the use of nuclear weapons has taken root around the world since 1945 (Tannenwald 1999). It is possible that this widespread nuclear taboo helps underpin the Nuclear Non-Proliferation Treaty of 1968 and its key organizational body, the International Atomic Energy Agency (IAEA).

Taboo
A strong and widely held normative condemnation against some form of behavior; in constructivist international relations theory.

Constructivists also have argued that norm entrepreneurs – essential in creating international laws – also play a key role in making those laws effective. We see this in the case of NGOs and the impact of international human rights law. Scholars have found that governments are more likely to abide by their commitments under the terms of international human rights conventions if their domestic societies possess robust nongovernmental organizations that are concerned about human rights and can monitor and press for full implementation of those treaties (Neumayer 2005).

The impact of domestic human rights organizations can be augmented significantly by the work of external NGOs such as Amnesty International or Human Rights Watch, and by the ability of the latter to pursue strategies of '**naming and shaming.**' Naming and shaming refers to the highlighting by national but especially international NGOs, through written reports and other publicly available media products, the presumed non-compliance of states with their obligations under international humanitarian and human rights laws, with the goal of compelling those states to react to the unfavorable depictions by bringing their behavior more in line with international legal norms.

Naming and shaming
Strategy of national but especially global NGOs to highlight publicly the possible non-compliance of states with their obligations under international humanitarian and human rights laws, with the goal of compelling those states to react to the unfavorable depictions by bringing their behavior more in line with international legal norms.

Levels of Analysis *Explanations for Efficacy of International Law and Organizations*

State	International
Liberal theorists argue that democratic states, by having more domestic veto-points and stronger domestic networks of NGOs than is observed in authoritarian states, are more likely to comply with the international laws they accept and to work more effectively with one another through international organizations.	Realists believe that states are more likely to adhere to cooperative commitments in the face of a common external threat and that a particularly strong state – a hegemon – can facilitate observance by partner-states with their international legal obligations by bearing associated costs and providing a secure environment for the partners.
	Constructivists believe that global NGOs, especially through a strategy of naming and shaming, can help domestic NGOs press governments to adhere to their international legal commitments.

REVISITING THE ENDURING QUESTION AND LOOKING AHEAD

This chapter began with the observation that states and other actors in contemporary world politics operate within a multitude of international rules and institutions. The United Nations, the World Trade Organization, the International Criminal Court – across the many domains of global affairs, sovereign states are deeply entangled in laws, norms, and organizations of their own making. The Westphalian state system and the modern system of international law have developed hand in hand. Out of these observations, this chapter has asked an enduring question: how important are international laws and organizations in a world of sovereign states? Are international laws and organizations simply tools of powerful states or do they have some independent role and impact in shaping and restraining the interaction of states? This chapter shows that there is not a simple or single answer to this enduring question, but also has illuminated the many realms and ways in which international laws and organizations play a role in world politics.

International law captures the many rights and obligations that states agree to as guides to how they will conduct their relations. As we have seen, many of the most important international legal obligations have emerged as customary law, including those relating to genocide, slavery, and the law of the sea. Over time, these obligations have become more systematic and formal. They also become embedded in international organizations, created by states to facilitate the implementation of legal obligations and commitments. Together, international law and organizations provide an institutional and normative infrastructure for international relations.

The chapter has shown that international law and organizations apply across a variety of international issues. There are normative and legal frameworks that specify the acceptable reasons under which states can go to war, the conditions under which states can intervene in other states to protect citizens from harm, and the rights of individuals. International law also regulates the use of oceans and other aspects of the natural environment. In each of these areas, international law and organizations help to define the terms by which states engage, cooperate, and settle conflicts with each other.

Finally, we explored the ongoing theoretical debate about how and why international laws and organizations matter. Liberals see laws and organizations as collective arrangements to help states manage their relations and realize mutual gains. Realists see laws and organizations primarily as instruments by which powerful states assert their domination over others. When states compete or when they enter into conflict, realists expect power and interests to matter more than laws and norms. Marxists tend to agree, although they see laws and organizations as tools of capitalism and the dominant class. Constructivists tend to agree with liberals that international laws and organizations are intrinsically important, giving shape to the norms and ideas that influence how states think about what is right, wrong, moral, and legitimate.

International laws and organizations never fully determine how and why states do what they do. But they provide important incentives and constraints that shape and guide states and their leaders. We will see international law and organizations in play in the next section of the book, which focuses on security relationships among states.

STUDY QUESTIONS

1. How is international law different from domestic law?
2. In which of the four substantive areas we highlight in this chapter are international laws and organizations most developed? In which are they least developed? Why?
3. Why do some scholars believe that the emphasis on human rights since World War II constitutes a 'revolution' in international law?
4. What are the main similarities and differences between liberal, constructivist, and realist thinkers on the causes and effects of international law and organizations?
5. How important is the domestic political system of a state in determining whether it abides by international law?

FURTHER READING

Bosco, David (2017) *Rough Justice: The International Criminal Court in a World of Power Politics* (New York: Oxford University Press). Bosco provides a detailed history of the ICC, focusing on the role of power politics in shaping prosecutorial behavior.

Bradley, Mark Philip (2017) *The World Reimagined: Americans and Human Rights in the Twentieth Century* (Cambridge: Cambridge University Press). Bradley explains, with reference to both elite and popular culture, how postwar Americans came to embrace the human rights revolution.

Glendon, Mary Ann (2001) *A World Made New: Eleanor Roosevelt and the Universal Declaration on Human Rights* (New York: Random House). Glendon tells the story of how a remarkable group of individuals, including US first lady, Eleanor Roosevelt, created the foundational document of the global human rights movement.

Hinton, Alexander (2016) *Man or Monster? The Trial of a Khmer Rouge Torturer* (Durham: Duke University Press). Hinton explores how a math teacher was transformed into a mass murderer during the Cambodian genocide of the 1970s.

 Visit www.macmillanihe.com/Grieco-IntroIR-2e to access extra resources for this chapter, including:

- Chapter summaries to help you review the material
- Multiple choice quizzes to test your understanding
- Flashcards to test your knowledge of the key terms in this chapter
- An interactive simulation that invites you to go through the decision-making process of a world leader at a crucial political juncture
- Pivotal decisions in which you weigh up the pros and cons of complicated decisions with grave consequences
- Outside resources, including links to contemporary articles and videos, that add to what you have learned in this chapter

Part II

War and Peace: An Introduction to Security Studies

Author Debates

 Visit **www.macmillanihe.com/Grieco-IntroIR-2e** to watch the authors debating the issues discussed in this Part.

Video 1: How important are diplomacy and military force in today's world?

Video 2: Are China and Russia 'revisionist states'?

6 War and Its Causes

Enduring question
Why is war a persistent feature of international relations?

Chapter Contents

Learning Objectives

By the end of this chapter, you will be able to:

→ Distinguish among the different kinds of international military conflicts, including their frequency and lethality.

→ Understand the different kinds of conflicts of interest between countries that can be the immediate cause of war.

→ Compare and assess the underlying causes of international military conflict at the individual level of analysis, with a focus on errors by national leaders arising from misperceptions, small-group dynamics, or a propensity toward overconfidence.

→ Recognize and analyze causes of conflicts at the state level of analysis, with a focus on domestic economic systems, political institutions, and governmental processes.

→ Evaluate the causes of military conflicts at the international level of analysis.

→ Identify the causes and effects of internal wars and understand their impact on the prospects for war and peace between states.

President George Bush of the United States and Prime Minister Tony Blair of the United Kingdom led a coalition of states in a war against Iraq in March 2003 because they believed that Iraq under Saddam Hussein was trying to build nuclear weapons. Just before the US invasion, US Deputy Secretary of Defense Paul Wolfowitz dismissed as 'wildly off the mark' an estimate by General Eric Shinseki, the US Army Chief of Staff, that, after the allies had defeated Saddam's military, hundreds of thousands of US troops might then be needed to occupy and pacify Iraq (Milbank 2005). As it turns out, there were no Iraqi nuclear weapons. The United States, the United Kingdom, and their allies did, as expected, readily defeat Iraq's military, but an insurgency soon threatened allied forces and the new Iraqi government, and the United States and its allies only achieved a modicum of stability in Iraq with a force that included 160,000 US troops. More than 165,000 Iraqi civilians, 4,400 American military personnel, and almost 200 British military personnel were killed during the Iraq war and the subsequent insurgency.

Turning to Europe, after several civil wars in the Balkans in the 1990s, and a Russian attack on Georgia in 2008, the continent entered the decade of the 2010s with reason for optimism. NATO and the EU had expanded to include much of Eastern and Central Europe, and there was almost no expectation that problems with Russia could bring about a new Cold War. Then things changed. When, in November 2013, Ukrainian president Viktor Yanukovych announced that he had decided not to sign an association agreement with the EU, violent civilian protests erupted in the Ukrainian capital of Kiev, and at the end of February President Yanukovych fled Ukraine for Russia. Russia then moved. Russian commando units without official insignia entered the Crimean Peninsula in early 2014 in the far south of Ukraine. Russian forces gave support to local Russian-speaking Crimean separatists who organized an internationally disputed referendum in mid-March 2014 that called for a unification of Crimea with Russia. President Putin signed into law the annexation by Russia of Crimea on March 18. For the first time since World War II, a European state had used force to seize territory of a neighbor. Russia also instigated a low-level separatist war in eastern Ukraine, even though in 1994 and 1997 Russia had signed agreements that recognized the inviolability of Ukraine's borders.

Why does a war like that against Iraq or Ukraine occur? Why, more generally, do wars remain a persistent feature of the world around us? We discussed in Chapter 5 how the UN Charter commits states to refrain from the use of military force in their international relations and, except for immediate self-defense, to use force only when authorized by the UN Security Council. Yet, states often do resort to arms and they do so without the authorization of the UN. We therefore devote this chapter to an exploration of the enduring question in international relations of why war is a persistent element of global affairs. In the chapter's first section, we establish a foundation about international military conflict by identifying the main types of conflicts that occur between countries and investigate how international military conflicts have varied across time in their incidence and severity. We then, in the chapter's second main section, discuss the kinds of disagreements between countries which can make them turn to military threats or violence. In the chapter's subsequent three main sections we examine the underlying causes of war and other serious military conflicts between states, using the levels-of-analysis framework, with its emphasis on arguments pitched at the level of the individual, the internal characteristics of countries, and the interstate system, to organize the discussion and the efforts by the main theoretical traditions in international relations to understand the causes of war.

In the chapter's last main section, we shift our focus from war *between* states and toward war *within* states, or internal wars. We highlight the reasons why students of international relations must understand internal wars; discuss different types of internal wars, as well as their incidence and severity; and identify and examine the range of causes that may bring about such wars within countries.

WARS BETWEEN COUNTRIES

Before we explore the immediate and underlying causes of international military conflicts, we first lay down three foundations: we define and examine different kinds of military conflicts that take place between countries, present information on the incidence of those different types of military conflicts that have taken place between countries over the past two centuries, and consider how lethal those conflicts have been in terms of deaths of combatants and civilians.

Types of Military Conflicts between Countries

We begin with interstate war, which occurs when two or more national governments direct military forces against each other in organized, sustained, and highly deadly clashes.

There are many types of **interstate war** (Levy and Thompson 2011). For example, several that we examined in Chapter 2 – the Thirty Years War and the wars against Napoleonic France, Germany under William II and Hitler, and Imperial Japan – were **general wars** or major wars in the sense that they involved many or all of the most powerful states in their respective historical eras. Some, such as the Napoleonic Wars and World War II, were also **hegemonic wars,** that is, their outcomes determined which states would have predominant influence in the international system for years and even decades. World War I and especially World War II were instances of **total war**, where warring governments sought to mobilize as much of their human and economic resources as possible, and some of the main belligerents systematically sought to weaken or kill the civilian populations of their enemies as a part of their war strategies.

Since 1945, there has been no total war between or among the most powerful states, that is, the United States, the Soviet Union (now Russia), the United Kingdom, France, and China. With the exceptions of large-scale US–Chinese clashes during the Korean War of 1950–53, and minor skirmishes between Soviet and Chinese forces on their mutual border in 1969, the major powers since 1945 have avoided fighting each other directly. One important reason for the lapse in total war and the absence of war between the major powers is the existence of nuclear weapons. During the Cold War, the Soviet Union and the United States (and two US allies, the United Kingdom and France) possessed large arsenals of nuclear weapons, and as we will see in Chapter 8, the fear of nuclear war contributed greatly to the prevention of World War III. Moreover, Japan and Germany, which under authoritarian and dictatorial governments were highly aggressive states during the first half of the twentieth century, became stable democracies in the wake of World War II, and, as we will see below, democracies are unlikely to fight among themselves. At the same time, these states were less likely to fight each other because they all found it necessary to work together to resist (but, in the face of nuclear weapons, not to fight) the Soviet Union during the Cold War.

This does not mean that the major states since 1945 have avoided all forms of military conflicts with one another or with other states. As we saw in Chapter 2,

Interstate war
When two or more national governments direct military forces against each other in organized, sustained, and oftentimes deadly clashes.

General war
A war that involves many or all of the most powerful states in a particular historical era. Synonymous with major war.

Hegemonic war
A war the outcome of which determines which states will have predominant influence in the international system in the coming years or even decades.

Total war
War in which belligerent states mobilize all resources and target civilians as part of their war strategy.

Photo 6.1 London under Air Attack
When Germany carried out air raids against London during World War II, residents found shelter in London subway (or 'tube') stations.

Source: Bettmann.

Limited war
Smaller war in which major powers avoid fighting each other directly, contrasted with general or major war.

during the Cold War the United States and the Soviet Union fought proxy wars against each other. Moreover, we have witnessed **limited wars** between one or more of the major states and less powerful countries, such as between China and India in 1962, or between less powerful states, including multiple wars between India and Pakistan and between Israel and Egypt and Syria.

There is in the field of international relations no universally agreed-upon threshold of violence that must take place between governments before that violence is classified as an interstate war. Many scholars, however, utilize a threshold proposed by the Correlates of War (COW) project, a data-collection program on different kinds of armed violence within and between countries. The COW data project stipulates that interstate wars are those organized clashes between the military forces of states that result in at least 1,000 combat fatalities during a 12-month period (Sarkees and Wayman 2010).

Militarized interstate dispute (MID)
An instance in which a state threatens or uses force against another state.

Interstate wars comprise the first of three COW-identified categories of international military conflicts. The second type is that of **militarized interstate disputes (MIDs)**. An MID is an international conflict in which states seek to win a dispute through military coercion. The concept of an MID covers a broad range of state actions: from the issuing by states of *threats* of military force against one another; to the making of *displays* of military power against one another, such as moving troops up to a common border; to the actual use of force by a state against an adversary, which in turn can run the gamut from using forces to seize territory, declaring war, or engaging in violent clashes with the adversary at levels below that of full-scale war (Ghosn, Palmer, and Bremer 2004).

Simulations: What would you do? Imagine you are the President of Peru, faced with threats from hostile and unstable neighboring states. Visit the companion website to see the scenario develop based on the decisions you make!

Extra-state wars represent the third COW category of international military conflicts. An extra-state war is a violent clash – resulting in at least 1,000 combat deaths – between the national government of a recognized state and an entity in a foreign territory that is not an internationally recognized state, or is a non-state actor located in a foreign state (we discuss non-state actors in more detail in Chapter 12). The conquests that European states undertook against African tribal communities during the 1800s were extra-state wars, as were the wars for independence that colonies such as Algeria and Vietnam undertook against France after World War II. More recently, the United States has undertaken extra-state wars particularly with remotely piloted armed drones and conventional aircraft against Islamic State targets in such countries as Iraq, Syria, Libya, and Afghanistan, as well as Al Qaeda or Al Qaeda-affiliated terrorist sites in Yemen, Somalia, and Pakistan. Given that the differences in power between states and foreign entities in extra-state conflicts are usually vastly in favor of the states, and in consequence of that the two sides often use very different strategies and tactics (for example, drone strikes versus terrorist attacks on civilians), this category of conflict is sometimes called asymmetrical warfare.

> **Extra-state war**
> A violent clash between the national government of a recognized state and an entity that is not an internationally recognized state, or a non-state actor located in a foreign state.

Modern international conflicts can often have both interstate and extra-state dimensions. For example, after the Al Qaeda attacks against the United States in September 2001, US forces destroyed the bases that terrorist organization had established in Afghanistan. The United States also helped indigenous Afghan groups topple the Afghan government, which was then under the control of the Taliban, an Islamist fundamentalist group that had given Al Qaeda a safe haven in Afghanistan. Two wars thus occurred at the same time during 2001 and 2002: that against Al Qaeda was an extra-state war, while that against Taliban-controlled Afghanistan was an interstate war. The Taliban soon recovered from their defeats in 2001–02 and utilizing bases in Pakistan and Afghanistan launched an insurgency against the US-backed government in Kabul. By consequence, since 2002 the United States, the United Kingdom, and several allied countries have fought an extra-state war against a resurgent Taliban in Afghanistan and in neighboring Pakistan. Similarly, the Iraq war that began in March 2003 began as an interstate war, but an extra-state war soon developed in which the United States and its allies fought Iraqi opposition groups and outside fighters, including some affiliated with Al Qaeda.

Incidence of International Military Conflicts

We are interested in understanding how often individual states make the decision to initiate military conflicts of different types with other states. Let us begin with full-scale interstate wars. There were 95 such interstate wars between 1816 and 2007, the period for which the COW research team now provides information.

Let us call each such decision by a state to initiate a war against another state a 'national war initiation' (NWI). It is possible, using the COW data set, to identify 165 such NWIs between 1816 and 2007. Our goal is to understand the variation in these 165 NWIs between 1816 to 2007, for doing so allows us to address the question, has the incidence of war initiations gone up, down, or stayed the same during the past two centuries?

To make such cross-temporal comparisons we need to take into account the fact that there are different numbers of years and different numbers of countries in what may be considered politically relevant time periods. To do so we follow the procedure employed by two prominent analysts of the onset of civil wars (Fearon and Laitin 2003). As can be seen in Figure 6.1, we divide the 1816–2007 timespan into five successive periods, and then show separately two periods consisting of the Cold War era and the immediate post-Cold War era. We then present the number of NWIs that took place per 100 country-years in each period. We calculated NWIs per 100 country-years in the following manner, using the immediate post-Cold War period as an example. From the COW data set we identified 13 NWIs in the immediate post-Cold War period of 1990–2007. We determined that there were 187 countries in existence on average during that 18-year period; we then calculated that there were 3,366 country-years in that period (18 years × 187 countries = 3,366 country-years). With that information we were then able to estimate that there were 0.4 NWIs per 100 country-years in that period, that is, (13 NWIs/3366 country-years)*100 country-years = 0.4 NWIs per 100 country-years. We have calculated the NWIs per 100 country-years in this manner for each period depicted in Figure 6.1, which permits us to make comparisons across the last two centuries as well as between the Cold War and post-Cold War eras in the propensity of states to initiate full-scale wars against one another.

As can be observed in the figure, the propensity of states to initiate wars against one another increased steadily from 0.8 NWIs per 100 country-years between 1816 and 1849 to 1.6 NWIs between 1850 and 1899 all the way up to 2.8 NWIs per 100 country-years between 1900 and 1949. However, national war initiations dropped dramatically from the middle of the last century onwards, plummeting to 0.6 NWIs per 100 country-years during 1950–99 and then to 0.2 NWIs per 100 country-years

Figure 6.1 National War Initiations, 1816–2007, and during and after the Cold War
In this chart, for each designated period, the bar represents the number of national war initiations (NWI) per 100 country-years. In this figure we can see that after steadily increasing between 1816 and 1949, NWIs declined during the second half of the twentieth century. This decline in NWIs that began during the Cold-War period appears to have been even more marked in the immediate post-Cold War years.

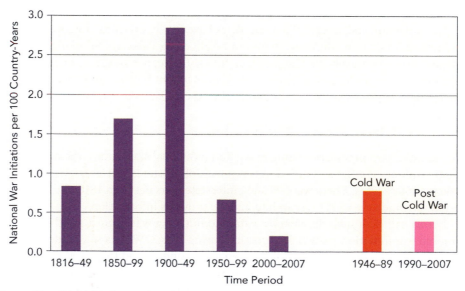

Source: Meredith Reid Sarkees and Frank Wayman (2010) *Resort to War: 1816–2007* (CQ Press). Data available at Correlates of War Project, COW War Data, 1816-2007 (v4.0), available at http://www.correlatesofwar.org/data-sets/COW-war.

during the first years of the current century. Close attention should also be paid to the two bars on the far right of Figure 6.1, which depict the incidence of war initiations during the Cold War and immediate post-Cold War eras, respectively. National war initiations went down by 50 percent across the two periods, from 0.8 to 0.4 NWIs per 100 country-years. Hence, it is possible that after a relentless upward trend in the use of war by states from the early nineteenth to the middle of the twentieth century, we are now seeing a reversal of that trend. We should be careful about drawing inferences about the prospects for war from either the Cold War era or especially the relatively short period of time that has passed since the end of the Cold War. However, going back to our enduring question, if this trend toward relative peacefulness were to hold it would raise doubts about whether war continues to be, in fact, necessarily a persistent feature of international politics (Mueller 2009). For that reason, it is a trend that is clearly worthy of continued attention in the years ahead.

We may now turn to the second type of military conflicts, MIDs. The COW data project has identified 2,586 MIDs between 1816 and 2010. Using the same method described above to assess trends in the propensity of states to initiate wars, we report in Figure 6.2 the propensity of states to undertake national MID initiations, or NMIs.

As with the launching of full interstate wars, there was a sustained uptick in the propensity of states to initiate MIDs from 1816 to 1949, with NMIs per 100 country-years increasing from about nine during the first half of the nineteenth century to 14 during the second half of that century, all the way up to almost 25 during the first half of the twentieth century. Then, as with full interstate wars, but to a relatively more attenuated degree, NMIs dropped after World War II, decreasing to 23.4 per 100 country-years during 1950–99 and to about 18 during the first decade of the current

Figure 6.2 National MID initiations, 1816–2010, and during and after the Cold War
In this chart, for each designated period, the bar represents the number of national MID initiations (NMIs) per 100 country-years. As with the initiation by states of wars, states since the middle of the 20th century have reduced their propensity to launch MIDs, although the decrease has not been as marked as it has been with national war initiations.

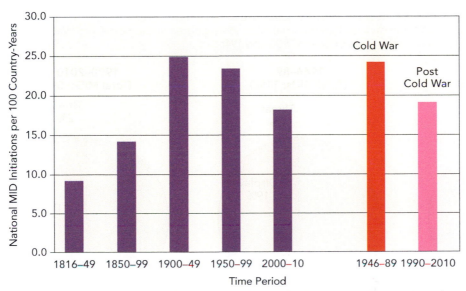

Sources: Palmer et al. (2015); and Faten, Ghosn and Scott Bennett (2003). Data available at Correlates of War Data Project, Militarized Interstate Dispute data set (v4.1), available at http://cow.dss.ucdavis.edu/data-sets/MIDs/mids.

century. Moreover, if we look to the right of the figure, and compare the Cold War and post-Cold War eras, we see, as we did with full-scale national war initiations, a decrease in national initiations of militarized disputes, but the decrease has not been as marked as it has been in the case of national war initiations. Moreover, it may be observed in the figure that NMIs have been taking place during the post-Cold War period at a rate that is higher than what we observe in the first half of the nineteenth century, controlling for the number of years and number of countries under review. It would seem then that while states may be becoming less reliant on full-scale war to resolve their international disagreements, they are still using lesser levels of military force to try to do so.

At the same time, it is possible that the relative severity of MIDs has decreased in the post-Cold War era. We can assess this possibility by reference to Figure 6.3. Consider the first pie chart in the figure. It reports the percentage of the 477 MIDs that occurred between 1900 and 1945 that took the form solely of threats issued by one state against another (5 percent of the total), the percentage that were more severe than threats, namely, displays of military force (24 percent), and finally, at the highest level of hostility, the percentage of MIDs that entailed the actual use of force between the contesting states, including violent clashes short of war (71 percent). Turning next to the second pie chart, we see that during the Cold War years of 1946–89, during which there were 1,150 MIDs, the percentage of that total that were of the most severe type, the use of force, reached 77 percent. Notice, finally, the third pie chart: it indicates that during the first 20 years of the post-Cold War period, during which there were 598 MIDs, 59 percent of that total entailed the use of force, substantially below that of both the Cold War era and the first half of the twentieth century. It would seem then that while the rate at which states launch MIDs has not declined very dramatically with the end of the Cold War, relatively fewer MIDs are reaching the highest level of severity. This mixed pattern of trends regarding MIDs certainly invites research in the years ahead.

Figure 6.3 Severity of Militarized Interstate Disputes, 1900–2010

Compared to the first half of the twentieth century, the actual use of force more typically characterized MIDs during the Cold War. The use of force during MIDs has abated to some degree in the post-Cold War period compared to the Cold War era or to the years between 1900 and 1945.

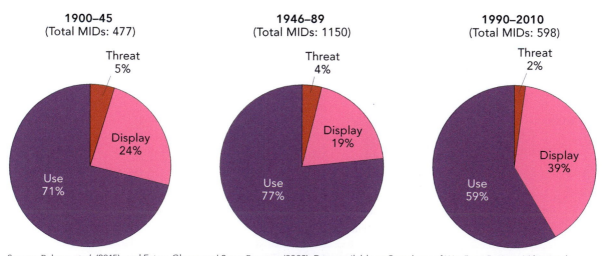

Source: Palmer *et al.* (2015); and Faten, Ghosn and Scott Bennett (2003). Data available at Correlates of War Data Project, Militarized Interstate Dispute data set (v4.1), available at http://cow.dss.ucdavis.edu/data-sets/MIDs/mids.

We next focus on extra-state wars. You will recall that extra-state wars differ from interstate wars and MIDs insofar as the latter two involve by definition only states. The COW research team has identified 163 such extra-state wars that took place between 1816 and 2007. States often have been the initiators of extra-state wars: France, Britain, Russia, and the Netherlands did so repeatedly in the nineteenth century as they colonized foreign peoples. However, such wars also have resulted from military efforts by a non-state actor, such as a national liberation movement, to expel a colonial occupying force, as we see, for example, in the armed nationalist movements that expelled France from Indochina between 1946 and 1954 and from Algeria between 1954 and 1962. Therefore, below we focus on the relative frequency with which states fought in extra-national wars either as initiators or respondents.

Figure 6.4 reports this incidence of national extra-state war participation per 100 country-years during different time periods between 1816 and 2007. This type of war involvement very much reflects what we discussed in Chapter 2: imperialism and resulting extra-state war participation by mainly European states were both high throughout the nineteenth century, and war participation declined in the twentieth century, first, as the imperial states succeeded in consolidating their foreign holdings and then as colonial peoples acquired their independence, sometimes but not always through armed struggle. However, extra-state wars have once more become a prominent element of world conflict. We saw this in first instance in the wars against international terrorism, such as the US and allied invasion of Afghanistan in 2001 to

Figure 6.4 State Participation in Extra-State Wars, 1816–2007, and during and after the Cold War
For each designated time period, the bar represents the frequency per 100 country-years with which states became involved in extra-state wars. States were relatively highly involved in such wars during the imperialist nineteenth century, but then became involved in fewer extra-state wars during the first and especially the second half of the twentieth century, reflecting first the consolidation and then the end of colonialism during that century. However, in very recent years states have become involved in relatively more extra-state wars as a result, in part, of wars against the Al Qaeda terrorist group and its Afghan national host, as well as resistance to the occupation and pacification of Afghanistan and Iraq.

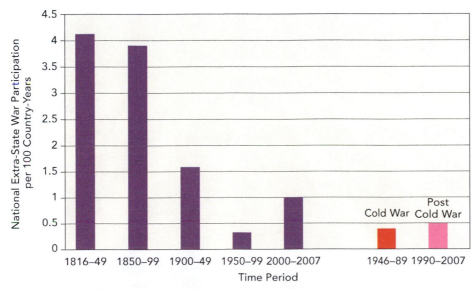

Source: Meredith Reid Sarkees and Frank Wayman (2010) *Resort to War: 1816–2007* (CQ Press). Data available at Correlates of War Data Project, Extra-State Wars (v4.01), available at http://www.correlatesofwar.org/data-sets/COW-war/extra-state-war-data-v4-0.

fight Al Qaeda and its Taliban hosts after the September 11 attacks. We also observed this in the sustained armed struggle in Iraq between numerous intervening states and various resistance forces following the US-led invasion of that country in 2003. More recently there has been a US campaign, undertaken together with a coalition of allies, against Islamic State in Iraq, Syria, Libya, and Afghanistan, together with a US-France operation against IS in the Sahel countries of Mali, Mauritania, Burkina Faso, Niger, and Chad.

Lethality of International Wars

The COW data project does not present battlefield fatalities for each MID, but we do have reasonable estimates for such deaths that were incurred during interstate and extra-state wars. At least 32 million combat deaths resulted from the 95 interstate wars that were fought between 1816 and 2007. Of that total, more than 8 million combat deaths occurred during World War I, and 16 million during World War II. Approximately 2.1 million or more combatants were killed during that period in extra-state wars.

As we can see in Panel A of Figure 6.5, the lethality of interstate wars almost doubled from the first to the second half of the nineteenth century, and then exploded in the first half of the twentieth century. More powerful weapons, such as heavy artillery, tanks, and machine guns; industrialization and thus the ability of states to produce vast quantities of those weapons; and a stronger capacity of governments to mobilize national populations and to put together ever larger militaries: these factors combined during the 1900–49 period to produce armed forces that could inflict truly massive casualties on one another. Thereafter, reflecting perhaps the fact that the major powers avoided direct war with one another because of nuclear weapons and

Photo 6.2 Battle of the Somme, 1916
A view of military graves illuminated to mark the 100th anniversary of the beginning of the Battle of the Somme at the Thiepval Memorial to the Missing on June 30, 2016 in Thiepval, France, where 70,000 British and Commonwealth soldiers with no known grave are commemorated.

Source: Gareth Fuller - Pool/Getty Images.

democracies, wars on average dropped in lethality. We can also see that the wars that have occurred in the post-Cold War era (India-Pakistan in 1999, the US-led wars against Iraq in 1992 and 2003) were less lethal for combatant forces than were the wars that took place during the Cold War.

Figure 6.5 Battlefield Deaths in Interstate and Extra-State Wars, 1816–2007, and during and after the Cold War
For each designated time period, the bar represents the average number of battlefield deaths that occurred during the wars (interstate in Panel A and extra-state in Panel B) during the period; the number in parentheses is the total number of such wars that began during the period.

(a) Interstate Wars

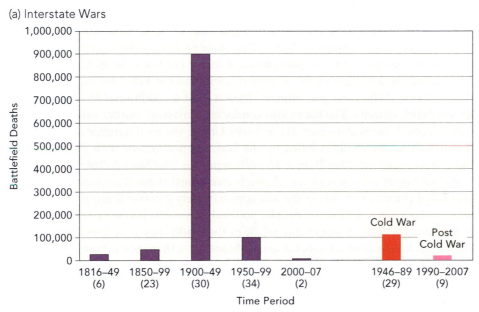

(b) Extra-State Wars

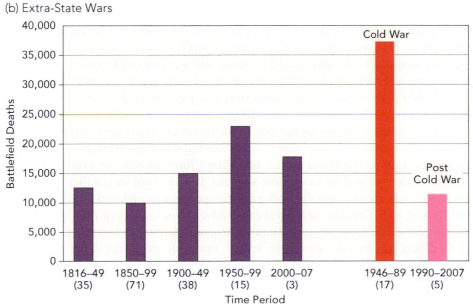

Source: Meredith Reid Sarkees, and Frank Wayman (2010) *Resort to War: 1816–2007* (CQ Press). Data available at Correlates of War Project, COW War Data, 1816-2007 (v4.0), available at http:// www.correlatesofwar.org/data-sets/COW-war, and Extra-State Wars (v4.01), available at http://www .correlatesofwar.org/data-sets/COW-war/extra-state-war-data-v4-0.

We may also observe in Panel B of Figure 6.5 that extra-state wars became more lethal during the twentieth as opposed to the nineteenth century. Wars of decolonization could be especially lethal: for example, some 270,000 combatants were killed during France's unsuccessful war to hold on to Vietnam, and 34,000 combatants were killed during France's failed bid to retain Algeria. There appears to have been a decrease in the lethality of extra-state wars with the end of the Cold War.

Interstate wars also have caused vast numbers of non-combatant deaths (Downes 2008). Perhaps 50 million civilians were killed during the wars of the twentieth century. At least 30 million civilians were killed in World War II alone. Many civilians died during that war due to malnutrition or disease or as a result of air bombings that were conducted by the Germans as well as the British and the Americans. World War II also witnessed genocide in the form of the Holocaust – the highly organized campaign by the Nazi state to destroy the Jewish community throughout Europe. That campaign resulted in the Nazi murder of 6 million Jews. Approximately 3 million of the 6 million Jewish people killed by the Nazis were Polish citizens. The Nazi government killed at least an additional 1.9 million non-Jewish Polish citizens. The Nazis also conducted a massive murder campaign when they occupied the western part of the Soviet Union: the total number of Jewish and non-Jewish Soviet civilians killed by the Nazis is not known with precision, but estimates range from 13 million to 15 million people. The Nazis killed an additional 5 million Soviet prisoners of war through intentional mass starvation. The Nazis also killed prior to and during the war approximately 200,000 Roma (Gypsies), and tens of thousands of disabled people, political prisoners, homosexuals, and other individuals the Nazis thought did not fit in the world they were seeking to create. Such mass killings and attempts at genocide are not a thing of the past: since World War II, perhaps 2 million or more civilians have been killed during interstate wars such as the Korean and Vietnam wars.

IMMEDIATE CAUSES OF WAR

To this point we have sought in the main to *describe* international military conflicts: their types, incidence, and lethality. Now we shift our attention to developing a capacity to *explain* why such conflicts occur. We will proceed in two steps: in this section we will identify the immediate causes of war, and in the next section we will identify possible underlying causes of military conflicts. An **immediate cause of a military conflict** consists of the disagreement, or the conflict of interest, that causes one state or another to escalate to the threat or actual use of military force. An **underlying cause of a military conflict** is the set of circumstances that made such escalation to the threat or use of military force possible or even inevitable. In this section we will focus on how a strong disagreement or conflict of interest between states about a specific issue can prompt them to undertake MIDs or even full-fledged wars. Conflicts of interest can revolve around economic resources, policy disagreements, political regimes, ethnic or religious identity, and territory.

Conflicts of interest involving scarce *economic resources* have served to foment militarized violence between states (Gleditsch *et al.* 2006). For example, disagreements between Israel and its Arab neighbors over water resources may have helped set the stage for one of the major Arab–Israeli wars in June 1967. When, in 1964, Israel began to draw water from the Jordan River, Egypt's President Nasser coordinated an Arab plan that would effectively divert water flows in Jordan, Syria, and Lebanon away from Israel. Israel responded with military strikes against the

Immediate cause of a military conflict
Disagreement, or the conflict of interest, that causes one state or another to escalate to the threat or actual use of military force.

Underlying cause of a military conflict
The set of circumstances that made escalation to the threat or use of military force possible or even inevitable.

construction sites for this project in Syria three times during 1965 and 1966 (Cooley 1984; Amery 1997).

Economic conflicts involving energy have also led to militarized conflicts. As we noted in Chapter 1, China and its neighbors have been locked into a struggle for control of the oil and natural gas resources that may lie beneath the South China Sea, and this conflict of interest has produced low-level MIDs. Saddam Hussein justified Iraq's August 1990 invasion of neighboring Kuwait in part with the claim that oil companies were using lateral drills to steal Iraqi oil. The United States then led an international coalition to expel Iraq from Kuwait. The United States decided to invade Iraq in 2003 in part because it worried that if Iraq had nuclear weapons, it would use them to dominate the Middle East and its economically crucial oil resources. This fear was expressed in July 2002 by Vice President Dick Cheney:

> Armed with an arsenal of these weapons of terror, and seated atop ten percent of the world's oil reserves, Saddam Hussein could then be expected to seek domination of the entire Middle East, take control of a great portion of the world's energy supplies, directly threaten America's friends throughout the region, and subject the United States or any other nation to nuclear blackmail. (Cheney 2002)

Policy disagreements can also produce conflicts of interest between states that have the potential for military conflict. In early September 2007, Israeli warplanes destroyed what appears to have been a nuclear reactor that Syria had under construction. Israeli leaders had concluded that the Syrian government intended to employ the reactor to build nuclear weapons, which they deemed an unacceptable possible threat to Israel. In this instance, Israel's intolerance of Syria's possible policy of acquiring nuclear weapons produced a militarized interstate dispute. It did not produce an interstate war because Syria chose not to escalate by retaliating against Israel.

States can also find themselves in serious conflicts of interest due to disagreements about one or another's *political regime*. As we explore in Box 6.1, in two very different instances, one at the outset of the modern era and one much more recent, disputes between states over political regimes have led to war.

Issues of *ethnic identity* can also lead states into serious conflicts of interest. By ethnic identity, we are referring to the linguistic, cultural, and religious beliefs and practices, common ancestral or kin ties, or other historical experiences that people believe they share and that cause them to believe that they constitute a community. In 1999, members of the NATO alliance attacked the Balkan country of Serbia. Why? Ethnic Albanians, who comprise the majority of residents in Kosovo, then a province in the south of Serbia, were pressing for greater self-governance, which they felt had been long denied to them while they remained part of Serbia. In the late 1990s, an ultra-nationalist Serbian government under the leadership of Slobodan Milosevic abused and murdered Albanian civilians in Kosovo as a part of an effort to suppress an armed Albanian secessionist movement, the Kosovo Liberation Army. The United States and its NATO allies became concerned that Milosevic might unleash a war aimed at '**ethnic cleansing**,' that is, the Serbs might murder and commit atrocities against residents of Albanian background with the goal of inducing the survivors to flee and thus leave Kosovo open for Serbian control. Between March and June 1999, the United States and its NATO allies launched air strikes against Serbia to compel the Milosevic government to cease its anti-Albanian campaign and accept a NATO peacekeeping force in Kosovo. Kosovo has since declared its independence from Serbia and is today administered by the United Nations.

Ethnic cleansing
Sustained, organized violence perpetrated against a particular ethnic group with the goal of eradication of that group.

6.1   MAKING CONNECTIONS
Then and Now

Conflict of Interest over Domestic Political Regimes: The French Revolutionary Period in the 1790s and the Buildup to the US Invasion of Iraq in 2003

Then: Austrian Rationale for Fearing a Democratic Regime in France, 1791

In the early 1790s, a top Austrian official, Baron Thugut, feared that the democratic character of revolutionary France would undermine the Habsburg dynasty. He said:

> Austria has certainly fought more wars in which threatening danger was much closer. But one cannot compare those with such an all-embracing struggle that we are now in … Just as [earlier] wars weakened us, so they weakened the enemy, and at the end military victory or a more or less advantageous peace would bring them to a halt. But now this House [the Habsburgs] … must fight a nation which has not only become utterly fanatical but which tries to drag along with it other peoples and which has prepared its current efforts for a long time in all of Europe through the voices of its prophets.
>
> Source: Baron Thugut, in the summer of 1791, who became Foreign Minister of Austria in 1793, quoted in Roider (1987): 129.

Now: American Rationale for Overthrowing Iraq's Authoritarian Regime, 2003

In 2003, the United States launched a war against Iraq in part because President George W. Bush and his advisors believed that Saddam Hussein's dictatorship in Iraq represented a threat both to the region and to the United States and the replacement of Hussein's regime with a democratic regime would yield a more peaceful Iraq and a more stable Middle East. President Bush at that time said:

> The success of a free Iraq will be watched and noted throughout the region. Millions will see that freedom, equality, and material progress are possible at the heart of the Middle East. Leaders in the region will face the clearest evidence that free institutions and open societies are the only path to long-term national success and dignity. And a transformed Middle East would benefit the entire world, by undermining the ideologies that export violence to other lands. Iraq as a dictatorship had great power to destabilize the Middle East; Iraq as a democracy will have great power to inspire the Middle East. The advance of democratic institutions in Iraq is setting an example that others, including the Palestinian people, would be wise to follow.
>
> Source: Bush (2003b).

In two very different historical eras, leaders and officials have been similarly motivated to go to war out of concern about the domestic political regimes of other countries. Sometimes they may go to war either because they want to prevent a foreign country from attaining a particular regime (Thugut feared democracy) or to impose a regime on a foreign country (Bush wanted to impose democracy on Iraq).

Finally, conflicts of interest regarding territory have a high potential for engendering military conflict (Senese and Vasquez 2005). Territorial disputes are fraught with the risk of war for three reasons. First, as discussed above, the territories in dispute may possess important economic resources. Second, countries may assign military importance to a borderland. For example, separated from Russia and wedged between Lithuania and Poland, the Russian area of Kaliningrad serves as the base for the Russian Baltic fleet, and as such provides Russia with a strategic position vis-à-vis NATO.

Third, in circumstances in which countries border one another and contain populations with similar ethnic characteristics, one side or the other might be tempted to go to war to 'unite the nation' under the rule of one sovereign state. Decolonization and the onset of the Cold War often divided similar cultural groups into separate states. After the new states were established, one often sought reunification with the other through military conquest. Examples of this type of culture-based international territorial conflict include the two Koreas, where unification has not occurred; the two Vietnams, where unification eventually took place in 1975. Taiwan and the People's Republic of China (PRC), where the outcome of a long-standing territorial problem is unknown but will greatly determine the future of peace in East Asia, are locked into a fundamental conflict of interest regarding the status of Taiwan. As is highlighted in Box 6.2, there are radically differing perspectives on the part of Taiwanese and PRC officials on the status of the island, notwithstanding the ethnic similarities of the two nations – or perhaps because of them.

Most states resolve conflicts of interest with other states through diplomacy. Thus, the presence of a conflict of interest cannot by itself explain the onset of war. When we see the onset of an MID or a war, there must be, in addition to an immediate conflict of interest, the operation of one or more underlying or fundamental causes of war. What are those underlying or fundamental causes? It is to that question that we now direct our attention.

Photo 6.3 Strategically Important Territory: Kaliningrad
Although separated from Russia and wedged between Lithuania and Poland, Kaliningrad is Russian territory and serves as the base for the Russian Baltic fleet.

Source: Knut Müller/ullstein bild via Getty Images.

6.2 DIFFERING PERSPECTIVES

Conflict of Interest over Territory: Taiwan, China, and the Risk of Military Conflict in East Asia

Perspective of the People's Republic of China (PRC), 1993

From People's Republic of China, 'White Paper on Taiwan, "The Taiwan Question and Reunification of China," ' August 31, 1993:

> There is only one China in the world, Taiwan is an inalienable part of China, and the seat of China's central government is in Beijing…. Peaceful unification is a set policy of the Chinese Government. However, any sovereign state is entitled to use any means it deems necessary, including military ones, to uphold its sovereignty and territorial integrity. The Chinese Government is under no obligation to undertake any commitment to any foreign power or people intending to split China as to what means it might use to handle its own domestic affairs.

Perspective of the Republic of China (ROC), 2002

Statement by Taiwan's President Chen Shui-bian, Opening Address to the 29th Annual Meeting of the World Federation of Taiwanese Associations (in Tokyo, Japan) via live video link:

> Taiwan is our country, and our country cannot be bullied, diminished, marginalized, or downgraded as a local entity. Taiwan does not belong to someone else, nor is it someone else's local government or province…. China's so-called 'one China principle' or 'one country, two systems' would change Taiwan's status quo. We cannot accept this, because whether Taiwan's future or status quo should be changed cannot be decided for us by any one country, any one government, any one political party, or any one person. Only the 23 million great people of Taiwan have the right to decide Taiwan's future, fate, and status.

Source: Kan (2007): 50–1, 72.

Levels of Analysis *International Military Conflict*	
Individual	International
Individuals are the main victims in war, either as combatants or as civilians.	Interstate wars involve two or more states in intensely violent military conflict; MIDs also take place between states; and extra-state wars involve states and non-state actors.

UNDERLYING CAUSES OF WAR: THE INDIVIDUAL LEVEL OF ANALYSIS

Individuals must be at the heart of the study of the causes of war, for leaders and other policy makers are the actors who ultimately make the decision for or against war. In this section we examine important examples of scholarship that emphasize the role of leaders (and their policy subordinates) in causing wars.

This scholarship is important in terms of our theoretical understanding of international relations. Realist international theory, which we examined in Chapter 3, assumes that states are rational and unitary actors. That is, realist theory works with the assumption that when we analyze international affairs we need not consider the preferences, beliefs, and decision-making procedures of individual leaders and their policy officials. Instead, realist theory works with the assumption that states are unitary actors, that is, they act as if they were integrated, coherent entities. Government leaders may be assumed to react more to their international circumstances than to their personal characteristics. In addition, realist theory assumes states (including their leaders) are rational: they perceive international circumstances correctly and act after a full and careful search for and assessment of policy options. Those states that do not do so suffer costs and adjust, or make so many mistakes, and suffer so many costs, that they are ultimately selected out of the international system.

In this section we examine different lines of scholarship on the impact made by individual leaders and their policy officials on the probability of war. These lines of scholarship differ among themselves, but they are united by a rejection of the realist view that states are rational unitary actors. Instead, they put forward arguments that emphasize that to understand the sources of war we need to understand how state leaders may find it difficult, if not impossible, to act in accord with perfect rationality as assumed in realist theory. Then, in the next major section, we will see in the scholarship on domestic institutions how the assumption of states as unitary actors is also highly questioned in the field of international relations.

Misperception, Stress, and 'Motivated Biases'

A national leader may go to war because of misperceptions: that is, he or she may perceive something about the world that is factually incorrect (Jervis 1988; Leng 2004). As we noted in the previous section, US leaders thought Saddam Hussein had a threatening nuclear program, but he did not; at least some US leaders thought a US occupation of Iraq would be easy to accomplish, and it was not. Under what circumstances are leaders more likely to succumb to misperceptions in a way that propels their countries toward war?

One possibility is stress. Scholars have suggested that when national leaders and their subordinates find themselves in a diplomatic crisis and perceive that the risk of war is present and growing, they are likely to experience severe physical and emotional stress. That stress could cause them to make mistakes in how they perceive their own policy options and those of their adversaries. These stress-induced misperceptions and mistakes, in turn, could increase the risk that the crisis might escalate to war.

Political scientist Ole Holsti (1972) has produced the classic work on the possible link between stress, impaired decision-making, and the decision for war. Holsti argues that, during the diplomatic crisis of July–August 1914 that led to the outbreak of World War I, discussed in Chapter 2, a dramatic upsurge in communications between the United Kingdom, France, Germany, and Russia in a short period of time appears to have contributed to rising stress among the leaders of those countries. That stress led the leaders to believe that time was working against them and their options in the crisis were decreasing in number, while the policy options of their adversaries were still wide open. Each leader began to say that it was up to the adversary to resolve the crisis before war engulfed Europe. As a result of this stress-induced tendency to perceive that others had more options, the main European leaders all inferred that it was not their responsibility, but that of others, to take decisive steps to stop the crisis that was moving toward war. Since none acted, the crisis spiraled out of control.

Stress may not be the only source of misperceptions. Cognitive psychologists have also identified a tendency for individuals to have 'motivated biases.' A motivated bias is any belief or attitude that a person holds because it advances or protects some interest, desire, or preference. Such motivated biases can impair the capacity of a decision maker to revise his or her beliefs in the face of new information. For example, one study has found that, during a crisis between Germany and the UK over Morocco in 1906, those German decision makers who had initially sought a confrontation with the UK were more reluctant to change course as the crisis began to take a turn against Germany than were German decision makers who had not made a commitment to the initial course of action leading to the crisis (Kaufman 1994). Motivated biases may account for the difference in views about how many US forces would be needed for Iraq in 2003, a matter we highlighted in the introduction to this chapter. Deputy Secretary Wolfowitz had been the main early proponent for the invasion, and so might not have wanted to anticipate how hard the invasion would be; General Shinseki appears to have played a less central role in deciding to attack Iraq, and therefore might have been more dispassionate in estimating what it would take to stabilize the country.

Social Psychology of Small Groups: Groupthink

Groupthink
Psychological need on the part of individuals to be accepted by colleagues that can cause national leaders and advisors to make serious errors during a foreign policy crisis.

The capacity of leaders and officials to process information and make sound judgments in the midst of a crisis might be impaired not just because of stress, but also as a result of psychological needs that those leaders and officials bring to their jobs. The **groupthink** thesis (Janis 1982) suggests that a psychological need on the part of individuals to be accepted and liked by their work colleagues can lead national leaders and especially their advisors to make serious errors of analysis and judgment in the midst of a foreign policy crisis. For example, in April 1961, the new US president, John F. Kennedy, decided to press ahead with a Central Intelligence Agency (CIA) plan that had been developed in the last years of the Eisenhower administration to overthrow Cuba's pro-Soviet regime under Fidel Castro. The operation involved transporting about 1,500 anti-Castro rebels to beaches in Cuba called the Bay of Pigs, who were supposed to instigate a larger uprising by Cubans against their government. Cuban military forces quickly surrounded and attacked the anti-Castro force; Kennedy ceased support for the rebels, who were soon killed or captured; and Castro's victory fortified his grip over Cuba.

Several senior advisors to President Kennedy had doubts about the Bay of Pigs operation but failed to express them. From the groupthink perspective, this silence was because the doubters liked belonging to an elite group of advisors, and since most of those advisors *seemed* to support the operation, the doubters stayed quiet rather than jeopardize their positions in the group. Arthur Schlesinger, one of the doubters, recounted later that he did not want to appear soft while the other members of Kennedy's new team were expressing a strong 'we can do it' attitude.

The groupthink thesis may shed some light on why Kennedy's advisors failed to give the President their full assessment of the prospects for success of the Bay of Pigs operation. However, constructivist IR theory and feminist IR theory might suggest that the groupthink thesis raises at least as many questions as it answers. We take up this engagement of the groupthink thesis by those two perspectives in Box 6.3.

One study (Kramer 1998) has suggested that the Bay of Pigs failure occurred not because of groupthink but because President Kennedy made the political calculation that if he canceled an operation that President Eisenhower had already approved, and this became known, Kennedy would suffer a serious loss of confidence both at home and abroad. On the other hand, and in seeming support of the groupthink thesis, a recent US Senate Intelligence Committee report invoked the groupthink thesis to explain how, in the lead-up to the Iraq war of 2003, the CIA overrated the status of Iraq's nuclear, biological, and chemical weapons programs. Commentaries on the Senate report emphasize that CIA analysts likely made errors in their assessments because they knew that national decision makers wanted to be told that Iraq had large-scale programs directed toward weapons of mass destruction (Phythian 2006).

6.3   DIFFERING THEORETICAL APPROACHES

Constructivist and Feminist Interpretations of Groupthink and the Bay of Pigs

Background

President John F. Kennedy approved in April 1961 a CIA-backed invasion of Cuba by a force of Cuban exiles, an operation that ended in failure.

Groupthink Explanation

Prior to the final go-ahead, advisors to President Kennedy who otherwise harbored doubts about the chances of success of the operation remained silent because they worried that if they expressed their doubts they would lose the respect and esteem of colleagues and the President. The result was that the advisors, by staying silent, helped propel Kennedy and the United States into a serious military debacle.

Constructivism

For a constructivist scholar, the groupthink argument raises but fails to resolve a question about the dynamics of groupthink. The constructivist would ask: why did Kennedy's advisors believe that expressing doubts would lead to a loss of esteem with their colleagues and access to the President? A constructivist would suggest that the foundation for that fear was a network of shared understandings among the advisors and between them and the President. They all shared the view that Castro presented a serious threat to the United States, and that covert operations like the Bay of Pigs presented at least some prospect of success. The advisors knew that colleagues and the President had these ideas and, knowing that, they feared that voicing doubts meant revolting against the group, which in turn would trigger exclusion. Hence, a constructivist would say that to understand how groupthink operated and contributed to the Bay of Pigs disaster, it is necessary to understand that the advisors and the President shared common understandings, namely, about the character of threats facing the United States and the prospects for success of a military response to those threats.

Feminism

A feminist IR scholar might criticize the constructionist viewpoint on the same grounds that a constructivist criticizes the groupthink thesis; namely, that the constructivist argument is helpful but insufficient, for it raises but fails to answer several key questions. In particular, why did Kennedy's advisors believe that Castro was a threat to the United States, why did they believe that a covert military operation would have any prospect of success, and perhaps most importantly, why did they each feel so strongly that they could not risk losing the comradeship of their colleagues and access to the President as a result of expressing doubts about the whole enterprise? A feminist IR scholar would suggest that gender might be a part of the story, for not only was Kennedy a male, but so too was each one of his advisors on the Bay of Pigs. Perhaps Kennedy and his advisors, by virtue of how they were socialized as males, and perhaps because of their male-based psychological make-up, were more inclined than was objectively true to see an independent and non-pliable Castro as a fundamental threat to them and the United States, and to believe that it was entirely appropriate and rational to think of using violence to deal with the problem of Castro. Most crucially, the feminist IR scholar might suggest, it could be the case that men have an especially high need for approval from other men, and a particularly great desire for proximity to power. Thus, Kennedy's advisors might have been prone to think that violence was the answer to Castro, and may have been fearful that expressing doubts about that answer would lead to their expulsion from the group. Those male advisors were essentially biased by their gender both to make a recommendation to use violence and paralyzed in expressing doubts about that approach to the Castro challenge.

Personality Trait of Leaders: Over-Optimism

As can be observed in the comments by US Vice President Dick Cheney in the days in 2003 just before the United States invaded Iraq (see Box 6.4), leaders have often believed – falsely as it turns out – that if war were to occur their side would win a quick and easy victory, and thus be more willing to fight. One scholar has gone so far as to suggest that a crucial clue to understanding the causes of war is the 'optimism with which most wars were commenced by nations' leaders' (Blainey 1988: 35).

6.4 MAKING CONNECTIONS
Aspiration versus Reality

Pre-Conflict Aspirations of Leaders and the Realities of War

The United States Invades Iraq, March 2003

Aspiration

On March 16, 2003, three days before President George Bush announced that the United States would invade Iraq, Vice President Dick Cheney predicted that 'I think things have gotten so bad inside Iraq, from the standpoint of the Iraqi people, my belief is we will, in fact, be greeted as liberators.' When asked if he thought Americans were ready for a 'long, costly and bloody battle,' the Vice President replied that 'Well, I don't think it's likely to unfold that way. . . . [the Iraqi people] want to get rid of Saddam Hussein, and they will welcome as liberators the United States when we come to do that.'

Reality

The United States readily defeated Iraqi regular military forces. However, an insurgency soon took hold and required several years to contain and entailed the loss of more than 4,000 US military personnel, including 3,500 combat deaths. It was not until December 2009, more than six years after the war had begun, that the United States did not sustain a combat fatality during a month. US forces were unable to withdraw from the country until 2011.

Sources: NBC (2003); GlobalSecurity.org (undated).

Scholars have identified at least three reasons why leaders may be overly optimistic in estimating what they can achieve with military force. First, individuals in general may be prone to **positive illusions** – what we think we can accomplish is often greater than what we would expect to achieve if we had a truly accurate picture of our capabilities (Johnson 2004). Individuals may be prone toward positive illusions because they inspire confidence and confidence impels us to strive harder than we otherwise would. National leaders may be particularly prone toward positive illusions. Optimism and a 'can-do' attitude are among the characteristics that cause an individual to attract and instill confidence in others, and thus they are an attribute of successful leadership. The characteristics that make a person attractive and effective as a leader, in fact the very characteristics that helped that person ascend to power in the first place, might also make that person prone toward overestimating what can be achieved in a foreign crisis through different policy instruments, including the use of military force.

> **Positive illusions**
> The idea that what we think we can accomplish is often greater than what we would expect to achieve if we had a truly accurate picture of our capabilities.

Second, it is possible that sudden increases in a country's military power may cause at least some of its leaders and policy makers to become more belligerent. For example, Pakistan's successful testing of a nuclear weapon in May 1998 may have contributed to its decision to use force against India later that year. A scholar of nuclear proliferation, Scott Sagan (Sagan, Waltz, and Betts 2007: 139), notes that:

> When Pakistan acquired nuclear weapons there were many inside its military who said, 'This is our chance to do something about Kashmir,' so they misled then-Prime Minister Nawaz Sharif into approving an operation which sent Pakistani soldiers disguised as Mujahedeen guerillas to conduct low-level military actions in India-controlled Kashmir near the town of Kargil in the winter of 1998.

This infiltration in turn sparked a war between Pakistan and India, also in possession of nuclear weapons, between May and July 1999. Hence, the Pakistani military may have been emboldened by its acquisition of nuclear weapons, and this may have contributed to Pakistani aggression against India.

Feminist international theory suggests that men and women might differ systematically in the way they view and approach international relations. One specific way in which this might occur is through gender's role in the generation of positive illusions (Johnson *et al.* 2006; McDermott *et al.* 2009; Rosen 2005). As you will recall from Chapter 3, Dominic Johnson and his co-authors conducted a study on the confidence of individuals prior to playing a computer-based conflict simulation game that included different ways of resolving disputes with other players, including the launching of 'wars.' Among the findings the study revealed were (a) prior to playing the game, males in the study were much more likely than females to predict that they would achieve above-average scores; (b) individuals who were overconfident before the game started were substantially more likely to launch wars as a way of trying to win the game; and (c) males who were especially confident prior to the game were especially likely to launch wars. From these findings, the research team concluded that males may have a propensity toward overconfidence and this overconfidence may have led males to tend to launch wars to win the game. The research team could not identify what it might be about males that seemed to link them to overconfidence and then to the tendency to launch wars, and this question demands future research. However, the study does point to the possibility that there may be connections between gender, overconfidence, and decisions for war.

In sum, and in strong contention with the realist view that individual characteristics can be put aside in the analysis of war, scholars have found that a range of individual-level factors – misperceptions, groupthink, and positive illusions – may contribute to the risk of war between states.

UNDERLYING CAUSES OF WAR: THE STATE LEVEL OF ANALYSIS

Realist theory suggests that we can obtain good insights into international affairs by assuming that states act as unitary actors. That is, we may assume that state leaders act in the foreign domain more in reaction to circumstances in that domain, and not so much if at all in response to domestic institutions or conditions. Many scholars challenge this realist approach to international analysis. They suggest that domestic institutions and policy processes within countries shape the way leaders deal with international problems and, apart from and in addition to the impact of individual-level factors, might contribute to decisions by leaders to go to war. As we will see below, these scholars focus on a variety of domestic economic, political, and policy-making features of countries that may influence the risk of war.

Domestic Economic Systems and War

Some scholars, drawing often from the Marxist tradition that we described in Chapter 3, have suggested that the economic organization of a country, and whether the country has a capitalist or socialist economy, may determine whether that country is more or less inclined to use military force to resolve foreign conflicts of interest. As we saw in Chapter 3, in a capitalist economic system (or market-based economy) consumers, enterprises, and workers interact in relatively unregulated markets. This interaction determines which goods and services a country produces and consumes, how much workers are paid, and how much money is used for consumption as opposed to saving and investment. In contrast, in a socialist economic system the government plays a central role in the organization and coordination both of the supply of the factors of production, such as the number of workers in a particular industry, and the quantity of goods and services that are produced in that industry.

As noted in Chapter 1, Russian Bolshevik leader Vladimir Lenin suggested that the main cause of World War I was the fact that the European states had capitalist economies. He argued that these capitalist countries necessarily underpaid their workers and, consequently facing insufficient demand at home, they competed for colonies abroad and thus ultimately came to war against one another. More recent work in international relations (Rosecrance 1999; Gartzke 2007) suggests that, in fact, there exists what Gartzke calls a 'capitalist peace,' that is, capitalist countries are particularly likely to remain at peace with one another. Such countries avoid conflict with each other because they want relatively open trade and a stable international monetary system, and territorial issues among them have ceased to matter because they mutually recognize that they can obtain economic prosperity much more readily through trade and financial integration than through conquest of each other or other countries.

Domestic Political Institutions and Governmental Processes

The most important challenge to the realist view about the immateriality of domestic factors in world politics is situated firmly in the liberal tradition: it is the democratic peace thesis, that is, democracies almost never fight each other. As we discussed in Chapter 3, scholars have suggested that two sets of causes account for the democratic peace: the first relates to institutional constraints (Russett 1993); the second to normative constraints (Owen 1994). We now examine in more detail how these two causal processes may produce the democratic peace.

Institutional constraints are the constitutional or customary checks within a country that impede, slow, or limit the capacity of a leader unilaterally to undertake some action. Citizens of democratic states, knowing they and their children will pay most of the costs of war, use their political influence – and especially their right to elect leaders – to constrain leaders from going to war except in the direst of circumstances. By contrast, authoritarian leaders can use coercion to shift the costs of war onto the general public rather than their immediate supporters: we see this, for example, in Italian dictator Benito Mussolini's ability to send conscripts to fight in Africa and Russia during World War II rather than fascist party members. Indeed, authoritarian leaders like Mussolini may positively embrace war as a way of seeking power and glory for themselves, and to divert the attention of citizens from domestic problems (Chiozza and Goemans 2011). Thus, authoritarian leaders may have a greater motive and ability to start wars than is true of democratic leaders, although Box 6.5 suggests a possible qualification to this argument.

Normative constraints are the beliefs, values, and attitudes that inform and shape the behavior of a leader. The normative constraints on democratic leaders might give democracies time and political space to solve their problems with each other. The kind of person who is likely to rise to power in a democratic state must demonstrate that she or he values compromise over total victory, peaceful change over violence, and the rule of law over the use of force to solve disputes. Exactly the opposite characteristics are likely to propel a person to the top leadership position in an authoritarian state. Authoritarian leaders often gain and maintain power using violence. Both kinds of leaders are likely to bring their very different orientations to political life to foreign policy interactions. If that is so, then leaders of democratic states will likely find it much easier to amicably resolve any conflicts of interests with leaders of other democratic states than they would with leaders of autocratic countries. Moreover, leaders of autocratic states would have grave difficulties in reaching peaceful accords with each other if they faced serious conflicts of interests.

Democratic institutions and norms may be doing more than maintaining the democratic peace. They may also be serving as brakes on the possible risk that military conflict abroad might undermine those democratic institutions. In January 1961, Dwight D. Eisenhower, in his farewell address as President, warned that a **military-industrial complex**, a growing US military bureaucracy together with a network of large American defense-related firms, was acquiring too much influence over US national security policy. Eisenhower (1961) also warned that 'In the councils of government, we must guard against the acquisition of unwarranted influence, whether sought or unsought, by the military industrial complex. The potential for the disastrous rise of misplaced power exists and will persist ... We must never let the weight of this combination endanger our liberties or democratic processes.' Sociologist Harold Lasswell (1941) had issued a similar warning when he suggested that there might be emerging at that time what he termed the '**garrison state**,' that is, highly militarized countries in which governments controlled economic, social, and

Institutional constraints
The constitutional or customary checks within a country that impede, slow, or limit the capacity of a leader unilaterally to undertake some action.

Normative constraints
The beliefs, values, and attitudes that inform and shape the behavior of a leader.

Military-industrial complex
A large military bureaucracy and a powerful network of defense firms, united to exercise influence over national security policy (generally applied to the United States).

Garrison state
A highly militarized state in which the government controls economic, social, and political life in order to maximize military power.

6.5   RESEARCH INSIGHT

Beyond the Democratic Peace Thesis: Some Authoritarian States May Be as Peaceful as Democracies

The Problem

Since the pathfinding work of Michael Doyle (1983a, 1983b), scholars in international relations have focused on how democratic and non-democratic states may differ in their propensity to launch military conflicts with other states. The main finding of the resulting work is that democracies are less likely to start military trouble against one another than are authoritarian states either against other authoritarian countries or against democracies. Yet, at least some non-democracies, such as Mexico prior to 1997, studiously avoid becoming embroiled in military disputes. Why, in spite of the seeming absence of domestic constraints, do some authoritarian states appear to avoid military fights with other countries?

The Research Insight

Weeks (2012), building on the work of Geddes (2003) and Slater (2003), has suggested that authoritarian regimes can be differentiated on the basis of two dimensions: the first concerns whether the relevant authoritarian leader is constrained or unconstrained in their personal rule, and the second focuses on whether the regimes are led by civilians or the military. Using these two dimensions Weeks identifies four distinct kinds of authoritarian states: civilian-based party-machines (today's China), bosses (Cuba under Castro), juntas (Nigeria for a part of its post-World War II history), and strongmen (Egypt under Nasser). She then argues that, compared to bosses, strongmen, and juntas, leaders in authoritarian party-machines are relatively accountable to an audience of civilian supporters, and those supporters are as vulnerable to the costs of war and thus are as unenthusiastic about starting military conflicts as are civilians in democracies. She then undertakes a statistical test of the initiation by states of high-intensity MIDs (that is, those that resulted in combat fatalities) during the years between 1946 and 1999. Not only does she find that authoritarian states that are ruled by civilian party-machines are less likely to initiate such MIDs than are states with bosses, juntas, and strongmen, but she also finds that party-machines are no more likely to initiate high-intensity MIDs than are democracies. This raises the possibility that we might have peace between countries even when they are not all democracies. From a policy viewpoint there is an equally interesting inference: perhaps China can have peaceful relations with its neighbors and with the United States if, and perhaps even because, it retains an authoritarian civilian party-machine form of government.

political life to maximize military power. Yet, the US system of political checks and balances, together with a widespread skepticism about government, have interacted to ensure that the United States has retained its republican character and has not become a garrison state working at the behest of a military-industrial complex (Friedberg 2000).

The democratic peace thesis is persuasive. However, we should keep in mind three points of caution. First, democracies rarely go to war with each other, but they often become involved in militarized conflicts with non-democratic states. Second, while there is strong empirical support for the democratic peace, there is yet no consensus on why we observe it. Third, almost all of the scholarly work on the democratic peace to date has drawn a sharp contrast between democratic and non-democratic states, with the former cast as peaceful among each other and the latter as uniformly disposed to starting military conflicts with other countries. However, as we discussed in Box 6.5, recent scholarship suggests that authoritarian regimes of at least one type, namely, civilian-based party regimes, may be as disinclined to start military conflicts with other countries as are democracies.

Finally, even in democracies, there are some occasions when policy subordinates may misinterpret – possibly even purposely – the directives of leaders and essentially begin to pursue something approaching their own foreign policies. During a political-diplomatic crisis such policy incoherence can contribute to the risk of war, as can be observed in the example in Box 6.6.

6.6 MAKING CONNECTIONS
Theory and Practice

Institutional Politics and War: The US Oil Embargo against Japan, 1941

Theory: The Unitary-Actor Assumption in Realist International Theory

Realist international theory assumes that states are unitary actors. That is, having established a national strategy, top state leaders can then execute it in the manner that reflects their preferences and ideas by effective orchestration and control of the actions of various parts of the national government. According to this assumption, state leaders have a high capacity to monitor and control subordinate officials.

Practice: The US Oil Embargo against Japan, 1941

In response to Japan's invasion of French Indochina (today's Vietnam, Cambodia, and Laos), President Franklin Delano Roosevelt on July 24, 1941 ordered a freeze on Japanese financial assets in the United States. When Roosevelt announced the freeze, he promised that Japan could apply to the US government for licenses to import oil, that such licenses would be issued, and that funds held by Japanese importers in the United States would be released so the Japanese could pay for licensed oil sales. Assistant Secretary of State Dean Acheson (who later, under President Harry Truman, served as Secretary of State), the official responsible for releasing Japanese funds, refused to do so in the first weeks of August, while Roosevelt was out of the country. When Roosevelt returned at the end of August and learned of Acheson's refusal to release the funds, the President apparently decided he could not reverse Acheson's actions. Thus, a financial sanction that Roosevelt wanted to exclude oil came to include oil, as Acheson had wanted. The oil embargo contributed to the Japanese decision to attack Pearl Harbor in an ill-conceived effort to achieve a quick victory against the United States.

Acheson later claimed that even though Roosevelt had said he wanted the oil shipments to go through, Acheson knew that what Roosevelt really wanted and what the US national interest really required was a total embargo of oil shipments to Japan. Acheson suggested that '[If] President Roosevelt lacked decisiveness in the degree his successor [President Truman] possessed it, he had a sense of direction in which he constantly advanced. It seemed to those in government [that is, Acheson] that our most useful function was to increase in so far as we could the rate of that advance.'

Source: Sagan (1994): 70.

Nationalism and War

Patriotism
Absolute value an
individual assigns to that
person's state, including
its history, culture,
and political system,
independent of how that
person feels about other
states.

Nationalism
Relative value that an
individual assigns to that
person's state; a person
is nationalistic if that
person thinks his or her
country is superior to
other countries.

Patriotism is the *absolute* value an individual assigns to that person's state, including its history, culture, and political system, independent of how that person feels about other states and their histories, cultures, and political systems. It is quite possible that a Canadian may have patriotic sentiments while also being very fond of France. In contrast, **nationalism** is the *relative* value that an individual assigns to that person's state, that is, how much that person values his or her country relative to other countries (Machida 2017: 89). We say a person is nationalistic if that person not only loves his or her country but thinks it is superior to other countries.

Nationalism and patriotism are attitudes possessed by an individual. However, either sentiment may be shared by many individuals who are either members of the elite or the general public of a society, and such sentiments might motivate their efforts to shape the foreign policy of their country. We may say, then, that relative levels of patriotism and nationalism are country-level characteristics of different states at a given point in time.

Patriotism and nationalism may have very different effects on the prospects for war between states. For example, in a recent survey experiment of the conditions under which a sample of Japanese respondents expressed support or not for the use of military force by Japan against China to preserve Japan's possession of what in Japan are called the Senkaku Islands (known in China as the Diaoyu Islands), possession by respondents of patriotic sentiments had no discernible effect on the likelihood that the respondents would support the use of force on behalf of the islands, but possession of nationalistic sentiments was highly associated with expression of support for the use of force to defend the islands (Machida 2017).

Nationalism has been found to be generally associated with a higher propensity on the part of states to launch wars against other states (Schrock-Jacobson 2012). Moreover, different forms of nationalism may vary in their impact on the propensity of states to be warlike. For example, war initiation appears to be more closely associated with a form of nationalism that relies on claims to a common ethnic, cultural, or historical background than is true of a type of nationalism that is defined in terms of protecting a revolutionary regime (Schrock-Jacobson 2012; also see Snyder 2000). This is a potentially alarming finding, for in China, Russia, and the United States we can observe today elements of the governing elites seeking to employ at home precisely the kind of ethno-cultural nationalistic rhetoric that may be associated with more bellicose behavior abroad.

It should be noted that nationalistic sentiments within a country might in particular circumstances help a state bring about a peaceful (albeit one-sided) resolution to a conflict of interest with other states. Between 1985 and 2012, for example, the Chinese Government permitted and controlled nationalistic public protests in China during disputes with the United States as a way of extracting concessions from the latter (Weiss 2013). On the other hand, nationalism might constrain the capacity of its government to find a diplomatic solution to a crisis. For example, very late in the crisis of 1914 German leaders appear to have considered but retreated from a peaceful solution because they feared a hostile reaction from nationalistic segments of German middle-class society – segments whose nationalistic sentiments the German government had itself helped stoked (Snyder 1991: 66–111).

In sum, economic and political systems of countries, as well as the degree to which domestic societies are characterized or not by high levels of nationalism, play a large role in inclining those countries toward peace or war with each other in the context of a serious conflict of interest.

Societal Gender Relations and International Conflict

We will see below that many scholars suggest that the fact that states are co-located in a political environment without a centralized, effective international government – that is, they find themselves in an anarchical political structure – is a structural condition that itself may push states toward war, or at least fail to stop them from resorting to war. However, feminist international theory argues that unequal gender relations within nations, and widespread violence toward women in many societies, produces a societal structural condition, in the sense that gender problems are persistent and deeply embedded within societies, that itself can also promote war (Tickner 1988; Sjoberg 2012).

Recent studies have in fact identified significant empirical associations between the status of women within different societies of different states and the likelihood of those states becoming embroiled in military conflicts with other countries. For example, one study (Caprioli and Boyer 2001) finds that states with higher levels of societal gender equality tend to use less military violence in military crises than do those states with lower levels of gender equality. More recently, two related teams of scholars have found that societies in which there is greater domestic insecurity for and violence against women are also more likely to launch violent conflicts with other countries (Hudson *et al.* 2008/2009; Hudson *et al.* 2014). This line of inquiry suggests that progress toward gender equality and security within the societies of nations may translate into less violence by states in the international system.

Levels of Analysis *The State as the Cause of War*

 State

Democratic states may be less likely to fight each other than other kinds of pairings of countries (mutually non-democratic or mixed) because they possess a wider and more potent range of institutional and normative constraints on the use of force.

Domestic economic conditions within countries may increase their bellicosity in world affairs.

Nationalism may increase the risk that the country will be belligerent toward others.

In all states, intra-governmental policy dynamics, including overly aggressive officials, can increase the risk of war.

Gender relations within a state's society may influence the probability that that state will engage in violence internationally.

UNDERLYING CAUSES OF WAR: THE INTERNATIONAL LEVEL OF ANALYSIS

For realists, international anarchy may act as a permissive cause of war – it may enable factors situated at other levels of analysis to induce states to be inclined toward war. Scholars who often but not always subscribe fully to realist theory also emphasize that anarchy may serve as an active cause of war, that is, it might positively propel states to do things that increase the risk of war between them.

Anarchy as a Permissive Condition for War

If international anarchy always inclined states to fight when they found themselves in diplomatic crises, then every time states encounter such a crisis we should also see those states go to war. As we have seen in this chapter, most diplomatic crises do not end in war. Hence, anarchy by itself cannot cause states to go to war with each other.

International anarchy might instead give free rein to individual-level and state-level factors that push states toward war (Waltz 1959). The United Nations is available to offer a helpful framework for diplomatic resolutions of disputes, and in doing so it has probably helped states resolve disagreements before they escalated to war (see Chapter 5). However, the UN cannot itself provide protection to a state if it is attacked, or penalize a state that turns to violence. Because then there is no reliable international government, the risk of war weighs on state leaders in the midst of a crisis. If those leaders experience stress or groupthink or overconfidence and begin to make errors, no outside agency exists that can, with a high level of reliability, stop them from going over the brink to war.

Anarchy as a Propellant of International Conflict

Private information problem
Conflict-exacerbating tendency of states to overstate their resolve and capabilities during a crisis because no international authority forces them to reveal truthful information.

International anarchy may not just allow other factors to move states toward conflict, it may itself positively and independently propel states to initiate military crises and even war (Fearon 1995). Anarchy may, in the first place, generate what international relations scholars call the **problem of private information**. Because there is no international authority to force states to reveal their true preferences, intentions, and capabilities, they have the capacity and thus the incentive to overstate their resolve and capabilities during a diplomatic or military crisis. This tendency toward bluff could make a diplomatic resolution more difficult to attain and war more likely to occur by each side pressing too hard with threats and counter-threats. For example, after he was soundly defeated in the first Iraq war of 1991, Saddam Hussein sought to maintain power at home and security abroad by *seeming* to have a nuclear weapons program and taking actions that seemed to hide such activities from Western intelligence agencies and the International Atomic Energy Agency (IAEA). Hussein had ceased serious efforts to develop a nuclear military capability sometime during the 1990s, but US, British, and other intelligence services were convinced that he was going for the bomb. Toward the end of the crisis of 2002–03 that culminated in the second Iraq war, Hussein's government sought to signal that Iraq really had no nuclear weapons program, but by then it was too late. US and British leaders were convinced that Hussein was lying, and the only way to eliminate Iraq's nuclear threat was to invade and destroy his regime.

Commitment problem
A state's fear that an agreement with an adversary that is reached today will be violated at some point in the future when that adversary is stronger.

Second, anarchy may produce what is often called the **commitment problem**. Given the absence of an international government, states must fear that any diplomatic agreement they reach with an adversary to stave off a war might be violated at some point in the future when that adversary is in a position to be more deadly and demanding. In those circumstances, one or both sides may decide that it may be better to fight today rather than be cheated upon and attacked at a moment of weakness in the future. For example, as noted above, it is quite likely that US and allied leaders in 2002 and early 2003 simply ceased to believe that Saddam would keep his word if he signed an agreement to make no future demands on Kuwait and to refrain from reconstituting his nuclear program. Without that trust, or a capacity to ensure compliance, it seemed a safer path for the US and allied leaders to invade and remove Saddam from power once and for all.

You will recall from Chapter 5 our discussion of the Prisoner's Dilemma and the problem that states are likely to encounter in single-play interactions without strong international law and organizations inducing them to think very much about the future. That appears to have been to a great deal the situation that Iraq and the United States encountered as they faced off against one another in the lead-up to war in 2003. Prior to the outbreak of hostilities, the two sides might have considered making the following deal: Iraq would forego any future nuclear weapons program or aggressive designs on Kuwait or other neighbors, and the United States would agree not to invade the country and to lift economic sanctions that had been in place since the early 1990s. The two sides in this instance would grudgingly have to live with each other, but they would avoid a costly war. This arrangement would correspond to the cooperate–cooperate outcome in the Prisoner's Dilemma. However, the United States would worry that if it lifted sanctions and forswore attacking Iraq, the latter might be tempted to develop nuclear weapons secretly, and after it had those weapons it might become extremely dangerous toward Kuwait and other countries in the Middle East. Iraq on the other hand would worry that if it adhered to the agreement, the United States would find some other pretext at a later date to undermine it: in other words, the United States would renege on the cooperative arrangement aimed at averting war. Hence, for both sides, a war – what would constitute the mutually very costly defect–defect cell in the Prisoner's Dilemma game – is clearly costly but at least it gives each the hope that it can avoid its worst outcome, that is, making a deal but then later being cheated upon by the other. The mutual fear of the United States and Iraq of defection is being driven by the absence of an effective international government to enforce agreements, that is, international anarchy.

In sum, international anarchy may establish a context in which states overstate their claims and resolve, and fear that a deal to avert war today might lead to a situation in the future that is actually worse than commencing a war. In these two ways, international anarchy might propel states with a conflict of interest toward war.

Scholars who view international anarchy as a strong propellant or a permissive condition for war believe that factors from the other levels of analysis may contribute to war, but anarchy is such a strong structural condition that animates international conflict that its effects operate regardless of the operation of factors situated at other levels of analysis. That is, they propose that, regardless of the societal conditions of states or the characteristics of individual leaders, the anarchical context of international relations itself systematically and persistently either fails to prevent wars or positively moves states toward them. Yet, proponents of the democratic peace thesis might ask, do democratic states really react to anarchy the same way as do authoritarian nations? Feminist theorists ask, as we noted above, is it the structural condition of international anarchy that drives state leaders to war, or is it the permeation of societies with masculine attitudes and male leaders that together constitute an alternative structural constant in world affairs that produces an ongoing risk that conflicts of interests between nations are resolved through violence rather than reason (Tickner 1988; Sjoberg 2012)? These are the kinds of questions that continue to make the study of anarchy and war an open-ended and interesting feature of the study of world politics.

Interstate war and other forms of interstate military conflict are persistent and highly dangerous elements of world politics. While there are some promising signs that such conflicts are decreasing in incidence in recent decades, the risk of their occurrence remains distressingly dogged: witness, for example, the recent invasion of Ukraine by Russia and the widespread extra-state wars covering much of Central Asia, the Middle East, Northern Africa, and the Sahel. Such conflicts have immediate causes, such as disputes over policy, political regimes, and especially territory, and they have deep-rooted underlying causes, including the psychology and character of leaders, the domestic institutional characteristics of nations, and the interstate system. War and other forms of military struggle among nations appear to be hard-wired in the human condition, although the variability in such struggles suggests there may be ways to control them. We return to and focus on this possibility in the next chapter, on pathways to peace. Before we pursue that possibility, we must turn to a second widespread form of mass human conflict, those that take place within countries.

INTERNAL WARS AND THEIR CAUSES

The enduring question of this chapter does not limit itself to wars between nations, and students of international relations have good reasons to be interested in internal wars, and especially civil wars. In general, an **internal war** is an instance in which politically organized groups within a country, including most often the national government, become engaged in sustained military operations against one another.

Internal war
Any war within a state, contrasted with war between two or more states.

Internal Wars and Their Impact on International Peace and Security

Internal wars may have important repercussions for international peace and security. An internal war may spread to other countries, it may cause the state experiencing the internal war to be more aggressive toward other states, or it may cause other states to become hostile toward the state experiencing domestic violence.

An internal war in one country can instigate international violence through at least three different pathways. First, an internal war in one country can bring about **contagion**, that is, it can spread to neighboring countries (Buhaug and Gleditsch 2008; Braithwaite 2010). Rebels in one country often find shelter in a neighboring country, and they sometimes begin to fight the government of that country. The Taliban, who originally held power in Afghanistan, moved in large numbers to Pakistan after the US invasion of 2001, and in recent years have been conducting an insurgency against the US and the US-supported government in Kabul while also

Contagion
The spread of an internal war in one country to another, often caused by rebels seeking shelter in a neighboring country and beginning conflict there.

fighting an insurgency aimed at Pakistan's central government. Alternatively, refugee flows from a war-torn country into a neighboring country can lead to instability and the outbreak of violence in the latter country, as occurred in the mid-1990s when refugees from Rwanda's civil war fled to neighboring Zaire and overwhelmed its infrastructure, which in turn contributed to the onset of a civil war in that country. It is also possible that an internal war will draw in foreign fighters, who in turn become a security threat when they return to their home countries: we have witnessed this in the case of French and British nationals who were drawn to Syria after 2011 to fight in that country's civil war on behalf of Islamic State, and upon their return to France and the UK have become active in terrorist operations in those countries.

Second, a state that has experienced an internal war and political change arising from that war may for a time become more aggressive toward other states. Consider, for example, how France, in the wake of its revolution in 1789, and fearful that Austria and Prussia might become the bases for counter-revolutionary forces, declared war on those two countries in 1792. A revolutionary state may do so either out of a fear that other states are hostile to it, or to divert domestic attention from the problems the new government is having in establishing the legitimacy of its rule as well as domestic order and stability (Maoz 1989; Walt 1996; Colgan 2013).

The third pathway by which internal war within a country might lead to international military conflict is that a state experiencing violence at home might attract invasions or other military confrontations from abroad. This could take place in at least two ways. On the one hand, a foreign state may believe that the country experiencing internal war may be vulnerable and easy to defeat militarily. Saddam Hussein appears to have made this calculation when he decided to invade Iran in September 1980, just as Iran was enmeshed in revolutionary change. As it turned out, the war dragged on for eight years and ended in a stalemate that favored Iran.

Another form of international military intervention against a state involved in internal war might arise from outrage by other states about the way domestic violence is taking place within the country. Internal wars often produce social chaos, mass hunger, and a collapse of medical care, and combatants often deliberately kill massive numbers of civilians. Combatants sometimes commit war crimes during these conflicts – mass killings of civilians, using rape as a military strategy, or employing children as soldiers – as has happened in numerous internal wars in recent years in the Balkans (for example, in Bosnia-Herzegovina and Kosovo) and in sub-Saharan Africa (such as in Sierra Leone and the Central African Republic), in Asia (for example, in Sri Lanka), and North Africa (Libya in 2011). As we discussed in Chapter 5, in some of those instances, one or more outside states have reacted to the atrocities by intervening militarily to try to bring the internal strife to an end.

Given their repercussions for international relations, we need to understand internal wars. It is to that task that we now direct attention.

Internal Wars: Types and Trends

There are many types of internal wars. The most prevalent form is **civil war**. A civil war is a sustained clash between forces that are controlled by the national government and forces that are controlled by an organized opposition group within the country. Those opposition groups typically have one of two goals. First, they may seek to overthrow the current regime and seize control of the central government, especially its military and national police. Several 'Arab Spring' revolutions that swept through North Africa and the Middle East in 2011–12 are in this class of civil wars. The Libyan civil war that began in February 2011 was complex in its origins and

Civil war
A sustained clash between forces that are controlled by the national government and forces that are controlled by an organized opposition group within the country.

conduct but was essentially a military struggle on the part of several loosely allied domestic opposition forces, supported by a coalition of outside powers that fought to overthrow Colonel Muammar Gaddafi and his dictatorship. It ended with the defeat of forces loyal to Gaddafi, the fall of the dictatorship, the formation of a transitional government that was recognized by the United Nations in September 2011, and the capture and killing of Gaddafi the following month.

Sometimes the opposition group or coalition does not wish to seize control of the national government, but instead to bring about the secession of a part of a country to form a new state. An example of such a **secessionist civil war** concerns Sudan. Forces in the southern part of Sudan fought two prolonged civil wars (1955–72 and 1983–2005) against the central government in Khartoum, and in 2012 finally achieved independence and became the sovereign state of the Republic of South Sudan. Different opposition groups in Darfur, in the western part of Sudan, have also fought a civil war aimed at secession since 2003, but have not succeeded in breaking away from the central government.

Civil wars constitute about 92 percent of the 334 internal wars that occurred between 1816 and 2007, according to the COW research team. Two other types of internal wars do not involve the central government fighting an opposition group. The first type consists of **inter-communal wars**: they constitute about 5 percent of COW-identified internal wars and take place when members of different religious communities in a country become embroiled in large-scale organized violence. For example, several militias that fought one another during the civil war in Lebanon between 1975 and 1990 were organized along sectarian lines – among others there were several different Shia Muslim, Sunni Muslim, and Maronite Christian fighting forces. Finally, in a few instances – about 3 percent of the total – internal conflicts have consisted of violence between military forces of governmental entities below the national level and nongovernmental entities. For example, in 1967, fighting broke

Secessionist civil war
A civil war in which the rebel group seeks to bring about the breaking away of a part of the territory of a country to form a new, separate state.

Inter-communal war
A war in which members of different religious communities in a country become embroiled in large-scale organized violence.

Photo 6.4 Arab Spring Uprisings, 2011
In the spring of 2011, mass protests and uprisings against authoritarian leaders began in several Arab countries, including in Cairo's Tahrir Square in Egypt.

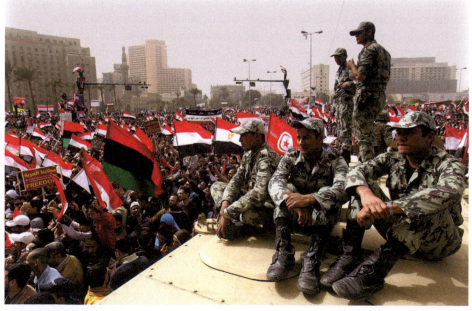

Source: KHALED DESOUKI/AFP/Getty Images.

out in China between Red Guard radicals and regional military forces during the Cultural Revolution that communist leader Mao Zedong sought to instigate against what he thought were increasingly conservative party comrades.

In Figure 6.6 we present the relative incidence of internal wars per 100 country-years that occurred in different periods of time between 1816 and 2007. In developing this figure we employ the same methodology in mapping the incidence of international conflicts, that is, we normalize both for the different number of countries and the different numbers of years in the time periods we examine. In general, internal wars occurred with moderate frequency in the nineteenth century, and became relatively rare during the twentieth century, a trend that appeared to continue at least in the first years of the current century. The end of the Cold War, we can observe in the two bars to the far right of the figure, does not appear to date to have had a large effect on the propensity of states to experience internal wars, as we shall discuss later in this chapter.

We present in Figure 6.7 tentative estimates of trends in the lethality of internal wars. These are rough estimates because good data on battlefield deaths during internal wars is much less systematic than what is available on interstate or extra-state wars. Keeping that note of caution in mind, we are able to observe that at least 6 million combatants were killed in internal wars between 1816 and 2007, the vast majority of whom were killed in the civil wars of the twentieth century. In more recent times, the lethality of internal wars appears to have gone down, both in terms of total killed and killed per war.

Internal wars may be at least as lethal for non-combatants as the various types of international wars. Civilian deaths during internal wars are often due to intentional

Figure 6.6 Incidence of Internal Wars, 1816–2007, and during and after the Cold War
For each designated time period, the bar represents the number of internal wars that commenced per 100 country-years. Over time, internal wars have generally become a relatively rare event in world affairs.

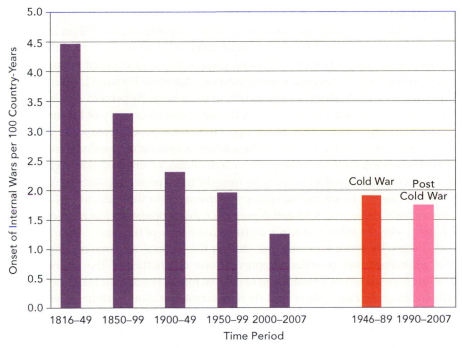

Source: Meredith Reid Sarkees, and Frank Wayman (2010) *Resort to War: 1816–2007* (CQ Press). Data-set available from Correlates of War, Intra-State War Data (v4.0), at http://www.correlatesofwar.org/.

Figure 6.7 Lethality of Internal Wars, 1816–2007, and during and after the Cold War
For each designated time period, the bar represents the average number of battlefield deaths that occurred during the period; the number in parentheses is the total number of internal wars that began during the period.

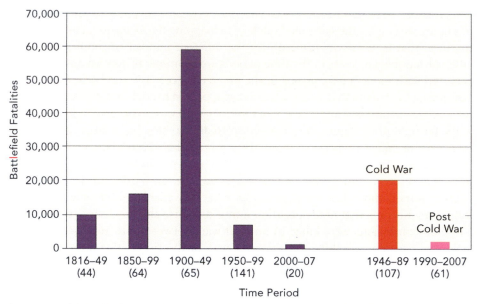

Source: Meredith Reid Sarkees, and Frank Wayman (2010) *Resort to War: 1816–2007* (CQ Press). Data-set available from Correlates of War, Intra-State War Data (v4.0), at http://www.correlatesofwar.org/.

wartime killings by one or more sides involved in the war (Kalyvas and Kocher 2009). For example, a 2004 study identified 115 civil wars during the years between 1945 and 2000, and it found that during 27 of those wars at least one of the warring sides carried out a strategy of mass civilian killings (Valentino, Huth, and Balch-Lindsay 2004).

There have been numerous instances in which civil wars spark civilian killings on an enormous scale. In Cambodia, the Khmer Rouge rebel force overturned the central government in Phnom Penh in 1975, and then began what it called a 'purification' campaign that, by 1979, resulted in the murder of somewhere between 1.5 and 2 million men, women, and children, or something approaching 20 percent of Cambodia's population in 1975. Just 19 years later, in the sub-Saharan country of Rwanda, a civil war began during which government-supported armed groups composed mainly of individuals from one tribal group, the Hutu, killed in a matter of months approximately 800,000 unarmed civilians belonging to individuals of another tribal group, the Tutsi, or other Hutu civilians who were thought to be protecting Tutsi or who were thought in one way or another to oppose the massacre. In that case, as in Cambodia, approximately 20 percent of Rwanda's prewar civilian population was murdered.

Internationalization of civil war
During a civil war, one or more foreign states intervenes and supports one or another of the warring sides with equipment or troops.

Finally, with the aid of Figure 6.8 we turn to the issue of the **internationalization of civil wars**, by which we mean that, during the internal war, one or more foreign states intervened and provided support to one or another of the warring sides, including sometimes the introduction of combat forces, but did not take over the bulk of the fighting. We can make at least three observations about external interventions in internal wars from the data in the figure. First, for reasons that scholars have not yet identified, international interventions do not take place in connection to all civil wars. Second, such interventions are not a new phenomenon: they occurred during the nineteenth and twentieth centuries and have continued in the twenty-first

Photo 6.5 Genocide after the Cambodian Civil War, 1975–79
Photos of the victims of the Khmer Rouge are displayed at the Tuol Sleng Genocide Museum, in Phnom Penh, the capital of Cambodia. The site is a former high school that was used by the Khmer Rouge as a torture and killing center.

Source: iStock.com/Alatom.

century. Third, the frequency with which foreign states intervened in internal wars was much higher during the second half of the twentieth century, and in particular during the Cold War, than in earlier periods, or since the end of the Cold War. Part of the explanation is that the Cold War was conducted through a series of proxy wars consisting of interventions by one or both superpowers, and other allied great powers, in civil wars and other internal military conflicts in the Third World. For example, during the 1970s and much of the 1980s, Cuba and the Soviet Union supported one of the main rebel armies, while China, the United States, and South Africa supported another.

Causes of Internal Wars

Just as the levels-of-analysis framework helps us learn about the causes of interstate war, it is also helpful in exploring what observers have suggested might be the causes of internal and civil wars.

The Individual and Internal War

Many of the factors discussed above that prompt individual national leaders to go to war probably operate on the leaders of factions in internal wars. Beyond that, scholars have suggested that at least two additional individual-level mechanisms may increase the likelihood of internal wars, namely, greed and grievance (Collier, Hoeffler, and Rohner 2009). By **greed** we mean a person's intense desire to possess goods or money, and by grievance we mean a person's belief that he or she is being victimized by or excluded from important institutions in a country. Individuals may believe they are being victimized or excluded for many reasons, including their religion, race, ethnic background, gender, or social class.

Greed
A person's intense desire to possess goods or money. On the individual level of analysis, a primary mechanism that increases the likelihood of internal war.

Figure 6.8 International Interventions in Internal Wars, 1816–2007, and during and after the Cold War

For each designated time period, the bar represents the percentage of internal wars during the time period that witnessed an international intervention. The international interventions and the total number of internal wars are reported in the parenthesis under the time period. For example, as can be seen on the far right of the figure, between 1990 and 2007 there were 61 internal wars and 14 external interventions, producing an estimated international-intervention rate of 23%, depicted in the bar for that period.

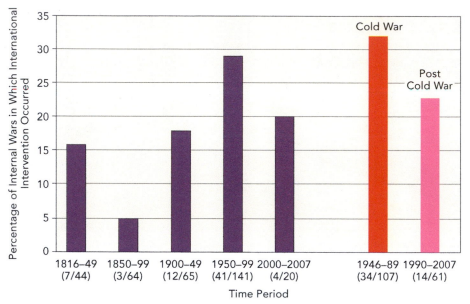

Source: Meredith Reid Sarkees, and Frank Wayman (2010) *Resort to War: 1816–2007* (CQ Press). Data-set available from Correlates of War, Intra-State War Data (v4.0), at http://www.correlatesofwar.org/.

Lootable wealth
Natural resources that can be readily acquired, transported, and sold for cash. In some countries, greed and lootable wealth combine to make internal conflict more likely.

Grievance
A person's belief that he or she is being victimized by or excluded from important institutions in a country; a primary mechanism that increases the likelihood of internal war.

Greed may be a part of what motivates individuals in internal (and international) wars of all sorts, but it may play a particularly large role in countries that possess natural resources that can be readily acquired, transported, and sold for cash. Such resources, sometimes termed **lootable wealth**, may include diamonds, gold, minerals, timber, narcotics, and oil. Countries where lootable wealth has played a role in prompting or prolonging civil wars are concentrated in sub-Saharan Africa, including Angola, Congo, Liberia, and Sierra Leone (Weinstein 2005).

In addition to greed, **grievance** might be a powerful individual-level factor in prompting internal wars. Scholars in recent years have found that ethnicity-based grievances have played a key role in motivating individuals to take up arms in civil wars (Cederman, Wimmer, and Min 2010). Ethnic identity-based grievances were very much a part of the tensions that led to the civil war between the Hutu and the Tutsi in Rwanda, for example. More generally, perhaps 60 ethnicity-based conflicts occurred between 1946 and 2005 and reached the COW standard for a civil war, namely, 1,000 battlefield deaths within 12 months, which suggests that ethnic conflicts made up a substantial portion of all civil wars during the second half of the twentieth century.

Competition over natural resources can interact with ethnic differences and contribute to individual and ultimately group-level grievances and the onset of an internal war. One example of this dynamic can be observed in the secessionist civil war in the Darfur region of Sudan. That civil war, which began in 2003 and was ongoing in 2018, has pitted the central government in Khartoum and local Arab militias called the Janjaweed against two indigenous rebel groups, the Sudanese Liberation Movement/Army (SLM/A), and the Justice and Equality Movement (JEM). The war has been brutal: perhaps 450,000 civilians have been killed and 2.75 million persons displaced from their homes. The United Nations since late 2007 has undertaken a peacekeeping mission in the region, replacing an earlier effort by the African Union, but periodic violence has continued. The United States and other countries have accused the central government in Khartoum of perpetrating genocide in Darfur, and the International Criminal Court (ICC) has issued an international arrest warrant for Sudan's president, Omar Hassan Ahmad Al Bashir, for directing war crimes and crimes against humanity in Darfur.

The continuing civil war in Darfur has many roots, and among them has been the overlay of ethnicity and competition over scarce resources. At the heart of the Darfur war is a dispute between African farmers who wish to settle and cultivate land and Arab semi-nomadic livestock herders who want periodic access to that land. The latter group has been supported by the Khartoum government. Herder–farmer tensions had long been present in Darfur. However, a drought that began roughly in the mid-1980s and was still in effect in the mid-2000s sharpened the competition between farmers and herders over scarce land and water resources, making the settlement of this underlying resource dispute more difficult and turning it into a driver of what has become an interethnic war in that region (Straus 2005).

The State and Internal War

Three characteristics of countries at the state level of analysis may play a role in the outbreak of internal wars, namely, clans and the associated issue of the status of women, the degree of inclusiveness of different elements of society in the control of the state, and the capacity of the state.

First, violence within many countries results from the interaction of clans, that is, extensive family networks. Recent scholarship has found that these clans often produce and depend upon the subordination of women (Hudson, Bowen, and Nielsen 2015). This work suggests further that it is this subordination of women that is a key motor of inter-clan violence, by way of animating such intermediate mechanisms as promoting government corruption and contributing to very fast escalation of inter-clan disputes to ever-increasing levels of violence. Improvements, then, in the status of women in many countries may abate inter-clan competition and thus intranational violence.

Second, governments in ethnically divided societies that favor one ethnic group, and systematically discriminate against other groups, are much more likely to induce the latter to take up some form of resistance, perhaps leading to a secessionist war. The degree of inclusion or exclusion based on ethnicity by a national government is an important state-level contributor to civil peace or civil war. The presence of democratic political institutions does not appear to reduce the likelihood of civil wars, so while inclusiveness is important it appears that there may be several political arrangements whereby that goal can be achieved (Fearon and Laitin 2003; Collier, Hoeffler, and Rohner 2009).

Third, the capacity of the government to resist an armed insurgency has a strong influence on the likelihood that a country will experience some form of internal war (Fearon and Laitin 2003). Failed states, something we discuss in Chapter 12, are prone to civil wars, while on the other hand several statistical studies have shown that wealthy countries are markedly less likely to experience internal wars. Such countries may be characterized by less severe or widespread grievances on the part of individuals within those countries. In addition, a country's wealth creates the basis for the strength of its government. If the society is wealthy, then the government will have a relatively larger pool of tax revenues and a more sophisticated and educated work force. This strong government in turn will be able to reduce the risk that the country will experience a civil war. For example, it will have sophisticated military and police intelligence resources, so it can identify and suppress domestic dissident groups that might have the potential to turn to arms. It is also likely to have built a network of roads, and these roads give government military leaders an advantage in moving troops to trouble spots, overcoming possible terrain advantages that rebels might otherwise enjoy, such as mountainous regions, and suppress early signs of rebellion. A strong government is also better able than a weaker government to conscript fighters to defeat insurgencies before the latter reach a high level of effectiveness.

In sum, characteristics of governments – whether they are inclusive or exclusive, and, perhaps most important, whether they have strong and effective societal-control capabilities – play an important role in the incidence of internal wars.

The International System and Internal War

At least two conditions at the international level may affect the onset of internal wars: interstate wars on the one hand and colonialism and its aftermath on the other. A third factor, the Cold War, did not affect the incidence of internal wars, but it may have affected the way they were fought.

Wars between states can increase the chances of a civil war in one or the other combatant state. Political scientist Theda Skocpol (1974) has shown how the multiple wars that the French kings fought in the eighteenth century, and Russian monarchies fought during the nineteenth and early twentieth centuries, alienated important domestic groups, weakened the regimes, and pushed them toward revolution and civil war. China's defeat by Japan in 1895 caused the Ch'ing dynasty to undertake a number of political and administrative reforms, but those reforms themselves led to a weakening of central governmental authority and paved the way for a period of successive revolutions in China between 1911 and 1949. As noted above, Iran's civil war in 1979 made it a more tempting target for Iraq (the two had been mired in maritime territorial disputes going back to the late 1960s), which launched a war against the new revolutionary regime in 1980.

Since World War II, ex-colonies have been at a high risk of internal war. Colonialism may be a risk factor for internal war for three reasons. First, European great powers drew colonial borders not based on the ethnicity of the peoples in the colonies, but the relative power and degree of competition among the great powers themselves. In sub-Saharan Africa, for example, the countries that therefore emerged from colonialism had highly diverse ethnic populations, with members of the same ethnic group often located in two or more neighboring states. This mismatch between borders and ethnicity in post-colonial Africa may have made domestic stability more difficult to attain and maintain (Englebert, Tarango, and Carter 2002).

In addition, colonial powers in sub-Saharan Africa focused mainly on extracting natural resources, and did little to create institutions, such as courts systems, that would promote long-term economic growth (Acemoglu and Robinson 2012). The countries that emerged from colonialism in that region were hence weak economically, and thus less able to co-opt or defeat anti-regime opposition groups. Third, the colonial powers maintained order through the deployment of their own military and police forces. Once those forces were withdrawn, the newly independent countries had weak armies at their disposal: the door was left open to civil war (Fearon and Laitin 2003: 81).

We can observe in Figure 6.6 that the average annual incidence of internal wars during the Cold War years 1946–89 was roughly the same (2.0 per 100 country-years) as that during the first half of the twentieth century, that is, 1900–49 (2.3 per 100 country-years). Hence, we cannot say that the Cold War brought about an increase in internal wars. At the same time, it may be recalled from the discussion above that the lethality of internal wars has declined in the wake of the Cold War. It is possible, given a recent analysis of the changing character of civil wars after the end of the Cold War, that the end of that conflict has meant internal war combatants – both governments and the opposition – in recent years have been fighting with relatively fewer heavy armaments, since they have lost their Soviet and US suppliers, and as a result they are less able to inflict heavy casualties on each other (Kalyvas and Balcells 2010).

In sum, international factors, particularly interstate wars, colonialism and its legacy, and the end of the Cold War, have all played a role in the onset and character of internal wars in the contemporary era.

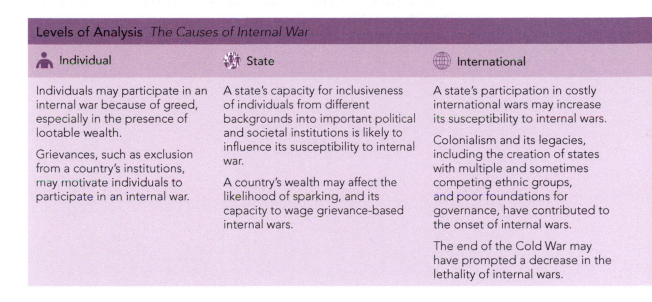

Levels of Analysis *The Causes of Internal War*		
👤 Individual	👥 State	🌐 International
Individuals may participate in an internal war because of greed, especially in the presence of lootable wealth. Grievances, such as exclusion from a country's institutions, may motivate individuals to participate in an internal war.	A state's capacity for inclusiveness of individuals from different backgrounds into important political and societal institutions is likely to influence its susceptibility to internal war. A country's wealth may affect the likelihood of sparking, and its capacity to wage grievance-based internal wars.	A state's participation in costly international wars may increase its susceptibility to internal wars. Colonialism and its legacies, including the creation of states with multiple and sometimes competing ethnic groups, and poor foundations for governance, have contributed to the onset of internal wars. The end of the Cold War may have prompted a decrease in the lethality of internal wars.

REVISITING THE ENDURING QUESTION AND LOOKING AHEAD

Military conflicts, including full-scale wars, have been and remain a central feature of international politics. Why do they happen, given that they are often horrifically costly in terms of the deaths of both combatants and civilians? This is the enduring question that we pursued in this chapter. We have shown that wars and other types of military conflicts between states, and within them, are rare but have taken place persistently through history. We also showed that war occurs in the most immediate sense because states have conflicts of interest with one another. Yet, that explanation is not satisfactory by itself, because states often have conflicts of interest and their disagreements over those interests do not end in war.

Why, then, do some disagreements between states, and the conflicts of interests on which those disagreements rest, escalate to MIDs or even full-fledged wars? Given that arguments that stress the immediate causes of wars are not sufficient, we then shifted our focus to different possible underlying causes of wars and other violent conflicts between states. These causes are situated and operate at the individual, state, and international level of analysis, and many of them are emphasized by realist, liberal, constructivist, and feminist theories of world politics. Those theories and the causes they identify provide us with a quite substantial menu of possible fundamental causes of war.

We also discussed wars within countries. We examined why internal wars matter on their own terms, for example, in respect to their lethality for civilians, and by their capacity to affect international relations. We also explored different types of internal wars and sought to understand the multiple causes for such wars, causes that again are situated at the individual, state, and international levels of analysis.

War is a persistent and dangerous part of the international domain. Yet, consider the case of France and Germany during the past 150 years. These two countries fought each other in three major wars between 1870 and 1945. During most of that period, when they were not actually fighting each other, they were bitter diplomatic adversaries. Yet, after 1945 these two countries reconciled and became close partners in the European Union. Just as there are many pathways to war, there must be factors in world politics that provide states with pathways to peace. We turn to this possibility in the next chapter.

STUDY QUESTIONS

1. Is war an inevitable feature of international relations?
2. What one thing would you change about the internal features of a specific country that you believe would decisively lower the risk of war in the modern era?
3. How does a constant, like international anarchy, possibly influence the onset of interstate wars, which vary across time?
4. Is there a link between gender and war?
5. Given what we know about internal war, what can be done to reduce its incidence and severity?

FURTHER READING

Blainey, Geoffrey (1988) *The Causes of War*, 3rd edn (New York: Free Press). Blainey identifies the main theoretical arguments about the causes of war, and provides a superb critique of them.

Gurr, Ted Robert (2011) *Why Men Rebel: Fortieth Anniversary Edition* (Boulder: Paradigm Publishers). This book pioneered the systematic study of internal war, and remains a helpful intellectual gateway to this important subject.

Jervis, Robert (1997) *Perception and Misperception in International Politics* (Princeton: Princeton University Press). This book remains the best overview of different forms of misperceptions and their impact on the risk of war. It also presents a superb discussion of the levels-of-analysis framework for the study of international relations.

Pinker, Steven (2011) *The Better Angels of Our Nature: Why Violence Has Declined* (London: Allen Lane). Pinker puts forward the provocative thesis that human beings in general are becoming less violent toward one another, of which one manifestation is a decline in war.

Waltz, Kenneth (1959) *Man, State, and War: A Theoretical Analysis* (New York: Columbia University Press). This is the seminal work on viewing the causes of war from the perspective of factors situated at the individual, state, and interstate levels of analysis, or what Waltz himself termed 'images.'

Visit **www.macmillanihe.com/Grieco-IntroIR-2e** to access extra resources for this chapter, including:

- Chapter summaries to help you review the material
- Multiple choice quizzes to test your understanding
- Flashcards to test your knowledge of the key terms in this chapter
- An interactive simulation that invites you to go through the decision-making process of a world leader at a crucial political juncture
- Pivotal decisions in which you weigh up the pros and cons of complicated decisions with grave consequences
- Outside resources, including links to contemporary articles and videos, that add to what you have learned in this chapter

7 Pathways to Interstate Peace

Enduring question
What factors make it more likely that states can resolve their differences and avoid war?

Chapter Contents

Learning Objectives

By the end of this chapter, you will be able to:

→ Recognize how two very different distributions of international power may contribute to peace among states: the balance of power and hegemony.

→ Analyze the two most important policies that governments have used to promote peace: diplomacy and power balancing.

→ Identify and evaluate the ways international law and institutions may promote peace.

→ Examine the capacity of transnational interactions, such as economic interdependence, the spread of democracy, and peace movements and civil society, to prompt states to resolve their disputes in peaceful ways.

→ Discuss the importance that leaders and especially ordinary people have assigned to peace.

War has been a constant feature of world politics over the centuries – but so too has been the search for peace. As soldiers have marched across distant battlefields and generals have plotted their military campaigns, diplomats and scholars have pondered the best ways to prevent war and establish stable international order. As we saw in Chapter 6, wars have come in many shapes and sizes. So too have the visions and strategies of peacemaking.

What scholars and policy makers believe will work to promote peace depends on their assumptions about what causes war. For example, if you believe that dictators are likely to be prone to war, you might favor the creation of democratic communities as a solution to the war problem. If you believe the real problem is the existence of nation-states in anarchy, you might be inclined to favor the much discussed yet never realized alternative of world government, or even the elimination of sovereign states. If men cause war, then a practical solution might be to have more female leaders in power. The point is not that any of these claims is necessarily correct; it is that the solution to a problem such as war must go hand in hand with analysis, or one's argument about the causes of war.

This chapter traces the various ways that peoples and governments throughout history have attempted to construct a stable and peaceful international system. We begin by looking at the background conditions that allow for a stable peace: a balance of power on the one hand or hegemony on the other. After this, we go on to examine the different strategies or instruments of peacemaking. The strategy that perhaps comes to mind most immediately is diplomacy. But often diplomacy is not enough. Nation-states also form alliances or collective security arrangements to deter potentially aggressive states. Moreover, states over time have developed a series of international laws and institutions to avert war and promote peace, and building on Chapter 5, we will look at ways that laws and institutions are used as tools of peacemaking. We will also move beyond states and state leaders and focus on three transnational forces that may promote peace, namely, economic interdependence, the possible emergence of a community of democratic nations, and the efforts of nongovernmental actors who together constitute elements of a transnational civil society.

THE INTERNATIONAL DISTRIBUTION OF POWER AS A CONDITION FOR PEACE

The distribution of power among states influences the prospects for peace. Two possibilities regarding peace and the distribution of power have been investigated by scholars: one is that peace is more likely in periods when there is a roughly equal distribution of capabilities among a number of states, while the other, in a completely different line of analysis, is that peace is more likely when there is a single overwhelmingly powerful state in the international system.

Balance of Power

In a situation of a balance of power, a rough equality of power exists between the major states in the international system at a given moment in time. If several great powers are roughly equal in their material capabilities, the balance of power has taken the form of a multipolar system. In those circumstances, peace and stability may be attained because coalitions of states form alliances or partnerships to ensure that no single state – or coalition of states – gains dominance. When two states overshadow all others – as the United States and the Soviet Union did during the Cold War – the balance of power is established through bipolar balancing. Each of the two superpowers gathers allies and seeks to muster sufficient collective capabilities to counterbalance the other side.

In both bipolar and multipolar settings, peace is maintained when there is a rough equilibrium of power. After the European wars of the eighteenth and nineteenth centuries, the balance of power was the dominant condition for re-establishing peace. During the Cold War, the balance of power was again a crucial mechanism for preserving stability. The United States and the Soviet Union were each convinced by the power of the other side that war was not worth the risks. Nuclear weapons and the threat of retaliation against a 'first strike' figured prominently in this calculation (see Chapter 8). Each side went to considerable efforts to establish the credibility of its own power position to ensure that the other side would indeed make sober calculations of restraint.

Hegemony

Hegemony, or the dominance of one state over other states, is a second condition that can allow for stable peace. In this situation, the ability of a powerful state to organize and enforce order creates peace among states. Over the centuries, there have been several occasions when a powerful state has been able to organize and rule over large parts of the world. The historian Edward Gibbon coined the term *Pax Romana* to refer to the Roman Empire of the first and second centuries CE, when Rome maintained political control over vast reaches of Europe and Northern Africa (Gibbon 1996). Rome's extended imperial order existed in relative peace and tranquility, undisturbed by internal civil war or foreign invasions. China – beginning with the Han Dynasty in 200 BCE to 200 CE – dominated East Asia and established a stable peace that lasted for centuries. This era of peace, known as the *Pax Sinica*, involved the establishment of hierarchical relations of status – the so-called tribute system – between China and its Japanese, Korean, and Vietnamese neighbors (Kang 2010; Fairbanks 1992).

Map 7.1 The Roman Empire in 116 CE
The Roman Empire experienced great prosperity and stability prior to its fall. The *Pax Romana* was one of the earliest examples of what scholars call hegemonic stability.

Later, scholars characterized the British leadership and dominance of the international system in the nineteenth century, and American leadership and dominance within the non-Communist world of the latter half of the twentieth century, as similar eras of international peace. Peace was established not through a balance of power – at least in large parts of the world that the United Kingdom and the United States dominated – but by the hegemonic presence of the major power. Hegemonic peace here was not derived through direct imperial control but through leadership. States within the British and American hegemonic orders became willing partners, as these leading states used their economic, political, and military capabilities to establish and maintain order – and ensure the peace. For example, after World War II, Western European countries and Japan joined the United States to jointly manage the capitalist world economy. Cooperation between these countries was not simply a result of American power. It was also manifest in their common interests and values and the way they shared leadership responsibilities. During the decades of the Cold War, this American hegemonic order coexisted with a global balance of power between the United States and the Soviet Union. In this way, global order was built on both hegemony and power balance.

Levels of Analysis   *The Distribution of Power as a Source of Peace*

 International

A balance or equilibrium of power among states can be a source of stable and peaceful order.

The dominance of a single state can also be a source of stable and peaceful order.

STATE STRATEGIES FOR ACHIEVING INTERSTATE PEACE

To promote peace, policy makers within states rely on diplomacy as a key foreign policy instrument and power balancing as a key foreign policy strategy.

Diplomacy

One of the oldest and most time-honored peacemaking instruments that states employ for a variety of reasons is diplomacy. Diplomacy, as noted in Chapter 3, primarily consists of actions that governments undertake as their representatives negotiate with representatives of other governments to resolve disputes and establish collaborative bilateral or multilateral arrangements through which their countries can mutually achieve individual gains. The British scholar-diplomat, Harold Nicolson, defined diplomacy as 'the process and machinery by which … negotiation is carried out' (Nicolson 1963). The historian Jeremy Black describes diplomacy as the activities that states undertake to manage their relations abroad, particularly as they make representations, acquire information, and conduct negotiations (Black 2010). Diplomacy, then, is what states do when they engage in dialogue and negotiation. Diplomacy can be used by states for many purposes – but perhaps its most important use is the search for peace.

The tradition of diplomacy dates to the rise of the system of states in early modern Europe, beginning in the sixteenth century with the development of permanent representatives among the city-states in northern Italy (Black 2010). The small Italian states posted diplomats in neighboring city-states and used them to collect and disperse information and conduct negotiations relating to war and peace. This practice spread throughout the European continent as states became sovereign political entities and began to conduct foreign policies. By the nineteenth century, this formal system spread worldwide, with governments dispatching official representatives – ambassadors – to the other capitals of the world. Embassies and diplomatic staffs were established, and rules, protocols, and traditions of diplomacy gradually emerged, providing mechanisms for states to communicate their intentions and exchange information (Mattingly 1988).

At the heart of this modern system of diplomacy were the evolving norms of state sovereignty in which states recognized and respected each other as independent and self-governing political entities. States existed in a world of states – and diplomacy was the institutional network of offices and officials that provided the means for the management of these interstate relationships (Bull 1977).

The breakthrough in this system of sovereign statehood, as noted in Chapter 2, came with the Treaty of Westphalia of 1648, the peace settlement that followed the bloody Thirty Years War in which Protestants and Catholics fought to impose their religious views on each other. The victorious states in the war – particularly France and Sweden – disavowed and sought to undermine the religious universalism and hierarchical control of the Holy Roman Empire. As Kalevi Holsti argues, Westphalia 'represented a new diplomatic arrangement – an order created by states, for states – and replaced most of the legal vestiges of hierarchy, at the pinnacle of which were the Pope and the Holy Roman Empire' (Holsti 1991). The treaty countered Europe-wide religious-imperial domination by strengthening the legal and political autonomy of territorial rulers to achieve a stable peace. Power was dispersed into the hands of sovereign states, and the international order was organized around sovereign states that acknowledged one another as legal equals. Territorial rulers were given the right to choose their religion for themselves and their territories. A state system managed through diplomacy and statecraft was the pathway to peace.

Over time, rules and norms have evolved to govern the ways ambassadors and other state officials represent their governments abroad. In the seventeenth century, when European states began the practice of posting permanent diplomatic representatives in foreign capitals, delegations were small, typically consisting of only an ambassador and a small staff. After the Napoleonic wars of the early nineteenth century, European diplomats meeting in Vienna agreed to formalize the roles and rankings of diplomatic representatives within international law. By the twentieth century, the world's leading states had established large embassies in major world capitals with hundreds of ministers and staff. These embassies have continued to grow, with ministers and officers charged with contacting foreign governments in areas such as business, military, energy, environment, labor, human rights, law enforcement, and cultural affairs. In recent decades, diplomacy has also been increasingly carried out in a wide range of settings – summit meetings, international conferences, and other multilateral gatherings.

In capitals around the world, this far-flung diplomatic system of ambassadors and embassies is visibly on display through imposing headquarters often grouped together in a particular area. Under international law, these embassies are the 'territorial sovereignty' of the foreign government and, as such, are above the law of the local host country. The privileges and immunities granted to the ambassador and the embassy staff exempts them from the full force of local laws. This principle of **diplomatic immunity** – accepted by governments on a reciprocal basis – developed to allow the foreign state to maintain government relations and the chain of authority over its overseas embassies, necessary if the ambassador is to truly speak for the sovereign or head of government. Although this practice of diplomatic immunity is deeply rooted in international law and historical tradition, average citizens of

Diplomatic immunity
The privileges and immunities granted by a host country to foreign ambassadors and embassy staff, exempting them from the full force of local laws.

countries often find out about it in less lofty ways. For example, residents of New York City, which hosts the United Nations and thousands of foreign embassy officials, periodically read newspaper reports about how these officials never pay their parking tickets. Disgruntled New Yorkers have discovered one of the practical implications of diplomatic immunity.

Although diplomacy between states has been institutionalized into a worldwide system of embassies, ambassadors, norms, and traditions, it has also grown beyond this system. Traditionally, the Foreign Ministry (or in the United Kingdom, the Foreign Office, or in the United States, the Department of State) has carried out diplomacy. But in certain, typically politically sensitive situations, leaders rely on 'personal envoys' to conduct diplomacy. In 1974, Zambian President Kenneth Kaunda sent a private advisor (Mark Chona) to Pretoria, the capital of South Africa, to explore the possibility of improving ties between two countries that considered each other adversaries. Similarly, in 1971, President Nixon turned to his White House foreign policy advisor, Henry Kissinger, to undertake a secret trip to China to explore the possibilities of opening relations between two Cold War enemies. Nixon did not just bypass the State Department in this groundbreaking diplomatic overture; he did not even inform the department about it. Sometimes diplomacy is even further removed from traditional channels. In efforts to improve relations with other countries, governments have encouraged private groups – orchestras or sports teams, for example – to help break the ice. In 2008, the New York Philharmonic Orchestra visited and performed in North Korea as a gesture of goodwill and friendship between American and North Korean peoples. More dramatically, in 2018 North and South Korea agreed to create a unified women's hockey team to participate in the Pyeongchang winter Olympics. South Korea, the host country, suggested this diplomatic initiative and advertised the games as the 'Peace Olympics.' In previous centuries, diplomacy was a more scripted

Photo 7.1 Peace Diplomacy through World Sporting Events
During the 2018 Winter Olympic Games held in Pyeongchang, South Korea, North and South Korea formed one Olympic women's hockey team to symbolize cooperation and unity.

Source: Woohae Cho/Getty Images.

craft, with diplomats conducting formal state-to-state dialogues. In today's world of growing economic interdependence and open democratic societies, diplomacy has become more multifaceted (see Box 7.1).

7.1 MAKING CONNECTIONS
Then and Now

The Growth of Modern International Diplomacy

Over the last hundred years, the number of nation-states in the global system has grown dramatically and their diplomatic interactions have intensified. One way of seeing this intensification of diplomacy is the expansion in nongovernmental organizations and international bodies. Nation-states are doing more diplomatic business with each other and more nongovernmental groups are linking these states together. For those seeking to build a more peaceful world, this growth in diplomatic exchange and nongovernmental linkages are a hopeful development.

Figure 7.1 International Organizations by Year and Type, 1909–2013

Source: Data from Union of International Associations, 'Statistics: Number of International Organizations by Year and Type, 1909–2013'.

The most dramatic – and high stakes – moments for diplomacy occur when states appear to be on the brink of war. Diplomacy then becomes a tool to try to defuse the conflict and prevent war. The border between North Korea and South Korea is the most militarized in the world, and the United States, South Korea, and Japan – joined by China – have periodically pursued negotiations with North Korea to avert a military clash. When North Korea took steps in the 1990s to build nuclear weapons, the United States launched intensive negotiations to end these efforts, offering energy and food aid in exchange for North Korean promises to step back from the nuclear brink. In the early twenty-first century, North Korea relaunched its nuclear programs and tested nuclear weapons devices. In response, the United States, China, North Korea, Japan,

Russia, and South Korea initiated the Six-Party Talks to explore a settlement of the nuclear standoff. These talks – now suspended – attempted to draw North Korea into an agreement under which it would agree to end its nuclear program in exchange for normalization of relations with the outside world. In 2018, the crisis on the Korean Peninsula has led to new diplomatic efforts, including summit meetings between the leaders. Frustration has been a consistent theme in these negotiations, but the states of Northeast Asia see few options besides patient diplomacy.

 Simulations: What would you do? Visit the companion website and participate in a foreign affairs crisis in Oman that threatens peace and stability. You must choose wisely to avoid war breaking out!

The Clinton administration also engaged in diplomacy in 1998 to avert war between India and Pakistan over Kashmir, when Pakistani and Kashmiri insurgents moved across the border into India and armed conflict followed (see Map 7.2). Long-standing disputes over territory and the status of Kashmir increased the risk that these clashes would escalate into a major war. Indeed, the United States received evidence that Pakistan had moved nuclear weapons into forward positions, in anticipation of a general war. The Pakistani government appealed for American assistance to end

Map 7.2 The Dispute over Kashmir
The region of Kashmir is the world's most militarized, with roughly 750,000 soldiers present. India controls 45% of Kashmir, Pakistan controls 35%, and China 20%.

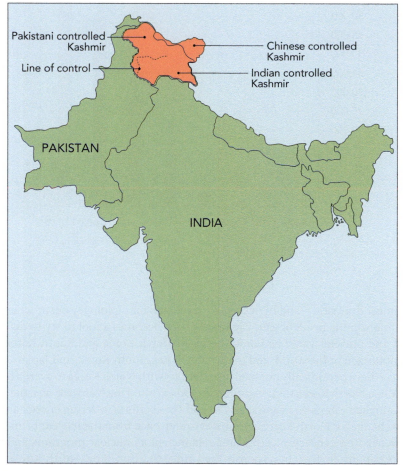

Source: Stanislas Giroux.

Photo 7.2 Diplomacy to Avert War and Resolve a Crisis
US President Bill Clinton greets Pakistani Prime Minister Nawaz Sharif in July 1999 in Washington, DC, for talks on ways to end fighting in Kashmir. Clinton's diplomacy was instrumental in helping India and Pakistan avoid war over Kashmir in 1998.

Source: BALTI/AFP/Getty Images

the crisis, and the Clinton administration agreed, but only after Pakistani troops withdrew from across the Indian border. The diplomatic intervention of the United States helped defuse the situation. Clinton officials facilitated a settlement of the dispute by identifying steps that each side could take to reduce tensions, and applied pressure on Pakistan, which relied on the United States for foreign aid and military assistance. Diplomacy made a difference.

Diplomacy, however, does not always work. For example, it failed during the run-up to the first Gulf War in 1990. In 1990, Iraq – led by President Saddam Hussein – charged Kuwait with **economic warfare** by overproducing oil and stealing oil from Iraqi fields near the border. In August 1990, roughly 100,000 Iraqi troops invaded Kuwait and within a day seized control of the country. The United Nations Security Council voted to impose sanctions on Iraq, and the United States, the United Kingdom, and France began a military buildup in the region, deploying troops to Saudi Arabia and imposing a naval blockade against Iraq. An international military coalition had been assembled, and the George H.W. Bush administration was committed to a war to push Iraq out of Kuwait. But the United States made one last attempt to convince the Iraqis to leave without a fight. In early 1991 US Secretary of State James Baker began talks with Iraqi Foreign Minister Tariq Aziz about the withdrawal of Iraqi forces from Kuwait. In his memoirs, Baker recalled the thinking behind the American proposal for direct talks with Aziz:

Economic warfare
Aggressive actions by a state intended to damage another state economically.

> A face-to-face meeting might create its own psychological and political imperatives that could lead Saddam to withdraw. It certainly would give him an opening he could use to avoid war if he were seeking one. And if we could not convince Iraq to withdraw in direct talks, then no one would be able to question that we had done all we could. This would also help us with the Soviets and others who were reluctant to see force used. (Baker 1995)

In the end, the Iraqis were unwilling to use this opening to withdraw from Kuwait and avert war. Operation Desert Storm began a week later, and by the end of February 1991, the Iraqis had been expelled from Kuwait and the war was over.

In reflecting on the relationship between diplomacy and war, we might say that in one sense, the two activities are alternatives. Diplomacy is the tool a state uses to alter the actions of other states short of war. Prussian theorist of war Carl von Clausewitz famously argued that war is the pursuit of diplomacy by other means. But war and diplomacy are also complements. Diplomacy can be an important tool for state leaders who find themselves on the road to war. In the first Gulf War, as noted earlier, the Bush administration found that offering diplomatic contact with Iraq was

Power balancing
Efforts by states to protect themselves in a dangerous world by arraying power against power, consisting of both internal balancing and external balancing.

Internal balancing
The process by which states muster their own power to balance rival states by mobilizing their economy and increasing their defense capabilities.

External balancing
The process by which states enter into security alliances with other states to balance the power of a particularly strong state or coalition of states.

a way to build support – both internationally and at home – for military action. The message that the United States was seeking peace and wanted a settlement made other states more willing to acquiesce. Moreover, war itself is rarely total. Wars are aimed at specific objectives, and even if the use of force is successful, diplomacy is typically a necessary tool in the aftermath of war to ratify the result of the war and rebuild peace.

Power Balancing

Diplomacy is a policy instrument whereby states seek advantages and settle disputes short of war. States also pursue a more general strategy, that is, a goal and associated policy instrument that can promote peace, namely, **power balancing**, which consists of efforts by states to protect themselves in a dangerous world by arraying power against power. States can attempt to counteract powerful or threatening states through internal and external balancing. **Internal balancing** is the process by which states muster their own power by mobilizing their economy and increasing their defense capabilities. In **external balancing**, states enter security alliances with other states. In amassing counterbalancing force, states seek to dissuade other states from resorting to war. If a state knows that its power will be met with resistance – if it knows that its capabilities on the battlefield are no greater than those of its enemies – it

Map 7.3 The Wars of German Unification, 1866–71
During the late nineteenth century, Bismarck unified the German states through a series of wars. This unification led Britain to pursue a strategy of balancing against Germany, eventually leading to the world wars of the twentieth century.

will hesitate to start a war. In an international system in which power is balanced, states have incentives to act with restraint and caution. According to this logic, a world in which power is balanced is a world that will tend toward peace.

Much of international politics in the modern era has involved states using balancing strategies to advance their interests. In the late eighteenth and nineteenth centuries, Great Britain pursued a strategy of power balancing to prevent the European continent from being dominated by a hostile hegemonic state. This strategy involved staying 'off shore' and watching over developments on the continent. If and when a continental great power became too powerful or sought to dominate Europe as a whole, Great Britain would endeavor to organize a balancing coalition to undercut the challenger. In the late eighteenth century, Napoleonic France made a bid for European dominance, and Great Britain assumed leadership of the coalition of states that fought and eventually defeated Napoleon. In the late nineteenth century, Britain again cast a wary eye on the rise of Germany, led by 'Iron Chancellor' Otto von Bismarck. The British Foreign Office codified this balancing strategy in strategic documents, and it was reflected in Lord Palmerston's famous dictum that Britain had 'no permanent friends, no permanent enemies, only permanent interests.' This balancing strategy had as its objective the use of British power to maintain the balance between the great powers on the European continent, undercutting efforts by any state to make war and try to dominate the region.

During the Cold War, the United States and the Soviet Union employed power balancing as a tool for managing their relations with each other. For both superpowers, the internal strategy involved mobilization of their economies, reflected in investments in research and development, education and training, and massive expenditure to boost military capacities. On the American side, external balancing took the form of building alliances, providing foreign and military assistance, and championing economic and political cooperation within the non-communist world. The Soviet Union also built a European alliance, the Warsaw Pact, and cultivated relationships with allies globally including North Vietnam, Cuba, Angola, and Nicaragua. This so-called bipolar power balancing lasted for decades and, in retrospect, it appeared to play an important role in preserving peace between the two superpowers, although proxy wars were fought in other countries (as we discussed in Chapter 2).

States today still often pursue a strategy of balancing, either directly or indirectly. The rise of China has led countries in Asia to explore ways to counter or guard against the possibilities of China's domination of the region. India, another large and growing Asian country, has looked warily at the rise of China – and has taken steps to strengthen its military capacities and political relations in the region as countermeasures. In recent years, India has strengthened its ties with Japan, Australia, and other countries in the region. Southeast Asian countries, such as Singapore, Australia, and the Philippines, seek to engage China and benefit from good political and economic relations. But indications suggest that at least some of these countries also want the United States to remain in the region as a balance against Chinese power. The United States has responded to this situation by reassuring East Asian states of its security commitments and leadership in the region. The announcement by Secretary of State Hillary Clinton in the summer of 2010 that the United States would play an active role in brokering territorial disputes in Southeast Asia – disputes that pit China against the smaller states – reflects this use of power balancing as a tool of diplomacy. The Trump administration has sent more mixed signals about its commitment to its East Asian alliance partners. China, in return, has adopted a strategy of diplomacy, reassuring its neighbors and offering to participate in various regional economic and security institutions to mitigate the worries that other states have about a rising China, thereby undercutting the urge these states might have to seek to balance power against China. China's recent establishment of the Asian

Infrastructure Investment Bank, a source of development lending, and its ambitious Belt and Road Initiative, which proposes to develop economic infrastructure across the expanse of Eurasia, are examples of China's use of economic instruments as a way to engage its neighbors and make its growing power in the region more acceptable.

Bandwagoning
When smaller, weaker states ally with a larger, powerful state for protection. Contrasts with balance of power.

We can contrast balancing with **bandwagoning**. If balancing involves aggregating capabilities to resist the threats of an increasingly powerful rival state, bandwagoning occurs when smaller states flock to a state for protection. Rather than resist the power of a leading state, weaker neighbors affiliate with the more powerful state. Their strategy is to tie themselves to the leading state, thereby gaining protection and other benefits from it. States often pursue this strategy in conjunction with power balancing. So, for example, as the United States balanced against the Soviet Union during the Cold War, smaller states bandwagoned with the United States.

Levels of Analysis *State Strategies in Pursuit of Peace*

 State

States employ diplomacy and undertake balancing to advance their interests, and in doing so may bring about peace.

INTERNATIONAL LAW AND INSTITUTIONS AS MECHANISMS FOR PEACE

States have tried to establish stable peace by building systems of international law and institutions. As we discussed in detail in Chapter 5, international law consists of the body of rules, norms, and standards that states have crafted over time that give those states and other actors rights and obligations in their interactions with one another. International law specifies the rules and principles governing the relations among states, although in recent decades the scope of international law has been expanded to include relations between states and individuals and with international organizations. As we noted, the origins of international law date back to the seventeenth century. The Treaty of Westphalia was itself an effort to establish agreed-upon rules and norms for the conduct of relations among European sovereign states.

International law seeks to govern relations among states by setting out principles and standards of conduct that states are expected to obey. It seeks to establish a rule-based framework within which states expect each other to operate. In the contemporary world, international law is grounded in a multitude of rules and principles that cover all sorts of state action, including rules about war, human rights, and various aspects of international trade and finance. Champions of international law say that it offers a vision of world politics in which the laws of nations are expected to strengthen peaceful relations and provide a stable environment for states to cooperate and prosper.

We have noted that the great weakness of international law is that it is difficult – if not impossible – to enforce. However, international law does not totally lack enforcement. First, groups of states can impose economic sanctions on states that are seen to violate international law. Economic sanctions involve the curtailment of commercial, financial, and political relations with a target country with an aim of changing its behavior. Sanctions can involve various measures: travel bans, asset freezes, arms embargoes, capital restraints, foreign aid cut-offs, and trade restrictions. They can be comprehensive, involving a complete embargo of economic flows, seen in America's decades-long embargo of Cuba, or more selective sanctions that prohibit specific transactions aimed at specific substate individuals, groups, or organizations.

Second, states that join the International Criminal Court (ICC) and other international courts do – by their membership and ratification of these treaties – accept the authority of these courts. They acknowledge that these judicial bodies do have some authority to make decisions. Even though the ICC and other courts cannot force states to abide by their rulings, the authority of these bodies does put pressure on governments to comply. International court decisions can also make it easier for other governments to organize sanctions against the offending government or leaders. But enforcement is not binding. It is up to states to impose costs on other states and, in this sense, states – not the law – have the last word.

Since the nineteenth century, governments and international bodies have increasingly resorted to economic sanctions in efforts to alter the policies of states that threaten the peace or violate international norms. When diplomacy fails, it is often seen as the next step, in efforts to coerce, deter, or punish a state without resort to direct military force. The logic of collective security, upon which the League of Nations was built, depended on the ability of governments to cooperate in imposing sanctions on states engaged in aggression. In recent decades, the UN Security Council has depended on the authorization of economic sanctions as a tool for imposing costs and putting pressure on governments that are found to violate the United Nations Charter's norms and principles. For example, when Saddam Hussein invaded Kuwait in August 1990, the first response of the UN Security Council was to impose sanctions on Iraq.

In the post-Cold War period, economic sanctions have been a central tool that Western states have used to deal with security threats and challenges. For example, the United States and Europe have imposed a wide range of trade and financial sanctions on Russia in response to Moscow's annexation of Crimea and interventions in Ukraine to destabilize its pro-European government. Backed by United Nations Security Council resolutions, many states have employed escalating economic sanctions against North Korea, seeking to deter it from continuing development of its nuclear weapons capabilities. The effectiveness of economic sanctions is widely

7.2 MAKING CONNECTIONS
Theory and Practice

Realist Theory on International Law, Institutions, and Government Actions

Theory

Some realist theories suggest that international law, norms, and institutions are of little or no significance to states. Power rather than the rule of law or international institutions matters in how states act. Anarchy and competition for wealth and power create the conditions in which states operate. In world politics, power rules.

Practice

Governments in the modern era have spent an extraordinary amount of time and energy to create international institutions and enshrine their actions in international law. At critical moments, even when national security is at stake, governments care about acting according to international laws and norms. For example, during the Cuban Missile Crisis in 1962, the Kennedy administration sought the approval of the Organization of American States as a way of ensuring that the embargo and possible use of force was widely seen as consistent with regional and global law and norms.

debated – but most observers would agree that they have a mixed record. Even in the face of high economic costs, sanctions often fail to change the behavior of the target. For example, UN sanctions on Afghanistan in 2001 were severe, but the Taliban did not cooperate in the hunt for Osama bin Laden. Of course, the specific goals and circumstances of sanctions differ widely. Even if economic sanctions do not change a state's offensive behavior, the sanctions may nonetheless send a signal to others of the international community's commitment to shared norms of peace and security. (Hufbauer *et al.* 2009).

Across the centuries, statesmen, political activists, jurists, and peace-advocates have sought to foster peace by strengthening the fabric of international law and institutions (see Box 7.2). We can look at three of these modern efforts.

Three Experiences with International Law and Institutions: The League of Nations, the United Nations, and the European Union

During the past century, state leaders have made multiple efforts to build international institutions – again, the combination of laws and associated organizations – that would help keep the peace. The most ambitious of these have been the effort after World War I to establish a global collective security system, the League of Nations; then the creation after World War II of the United Nations; and finally, in Europe, a succession of institutions aimed at regional integration and peace, currently called the European Union.

Collective Security and the League of Nations

Collective security
Security provided by the members of an international cooperative institution in which, if any state threatened or actually used military force illegally against a member state, the other members pledged to form an overwhelming coalition to defeat the aggressor.

A peacemaking instrument that combines elements of international law and alliances/balancing is **collective security**. In this arrangement, member states agree to come to the aid of any member that is attacked by an aggressor from either within or outside the collective security arrangement. The basic idea is 'all for one and one for all' or 'safety in numbers.' Weaker states find collective security attractive because it offers the opportunity to lock stronger states into a commitment to protect them.

The classic example of collective security – and its problems – is the League of Nations, the international organization designed and proposed by US President Woodrow Wilson after World War I. In Wilson's vision of this universal membership organization, member states committed themselves to act in concert to protect territorial borders and enforce the peace. If a member of the League was attacked by another state, the other states in the League were to come to its defense. The idea of collective security was based on several assumptions. First, the League was to be a global organization in which membership would be near universal. All states would need to agree to uphold the commitments and obligations of membership. Second, states would not be able to veto or block actions of the organization. If they could, the collective security organization would likely find itself on the sidelines precisely when it was needed. Third, states would need to be sufficiently interdependent such that the threat of sanctions would be persuasive. Finally, all the states in the international system would need to be convinced that the members of the organization would indeed come to the aid of any member that was attacked. If these conditions held, as Wilson and other champions of the League of Nations argued, would-be aggressors bent on war would think twice.

The League of Nations was meant to embody this collective security idea and provide an institutional form to manage disputes around the world. The League's principal mission was the avoidance of war largely through arbitration and a reduction of armaments, and then, if necessary, the threat of collective sanctions. States would agree to act – imposing sanctions or employing force – when confronted with territorial aggression by an outlaw state. International relations scholar Inis Claude described the logic of collective security in this way:

> The twentieth-century hope that international organizations might serve to prevent war, or, failing that, to defend states subjected to armed attack in defiance of organized efforts to maintain the peace, has been epitomized in the concept of collective security ... Collective security can be described as resting upon the proposition that war can be prevented by the deterrent effect of overwhelming power upon states which are too rational to invite certain defeat. (Claude 1956)

In the League of Nations, states were to come together as equals. The League had an Executive Council but, adhering closely to the principle of the equality of states, the council's powers were simply to initiate investigations and make recommendations to the body of the whole. The League of Nations embodied a universal set of laws and principles intended to provide the foundation for a new era of peace and stability, reflecting Wilson's belief in the virtues of a world ordered by international law. As Wilson put it, 'the same law that applies to individuals applies to nations' (Wilson 1917). International law and the system of collective security anchored in the League of Nations would provide a socializing role, gradually bringing states into a 'community of power.' The League of Nations, with 42 founding members, held its first council meeting in January 1920, a week after the Treaty of Versailles came into force.

The League of Nations was weakened at the outset by the failure of the United States to join it. President Wilson campaigned across the United States for ratification of the Treaty of Versailles, which included membership in the League of Nations. But in a stinging defeat for Wilson and League of Nations supporters, the vote in the US Senate fell short. Part of the opposition came from conservative and isolationist senators who did not want the United States to be involved in foreign affairs. Other senators were willing to vote for the treaty but only with formal reservations that affirmed the Senate's constitutional right to decide when and if the United States would commit military forces abroad. For reasons that diplomatic historians still debate, Wilson was unwilling to compromise with these 'reservationist' senators who would have insured ratification of the treaty (Knock 1995). Ironically, the United States helped inspire the idea of the League of Nations – and the vision of world peace based on collective security – but was not part of its organizational founding.

Soon after the League of Nations was established, its ability to foster a peace system based on collective security was called into question. As we observed in Chapter 2, by the 1930s, the world was entering a global economic depression, and protectionism and nationalism were on the rise. In Asia, Japan responded by invading its neighbors and building an empire. This development put the League of Nations to the test. In 1931, Japan, a League of Nations member, invaded and occupied Manchuria, a part of China. League members initially debated imposing economic sanctions on Japan. But the world economy was weak, and many countries depended on trade with Japan, so there was little support for sanctions. Unable to penalize Japan, the League resorted to diplomatic persuasion. The League sent a delegation to study the problem, reporting back a year later. In 1933, after two years of deliberations, the League passed a resolution condemning the invasion and calling for Japan to withdraw from Manchuria. But the resolution did not commit members of the League to any specific actions, because member states could not agree on actions. Japan refused to leave Manchuria and instead withdrew from the League of Nations.

A second blow to the League of Nation's system of collective security came in 1935 with its inaction in response to Italy's invasion of Abyssinia (now Ethiopia).

Photo 7.3 Italy Conquers Abyssinia, 1935
The Italian Army triumphantly enters the capital city of Addis Ababa, Abyssinia (today's Ethiopia) in 1935 in defiance of the League of Nations.

Source: Popperfoto/Getty Images.

Both Italy and Abyssinia were members of the League of Nations. By the early 1930s, Mussolini's fascist regime ruled Italy and – as part of an aggressive foreign policy – it threatened Abyssinia with military invasion from its bordering imperial territory of Italian Somaliland. The Abyssinian Emperor, Haile Selassie, went to the League of Nations to appeal for help. The League initially proposed to give some of Abyssinia to Italy, but rather than work with the League, Mussolini simply invaded Abyssinia. As in the case of Japan's invasion of Manchuria, the League was unable to rally states to stop the aggression. Indeed, in the case of Abyssinia, two of the leading members of the League, the United Kingdom and France, secretly agreed to hand over Abyssinia to Italy. They chose not to stand up against Italian aggression, fearing that doing so would push Italy closer toward an alliance with Hitler's Germany. The fact that the United States was not a member of the League simply compounded these failings. By the mid-to-late 1930s, the promise of world peace based on collective security had disappeared, as the example in Box 7.3 further shows, and would fail entirely with the eruption of World War II.

The United Nations: A Modified Collective Security System?

After World War II, the United States and other countries again had an opportunity to build an international order – and again they sought to strengthen the role of rules and institutions as a basis for lasting peace. Between 1944 and 1950, the United States and other countries proposed a wide variety of postwar political, economic, and security institutions, including the United Nations, the Bretton Woods economic institutions, and the North Atlantic Treaty Organization (NATO). Like Wilson, President Franklin Roosevelt, his successor, President Harry Truman, and other American leaders in the 1940s wanted to build a system of order that would provide for a new era of peace. A global institution – the United Nations – was to be the cornerstone of this new attempt to create an open system built around collective security and the peaceful settlement of disputes.

7.3   MAKING CONNECTIONS
Aspiration versus Reality

Collective Security versus the British Abandonment of Czechoslovakia

Aspiration: Article X, League of Nations Covenant, 1919

In the Covenant of the League of Nations, members pledged to preserve the territorial sovereignty of fellow members of the League. The members of the League undertake to respect and preserve as against external aggression the territorial integrity and existing political independence of all members of the League. In case of any such aggression or in case of any threat or danger of such aggression the Council shall advise upon the means by which this obligation shall be fulfilled.

Reality: British Prime Minister Neville Chamberlain, September 1938

In practice, leaders of the world were more cautious and reluctant to go to the aid of other League members who faced military aggression. Prime Minister Neville Chamberlain, in an address to the British people during the crisis over Czechoslovakia, on September 27, 1938, said:

> How horrible, fantastic, incredible it is that we should be digging trenches and trying on gas masks here because of a quarrel in a far-away country between people of whom we know nothing … However much we may sympathize with a small nation confronted by a big and powerful neighbor, we cannot in all circumstances undertake to involve the whole British Empire in war simply on her account.

But with his vision, President Franklin Roosevelt also wanted to avoid the problems Wilson and the League of Nations had encountered. So, the United Nations (UN) was established as a 'modified' collective security system with several significant differences from the League of Nations. First, the UN gives the great powers a large role in managing international peace and security. The UN is composed of six principal organs (with numerous specialized funds and agencies in its wider system), but of most relevance to the issues of war and peace are: the General Assembly in which all member states participate on an equal basis; and the Security Council, with five permanent members (the United States, France, the United Kingdom, the Soviet Union, and China) along with an additional group of rotating temporary members. Second, these permanent members are given a veto over resolutions mandating UN action. This provision makes the great powers more likely to join the organization because actions without unanimous support would be vetoed. The League of Nations became discredited because it was not able to deliver on its basic promise to marshal the actions of all states in the face of territorial aggression. The UN would avoid this fate by allowing the major states to veto action where their interests were at stake. This veto power meant that the UN would not act in all instances, but only when the major states agreed that action was needed and when action was possible. Success or failure would hinge on the ability of the permanent members of the Security Council to cooperate.

While the UN avoided the fate of the League of Nations, it too gave way to the realities of power politics. The Cold War between the Soviet Union and the United States doomed Roosevelt's vision of the great powers collectively upholding peace and stability. Instead, the United States took on more direct responsibilities for organizing and leading the non-communist world and began building alliance partnerships – with Europe and East Asia – as an alternative pathway to international security.

NATO became the central mechanism for establishing security in Europe. In East Asia, the United States built bilateral security alliances with Japan and other states. These alliances did not provide collective security for all states in the international system. They only provided security – what might be called cooperative security – for those countries which were part of the alliances. The vision of a global system of collective security managed by the great powers narrowed to become a Western-oriented security community organized around cooperative security.

The UN did act – at least indirectly – in matters of war and peace as it assumed new responsibilities in the decades following World War II. First, the UN became the 'voice of the South' as it represented the states of the developing world. The UN was designed primarily to address the problems of war and peace, as had been experienced in the two world wars. Great-power wars in which a powerful state invaded another country were the preeminent threat to world peace, and the UN was the embodiment of the world community's desire to prevent such wars in the future. But in the post-World War II era, the struggles for security and prosperity in the developing world emerged as a new problem for the global system. The new problems focused on establishing political independence and stable order and grappling with the challenges of economic development. The UN gave these developing countries a forum for debate on development and governance. The UN was a 'great power club' but it was also a thriving venue for small and poor countries to advance their ideas.

Second, the UN became increasingly focused not just on peacemaking, but on peacekeeping. **Peacemaking** involves trying to end wars – an activity that states have pursued across history. In **peacekeeping** operations, UN-sponsored troops, drawn from various UN member states, are deployed in countries in the aftermath of war or civil violence to keep the warring groups apart and enforce the peace settlement. The Cold War and the stalemate between the Western powers and the Soviet Union meant that the UN Security Council would not be able to act, as its permanent members could not reach unanimous decisions. But the UN did play a role in deploying peacekeeping operations to keep war from recurring. The UN Charter gives the Security Council responsibility to take action to maintain peace and security. As a result, countries often come to the Security Council for help in implementing peace agreements. When the Security Council authorizes the deployment of peacekeepers, it draws upon military and civilian personnel from various countries to work together as a combined UN operation. Since 1948, the UN has sponsored 63 peacekeeping operations; 15 of these are ongoing.

In her exhaustive study of peacekeeping operations, Virginia Page Fortna shows that these UN-sponsored interventions are a very effective policy tool, dramatically reducing the risk that war will break out again. Fortna cites evidence to show that where civil war ceasefire agreements are backed up with peacekeepers, the peace tends to last much longer. Peacekeeping operations have several potential impacts. They can help raise the costs that combatants face if they choose to resume fighting, they can increase the confidence that each side has in the terms of the ceasefire agreement, and they help prevent accidental incidents that might spark a return to violence. The warring parties need to find some way to the

Peacemaking
UN action before war breaks out designed to prevent two states from going to war with each other by brokering peaceful settlements. Contrasts with peacekeeping, which occurs in the aftermath of war.

Peacekeeping
UN operations in which UN-sponsored troops are deployed in countries in the aftermath of war or civil violence to keep the warring groups apart and enforce the peace settlement.

Photo 7.4 UN Peacekeeping Operations
A Ghanaian peacekeeper with the UN Mission in Liberia (UNMIL) is pictured on guard duty. The United Nations Security Council has the authority to deploy peacekeepers. In doing so, it draws upon military and civilian personnel from various UN member states.

Source: UN Photo/Staton Winter.

peace table, but if they do get there – and agree to a ceasefire – UN peacekeepers can help keep the peace going (Fortna 2008).

The role and significance of the United Nations in world politics is a source of ongoing debate among international relations scholars. In Box 7.4, we compare liberal and realist views of the manner and extent to which the UN matters as a mechanism of peace.

7.4   DIFFERING THEORETICAL APPROACHES

The Role and Significance of the United Nations

Background

The United Nations is a large global institution that supports a wide array of activities. How important is this international organization in the promotion of peace and justice in world affairs? The theoretical traditions offer different answers.

Liberalism

Few liberal theorists argue that the United Nations has had a transformative impact on global peace and security, but they do emphasize its various contributions. The UN General Assembly provides a forum for debate, giving a louder voice to weaker states that might not otherwise be heard. The UN Security Council provides a venue for the great powers to consult – and possibility act – on questions of war and peace. In these ways, the UN offers space for diplomacy – and it is up to states to use it as they can to overcome differences and rivalries that can lead to war. Overall, liberals argue that the UN plays a valuable role as it enshrines a set of ideals and aspirations for the conduct of world affairs that in small ways or at critical moments can help states move away from armed violence and toward a stable peace.

Realism

Realists are more skeptical of what the UN can do in world politics. States act in their own interests whether they are making decisions at the United Nations or in their own capitals. The UN Security Council reflects this reality. It gives the great powers that created the UN – the United States, Russia, China, France, and the United Kingdom – a veto over UN resolutions. In effect, power politics can always trump UN action. The fact that the permanent members of the UN Security Council do not seem willing to give permanent Security Council membership to other powerful states – such as India, Germany, and Japan – only underscores the dynamics of power that lurk in the background of the global body.

The Rule of Law and Institutions: The Case of the European Union

Europe has developed the most elaborate form of stable peace through international law and institutions. After World War II, Western European countries began a decades-long process of building a cooperative regional order. The violence and destruction of World War II led postwar European leaders to search for new ways to create peace. Rather than return to a balance of power, these leaders chose a path of regional integration and institution building, beginning with the European Coal and Steel Community and later the European Economic Community (discussed in more detail later in this chapter). From a core group of countries, led by France and

West Germany, the European project both expanded to include most of the states of Europe and deepened relations by reducing trade barriers. In the 1990s, European states inaugurated the European Union with formal institutions such as the European Parliament, Court of Justice, and a Commission and created a common currency, the euro; these arrangements bind the countries together as a political community. Europe was the site for centuries of bloody war. The European Union can be seen as an historic effort to overcome old antagonisms and rivalries – particularly between Germany and France – and create a zone of peace.

The European Union is a new type of political community, a group of liberal democracies tied together by shared institutions and a commitment to governance through the rule of law. Like the League of Nations and the United Nations, it is an experiment in overcoming the age-old problems of conflict and war. Like these other experiments, the European Union has had its successes and failures. It has succeeded in building a framework for economic and political cooperation and at least limited joint governance. It has expanded its members across the European continent, integrating many of the countries from the former Soviet Union. However, it has struggled in recent years with its common currency and monetary order. The economic misfortunes of many member states – such as Greece and Spain – have put tremendous strains on the European Union. More recently, the United Kingdom has voted in a referendum to withdraw from the European Union, although the terms and conditions of what is being called 'Brexit' remain contested and unresolved. Like all efforts to build a system of peace and prosperity, the European Union is an ongoing experiment.

The various mechanisms that states have used to promote peace are not mutually exclusive. Interstate peace may be built on a combination of them. The peaceful order that emerged in Europe in 1815, after the Napoleonic Wars, was built around both the balance of power and an elaborate set of rules among the great powers. At the same time, the European great powers continued to dominate smaller states through empire and other forms of control. Likewise, the American-led order that emerged among the democracies after World War II combined all three structures – balance of power, hegemony, and international law and institutions. During the Cold War, the United States stepped forward to organize a Western or 'free world' order, doing so as it pursued a balance-of-power strategy against the Soviet Union. This order had characteristics of hegemony as well. The United States took the lead in organizing and running the order, providing security, and managing the open world economy as it built partnerships with other states in Europe and Asia. This American-led order was also characterized by multilateral rules and institutions that both reflected American power and also established limits and restraints on how power could be exercised within this order. The result was a distinctive political order – stretching across the Atlantic and Pacific oceans – that has provided stable peace (at a global level) for many decades, even after the end of the Cold War.

Levels of Analysis *International Law and Institutions as Mechanisms for Peace*

State	International
States have established international rules and institutions to facilitate cooperation and reinforce stability and peace.	International law may inform and constrain the behavior of states in ways that avert war and promote peace.
Western democracies have made repeated efforts to build global and regional systems of collective security and rule-based relations.	The European Union is the most successful example of how international institutions can promote peace.

TRANSNATIONAL MECHANISMS FOR PEACE

To this point we have discussed mechanisms for peace that mostly rely on states and national leaders. However, there are at least three pathways by which private individuals and nongovernmental actors can play a central role in promoting peace and averting/ending war, sometimes by pressuring national leaders. These three pathways relate to economic interdependence, a possible international community of democratic nations, and peace movements and global civil society.

Economic Interdependence

States have also sought to build peaceful international relations through the promotion of open trade and economic interdependence. The relationship between economics and peace is a complex one, and scholars continue to debate the specific ways in which the economic relationships that states pursue alter their conduct in matters of war and peace – if they do at all. Many liberal thinkers are convinced that extensive economic interdependence between countries creates domestic interests and constituencies that favor stable and peaceful relations. When countries are tied together in mutually beneficial trade and exchange, disrupting those relations is costly – and states should be sensitive to this consideration in their security relations. Others are more skeptical. Today, the rise of China – and its growing economic ties with Western states – provides a new test for the way in which economic interdependence influences the way states make decisions about security and cooperation.

Leaders of liberal democratic states such as Britain in the nineteenth century and the United States in the twentieth century and today have acted on this conviction. Both countries have had powerful economic incentives to do so – after all, they were the most advanced and productive economies of their day. But British and American leaders also promoted the building of an open world economy because of the more general effects this would have on international relations. As US Secretary of State Cordell Hull argued in the 1930s, 'if goods cross borders, soldiers won't.' Hull's logic was simple: trade fosters economic growth; growing and prosperous countries have fewer reasons to wage war. Moreover, the joint gains from trade and the mutually beneficial economic ties that would grow between countries would also create interests – and stakeholders – in these countries that favor peaceful and stable relations. Free trade creates expanding 'vested interests' that favor peace.

British economists and politicians made the first serious efforts to champion free trade to promote world peace in the early nineteenth century. The British free trade movement came on the heels of the ideas advanced by economist Adam Smith whose *Wealth of Nations* (1776) had argued in favor of the many virtues and benefits of free markets and international trade. Britain was just beginning to lead the world in a new stage of rapid industrialization. Business leaders and workers were a growing force in British politics – and they increasingly identified their interests with open markets. In a dramatic political battle, the British Parliament debated – and eventually repealed – the Corn Laws, which were key protectionist blocks to the free flow of goods across borders. In their speeches to Parliament, John Bright and Richard Cobden, two of the leading political figures who opposed the Corn Laws, made eloquent pleas for free trade, linking expanding markets and trade with the movement toward a more peaceful world.

Over the next decades, Britain and other countries lowered tariffs and established the first great age of an open world economy. By the end of the nineteenth century, goods and capital flowed throughout Europe and around the world. Steamships, telegraph wires, and railroads provided the new infrastructure for a global economy. But all this changed abruptly with the coming of World War I. Despite the extensive trade and financial ties between the European states, peace did not last. In *The Grand Illusion* (1909), British politician Norman Angell, reflecting the liberal conviction that economic interdependence would deter war, argued that economic integration had grown so extensive between the European states that war between them was utterly futile. Angell's thesis was not that war was impossible – after all, political leaders could do what they wanted to do – but that it was economically irrational. Nonetheless, a bloody world war did come, dramatically revealing the limits of the economic sources of peace.

In the years leading to World War II, the United States saw its geopolitical operating space shrink as the other great powers began to construct closed and competing regional blocs. Japan was establishing an imperial regional order in East Asia, the Soviet Union dominated its region, and Germany was seeking to dominate Western Europe. After the war's end, the United States hoped to build a peaceful world around trade and an open world economy and committed itself to rebuilding such an economy. US officials believed that a non-discriminatory commercial system would be the cornerstone of a stable peace. Open markets would provide the essential foundation for a wider multilateral system organized around the rule of law. This conviction about how to organize the global system brought together economic, ideological, and geopolitical strands of thinking among American policy makers.

Both the Roosevelt and Truman administrations championed a postwar effort to reopen the world economy. Free traders in the State Department, led by Secretary Cordell Hull, were at the forefront of this effort. Hull and his colleagues embraced economic interdependence, led by the United States, as the only way to ensure prosperity and stable peace. In a speech in November 1938 Hull said:

> I know that without expansion of international trade, based upon fair dealing and equal treatment for all, there can be no stability and security either within or among nations … I know that the withdrawal by a nation from orderly trade relations with the rest of the world inevitably leads to regimentation of all phases of national life, to the suppression of human rights, and all too frequently to preparations for war and a provocative attitude toward other nations. (Hull 1938)

Hull's emphasis was less on free trade than it was on non-discrimination and equal commercial opportunity. Open markets, according to this widely shared American view, would simultaneously advance two objectives. They would ensure that the United States would have access to markets and raw materials around the world. Open markets would also contribute to economic growth and interdependence, in turn creating shared interests among countries in a peaceful international order.

President Truman believed strongly that World War II had its roots in economics. It sprang from the rivalries and insecurities generated by protectionism, closed markets, and imperial blocs. If the world was to return to a period of stable peace, the barriers to free trade and non-discrimination would need to be swept away. Assistant Secretary of State Dean Acheson argued in April 1945 that there was 'wide recognition that peace is possible only if countries work together and prosper together. That is why the economic aspects are no less important than the political aspects of peace' (Acheson 1945).

The promotion of peace through the expansion of markets was a critical strategy that the United States and its European partners brought to bear on postwar Europe. In the first decade after 1945, American and European officials worried that Europe would become an economic and political failure. The memory of World War I and the economic depression that followed was still fresh in the minds of postwar leaders – and the lesson was clear: economic contraction, rising unemployment, and social hardship provided the ugly conditions of political radicalism and instability. The challenge was to rebuild Europe in a way that would allow Germany to integrate into the continent without reigniting old hostilities and insecurities. Economic integration became a key component of reconstruction policy. One part of this strategy was to tie together the old rivals – Germany and France – in new forms of economic cooperation. The European Coal and Steel Community was established to bind together these two industrial sectors in Europe's heartland. The 'industries of war' would no longer be national but European. The United States further pushed its postwar partners to create a Europe-wide common market. An integrated Europe that was growing together as a single whole would be less nationalist, militarist, and geopolitically divided.

7.5 RESEARCH INSIGHT

Economic Interdependence and Conflict

Liberal thinkers and liberal states believe free trade leads to peace, but the results of scholarly studies offer a mixed picture. There is empirical evidence for both the liberal view that economic interdependence can promote peace and the realist view that it does not. Economic interdependence does not – in itself – stop states from going to war. World War I remains the classic case that shows that statesmen do not always listen to businesspeople and bankers. There is no evidence that governments make straightforward decisions about war and peace based on simple calculations of economic gain or loss. War has many causes and so it is unrealistic to think that the presence of mutually beneficial economic ties, by itself, will stand as an absolute brake on war.

Nonetheless, there is evidence of some relationship. One scholar has discovered that since 1850 the level of international trade has been inversely related to the occurrence of major power war (Mansfield 1994). Another study of the period 1950–86 found a significant correspondence between increased interdependence and democracy, on the one hand, and a reduction in the incidence of military conflict on the other (Oneal and Russett 1997). On the realist side, scholars have found that during the early decades of the twentieth century, the costs of disrupting interdependence did not restrain countries from going to war (Blanchard and Ripsman 1996/97). One scholar looking at the full array of recent studies of interdependence and conflict found that ten supported the liberal position, four supported the realist position, and six found mixed results (McMillan 1997).

What seems to be most telling in recent research on economic interdependence and war is that what scholars call 'intervening variables' tend to matter (Mastanduno 1999). For example, economic interdependence does have impacts on domestic groups and political coalitions. Economic interest groups that benefit from trade will push for stable relations with other states, but whether they are influential will hinge on many factors, including the character of the governing elite's political coalition. Some scholars also point to how state leaders think about their future economic prospects, while others look at the more general security environment surrounding economic relations. In the end, these contingent factors seem to matter in determining the nature of the relationship between economic interdependence and conflict.

The American strategy for the wider postwar international order was also grounded in the opening and expansion of world markets. The United States took the lead in the 1940s in negotiating with Britain and other market democracies to establish trade and monetary rules. The system of agreements reached at the 1944 conference in Bretton Woods, New Hampshire, provided mechanisms for governments to manage economic openness, which we shall explore further in Chapter 9. In the decades that followed, the advanced democracies continued to liberalize trade, lowering tariffs and non-tariff barriers. Trade and investment grew steadily though the postwar decades. American and European multilateral corporations expanded their operations worldwide. After the end of the Cold War, the world economy expanded to include most of the developing and former communist world.

The globalization of the world economy does not in itself ensure a stable peace. But it does create incentives for countries to settle their differences short of war. The interconnectedness of countries increases the number of stakeholders committed to a stable, open system. Yet interdependence also creates new problems with which states must struggle collectively. Globalization brings with it such problems as transnational crime, drugs, and terrorism, and it makes countries more vulnerable to economic crises and upheavals in other parts of the world. But it also creates incentives for governments to develop rules and institutions – and international capacities – to manage their joint vulnerabilities.

A Possible International Community of Democratic Nations

As we saw in Chapter 6, liberal democracies tend not go to war against each other – and, in fact, they are unusually capable of working together to build cooperative relations. This simple insight lies behind one of the most celebrated and debated strategies of peacemaking, the democratic peace thesis, which focuses on democracy and the building of community among democracies. The characteristics of liberal democracies – the rule of law, free speech, private property, and leaders that are accountable to citizens – makes them predisposed to avoid war with other liberal democracies. It is not that liberal democracies are pacific states; they frequently attract and make trouble. But when democracies confront each other, they often find ways to settle their differences short of war. As democracy spreads around the world, so too does the **zone of peace** in world politics, that is, the number of countries and the geographic space they possess within which states do not want to use military force or believe it will be used against them.

Zone of peace
The number of democratic countries and the geographic space they possess within which states do not want to use military force or believe it will be used against them, in keeping with the democratic peace theory.

As we noted in Chapter 3, the German philosopher Immanuel Kant first advanced this argument in his 1795 essay, *Perpetual Peace*. Writing when democracies were just beginning to appear in the Western world, Kant suggested that what he called 'republics' – that is, countries with legal equality of citizens and representative government – would be driven to affiliate with each other and build peaceful forms of community. Kant's thesis was not only that republican states lack reasons to attack each other in war, but that they actually have incentives to draw closer together. Their market economies lead them to seek opportunities for trade and exchange, and their common political orientations make collaboration particularly easy. Kant argued further that building a democratic union would provide security in a world where democracies still faced threats from non-democratic states. Strength exists in numbers. A grouping of democratic states is more likely to withstand the assaults of other states than democracies operating individually on their own.

American leaders after World War II were determined to anchor the postwar international order in an alliance of democracies. While Roosevelt hoped that the

United Nations might provide the master mechanism for world peace, the other US leaders placed greater reliance on political, economic, and security cooperation with Europe and the wider free world community of democracies. As the Cold War loomed, American leaders made far-reaching commitments to build and manage the international order. The shared democratic traditions of its Western partners made it easier for the United States to honor these commitments. In arguing for economic aid to Europe in 1948, for example, Secretary of State George Marshall told a congressional committee that American assistance was necessary to prevent 'economic distress so intense, social discontents so violent, political confusion so widespread, and hopes for the future so shattered that the historic base of Western civilization, of which we are by belief and inheritance an integral part, will take on new forms in the image of the tyranny that we fought to destroy in Germany' (Marshall 1948). Europeans also invoked this notion of Western civilization in arguing for postwar cooperation. British Foreign Secretary Ernest Bevin argued for a European security alliance with the United States – what became NATO – as part of a 'spiritual union' that would link the Atlantic world. 'While, no doubt, there must be treaties or, at least, understandings, the union must primarily be a fusion derived from the basic freedom and ethical principles for which we all stand. It must be on terms of equality and it must contain all the elements of freedom for which we all stand' (Bevin 1948; Jackson 2003). The failure of peacemaking after World War I and the search by the United States for a stable group of like-minded countries with whom to build institutionalized relations made officials on both sides of the Atlantic receptive to these appeals to Western democratic solidarity (Jackson 2006; Hampton 1995; Hampton 1996).

After the end of the Cold War, the United States and the other leading democracies again affirmed their commitments to one another. Speaking at the United Nations in September 1991, President George H.W. Bush noted that the two great breakthroughs in the modern world had been the rise of individual enterprise and international trade. 'As democracy flourishes,' Bush said, 'so does the opportunity for the third historical breakthrough – international cooperation' (Bush, 1991). The Clinton administration also enshrined democratic community as the great reality of world politics after the Cold War – and its strategy of global peacemaking involved the 'enlargement' of this globalizing, democratic, market-oriented world system. The trade system was strengthened with the establishment of the World Trade Organization in 1995, which provided rules and dispute settlement mechanisms for the expanding world economy. In the late 1990s, the Clinton administration also supported the creation of the Community of Democracies, which was a forum for the leaders of the world's democracies to gather periodically to discuss ways to support and strengthen democratic institutions in transitional and developing countries.

The rise of China today will test these liberal ideas. As China becomes more powerful, will it peacefully integrate into the existing international order or seek to overturn it? Liberals and realists offer strikingly different visions of the future. Liberal thinkers argue that a 'peaceful rise' of China is possible if its domestic system evolves toward liberal democracy. In this view, China would follow a pathway similar to that of Japan after World War II. As a liberal capitalist state China will grow wealthier and gradually integrate into the world economic and political system. It will become a stakeholder in the existing order. Realist thinkers are more skeptical that democracy is a sufficient brake on conflict. For realists, the changing power position of China and the United States will matter more. China, regardless of its internal system, will seek to use its power to expand its influence and control over its region and perhaps the wider world. The United States, in turn, will resist China's quest for domination. Conflict – perhaps even war – will be the inevitable result.

7.6 DIFFERING PERSPECTIVES

Liberals and Realists on Interdependence and the Rise of China

Former President Bill Clinton, a Liberal Voice

- China should be brought into the World Trade Organization, because the more China trades with the West, the more likely that its domestic system will evolve toward democracy.
- The key to getting the China relationship right is to increase China's interdependence with the outside world. A more interdependent China will be a China with a more cooperative foreign policy, and one less inclined to undermine order regionally or globally.
- 'The world will be a better place over the next 50 years if we are partners, if we are working together.'

Political Scientist John Mearsheimer, a Realist Voice

- China will attempt to be a 'regional hegemon,' the undisputed power in its part of the world and will not tolerate meddling by an outside state like the United States.
- The rise of China – and its likely desire to dominate East Asia – will pose a fundamental threat to the United States in the near future.
- 'The best way to survive in this system is to be the biggest and baddest dude on the block ... Nobody fools around with Godzilla.'

Source: Swain (2008).

The United States and other advanced democracies believe strongly that a world of democracies is more likely to be peaceful than the alternative – a world of autocratic and authoritarian states. Many observers also believe that democracy – at least when it is deeply rooted within stable societies – facilitates other international developments that foster peace: international interdependence and the rule of law. Democracies are predisposed to trade with other states and collaborate to establish rules and institutions that allow them to collectively manage their relations.

Peace Movements and Global Civil Society

States make war – and so, not surprisingly, do states also take charge to make peace. But nongovernmental organizations (NGOs), that is, citizens' groups and political movements, have also played a role in pushing governments to the peace table, particularly over the last two centuries with the rise of liberal democracy and the increasingly destructive experiences of war. While these nongovernmental groups do not directly end wars or make peace agreements, they serve to draw attention to the costs of wars and to lobby governments to address issues of human suffering and social justice.

Before the twentieth century, citizen groups were not a major presence when states went to war. In both Europe and the United States, pacifist groups formed to seek alternatives to war and made small acts of resistance. For example, in the United Kingdom, the National Peace Council, established in 1908, brought together citizens from voluntary groups around the country to seek disarmament and the peaceful resolution of disputes. With World War I, however, large-scale groups of citizens organized to oppose government policy. During and after the war, peace activists in the United Kingdom and the United States also put forward ideas about world peace, offering proposals for a world organization that would promote peace – ideas that Woodrow Wilson drew from in his proposal for a League of Nations. The massive outpouring of people into the streets of cities across Europe to greet Wilson on the eve of the Paris peace talks lifted and reinforced Wilson's peacemaking agenda.

The devastation of the two nuclear bombs dropped on Japan at the end of World War II provided the political and symbolic catalyst for a new generation of peace activism, which gained additional participants in the early decades of the Cold War. The dangers of nuclear war provided the focal point for these peace campaigns. Political activists, philosophers, theologians, and public intellectuals were active participants in the worldwide Cold War peace movement. Even nuclear scientists who had helped in inventing atomic weapons became involved in the search for arms control and disarmament. In 1957, for example, a group of scientists from both sides of the Cold War divide met in Pugwash – a remote location in Canada – to promote understanding and reconciliation between Western and Communist countries. The Pugwash Conferences, so named for that first meeting, continue today to bring together scholars and public figures to seek to reduce the dangers of armed conflict and find cooperative solutions to global problems.

Peace movements have had many different specific aims. In the United States, the Vietnam War triggered the most organized and vocal peace movement in the country's history. Hundreds of thousands of protesters marched on Washington on various occasions to demand that the United States withdraw from the war and bring the troops home. Opposition to the Vietnam War sparked protest demonstrations at the 1968 Democratic National Convention in Chicago, culminating in violence and hundreds of arrests. The antiwar movement touched many facets of life – music, art, education, and lifestyle. Rock groups such as the Grateful Dead and the Beatles incorporated messages of peace in their music, spreading those sentiments within American and international youth culture. The anti-Vietnam War movement ended when American troops finally left Vietnam in the spring of 1972.

In the 1980s, the American and European peace movements came to life again in protests over the escalation of hostilities between the United States and the Soviet Union. Huge crowds in the major capitals of Europe protested the decision by the Reagan administration to introduce new mid-range nuclear missiles on the European continent. Campaigns for nuclear disarmament that had been active during the earlier decades of the Cold War resumed. Church groups – including Catholic bishops, and doctors – through an organization called Physicians for Social Responsibility – issued statements about the catastrophic loss of life that nuclear war would bring to the planet.

More recently, the 2003 American war in Iraq also triggered an outpouring of antiwar protests in the United States, Western Europe, Japan, Turkey, and around the world. Protests began in 2002, even before the war was launched, and continued thereafter. Hundreds of thousands of people flooded into public squares to demonstrate

Photo 7.5 Protesting the US-Led Intervention in Iraq, 2003
More than 2 million peace protesters, some wrapped in rainbow peace flags, flooded the center of Rome, Italy on February 15, 2003 to protest the war in Iraq.

Source: Eric VANDEVILLE/Gamma-Rapho via Getty Images.

against the war in cities such as Washington, DC, Paris, Berlin, and London. In Rome, on February 15, 2003, more than 2 million people came out to demonstrate against the war, which might be the largest antiwar rally in history. On the same day, antiwar protests were held in nearly 600 cities worldwide.

It is difficult to measure the influence of the peace movement on the actions of governments. Peace demonstrations likely played some role in helping to pressure the US government to end its involvement in Vietnam. In the 1980s, the Western peace movement provided the backdrop of the diplomacy between the United States and the Soviet Union, which ultimately brought the Cold War to an end. The antiwar demonstrations against the American war in Iraq – and the widespread opposition to the war particularly in Western Europe – made it easier for elected leaders to criticize US policy and oppose the war in places such as the United Nations. The peace movement does not rely simply on demonstrations, although they have been important across the last century. In individual countries, peace movement groups are active in electoral politics and public affairs, urging their governments to seek diplomatic settlements for global trouble spots.

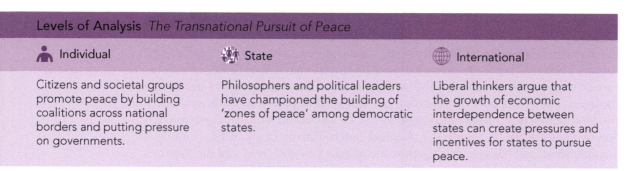

Levels of Analysis *The Transnational Pursuit of Peace*

👤 Individual	👥 State	🌐 International
Citizens and societal groups promote peace by building coalitions across national borders and putting pressure on governments.	Philosophers and political leaders have championed the building of 'zones of peace' among democratic states.	Liberal thinkers argue that the growth of economic interdependence between states can create pressures and incentives for states to pursue peace.

REVISITING THE ENDURING QUESTION AND LOOKING AHEAD

As the weapons of war have become more destructive over time, the search for stable peace among states has also gained ground. Over the centuries, states have traveled many different pathways to peace. Until the sources of war completely disappear, the search for peace will remain a persistent feature of world politics.

Two international distributions of power may influence the prospects for peace: a balance of power and hegemony. Diplomacy and power balancing represent actions by states to advance their interests but may also help promote peace. International law and institutions, and in particular the European Union, may offer important new opportunities for peace. The extension of democracy to more countries, the intensification of trade and investment across the world, and the rise of peace movements and international civil society have also helped maintain international peace, particularly among democratic states.

Nuclear weapons have also perhaps had a pacifying effect on world politics. Indeed, nuclear weapons are so important that it is sometimes suggested that they brought about a revolution in the very character of world affairs. It is to that possibility that we now turn our attention.

STUDY QUESTIONS

1. Among the forces for peace today are democracy, economic interdependence, diplomacy, and international law. Which of these do you consider the most powerful force for peace today? Could it be some other force? On what grounds are you basing your answer?

2. As noted in this chapter, a single big power, a hegemonic state, might be a force for peace. If you live in a small country that neighbors that hegemonic state, what questions might you pose to the leaders and citizens of the hegemonic state about their intentions as they bring peace into being?

3. A Roman writer of the fourth century CE advised: 'If you want peace, prepare for war.' To what extent do you find his advice persuasive?

4. In today's international system, how much overlap do you perceive among the two main power structures which reinforce stable peace – balance of power and hegemony?

5. With the advent of the internet and new forms of social media, do you expect the role of citizens as a source for peace to increase or decrease in the years ahead? Explain your reasoning.

FURTHER READING

Claude, Inis (1956) *Swords into Plowshares: The Problems and Progress of International Organizations* (New York: Random House). A classic study of the efforts by states in the modern era to build international peace organizations, with a focus on the League of Nations and the United Nations. Claude provides one of the best statements of the logic of collective security.

Falk, Richard A., Friedrich V. Kratochwil, and Saul Mendlovitz (eds) (1985) *International Law: A Contemporary Perspective* (Boulder: Westview Press). Essays in this volume discuss the various ways that international law is useful in the pursuit of peace and justice in world affairs.

Hamilton, Keith and Richard Langhorne (2010) *The Practice of Diplomacy: Its Evolution, Theory, and Administration*, 2nd edn (New York: Routledge). A survey of the rise of diplomacy among states as a tool for managing relations and establishing the conditions for peace and problem-solving. The book also looks at the current experience of diplomacy in the areas of climate change, human rights, and the activities of NGOs.

Ikenberry, G. John, Michael Mastanduno, and William C. Wohlforth (eds) (2011) *International Relations Theory and the Consequences of Unipolarity* (New York: Cambridge University Press). This book features various scholars exploring the consequence of a unipolar or hegemonic organization of world politics, particularly on international peace and stability.

Kaufman, Stuart, Richard Little, and William C. Wohlforth (2007) *Balance of Power in World History* (New York: Palgrave Macmillan). A sweeping study of the role of balance of power and empire across world history.

Wooley, Wesley T. (1988) *Alternatives to Anarchy: American Supranationalism Since World War II* (Bloomington: Indiana University Press). A vivid portrait of the ideas of postwar globalists and peace activists and their political efforts to usher in radical shifts in the governance of the global system to overcome the dangers of war and geopolitical conflict.

 Visit **www.macmillanihe.com/Grieco-IntroIR-2e** to access extra resources for this chapter including:

- Chapter summaries to help you review the material
- Multiple choice quizzes to test your understanding
- Flashcards to test your knowledge of the key terms in this chapter
- An interactive simulation that invites you to go through the decision-making process of a world leader at a crucial political juncture
- Pivotal decisions in which you weigh up the pros and cons of complicated decisions with grave consequences
- Outside resources, including links to contemporary articles and videos, that add to what you have learned in this chapter

8 Technology, the Use of Force, and Weapons of Mass Destruction

Enduring question
How have weapons of mass destruction, and in particular nuclear weapons, changed the practice of international relations?

Chapter Contents

Learning Objectives

By the end of this chapter, you will be able to:

→ Appreciate the relationship between technological change and the use of force.

→ Recognize the unprecedented destructive capacity of nuclear weapons and their influence on modern international relations.

→ Analyze the peculiar logic of nuclear deterrence and its impact on governmental policy.

→ Understand the spread of nuclear weapons and evaluate efforts to halt it.

→ Analyze the dangers posed by chemical and biological weapons for modern society.

→ Demonstrate the connections between non-state actors, terrorism, and weapons of mass destruction.

→ Recognize how today's new technologies affect the use of force.

Although it may seem counterintuitive, the best way for two countries to avoid a nuclear war is for each one to try *not* to defend its own people in the face of a possible nuclear attack. This curious conclusion has been reached by many scholars and strategists who have thought long and hard about the connection between nuclear weapons and world politics. Nuclear weapons are so destructive that a nuclear war is unwinnable. The best way to avoid a nuclear war is to prevent countries from having nuclear weapons. But once countries have them, the best strategy may be to make sure no country sees a possible way to use nuclear weapons without facing massive destruction itself.

This chapter explores the relationship between technology and the use of force. We pay particular attention to nuclear weapons because these weapons have created a revolution in the way we think about technology and warfare. It is common to think that governments develop weapons to be used in war. But nuclear weapons are different, so different that their existence has changed the way most governments think about war itself. These are weapons not to be used in war, but to be used instead to deter war. Prior to the nuclear age, the great powers of the international system fought major wars with other each to settle their differences. In the nuclear era, however, the type of great-power wars the world witnessed between 1914 and 1945 has not taken place. Do nuclear weapons constitute an extraordinary 'pathway to peace' for nation-states? Have they changed fundamentally the relationship between diplomacy and warfare? This latter question has been an enduring and consequential one in international relations since the dawn of the nuclear age.

We will look first at the interplay between technology and warfare prior to the nuclear age. Then we examine what nuclear weapons are, how they work, and that peculiar logic of nuclear strategy that says the best way to avoid war is not to be prepared to fight it. That logic applied to the United States and Soviet Union who had massive nuclear arsenals facing each other during the Cold War. But does it also apply to countries like India and Pakistan, who face each other today with smaller nuclear arsenals? Or to countries that possess nuclear arsenals of vastly different size and sophistication, such as the United States and North Korea? More generally, does it apply to a world of nuclear proliferation in which many countries including North Korea and Iran, and perhaps their neighbors, are either developing or contemplating nuclear capabilities? We will also examine other weapons of mass destruction – weapons designed to kill very large numbers of civilians or armed forces, such as biological and chemical weapons – and explore the ongoing efforts by the international community to control the spread of all types of destructive weapons. We will look at the role of non-state actors and the special problem of terrorism and weapons of mass destruction. Finally, we consider how the new technologies of today, such as drones and cyber capabilities, may be reshaping the use of force.

TECHNOLOGY AND THE HISTORICAL EVOLUTION OF WARFARE

Across time, technology has shaped the nature of warfare and technological innovations have enabled states to use force in new ways. During the seventeenth and eighteenth centuries, military technology changed very slowly. Military capability was largely a function of the size of a country's professional standing army. 'Arms races' typically involved efforts by dynastic leaders to accumulate enough money to grow their own army faster than those of their neighbors or competitors. During the Napoleonic era (1799–1815), France overcame that constraint and transformed the nature of warfare through universal conscription, or the practice of requiring all physically capable citizens of a certain age (as opposed to paid professionals) to fight for the state. France created a 'nation in arms' and set in motion a transition from the wars of kings to the wars of peoples (Osgood 1983). Universal conscription enabled Napoleon to take on multiple adversaries in his bid for European hegemony; he remarked in 1813 that 'a man like me troubles himself little about the lives of a million men' (Woloch 1986: 101).

In the latter part of the nineteenth century, Germany rose to great-power status and took advantage of emerging technologies to gain decisive victories against Austria in 1866 and France in 1871. Germany mobilized and concentrated its forces by exploiting a new communications technology, the telegraph, which allowed instant communication over long distances and meant military commanders no longer had to rely on the speed of a horseman to send messages and issue commands. By making military use of a transportation technology that had developed over several decades, the railways, Germany managed to mass its forces quickly at the frontier so that its troops were ready for war, and took to the offensive, before their adversaries were fully prepared.

As we discussed in Chapter 2, the great lesson drawn from Germany's victories was the 'cult of the offensive,' or the widespread belief that the quicker a state mobilized for war and went on the offensive, the better its chances of victory (Van Evera 1984). European military staffs carried this belief into World War I. But technology had evolved in a way that confounded offensive military strategies. Armies built defensive trenches and used a relatively new weapon, the machine gun, to mow down the rapidly advancing forces of their enemies. What European governments expected to be a short war turned into a long, brutal stalemate in which each side took massive casualties.

Although World War II was fought only 20 years later, technology shifted again, and with a decisive impact on the use of force. Germany relied on a tactical military innovation called *Blitzkrieg*, or lightning war; it massed tanks and artillery in a concentrated space to push through enemy lines. The major combatants made extensive use of military aircraft, not only to diminish each other's forces, but also to bomb cities to demoralize enemy populations. By the end of the war the United States had developed, and used, an entirely new type of military technology and weapon, one that ultimately would reshape not only warfare but international relations as well, the nuclear bomb.

Levels of Analysis *Technology and the Evolution of Warfare*		
Individual	**State**	**International System**
The practice of universal conscription, that is, requiring citizens to fight for the state, began during the Napoleonic era.	Great powers in any era take advantage of innovations in military technology.	Technology affects the duration and intensity of war and, in the nuclear era, the likelihood that great-power war will take place.

NUCLEAR WEAPONS AND THE NUCLEAR REVOLUTION

We use the word 'blockbuster' today to describe a big event, such as a hit movie. The term was popularized during World War II, when the largest conventional bombs the combatants used were called blockbusters because they were powerful enough to destroy an entire city block. The original blockbusters that US and British forces dropped on their enemies contained *two tons* (4,000 pounds/over 1800kg) of high explosive. Blockbusters were designed to blow the roofs off buildings so that smaller bombs could be dropped to destroy building interiors.

On July 16, 1945, the United States detonated a very different type of bomb at a remote testing site near Alamogordo, New Mexico. That device – by today's standards, a very simple and crude nuclear bomb – released the energy equivalent of *19,000 tons* of TNT. The explosion in the New Mexican desert, which American nuclear scientists labeled the Trinity test, ushered in a new era for military technology and international politics (Rhodes 1986).

The Devastating Effects of Nuclear Weapons

Manhattan Project
The secret project that brought together expert scientists to build a super-weapon, culminating in the creation of the first atomic bomb.

The Trinity test was the culmination of a secret project that began just as America entered World War II. Codenamed the **Manhattan Project**, it brought together some of the best scientific minds of the United States and Europe to develop a super-weapon that would take advantage of recent discoveries in atomic physics. Albert Einstein, whose work on relativity served as the foundation of nuclear physics, helped to prompt the Manhattan Project by sending a letter to President Franklin Roosevelt in 1939 to alert him that German scientists were trying to exploit these key findings for military purposes (E-World 1997). Manhattan Project scientists worked to design a weapon that could harness and then release the tremendous energy created by **fission**, or an atom-splitting chain reaction, before the Germans did.

Fission
An atom-splitting chain reaction that is central to the working of a nuclear weapon.

On August 6, 1945, a US Air Force B-29 plane dropped a nuclear weapon called Little Boy on the Japanese city of Hiroshima. Three days later, a second bomb known as Fat Man was detonated over Nagasaki. The destructive effects were startling. The Hiroshima bomb killed between 70,000 and 80,000 people and injured 70,000 others.

Photo 8.1 Hiroshima after the Nuclear Attack
This building, today called Atomic Dome and 260 meters from the Hiroshima atomic bomb epicenter, is seen in September 1945 in Hiroshima, Japan. The world's first atomic bomb was dropped on Hiroshima on August 6, 1945, killing an estimated 70,000 people instantly. Over time, considering the effects of radiation, the total number of the victims is estimated at 340,000 people.

Source: Eiichi Matsumoto/The Asahi Shimbun via Getty Images.

The Nagasaki bomb exploded over a relatively isolated part of the city, resulting in about 40,000 killed and 40,000 injured. Japan surrendered shortly after the nuclear attacks on Hiroshima and Nagasaki, effectively ending World War II. As we show in Box 8.1, historians continue to debate the morality of the nuclear attack and whether it was truly necessary to cause the Japanese surrender.

America's nuclear monopoly did not last very long. In 1949, the Soviet Union shocked the world by successfully testing its own version of a fission atomic bomb. By 1952, the United States had developed an even more powerful and sophisticated device – a **thermonuclear**, or **fusion bomb**, also known as the hydrogen or 'H' bomb. Fusion bombs rely on the power of a contained fission explosion to trigger the fusing of hydrogen particles, a process that yields even greater amounts of destructive energy than a fission reaction alone. The United States tested its first fusion bomb in November 1952, and the explosion released 10.4 megatons, or millions of tons of TNT equivalent. That blast, more than 500 times more powerful than the Trinity test, vaporized an entire South Pacific island and replaced it with a crater 6,000 feet across and 164 feet deep.

That first thermonuclear device was too cumbersome to be used as a weapon. It was the size of a small building and weighed about 70 tons. As countries mastered nuclear technology, however, they abandoned the 'bigger is better' theme and sought to make nuclear devices smaller, more efficient, and able to penetrate enemy defenses and deliver weapons more accurately to chosen targets.

Thermonuclear bomb
A type of nuclear weapon, even more powerful than a conventional nuclear weapon, that relies on the power of a contained fission explosion to trigger the fusing of hydrogen particles, a process that yields even greater amounts of destructive energy than a fission reaction alone. Also known as a **fusion bomb**.

8.1   DIFFERING PERSPECTIVES

Were Nuclear Attacks on Japan Needed to End World War II?

Background

During August 1945, the United States dropped two atomic bombs on Japan, the Soviet Union declared war on Japan, and Japanese leaders surrendered to the United States and its allies. For decades, scholars and scientists have debated whether the use of atomic weapons was necessary to end the war and morally justifiable. Newly declassified materials and other primary source documents have gradually become available to stir the debate (Burr 2007).

Supporters of President Truman's historic decision believe that the use of nuclear weapons was the most viable way to force a Japanese surrender short of a long and costly invasion. The Japanese fought with almost fanatical resistance and signaled a determination to fight to the last man rather than surrender. Supporters argue that an invasion of Japan would have resulted in casualties far exceeding those caused by the attacks on Hiroshima and Nagasaki. The shocking effect of the dramatic new weapon convinced Japan's unyielding leaders to surrender, and ended the war quickly enough that the Soviet Union could not make any plausible claim to occupy Japan jointly with the United States.

Critics argue that the United States had viable alternatives to nuclear attack on two cities filled with Japanese civilians. They believe that by August 1945 Japan was already close to surrender due to the destruction by conventional bombing of over 50 of its cities, the blockade of its territory by the US Navy, and the fact that the Soviet Union had now joined the war against it. The threat of a final invasion under these circumstances should have been credible and sufficient to prompt capitulation. Moreover, if US leaders believed the shock effect of the nuclear device was really needed to prompt Japanese surrender, they could have detonated a weapon over Tokyo Harbor or a similarly visible location in order to achieve the desired political response while minimizing civilian casualties. Critics of Truman's decision suspect that US leaders were more interested in containing Soviet ambitions in the Pacific, or perhaps seeking to justify the massive costs associated with developing the atomic weapon, than in finding the least costly way to end the war.

Henry Stimson, US Secretary of War in 1945

I felt that to extract a genuine surrender from the Emperor and his military advisers, they must be administered a tremendous shock which would carry convincing proof of our power to destroy the empire. Such an effective shock would save many times the number of lives, both American and Japanese, than it would cost... The decision to use the atomic bomb was a decision that brought death to over one hundred thousand Japanese. No explanation can change that fact and I do not wish to gloss over it. But this deliberate, premeditated destruction was our least abhorrent choice. The destruction of Hiroshima and Nagasaki put an end to the Japanese war. It stopped the fire raids, and the strangling blockade; it ended the ghastly specter of a clash of great land armies.

Source: Stimson (1947): 101.

Admiral William D. Leahy, Chief of Staff to President Truman

It is my opinion that the use of this barbarous weapon at Hiroshima and Nagasaki was of no material assistance in our war against Japan. The Japanese were already defeated and ready to surrender because of the effective sea blockade and the successful bombing with conventional weapons ... The lethal possibilities of atomic warfare in the future are frightening. My own feeling was that in being the first to use it, we had adopted an ethical standard common to the barbarians of the Dark Ages.

Source: Leahy (1950): 441.

Intercontinental ballistic missile (ICBM)
Missile that in under an hour can travel thousands of miles through outer space and release multiple nuclear warheads, each carrying a payload of several hundred kilotons and independently guided to explode within several hundred feet of a separate target.

Submarine-launched ballistic missile (SLBM)
Missile that can produce much the same effect as an intercontinental ballistic missile (ICBM) from a platform deep beneath the ocean's surface.

Cruise missile
Missile, capable of being launched from land, air, or sea, that can travel below radar detection and guide itself around obstacles to deliver the warhead it carries.

Today's most sophisticated nuclear arsenal belongs to the United States and contains an array of compact and miniaturized nuclear weapons that can be delivered from land, sea, and air. Weapons may be dropped from 'stealth bombers,' or planes that can fly up to 6,000 miles without refueling and are invisible to enemy radar despite their large size. In less than one hour, **intercontinental ballistic missiles** (ICBMs) can travel thousands of miles through outer space and release multiple nuclear warheads, each having a yield of several hundred kilotons and independently guided to explode within several hundred feet of a separate target. **Submarine-launched ballistic missiles** (SLBMs) can accomplish the same mission, with a similar degree of accuracy, from a platform deep beneath the surface of the world's oceans. **Cruise missiles**, measuring about 20 feet long, can travel 'below the radar' at low altitudes, and possess a terrain-matching guidance system that enables them to fly across valleys and around mountains to deliver their nuclear warheads. Cruise missiles may be launched from the ground, aircraft, or ships (Schwartz 1998).

Regardless of how they are delivered, the distinctive feature of nuclear weapons is their unprecedented destructive capacity. Never in history have humans created a weapon that could destroy property and people so easily and quickly, with little discrimination between combatants and civilians.

Nuclear explosions create blast, heat, and radiation effects. An authoritative study by the Office of Technology Assessment (OTA) for the US Congress in 1979 found that the **blast effect** of a one-megaton explosion would be sufficient to level all buildings not specially reinforced within a four-mile radius (Office of Technology Assessment 1979). People near 'ground zero' would be crushed by debris or experience fatal collisions with nearby objects due to winds of up to 180 miles per hour. The heat or **thermal effect** of a one-megaton blast would cause third-degree burns on exposed skin up to five miles away from the explosion. Because a nuclear explosion causes dirt and air particles to become radioactive, the radiation or **fallout effect** would spread much further, with the potential to expose people hundreds of miles from the blast site to fatal cancers over time. Figure 8.1 shows the radius of the firestorm that would result from a nuclear detonation over the city of New York.

The OTA study estimated the likely effects of a variety of hypothetical nuclear exchanges between the United States and the Soviet Union during the Cold War. An attack of one nuclear weapon on a US or Soviet city (the OTA modeled Detroit and Leningrad as the hypothetical targets) would result in up to 2 million deaths immediately. A limited nuclear exchange in which each side fired ten missiles at oil refineries would result in the loss of about two-thirds of each country's oil capacity and the deaths of 1 to 5 million people. An all-out exchange utilizing large fractions of the nuclear arsenals of the two sides would result in between 20 and 160 million deaths and 'incapacitating psychological trauma and the breakdown of social order.' During the 1980s scientists speculated that a large-scale nuclear war might even result in a **nuclear winter**, as the smoke and soot resulting from explosions blocked out the sunlight from the earth's surface for extended periods of time.

Blast effect
The immediate explosive effect of a nuclear weapon. Can be powerful enough to level all buildings in a several-mile radius and to produce destructive winds of between 100 and 200 miles per hour.

Thermal effect
The secondary effect of a nuclear explosion, in which the heat waves from the explosion can cause third-degree burns up to five miles from the detonation site.

Fallout effect
The tertiary effect of a nuclear explosion. Because nuclear weapons cause dirt and air particles to become radioactive, an explosion can expose people hundreds of miles from the blast site to fatal cancers over time. This exposure to radiation is the fallout effect, and affects a much wider range than the blast or thermal effects.

Nuclear winter
A situation, feared by many scientists in the 1980s, in which the smoke and soot resulting from numerous nuclear explosions blocked out the sunlight from the earth's surface for extended periods of time.

Figure 8.1 Nuclear Firestorm
An 800 kiloton nuclear weapon detonated about one mile above Manhattan would create a huge firestorm in a heavily populated area.

Source: Starr, S., Eden, L. and Postol, T.A (2015), 'What would happen if an 800-kiloton nuclear warhead detonated above midtown Manhattan?' *Bulletin of Atomic Scientists*, https://thebulletin.org/2015/02/what-would-happen-if-an-800-kiloton-nuclear-warhead-detonated-above-midtown-manhattan/

Table 8.1 Ten Bombs on Ten South Asian Cities

A nuclear war between states that possess even modest stockpiles would result in several million persons killed or wounded.

Estimated nuclear casualties for attacks on ten large Indian and Pakistani cities				
City name	Total population within 5 kilometers of ground zero	Number of persons killed	Number of persons severely injured	Number of persons slightly injured
India				
Bangalore	3,077,937	314,978	175,136	411,336
Mumbai	3,143,284	477,713	228,648	476,633
Kolkata	3,520,344	357,202	198,218	466,336
Chennai	3,252,628	364,291	196,226	448,948
New Delhi	1,638,744	176,518	94,231	217,853
Total India	14,632,937	1,690,702	892,459	2,021,106
Pakistan				
Faisalabad	2,376,478	336,239	174,351	373,967
Islamabad	798,583	154,067	66,744	129,935
Karachi	1,962,458	239,643	126,810	283,290
Lahore	2,682,092	258,139	149,649	354,095
Rawalpindi	1,589,828	183,791	96,846	220,585
Total Pakistan	9,409,439	1,171,879	614,400	1,361,872
India and Pakistan				
Total	24,042,376	2,862,581	1,506,859	3,382,978

Source: NRDC, Natural Resources Defense Council, 2002, http://www.nrdc.org/ nuclear/southasia.asp. Reproduced with permission.

In 2002, the National Resources Defense Council produced an estimate of the effects of a 'small' nuclear war between India and Pakistan. They simulated India and Pakistan each exploding five nuclear bombs over five major cities of their neighbor. Each bomb in the Indian and Pakistani arsenals is about the size of the Hiroshima weapon. In this scenario, almost 3 million Indians and Pakistanis would be killed instantly, and another 1.5 million would suffer severe injuries (National Resources Defense Council 2002). Table 8.1 presents the cities targeted and the specific casualties estimated for each one.

Thankfully nuclear weapons have not been used since the attacks on Hiroshima and Nagasaki. But the **nuclear club** of nation-states believed to have possession of nuclear weapons has grown gradually to include nine members (see Table 8.2). The United States possesses the world's most diverse and technologically sophisticated nuclear arsenal, totaling roughly 7,000 nuclear warheads, of which about 1,800 are 'active' or operational. Although its former Cold War capacity has been diminished, Russia remains a major nuclear power with a similar stockpile of 7,000 warheads, of which 1,950 are operational. It inherited the nuclear arsenal of the former Soviet

Nuclear club
The group of states believed to possess nuclear weapons.

Table 8.2 World Nuclear Forces, 2017
Today there are nine nuclear weapons states, and even with the end of the Cold War, the nuclear arsenals of the former superpowers are still very large.

Country	Year of first nuclear test	Deployed* warheads	Stored warheads	Other warheads	Total inventory
United States	1945	1,800	2,200	2,800	6,800
Russia	1949	1,950	2,350	2,700	7,000
United Kingdom	1952	120	95	–	215
France	1960	280	10	10	300
China	1964	–	270	–	270
India	1974	–	120–130	–	120–130
Pakistan	1998	–	130–140	–	130–140
Israel	–	–	80		80
North Korea	2006	–		10–20	10–20
Total		4,150	5,275	5,510	14,935

Source: Kristensen, H. M. and Kile, S., 'World nuclear forces', *SIPRI Yearbook 2017* (Oxford University Press). Reproduced with permission of SIPRI.

*: 'Deployed' refers to warheads placed on missiles or operational on military bases. 'Stored' warheads would require preparation before they could be deployed and used. In the 'Other warheads' column, the United States and Russian holdings are warheads scheduled to be dismantled. The North Korean number reflects uncertainty over both how many exist and whether they are deployed. North Korean warheads are not included in the total, and for India and Pakistan, the higher estimate has been included in the totals.

Union; former Soviet republics such as Belarus, Ukraine, and Kazakhstan transferred nuclear weapons left on their territory after the collapse of the Soviet Union to Russia during the 1990s. The United Kingdom, France, and China were the third, fourth, and fifth nation-states to test a nuclear weapon, in 1952, 1960, and 1964 respectively. Each country currently possesses an arsenal of several hundred warheads.

It is difficult to make precise estimates of the holdings of other members of the nuclear club. Israel is widely thought to possess at least 80 warheads, even though it has not conducted a public test and refuses to acknowledge the existence of its arsenal. Nuclear experts believe India and Pakistan each possess about 125 warheads. North Korea first tested a nuclear weapon in 2006 and conducted five other tests between 2009 and 2017 and is believed to have sufficient nuclear material to construct up to 20 warheads. South Africa was a member of the nuclear club, having produced six warheads during the 1980s, but it dismantled its program and weapons in 1991 after its *apartheid*, or racially segregated, regime was overthrown in a popular revolution.

You now have a good grasp of what nuclear weapons are, how they work, and who has them. In the next section, we explore the implications of these weapons for international relations.

The Nuclear Revolution

The traditional purpose of military innovation has been to create new and more effective weapons that can be used to defeat an enemy in wartime. The machine gun, battle tank, aerial bomber, and submarine each played key roles in the world wars of the twentieth century. Nuclear weapons are qualitatively different and cannot be thought of as simply the next generation of war-fighting instruments. Bernard Brodie, one of the first military theorists of the atomic age, put it succinctly in 1946: 'Thus far the chief purpose of our military establishment has been to win wars. From now on its chief purpose must be to avert them. It can have almost no other useful purpose' (Brodie 1946: 76). Brodie captured the paradoxical essence of the nuclear revolution – nuclear weapons are so powerful that they cannot be used. As noted in Chapter 7, the nineteenth-century German strategist Carl von Clausewitz famously stated that warfare is 'the continuation of politics by other means.' Warfare, in other words, is a rational instrument of statecraft to be used by policy makers to achieve political goals. Warfare and diplomacy are two sides of the same coin; where diplomacy fails, military action might succeed. Even the all-out world wars of the twentieth century fit Clausewitz's model; military power was used to achieve a politically meaningful objective, even if at great cost. But nuclear weapons seem to nullify Clausewitz's rule. It is hard to imagine a politically meaningful purpose being served by an all-out nuclear war, or even by a 'limited' one. As Nina Tannenwald (2008) points out in an important constructivist study, much of the international community has internalized this understanding; a 'nuclear taboo' developed gradually after 1945, prompting most states to embrace the non-use of nuclear weapons as a political and moral imperative.

Nuclear deterrence
Using the threat of retaliation to protect oneself from an attack. Nuclear states use the threat of nuclear retaliation to deter other states from attacking them.

If nuclear weapons are not useful as weapons of war, then what purpose might they serve? The most basic answer is **nuclear deterrence** (Freedman 2004; Jervis 1989a). Instead of being used to fight wars, these weapons may be used to deter

Map 8.1 Israel, Iran, and the Middle East
Although it struck a separate peace with Egypt in 1979, Israel continues to view some of its neighbors, in particular Iran, as implacably hostile. Iran and other regional actors such as Hamas (which governs the Gaza Strip), in turn, question Israel's right to exist and view it as a regional aggressor that continues to occupy Arab lands, and to repress Palestinian peoples. These actors also resent that powerful Western states seem willing to tolerate Israel's nuclear arsenal while seeking to prevent Iran and others from acquiring nuclear weapons.

war or other types of behavior government leaders might find unacceptable. The nuclear strategy of the United States, for example, is designed to deter a nuclear attack on America, and to deter a nuclear or even a non-nuclear attack against America's closest allies. Many analysts believe that the purpose of the Israeli nuclear force has long been to deter any kind of attacks from an array of hostile neighbors, including Syria, Iran, and, prior to the 2003 war between Iraq and the United States, Saddam Hussein's Iraq. Iran, in turn, may be acquiring nuclear weapons to deter what it perceives as potentially aggressive Israel and United States (see Map 8.1). North Korea's determined nuclear effort is designed to deter the United States from attempting regime change, or the overthrow of the Kim family dynasty. Recall the importance of viewing the world from multiple perspectives: any state's nuclear program might be viewed as prudent and defensive by its leaders, yet as aggressive and alarming by its neighbors.

Assured Destruction and the Peculiar Logic of MAD

To understand nuclear deterrence theory, consider the simplified situation of two states, each with sizable nuclear forces. The United States and Soviet Union during the Cold War inspired this model. What was required for the United States to effectively deter the Soviet Union from attacking America with nuclear weapons? First, the United States needed the ability to retaliate and deliver nuclear weapons against the territory and population of the Soviet Union even after the Soviet Union had struck the United States first. Second, the threat of US retaliation had to be credible; Soviet leaders had to believe the United States would retaliate. Third, the costs of retaliation had to be judged by the Soviet leadership as unacceptably high. In other words, even after being struck first, the United States had to have sufficient forces remaining, and the will and capacity to deliver them, to inflict unacceptable damage on the Soviet population and territory.

Unacceptable damage is difficult to define precisely. For some countries, the prospect of a single nuclear attack against one city might be sufficient to deter them. Others, depending on the stakes involved in a conflict, might be willing to contemplate far greater losses in order to achieve a particular political objective. During the Cold War, American military planners tended to apply 'worst-case' analysis and presumed that the Soviet threshold for unacceptable damage was high. In the early 1960s, the United States government developed a nuclear arsenal with the premise that, to deter a possible Soviet first strike, the level of damage the United States had to inflict in a second strike was approximately 25 percent of the Soviet population and about 50 percent of the country's industry.

Once the United States possessed the ability and will to inflict unacceptable damage on the Soviet Union – even after the Soviets hit first with their best nuclear attack – it had what nuclear strategists call a **second-strike capability**. This is also called an assured destruction capability. Once the Soviet Union also acquired a comparable second-strike capability in relation to the United States, the two countries were in a situation of **Mutual Assured Destruction**, or **MAD**.

In the terminology of nuclear deterrence theory, a **first-strike capability** is the negation of another country's second-strike capability. In other words, if the United States possessed a first-strike capability (as it did during the early 1950s, when the Soviet Union had a small number of nuclear weapons and vulnerable delivery systems) it could strike the Soviet Union first in a nuclear attack, and the Soviets would not have sufficient residual nuclear forces to strike the United States in response and inflict unacceptable damage.

Unacceptable damage
The level of damage that a state is absolutely unwilling to sustain.

Second-strike capability
The ability and will to inflict unacceptable damage on an adversary – even after the adversary hits first with its best nuclear attack. Also known as **assured destruction**.

Mutual Assured Destruction (MAD)
A situation in which two adversaries each possess assured destruction capability, meaning that a nuclear conflict would likely inflict unacceptable damage on both countries.

First-strike capability
The negation of another country's second-strike capability.

Assuming two countries have sizable and dispersed nuclear forces, it is difficult to achieve a first-strike capability. But we can conceive of ways it might be accomplished. For example, one country's nuclear forces could become so accurate that they could locate and destroy most or all of the nuclear weapons of their adversary in a coordinated first strike. Second, a country might figure out how to defend its own territory and population from nuclear attack, perhaps by developing a space-based defensive system that would shoot down the other side's nuclear warheads before they could detonate on their targets. Since the early 1970s, the United States government has spent billions of dollars to research the possibility of a missile defense system that might thwart a nuclear attack against the United States. For example, Walt discusses a proposed space-based defense system with a 'railgun' that would electronically launch 'smart' projectiles to destroy incoming missiles (Walt 2000). Critics of missile defense argue that it is impossible to stop a determined nuclear attack because if even one or several warheads get through, they will render unacceptable levels of damage on the target. Critics also worry that if any state believes it might be able to defend itself against a nuclear attack, it may be more tempted to use nuclear weapons itself in a conflict with an adversary.

Most nuclear deterrence theorists believe that second-strike capabilities are desirable and first-strike capabilities are undesirable. They believe, in fact, that MAD is the best of all possible nuclear worlds. The reasoning is simple yet powerful. If two adversaries each have secure second-strike capabilities, neither has any incentive to start a nuclear war. No matter how good your initial nuclear attack might be, your adversary will still be able to destroy your territory and society in retaliation. MAD represents stability because no one can win a nuclear war, even if you catch your adversary by surprise.

In contrast, first-strike capabilities create instability. If the United States or any other country achieves a first-strike capability, they might be tempted in a crisis or a war to use nuclear weapons, on the assumption that they might be able to limit damage to their own society and perhaps 'win' a nuclear war. The situation is most unstable if two adversaries *each* believe they have a first-strike capability. In that case, there are great incentives to 'go first,' because the state that launches its nuclear forces first has the potential to come out of any conflict in a relatively advantageous position. Mutual first-strike capability gives each side the incentive to be 'trigger happy.' This is especially troubling in times of crisis, when government leaders are under considerable stress.

The policy implications are counterintuitive if one follows the logic of MAD. The most important advice for policy makers is to protect their weapons instead of their people. If governments can retaliate effectively and credibly, their adversaries will have no incentive to attack them with nuclear weapons. Policy makers should also avoid deployments that might enhance their own first-strike capability, because the appearance of a first-strike capability will only heighten the anxiety of adversaries and give them incentives to develop their own in response. For this reason, proponents of MAD oppose missile defense systems; any efforts to develop an effective defense might tempt a country into thinking it could combine offensive and defensive measures to limit damage to its territory in a hypothetical nuclear war. The most striking policy implication of MAD logic is that governments should not try to defend their populations from nuclear attack. In the logic of MAD, keeping the American and Soviet populations as 'mutual hostages' during the Cold War, and by implication, keeping the Chinese and American populations as mutual hostages today, represents the best way to ensure that no government is tempted to use its nuclear arsenal.

Should Governments Prepare to Fight Nuclear War?

As Box 8.2 indicates, not everyone is convinced by the logic of MAD. Beginning in the 1980s, a small group of scholars and practitioners in the US defense community, some of whom were close advisors to US President Ronald Reagan, argued that MAD is impractical and urged the United States to enhance its nuclear war-fighting capabilities (Gray 1979). MAD proponents dubbed adherents to this view as **Nuclear Utilization Theorists**, or **NUTS** (Keeny and Panofsky 1981–82). It is important to understand their perspective to gain a fuller appreciation of the logic and consequences of nuclear deterrence.

Nuclear Utilization Theory (NUTS) Contrary to MAD proponents, many Cold War policy makers followed this strategy, which argues that the United States should do everything it can to be prepared to fight a nuclear war.

8.2   MAKING CONNECTIONS
Theory and Practice

The Logic of MAD versus the Cold War Nuclear Strategies of the United States and Soviet Union

Theory: The Inescapable Logic of MAD, as Described by Robert Jervis, Professor of Political Science, Columbia University

A rational strategy for the employment of nuclear weapons is a contradiction in terms. The enormous destructive power of these weapons creates insoluble problems. For this reason, much of the history of nuclear strategy has been a series of attempts to find a way out of this predicament and return to the simpler, more comforting pre-nuclear world in which safety did not depend on an adversary's restraint. Short of developing an effective defense, however, these efforts cannot succeed. Instead, they can only produce doctrines which are incoherent and filled with contradictions, which though they are superficially alluring, upon close examination do not make sense.

Source: Jervis (1984): 19.

Jervis's point is the core of nuclear deterrence theory, which holds that it is both futile and dangerous for states to try to escape the logic of MAD. It is futile because there is no practical way to limit damage from a nuclear attack, and dangerous because the attempt to limit damage only increases the incentive to use nuclear weapons. Nevertheless, in practice countries do try to escape the logic of MAD, as Soviet and American nuclear strategy during the Cold War demonstrates.

Practice: American Nuclear Strategy during the 1980s

American strategy for the past several years – the 'countervailing strategy' – has assumed that what is crucial is the ability of American and allied forces to deny the Soviets military advantage from any aggression they might contemplate. The US must be prepared to meet and block any level of Soviet force. The strategy is then one of counterforce – blocking and seeking to destroy Soviet military power.

The nuclear policy of the Reagan administration – which is essentially the same as that of the Carter administration and which has its roots in the developments initiated by even earlier administrations – is particularly ill-formed … the strategy rests on a profound underestimation of the impact of nuclear weapons on military strategy and attempts to understand the current situation with intellectual tools appropriate only in the pre-nuclear era.

Source: Jervis (1985): 85.

Civil defense
Defenses, such as fallout shelters, designed to protect civilians in case of a nuclear strike from an adversary.

Photo 8.2 Civil Defense Planning Early in the Nuclear Era
These illustrations, taken from a 1961 US Defense Department publication, show two proposed models of family bomb shelters during the Cold War. The logic of MAD suggests governments should not attempt civil defense against a nuclear attack.

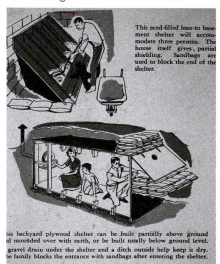

This sand-filled lean-to basement shelter will accommodate three persons. The house itself gives partial shielding. Sandbags are used to block the end of the shelter.

This backyard plywood shelter can be built partially above ground and mounded over with earth, or be built totally below ground level. A gravel drain under the shelter and a ditch outside help keep it dry. The family blocks the entrance with sandbags after entering the shelter.

Source: Hulton Archive/Getty Images.

Proponents of nuclear war fighting argued that MAD left the United States with an immoral and impractical response to the threat of a Soviet nuclear attack. MAD was immoral because the responsibility of the federal government was to protect the US population from attack, but the logic of MAD suggested that the government abdicate that responsibility and leave the population exposed. MAD was not credible because, in the event of a limited Soviet nuclear attack, it left the United States with a retaliatory choice of 'all or nothing.' If the Soviet Union launched even one or two nuclear weapons at US targets, would US leaders unleash the full US arsenal in response, knowing full well that the Soviets could then do the same? According to Nuclear Utilization Theorists, the Soviets were less likely to be deterred by non-credible threats to destroy the planet than by the realization that the United States was prepared to fight and try to win a nuclear war even though it had no intention of starting one.

The policy implications of nuclear war-fighting logic meant that the United States needed to get as close as possible to a first-strike capability. It needed to emphasize weapons that could target and destroy Soviet nuclear forces and develop strategies to eliminate the Soviet leadership and disrupt communications in the event of war so that the Soviets could not retaliate. And it needed to do its best to protect the US population by developing space-based missile defense technologies and enhancing **civil defense** (for example, underground bomb shelters) to protect against any Soviet warheads that reached US territory.

The debate between proponents of MAD and NUTS mirrored an important dichotomy within both the US and Soviet (now Russian) governments during and after the Cold War. The *civilian leaders* of each country have embraced, in their public statements, the logic of MAD. American and Russian leaders have argued consistently that there could be no winners in nuclear war; the only outcome was mutual annihilation. At the same time, however, the American and Russian *military establishments* have been preparing to fight a nuclear war in the event one occurred.

Each side developed accurate land-based missiles that could be used in a first strike against the land-based forces of the other side. They targeted each other's command and control systems and spent billions of dollars and rubles conducting research on missile defense systems. Civilian leaders have aspired to avoid war, but the job of professional militaries is to prepare for war, and develop strategies for winning in the event war takes place.

Reflecting on these nuclear debates in 1989, political scientist Robert Jervis observed that 'MAD is a fact, not a policy' (Jervis 1989b). He sought to remind us that nuclear weapons are so profoundly destructive that it is an illusion for any country, facing an adversary with sizable nuclear forces, to escape the logic of MAD. It takes so very few nuclear weapons to inflict a level of damage on a territory or population that most reasonable governments would consider unacceptable. A space-based defense system might be flooded with warheads or fooled by decoys. An effective civil defense would require people to behave calmly and rationally while cities were being destroyed and hundreds of thousands, if not millions, of their fellow citizens were being killed or irradiated. Box 8.3 shows the difficulties US governing authorities faced, even though they had considerable warning time, in trying to respond to a local crisis – Hurricane Katrina that struck New Orleans in 2005. Just imagine the difficulty of responding to a nuclear attack with little or no warning that devastated dozens of US cities at the same time.

8.3   MAKING CONNECTIONS
Aspiration versus Reality

Government Advice on Preparing for Nuclear War versus Government Response to Hurricane Katrina

Aspiration

In 1977, the US Defense Civil Preparedness Agency published a pamphlet entitled 'Protection in the Nuclear Age' (US Department of Defense 1977). This pamphlet was written for ordinary citizens with the purpose of reassuring them that in the event of a nuclear war, the US government at all levels would be there to help and protect them. The pamphlet was circulated among public libraries and opened with the following:

> If an enemy should threaten to attack the United States, you would not be alone. The entire Nation would be mobilizing to repulse the attack, destroy the enemy, and hold down our own loss of life. Much assistance would be available to you – from local, State, and Federal governments, from the US armed forces units in your area, and from your neighbors and fellow Americans. (p. iii)

Chapter One explains blast, heat, and radiation effects of a nuclear attack, and subsequent chapters provide detailed instructions and diagrams for constructing a fallout shelter in the basement of one's home, including advice on how much dirt would need to be packed around the home foundation to absorb radiation produced by exploded nuclear warheads. It advised citizens that they should, upon hearing a warning signal from their local government: 'go immediately to a public fallout shelter or to your home fallout shelter. Turn on a radio, tune it to any local station that is broadcasting, and listen for official information. Follow whatever instructions are given' (p. 12). The authors anticipate that nuclear war could prompt tense moments and antisocial temptations. They instruct: 'If you get caught in a traffic jam, turn off your engine, remain in your car, listen for official instructions, and be patient. Do not get out of the line to find an alternate route. All routes will be crowded. Be sure you have adequate gasoline when you start out. DO NOT BUY ANY MORE GAS THAN YOU WILL NEED' (p. 54, caps in original). The pamphlet shows a picture of one motorist offering a can of gasoline to another whose car is stalled. Upon arrival at a public fallout shelter, it advises people to 'elect a leader and form working groups' for tasks such as cooking, maintaining order, caring for the injured, and 'organizing recreation and religious activities' (p. 55).

Reality

The desire of any government to try to prepare its citizens for disaster is understandable. Our point is not to criticize that effort but to highlight the almost certain futility of it. An actual nuclear attack would pose individual, social, and organizational challenges that are virtually unimaginable. Instead of following plans and instructions, people would likely panic, chaos would reign, and government agencies, to the extent they still exist, would be incapable of developing strategies and directing citizens to respond in a calm and orderly fashion.

To appreciate the gap between aspiration and reality, consider the public response to Hurricane Katrina, which battered New Orleans in 2005. Katrina was one of the deadliest natural disasters in US history, with nearly 2,000 people losing their lives in the hurricane and subsequent flooding. Although there was ample warning, government response at the local, state, and national level is widely regarded to have been a dismal failure. According to a congressional report following the crisis, entitled 'A Failure of Initiative,' government officials neither executed emergency plans nor shared information that would have saved lives (Hsu 2006).

The report cited 90 failures at all levels of government including that the White House failed to act on the collapse of the New Orleans levee system which led to catastrophic flooding; that the US military and the Federal Emergency Management Agency (FEMA) set up rival and conflicting chains of command on site; that the Secretary of Homeland Security, Michael Chertoff, and the Governor of Louisiana, Kathleen Blanco, could neither cooperate effectively nor agree on who should have primary responsibility for response to the crisis; and that inadequate training, lack of qualified emergency personnel, and poor communication among first responders hampered rescue and relief efforts. The report asserted that 'blinding lack of situational awareness and disjointed decision making needlessly compounded and prolonged Katrina's horror.'

The evacuation plan initiated by New Orleans Mayor Ray Nagin did not account for the fact that 100,000 city residents had no cars and relied on public transportation. Shelter sites were overwhelmed; the Louisiana Superdome was intended to host fewer than 1,000 evacuees, but more than 30,000 showed up.

The congressional report found that the single biggest government failure was in not fully anticipating the consequences of the storm.

Living with MAD: Arms Control Efforts

Recognition that there would be no winners in nuclear war helped to inspire governments to undertake nuclear arms control efforts that have spanned more than five decades. The Cuban Missile Crisis of 1962, which brought the world as close as it has ever been to nuclear war, was a key catalyst. In 1963, the Soviet Union, United States, and the United Kingdom signed the Partial Test Ban Treaty, which prohibited tests of nuclear devices in the atmosphere, outer space, and under water, but allowed them deep underground. Over 100 countries subsequently signed and ratified the treaty. The signatories of the Test Ban Treaty acknowledged both the danger of nuclear weapons and their potential to contaminate the natural environment.

 Simulations: What would you do? Imagine you are President John F. Kennedy during the Cuban Missile Crisis. Visit the companion website and choose from a range of options. How would you handle this nuclear threat?

By 1969, the two superpowers were prepared to take the next step and begin placing limits on nuclear capabilities. The first Strategic Arms Limitation Treaty (SALT I) was signed in 1972. It froze US and Soviet land-based and submarine-based ballistic missiles at their then current levels. The Anti-Ballistic Missile (ABM) Treaty, also signed in 1972, prohibited the development, testing, and deployment of comprehensive missile defense systems. SALT I was followed by SALT II, a more complicated treaty that sought to limit the arms race types of nuclear warheads and delivery systems. SALT II allowed the United States and Soviet Union to each field no more than 2,400 ICBMs, SLBMs, and strategic bombers.

Many proponents of arms control in the United States complained that the SALT process did not actually limit or stop the nuclear arms race; by setting ceilings on the number of weapons each side could have, it simply provided incentives to American and Soviet planners to develop more sophisticated and potent nuclear weapons. As we saw in Chapter 7, a mass movement during the early 1980s including peace activists, politicians, scientists, and religious leaders emerged in support of a **nuclear freeze**. The idea of the freeze was to avoid complicated negotiations and simply stop the arms race where it was by preventing the superpowers from developing or deploying any new warheads or delivery systems.

Nuclear freeze
A plan that would stop an arms race in its place by simply preventing two adversaries from developing or deploying any new warheads or delivery systems.

Although the nuclear freeze was never implemented, it influenced politics in the United States. The administration of President Ronald Reagan responded with its own idea for a new agreement with the Soviets – the Strategic Arms Reduction Treaty or START. Reagan presented START as an improvement over SALT because it called for actual reductions in superpower arsenals, rather than setting high limits to which each side could legally race. Soviet leaders were initially skeptical of START because they did not want to reduce their arsenal while the United States was simultaneously exploring the possibility of a sophisticated, space-based missile defense system, popularly known as the Reagan Star Wars plan. But the Soviet position softened as the end of the Cold War drew near and it became clear that an effective space defense against thousands of missiles and decoys would be almost impossible to accomplish. In 1991 START I was signed, calling for the United States and Soviet Union to each reduce their strategic nuclear arsenals to no more than 6,000 warheads on a maximum of 1,600 land-based and sea-based missiles and nuclear-capable aircraft. START I did produce a radical reduction in forces. By the deadline for implementation in 2001, the two sides destroyed over half of their strategic nuclear weapons.

A START II treaty was signed by US President George W. Bush and Russian President Boris Yeltsin in 1993. The treaty required each side to reduce their deployed nuclear warheads to 3,500 and banned the use of MIRVs (Multiple Independently Targetable Re-entry Vehicles, or missiles that could deliver multiple warheads to different targets at the same time) on land-based missiles to discourage each side from having a potent means to attack the land-based missiles of the other. However, START II was never implemented due to Russia's objections to US plans to develop a limited missile defense system. US diplomats emphasized that this missile defense initiative was not directed at Russia, but at rogue states such as Iran and North Korea, or terrorist groups, whose leaders might not be deterred by the threat of retaliation. Nevertheless, when in December 2001 the United States notified Russia (as per the terms of treaty) that it was withdrawing from the ABM Treaty, Russia announced that it no longer considered itself bound by the provisions of START II.

Table 8.3 Timeline of Nuclear Arms Control Agreements and Treaties
Negotiations to control, limit, or reduce nuclear weapons have been a part of world affairs for half a century.

1959	Antarctic Treaty
1963	Treaty banning nuclear weapon tests in the atmosphere, in outer space, and under water (LTBT)
1967	Treaty for the prohibition of nuclear weapons in Latin America
1968	Non-Proliferation Treaty (NPT)
1972	First round of Strategic Arms Limitation Talks (SALT I) ends Treaty between the US and the USSR on the limitation of underground nuclear weapons tests (TTBT) Interim agreement on Strategic Offensive Arms (SALT I Treaty)
1974	Treaty between the US and the USSR on the limitation of underground nuclear weapon tests (TTBT)
1976	Treaty between the US and the USSR on underground nuclear explosions for peaceful purposes (PNET)
1979	Treaty between the US and the USSR on the limitation of Strategic Offensive Arms, together with agreed statements and common understandings regarding the treaty (SALT II Treaty)
1985	South Pacific Nuclear-Free Zone Treaty (Treaty of Rarotonga)
1987	Treaty between the US and USSR on the elimination of their intermediate-range and shorter-range missiles (INF Treaty)
1991	Treaty between the US and the USSR on the reduction and limitation of Strategic Offensive Arms (START I Treaty) Presidential nuclear initiatives
1993	Treaty between the US and the Russian Federation on further reduction and limitation of Strategic Offensive Arms (START II Treaty)
1995	Treaty on the Southeast Asia Nuclear Weapon-Free Zone (Bangkok Treaty)
1996	African Nuclear Weapon-Free Zone Treaty (Pelindaba Treaty) Comprehensive Test Ban Treaty (CTBT)
2002	The Moscow Treaty on Strategic Offensive Reductions (SORT)
2010	The New START Treaty between Russia and the US
2017	Treaty on the Prohibition of Nuclear Weapons (passed in the UN in July 2017 but not in effect as of May 2018)

Arms control efforts continued, however, and a so-called New START Treaty was signed by the United States and Russia and ratified by the US Senate at the end of 2010. The Treaty limits each side to 1,550 deployed strategic warheads (warheads placed on missiles and planes and ready to be used), and 700 deployed land-based missiles, sea-based missiles, and strategic bombers. It also allows each side to have up to 100 *non-deployed* missile launchers and bombers. The Treaty stipulates that these limits will stay in effect until the Treaty expires in February 2021. Each side also gets to conduct on-site inspections to ensure the compliance of its partner.

Critics pointed out that the counting rules of the New START Treaty actually allow for each side to deploy many more nuclear weapons than it first might appear. This is because every bomber equipped with nuclear weapons counts as one warhead under the terms of the treaty. In other words, heavy aircraft could carry many nuclear warheads even though each aircraft counts as only one. Arms control proponents were also disappointed that the treaty did not place significant limitations on missile defense systems.

Arms control efforts have come a long way since the Cold War, notwithstanding the strengths or weaknesses of particular agreements. As late as 1986, the United States had over 23,000 nuclear warheads and the Soviet Union had over 40,000. Currently the United States and Russia each deploy fewer than 2,000. Given the destructive capacity of nuclear weapons, the principle of MAD continues to apply even at these relatively smaller force levels. It is important to emphasize, however, that the logic of nuclear deterrence and its associated arms control efforts were developed in a world of two major nuclear powers. But what are the implications as more and more states possess nuclear weapons, and with arsenals that vary in size and sophistication? We turn next to that important question.

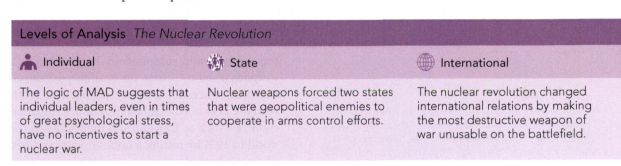

Levels of Analysis *The Nuclear Revolution*		
👤 Individual	👥 State	🌐 International
The logic of MAD suggests that individual leaders, even in times of great psychological stress, have no incentives to start a nuclear war.	Nuclear weapons forced two states that were geopolitical enemies to cooperate in arms control efforts.	The nuclear revolution changed international relations by making the most destructive weapon of war unusable on the battlefield.

NUCLEAR PROLIFERATION AND EFFORTS TO HALT IT

For the first 40 years of the nuclear era, the possibility of all-out nuclear war between the superpowers preoccupied international relations scholars and practitioners. Today, the more important concern is the spread of nuclear weapons and the possibility that, as more actors obtain them, nuclear war becomes more likely either by accident or design. In this section, we explore how difficult it is to obtain nuclear capability and why some states choose to make that effort. We also examine different perspectives on the dangers of nuclear proliferation. Finally, we look at efforts to halt the spread of nuclear weapons and abolish them altogether.

Obtaining Nuclear Capability: Difficult but Not Impossible

The basic design features of a nuclear weapon are readily available to anyone with a computer or access to a good public library. Fortunately, understanding the basic idea of how to build a nuclear weapon is very different from obtaining the materials and configuring the device with the necessary precision so that it works. It is very difficult, but not impossible, for a state or non-state actor to develop a viable nuclear weapon.

The highest hurdle is to obtain fissionable material. The only materials that can achieve a self-sustaining, atom-splitting chain reaction in the core of a nuclear bomb are **plutonium** and **uranium**. Neither is easy to produce in *weapons-grade* form. Plutonium is rarely found in nature but created as a by-product when energy is generated by a nuclear power plant. Plutonium needs to be extracted and then *reprocessed* or refined in a technically demanding procedure to become weapons grade. Uranium does occur in nature, but the predominant isotope (U-238) is unsuitable for nuclear weapons use. It needs to be *highly enriched* in a sophisticated technical facility to concentrate the minority isotope (U-235) that can sustain a chain reaction. Facilities to enrich uranium or reprocess plutonium are large and the processes are complicated.

Reprocessed plutonium or highly enriched uranium form the core of a nuclear weapon. But for the chain reaction to become self-sustaining, the core material must be placed under incredible pressure. Typically, this is done by surrounding the nuclear core with an outer ring of conventional high explosives, which must be detonated at precisely the same time so the pressure on the nuclear material is intense and uniform. Thus, in addition to uranium or plutonium, the nuclear shopping list would include air pressure measuring equipment, detonating heads, explosive charges, fuses, lead shields, neutron deflectors, and a team of scientists who could put it all together without destroying themselves and their facility in the process.

Countries that already possess nuclear weapons do not sell them to others on the open market. They also guard their nuclear arsenals carefully, so weapons are not lost or stolen. If it is not possible to buy one or easily steal one, how do countries develop nuclear weapons? Since fissile material is the key ingredient, a typical starting point is to develop a civilian nuclear power capability to generate energy. The expertise, equipment, and materials gained from this peaceful application of nuclear technology could subsequently be diverted to a weapons program. India, for example, developed a civilian nuclear capability during the 1960s with the help of companies from more advanced countries such as Canada, and then shocked the world in 1974 by testing a nuclear weapon it had obviously been developing as a by-product of its peaceful activity.

Israel, Pakistan, and Iraq attempted similar strategies with varying success. Israel developed, allegedly for peaceful purposes, a large nuclear complex near the city of Dimona, with French assistance, beginning in the late 1950s. Israel's diversion from nuclear power research to weapons production is assumed from the pattern of activity at that complex and satellite pictures of weapons bunkers and launch sites. Pakistan began during the 1970s with a nuclear power plant near Karachi that led to a diversion of material over several decades, with considerable help from China, before testing its weapon in 1998. China, which during the Cold War believed the two superpowers should not monopolize nuclear

Plutonium
Along with uranium, one of the two materials that can be used to create a nuclear weapon. Rarely found in nature, plutonium is found as a by-product when energy is generated by a nuclear power plant and must then be extracted and reprocessed to become weapons grade.

Uranium
Along with plutonium, one of two materials that can be used to create a nuclear weapon. Unlike plutonium, uranium can be found in nature, but is not suitable in that form (U-238) for nuclear weapon use. It needs to be highly enriched in a sophisticated technical facility to produce the concentrated uranium (U-235) that can sustain a chain reaction.

Photo 8.3 'Ivy Mike' Thermonuclear Explosion in the Marshall Islands
A mushroom cloud rises from the Ivy Mike test on Enewetak Atoll in the Marshall Islands, South Pacific Ocean. Operation Ivy was the code name given to America's plan to develop a hydrogen bomb. 'Mike' was shorthand for 'megaton' explosion.

Source: Science Photo Library.

capability, transferred to Pakistan nuclear weapon designs, technical expertise, and some of the sophisticated ancillary equipment.

Iraq's nuclear ambitions were frustrated in 1981, when Israel destroyed an Iraqi nuclear reactor that Israel claimed was being used to produce weapons-grade fuel. It became apparent after the first Gulf War (1990–91) that Saddam Hussein had revitalized the Iraqi nuclear program, only to have it destroyed by international inspection teams as part of the surrender terms after the war. The US attack against Iraq in 2003 was premised, in part, on the belief that Saddam Hussein still possessed and was hiding a nuclear weapons program. No evidence was found to support this suspicion, leading many countries, including close allies of the United States such as Germany and France, to question US motives and protest its decision to attack Iraq.

Globalization has increased opportunities for nuclear aspirants to obtain the necessary materials, equipment, and expertise. In 2003, the world discovered that Abdul Qadeer Khan, the 'father' of Pakistan's nuclear program, had been orchestrating a global black market in nuclear technology for years. Khan's network stretched across Europe, Russia, the Middle East, and Southeast Asia. He apparently assisted North Korea, Iran, and Libya in furthering their nuclear programs. Like any good salesman, Khan even published brochures and catalogues advertising the materials and services his 'team' could offer to clients. His ring was broken up in 2004, but he remained defiant in justifying his activities as appropriate to enhance the security needs of developing countries.

Iran and North Korea: A Nuclear Deal and a Nuclear Standoff

In recent years the problem of nuclear proliferation has centered on the programs of two countries, Iran and North Korea. Sanctions and negotiations led to an international agreement to stall, if not eliminate, Iran's proliferation effort. In the case of North Korea, diplomacy and sanctions failed and 2017 brought a nuclear standoff between the leader of North Korea, Kim Jung-un, and the President of the United States, Donald Trump.

Iran raised concerns when international inspectors discovered a uranium enrichment plant south of the capital, Tehran, in 2002. In 2004, Iranian leaders agreed to suspend nuclear enrichment activity, but they resumed those activities in defiance of the UN in 2005, claiming that their nuclear facilities were intended solely to produce electricity. Western countries responded with international sanctions, but Iran continued its efforts.

The sanctions took their toll. Between 2012 and 2014 Iran's economy shrank by about ten percent. Its oil exports fell from 2.5 million barrels per day (mbd) to 1 mbd, investments in its energy sector were curtailed, and Iran lost access to $120 billion in reserve assets held in foreign banks (Katzman 2018). The sanctions, and the election of a more moderate leader, Hassan Rouhani, brought Iran to the negotiating table. It struck an agreement in 2015 with the P-5 (the United Kingdom, the United States, Russia, China, and France) plus Germany. The deal allowed Iran, for 15 years, to enrich uranium, but only to the extent required to fuel nuclear power plants. Iran also eliminated its existing stockpile of weapons-grade enriched uranium. In exchange, its negotiating partners relaxed sanctions and allowed Iran access to its frozen assets. In the United States, the deal was negotiated under President Obama and harshly criticized by incoming President Trump. Trump was skeptical (despite confirming evidence from intelligence agencies) that Iran was complying with the letter of the agreement and felt that Iran violated the spirit by supporting terrorism and acting aggressively in the Middle East and Persian Gulf. Trump abandoned the agreement in 2018, but other signatories defended it as at least a temporary solution to the Iranian nuclear problem and as vital to the maintenance of regional peace.

The North Korean proliferation dispute has proved less tractable. In 1994 North Korea agreed to suspend its nuclear weapons efforts in exchange for international aid and access to new civilian nuclear reactors. A decade later the United States offered evidence that North Korea had been operating a covert nuclear program in violation of the 1994 deal. North Korea responded by declaring itself a nuclear weapons state and by testing a device in 2006. It subsequently agreed, after Six-Party Talks with China, Japan, Russia, the United States, and South Korea, to abandon its program in exchange for economic and energy assistance. But the deal fell through and North Korea continued to enrich uranium, test weapons, and develop medium- and long-range ballistic missiles capable of delivering the weapons. The UN Security Council responded by isolating North Korea diplomatically and imposing economic sanctions of increasing severity.

Sanctions proved less effective in this case. Although it objected to North Korean nuclear activities, China, North Korea's principal economic partner, was reluctant to cooperate fully with sanctions and apply maximum economic pressure. For China, the possible collapse of the North Korean regime and the accompanying flood of refugees into China were bigger concerns than North Korea's nuclear program. China also worried that, in the event of regime collapse, the two Koreas might be reunified as an ally of the United States.

China's calculation created a predicament for the United States. Without full Chinese cooperation, sanctions could not pressure North Korea to change its behavior. The alternative to sanctions, military force, was of high cost and questionable utility given that Seoul, the capital of America's South Korean ally, is uncomfortably close to North Korea and would likely experience significant damage and casualties in any military conflict on the peninsula. The predicament took on increasing urgency as it became clear by 2017 that North Korea was making rapid progress not only in weapons development but in the means to deliver them even to the west coast of the United States.

A possible diplomatic resolution was complicated by the unpredictability that developed personally between Kim and Trump. In 2017 the two resorted to an escalating war of words including personal insults and parallel threats to destroy each other. Analysts warned that the situation resembled the Cuban Missile Crisis, albeit in slow motion (Sagan 2017). Equally troubling, neither leader appeared prepared to apply a key lesson of the earlier nuclear crisis and offer his counterpart a face-saving way to back down from conflict. In 2018, however, both Kim and Trump adopted a more cooperative stance and even agreed to meet personally at a summit in Singapore. The key issues involve whether North Korea will give up its nuclear program, as demanded by the United States, in exchange for recognition, security guarantees, and economic assistance, as expected by North Korea.

Why Do States Want Nuclear Weapons?

Given the insecurity of an anarchical international system and the potency of the 'ultimate' weapon, we might expect every country to follow Iran and North Korea in hot pursuit of a nuclear capability. Surprisingly, most are content to be non-nuclear weapon states. Only a relatively small number of states are determined to join the nuclear club, and it is important to understand why. We should resist the temptation to conclude that, beyond the 'responsible' states that already possess them, only 'irrational' states or leaders seek nuclear weapons.

We can identify at least three general reasons why states might be willing to bear the substantial financial costs and risk the disapproval of the international community by pursuing nuclear weapons. Conflicts with neighboring states or geopolitical rivals constitute the most important rationale for proliferation efforts.

India and Pakistan are long-standing rivals. Once India tested the bomb, Pakistan's leaders felt that nuclear capability was essential to deter and prevent intimidation by India. Resource-poor Pakistan was determined to match India even if the effort took decades. Israel's not-so-secret nuclear weapons program clearly inspired some of its regional rivals – Iran, Syria, Libya, and Iraq – to pursue their own projects. Not surprisingly, Iran's leaders find it hypocritical that powerful Western countries tolerate Israel's nuclear program – presumably because Israel faces hostile neighbors – but refuse to tolerate Iran's, even though Iran, too, faces a hostile neighbor, Israel.

A second motivation concerns status or prestige. Nuclear weapons, like a space program, confer great-power status or, in a regional context, major-power status on their holders. The great powers of an earlier era, the United Kingdom and France, developed and maintained their own nuclear forces after World War II to signal that they still merited great-power status despite their decline in relative influence and membership within the NATO alliance. British Prime Minister Winston Churchill famously remarked that the cost of maintaining nuclear weapons was the price the United Kingdom paid to 'sit at the top table.' France's nuclear forces both conferred prestige and gave France a degree of independence from their dominant ally, the United States. Iraq's nuclear program was clearly tied to Saddam Hussein's ambition to make Iraq a dominant regional power, the self-appointed leader of Arab states mobilizing against the common enemy of Israel. China and India each had plausible geopolitical reasons (including fear of each other) to develop nuclear weapons, but also sought respect as large, emerging great powers in the international system.

Third, nuclear weapons are great equalizers, and are especially attractive to states or regimes that perceive themselves as facing threats to their very existence. Israel, at least initially, perceived itself as weak and vulnerable in a neighborhood of hostile Arab states that did not accept its right to exist. South Africa developed nuclear weapons during the decades it was treated as a pariah state; the *apartheid* regime was widely challenged by neighboring black states and the international community. North Korea, particularly after the fall of communism globally, views itself as a fragile state in a precarious position in part because the United States has expressed its desire for the regime to collapse.

We should also ask why states with the clear potential to develop nuclear weapons refrain from the attempt or abandon it. **Extended deterrence** – the threat by one country to use its nuclear forces to protect other countries – is one key reason. Many of America's allies in NATO and others, including Japan and South Korea, are technologically capable of joining the nuclear club, but instead have relied on the protection provided by the US 'nuclear umbrella.' The United States has committed to protecting them, with nuclear weapons if necessary, from attacks by neighboring states who themselves may possess nuclear weapons. One important reason for America's continued military presence in East Asia after the Cold War is to discourage nuclear proliferation. If the United States abandoned its commitment, Japan and South Korea, surrounded by nuclear-capable states (China, North Korea, Russia, and India) might feel compelled to develop their own nuclear equalizers.

Some states recently abandoned well-developed nuclear programs to earn approval and material benefits from other states. South Africa produced six nuclear weapons by the end of the 1980s yet dismantled them with the collapse of the *apartheid* regime. Giving up the weapons was part of a larger strategy for South Africa to integrate into an international community that had long considered it an outcast. Libya suddenly announced in 2003 that it would terminate its nuclear weapons program. It had been subject to international economic sanctions since the late 1980s for support of terrorism and development of weapons of mass destruction. Libya had not yet

Extended deterrence
The threat by one country to use its nuclear forces to protect other countries.

developed warheads but had acquired the technology and materials needed to enrich uranium. Its renunciation of nuclear weapons helped to end its isolation and expose the smuggling ring of A.Q. Khan. Three countries – Ukraine, Kazakhstan, and Belarus – inherited nuclear weapons (respectively 5,000, 1,400, and 81) stationed on their territory when they became independent states after the Soviet Union collapsed. All three new states eventually transferred their nuclear holdings back to Russia in the mid-1990s; in exchange, they received economic aid and diplomatic support from many other states.

Giving up nuclear weapons brings international approval, but might it make weaker states more vulnerable to attack? This question was raised in 2011, with the decision by NATO countries to intervene in Libya's civil war in support of rebel forces seeking to overthrow Libya's government. Libya had given up its nuclear program in 2003 in exchange for Western diplomatic and economic concessions; in 2011, Western countries saw the Libyan civil war as an opportunity to oust Libya's dictatorial government. North Korea observed these events, and the North Korean official news agency released a statement in March 2011 suggesting that Libya had been deceived by the West when it gave up its nuclear program. A North Korean Foreign Ministry official called the West's earlier bargain with Libya 'an invasion tactic to disarm the country' (McDonald 2011). These comments appeared to be intended to signal to the international community that North Korea would refuse to abandon its own nuclear quest.

The reasons why states seek to acquire, or not acquire, nuclear weapons capabilities are debated by scholars from different theoretical perspectives. In Box 8.4, we examine recent academic scholarship on an important question: do nuclear weapons bring greater influence in foreign policy disputes to the states that possess them?

8.4   RESEARCH INSIGHT

Does Having the Bomb Provide Foreign Policy Benefits?

Some states are determined to acquire nuclear weapons even at high cost, including the possibility that more powerful states will respond with economic sanctions and efforts to force regime change. Is the quest for nuclear weapons worth it? Recent scholarship in international relations suggests the answer is probably yes (Gartzke and Kroenig 2016).

For example, two scholars examined crisis outcomes from 1945 to 2000 and found that nuclear-armed states are more likely to prevail in crisis conflicts with non-nuclear states (Asal and Beardsley 2009). When a nuclear and non-nuclear state are involved, crises also tend to be of shorter duration than when they involve two non-nuclear states. The authors also show that adversaries of states with nuclear programs show more restraint in their use of military measures.

Two other recent studies offer somewhat contradictory evidence on the foreign policy utility of nuclear arsenals. Kroenig's (2013) study of 52 crises found that states with nuclear *superiority* were both more likely to take risks and more likely to prevail in interstate conflicts. But Sechser and Furmann (2013) found, in a study of 200 attempts to take or hold territory, that having nuclear weapons does not increase the probability of success. One possible way to reconcile these contradictory findings is to distinguish deterrence from compellence (Sechser and Furmann 2017). Possessing nuclear weapons may be more useful for states looking to deflect threats from others than for those looking to change the territorial status quo in their favor.

8.5   DIFFERING THEORETICAL APPROACHES

Why Don't More States Pursue Nuclear Weapons?

Nuclear weapons are regarded by many as the 'ultimate' weapon. When a state possesses them, it can deter potential adversaries, even more powerful ones, from attacking it. A relatively small number of states have pursued nuclear capability with determination. But many others have decided to pass up the opportunity to develop the ultimate weapon. Constructivists, liberals, and realists can offer different insights, highlighting different explanatory factors, into why states forego nuclear weapons.

Constructivism

Constructivists emphasize the development and spread of international norms in shaping state behavior. The 'nuclear taboo' and 'chemical weapons taboo' are clear examples of norms that have developed over time and been embraced by most member states in the international community. Constructivists might note that even states that developed or inherited nuclear weapons, for example South Africa and Ukraine, were willing to give them up to conform to international normative expectations.

Liberalism

Liberals share with constructivists a belief in the power of international norms but emphasize even more strongly the importance of international institutions. For liberals, the nuclear non-proliferation regime provides an institutional framework to enable states to forego weapons, for example by rewarding states willing to give up nuclear weapons with access to civilian nuclear technology. In other words, the institutional agreement, backed by United Nations monitoring and verification, is that if a state gives up nuclear weapons programs it can gain the technology to develop and run nuclear power plants.

Realism

Realists emphasize calculations of power and interest. Technologically capable states might bypass their own nuclear forces if they are confident that the 'nuclear umbrella' of a stronger ally will protect them by deterring potential aggressors from attacking them. Many realists expect Japan, for example, to continue to forego nuclear weapons as long as the United States remains credibly committed to protecting Japan. Constructivists see it differently and would argue that Japan's nuclear reluctance is more a function of a political culture shaped by Japan's difficult history as both an international aggressor and a victim of nuclear attack itself.

Box 8.5 showcases constructivist, liberal, and realist views on why technologically capable states might forego nuclear weapons.

How Dangerous Is Nuclear Proliferation?

The answer to this question might seem obvious, but it is not to all political scientists. Kenneth Waltz and Scott Sagan published a book that debated whether the gradual spread of nuclear weapons would have a stabilizing or destabilizing effect on international politics. Waltz argued that more may be better, while Sagan worried that more will be worse (Sagan and Waltz 2002).

Waltz's counterintuitive argument rests on a belief in the strong deterrent effect of nuclear weapons. Because they are so destructive, nuclear weapons make states act cautiously. Once a state has nuclear forces – even a small amount – its rivals become wary of attacking because the possibility of nuclear retaliation is such a costly outcome. Would the Bush administration have invaded Iraq in 2003 if Saddam Hussein had even a small handful of nuclear weapons, or would it have decided that the risk of even one retaliatory strike against the United States was too great to bear? Waltz believes the United States would have reconsidered. He also believes that India and Pakistan, bitter rivals who have fought wars in the past, will be less likely to fight any kind of war with each other now that both are nuclear powers.

In Waltz's view, nuclear weapons make their holders responsible as well as cautious. He detects a Western bias in the belief that a nuclear-armed United States will act more responsibly than a nuclear-armed Iran or North Korea. States learn by doing, and the very act of developing and deploying nuclear weapons instills a sense of responsibility in the holder who learns to protect the force and avoid accidental use. Waltz reminds us that during the 1950s and 1960s China was considered a revolutionary state determined to upset the international status quo. China acquired nuclear weapons and has possessed them for over four decades without using or losing them. Today China would hardly be considered an irresponsible state or dangerous nuclear power.

Sagan and other critics accept the logic of deterrence but believe that Waltz underestimates the dangerous characteristics and circumstances of states that have recently acquired or are likely to acquire nuclear weapons. One problem is that not all states have stable, civilian-run governments. Some have weak civilian governments or military rulers, while others, like Pakistan, flip back and forth between civilian and military rule. Recall our earlier discussion of US and Soviet nuclear strategy; civilian leaders were more inclined to stress deterrence, while military leaders placed greater emphasis on being ready and able to fight nuclear wars if necessary. The lack of robust civilian control of the military in a new nuclear state could mean a greater likelihood of using these weapons, especially under the pressure of a crisis.

Second, deterrence works best when the states involved have large forces with secure second-strike capabilities. But what if rival states had small forces that might be vulnerable to attack? If India and Pakistan each had several thousand weapons deployed on land, in the air, and under the oceans, neither side's military might feel a nuclear first strike would be a viable strategic option. But what if each side had only several dozen weapons, believed to be stored at a few military sites? In that scenario, a government might be tempted, in a crisis, to try to eliminate its rival's nuclear forces. The danger is heightened by the fact that nuclear weapons tend to spread unevenly to rival states. India had the bomb long before Pakistan. Israel is in a similar position with respect to Iran, and tensions between the two countries have led many analysts to wonder whether Israel will seek to destroy Iranian nuclear capability preemptively to deny its adversary the nuclear equalizer. Similar questions arise in the standoff between the United States, the world's leading nuclear power, and North Korea, the newest and arguably most vulnerable member of the club.

Sagan also worries that, as more states obtain them, the possibility of nuclear accidents increases. We cannot assume that new nuclear states who develop their weapons programs covertly will simultaneously figure out how to safeguard those weapons from unauthorized use or premature detonation. UN inspectors poring over

Iraq's nuclear program in the early 1990s speculated that an Iraqi bomb would have been so unstable it might have detonated if it fell off a desk. Even if we could be confident that new members of the nuclear club would develop safeguards over time, the learning period might still be precarious. Nuclear weapons, Sagan tells us, are controlled by 'imperfect human beings in imperfect organizations.' The potential for error accumulates as more imperfect humans in imperfect organizations gain access to the ultimate weapon.

The possession of nuclear weapons may make your neighbor think twice before attacking you. But a world of many nuclear states might encourage more risk taking in overall terms. More aggressive states might believe they can take advantage of the fact that other states, fearing nuclear escalation, will be cautious and back down rather than risk war over something relatively small. This is the seductive logic of 'chicken,' the dangerous game in which two drivers speed directly at each other to determine who will be more frightened and swerve first. The game often ends sensibly, with one or both drivers swerving. But sometimes each miscalculates, assuming the other will swerve, and they find themselves in an avoidable but tragically fatal head-on collision.

Efforts to Halt Proliferation: The Grand Bargain

The potential dangers of proliferation were recognized early in the nuclear era. In 1968, the Nuclear Non-Proliferation Treaty (NPT) was signed by 98 countries. As of 2016, there were 191 signatories, making the NPT almost universally accepted in the international system (as discussed below, some key states have not signed the treaty or have signed, but are not in compliance). The NPT is sometimes called a grand bargain because it offers benefits and demands obligations from nuclear and non-nuclear states.

Non-nuclear signatories agree to renounce nuclear weapons and refrain from developing, obtaining or deploying them. In exchange, they are entitled to receive civilian nuclear technology, such as nuclear power plants and the know-how to produce nuclear energy for peaceful purposes, from nuclear weapon possessing states, as well as other advanced industrial states. Non-nuclear states also agree to allow their peaceful nuclear operations to be monitored and inspected to ensure that diversion to weapons programs is not taking place. An international organization under the UN known as the International Atomic Energy Agency (IAEA) is charged with carrying out this monitoring function.

The major benefit for nuclear weapon possessing states is the stability derived from maintaining a selective nuclear club. The treaty legitimizes a division between nuclear haves and have-nots. In exchange, the nuclear weapons states must commit to transferring civilian nuclear technology to non-nuclear signatories in compliance with the terms of the NPT. Nuclear weapon possessing states also pledged to take effective measures to reduce their own nuclear arsenals and work toward disarmament. This disarmament provision is a key component of the NPT because it provides some political cover for non-nuclear states to sign on without having to accept that a world of similarly sovereign states will be divided by international law into those states who can have the ultimate weapon and those who cannot.

The effectiveness of the NPT has been mixed and reflects both the promise and limits of international law as discussed in Chapter 5. On one hand, the NPT has established and institutionalized an international norm that nuclear proliferation, like nuclear use, is unacceptable. It has created legitimacy for nuclear weapon possessing states, working through the IAEA, to intrude upon the sovereignty of non-nuclear states and inspect their facilities and activities. By creating the expectation of civilian technology transfer, the treaty gives states a plausible economic rationale to renounce an option for protecting their security. The NPT also provides reassurances to some states that if they deny themselves nuclear weapons they won't be at a disadvantage relative to their neighbors. Latin American rivals Brazil and Argentina, for example, decided during the 1990s to give up their respective nuclear weapons efforts and join the NPT. They also signed the Treaty of Tlatelolco, which bans nuclear weapons from Latin America.

On the other hand, the clear problem with the NPT is that those countries most determined to proliferate will either not sign the treaty, or, if they do sign, at some point exercise the option to renounce it. Israel, India, and Pakistan, now members of the nuclear club, never signed. North Korea did sign the NPT, but in 2003 withdrew, announcing that it was on the verge of testing a nuclear weapon. Iran was found in non-compliance with the NPT in 2003 for its failure to declare its uranium enrichment program.

The NPT is not well designed to prevent 'hard' cases from proliferating. The treaty lacks adequate enforcement measures; for example, it does not call for collective sanctions against violators. Furthermore, even states that make compliance and inspection agreements with the IAEA can find room to maneuver if they are covertly pursuing nuclear weapons. It became clear after the Gulf War of 1990–91 that, during earlier decades, Iraq had been allowing inspectors to view some nuclear facilities but was developing weapons at other sites not subject to inspection. North Korea sounded a similar alarm in 1993 when it asserted its sovereignty and refused to allow international inspectors to view its plutonium reprocessing facilities.

If the NPT, despite its significant benefits, cannot achieve it, is there any way for interested states to stop the small number of determined proliferators? Several strategies are available, though none guarantees success. Collective economic sanctions and diplomatic isolation sometimes work if applied consistently over an extended period. Libya might be considered a successful case – it had not been a signatory to the NPT, but joined the effort in 2004 when it announced that it would abandon its nuclear weapons efforts. As discussed above, sanctions and isolation have worked more effectively in the case of Iran than in that of North Korea.

As the NPT suggests, it is important to recognize that 'carrots' as well as 'sticks' are valuable instruments in preventing proliferation. After the Soviet Union collapsed, the United States passed the Soviet Nuclear Threat Reduction Act (also known as the Nunn–Lugar program, after its sponsors, Senators Sam Nunn of Georgia and Richard Lugar of Indiana), which authorizes the United States to spend billions of dollars helping its former Soviet-bloc enemies to destroy nuclear, chemical, and biological weapons and establish verifiable safeguards to prevent their proliferation. Nunn–Lugar has involved retraining thousands of Soviet-era nuclear scientists and helping them find civilian sector jobs, so they might resist the temptation to peddle their nuclear weapons skills on the black market.

Export control efforts are also an important strategy to halt proliferation. The Nuclear Suppliers' Group (NSG) was created in 1985 to establish guidelines restricting the export of nuclear-related equipment and technologies to non-nuclear states pursuing or contemplating a weapons program. As the A.Q. Khan ring demonstrated, the NSG is hardly leak-proof, but it does provide a way for the principal nuclear supplier states to exchange information and coordinate efforts to restrict technology transfer. A similar arrangement, the Missile Technology Control Regime, was established in 1987 to stem the proliferation of missiles that could deliver weapons of mass destruction.

Preemptive military action is a controversial non-proliferation strategy open to the selected states with the means to employ it. We noted earlier that Israel destroyed an Iraqi nuclear reactor in 1981. It employed a similar strategy against Syria in 2007, bombing what it claimed was a nuclear reactor under construction. The strike followed a visit to Syria by a North Korean ship suspected of delivering reactor components.

A similarly controversial strategy is missile defense. As a response to proliferation, the United States continues to pursue a missile defense system designed to prevent limited attacks by nuclear states using short- or medium-range ballistic missiles. Both the Bush and Obama administrations worked on missile defense with selected allies such as Turkey, Romania, and Poland to protect against a possible future attack from Iran. Although these defense plans are ostensibly aimed at Iran, they have created anxiety in Russia whose leaders worry that NATO-based missile defense could one day, if successful, compromise Russia's nuclear deterrent. For similar reasons, China objects to US plans to develop missile defense in collaboration with Japan and South Korea. Although the stated purpose of such collaboration is to deflect a possible North Korean attack, China fears any effective system would be detrimental to its own deterrent.

One of the most significant constraints on non-proliferation efforts for policy makers is the fact that non-proliferation may compete with other foreign policy priorities. This problem is evident in US policy toward recent entrants to the nuclear club. For some time, the United States proved willing to tolerate Israel's nuclear development because Israel is a close ally of the United States. The fact that Israel proliferated silently, without an obvious public test of a nuclear weapon, made it easier for the United States to maintain what many view as a hypocritical stance. US non-proliferation efforts have been inconsistent with respect to Pakistan. At times, US policy makers have imposed sanctions but, at other times, they have quietly reduced the pressure in exchange for Pakistan's cooperation on issues of importance to the United States. Pakistan helped the United States provide support to insurgents resisting the Soviet occupation of Afghanistan during the 1980s and assisted the United States in the war on terrorism after 2001. With the rise of China in East Asia, the United States has been strengthening existing alliance relationships and cultivating new ones, particularly with China's long-standing rival, India. Even though India had defied the NPT and developed nuclear weapons, in 2005 the United States recognized it as a 'responsible state' possessing nuclear technology, paving the way for full nuclear cooperation between the two countries.

France significantly assisted Israel's quest for nuclear weapons. The French feared Arab nationalism; in 1956 they cooperated with Israel and the United Kingdom to gain control of the Suez Canal. That attempt failed (in part due to opposition from the United States), and subsequently the French provided technical assistance to the Israeli nuclear effort to counter the Arab nationalist movement led by Egypt's Gamal Nasser. China, although it joined the NPT in 1992, continued to provide nuclear assistance to Pakistan because Pakistan was the enemy of China's enemy, India.

Given their danger to human beings and the international system, can nuclear weapons ever be abolished? Most scholars would argue that the nuclear genie cannot be put back into the bottle. Nuclear weapon states may be willing to control or reduce their arsenals, even substantially, but unwilling to give them up completely. Aspiring nuclear states would be reluctant to forego the influence and prestige that comes with nuclear weapons, and the ability to deter neighbors they do not trust. Even if we could find a way to achieve the improbable feat of getting all states to agree to eliminate nuclear weapons, the production and deployment knowledge would remain, with the potential to be exploited by states or groups seeking to take advantage of the restraint of others.

Despite these practical difficulties, the idea of 'getting to zero,' or total nuclear disarmament, remains alive and well and has been with us throughout the nuclear era. The idea has obvious appeal to pacifists and antiwar activists. But, as Box 8.6 shows, it also attracts less likely proponents, such as the conservative US President Ronald Reagan and the veteran realist statesman and writer, Henry Kissinger. Kissinger, along with former Senator Sam Nunn, former Secretary of State George Shultz, and former Defense Secretary William Perry, formed a nongovernmental organization called the Nuclear Security Project to mobilize global action to reduce nuclear threats and build support for eventually eliminating nuclear weapons.

Nuclear weapons are the most significant but not the only weapons of mass destruction. We next turn to chemical and biological weapons and efforts to control them.

8.6 MAKING CONNECTIONS
Then and Now

Proposals from US Political Elites for a Nuclear-Free World

Then: 1946, The Baruch Plan

Bernard Baruch was an American financier and close advisor to Presidents Woodrow Wilson and Franklin Roosevelt. President Truman appointed Baruch as US representative to the newly created United Nations Atomic Energy Commission. At its first meeting in June 1946, Baruch proposed that the United States would turn over its nuclear weapons and the designs to produce them to the United Nations, on the condition that all other countries pledged not to produce atomic weapons and subjected themselves to an effective system of inspection. Americans perceived this as a generous offer since, at that time, the United States enjoyed a nuclear monopoly. Stalin's Soviet Union rejected the Baruch Plan because it felt the United Nations would be dominated by the United States and its allies and could not be trusted to implement the plan fairly. Lacking Soviet agreement, the Baruch Plan was not viable.

Then: 1986, Ronald Reagan and the Reykjavik Summit, October 20, 1986

> It is my fervent goal and hope...that we will someday no longer have to rely on nuclear weapons to deter aggression and ensure world peace. To that end the United States is now engaged in a serious and sustained effort to negotiate major reductions in levels of offensive nuclear weapons with the ultimate goal of eliminating these weapons from the face of the earth.

As President, Ronald Reagan intensified the Cold War with the Soviet Union, but also surprised many people by arguing forcefully for the elimination of nuclear weapons. Reagan shocked his own advisors in 1986 by proposing, at a summit meeting with then Soviet leader Mikhail Gorbachev, that the two superpowers work together to reduce and then eliminate completely their nuclear arsenals.

Gorbachev was receptive, but ultimately resisted when it became clear that Reagan was unwilling to give up American efforts to develop his Strategic Defense Initiative to defend the United States from nuclear attack.

Now: 2007, The 'Gang of Four' Calls for a Nuclear-Free World

On January 4, 2007, George Shultz, William Perry, Henry Kissinger, and Sam Nunn published an essay called 'A World Free of Nuclear Weapons' (Shultz et al. 2007). Each played an important role in US national security policy during the Cold War; Shultz and Kissinger as former Secretaries of State, Perry as former Secretary of Defense, and Nunn as a prominent Senator from Georgia. They wrote:

'Nuclear weapons today present tremendous dangers, but also an historic opportunity. US leadership will be required to take the world to the next stage – to a solid consensus for reversing reliance on nuclear weapons globally as a vital contribution to preventing their proliferation into potentially dangerous hands, and ultimately ending them as a threat to the world.' They argued that reliance on nuclear weapons only increases the chances of accidents, misjudgments, and catastrophic terrorism. They called for substantially reducing the size of nuclear forces in all states, providing the highest possible standards of security for all stocks of weapons and weapons-grade plutonium and uranium, and halting the production of fissile material for weapons globally. They concluded that 'we endorse setting the goal of a world free of nuclear weapons and working energetically on the actions required to achieve that goal.'

Levels of Analysis Nuclear Proliferation	
State	International
Many countries have relied on nuclear deterrence as well as physical defense to prevent attacks against their territory and people.	The NPT is an important example of global governance – an effort by many states to find cooperative solutions to the dangers posed by nuclear weapons.
	The NPT also reflects the inequality of nations in that it reinforces that some states have nuclear weapons and others do not.

CHEMICAL AND BIOLOGICAL WEAPONS

Nuclear weapons are by far the most destructive weapons ever created. But other types of weapons also qualify as weapons of mass destruction or weapons with the ability to do significant harm to massive numbers of people. Many analysts place chemical and biological weapons within this category.

How They Work and Efforts to Control Them

Chemical weapons use manufactured chemicals to kill people. Common examples include chlorine gas and mustard gas, both of which were used by combatants in World War I. These chemicals do their damage by blistering lung tissue. More sophisticated chemical weapons include sarin gas, a nerve agent that causes suffocation through uncontrollable muscle contraction. One milligram of sarin in the lungs is sufficient to kill someone, as compared to ten milligrams of mustard gas. In 1995, a Japanese group of extremists named Aum Shinrikyo released sarin in the Tokyo subway

Chemical weapons
A category of WMD that uses manufactured chemicals to kill people.

Photo 8.4 Aftermath of a Chemical Weapon Attack in Japan
Tokyo Fire Department after decontamination work at Kasumigaseki Station on March 20, 1995 in Tokyo, Japan. The chemical terrorist attack by Japanese cult Aum Shinrikyo happened almost simultaneously on five subway lines during the morning commute, killing 13 people.

Source: The Asahi Shimbun via Getty Images.

system, killing 12, injuring thousands, and causing mass terror. An even more lethal form of sarin is called VX. In a 1996 film, *The Rock*, a renegade US Marine threatens to launch a missile containing VX nerve gas into San Francisco (Sean Connery and Nicholas Cage help to save the day).

Biological weapons kill people by spreading bacteria or viruses. Examples of potential bioweapons include smallpox, a highly contagious virus that has been eradicated worldwide but could be recreated in new strains for destructive purposes. Botulism is a highly lethal bacterium that kills by causing muscle paralysis. Anthrax is a durable bacterium, and if anthrax spores find their way into a person's lungs they can create a fatal toxin. Americans learned first-hand just how dangerous anthrax can be: just after the September 2001 Al Qaeda attacks against the Twin Towers and the Pentagon, an Army bioweapons expert (who later committed suicide) mailed letters containing anthrax to the offices of two US senators in Washington, DC, as well as to several news media offices in New York City, and caused five deaths.

Chemical or biological agents may be delivered in various ways. Low-flying crop duster planes could spray a lethal agent from the air, just as a truck equipped with a fire hose could spray a fine mist on the ground. Chemical or biological agents could be placed in a bomb to explode in a populated area, or perhaps used to contaminate a water supply. Aum Shinrikyo used several small explosive canisters in their Tokyo subway attack.

Chemical weapons have a long history, both on the battlefield and at the negotiating table. The Hague Conventions of 1899 and 1907 banned the use of poisonous weapons in warfare. These prohibitions were ignored during World War I, as both France and Germany made extensive use of chlorine and mustard gas. Other

Biological weapons
A category of WMD that kills people by spreading bacteria or viruses.

agreements – the Washington Arms Conference Treaty of 1922 and the Geneva Protocol of 1929 – subsequently prohibited chemical weapons use, again with limited effect. Japan's army used chemicals against Asian populations it sought to subjugate before and during World War II. On the European front, both Allied and Axis powers developed and deployed chemical agents, though neither side relied on chemical warfare in part because any state that used chemical weapons would have its own forces or population subject to chemical attacks in response.

The most extensive use of chemicals in the postwar era took place during the Iran–Iraq War of 1980–88. Iraq deployed mustard gas and other agents against advancing Iranian forces and Kurdish groups within its own population. In one such attack in March 1988, 5,000 civilians, mostly women and children, perished in the Kurdish town of Halabja. Ali Hassan al-Majid, known as 'Chemical Ali,' was condemned to death in 2010 by an Iraqi court that found him guilty of masterminding the massacre. Many feared that Iraq might use chemical weapons against coalition forces or Israel during the 1990–91 Gulf War. Those attacks never materialized, possibly because the United States threatened nuclear retaliation in the event of a chemical attack.

However, despite this, a second tragic use of chemical weapons occurred more recently, in the context of Syria's civil war. In August 2013, rockets containing sarin killed hundreds and possibly thousands of Syrian civilians, and several dozen Syrian opposition fighters, in the Ghouta suburbs of the Syrian capital, Damascus. The Syrian government of Bashar al-Assad and the rebel forces seeking to overthrow it blamed each other for the chemical attack. (al-Assad's government claimed the rebels launched the attack and even killed some of their own forces to frame the Syrian government and prompt international outrage against it.) After a UN investigation, the European Union, United States, and neighboring Arab countries concluded that the attack had been carried out by forces loyal to the Syrian government. In September 2013, Russia and the United States announced an agreement that resulted in the elimination of Syria's remaining chemical stockpile by the middle of 2014. The deal drew both praise and criticism – praise because it avoided outside military intervention and convinced Syria to agree to give up its chemical weapons; criticism because the deal left the dictator al-Assad in power, gave him international legitimacy as a negotiating partner, and left his forces to continue killing tens of thousands of Syrian civilians using conventional weapons in the ongoing and brutal Syrian civil war.

The Iraq and Syria experiences helped to strengthen the international consensus on the desirability of banning chemical warfare and eliminating chemical weapons. A major international treaty, the Chemical Weapons Convention (CWC), was established in 1993 and came into force in 1997. As of 2017, 192 countries were bound by the Convention and 188 had signed the treaty. The CWC forbids outright the production and possession of chemical weapons. Signatories must destroy their existing stockpiles and must allow a UN entity, the Organization for the Prohibition of Chemical Weapons (OPCW), access to their territories to inspect plants designed to produce chemicals for civilian uses such as fertilizers. Because of the Russia-US agreement noted above, Syria joined the CWC in 2013 and allowed the OPCW access to its territory to locate and eventually dismantle its chemical weapons.

The CWC is a major arms control accomplishment in that it completely forbids an entire category of lethal weapons. Its implementation is not straightforward because the destruction of existing stockpiles is costly and requires complicated safety precautions to be carried out effectively. By 2017, however, about 90 percent of the world's declared stockpile had been verifiably destroyed. Russia announced it had destroyed its entire stockpile and called on the United States to do the same by the deadline of 2020. The next challenge is to persuade states with probable or definite chemical programs (such as Egypt and North Korea) to sign the treaty, and to convince Israel, which has signed it, to ratify it.

Biological weapons have an even longer history of use in warfare. In ancient times, city-states at war would use biological agents to poison the food and water supplies of their enemies. Beginning in the 1930s, both Nazi Germany and Imperial Japan conducted extensive experiments on human subjects using lethal biological agents. Biological weapons did not play a major role during World War II, although in 1940, the Japanese Air Force dropped ceramic bombs on China that contained fleas carrying botulism. The Soviet Union and United States developed bioweapons programs during the war and carried out extensive research and production during the Cold War. The United States had bioweapons ready for battlefield delivery in aerosol spray cans, cluster bombs, or missile warheads, in the event bioweapons were used by an adversary.

As in the case of chemical weapons, an international consensus formed during the Cold War that biological weapons should be outlawed. The Biological and Toxic Weapons Convention (BWC) of 1972 reflected this sentiment, and banned the development, production, and stockpiling of microbes except in the small amounts needed for peaceful research. As of 2018, 180 states (including Palestine) had ratified the treaty. In 1992, the head of the former Soviet Union's biological weapons effort, Ken Alibek, defected to the United States and revealed that the Soviet Union, despite signing the BWC, secretly continued research and production of biological weapons until its collapse in 1989. The BWC is weaker than the CWC because it has no provisions for monitoring or verifying compliance and implementation.

Comparing Nuclear, Biological, and Chemical Weapons

Although nuclear, chemical, and biological weapons are commonly lumped together under the heading of weapons of mass destruction, we should recognize significant differences across these categories. Most importantly, nuclear weapons are qualitatively different in terms of their destructive power because a few weapons can do so much damage to lives and property. Biological weapons have great potential to be lethal, but their success depends on the widespread yet precise distribution over an exposed population. They must be spread carefully, and survival depends on environmental conditions. Similarly, chemical weapons can be lethal but only under specific conditions. The attacker must disperse a large amount of chemical agent to kill a great number of people and must recognize that dispersal of the agent may be hard to control. Shifting winds, for example, may carry chemical agents beyond the range of intended target populations or may blow chemical agents back upon the attackers themselves. During the World War I Battle of Loos, in France in September 1915, British soldiers released chlorine gas intended for the Germans, but some of the gas was carried back by the wind onto the United Kingdom's own soldiers who were deployed in trenches.

There are also significant differences across these weapons categories regarding the possibility of defense. We argued earlier that it is almost impossible to defend effectively against a nuclear attack. Defense against biological and chemical agents is not easy, but it is possible. Troops can be equipped with gas masks and protective clothing when operating in a military environment under the threat of chemical attack. Even civilians may be offered some protection in anticipation of attack; the Israeli government distributed gas masks to its citizens during the 1990–91 Gulf War in case Saddam Hussein launched missiles with chemical warheads at Israel in retaliation for the US-led attack against his forces in Kuwait. In the face of biological warfare, preventive vaccination has some potential to be effective, yet only if one is certain of the type or strain of the agent in question. US troops were vaccinated against possible anthrax attacks during the Gulf War.

Nuclear weapons are also more difficult to develop than biological or chemical weapons. Reprocessed plutonium and enriched uranium require a complex technical infrastructure to produce. In contrast, the basic building blocks of chemical weapons are more readily available. Chlorine, for example, is a common chemical used to kill bacteria in water systems. Anthrax may be found in nature and grown in laboratories from existing spores. This is not to suggest that developing a biological or chemical weapon is a simple task, only that it is a more achievable task than developing a nuclear weapon.

International legal norms governing these classes of weapons also differ. Biological and chemical weapons are completely outlawed. The consensus codified by international law is that no state, great power or otherwise, should be allowed to use them, deploy them, or even stockpile them. International law regarding nuclear weapons divides the world into have and have-not states. A handful of states have the legal right to possess and deploy the weapons while the great majority of states do not. A state that 'crosses the line' in defiance of legal norms might later try to become accepted as a legitimate member of the club, as India has recently attempted with the support of the United States. Arms control advocates hope the more universal prohibitions that apply to chemical and biological weapons will one day apply to nuclear weapons.

Weapons of mass destruction in the hands of numerous nation-states are a cause of great concern in international politics. The same holds true for non-state actors, and below we discuss the connection between terrorism and weapons of mass destruction.

Levels of Analysis *Chemical and Biological Weapons*	
State	International
A small number of states use chemical weapons, in defiance of international norms and agreements, against military and civilian populations.	The CWC and BWC are landmark arms control agreements in that each completely forbids an entire category of WMD.

WEAPONS OF MASS DESTRUCTION, NON-STATE ACTORS, AND TERRORISM

The attacks of September 11, 2001 in the United States, the 2002 bombings in Bali, Indonesia, the 2004 train bombings in Madrid, and the July 2005 bombings in London greatly heightened the fear of terrorism around the world. After these attacks, it was natural to ask the horrifying question of what might happen if terrorists managed to gain control of chemical, biological, or nuclear weapons.

Violent non-state actors have been relatively most successful in acquiring and using chemical weapons. The 1995 Aum Shinrikyo attack in Tokyo using sarin gas, discussed above, killed 12 and injured thousands of people. Western intelligence sources believe Hamas and Al Qaeda have active chemical weapons research programs. Beginning in 2015, Islamic State (ISIS) regularly employed chemical weapons, carrying out 76 attacks against civilians and military forces (e.g., Kurdish units) in Iraq and Syria. Some of these attacks injured up to 2,000 soldiers or civilians.

Islamic State first relied on chemical stockpiles it captured from the former Ba'athist regime in Iraq, but later developed its own production facility in Mosul, Iraq and the means to deliver chemical agents with rockets and mortars (Strack 2017). Although it lost its production capability in July 2017 when coalition forces recaptured Mosul, it is fair to assume that Islamic State retains both the aspiration and expertise to produce and use chemical agents.

Biological attacks have been harder for terrorists to master. Before its successful 1995 chemical attack, Aum Shinrikyo attempted several biological attacks that proved unsuccessful due to its failure to isolate and disperse the most virulent form of the toxin it chose (Enemark 2006). No other terrorist group has carried out a successful bioweapons attack. Nevertheless, concern that a terrorist group might effectively combine the expertise and aspiration to carry out such an attack in the future remains high. The Ebola outbreak that began in 2013, which claimed over 10,000 lives, served as a sober reminder to governments of how rapidly deadly infectious diseases could develop and spread, and how relatively unprepared governments (and the World Health Organization) are to combat them.

Given their massive destructive capability, with possible casualties measured in the hundreds of thousands or millions, the prospect of a terrorist group gaining control of a nuclear weapon is the most profound and disturbing scenario. As discussed above, deterrence theory holds that the use of nuclear weapons may be effectively deterred by the threat of nuclear retaliation. The problem is that terrorist groups may be harder than nation-states to deter. Deterrence against nation-states rests on the threat of inflicting unacceptable damage on something of value to the nation-state in question, such as its territory, population, national identity, or sovereign integrity. Terrorists are usually stateless; they have no fixed territory to defend, and no population that might credibly be held hostage by the threat of nuclear retaliation. It is often said that terrorist groups have 'no return address,' or no specific home to direct the threat or actuality of retaliation.

One could, of course, threaten to retaliate against states that harbor terrorists. The United States followed this logic by invading Afghanistan because the Taliban regime provided sanctuary for Al Qaeda prior to the September 11 attacks. Threatening the host state might cause the host government to think twice about harboring terrorists on their territory. Yet that same threat might be less effective in deterring the terrorist group operating within the borders of the host state. The host territory itself might not be of sufficient value to the terrorist group; it could simply move its operation to a different host or to multiple hosts. Retaliation against populations which are sympathetic to the terrorist groups in question might be another alternative, but the pitfalls here are obvious; the threat would be made against innocent civilians and the threat itself might serve to mobilize political sympathy for the terrorist group. In short, the usual reassuring rules of deterrence do not operate as easily in the case of a terrorist threat.

A terrorist group in possession of nuclear weapons may be difficult to deter, but how likely are terrorist groups to acquire nuclear weapons? The difficulties nation-states face in developing a nuclear capability apply even more forcefully to stateless groups. As we have seen, developing nuclear weapons, as opposed to chemical weapons, requires a far-reaching technical infrastructure and support system; it is not something that can be accomplished in one's basement or backyard. Terrorists typically do not have the resources – appropriate and ideally hidden facilities, sophisticated equipment, scarce raw materials, scientific talent, and ample time (measured in decades) – to put it all together. Press reports occasionally speculate that terrorists would not need a missile or other sophisticated delivery system and instead could rely on a small 'suitcase' bomb. But to develop a *small* nuclear weapon that works effectively is an even more demanding task technologically; the first nuclear weapons developed by determined nation-states were large and cumbersome.

The difficulty of developing a nuclear weapon does not imply that the problem of nuclear terrorism is trivial. If terrorists cannot do it alone, there is always the possibility of stealing an existing weapon, or having one transferred voluntarily from a nuclear weapon possessing nation-state. The United States invaded Iraq in 2003 in part because it feared Iraq might possess nuclear weapons (it did not turn up evidence to confirm that fear), and out of fear that Iraq might one day share its nuclear capability with a terrorist group. Leaving aside the political particulars (Al Qaeda and Saddam Hussein were not allied), deterrence theory suggests that the nation-state sharing nuclear weapons with a terrorist group would at least have to take into account the possibility of being the target of retaliation – the return address – in the event the nuclear hand-off was traced back to it.

The most likely route to a terrorist nuclear capability involves the so-called '**dirty bomb**,' or radiological dispersal device. This would be a device that, without the profound power of a nuclear explosion (and its attendant heat and blast effects), disperses some type of radioactive material. The damage from a successful dirty bomb would be far less than from a nuclear weapon, and the effects (radiation poisoning) would likely be long term instead of immediate. The most important effect would be psychological; the detonation of a radiation dispersal device would surely terrorize any population it victimized.

In a recent book, Graham Allison (2004) describes nuclear terrorism as 'the ultimate preventable catastrophe.' He urges nation-states to cooperate in a global alliance to guard against the theft of weapons or weapons-grade material, ban the new production of highly enriched uranium or reprocessed plutonium, and ensure that no other states join the nuclear club.

'Dirty bomb'
A device that, without the profound power of a nuclear explosion (and its attendant heat and blast effects), disperses some type of radioactive material.

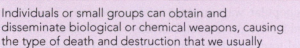

Levels of Analysis *Terrorists and Weapons of Mass Destruction*	
Individual	🌐 International
Individuals or small groups can obtain and disseminate biological or chemical weapons, causing the type of death and destruction that we usually associate with the armed forces of sovereign states.	The logic of deterrence applies differently to state and non-state actors.

NEW TECHNOLOGIES AND NEW CHALLENGES: DRONES AND CYBER-WARFARE

We opened this chapter by observing that technologies and their military applications continue to evolve. Although not every technological innovation is as dramatic as that which brought the nuclear revolution, two recent developments are highly significant. One has already transformed the battlefield of the twenty-first century, and the other has implications that are still uncertain but potentially far-reaching.

Drones

Unmanned Aerial Vehicles (UAVs), or more commonly drones, are pilotless vehicles that can be operated and targeted by remote control (Kreps 2016). Drones have both a variety of possible commercial applications (e.g., photography, package delivery)

Unmanned Aerial Vehicles (UAVs)
More commonly drones, are pilotless vehicles that can be operated and targeted by remote control.

Photo 8.5 A Drone Control Room in Nevada, USA
Drone pilots often 'commute' to war. They sit in control rooms and operate drones across the world using satellite links.

Source: Isaac Brekken/Getty Images.

as well as military applications. The most sophisticated military drones can travel undetected and observe a landscape for a full day or more, selecting and tracking an individual or individuals as a target. The controller can at any point be directed to release the drone's missiles or bombs in a precision-guided attack on the target.

The United States has the largest and most advanced force of military drones. The vehicles fly from bases and airstrips, mostly within Afghanistan or North Africa, and are controlled remotely by drone operators based either in the United States or abroad. During the Obama administration, drones became the weapon of choice in the war on terrorism. After 2001, the United States fought long, costly, inconclusive, and unpopular wars in Afghanistan and Iraq. The Obama administration opted instead for a 'light footprint' strategy based on drones in the air and operations by special-forces on the ground (Sanger 2012). Between 2009 and 2016 the United States launched over 3,000 drone strikes to target and kill terrorist leaders and mid-level operatives, primarily in Afghanistan and Pakistan but elsewhere as well.

The routine reliance on drone warfare has raised difficult legal questions. Since the 1970s, US policy has prohibited the government from undertaking targeted political assassinations of foreign leaders. In what ways does killing an Al Qaeda official with a Hellfire missile launched from a drone differ from hiring a team of assassins to blow up a leader's car or poison his or her food? Does it matter if the target is the leader of a foreign government, as opposed to an operative for a non-state actor? There are ethical dilemmas as well. Although drone strikes can be exceptionally precise, with operations occurring so routinely it is inevitable that civilian casualties will be taken, either by mistake or because at times it proves too difficult to distinguish combatants from non-combatants. There is also the political question of the extent to which drone strikes, which often do kill terrorist targets effectively, also serve as a recruiting tool for terrorists who can mobilize popular resistance to a foreign power using superior technology remotely to destroy homes and family members.

Proliferation is an equally pressing concern. Compared to fighter aircraft, drones are relatively cheap to produce and operate. By 2017 nearly two dozen countries, including China, Russia, Israel, Iran, India, Nigeria, and South Africa possessed military drone capabilities of varying size and sophistication. China has played a key role in facilitating proliferation by designing, producing, and selling less expensive drones in a political environment unconstrained by regulations or legal restrictions. The geopolitical implications of a world in which many states, and presumably non-state actors, possess and deploy drone arsenals are not yet fully appreciated.

The Emergence of Cyber-Warfare

We should also recognize the destructive potential of an even newer technological threat, that of **cyber-warfare**. Cyber-warfare is a form of information warfare; it is the use of the internet and related technologies by governments to damage or disrupt the activities or systems of an adversary or a private entity of value to an adversary. A related term, cyber-terrorism, refers to the use of cyber-warfare techniques by groups or individuals operating independently of national governments.

Several states, including Israel, the United States, Iran, China, and Russia have indicated that they have active cyber-warfare programs. Intelligence analysts believe that Iran's cyber-warfare was behind a string of attacks in 2012 that disabled the websites of numerous US banks and disrupted the operations of the Saudi Arabian oil company Aramco. For their part, US and Israeli operatives developed a computer virus named Stuxnet that was secretly targeted against Iran's nuclear enrichment facility at Natanz. Stuxnet damaged Iran's facility and was only detected when it presented on the internet because an Iranian nuclear technician inadvertently transferred the virus from Iran's nuclear facility through his personal computer. Russia relied on control of the 'information space' (that is, the internet and other mechanisms of communication) in its recent annexation of Crimea. Based in part on that successful intervention, Russian military doctrine has begun to place emphasis on **hybrid warfare**, or the blending of conventional warfare, using regular and irregular armed forces, with informational warfare, including the spreading of fake news and the disruption of normal political functions (for example, elections) in target countries.

Is cyber-warfare an anti-proliferation device, an information-intensive supplement to conventional war tactics, or a potential new weapon of mass destruction? It is too early to tell, but some scientists see eerie parallels to the dawn of the nuclear age (Kemp 2012). As we saw at the beginning of this chapter, nuclear weapons were developed in an environment of interstate competition and used by one government without a full appreciation of their implications. Although the destructive potential may differ, governments developing cyber-warfare may be heading down a similar path, creating weapons that could possibly destroy stock markets and banking systems, flood dams, and poison water supplies. The extent to which cyber-warfare 'arms races' take place and whether the international community will seek to control or ban their use remain to be seen.

Cyber-warfare
The use of the internet and related technologies by governments to damage or disrupt the activities or systems of an adversary or a private entity of value to an adversary.

Hybrid warfare
The blending of conventional warfare with informational warfare, including the spreading of fake news and the disruption of normal political functions (for example, elections) in target countries.

Levels of Analysis *Drones and Cyber-Warfare*

 State

Some states have adopted drones and cyber-warfare as new forms of military statecraft, with uncertain implications for diplomacy and warfare.

REVISITING THE ENDURING QUESTION AND LOOKING AHEAD

This chapter examined how new technologies shape the use of force and relations among states. We focused on the most important military innovation of the modern era, nuclear weapons, and the extent to which they have transformed international relations. Nuclear weapons may have an important stabilizing effect – they discourage great powers from fighting the kind of all-out wars that characterized the pre-nuclear history of the international system. The spread of nuclear weapons to additional states and potentially to non-state actors and terrorist entities, however, raises a host of concerns about the potential for international conflicts to escalate in truly destructive ways. The existence of nuclear weapons makes war less likely, yet potentially more catastrophic should it occur. Although they have less destructive capacity, the same argument applies to biological and chemical weapons. The systemic effects of the newest military technologies, drones and cyber-warfare, are not yet fully appreciated.

In these last three chapters we have explored the enduring problem of war, the strategies statesmen and citizens have employed in pursuit of peace, and the special challenges posed by nuclear and other weapons of mass destruction. The questions of what causes war and what are the conditions for peace are among the most fundamental in world politics. But international relations, both in the sense of what is happening in the international domain and as a field of study, are not just defined by the military dimensions of war and peace. International relations are also vitally concerned with international commerce and finance, the exchange of goods and services between countries, and the investing of money across borders. Those economic relations, the political conditions that hinder or facilitate those relations, the impact of economics on politics and military affairs, and the special question of whether international economic ties help or hurt the prospects of poorer countries, constitute the study of international political economy (IPE).

IPE is vital to our understanding of international affairs, and we now turn to it. We explore how international politics and economics interact, and why economic relations often inspire international cooperation and sometimes lead states to conflict. We examine why some states develop their economies more rapidly than others, and what that implies for the stability of the international system.

STUDY QUESTIONS

1. Imagine that, during the 20 years after 1945, neither the United States nor the Soviet Union possessed nuclear weapons. Do you think those two countries would have gone from a Cold War to major hot war during that period?

2. How many nuclear weapons do you think the United States needs to deter any potential nuclear weapons state from using its arsenal against America? 200 warheads? 500 warheads? More? Fewer? Explain your answer.

3. Imagine this world: your home country does not have nuclear weapons and is a signatory to the NPT. All other countries in your region now possess nuclear weapons. In this imaginary world, would you favor or oppose the acquisition of nuclear weapons by your country, even if it had to break its obligations under the NPT? Why or why not?

4. Are nuclear weapons morally justifiable?

5. To what extent are biological and chemical weapons substitutes for nuclear weapons?

6. Do you think the threat of terrorism will increase international efforts to contain nuclear proliferation and the spread of biological and chemical weapons? Why or why not?

7. Can you imagine any ways to develop arms control agreements for the newest types of military technologies, drones, and cyber-warfare?

FURTHER READING

Alibek, Ken (2008) *Biohazard: The Chilling True Story of the Largest Covert Biological Weapons Program in the World* (New York: Random House). A physician and microbiologist, Alibek ran the Soviet Union's massive bioweapons program during the Cold War. He emigrated to the United States in 1992 and provided a full account of this ongoing program to the US government.

Allison, Graham (2004) *Nuclear Terrorism: The Ultimate Preventable Catastrophe* (New York: Times Books). Allison assesses the dangers of nuclear terrorism – who might attempt it and how they might obtain the weapon. He views the threat as preventable assuming a broad coalition is willing to work together to control weapons-relevant materials at the source.

Cohen, Avner (1988) *Israel and the Bomb* (New York: Columbia University Press). Cohen provides a detailed account of when, how, and why Israel developed its nuclear capability. He draws on interviews and declassified documents to piece together this important political history.

Hersey, John (1946) *Hiroshima* (New York: Alfred Knopf). A war correspondent during the 1940s, Hersey tells the horrifying story of the impact of the world's first nuclear explosion on ordinary people. He also traces the path of a handful of Japanese who survived the attack.

Kaplan, Fred (1991) *The Wizards of Armageddon* (Stanford: Stanford University Press). This is a readable account of the lives and times of the civilian architects of the nuclear age. Kaplan explores the role and impact of key scientists and policy makers who developed the field of nuclear strategy after World War II.

Kreps, Sarah (2016) *Drones: What Everyone Needs to Know* (New York: Oxford University Press). An introduction to the technical operation and political implications of this important new military technology.

Tannenwald, Nina (2008) *The Nuclear Taboo: The United States and the Non-Use of Nuclear Weapons since 1945* (Cambridge: Cambridge University Press). Tannenwald makes the constructivist case that a nuclear taboo, or the shared social inhibition against nuclear use, is more important than the standard arguments about deterrence in accounting for why no state has used nuclear weapons since 1945.

 Visit **www.macmillanihe.com/Grieco-IntroIR-2e** to access extra resources for this chapter, including:

- Chapter summaries to help you review the material
- Multiple choice quizzes to test your understanding
- Flashcards to test your knowledge of the key terms in this chapter
- An interactive simulation that invites you to go through the decision-making process of a world leader at a crucial political juncture
- Pivotal decisions in which you weigh up the pros and cons of complicated decisions with grave consequences
- Outside resources, including links to contemporary articles and videos, that add to what you have learned in this chapter

Part III

Wealth and Power: An Introduction to International Political Economy

Author Debates

 Visit **www.macmillanihe.com/Grieco-IntroIR-2e** to watch the authors debating the issues discussed in this Part.

Video 1: What does globalization mean today, and what are its effects and challenges?

Video 2: How does the global economy help (or hinder) poorer countries?

9 International Economics: Basic Theory and Core Institutions

Enduring question
How does international politics shape the global economy?

Chapter Contents

Learning Objectives

By the end of this chapter, you will be able to:

→ Understand the basic concepts of international trade theory and appreciate why governments sometimes embrace trade and sometimes seek to insulate their economies from it.

→ Recognize how exchange rates between national currencies are determined, why governments change them, and how they matter to international trade and investment.

→ Understand the characteristics of multinational enterprises and assess their importance in the world economy.

→ Appreciate the relationship between world politics and the international institutions that govern the world economy.

Photo by Adam Jang on Unsplash

In 2016, trade between the United Kingdom and Vietnam reached about $5.6 billion. Two important products Vietnam supplies to UK residents, tea and coffee, cannot readily be produced in the British Isles, but one of the major products that Vietnam sells to the UK is shoes. Why does the UK need or want to buy shoes from Vietnam, rather than making them at home? At the same time, a major British export to Vietnam is prescription medications. Why doesn't Vietnam develop and rely upon its own pharmaceutical industry? To address these and a host of other important questions relating to the international economy, we turn in this section to the subfield of International Relations that is called International Political Economy (IPE).

We begin our exploration of IPE with a brief overview of basic ideas from the discipline of economics that help us understand why countries undertake international trade and international financial transactions. We also provide you with an introduction to one of the most important agents in the international economy, the multinational enterprise (MNE). We then turn our attention to an overview of the main international institutions that states have created since World War II to help them both expand the international economy and cope with some of the problems that have been engendered by that expansion.

Our goal in this chapter is to provide you with an understanding of the economic and political dynamics through which countries have created an international economy. We then, in Chapter 10, examine how states sometimes utilize their international economic linkages to advance their political interests, including an enhancement of their overall power, or sometimes seek to limit their exposure to the international economy for fear that such exposure hinders the attainment of their national interests abroad and even curtails their internal economic and political autonomy. To understand how international economic linkages create political opportunities and also political risks for countries, it is vital first to understand why those countries engage with that international economy, why they have the particular kinds of interactions that they have – for example, why Vietnam exports shoes and imports pharmaceutical products, while the United Kingdom does the opposite – and what are the basic international institutions that states have created so that they can work together on international economic matters.

BASIC ELEMENTS OF INTERNATIONAL TRADE THEORY AND POLICY

Autarky
The separation of a country from the world economy in an effort to protect its economy from the effects of the global market.

During much of international history, governments either avoided trade by pursuing **autarky**, the separation of the country from the world economy, or they pursued mercantilism – efforts by governments to supervise and manipulate international economic contacts with the aim of maximizing exports, minimizing imports, and acquiring gold in exchange for exports to pay for a stronger military. Yet, between the mid-1700s and the mid-1800s Adam Smith and then David Ricardo put forward a critique of mercantilism and provided the intellectual underpinning for a gradual turn first by the Great Britain and then other countries toward freer trade, that is, the relaxation by governments of controls on private commerce both within and between countries.

Subsequent generations of economists have elaborated on the central ideas of Smith and Ricardo. Most economists argue, as we will see below, that trade encourages and allows countries to use their national resources more efficiently, and it allows them to consume more goods than would be possible if residents could only buy things that are produced at home. Trade, in short, makes good sense economically for the country as a whole. But as we shall see, trade does not always seem beneficial to every individual or all groups of individuals within a country, and those individuals and groups have a rational incentive to enter the political realm to push back and reverse, or at least seek protection from, freer trade. Politics thus is at the heart of trade: it can facilitate it, but it can also serve as a brake on it.

Building Blocks for Analysis: Consumption and Production

We begin with the individual person. Economists assume that an individual attains utility, or wellbeing, by consuming goods and services. Economists further assume that an entire country, just like an individual, enjoys greater wellbeing if it can somehow consume more goods and services. Economists have put forward a theory that suggests a country can improve its consumption of goods and services by engaging in trade rather than by practicing autarky. This outcome explains why countries undertake trade.

For goods and services to be consumed, they must first be produced. To understand what a country can produce, economists employ a model they call the **production possibilities frontier (PPF)**. A production possibilities frontier is a graphical representation of the different combinations of goods that a country may produce during some period, for example, a year, with the resources it has in its possession. When we refer to productive resources, we usually mean the land, labor (working people and managers), capital (factories and equipment), and technology located in the country.

To see what a hypothetical PPF looks like, let us imagine that the United States produces only two goods, computers and shoes, and that, given its endowment of productive resources, it has the PPF depicted in Figure 9.1.

Notice that the US production possibilities frontier in Figure 9.1 drops downward as we move from left to right. This downward slope represents the existence of what economists call an **opportunity cost** in the production of either computers or shoes, that is, an increase in the production of one of the goods requires foregoing some amount of the other. To see why, imagine that the United States is devoting *all* its productive resources to shoe manufacturing. In the figure this is represented by point P, at which the United States is producing and consuming OP pairs of shoes and zero computers. If the United States decides it wants a different combination of the two goods depicted in the figure – for example, it would like to be at point E, at which it is producing and consuming OM pairs of shoes and OR computers – it needs to reduce its production of shoes by MP pairs of shoes and move the productive resources thus released into computer manufacturing. Hence, for computer manufacturing to go up, shoe output must go down, and thus we have the downward slope in the PPF. Note that if we had said that the PPF in Figure 9.1 was that for the United Kingdom, Canada, India, or Sweden, those PPFs would also be downward sloping: economists argue that opportunity costs in the production of goods hold for all countries.

Although all countries have downward-sloping PPFs, the extent to which they must reduce one good to produce more of another is likely to be different, sometimes radically so. As we will see in a moment, these *differences* in opportunity costs between countries make possible the establishment of mutually beneficial trade between countries.

Production possibilities frontier (PPF)
A graphical representation of the different combinations of goods that a country may produce during some period of time with the resources it has in its possession.

Opportunity cost
The cost of producing more of a certain good in foregone production of another good. Opportunity costs are crucial in considering comparative advantage and the possibility for mutual gains from trade.

Figure 9.1 Hypothetical US Production Possibilities Frontier
This production possibilities frontier illustrates what the United States hypothetically could produce if it put all its productive efforts into making shoes, computers, or different combinations of shoes and computers.

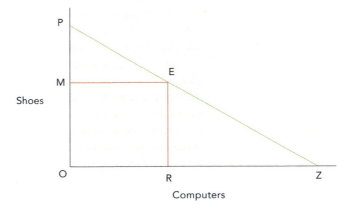

Comparative Advantage

Recall that the benchmark for evaluation of whether trade is worthwhile is greater consumption by each country. If we can show that two countries, for example, Vietnam and the United Kingdom, each achieve greater consumption because of trade, we can understand not only why those two countries trade with each other, but in general how trade can be beneficial to any trading partners, which explains why those partners engage in trade. The United Kingdom in the discussion below stands in for a range of advanced industrial countries that includes, for example, Japan, Germany, Sweden, and the United States; Vietnam is standing in for many developing countries, a group that includes among others Bangladesh, India, and Kenya.

We present our analysis of why countries trade with one another with the aid of four assumptions. These assumptions are by no means an accurate depiction of real-world countries, but they do help us focus on how countries can gain from trade. The four assumptions are:

- The United Kingdom and Vietnam each produces two and only two goods, pharmaceutical products (that is, prescription medications) and shoes.
- Labor is the only productive resource that is required to produce either product.
- Each country has 1 million workers, and so each country has available to it 1 million labor-years of work.
- Because UK workers are living in a technologically advanced country, they tend to be more efficient in manufacturing, and thus we may assume that any one UK worker can produce more bottles of prescription medications each year than any one worker can in Vietnam (500 bottles in the UK to 50 in Vietnam), and any one UK worker can also produce more pairs of shoes than a Vietnamese worker (200 to 175 pairs).

Absolute advantage
A situation in which one state has a productive advantage over another in two (or more) goods, but trade can still be mutually beneficial due to the principle of comparative advantage.

The last assumption means that in respect to prescription medications and shoes the United Kingdom has an **absolute advantage** over Vietnam – it is a more efficient producer of both goods. In these circumstances, we might reasonably ask, how could the UK possibly gain from trade with Vietnam?

The reason why the United Kingdom and Vietnam can both gain through trade despite the UK's absolute advantage in pharmaceutical products and shoes is that there are *differences* in the opportunity costs between the two countries in the production of those medications and shoes. As we can see in Table 9.1, a UK worker in one year can produce either 500 bottles of prescription medications or 200 pairs of shoes, so the UK opportunity cost to produce one additional pair of shoes is 2.5 bottles of medications (500 bottles of medication given up/200 extra pairs of shoes made = 2.5 bottles given up for each additional pair of shoes). By the same logic, the UK opportunity cost for one additional bottle of prescription medications is 0.4 pairs of shoes (200 pairs of shoes given up/500 bottles of medications fabricated = 0.4 pairs of shoes foregone for each additional bottle of medications). We can also see in the figure that any one worker in Vietnam can produce either 50 bottles of prescription medications or 175 pairs of shoes. The opportunity cost of making one additional pair of shoes in Vietnam is about 0.3 bottles of medications (50 bottles foregone/175 shoes made = about 0.3 bottles of medications foregone for each extra pair of shoes produced). The opportunity cost of producing one additional bottle of prescription medications in Vietnam is 3.5 pairs of shoes (175 pairs of shoes foregone/50 additional bottles of medications produced = 3.5 pairs of shoes given up for each additional bottle of medication).

Comparative advantage
One country has a comparative advantage over another in the production of a good if, in order to make one more unit of that good, it has to forego less of another good.

This example illustrates the concept of **comparative advantage**. One country has a comparative advantage over another in the production of a good if, to make one

Table 9.1 Hypothetical Output and Opportunity Costs, Bottles of Medications and Pairs of Shoes, UK and Vietnam
This table shows how countries can differ in opportunity costs in production, and thus differ in the goods for which they have a comparative advantage.

	Worker Output per Year		Opportunity Cost	
	Bottles of Rx	*Pairs of Shoes*	*1 Bottle Rx*	*1 Pair Shoes*
UK	500	200	0.4 pairs shoes	2.5 bottles Rx
Vietnam	50	175	3.5 pairs shoes	0.3 bottle Rx

more unit of that good, it must forego less of another good. In our example, although the UK has an absolute advantage over Vietnam both in prescription medications and shoes, Vietnam has a comparative advantage in shoes. This is because it is *relatively* cheaper to produce an additional pair of shoes *in terms of foregone bottles of prescription medications* in Vietnam (0.3 bottles) than in the United Kingdom (2.5 bottles). Another way of making the same point is to observe that the cost of producing an extra pair of shoes in Vietnam in terms of bottles of medications foregone is about one-eighth the amount that is required in the United Kingdom. At the same time, the UK has a comparative advantage over Vietnam in prescription medications. This is because it is *relatively* cheaper to produce an additional bottle of prescription medications *in terms of foregone shoes* in the UK (0.4 pairs) than in Vietnam (3.5 pairs). Put another way, in the United Kingdom the cost of producing one additional bottle of prescription medications in terms of shoes foregone is about one-ninth the amount that must be foregone in Vietnam.

The Gains from Trade

Even if it is true that, due to differences in opportunity costs in the two countries, the UK enjoys a comparative advantage in prescription medications, and Vietnam enjoys a comparative advantage in shoes, how exactly do both of those countries do better by trading with each other? We are now able to answer that question. Figure 9.2 illustrates how such a mutually beneficial trading situation can arise.

Figure 9.2 Specialization and Trade: The United Kingdom and Vietnam
The theory of international trade suggests that differences in opportunity costs in the United Kingdom and Vietnam, specialization by each based on comparative advantage, and mutually voluntary exchange between them, can combine to allow both countries to improve their consumption and thus their national wellbeing.

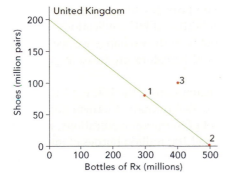
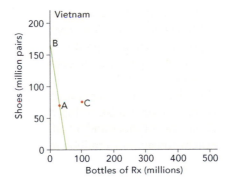

Let us begin with both countries in autarky. Each country's production possibilities frontier – depicted for the UK on the left side of Figure 9.2, and for Vietnam on the right side – dictates its consumption opportunities, since each country in autarky can consume only what it itself produces. Let us assume that in autarky each country allocates 600,000 labor-years to producing pharmaceuticals and 400,000 labor-years to making shoes. In these circumstances, the UK in autarky is at point 1 in the left panel of Figure 9.2: it produces and consumes 300 million bottles of prescription medications and 80 million pairs of shoes. Vietnam in autarky is at point A in the figure's right panel: it produces and consumes 30 million bottles of prescription medications and 70 million pairs of shoes.

What happens if trade becomes possible? The UK first specializes based on its comparative advantage: it entirely stops making shoes and increases its production of medications from 300 million to 500 million bottles. This is represented by the movement from point 1 to point 2 in the left side of Figure 9.2. Vietnam also specializes: it stops making pharmaceuticals altogether and increases its shoe production from 70 million pairs to 175 million pairs; this is noted by the movement from point A to point B in the right side of the figure.

Each country can now offer to exchange some of the good it makes for the good it no longer produces. To make an exchange, the two countries must agree on the **terms of trade**, that is, the rate at which UK bottles of prescription medications will be exchanged for Vietnamese shoes. Imagine that Vietnam and the UK each send a representative to negotiate on behalf of their respective country on this matter of the terms of the trade. Let us also imagine that the Vietnamese representative in the first instance offers less than 0.4 pairs of shoes for each bottle of prescription medications it receives (for example, the representative suggests terms of trade of three bottles per pair of shoes, which translates into 0.33 pairs of shoes per bottle). In those circumstances, the UK representative declines to agree to trade, for at anything less than 0.4 pairs of shoes per bottle the UK can acquire shoes more cheaply by shifting UK labor back into shoes and then obtaining 0.4 pairs for each bottle of medications it foregoes. On the other hand, if the UK representative were to propose a terms of trade that required Vietnam to give up more than 3.5 pairs of Vietnamese shoes per UK bottle of medications then the Vietnamese representative declines to trade, for it would be cheaper for Vietnam to shift labor out of its production of shoes and into the manufacturing of prescription medications and thereby obtain bottles of domestically made medications at an opportunity cost of 3.5 pairs of shoes.

The opportunity costs in the two countries require that the terms of trade must fall somewhere between 0.4 pairs of Vietnamese shoes for one bottle of UK prescription medications and 3.5 pairs of Vietnamese shoes for one bottle of UK medications. Let us assume that the United Kingdom and Vietnam mutually agree to set the terms of trade at one pair of shoes for each bottle of medications, and they agree further to a trade whereby Vietnam provides 100 million pairs of shoes in exchange for which it receives 100 million bottles of UK medications. Returning to Figure 9.2, Vietnam produces at point B, but with the exchange we just described above it now consumes at point C; the United Kingdom produces at point 2 but consumes at point 3.

In Table 9.2 we present the changes in consumption by the UK and Vietnam that their new trading relationship makes possible. Before trade, Vietnam consumes 70 million pairs of shoes and 30 million bottles of prescription medications; with trade, Vietnam consumes 75 million pairs of shoes and 100 million bottles of medications. Vietnam, by specialization and exchange, increases not only its consumption of

Terms of trade
The rate at which goods will be exchanged between two states.

Table 9.2 UK–Vietnam Trade: Gains in Consumption

In this hypothetical scenario, both the UK and Vietnam enjoy increases in their consumption of prescription medications and shoes, which for international trade theory explains why they undertake trade with one another.

Consumption	United Kingdom		Vietnam	
	Bottles Rx	*Pairs Shoes*	*Bottles Rx*	*Pairs Shoes*
After Trade	400	100	100	75
Before Trade	300	80	30	70
Gain from Trade	100	20	70	5

Note: all figures are in millions.

prescription medications by 70 million bottles, but it also increases its consumption of shoes by 5 million pairs. For its part, in autarky the UK consumes 300 million bottles of medications and 80 million pairs of shoes; with specialization and trade, the UK consumes 400 million bottles of medications and 100 million pairs of shoes. With specialization and trade the UK not only consumes 20 million additional pairs of shoes, it is also able to consume an additional 100 million bottles of prescription medicines.

Thus, for economists, there is a strong theoretical case for the proposition that countries benefit in terms of total consumption if they pursue specialization based on their comparative advantage and they undertake trade. All countries, according to this logic, have a pure economic interest in specialization and trade. Yet, as we will see below, political considerations intrude into the calculations and actions of states either to promote or impede trade and thereby shape the global economy.

Why Do Countries Protect Themselves from Trade?

While trade theory's depiction of the benefits of trade is elegant and persuasive, almost every government at one time or other places restrictions on goods coming into its territory, that is, it pursues some form of **protectionism**. Why does this occur? Governments turn to protection either because of their understanding of what constitutes the interests of the country, or because of pressures they may receive from some groups in society that are harmed by trade.

Protectionism
Any of a number of policies in which a country puts restrictions on incoming goods in an effort to protect the domestic economy.

Let us consider how governments might decide that, from the viewpoint of the country as a whole, protectionism is a necessary policy. In the example above, Vietnam improves its total consumption if it specializes in shoes and buys prescription medications from the United Kingdom. From the viewpoint of liberal international theory, which we reviewed in Chapter 3, this opportunity for absolute gains in consumption is sufficient to motivate Vietnam's government to open its country to trade based on comparative advantage.

Yet, Vietnam's government might face incentives and constraints highlighted in realist theory. For example, the Vietnamese government might worry that if it allows UK prescription medications into its market, Vietnam will have no prospect of ever having a local pharmaceutical industry. Given that the UK has had a head start in that industry, free trade would simply lock in its advantage and doom the formation of an indigenous Vietnamese industry in that important field. The Vietnamese government might calculate that such free trade will prevent Vietnam from developing a strong research capacity in chemistry and the chemicals industry, which might have implications for Vietnamese national security. The Vietnamese government might also calculate that trade based on current comparative advantage industry would make Vietnam dangerously dependent on the UK for medicines. Given how important pharmaceuticals are to modern life, Vietnamese leaders might fear that if they become dependent on the UK in that area they will be open to British pressure or even blackmail if those two countries found themselves in a dispute and the UK threatened to apply economic sanctions if Vietnam did not comply with its diplomatic demands.

Infant-industry protection
A policy in which imports of a certain type of good are restricted (in theory temporarily) to allow for the development of the capacity to produce that good domestically.

To address these concerns, Vietnam might adopt **infant-industry protection**, a policy by a government of restricting imports of a good so that potential or actual domestic producers of that good have a large enough domestic market that they can grow and become efficient and thus eventually not need trade protection. The Vietnamese government's goal would be to restrict UK medications and thereby to create a temporarily sheltered market for its own pharmaceutical industry to allow it to develop. The ultimate goal would be that the Vietnamese pharmaceutical industry could stand on its own in its home market and perhaps even to be able to engage in international competition. Of course, while the protection was in place, Vietnamese consumers would need to pay more for 'home-grown' prescription medications, and the country would not be using its economic resources most efficiently. In this case, Vietnam's government would believe that the country's long-term economic and political interests would need to override the economic interest of its consumers.

An example where infant-industry protection has worked in modern history is the United States, which was highly protectionist until well into the early twentieth century precisely to allow US industry to develop. The examples of Japan and South Korea in the second half of the twentieth century provide further evidence that infant-industry protection can sometimes be effective. We will return to this issue in Chapter 11; for the moment, we present differing views on this contemporary debate in Box 9.1.

Governments might also turn to protectionism to address the concerns of societal groups that are made economically vulnerable because of foreign competition. Liberal theory emphasizes that individuals and domestic interest groups drive foreign policy. While there are many grounds to believe that individuals and groups press democratic governments in peaceful directions, there are also good reasons to believe that, in international economic matters, different interest groups often pressure governments in different directions, some pressing for openness while others press for closure, with trade policy usually in consequence possessing both free-trade and protectionist elements.

In the above discussion of trade, we can imagine that UK pharmaceutical producers would press for freer trade with Vietnam. However, UK workers in British shoe factories might reasonably see imports of Vietnamese shoes as a threat to their jobs, livelihoods, and way of life. For those workers, it is largely impractical to believe they can give up making shoes and return to school for retraining to learn how to produce prescription medicines, so they might pressure politicians to restrict Vietnamese imports of shoes. If these UK shoe makers and their friends and families are clustered in politically sensitive parts of the United Kingdom, politicians in those districts might indeed press for protectionism, and they might prevail over the preferences of pharmaceutical manufacturers, or at

9.1   DIFFERING PERSPECTIVES

Infant-Industry Protection in Developing Countries

In her presidential address to the American Economic Association, Anne O. Krueger, a former World Bank Chief Economist and Deputy Managing Director of the International Monetary Fund (IMF), argued that infant-industry policies are typically unsuccessful; in contrast, a UN international panel headed by former Mexican president Ernesto Zedillo argued that there remains a place for them.

The Argument against Infant-Industry Policies in Developing Countries: Economist Anne O. Krueger

A second misapplication of good theory arose because of the nonoperational nature of the theory itself, and the failure to identify circumstances under which policy implementation might be incentive compatible and potentially increase welfare. A key culprit in this was the interpretation of the infant industry argument ... [it was] generally recognized as a 'legitimate' case for a departure from free trade ...The problem with the argument, as a basis for policy, is that it fails to provide any guidance as to how to distinguish between an infant that would grow up and a would-be producer seeking protection because it is privately profitable.

Source: Krueger (1997): 11–12.

The Argument for Infant-Industry Policies in Developing Countries: UN International Panel Headed by Former President of Mexico Ernesto Zedillo

However misguided the old model of blanket protection intended to nurture import substitute industries, it would be a mistake to go to the other extreme and deny developing countries the opportunity of actively nurturing the development of an industrial sector. A requirement for international approval of such protection could be a help to the governments of developing countries in resisting excessive demands from their domestic lobbies (and from multinationals considering local investment).

Source: United Nations (2001): 41.

For Krueger, the liberal economist, governments are ill-suited to pursuing protection based on infant-industry ideas because they do poorly at identifying industries that merit protection. Zedillo, the Mexican politician, believes it is important to maintain the option for infant-industry protection and suggests that Krueger's problem might be addressed through external assistance that would be tied to international approval of such national protection based on infant-industry claims.

least slow the rate at which UK–Vietnamese trade is liberalized. Although it might make economic sense for the United Kingdom as a whole to import most of its shoes, a regional political logic in which domestic interest groups have political influence might dictate that the UK avoids completely free trade in that industry. For a striking example of how economically inefficient yet politically powerful producers have used government restrictions to further their parochial interests, see Box 9.2 on rice farming in Japan.

9.2   MAKING CONNECTIONS
Theory and Practice

The Economic Logic of Specialization and Trade versus the Political Power of Domestic Interest Groups

Theory

The economic logic of comparative advantage holds that countries should specialize in what they produce most efficiently based on their factor endowments of land, labor, and capital, and trade with other countries to obtain goods and services that they produce less efficiently.

Practice

Countries often provide trade protection to their less efficient but politically sensitive producers. A good example is rice farming in Japan. Rice is produced cheaply and efficiently in Southeast Asian countries and other parts of the world. In Japan, due to the country's mountainous terrain and rice's cultural significance, rice is produced inefficiently and at high cost by a multitude of farmers tending very small plots, typically less than three hectares and often less than one hectare (one hectare equals approximately 2.5 acres). Japanese rice farmers are also part-time farmers, deriving less than half their income from this activity.

Nevertheless, Japanese rice has long enjoyed special protection from trade competition. Many in Japan consider rice a sacred cultural commodity because it is the key staple in the Japanese diet. Rice farmers have long been a key constituency of the Liberal Democratic Party, which ruled Japan from 1955 to 1993, from the mid-1990s to 2009, and from 2012 to 2018. Liberal Democratic politicians insisted on protecting Japanese rice producers and, until the 1990s, would not allow, in the words of one politician, 'a single grain of rice' to enter Japan from abroad. In return, rice farmers and their communities served as a loyal voting bloc to help Liberal Democrats maintain power.

In the 1990s, and under intense pressure from its trading partners, Japan reluctantly agreed to allow some foreign-produced rice into the country. The government also provided subsidies to make sure that most of the high-cost Japanese rice farmers could stay in business. One result is that Japan in recent years has found itself with more rice than it could consume, and it holds the surplus in storage. As of 2014, the Japanese tariff on imported rice remained at a very steep rate – 788 percent!

Protectionist pressures remain very strong in some sectors even in countries that rely heavily on international economic integration.

Photo 9.1 The Importance of Rice to Japan
Japanese Prime Minister Morihiro Hosokawa inspects a rice paddy in October 1993 in Fukushima, Japan. Rice has deep cultural significance in Japan and the country has faced international pressure to open its home market for rice to international competition.

Source: The Asahi Shimbun via Getty Images.

Forms of Protectionism

Protectionism itself can take many forms. Until quite recently, governments routinely employed **tariffs**, which is a tax collected by the government on goods coming into the country. Governments around the world quite often deploy one or another **non-tariff barrier (NTB)** to trade, which in general is a government policy that restricts the supply of imported goods and gives market advantage to home producers. As tariffs have come down since World War II, something we will discuss below, non-tariff barriers have become more important both as a government policy instrument and as a subject of international trade negotiation.

There are many types of NTBs. A particularly important and pervasive type involves the anti-dumping practices of importing countries. Dumping is the sale of goods by producers in a foreign market at prices that are lower than what those producers charge in their home market. Producers might engage in dumping to gain market share in the targeted foreign markets, or to drive out local producers in those markets, and having done so then increase prices and obtain very high profits. In most countries, governments have procedures through which local producers can claim that foreign producers are engaged in dumping. If the governments find merit to such claims, they can impose anti-dumping duties, that is, tariffs that offset the price cuts offered by foreign suppliers below what they charge in their own markets.

Anti-dumping is allowed under international trade law. However, suppose, returning to our UK–Vietnam example, that the British government puts into place anti-dumping procedures whereby it would be extremely easy and inexpensive for UK shoe makers to press any anti-dumping claims they might wish to make against Vietnamese shoe exporters. If UK shoe makers took advantage of the new and, from their viewpoint, easier procedures, then Vietnamese shoe exporters would need to hire lawyers and undertake lengthy and expensive efforts to demonstrate that they were not dumping. Those exporters might decide that, even if they were not in fact dumping their shoes in the UK market, it might still make sense to avoid the legal expenses and business uncertainty that would flow from an anti-dumping dispute and instead simply to raise their prices for shoes sold in the UK, or to turn away from the British market and instead to focus on other foreign markets. Anti-dumping procedures that are tilted in favor of domestic producers in this instance would serve to provide undue protection to UK shoe producers and thus would constitute a non-tariff barrier to trade.

A second type of NTB involves government procurement, that is, the purchase by government agencies of goods and services from private suppliers. Given that government expenditures can run into the hundreds of billions of dollars per year, how the government awards purchasing contracts can either promote or hamper international trade. For example, the American 2009 stimulus package, totaling almost $900 billion, included 'Buy America' provisions that required US infrastructure spending programs (for example, roads, tunnels, and public transportation) to give preference to US over foreign suppliers.

Import quotas represent a third type of NTB. Import quotas are government-imposed numerical limits on how much of a good or service may be imported during some period. Returning to our illustration of trade theory, to mollify the concerns of British manufacturers and unions in the shoe industry, the UK government could impose annual quotas on Vietnamese shoe imports. If British consumers want to buy 5 million pairs of shoes from Vietnam each year, but the UK government allows only 2 million pairs to be imported, customers will bid up the price of those shoes, forcing customers to look for alternatives – including UK domestically produced shoes.

The use of import quotas is restricted under international trade law because it keeps goods out of the market instead of (as through tariffs) letting them in at higher

Tariff
A tax collected by the government on goods coming into the country.

Non-tariff barrier (NTB)
Policies, such as anti-dumping duties, import quotas, or controlled government procurement, by which a state can control imports and import prices without imposing tariffs.

prices. To get around this restriction, governments sometimes employ Voluntary Export Restraints (VERs). Imagine that the British government announces that if Vietnam does not reduce its shoe exports to the UK, then the British government will impose quotas not just on shoes, but on other Vietnamese products, such as clothing. The Vietnamese government might then persuade or compel Vietnamese shoe manufacturers to agree 'voluntarily' to restrict their sales in the UK.

In sum, international trade theory helps us understand why states engage in trade. But, returning to our enduring question, the study of politics helps us understand how governments may turn to protectionism. Politics can also bend the logic of international monetary affairs, to which we turn next.

Levels of Analysis *International Trade Theory*		
👤 Individual	State	🌐 International
Individuals, alone and as members of households, are at the heart of international trade theory, for it is their preference for consumption that animates specialization and trade.	States can improve their consumption opportunities from trade, and this explains why countries trade. Workers and producers in import-competing industries can lose out from trade and thus pressure their governments for protectionism.	States may turn away from freer trade and pursue infant industry and other forms of protection to promote national autonomy or strengthen national defense.

 Simulations: What would you do? Visit the companion website to step into the shoes of a Finance Minister tasked with setting up a country's financial system. Watch the scenario develop with every decision you make!

BASIC ELEMENTS OF INTERNATIONAL MONEY

In the previous section, Vietnam and the United Kingdom literally exchanged pairs of shoes for bottles of prescription medications. Yet, in the real world, UK pharmaceutical exporters want to be paid in British pounds sterling, and Vietnamese shoe exporters want to be paid in their national currency, the dong. Moreover, if foreign investors want to invest in the UK, they need pounds sterling to do that, just as non-Vietnamese investors who wish to invest in Vietnam need dong. Consider these investment transactions, and notice how each requires the investor to acquire the currency of the country in which the investment is taking place:

- *Foreign Direct Investment*: Residents in one country – most typically multinational enterprises, about which we say more below – may establish wholly owned foreign subsidiaries or buy enough shares of a foreign firm to control the operations of that firm. For example, Volkswagen, a large manufacturer of automobiles, is headquartered in Germany, but in 2016 about 55 percent of its 626,000 employees worked in Volkswagen-owned factories around the world.
- *Portfolio Investment*: Residents in one country – individuals, mutual funds acting on behalf of individuals, or firms acting on their own – may purchase foreign securities such as bonds, or purchase equities of foreign firms in amounts that do

not confer managerial control. Large US and UK financial services firms – such as Vanguard and Fidelity in the former, and Aberdeen Asset Management and Barclays in the latter – offer to investors a wide range of funds that invest partly and even wholly in foreign firms.

- *Bank Deposits and Lending*: Banks headquartered in one country might extend loans to a foreign individual or enterprise. For example, if Deutsche Bank lends euros to a Vietnamese shoe manufacturer, that represents a German loan to a Vietnamese enterprise.

A person, household, or firm that wishes to acquire the currency of a foreign country typically does so through a purchase of the relevant currency on what is termed the **foreign exchange market**, that is, the marketplace (important locations are in London, New York, Frankfurt, and Tokyo) in which individuals, firms, and even governments sell and buy foreign currencies. Through a process of offering and bidding foreign currencies, market participants establish foreign currency **exchange rates**, that is, the amount of one currency that must be offered to purchase one unit of a foreign currency. So, for example, in late May 2018, based on the demand and supply conditions at that time, if you possessed Indian rupees and wanted to purchase some US dollars, you would go to a bank or some other foreign-currency retail outlet and pay roughly 67.5 rupees for each dollar you wished to purchase, and we would say that the rupee-dollar exchange rate for your transaction was 67.5 rupees to the dollar. Alternatively, if you possessed US dollars and wanted to purchase Indian rupees in late May, you would pay roughly 1.5 US cents for each rupee you wished to purchase. Note that the dollar-rupee exchange rate for any given time is the inverse of the rupee-dollar exchange rate, that is, in this example it would be in late May about 1.5 US cents to the rupee. For a fuller picture of exchange rates in late May 2018 that is similar in form to what you can see each business day in many newspapers, see Table 9.3.

Foreign exchange market
The marketplace in which individuals, firms, and even governments sell and buy foreign currencies.

Exchange rate
The amount of one currency that must be offered to purchase one unit of a foreign currency.

National Exchange-Rate Systems

If a government allows supply and demand in foreign exchange markets to determine the exchange rate for its currency, then the government is pursuing a **flexible (or floating) exchange-rate system**. Examples of countries that utilize largely flexible exchange-rate systems include the United States, the United Kingdom, Canada, and Switzerland. The alternative is for a government to establish a **fixed (or pegged) exchange-rate system**. In that instance, a government announces that its currency will trade at a specific rate or within a band of values against a foreign currency or group of currencies. The government is then obliged to intervene in the foreign exchange market or to take policy measures to maintain the pegged rate. These measures include monetary policy (efforts usually by the country's central bank to raise or lower interest rates or buy or sell foreign currencies) or fiscal policy (government decisions on spending and taxes). China today is an example of a country that has a largely fixed exchange-rate system.

Flexible (or floating) exchange-rate system
A system in which a government allows supply and demand in foreign exchange markets to determine the exchange rate of its national currency.

Fixed (or pegged) exchange-rate system
A system in which a currency trades at a government-specified rate against a particular currency or a group of currencies, and the government intervenes in the foreign exchange market or takes monetary or fiscal policy measures to keep those rates in place.

Flexible Exchange-Rate Systems

Both Canada and Switzerland allow their currencies to float against each other. We can see how the exchange rate between their two currencies, the Canadian dollar (often called the CAD by participants in foreign exchange markets) and the Swiss franc (often called the CHF) is determined, and can change, in Figure 9.3.

Table 9.3 Selected Currency Rates, September 2018

This chart depicts the rates of exchange, as of September 6, 2018, among a range of currencies. To read the chart, consider the second row, which reports how many units of each of the currencies listed in that row needed to be paid that day to buy one euro. You will observe that, to purchase one euro, a person that day would have had to pay about 1.16 U.S. dollars, 0.9 UK pounds, 17.8 South African rand, 128.7 Japanese yen, 7.9 Chinese renminbi, 22.5 Mexican pesos, or 83.6 Indian rupees. Some version of this chart may be found daily in the business section of most national newspapers.

	USD	EUR	GBP	CHF	AUD	ZAR	JPY	CNY	SGD	HKD	RUB	MXN	AED	INR
1 US dollar =	–	0.86	0.77	0.97	1.39	15.33	110.73	6.84	1.38	7.85	69.40	19.34	3.67	71.99
1 euro =	1.16	–	0.90	1.12	1.62	17.83	128.69	7.94	1.60	9.12	80.62	22.47	4.27	83.65
1 pound =	1.29	1.11	–	1.25	1.80	19.84	143.25	8.84	1.78	10.15	89.72	25.01	4.75	93.09
1 Swiss franc =	1.03	0.89	0.80	–	1.44	15.86	114.57	7.07	1.42	8.12	71.75	19.99	3.80	74.45
1 Australian dollar =	0.72	0.62	0.56	0.70	–	11.02	79.70	4.92	0.99	5.65	49.91	13.90	2.64	51.79
1 South African rand =	0.07	0.06	0.05	0.06	0.09	–	7.23	0.45	0.09	0.51	4.53	1.26	0.24	4.70
1 Japanese yen =	0.01	0.01	0.01	0.01	0.01	0.14	–	0.06	0.01	0.07	0.63	0.17	0.03	0.65
1 Chinese renminbi =	0.15	0.13	0.11	0.14	0.20	2.24	16.21	–	0.20	1.15	10.15	2.83	0.54	10.53
1 Singapore dollar =	0.73	0.63	0.56	0.70	1.01	11.14	80.55	4.97	–	5.71	50.43	14.05	2.67	52.33
1 Hong Kong dollar =	0.13	0.11	0.10	0.12	0.18	1.95	14.12	0.87	0.18	–	8.84	2.46	0.47	9.17
1 Russian ruble =	0.01	0.01	0.01	0.01	0.02	0.22	1.60	0.10	0.02	0.11	–	0.28	0.05	1.04
1 Mexican peso =	0.05	0.04	0.04	0.05	0.07	0.79	5.74	0.35	0.07	0.41	3.59	–	0.19	3.73
1 UAE dirham =	0.27	0.23	0.21	0.26	0.38	4.17	30.17	1.86	0.37	2.14	18.88	5.26	–	19.60
1 Indian rupee =	0.01	0.01	0.01	0.01	0.02	0.21	1.54	0.09	0.02	0.11	0.96	0.27	0.05	–

Source: Data from Bloomberg Cross Rates, https://www.bloomberg.com/markets/currencies/cross-rates, 6th September 2018.

Figure 9.3 Determination of Exchange Rates: Canadian Dollar and Swiss Franc
This figure shows how the interplay between demand and supply determines exchange rates.

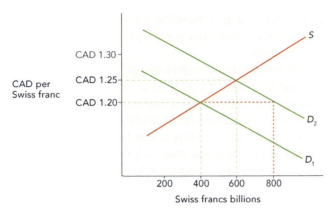

In Figure 9.3, we use **demand curves** and **supply curves** to explain how, because of market forces, the exchange rate is established between the Canadian dollar and the Swiss franc. A demand curve specifies the quantity of a good that consumers wish to purchase at different prices; a supply curve specifies how much producers are willing to offer at different prices. In Figure 9.3, D_1 and D_2 represent two hypothetical demand curves that Canadian residents have for Swiss francs over some period of time, for example, a year, while S represents the number of Swiss francs that Swiss residents are willing to offer during that same period at different rates of exchange against the Canadian dollar.

Notice that both Canadian demand curves are downward sloping. Assume that a Swiss watch sells for 100 francs in Switzerland. At an exchange rate of CAD1.20/ 1 Swiss franc, the watch costs CAD120 in Canada; if it only costs one Canadian dollar to buy a Swiss franc, the watch costs CAD100. As the price of a Swiss franc declines, Swiss watches become less expensive in Canada; more Canadian residents want to purchase them, and therefore, Canadian demand for Swiss francs will be greater. Notice also that the supply curve for Swiss francs, S, is upward sloping. As the Swiss franc becomes more valuable in terms of the Canadian dollars it can purchase, Canadian goods fall in price in terms of Swiss francs; Swiss residents will offer more of their currency so they can buy those cheaper Canadian goods.

In Figure 9.3 we assume that, at first, Canadian demand for and Swiss supply of Swiss francs equals one another at CAD1.20 per Swiss franc. How might this exchange rate change? Imagine that Canadian residents wish to purchase more Swiss products or financial assets, and therefore they demand, *at any given exchange rate*, more Swiss francs. This across-the-board increase in Canadian demand for Swiss francs is represented by a shift in the Canadian demand curve from D_1 to D_2. The new exchange rate where demand equals supply is CAD1.25 per Swiss franc.

In a flexible exchange-rate system, currency values are determined on the market, without government manipulation. Yet, even governments that normally prefer a flexible exchange-rate system occasionally intervene in currency markets. For example, in 2011, many individuals and companies began to sell euros (the common currency of several European countries, about which we will say more in a moment) for Swiss francs. The Swiss National Bank, the official central bank for that country, became alarmed that the resulting appreciation of the Swiss franc was making Swiss exports uncompetitive. It entered the foreign exchange market, offered Swiss francs for euros, and thereby capped the former's rise against the latter.

Demand curve
A demand curve specifies the quantity of a good that consumers wish to purchase at different prices. Along with supply curves, demand curves can show the likely price of goods, including currencies, in international markets.

Supply curve
A curve specifying how much producers are willing to offer of a good at different prices. Along with demand curves, supply curves can show the likely price of goods, including currencies, in international markets.

Fixed Exchange-Rate Systems

A government will sometimes try to maintain its currency at a fixed value relative to one or more other currencies. For example, in the 1990s, the Mexican government sought to keep the peso fixed against the dollar. China today pegs its currency against the dollar, although in recent years it has permitted some increase in the value of that currency relative to the dollar.

To see how a fixed exchange rate operates, imagine that the Canadian government wishes to fix the CAD-CHF rate at CAD1.20 to one Swiss franc. That rate would be the *official exchange rate* between the Canadian dollar and the Swiss franc, and the Canadian government would commit to maintain it through **currency market interventions** (purchases or sales of currency by the Canadian government), or by making changes in Canadian fiscal and monetary policy. What would happen if the Canadian government wanted the exchange rate to stay at CAD1.20 to the Swiss franc even if Canadian demand for Swiss goods and financial assets increased from D_1 to D_2? Returning to Figure 9.3, imagine if Canadian residents wished to import Swiss goods and buy Swiss financial assets at an annual rate totaling CHF 800 billion (see the dashed lines in the figure), while the Swiss supply of francs to buy Canadian goods and financial assets was CHF 400 billion. In those circumstances, Canada would soon experience a deficit in its current account.

Let us explain what we mean by a nation's current account. To do that, we need to introduce to you the idea of a country's overall **balance of payments**, and to the way a country can experience a balance-of-payments deficit or a balance-of-payments surplus. The balance of payments for a country is a summary of the international transactions of its residents, including individuals, households, private enterprises, and the government, with residents in the rest of the world during some fixed period, usually a quarter (three months) or a year. One key part of the balance of payments is the **current account**. The current account consists of the country's balance of trade in goods and services (the value of exports minus the value of imports), plus its income receipts such as the receipt of earnings from past investments abroad or the payment of such earnings to foreigners, and other transfers such as remittances that workers send out of the country or residents receive from abroad.

Imagine Canada has a fixed exchange-rate system and begins to run a current-account deficit with Switzerland. Without intervention by the Canadian government the Canadian dollar would drop in value, reaching perhaps CAD1.25 per Swiss franc rather than the official peg of CAD1.20. To prevent that, the Canadian government would need to use some of its holdings of Swiss francs to buy Canadian dollars and thereby bid up their price so that the market rate would stay at the official rate of CAD1.20 to the Swiss franc. As we will see below, a very wealthy country like Canada can do that for quite some time; a poorer country is likely to find itself more severely constrained in its capacity to maintain a peg in the face of a persistent current-account deficit.

There are two other policy options available to governments when it comes to their national currencies. First, governments may agree to establish a currency union, the giving up by countries of their respective national currencies in favor of a common currency. The most prominent currency union today is the **eurozone**. As of 2017, 19 of the 28 member states of the European Union had converted their national currencies to the euro (see Map 9.1). A second monetary policy option is when a country substitutes a foreign currency for its own in its home market. This practice is called dollarization because, as discussed in Box 9.3, the foreign currency most likely substituted has been the US dollar.

Currency market intervention
The purchase or sale of currency by a state government in international markets to maintain a constant exchange rate between that government's currency and another currency.

Balance of payments
A summary of the international transactions of a state's residents, including individuals, households, private enterprises, and the government, with residents in the rest of the world during some fixed period, usually a quarter (three months) or a year.

Current account
The current account consists of the country's balance of trade in goods and services (the value of exports minus the value of imports), plus its income receipts such as the receipt of earnings from past investments abroad or the payment of such earnings to foreigners, and other transfers such as remittances that workers send out of the country or local residents receive from abroad.

Eurozone
The world's most prominent currency union, consisting of 19 countries in Europe all using the euro as a national currency.

Map 9.1 Members of the European Union Using the Euro, 2017
A wide range of EU countries have elected to utilize a common currency, the euro.

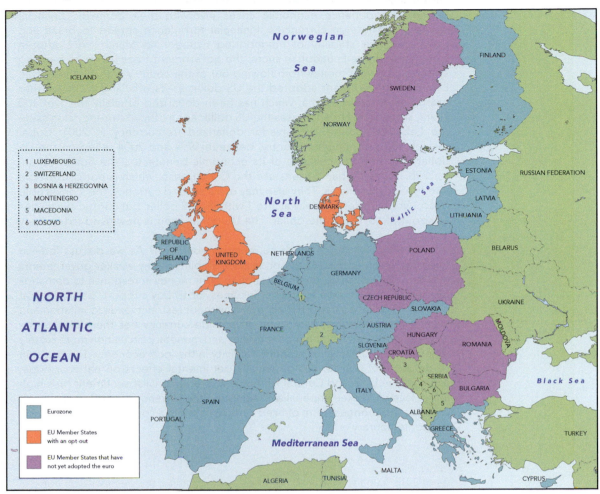

Legend:
- Eurozone
- EU Member States with an opt-out
- EU Member States that have not yet adopted the euro

1 LUXEMBOURG
2 SWITZERLAND
3 BOSNIA & HERZEGOVINA
4 MONTENEGRO
5 MACEDONIA
6 KOSOVO

9.3 MAKING CONNECTIONS
Aspiration versus Reality

Dollarization in Central and South America

Aspiration: Governments Must Defend the Value of Their Currency

For most governments, the national currency is an important symbol of sovereignty and power. They must also defend the value of their currency so that their own citizens, as well as investors abroad, have confidence in it as a store of value.

Reality: Not Every Government Manages to Create and Defend a Viable National Currency

Some governments decide, informally or formally, to allow their citizens to use a foreign currency either alongside or as a substitute for the local currency. This process is called 'dollarization' because, especially since the end of World War II, the US dollar has been the currency of choice as a substitute for local currencies in trouble. For example, in the late 1990s, many Asian countries began to experience economic crises involving their domestic financial markets and foreign currencies. Financial turbulence spread to Brazil and threatened the stability of neighboring Ecuador. In March 1999, after a steep drop in the Ecuadorian sucre, the government froze its entire banking system to prevent money from flowing out of the country. Shortly thereafter, Ecuador's government adopted the US dollar as its official currency. Other examples include Panama, which has been dollarized officially for over 100 years, since 1904. Lebanon uses the US dollar as an official currency alongside the Lebanese pound. El Salvador dollarized its currency in 2001. Cuba, though still a communist country, between 1994 and 2004 relied on the US dollar following the collapse of its economic benefactor, the Soviet Union, in 1990. Today, Cuban citizens use the Cuban peso, which is not convertible into foreign currencies. They also may use a second currency, the 'convertible peso,' which trades officially at 1 to 1 with the US dollar, but unofficially trades at about 25 to 1 with the dollar. The US dollar itself is now used extensively in Cuba.

Why adopt someone else's currency as your own? As we discuss later in this chapter, an important reason is price stability. Many weaker governments may be unable to resist the temptation to print money in response to demands by citizens and workers for higher incomes, or to buy support, particularly at election time. Of course, printing money without restraint leads to inflation and even bigger problems. Relying on an outside currency ties the hands of the government; it can no longer print money and monetary circulation more closely reflects the actual level of economic activity in the local economy. The decision to dollarize, of course, has potentially detrimental effects on national pride, especially in Latin and Central America, where nationalist sentiment runs high in the face of 'Yankee imperialism.' Adopting the currency of another country is perhaps the strongest form of fixed currency system a country can undertake in the contemporary era.

Photo 9.2 One Country, Two Currencies
As of 2018, Cuba still had two currencies in circulation, the peso, or CUP (for locals) and the convertible peso, or CUC (for tourists). The CUC is the stronger and more valuable currency. You can tell them apart because the CUC has pictures of monuments and the CUP has pictures of people.

Source: ADALBERTO ROQUE/AFP/Getty Images.

Fixed Exchange-Rate Systems: Benefits and Problems

Governments that peg their exchange rates often find it necessary to intervene in the foreign exchange markets or to adjust their monetary and fiscal policies to maintain their desired official rates of exchange. But why would a government want to have a fixed rate in the first place? Let's look at the benefits and risks of fixed exchange-rate systems.

One reason governments may fix their exchange rates is to fight **price inflation** (usually simply the term 'inflation' is employed) where too much money is chasing too few goods, pushing up prices of goods and services. If a government has had a poor track record in controlling inflation, it may stoke inflationary expectations, the belief on the part of individuals, firms, unions, and other economic agents that price increases are always just around the corner. In those circumstances, domestic and foreign holders of that country's currency are constantly on the lookout for any signs of inflation, and if they see them they sell their holdings of the currency, causing its value to drop on currency markets, and by so doing increasing the price of imports and therefore actually bringing on more price inflation.

Governments in the first place often try to counteract inflation and inflationary expectations through a policy of **austerity**; by raising interest rates, or by reducing government spending and increasing taxes, governments seek to discourage consumption and investment at home, and by dampening domestic demand also reduce inflationary pressures in the economy. However, another way a government can signal that it is resolved on fighting inflation is to fix the exchange rate of its currency against the currency of a slow-inflation country, and announce it will maintain the fixed rate, even if this means using fiscal and monetary policies that will slow a nation's economy and thereby keep inflation in check. A second reason a government might seek to peg its currency below what would be the free-market rate is to spur exports by its domestic producers. For example, the US government has claimed for many years that the Chinese government has pegged its currency, the renminbi (which is also known as the yuan, and whose trading symbol on foreign exchange markets is CNY), at an official rate below the free-market rate, precisely to promote Chinese exports.

Although fixed rates provide price stability and export advantages, they also carry risks. Consider the case of China and the possible undervaluing of the renminbi against the US dollar. China, with an undervalued currency, sells more goods to the United States than it purchases from that country; China in turn experiences large current-account surpluses; and, over time, it accumulates a large holding of US dollars – in recent years, something like $3 trillion.

There are three risks with this strategy. First, persistent large current-account surpluses accentuate the risk of Chinese domestic price inflation. As Chinese firms earn US dollars and other foreign currencies, they submit them to the Chinese central bank (that is how China's government has amassed $3 trillion); in return they receive renminbi. The firms deposit these renminbi in Chinese banks, which in turn lends them to Chinese residents to start new businesses, buy homes, or buy other goods and services. More and more renminbi thus move through the Chinese economy, and if the growth in the domestic supply of goods in China does not grow at the same rate as the growth in the currency, price inflation is likely to go up in China.

Second, Chinese monetary officials use the US dollars they accumulate to purchase US Treasury bonds. A bond is a financial instrument which has written terms whereby a borrower (usually a person, firm, or government) receives cash today from a lender (a person, firm, or government) in exchange for a promise that

Price inflation
A situation in which too much money is chasing too few goods, pushing up prices of goods and services.

Austerity
A policy by which governments raise interest rates or reduce government spending in an effort to discourage consumption and investment at home and, in so doing, reduce inflation and inflationary pressures.

the borrower will pay the cash back to the original lender at some specified time in the future (usually specified as a certain number of days, months, or years) and in the meantime the borrower promises to pay the lender some amount of money per month or quarter or year as a form of rent on the borrowed cash. Chinese purchasers of bonds issued by the US government need to believe that the latter will maintain the value of those bonds. Think of it this way: if you are holding $3 trillion in bonds, and the dollar's value falls 10 percent against major currencies, your bonds are worth $300 billion less when expressed in those other currencies. Chinese monetary authorities must sometimes wonder if their faith in the United States is entirely well placed. Since 2012, Chinese authorities have begun to diversify their official reserve portfolio by holding fewer US dollars and more Swiss francs, Japanese yen, and euros.

Finally, utilizing a fixed exchange-rate system to attain a competitive edge will work so long as a country's trading partners do not take some form of retaliation to offset the edge gained through a government-maintained undervalued currency. China's exchange-rate system has not prompted strong retaliation from major trading partners like Japan or the European Union. However, there have been persistent criticisms of China's currency peg in the US Congress. China also came under intense pressure regarding its currency peg at the April 2011 meeting of the Group of 20 Finance Ministers. The risk then of retaliation by trading partners, together with possible Chinese fears about domestic price inflation, may help explain why the Chinese government has begun to allow the renminbi to appreciate slowly against the dollar, as can be observed in Figure 9.4. However, there remain concerns about China's exchange-rate policy and its international competitiveness: in the spring of 2018, for example, President Donald Trump was making increasingly severe threats to impose high tariffs on Chinese goods entering the US market.

Fixed exchange-rate systems create challenges for countries with current-account surpluses. They can be much, much harder on countries that begin to experience serious current-account deficits, for example, Mexico in the mid-1990s and Argentina in the early 2000s. As we saw in the hypothetical case of Canada and Switzerland, a country that wants to maintain a peg when its current-account deficit is growing must intervene in the currency markets and buy its own currency with its holdings

Figure 9.4 US Dollar/Chinese Renminbi Exchange Rate, 2000–16

The Chinese government has allowed the renminbi, or CNY, to appreciate against the US dollar in recent years. While the exchange rate was fixed between 2000 and 2005 at 8.3 CNY per dollar, the CNY gradually began to appreciate from 2006 onward (fewer CNY were needed to buy one US dollar), and by 2016, and even with a modest depreciation that year of the Chinese currency, only 6.6 CNY were needed to purchase one dollar. This general movement toward a more valuable CNY may have been due to US pressure on China to allow its currency to float upward.

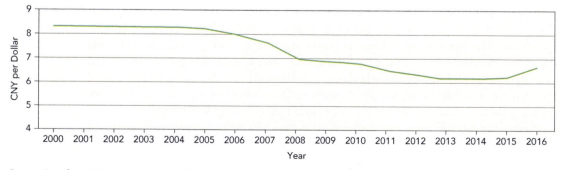

Source: Data from IMF, DataBank, World Development Indicators, available at http://databank.worldbank.org/data/reports. aspx?source=world-development-indicators#.

of foreign currency. That strategy is limited by two powerful constraints: its holdings of foreign currency, and its ability to borrow foreign currency to purchase its own currency.

In time domestic and foreign investors may come to question whether the central bank of a deficit country might run out of currency reserves or can borrow them from foreigners. Fearing that the government must finally allow the currency to devalue, holders of the currency – both local and foreign – might begin to sell assets they hold in the country and buy foreign currency and assets. The result is that local stock markets and real-estate markets fall, and the supply of the local currency on foreign exchange markets grows even faster, making it even harder for the country to maintain the peg. The government then faces a hard choice: either extreme austerity even as the national economy is already contracting, or going off the peg, which will in the short-term prompt even more currency sales and a sharper domestic economic contraction.

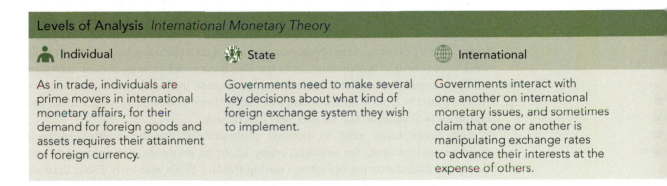

Levels of Analysis *International Monetary Theory*		
👤 Individual	👥 State	🌐 International
As in trade, individuals are prime movers in international monetary affairs, for their demand for foreign goods and assets requires their attainment of foreign currency.	Governments need to make several key decisions about what kind of foreign exchange system they wish to implement.	Governments interact with one another on international monetary issues, and sometimes claim that one or another is manipulating exchange rates to advance their interests at the expense of others.

MULTINATIONAL ENTERPRISES AND INTERNATIONAL POLITICAL ECONOMY

We will explore multinational enterprises (MNEs) and their important role in world affairs in three steps: first, we will provide a definition of such firms and examine their key characteristics; second, we will examine their economic importance in the modern global economy; and third, we will examine several ways in which they are important political actors.

Definition and Characteristics of Multinational Enterprises

Multinational enterprises (MNEs) are firms that have their headquarters in one country and ongoing business operations in one or (more typically) several other countries. Do note that there are other terms for MNEs that are often employed; two are multinational corporations (MNCs) and transnational corporations (TNCs). Each term refers to the same important type of business firm with global operations. Those operations can indeed be far-reaching in scope. For example, as can be seen in Map 9.2, at the outset of 2014 the Ford Motor Company owned and operated manufacturing facilities in 21 countries outside its home country of the United States.

Multinational enterprises often own substantial assets (property, equipment, financial assets, and intellectual property), generate a great deal of their total sales, and have large numbers of their employees in countries outside the country in which they are headquartered. For example, the Nestlé Corporation in 2016 had most of its assets outside its home country of Switzerland ($106 billion out of a total

Multinational enterprise (MNE) A firm that has its headquarters in one country and ongoing business operations in one or (more typically) several other countries.

of about $129 billion). Most of its sales were in foreign markets (about $89 billion out of a total of $91 billion), and most of its employees were based in foreign countries (318,000 out of 328,000).

Why do firms not just stay at home and simply export from their home countries to foreign markets? Why do they instead sometimes become multinational enterprises? As a purely business matter, some firms due to their industry must go abroad: international petroleum firms such as Exxon Mobil and BP long ago become global in order to explore and exploit oil deposits in the Middle East, Latin America, and Africa. MNEs in manufacturing industries may decide that placing manufacturing or research and development facilities in foreign markets allows them to understand better what the customers in those countries want. For example, Nestlé's global presence allows it to observe changes in consumer tastes more quickly than would be true if it relied on exports alone. Taking on international operations also allows firms to take advantage of skills that might be particularly widespread in those countries. For example, US auto firms that produce in Germany can take advantage of that country's highly effective apprenticeship system for the training of young people in machine-tool operations. Japanese auto firms such as Honda and Nissan can benefit from an entry point into European markets, an English-speaking base, and a flexible workforce through their investment in the UK. Sometimes moving abroad allows an MNE to employ labor that costs less than is the case in their home markets: many MNEs from the United States, Japan, and Europe have moved to Mexico, China, and countries in Southeast Asia for precisely this reason.

Sometimes firms elect to become multinational due to changes in their political environment. For example, many US firms established or enhanced their European manufacturing operations during the late 1950s and early 1960s because of the establishment in 1957 by Germany, France, Italy, Belgium, Netherlands, and

Map 9.2 A Multinational Enterprise: Ford Motor Company's Worldwide Operations, 2014
In 2018 the Ford Motor Company had manufacturing facilities in 21 countries outside its home country of the United States (purple-colored segments).

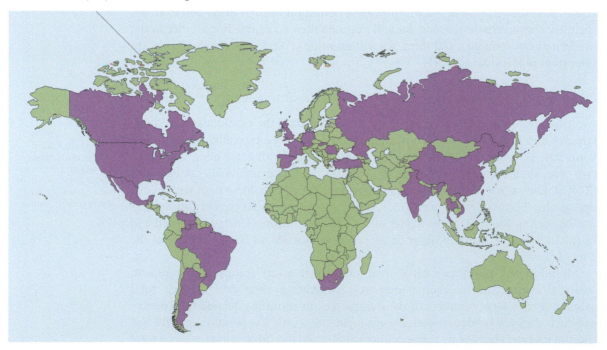

Luxembourg of the European Economic Community (EEC). The EEC established a common external tariff (CET) to imports of a variety of goods. However, the United States persuaded the European governments to include in the EEC founding treaty a **national treatment** clause so that European subsidiaries of US firms were treated as if they were national firms of one or another of the EEC members. By this national treatment provision in the EEC treaty, the subsidiary of General Motors (GM) incorporated in Germany would be treated by the German government and the EEC exactly as each would treat Volkswagen (VW) or BMW. That meant that GM automobiles manufactured in Germany could enter Italy with the same favorable EEC tariff treatment (compared to tariffs imposed on autos coming in from outside the EEC) as automobiles made by VW or BMW or Mercedes.

A firm might also decide to develop international operations to overcome non-tariff barriers. Japanese firms like Honda and Toyota responded to an automobile Voluntary Export Restraint (VER) agreement that the United States imposed on Japan in the late 1970s by establishing large manufacturing and assembly plants in the United States. The VER was designed and implemented in such a way as to only limit cars imported directly from Japan, not cars made in the United States by Japanese-owned automobile manufacturers.

National treatment
A clause in the EEC (non-EU), negotiated by the United States, that allows for American firms to be treated as though they are European firms.

Importance of MNEs to the World Economy

We can observe the importance of MNEs to the world economy in Figure 9.5, which shows how MNEs have been responsible for substantial proportions of global capital formation, global output of goods and services, and global trade.

Fixed capital is the value of assets a company utilizes in an ongoing way in the production of a good or service: we can think of fixed capital as what remains at a production site after everyone goes home at night: buildings, computers, and machinery used for production. **Gross fixed capital formation** represents the total increase in fixed capital that occurs in a country or in the world during a given period, usually a year. Foreign direct investment (FDI) that flows into a country is usually associated with the formation of new fixed capital, since it often entails the building of a new factory, or the introduction of new equipment for an existing factory. As we can observe in Figure 9.5, FDI inflows accounted for roughly 4 percent of capital

Fixed capital
The value of assets a company utilizes in an ongoing way in production of a good or service.

Gross fixed capital formation
The total increase in fixed capital that occurs in a country or in the world during a given period of time, usually a year.

Figure 9.5 Global Economic Significance of MNEs, 1990–2016
The global operations of multinational enterprises have for some time accounted for a large proportion of world trade, and since 1990 they have accounted for a significant proportion of global capital formation and world output.

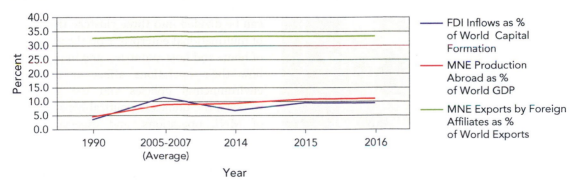

Source: UNCTAD, *World Investment Report 2017: Investment and the Digital Economy*, Table I.4, p. 26, available at http://unctad.org/en/PublicationsLibrary/wir2017_en.pdf.

formation throughout the world in 1990. It then almost tripled by the years prior to the Great Recession of 2008–09, and still represented almost 10 percent of world capital formation up to 2016.

Gross domestic product (GDP)
The world's GDP is the total monetary value of all goods and services produced by all countries of the world in a year. A country's gross domestic product is the monetary value of goods and services produced within its borders in a year.

MNEs also play a large and growing role in the production of the world's **gross domestic product (GDP)**, the total monetary value of all goods and services produced by all countries of the world in a year. (A country's gross domestic product is the monetary value of goods and services produced within its borders in a year.) As we can see in Figure 9.5, the total output by foreign affiliates of MNEs has gone from about 5 percent of world GDP in 1990 to about 11 percent in recent years. In 2016 the value of goods and services produced around the world totaled about $75 trillion; of that total, about $8.3 trillion was produced by foreign affiliates of MNEs. The foreign production efforts of MNEs are a significant piece of the production of goods and services around the world.

Finally, consider MNE exports relative to global exports, or the sum of all exports by all countries of the world. During the past 25 years, exports by MNE foreign affiliates have accounted for about one-third of total world exports. Global exports totaled a bit more than $20 trillion in 2011, and of that total, about $6.8 trillion consisted of exports by the foreign affiliates of multinational enterprises.

Intra-firm trade
The cross-country movement of different components that are put together at one or more final assembly plants in one or more countries.

Many of the exports by MNE foreign affiliates represent **intra-firm trade**, or the movement across countries of different components that are put together at one or more final assembly plants. For example, Ford Motor Company produces automobile engines at a Ford-owned plant in Chihuahua, Mexico. If that plant then ships those engines to Ford USA, this transfer takes place as an intra-firm sale and it appears as an export from Mexico to the United States. Intra-firm trade accounts for many of the exports by MNE foreign affiliates, and it has been for several decades an important feature of the world trading system.

Political Issues Surrounding MNEs

Multinational enterprises have attracted close attention and oftentimes strong criticisms on a range of issues from scholars, civil society activists, national governments, and international institutions. A great deal of attention is focused on whether multinational enterprises help or hinder poorer countries in achieving economic development, and we will devote substantial attention to that issue in Chapter 11. The important issues surrounding multinational enterprises that we will examine at present can be divided into three clusters: the effects of multinational enterprises on the autonomy of home and host countries, and in particular how their operations affect or constrain environmental policies and the status of workers; the domestic political consequences of MNE operations, and especially their effects on civil rights and the prospects for democracy around the world; and the impact that MNEs might have on the prospects for international peace.

Photo 9.3 Ford Production Line in Mexico, 2010
Ford and other foreign firms produce automobiles in Mexico and represent an important part of the operations of MNEs in that country. This assembly line is at the Ford plant in Cuautitlan Izcalli, Mexico.

Source: Susana Gonzalez/Bloomberg via Getty Images.

MNEs and National Autonomy: The Environment and Workers' Rights

Does the fact that multinational enterprises can move easily in and out of countries mean that governments lose some capacity to make independent choices in the kinds of policies they can pursue? Take, for example, a government that wishes to impose more stringent environmental rules or more robust health and safety rules in workplaces. These will necessarily generate costs for employers. The concern is that multinational enterprises already operating in the country, seeing their production costs go up, might be inclined to shift production to other countries where rules and standards may not be so high and expensive. The Canadian government, for example, might fear that if it brings into effect stronger environmental standards or health and safety rules for workers, Canadian firms might shift investments to countries with lower standards, such as Mexico or China. Thus, the Canadian government might be reluctant to put those stronger measures in place. Alternatively, Mexico and China, wanting to attract MNE investments and aware that they are competing with other developing countries such as Vietnam, might be reluctant to raise environmental or worker standards for fear of scaring away multinational investments. Governments around the world might find that they are engaged in a **'race to the bottom,'** that is, they put into place progressively lower policy rules and standards regarding the environment and workers' rights out of a fear of losing, and perhaps out of greed for attracting, foreign investments from multinational enterprises.

Moreover, there is some evidence (Pelc 2017) that MNEs respond to regulations by bringing unwarranted legal actions against national governments, and particularly democratic governments. The goal of these MNEs appears not to be to obtain compensation for undue costs they incur while seeking to be in accord with national health and safety regulations. Instead, MNEs might be seeking **'regulatory chill,'** that is, the use of legal proceedings to cause governments with strong safety and health regulations to incur such high legal costs in defending those regulations in various international arbitration venues that they, and other governments, will be deterred from instituting new and more ambitious regulations in the future.

Other recent scholarship presents a more mixed picture about MNEs and national policies on the environment and workers' rights. MNEs may be a positive force when it comes to workers' rights, but less than positive when it comes to the environment.

First, there is support for the thesis that MNEs seek out **'pollution havens,'** that is, countries that have low standards or lax enforcement of their environmental rules and regulations. Early work on the pollution-haven thesis (Eskeland and Harrison 2003) found no association between the location by MNEs of their production plants and the environmental laws and regulations of host countries. However, that scholarship tended to focus particularly on firms in 'heavy' industries such as mining, chemicals, and steel making. Plants in those industries are large and expensive to build, and so firms in them are likely to be resistant to moving in response to anything but the most extreme policy changes. More recent work (Kellenberg 2009) examines a wider range of firms, including those in 'footloose industries,' that is, firms whose plant costs are lower and plant mobility is therefore higher, such as in electronic components, computer assembly, and appliances. In that work it appears that MNEs in the years from 1999 to 2003 did increase their production in countries that were perceived to be lax in environmental policy enforcement.

On the other hand, multinational enterprises appear to bring about improvements in governmental labor policies, suggesting the possibility of a 'race to the top' among countries hosting MNEs (Mosley and Uno 2007). Three mechanisms might be producing this positive association between FDI and workers' rights and conditions

'Race to the bottom'
A situation in which two or more countries put into place progressively lower policy rules and standards regarding the environment and worker rights out of a fear of losing, and perhaps out of greed for attracting, foreign investments from multinational enterprises.

Regulatory chill
The possible strategy by MNEs to use trade and investment agreements to cause governments with strong safety and health regulations to incur such high legal costs in defending those regulations that they will be deterred from new and more ambitious regulations in the future.

Pollution haven
Countries that have low standards or lax enforcement of their environmental rules and regulations, which may attract foreign companies.

of employment. First, MNEs have a stake in law-governed business environments, for they themselves gain greatly from legal protection of their patents, trademarks, and investment in plant and equipment. Hence, in their own interests MNEs may press host-country governments to adhere to the rule of domestic and international law, including those regarding workers' rights. Second, MNEs may bring into a new country in which they become active relatively better policies that have become engrained in the way they do business, perhaps because these firms are aware that their operations are being scrutinized by nongovernmental organizations and activist groups. Finally, MNEs may be more interested in having high-quality rather than low-cost labor, and thus will tend to prefer to invest in countries where workers are accorded education, training, and generally favorable treatment.

Domestic Political Consequences of MNEs: Human Rights and Democracy

An important question about MNEs is whether their operations help improve the human rights situation in authoritarian countries and whether their presence improves the prospects for movement by those countries from authoritarian rule to democratic government.

Critics of multinational enterprises have suggested that multinationals in extractive industries such as oil or minerals, for example, provide authoritarian governments with tax revenues that they can use to purchase police and military capabilities to repress domestic dissent and retain authoritarian control over their countries. A more optimistic view is that foreign direct investment, like international trade, promotes economic development and a business community and middle class, and these two groups are ultimately powerful forces for democratization (Maxfield 1998; Maxfield 2000). A growing middle class wants its rights to be protected, and a responsive government is the best mechanism to ensure that. Integration through trade and finance promotes growth, growth promotes the emergence of a middle class, and this middle class, in order to attain an effective political voice, will ultimately move their respective countries toward democracy (Eichengreen and Leblang 2008).

It is possible to think of instances of authoritarian countries that became economically more open to the world and thereafter also became robust democracies: South Korea and Taiwan are two strong examples. More generally, statistical studies have identified a positive association between increases in trade and financial flows of *all types* and democratization (Eichengreen and Leblang 2008). However, it is not clear that FDI by multinational enterprises is by itself a force for improved human rights or democratization. Political scientist Nita Rudra (2005) determined that while greater trade by and *portfolio* capital flows to developing countries from the early 1970s to the late 1990s were positively associated with improvements in human rights and democracy, FDI flows were not a reliable predictor of change in either political dimension. Moreover, in the case of China, it is possible that MNE operations have unintentionally delayed the prospects for democratization in that country by impairing the development of a large and politically unified Chinese business community (Gallagher 2002).

MNEs and International Peace

As we noted in Chapter 7, scholars in the liberal tradition have long argued that countries that share stronger economic ties via trade and foreign direct investment may be less likely to go to war with one another. There has been a lively debate about whether *trade* between countries leads to a reduced risk of war between them. Relatively less attention has been paid to the role that foreign direct investment may play in attenuating the risk of military conflicts. This is surprising, for two reasons:

first, there is a well-developed set of arguments as to why FDI might have at least as much, if not more of a pacifying effect on relationships between countries than trade; and second, in contrast to the mixed findings that we see in quantitative studies on the matter of trade and conflict, studies that use statistical techniques have been notably consistent in finding that FDI has the capacity to reduce the risk of military conflicts between countries.

Let's consider the theoretical argument that states might become less oriented to fighting each other as they become the homes and hosts of foreign direct investment. Writing from the liberal perspective, Richard Rosecrance (1999) has suggested that many states have learned that foreign investment affords them growth, welfare, and technological sophistication – in other words, they can attain all the attributes of success in the modern world. On the other hand, with that success comes a risk, a risk that the country might do something that frightens away foreign firms and with them access to foreign technology and markets. One way to so frighten foreign firms, Rosecrance points out, is for a country to become involved in military disputes. It will not just be firms from the countries involved in the dispute that will shun investing in one another's countries; instead, firms from countries other than those immediately involved will wish to avoid the disputants, given that they have become risky places in which to do business. Thus, Rosecrance argues, national governments have strong reasons to resolve their disputes with others peacefully. In fact, scholars have been consistent in finding that FDI may promote peace, at least since 1945, including through the amelioration of territorial disputes, which we showed in Chapter 6 to be among the most war-prone types of conflicts of interests between nations (Gartzke and Li 2003; Bussmann 2010; Lee and Mitchell 2012).

Levels of Analysis *Multinational Enterprises*	
State	🌐 International
MNEs can have significant effects on a wide range of domestic circumstances of countries, including their environmental policies, treatment of workers, human rights, and prospects for democracy.	Cross-border direct investments, typically by MNEs, may reduce the incentives of governments to use military force to solve diplomatic problems, including conflict-laden territorial disputes.

THE INSTITUTIONS OF THE WORLD ECONOMY

As we saw in Chapter 2, in the face of the Great Depression of the 1930s, major economic powers like the United Kingdom, France, Germany, and the United States turned to extreme protectionism both in trade and in money. The result was a dramatic downward spiral in the volume of world trade, as can be observed in Figure 9.6. Almost all countries imposed high national tariffs and extensive controls on capital, and the leading powers organized regional blocs they could dominate and use to gain preferential trade advantages. The United Kingdom and France each created an imperial preference system with their respective colonies: each colonial power and its colonies charged much lower tariffs against one another's imports than they charged for goods coming from countries outside the bloc. Germany organized and dominated economic relations with smaller countries in central Europe. Japan adopted a militarist and coercive strategy of conquering its Asian neighbors to ensure its access to vital raw materials. The United States and Soviet Union each turned their large domestic economies inward; the United States to recover from the Depression, and the Soviets to mobilize internal resources to catch up with the West industrially.

After the war, the United States and its allies made another effort to rekindle the international economy. The goal was not the immediate creation of totally free international markets in goods or money. Instead, and in accord with constructivist theory, leaders and officials in the two most powerful states that were active in the negotiations, the United States and the United Kingdom, shared a consensus that they and other governments should create relatively freer markets in trade and finance across borders over time. They believed, as well, in limited government intervention, but also in some controls over the level and tempo of that liberalization so that national governments could employ fiscal and monetary policies when needed to promote national employment (Ruggie 1982). To attain this goal of gradual economic liberalization, the major states created several international economic institutions. We will examine these international institutions in three categories: trade, money, and governance.

International Trade: From GATT to WTO to the New Regionalism

For three weeks, July 1–22, 1944, diplomats from 44 countries allied against Nazi Germany met at the small resort town of Bretton Woods, New Hampshire, USA to develop a plan for the reconstruction of the world economy after depression and war. The resulting **Bretton Woods system** was originally designed to include all countries of the world, but with the onset of the Cold War, the Soviet Union and its allies remained outside the system. The Bretton Woods system was the central

Bretton Woods system
The international system created in 1944 to encourage progressive trade liberalization and stable monetary relations between all the countries of the world. Although initial membership was fairly low due to Cold War tensions, membership in the resulting organizations steadily increased to include the vast majority of the world's countries. The ITO, GATT, WTO, IMF, and World Bank were all created as a result of the Bretton Woods system.

Figure 9.6 The Kindleberger Spiral of Declining World Trade
If you look at this spiral srarting in January 1929, you will see how, month by month, and year by year, the value of world trade became less and less. This was the result of slower global growth as a consequence of the Depression and government policies of protectionism in response to that slower growth. As the 'economic pie' became smaller, each government tried to preserve its share of it by imposing protection and devaluing its currency. The overall effect was that the pie became even smaller.

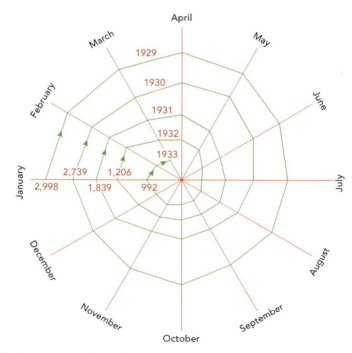

Source: *World in Depression, 1929–1939*, by Charles P. Kindleberger, © 2013 by the Regents of the University of California. Published by the University of California Press. Reproduced with permission.

focus for the development by countries of rules and norms governing international trade and monetary relations. Although parts of the original design have changed, the overall themes of progressive trade liberalization and stable monetary relations remain in place today and apply to almost all countries across the globe.

By 1947, international negotiations had produced an ambitious scheme for global trade management, the **International Trade Organization (ITO)**. The ITO reflected compromises among different national interests. The United States had the world's most dynamic and powerful economy and wanted international rules to maximize free trade. France and the United Kingdom, weakened by war, lobbied to retain their imperial preference systems. Less developed countries felt unprepared for open international competition and demanded infant-industry protection for their new manufacturing sectors and a host of other preferential arrangements. The ITO could only succeed with the support of the United States, but the Truman administration felt the final compromise departed significantly from US preferences and declined to submit the agreement to Congress for ratification. Without American participation, this first attempt to develop global trade rules was aborted.

A more modest trade initiative emerged in its place. The 1947 **General Agreement on Tariffs and Trade (GATT)** represented an initial attempt by the United States and other Western countries to lower their respective tariff rates on a wide variety of goods and to establish a first set of rules to resolve trade disputes among nations. Within the 1947 GATT agreement the participants agreed to extend any tariff reductions to which two or more members agreed, to all other members of the agreement. In the United States, this practice means conferring most-favored-nation status on various trading partners; those partners get the lowest or 'most favored' tariff rates that the United States offers to any country.

GATT became the nexus for a global trade order. GATT was given a home in Geneva, Switzerland, and its members entered a succession of negotiating rounds to reduce trade barriers. The GATT was upgraded in 1995 to an institution that enjoys a more formal legal status, the **World Trade Organization (WTO)**.

Diplomats have given each GATT (and now its successor organization, the WTO) negotiating round a name, such as the Geneva Round in 1947 and the Kennedy Round in 1962. By 1969, so much progress was made that tariff barriers were no longer a significant impediment to trade among advanced industrial countries. Tariff levels across the Atlantic dropped from an average of roughly 50 percent immediately after World War II to about 5 percent 25 years later. This period was the golden era for the GATT. After 1970, GATT rounds became more difficult to complete for two reasons. First, more countries joined the negotiating table as the world economy recovered. When the GATT was founded it had 23 member states; by the early 1960s the GATT had 62 members; and by 2016 there were 164 member states in the WTO. Second, as we noted above, the focus of trade negotiations has shifted from tariff to non-tariff barriers. Tariffs are easier to negotiate because they are quantitatively precise and transparent: they can take the form, 'I'll reduce my tariff on shoes from 50 percent to 40 percent if you reduce yours on computers from 35 percent to 25 percent.' Non-tariff barriers such as government procurement rules, anti-dumping procedures, health and safety standards, and border control policies are more varied, less quantifiable, less transparent, and subtler as means of trade protection. Such barriers are often deeply embedded in the domestic political and economic values of the countries around the table. Convincing France to reduce its tariffs on machinery by 10 percent is a lot easier than convincing French negotiators to relax domestic content restrictions on Hollywood-produced films when they believe that a thriving French film industry is essential to the national culture.

International Trade Organization (ITO)
An ambitious scheme for global trade management proposed in 1947. The ITO eventually failed because the United States refused to support it and was largely replaced by the less ambitious GATT.

General Agreement on Tariffs and Trade (GATT)
When the ambitious ITO fell through, GATT represented an initial, less ambitious attempt by the United States and other Western countries to lower their respective tariff rates on a wide variety of goods and to establish a first set of rules to resolve trade disputes among nations (finalized in 1947).

World Trade Organization (WTO)
Since 1995 the successor body to the GATT, with more explicit rules and guidelines than the GATT and a more highly developed mechanism for resolving trade disputes.

The Tokyo Round, so named to symbolize the importance of bringing Japan more fully under the rules of the liberal trading order, sought to discipline non-tariff barriers. Negotiations were protracted (the round began in 1973 and concluded in 1979) and results were modest. It took seven additional years for GATT members to even agree to begin a next round, called the Uruguay Round to symbolize the importance of bringing developing countries more fully under the auspices of GATT rules. The Uruguay Round took until 1994 to complete. It is no surprise that commentators came to refer to the GATT as the 'General Agreement to Talk and Talk.'

The Uruguay Round (1986–1994) was very ambitious. It sought a grand bargain between developed and developing countries for developed countries to reduce protectionist barriers in agriculture and textiles, two politically sensitive areas that had long been handled outside the GATT rules for free trade. For their part, developing countries agreed to consider liberalizing trade in new areas not previously covered by the GATT, including trade in services such as banking and insurance, and to develop new rules to protect intellectual property rights. For example, it would be illegal for developing country entrepreneurs to copy Western-made pharmaceutical products, movies, or music DVDs. In the end a deal was struck, although neither group was fully satisfied. Developing countries, led by India and Brazil, felt that the more powerful governments of the United States and European Union wrested concessions from weaker developing country negotiators without making sufficient concessions to open their own markets for food and clothing promptly and meaningfully.

An important institutional innovation did emerge from the Uruguay Round – the agreement to create the World Trade Organization (WTO), which on January 1, 1995 took effect as the successor to the GATT. The WTO has more explicit rules and guidelines than the GATT and involves the great majority of the world's countries as members. Most importantly, the WTO contains a more highly developed mechanism for resolving trade disputes among countries than was available under the GATT. This move toward stronger dispute-settlement procedures underscores, as discussed in Chapter 5, the liberal international view of the importance of international institutions to states in mitigating problems of compliance with agreements and the achievement thereby of mutually positive gains. Box 9.4 compares dispute settlement mechanisms in the GATT and now in the WTO.

The first multilateral trade negotiation that was held under the auspices of the WTO was the Doha Round, which was launched in 2001. However, for the first time since the end of World War II, the Doha Round failed to end in a large-scale multilateral accord, and the Doha talks were terminated in December 2015. Throughout the Doha Round industrialized countries, especially the United States and European Union, were reluctant to make concessions especially in the always-contentious agriculture sector. Developing countries, which believed they conceded too much in prior rounds, in turn declined to offer concessions to move the talks forward.

Nevertheless, most governments still recognize that a WTO-based global trade order is desirable. The WTO creates opportunities for states to resolve trade disputes and it has created a set of expectations among members that makes it difficult politically to impose new trade barriers. Yet, the advance of free trade also faces significant challenges. Key areas of world trade such as agriculture are still highly protected and others, such as trade in services, investment, and intellectual property, have only basic agreements in place and large gaps in coverage. New concerns have emerged at the intersection of trade and social policy. For example, environmentalists worry that free trade and investment agreements enhance the risk of something we noted in connection to MNEs, namely, a 'race to the bottom' in which developing countries relax environmental regulations to gain competitive advantage in the marketplace.

Despite its status as an improvement over GATT, the WTO has managed to attract passionate protests almost anywhere in the world that it holds a meeting.

The global trade order today is under serious stress. As discussed in Chapter 2, the most important challenges result from populism, or political movements that promise to support the rights and interests of common people as opposed to the interests of a

9.4   MAKING CONNECTIONS
Then and Now

Trade-Dispute Settlement in the GATT and WTO

Then: Dispute Settlement under GATT

The GATT had a procedure for settling trade disputes, but it was relatively ineffective. There were no fixed timetables, so dispute negotiations could drag on inconclusively for years. Rulings could only be adopted by consensus, which meant that any single country – even including the loser in the dispute – could object and block a ruling from taking effect. There was no effective way to enforce rulings that were accepted, and there was inadequate protection for third parties, or countries affected by the dispute but not directly part of it. It is not surprising that powerful countries tended to take matters into their own hands, seeking to resolve disputes outside of the GATT process. The United States was the most well-known practitioner of 'aggressive unilateralism,' or the attempt to coerce other states into changing trade practices that the US considered unfair. American trade legislation, generally referred to as Section 301 (originally part of the Trade Act of 1974) gave the President broad powers to single out unfair traders, force them into negotiations, and retaliate against them with protectionist measures if they refused to agree to US demands. Other members of the international trading community found it outrageous that the United States felt it had the right to act simultaneously as prosecutor, jury, and judge in trade disputes. The United States typically responded that it had no choice given the importance of opening markets abroad and the lack of an effective dispute settlement mechanism in the GATT.

Now: Dispute Settlement under WTO

The WTO sets out specific (though somewhat flexible) timetables for dispute settlement, emphasizing that prompt settlement is crucial for the WTO to function effectively. Countries are encouraged to settle disputes on their own, but if they cannot, a case may be brought to the WTO. Within 15 months, the WTO is expected to form an impartial panel of three to five experts from different countries to examine the evidence, have that panel deliberate, and issue a final report, allow the countries in question to appeal, and have the Dispute Settlement Body adopt the report. The 'losing' country is expected to change its practices to bring them in line with international expectations. If it cannot, for whatever reason, it must negotiate with the injured party to determine some type of mutually acceptable compensation. In the absence of acceptable compensation, the complaining side may ask the Dispute Settlement Body for permission to impose limited retaliatory sanctions against the offending member. The adoption of rulings is now far easier than it was under the GATT. Instead of requiring a consensus to adopt a ruling, the WTO requires a consensus to *overturn* a ruling. In other words, a country seeking to block a ruling must persuade all other WTO members, including its adversary in the case, to agree that the ruling should be invalidated. The robust dispute-settlement provisions and procedures under the auspices of the WTO constitute one of the most important developments in multilateral trade diplomacy to have occurred during the 1990s and the first decade of the 2000s.

privileged elite. Populists perceive the costs of global economic liberalization as high, especially in the wake of the Great Recession of 2008–09. As we discuss in Box 9.5, many countries introduced protectionist measures after 2008 and it has proven difficult to rescind those measures. Weak global aggregate demand, new business strategies of global corporations, and possibly the new national protectionism may be combining to produce an attenuation of the role of international trade in the global economy in recent years.

9.5   RESEARCH INSIGHT

Is Trade Becoming Less Important to Global Economic Growth?

The Problem

As we will see in greater detail in Chapter 10, we often think that we are living in a period of intense economic globalization. However, since the turn of the millennium, and particularly in the years since the Great Recession of 2008–09, there has been an observable slowdown in global trade integration. We can see this in Figure 9.7, which depicts the ratio of the growth in world trade to the growth in global output between 1981 and 2016. During that period, the average annual growth in trade has exceeded that of global output by about 50 percent. During the 1990s, growth in world trade was more than double that of global output. Truly that decade was one of remarkable economic globalization. The relationship between trade and global output during the first decade of the 2000s was about average, even with the marked drop in trade that occurred in 2009 (while not shown in the figure, trade contracted by almost 13 percent that year while world output dropped by about 2.5 percent). Notice, however, the 2011–16 period: the growth in trade during these recent years only matched the growth in global output. That is, trade was no longer growing faster than that national output. According to the WTO, this 'further slowing of trade relative to GDP remains a cause for concern' (Auboin and Borino 2017: 18).

Figure 9.7 Growth in World Trade Relative to Growth in World Output, 1981–2016
We see in this figure that, after a remarkable spurt in the growth in trade relative to world output during the 1990s, the growth in trade relative to world output has waned since 2000.

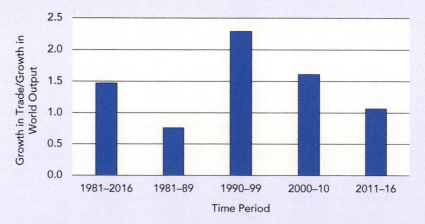

Source: Data from World Trade Organization, *World Trade Statistical Review 2017*, p. 18, available at https://www.wto.org/english/res_e/statis_e/wts2017_e/WTO_Chapter_03_e.pdf.

The Research Insight

One research team at the WTO has suggested that the slowdown in the growth of trade relative to world output in the immediate aftermath of the Great Recession was largely due to a cyclical factor, namely, weak global aggregate demand, as would be expected by macroeconomic theory (see, for example, Auboin and Borino 2017). It is also possible, a team of IMF economists has suggested, that longer-term structural changes in several key countries are operating: for example, as wages in China go up relative to those in the United States, US firms have less incentive to shift elements of their manufacturing chains to that country, and therefore even as world income goes up, trade goes up but at a slower rate (Constantinescu, Mattoo, and Ruta 2014). In addition to these cyclical and structural economic forces, it is also possible that protectionist policy measures put into place since 2008 may be dampening the growth of trade in recent years. For example, according to a recent report by the WTO, 1,671 protectionist measures were imposed between 2008 and October 2016 by countries belonging to the Group of 20 (see more in the main text); of those measures, only 408 had been withdrawn by the end of 2016 (WTO 2016: 2–4).

The rise of Donald Trump in the United States and, before that, the Brexit referendum in the UK, underscore the point that economic globalization lacks today the societal support it enjoyed during the 1990s and even the first years of the current century. The fundamental concern in the United States, UK, and parts of Europe is that cheaper labor and lax standards in developing countries are leading to the loss of high-quality working-class jobs at home. For their part, in developing countries the worry is expressed that global liberalization is stacked against them, and that the more advanced world is forcing them to accept free trade in domains where they are not ready for full competition, such as finance and information technology. Moreover, developing countries believe that they lack an effective voice in important global economic institutions. The bringing together of developed and developing countries under the auspices of the Group of 20, we will see below, marks an attempt by both groups of nations to address this ongoing problem.

Perhaps because global trade agreements through the GATT and now the WTO are increasingly difficult to complete, many countries have turned to regional trade agreements and bilateral free trade agreements (FTAs) as alternatives. In the early 1990s, the United States concluded the North American Free Trade Agreement (NAFTA) with Canada and Mexico. The United States has bilateral FTAs with at least 12 other countries, including Australia, Chile, Israel, Honduras, Morocco, and Singapore. In 2012, agreements with Columbia, Panama, and South Korea received congressional approval. In South America, Mercosur (the 'common market of the south' or Mercado Común del Sur) was formed in 1991 by Argentina, Brazil, Paraguay, and Uruguay. Chile and Bolivia were added later in the decade.

The European Union (EU) remains the world's most successful regional trade arrangement. In a series of progressively more ambitious agreements that began in 1951 with six countries forming the European Coal and Steel Community (ECSC), by 2017 the EU consisted of 28 countries participating in a single European market; that is, it has reduced almost all policy barriers to the flow of goods services, capital, and even labor among the partners. As discussed above,

19 of the EU countries have even gone beyond the creation of a single market and have formed a single currency, the euro, for use among what are termed the eurozone members, and a European Central Bank (ECB) to forge and manage a common monetary policy. No other region of the world has witnessed this level of institutional development.

As we discussed in Chapter 2, in June 2016 the EU experienced a massive shock. The British public voted, by a margin of 52 percent to 48 percent, to leave the European Union. This is the first time a member country has so decided to leave the EU. In March 2017 the British government formally initiated the two-year process of negotiations as envisioned in the main EU treaty to bring Brexit to completion. Those negotiations need to resolve a wide range of issues, such as whether and how much money the UK owes the EU upon its withdrawal, what legal status EU citizens who elect to remain in the UK will enjoy in the latter after the withdrawal, as well as the comparable status of Britons in EU countries, and what legal rules will shape EU-UK economic ties in a post-Brexit world. For example, the UK has a global competitive advantage in the financial services industry and has a particularly strong presence in European banking. It is not clear that the UK will have the same level of access to and success in European finance after it is no longer a member of the EU. More generally, as of mid-2018 it remained unclear whether the two sides would negotiate a 'soft' Brexit, one in which economic ties would remain highly robust, or end with a 'hard' Brexit, one in which the United Kingdom would lose most of its current favorable access to the EU.

Looking ahead, it is possible that regional trade and investment agreements will take precedence over WTO multilateral negotiations as the preferred vehicle with which countries will pursue heightened international economic liberalization. However, the track record in achieving regional accords is itself rather mixed.

For example, in 2011, the United States and the EU commenced negotiations on a Transatlantic Trade and Investment Partnership (TTIP). However, the negotiations stalled, most notably on whether TTIP provisions for the settlement of disputes between national governments and foreign investors would give US and other multinational enterprises the ability to evade the relatively strong environmental, worker-rights, and consumer-safety laws and regulations of many EU countries. By 2016, in the face of an upsurge in economic discontent in the United States, and with opposition growing too among European publics, especially in Germany, the TTIP negotiating process came to a stop. A similar fate befell plans for the Trans-Pacific Partnership (TPP), which would have constituted a major regional economic liberalization agreement among 12 countries in the Asia-Pacific region, including the United States, Japan, Canada, Australia, Vietnam, Malaysia, Singapore, and five other countries (but not, very notably, China). These countries successfully completed negotiations in October 2015 for the partnership. The process of approval of the TPP by the US Congress became bogged down during the election year of 2016 and came to a complete halt with the coming into office of the Donald Trump administration in January 2017. However, the countries that had negotiated the TPP, except for the US, signed in March 2018 a liberalization accord based largely on the original TPP agreement, and therefore it is possible that trans-pacific economic liberalization will move forward without the United States.

The Trump administration also insisted that NAFTA be renegotiated, and that its demand that Mexico pay for a wall between that country and the United States must be addressed in the negotiations for a revised NAFTA. The Mexican and Canadian governments have agreed that it would be useful to take a new look at NAFTA, but the former has made it abundantly clear that it will not contribute to the financing of any wall.

While the United States appears to be disinclined at least at present to pursue global economic liberalization either by way of the WTO or regional accords, other countries have begun to establish agreements not involving the United States. This process began in 2009 with negotiations between Canada and the European Union. Those talks resulted in 2014 in the finalization of an EU-Canada Comprehensive Economic and Trade Agreement (CETA), which in 2018 was well along in terms of garnering national ratifications and being prepared for implementation by member countries. CETA when in full effect will nearly eliminate tariffs between Canada and EU countries and will bring into effect the kind of investor-government dispute settlement rules that were envisioned in the TTIP. In addition, after five years of negotiations, the Japanese government and the EU countries announced in July 2017 that they had reached an agreement on what, if fully implemented, will be the world's largest regional free-trade area.

International Finance: Why Is the IMF so Controversial?

The main goal of the Bretton Woods negotiators was to create a new international monetary order. They recognized the close relationship between international trade and international monetary policy, and had fresh memories of how competitive currency devaluations, that is, downward changes in the *official* currency price by multiple countries seeking to make the price of their exports more attractive, helped destroy world trade during the Great Depression.

To prevent competitive currency devaluations in the future, American and British negotiators settled on a plan to create a system of exchange rates that were presumed to be fixed and could be changed only by mutual consent. Each government pledged to maintain a fixed rate for its currency relative to the US dollar. For example, the British government agreed to defend the rate of 1 pound sterling = $2.40, and the Japanese agreed to $1 = 360 yen (as an exercise you might wish to check business news websites to learn what the current exchange rates are between the dollar and pound sterling and the yen). Governments pledged that if the market value of their currencies moved too far from this official value, they would intervene in currency markets and buy or sell their own currencies in amounts sufficient to bring market prices back into line with official rates.

The negotiators at Bretton Woods created an international institution to facilitate and reinforce this postwar exchange-rate system, the **International Monetary Fund (IMF)**. The IMF, based in Washington, DC, began operations in 1946 and remains one of the world's most important international economic institutions. Bretton Woods planners created a sister organization for the IMF, the International Bank for Reconstruction and Development, more commonly known as the **World Bank**, which is also headquartered in Washington. The original purpose of the World Bank was to provide loans to countries to help them with economic recovery from the war. Today, the World Bank finances and manages projects – for example, the construction of a dam, the development of a communications grid, the building of highways – to foster the economic growth of developing countries.

The original role of the IMF was to assist governments – especially those running balance-of-payments deficits – in meeting their fixed exchange-rate obligations

International Monetary Fund (IMF)
An international institution created in 1946 to facilitate and reinforce the exchange-rate system created in the aftermath of World War II. The IMF remains one of the world's most important international economic institutions.

World Bank
The International Bank for Reconstruction and Development, initially created to provide loans to countries to help them with economic recovery from World War II, today finances and manages projects to foster the economic growth of developing countries.

under the Bretton Woods agreement. A country running deficits needed to use foreign reserves, or the currencies of other countries, to buy its own currency on international markets. But what if the government did not hold adequate amounts of foreign reserves in its central bank? The IMF held a fund of foreign reserves (mainly US dollars) that it could lend to countries in balance-of-payments distress. In return, IMF officials typically asked these borrowing governments to take certain steps in their domestic economies, such as reducing government spending to control inflation, as a condition for receiving the loan. This practice has become known as IMF conditionality.

But what if, despite repeated tries, the market price of a currency kept falling and the government could not buy enough of its own currency to defend its fixed rate? The more drastic next step would be devaluation, a downward change in the official price of the currency to more accurately reflect its market value. Devaluation would, however, also confer export advantages to the country in question, thus creating a temptation for them to do so under the guise of being unable to maintain an official exchange rate. Here the Bretton Woods agreement was critically important: countries could only devalue in the event of a 'fundamental disequilibrium' and only with the approval of the IMF. The IMF was there to ensure that countries only devalued as a last resort, and not to attain trade advantages against other countries.

What determines which states are especially powerful within the IMF? The IMF requires contributions from member states so that it has the funds on hand to lend out to countries with balance-of-payments problems. Member countries receive voting power in proportion to the contributions they make to the fund. In the early years of the IMF, when most other countries were still recovering from the war, the United States contributed about half the reserves. As a result, the United States at first had overwhelming power in IMF decision-making and could use the IMF as an instrument to influence the domestic economic policies of other governments. Today, the United States still has the relatively largest share of IMF votes, but the shares of other countries have moved up as well. Table 9.4 shows the voting shares of the ten largest contributors to the IMF in 2018.

The dollar played a special role in the Bretton Woods system, especially from the late 1940s to the late 1960s. Governments held dollars in their central banks for use in emergencies, to buy goods and services on world markets, and to buy back their own currencies when their exchange rates fell. Private individuals and companies also used the dollar in their international transactions. The US government, to reinforce everybody's confidence in the dollar, pledged to other governments that it would give them gold for dollars at a fixed rate, or $35 for one ounce of gold. With this pledge, the US government was essentially claiming that its paper currency was 'as good as gold,' and that others should treat it as the world's money.

Playing the role of banker to the world gave special privileges to the United States. If other countries were willing to hold its money as an 'IOU,' the United States could make international purchases without having to balance its payments right away. But if the United States abused this privilege and spent too many dollars abroad, other governments and private actors might begin to question whether the dollar was really as good as gold. This happened during the 1960s, when the United States spent more dollars abroad to provide foreign aid, paid the costs of stationing its troops in Europe and Asia, fought the Vietnam War, and bought more goods from its recovering Western trading partners. Some US allies, led by France, felt the United States was acting irresponsibly and should raise taxes or spend less on programs at home to

Table 9.4 Largest Voting Shares in the IMF by Individual Country, 2018
A relatively small number of states (10) in the international system provide the bulk (over 50%) of the lending resources at the disposal of the IMF, and therefore have a disproportionate voice in voting at the Fund.

Country	Voting Weight (Percent of Total)
United States	16.52
Japan	6.15
China	6.09
Germany	5.32
France	4.03
United Kingdom	4.03
Italy	3.02
India	2.64
Russia	2.59
Saudi Arabia	2.02
Total	**52.41**

Source: Data from IMF 2018.

help pay for the things it was doing abroad. They demanded gold in exchange for the dollars that were piling up in their national accounts. The United States claimed it was running national deficits because it was bearing the burden of Western defense. It argued that its Western allies were now sufficiently recovered to open their markets more fully to American goods and to pay more of the price of defending the West against the Soviet Union.

This conflict was finally resolved in August 1971 when the Nixon administration simply announced it would no longer meet its stated obligation of trading gold to other governments for US dollars. This decision, taken unilaterally by the United States, was so shocking to the world financial community that it became known as the 'Nixon shock.' The United States had created the fixed exchange-rate component of the Bretton Woods system, but 25 years later, when that component no longer served US interests, US officials ended it. If the United States was no longer committed to defending the value of its dollar relative to gold, then other governments would not defend their currency values relative to the dollar.

The world's leading economic powers transitioned during the 1970s, by default, to a flexible exchange-rate system. The IMF members revised the Fund's Articles of Agreement in 1976 to allow member states to follow whatever exchange-rate practices they chose, as long as they maintained reasonable price stability, took actions necessary to avoid or mitigate undue short-term fluctuations in exchange rates, and avoided the manipulation of exchange rates 'to gain an unfair competitive advantage over other members' (IMF 1976).

Exchange rates continue to be politically controversial, notwithstanding this general IMF guidance that countries be good international economic citizens. Economic partners of the United States have often complained that the US dollar is

Photo 9.4 Greek Citizens Protest Austerity Imposed by IMF and EU
In this February 2012 protest in Athens, Greece, thousands of demonstrators clashed with police as the Greek parliament prepared to vote on an EU/IMF austerity deal designed to help the country through its economic crisis.

Source: ARIS MESSINIS/AFP/Getty Images.

too strong, attracting money away from their countries, or too weak, thereby giving the United States unfair trade advantages. American officials in turn complained during the 1980s that Japan was manipulating its currency to obtain unfair trade advantages, and it makes a similar complaint about China today.

Members of the European Union, to insulate themselves from the effects of the powerful US dollar, went back to a fixed exchange-rate system among themselves during the 1980s and, as we discussed above, in the 1990s many of them (with some notable exceptions including the United Kingdom) abandoned their national currencies altogether for a common currency, the euro. The euro has been a mixed blessing for some of the more fragile economies of Europe, like that of Greece, which no longer have the option of allowing their currency to float downward to help ease the impact of balance-of-payments deficits. In the face of the 2008 financial crisis, the Greek government, at the urging of the IMF as well as the EU, cut government services and payments to workers, sparking a series of ongoing street riots.

The IMF and Its Critics Today

The IMF remains at the center of international political economy, continuing to serve as a fund for member countries in economic distress. Yet, as in the Greek example above, its lending practices frequently spark 'IMF riots' in recipient countries. If the IMF is there to help countries in need, why are its efforts so controversial? Many scholars, including some writing in ways consistent with the Marxist perspective we outlined in Chapter 3, have raised serious concerns about the operations of the IMF. They view the IMF as an instrument dominant capitalist countries use to impose their preferred economic arrangements on developing countries.

IMF conditionality – the conditions the IMF places on a government in exchange for its loans – is a main reason that critics are concerned about the IMF. The Fund generally prescribes what, to a country in distress, can appear to be harsh and bitter medicine. That medicine comes in the form of austerity or economic belt-tightening. A typical package of structural adjustments recommended by the IMF might include sharp reductions in government spending which affect the jobs and salaries of public sector workers, the benefits of the unemployed, and the pensions of retirees. If the government had been subsidizing necessities like food and electricity, complying with the IMF might require sharp price increases. The package might also call for interest rate hikes to slow inflation. But higher interest rates mean slower growth for the economy, and possibly even an economic recession. The IMF also urges governments to reduce the size of the state sector and liberalize trade and financial markets.

Governments, of course, could choose not to do business with the IMF. But another reason the IMF is so controversial is that it is so powerful. A country that is in financial distress may seek infusions of cash from international banks. But before lending, bankers often look to make sure that the country's policies have received the IMF 'seal of approval.' In other words, accepting the harsh medicine of the IMF is more likely to lead private money to flow into the economy, while defying the IMF might leave the country on its own.

The controversial policies often prescribed by the IMF – smaller state sectors, privatized markets, and liberalized trade and financial sectors – are policies preferred by the US government. During the 1980s, this collection of policies became known as the **Washington Consensus** – a consensus supported by the US Treasury Department and the Washington-based IMF and World Bank – and was put forth as the necessary path to prosperity for all countries to follow. The Great Recession of 2008–09, however, has cast considerable doubt on the desirability of the Washington Consensus. Governments and citizens around the world perceived these policies, and the idea of unregulated liberal capitalism, as the cause of the crisis rather than the necessary recipe for economic growth and prosperity. Moreover, for many very poor developing countries it has become impossible to repay all their foreign debts, as would be envisioned if they faithfully followed the Washington Consensus. Slowly, haltingly, the advanced countries have come to understand that debt repayment simply cannot be achieved by many especially poor developing countries and insisting that they do so condemns them to continued poverty. Between 2005 and 2006 the wealthy countries agreed to cancel the debts that as many as 40 especially poor countries, mostly in Africa but also in Central America as well as Afghanistan, had accrued to the IMF and the World Bank.

Washington Consensus
Controversial US-backed free-market policies set forth by the IMF as the necessary path to prosperity from the 1980s until the Great Recession of 2008–09, when the Consensus began to be widely questioned.

Global Governance: From the G-7 and G-8 to the G-20

The new controversies sparked by the IMF and Washington Consensus have highlighted a long-standing debate on the question: who should govern the world economy? As in other areas of international relations, the answer frequently raises a clash between aspirations and reality. Developing countries argue they should have a greater say in international economic governance because the world economy affects their development prospects so profoundly. More powerful countries tend to make the rules and manage the system. During the Bretton Woods era, the United States was powerful enough to not only make the rules, but also break them when they no longer served US interests. Since those days, international economic power has gradually diffused, first to other advanced industrial states and now even more broadly to newly emerging economies powers like China and Brazil.

After the collapse of Bretton Woods, the informal grouping that governed international economic relations was known as the **Group of 7 (G-7)**: the United States, the United Kingdom, France, Germany, Japan, Italy, and Canada. For many years the G-7 held annual summit meetings at which heads of governments, finance ministers, and the governors of central banks of these seven major industrialized countries sought to resolve international economic problems by coordinating their exchange rates and their domestic monetary and fiscal policies. The G-7 enjoyed notable achievements: the Plaza Agreement of 1985, for example, helped to ward off protectionism through coordinated efforts to increase the value of some currencies, such as the Japanese yen and German mark, and decrease the value of others, especially the US dollar.

After the end of the Cold War the G-7 countries began to invite Russia to participate in parts of their meetings, and thus was launched the **Group of 8 (G-8)**. The G-7 summits now take place among ministers of finance and central bank governors; Russia was ejected from G-8 after it invaded and seized Crimea from Ukraine in 2014. Alongside economic coordination, G-7 summits typically address pressing political issues, such as the war on terrorism or the proliferation of weapons of mass destruction.

Today, the G-7 is no longer the main locus of international economic governance. It has been supplemented and in time it might be replaced by a broader group, the **Group of 20**, or **G-20**, which includes the G-7 members along with newly rising developing countries like China and India, oil producers like Saudi Arabia, and middle powers such as Australia, Turkey, and Argentina. Table 9.5 displays the full membership of the G-20.

The G-20 was formed after the Asian financial crisis of 1997–98 and achieved substantial political prominence in the context of the deeper and broader global financial crisis that began in 2008. The rise of the G-20 reflects the diffusion of international economic power; the United States and its close allies are no longer powerful enough to shape the world economy by themselves. Moreover, it represents an attempt by the wealthier countries of the world to accord greater voice to a range of relatively more successful developing countries, something that was obviously lacking with the G-7. G-20 members represent 90 percent of global GDP, 80 percent of trade, and two-thirds of the world's population. The G-7, in contrast, represents only about 15 percent of world population, 65 percent of GDP, and 65 percent of world trade. The G-20's membership is more representative, but it is also more diverse. Whether this informal association of countries can provide effective leadership to the world economy remains to be seen; some of the main factors that are emphasized by different theories of IR in estimating how ambitious the G-20 policy agenda might become are highlighted in Box 9.6.

Group of 7 (G-7)
Seven countries (United States, United Kingdom, France, Germany, Japan, Italy, and Canada) that sought to govern international economic relations after the collapse of the Bretton Woods system by coordinating their exchange rates and their domestic monetary and fiscal policies.

Group of 8 (G-8)
The Group of 7 (G-7) plus Russia. In the aftermath of the Cold War, Russia was added as a symbolic move. Russia was suspended from the G-8 in 2014 in response to its annexation of Crimea.

Group of 20 (G-20)
The G-7, newly rising economic powers like China and India, oil producers like Saudi Arabia and Russia, and middle powers such as Australia, Turkey, and Argentina, which has replaced the G-7 in international economic decision-making.

Photo 9.5 Meeting of G-20 Finance Ministers

An important element of the G-20 is to facilitate dialogue among high-level government leaders from its member countries. This gathering of Finance Ministers and Central Bank Governors of the G-20 took place at the 2017 IMF and World Bank Annual Meetings in Washington, DC, USA on October 12, 2017.

Source: Samuel Corum/Anadolu Agency/Getty Images.

Table 9.5 The Group of 20

The G-20 brings together important industrial and emerging-market countries from all regions of the world. Together, member countries represent around 90% of global gross national product, 80% of world trade (including EU intra-trade) as well as two-thirds of the world's population. The G-20's economic weight and broad membership gives it a high degree of legitimacy and influence over the management of the global economy and financial system.

Membership
The G-20 is made up of 19 countries and the European Union

- Argentina
- Australia
- Brazil
- Canada
- China
- France
- Germany
- India
- Indonesia
- Italy
- Japan
- Mexico
- Republic of Korea
- Russia

- Saudi Arabia
- South Africa
- Turkey
- United Kingdom
- United States of America
- The European Union, which is represented by the rotating Council presidency and the European Central Bank, is the 20th member of the G-20.
- The Managing Director of the IMF and the President of the World Bank, plus the chairs of the International Monetary and Financial Committee and Development Committee of the IMF and World Bank, also participate in G-20 meetings on an *ex-officio* basis.

9.6   DIFFERING THEORETICAL APPROACHES

Realist, Liberal, and Constructivist Views on the Prospects for an Ambitious G-20 Agenda

The G-20 has a much larger and more diverse set of member countries than the G-7 and G-8. Given the larger membership, which includes all of the members of the original G-7 advanced industrialized countries, together now with not only Russia but also such countries as South Korea, China, India, and South Africa, it is possible that any policy decisions the G-20 makes will be more likely to be consequential for the world economy. On the other hand, it is also possible that large-group dynamics will make it more difficult for the G-20 to reach important decisions than was true for the G-7. What, then, are the prospects that, compared to the G-7 experience, the G-20 countries will be able to agree on bold initiatives in trade or monetary affairs? For different reasons, arguments emanating from the major theories of international relations share skepticism about the ability of the G-20 countries to pursue an ambitious international economic agenda.

Realism

A realist would not be optimistic about the G-20. The realist would argue that the G-7 countries during the 1970s and 1980s shared many common interests, including a common need to remain strong in the face of challenges from the old Soviet Union, and that this commonality of interests, including in the security domain, helped underpin the efforts by the G-7 countries to work together. In contrast, the G-20 countries include states that have relatively few foreign policy interests in common, and many of them are geopolitical rivals to one degree or another (India and China, the United States and Russia, China and the United States). The group includes at least one pair of countries that has had recent militarized international disputes (China and Japan). Given the heterogeneity in foreign policy interests of G-20 countries, the agreements they reach are likely to be very modest in scope.

Liberalism

A liberal with a domestic-institutions focus would have serious doubts about the capacity of the G-20 to embark on large initiatives. The issue for the liberal/domestic institutions theorist, as with the realist, is that the G-20 is characterized by too high a level of heterogeneity of interests. However, the liberal would argue that the problem is not just that there may be differing geopolitical interests among the G-20 countries that will impair their ability to reach agreements on trade and monetary matters, there is also the more fundamental problem that the G-20 includes countries with extremely different political systems, from highly authoritarian (China and Russia) to highly democratic (the United Kingdom, Canada, and Germany). Liberals with an international institutional perspective would argue that the G-7 worked reasonably well because there were numerous informal cross-country linkages among ministries of finance and central banks and that these linkages helped the G-7 embark on serious joint actions. The G-20 association lacks strong informal bonds such as the G-7 enjoyed and continues to enjoy, and it lacks the kind of formal organizational features – for example, a permanent secretariat and procedures for ensuring compliance with group decisions – that make bold action possible with such a large coterie of states.

Constructivism

A constructivist might also have doubts about the capacity for bold action by the G-7. That theorist would note that leaders and policy officials from the G-7 countries shared and continue to hold many ideas and beliefs in common. In particular, they all hold more or less similar beliefs about the proper role of government in the national and global economy, namely, that government should let market forces largely determine economic outcomes, but governments should intervene in limited ways when necessary to prevent sustained economic recessions. In contrast, the G-20 includes countries with radically different views about the role of government in the economy, from those that rely more on markets with limited government management (United Kingdom) to those that believe the government should be very directly active in the national economy (China and Russia). Countries with elites holding such different views are unlikely to be able to find common ground on how to address international economic challenges.

Levels of Analysis *Institutions of the World Economy*		
Individual	State	International
Individuals who worry about the effects of economic globalization and the power of MNEs and institutions like the IMF have participated in mass protest movements.	Civil society activist groups that are critical of modern economic globalization, including the operations of MNEs, have influenced national economic policies.	Major states, and especially the United States, but also the United Kingdom, both destroyed the international economy during the 1930s and created a new basis for international economic integration during the 1940s. Today, a wider range of states, including such countries as China, Japan, and India, play key roles in important international economic institutions as the IMF and the Group of 20.

REVISITING THE ENDURING QUESTION AND LOOKING AHEAD

This chapter has introduced you to the dynamics of international trade and money, and it has provided you with an introduction to some of the key international institutions, both private and public, that constitute and drive the world economy. With this knowledge you are well on your way toward engaging the enduring problem we presented at the outset of the chapter, how does international politics shape the global economy? You should also recognize and appreciate that the global economy, in turn, shapes international politics.

An understanding of international economic dynamics, such as the economic sources and effects of trade, or why we have exchange rates and how are they derived from market forces as well as government decisions and actions, is vital for making sense of both historical and contemporary international relations. We began by using concepts from the field of economics, most importantly comparative advantage, to show why countries trade. We also explained how both domestic and international political considerations sometimes lead states to disrupt the flow of trade. We examined the link between trade and money, again focusing on the political choices governments make to control (or not control) the price of their national currency, and the consequences that follow. We also paid substantial attention to a vitally important agent in the modern world economy, the multinational enterprise. Developing one further connection between international politics and economics, we examined key political international institutions that govern the world economy of today, the WTO, the IMF, and the G-20.

Chapter 10 moves more explicitly to the level of foreign policy analysis and continues our exploration of international political economy. We look in more detail at states and markets, and the tools and strategies that governments use in the world economy to provide economic benefits for their people at home as well as power and influence for their countries as they interact with one another on the international stage.

STUDY QUESTIONS

1. Trade theory assumes that countries gain from trade because, overall, they consume more goods and services through specialization and exchange. Why, then, would some countries prefer protectionism to freer trade?
2. The United Kingdom, Sweden, Canada, Australia, Switzerland, and the United States have sought to maintain a reasonably flexible exchange-rate system. What are the main benefits of having a flexible as opposed to a fixed exchange-rate system? Do you think it might be better to shift to a fixed exchange rate? Why or why not?
3. What are the main benefits that MNEs provide to the world economy? What are the main problems that they may pose for individuals and countries?
4. Does the IMF have too much power in international economic relations? If it does, how might you reform it?
5. As an instrument of international economic governance, is the G-20 an improvement over the G-7/G-8?

FURTHER READING

Brooks, Stephen (2005) *Producing Security: Multinational Corporations, Globalization, and the Changing Calculus of Conflict* (Princeton: Princeton University Press). Brooks develops in detail the thesis that, in the modern world, foreign direct investment by multinational enterprises ties countries together in ways that make military conflict between them irrational and unlikely.

Gilpin, Robert (2000) *The Challenge of Global Capitalism* (Princeton: Princeton University Press). This is a wide-ranging survey of the world economy at the turn of the twenty-first century, with attention to trade, finance, and foreign investment. Gilpin emphasizes the importance of a stable political foundation for international economic relations.

Lipset, Seymour Martin (1959) 'Some Social Requisites of Democracy: Economic Development and Political Legitimacy,' *American Political Science Review* 53 (1): 69–105. Lipset put forward an early and highly influential statement of the argument that a country that undergoes economic development is more likely also to follow a path of democracy. This essay is therefore essential for students who want to engage with the thesis that multinational enterprises and, more generally, international economic integration through trade and finance, are forces for democratization in the modern world.

Rivoli, Pietra (2009) *The Travels of a T-Shirt in the Global Economy* (Hoboken, NJ: John Wiley and Sons). Rivoli traces the creation of a cotton T-shirt all over the world, in an effort to gain understanding of the politics and economics of contemporary international trade.

Yarbrough, Beth, and Robert Yarbrough (2006) *The World Economy: Open-Economy Macroeconomics and Finance*, 7th edn (Mason, OH: Thomson/South-Western). This intermediate-level text provides a rigorous but accessible introduction to modern economic theory of international trade and finance.

 Visit **www.macmillanihe.com/Grieco-IntroIR-2e** to access extra resources for this chapter, including:

- Chapter summaries to help you review the material
- Multiple choice quizzes to test your understanding
- Flashcards to test your knowledge of the key terms in this chapter
- An interactive simulation that invites you to go through the decision-making process of a world leader at a crucial political juncture
- Pivotal decisions in which you weigh up the pros and cons of complicated decisions with grave consequences
- Outside resources, including links to contemporary articles and videos, that add to what you have learned in this chapter

10 States and Markets in the World Economy

Enduring question

How do governments manage international economic relations to further national political objectives?

Chapter Contents

Learning Objectives

By the end of this chapter, you will be able to:

→ Recognize and distinguish different schools of thought on how international politics and economics interact.

→ Understand the relationship between states and markets in the world economy.

→ Appreciate the economic choices of states in a geopolitically competitive world.

→ Identify ways that powerful states use economic tools to pursue foreign policy goals.

→ Explore the links between hegemony, open markets, and security.

→ Analyze the role of globalization, and challenges to it, in the current world economy.

Getty Images/Westend61

Even the most powerful states in the world – those with the largest military establishments and most destructive weapons – are deeply dependent on their economies to support such vast amounts of military power. At the same time, bankers and businesspeople around the world can engage in trade and exchange largely because states have created rules and institutions to support the free flow of goods and money. The world of international relations and power politics on the one hand, and the world of business and economics on the other, seem to be quite separate. Students tend to study these subjects in different classes and university departments. But, in fact, they are quite interconnected. Countries that are wealthy and fast-growing will tend to be more powerful on the world stage than poorer and slower-growing countries will be.

Chapter 9 addressed the enduring question of how international politics affects international economics, and introduced you to basic economic concepts: trade, monetary, and investment relations, and the core institutions of the world economy. This chapter takes you to the state level and more deeply into international political economy by exploring how states, the key political actors, and markets, the key economic mechanism, interact. The world of states and the world of markets coexist within the global system; they shape and influence each other. While diplomats and political leaders are pursuing foreign policy and national security, ordinary citizens are forming corporations, hiring workers, producing goods and services, and selling them in home markets and around the world. Citizens and corporations also invest heavily in sophisticated stock, bond, and currency markets across the global landscape. Businesspeople and traders depend on governments to support and uphold national and international economic rules and institutions. Governments depend on business; in the long run, states are only as powerful as their economies are wealthy and prosperous. And business depends on government to create the environment within which wealth and prosperity may be created. Both states and markets influence, and are influenced by, the global economy.

We will look first at the rise, decline, and re-emergence of an open world economy over the last two centuries. Then we examine the three great traditions of thinking about politics and economics – economic liberalism, economic nationalism, and Marxism. Each offers a different view about how states and markets shape and constrain each other. After this, we look at the ways in which states – as they compete for power and influence – seek both to foster economic growth and protect themselves from economic dependency. We look at the ways great powers seek to use markets – fostering the expansion of economic openness and integration – as tools for promoting their national interests and fostering global peace and security. We examine the role of leadership in maintaining an open system of trade and economic exchange, and at the end of the chapter raise the critical question: Is the postwar, liberal world economy headed once again into a cycle of decline?

TWO GREAT ERAS OF ECONOMIC GLOBALIZATION

As we saw in Chapter 9, economic relationships among sovereign nation-states may be relatively open and market-driven, or relatively closed with governments imposing many types of restrictions on cross-border economic activity. As noted in Chapter 2, globalization is the ongoing process of international economic and technological integration, made possible by advances in transportation and communication. Globalization involves greater openness and the broader and deeper movement of goods, capital, technology, ideas, and people within and across borders. In a striking development over the past 200 years, the world has witnessed two great eras of globalization characterized by the freer flow of economic transactions across state borders. World War I and, later, the Great Depression, brought the first era of globalization to an end, but after World War II, as Box 10.1 indicates, a second and even more intense wave of globalization took place, bringing unprecedented prosperity to the world economy. Today, growing economic nationalism and resistance to globalization raise questions about the durability of the current era of globalization.

In the late nineteenth century, Great Britain led the establishment of an open world economy in which goods, capital, ideas, and people moved relatively freely across Europe and beyond. By the beginning of the twentieth century, this system had generated unprecedented levels of economic interdependence within Europe, across the Atlantic, and between the more developed industrial core of the world economy in Europe and North America and the relatively less developed periphery of Asia, Africa, and Latin America. Multinational enterprises, discussed in Chapter 9, emerged as key actors in this interdependent world economy.

Map 10.1 The Dutch East India Company
The Dutch East India Company, founded in 1602, is considered by many to be the first multinational enterprise. During the seventeenth and eighteenth centuries, the company acted on behalf of European countries, especially Britain, in expanding markets to Asia.

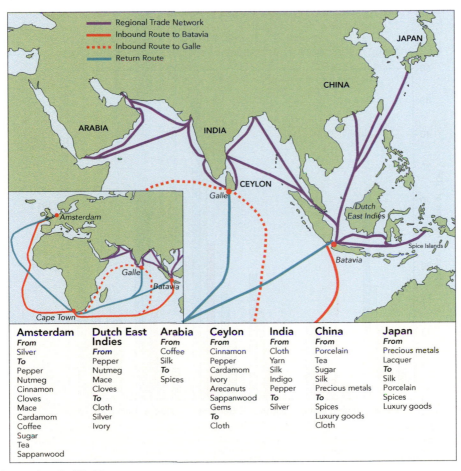

Amsterdam	Dutch East Indies	Arabia	Ceylon	India	China	Japan
From		*From*	*From*	*From*	*From*	*From*
Silver	*From*	Coffee	Cinnamon	Cloth	Porcelain	Precious metals
To	Pepper	Silk	Pepper	Yarn	Tea	Lacquer
Pepper	Nutmeg	*To*	Cardamom	Silk	Sugar	*To*
Nutmeg	Mace	Spices	Ivory	Indigo	Silk	Silk
Cinnamon	Cloves		Arecanuts	Pepper	Precious metals	Porcelain
Cloves	*To*		Sappanwood	*To*	*To*	Spices
Mace	Cloth		Gems	Silver	Spices	Luxury goods
Cardamom	Silver		*To*		Luxury goods	
Coffee	Ivory		Cloth		Cloth	
Sugar						
Tea						
Sappanwood						

Source: Jean-Paul Rodrigue.

359

10.1   MAKING CONNECTIONS
Then and Now

The Rise of a Liberal World Economy

Figure 10.1 measures exports as a percentage of Gross Domestic Product (GDP) across countries and time. It gives us a visual means to understand the evolution of the world economy in a more liberal direction since 1870.

Notice first the pattern for the entire world. Exports increased significantly between 1870 and 1913, during the first great wave of globalization. But between 1913 and 1950 – the era of two world wars and the Great Depression – world trade not only stagnated but declined. Since World War II, and particularly beginning in the 1990s, the world has experienced a second great wave of globalization as countries have become more dependent on trade as a percentage of their overall economic activity.

Note also that the United States, Germany, France, and the United Kingdom each follow roughly the same pattern over time. But the United States is relatively less dependent on trade in overall terms. US exports have grown significantly over time, but by 2007 still represented only about 12 percent of US GDP, while for Germany, the proportion in 2007 was about 45 percent, and for France and the United Kingdom, about 25 percent.

Figure 10.1 Merchandise Exports as Percent of GDP in 1990 Prices, five Countries and World, 1870–2007
The graph measures exports as a percentage of GDP across countries since 1870, showing the increasing importance of international trade over time.

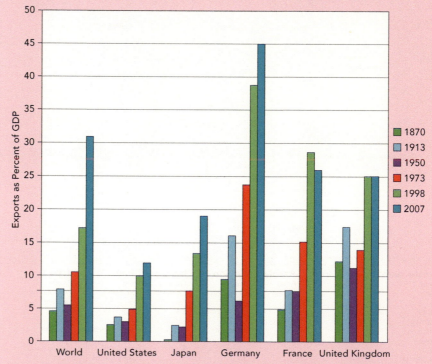

Source: For 1870 to 1998, see Angus Maddison, *The World Economy: A Millennial Perspective* (Paris, Organisation for Economic Co-operation and Development, 2001), Table F-5, p. 363. Both exports and gross domestic product are based on 1990 constant international dollars; for 2007 data, see International Monetary Fund, World Economic Outlook database for real GDP, April 2008, and for trade see World Trade Organization, 'International Trade and Tariff Data', available at http://wto.org/english/res_e/statis_e/statis_e.htm.

This open system collapsed in the wake of World War I and the economic depression of the 1930s. The United States led the way toward a second era of globalization after World War II. Trade tariffs were reduced. Currencies became **convertible**, which meant the paper money of one country could be exchanged at a market price for the paper currencies of other countries. Commerce and investment spread, first within the transatlantic world of Western Europe and the United States and gradually into other regions. In the 1980s, East Asian countries integrated more fully into this expanding world economy. After the Cold War, many countries from the former communist world, most importantly China, also pursued market reforms and joined the open world economy.

Convertible currency
A currency that can be exchanged at market price for the currency of another country.

By the turn of the twenty-first century, the world economy was truly a globalized system, encompassing all regions. The current 'center of gravity' of the world economy is shifting away from the Western economies toward Asia and the developing world. China is growing rapidly, and it could eventually overtake the United States as the world's largest economy. As we discuss in Chapter 11, India, Brazil, Indonesia, South Africa, South Korea, and other non-Western developing countries are also gaining a greater share of world economic activity. As Box 10.2 shows, emerging powers such as China may embrace some, but not all, of the principles of a liberal world economy.

Globalization has brought wealth and prosperity to millions of people around the world. But it also created new problems and pressures. The rapid flow of money into different economies has led to destabilizing currency crises, such as in Latin America in the 1980s, East Asia in the 1990s, and the entire world economy in the great financial crisis that began in 2008. The 2008 financial crisis and global economic recession has been particularly consequential because it began in the United States, the leader of the world economy and champion of open markets for the past 60 years. With the 2008 financial crisis and global economic slowdown, new debates have arisen over the virtues and dangers of open and relatively unregulated financial markets. Analysts have asked, for example, about whether banks should be allowed to engage in complex packaging of assets and loans that make it difficult to assess their risk and reliability (Johnson and Kwak 2010; Lewis 2010). In trade, globalization has triggered worries – and populist backlash politics – in the advanced industrial economies about the loss of high-paying jobs, as companies move their plants to lower cost countries and technology and automation disrupt the economy. The crisis has also raised questions in capitals around the world about the ability of the United States to continue to be the global economic leader, providing stability and support in times of economic turmoil.

Moreover, today's economic globalization has created anxiety over culture and identity; some Japanese, Americans, and Europeans worry about excessive immigration, some Europeans resist the fast food culture common in the United States, and some traditional groups and societies in the Middle East, Asia, and Africa are alarmed by the rapid spread of more permissive Western ideas about sex and lifestyle. In 2016, the British referendum decision to leave the European Union and the election of President Donald Trump in the United States were at least partly the result of political and cultural anxieties among some voters about immigration and open borders. Box 10.2 shows that the government of one of the world's largest economies worries about maintaining domestic political control while their people engage in more economic transactions around the world. China's trading partners, in turn, worry about whether seemingly unlimited supplies of Chinese labor will gobble up the world's natural resources and manufacturing jobs. Over these two great eras of globalization, states unleashed the dynamic forces of trade and investment to

10.2   DIFFERING PERSPECTIVES

The Chinese Government and Google

Google has become a part of many people's daily lives, providing users access to the world of information online. When people search the internet, they prefer access to the full range of information available so that they may individually pick and choose what to view.

The Chinese Government View

Officials within the Chinese government have a different agenda. The government allows the Chinese people increasing degrees of economic freedom, yet more closely restricts political freedom and freedom of speech. It fears that the Chinese people, with access to the full range of information available around the world, might come to question or even organize opposition to the Communist Party's monopoly over political authority. Google's interest in maximizing the free flow of public information and the Chinese government's interest in regulating the flow of information are at odds with each other.

Google's View

In 2006, Google set up business in China. It agreed to create 'filters' that would censor some search results. For example, if a Chinese user typed 'Tiananmen Square' or 'Dalai Lama' into Google, many of the sites that would otherwise be displayed were blocked. Google was unhappy with these restrictions but accepted them. A Google official said in 2006: 'Our decision was based on a judgment that Google.cn will make a meaningful – though imperfect – contribution to the overall expansion of access to information in China.' There were good business reasons to do so. China has more web users than any other country in the world – as many as 400 million users – and Google has made millions of dollars a year as a result (300 million dollars in 2009 alone, according to CNNMoney). In January 2010, however, the situation changed. Google announced that Chinese hackers had tapped into the Google Gmail accounts of Chinese human rights activists and conducted a 'highly sophisticated and targeted attack on our corporate infrastructure.' Google suspected that these hackers might have been acting with the support and encouragement of the Chinese government. In response, Google promised to stop censoring results in China unless the Chinese government changed its ways. It redirected Chinese Google users to Google's Hong Kong link which provides uncensored searches. A standoff occurred, and the Chinese government threatened not to renew Google's license to operate in China.

The Compromise

The two sides essentially both blinked. Google agreed not to automatically redirect Chinese users to the Hong Kong site. Users now need to actively click to transfer to the uncensored Hong Kong site. But Google did agree to the previous policy of filters on access. The Chinese government got the restrictions it wanted, and Google can claim that uncensored access to its search results is only a click away. Given the obvious conflict of interests, it is likely that this struggle will continue.

increase prosperity and power. The resulting expansion of global economic activity has generated power and wealth for some, and new challenges for all. To provide the framework for globalization, we will examine the major philosophies concerning the relationship between states and markets in the next section.

State	🌐 International
Britain in the nineteenth century and the United States in the twentieth century undertook efforts to liberalize trade and open world markets.	Great eras of world politics have been marked by both economic openness and closure.

STATES AND MARKETS: THREE GREAT TRADITIONS OF THOUGHT

Over the centuries, political thinkers have offered a wide array of perspectives about the relationship between states and markets and their effects on international relations. Understanding these different 'philosophies' will help to guide you through the arguments and debates of international political economy. Three major schools of thought on the relationship between politics and economics stand out: economic liberalism, economic nationalism (or statism), and the capitalist class theory of Karl Marx (Gilpin 1975). These philosophies of international political economy are linked respectively to the broader perspectives of liberalism, realism, and Marxism that we discussed in Chapter 3.

Economic Liberalism

The classical liberal view of international political economy dates to Adam Smith, a Scottish pioneer of political economics, and the early decades of capitalist growth in Britain in the late eighteenth century. Liberal economic thinkers believe in free markets, the harmony of interests between countries, and the positive effects an open world economy will have on politics and foreign policy. Because open economic relations bring so many positive benefits to all, Smith and other classical liberals argued that the role of the state in the national economy should be quite limited. The government should try to minimize its intrusions. The basic functions of the state were to provide property rights, enforce the rule of law, and provide for the national defense. According to Smith, the government was to be a 'night watchman,' standing guard over the economy to ensure that production and trade took place freely. In a similar way, we might think of the state in economic liberalism as a referee; it maintains and enforces the rules of the game without disrupting the flow of the game itself. The main players are private citizens as workers, producers, traders, and investors.

Smith speaks for an entire tradition of thinkers in emphasizing the natural and autonomous logic of markets. According to this view, people are inclined by nature to 'truck, barter, and trade' – that is, to buy, sell, and make deals. There is a deep human desire to build productive and commercial relations within and between nations. The appropriate role of the state is to provide a hospitable environment for these private deals and transactions to occur. Properly organized, commercial society will flourish.

Smith argued that a thriving world of commerce would generate wider benefits for society. He believed that the **invisible hand** of the marketplace – the uncoordinated behavior of individuals and firms acting in their own selfish interest – would lead to the best economic outcome for society as a whole. For liberals, economics is not a game in which some win while others lose; Smith and others believed in **absolute gains**, where economic interaction creates only winners, even if some benefit

Invisible hand
A term coined by Adam Smith to describe the uncoordinated behavior of individuals and firms acting in their own selfish interest in the marketplace.

Absolute gains
An important element of economic liberalism, absolute gains is the idea that economic interactions create only winners, even if some gain more than others. Contrasts with relative gains.

Photo 10.1 Adam Smith
Adam Smith's *The Wealth of Nations*, published in 1776, marks the foundation of classical economic theory. Smith advocated for an open economy with minimal government intrusion. His imagery of the invisible hand guiding the market is still widely utilized today.

Source: iStock.com/GeorgiosArt.

relatively more than others. Smith also believed that market society would bring out the best in people, providing a 'civilizing spirit' as people go about their pursuits. Smith's view was that people think rationally and understand their mutual interdependence and that this is true within and among nations. Trade among nations will leave all countries better off. It leads to the efficient allocation of resources and stimulates growth. And, as we discussed in Chapters 3 and 7, economic relations form an integral part of the liberal theory of international relations. Trade and economic interdependence create 'vested interests' in favor of stable and peaceful relations. Governments themselves, as Adam Smith suggests, should be encouraged to let these natural commercial impulses spread around the world. In doing so, the dangerous dynamics of power politics and security competition can be tamed. Open economic relations lead to prosperity for all and, as a bonus, promote peace as well.

Smith's logic was pushed a step further by another British political economist, David Ricardo, who developed the now-famous law of comparative advantage that we explained in detail in Chapter 9. Recall that the law of comparative advantage is the classic statement on why trade between two countries is advantageous to both, and why it makes sense for all countries to specialize and trade.

In the long run, liberals see states and societies adapting themselves to the imperatives of economic integration and wealth generation. This conviction has led the United States and other capitalist states around the world to pursue policies that promote open trade and exchange. In the view of liberals, economic growth is facilitated by specialization and the division of labor, leading businesspeople and traders to seek out ever-expanding geographical realms for the exchange of goods and services. As the technologies of communication and transportation improve, the scale and scope of markets will tend to expand outward. States will face pressure to reduce barriers and support the growth of markets. In this process, states will adapt, yielding to incentives for global political integration and cooperation (Neff 1990).

Economic Nationalism

We might think of economic liberalism as believing that states should make way for markets. A second great tradition reverses the relationship and emphasizes the key role of the state in shaping market relations to national advantage. In American economic history, this worldview is associated with Alexander Hamilton and other early industrial 'state builders' who focused on the political dynamics of state competition. Hamilton was an American founding father who championed a strong federal government that actively promoted economic development to help a young and vulnerable United States increase its chances of survival in a world of powerful European nation-states. In the nineteenth century, the cause of economic nationalism was taken up by German thinkers, especially Friedrich List, who worried that Germany would never compete economically with Great Britain unless the German state protected and nurtured Germany's infant industries (Earle 1971).

Economic nationalists, unlike liberals, do not trust in the magic of Adam Smith's invisible hand. They emphasize the importance of states as facilitators of economic growth. Economic development and the benefits of international trade do not in their view happen automatically; governments must build banks, nurture industries, and plan institutions to facilitate economic advancement at home and assure that the nation-state gets the best deal from engaging economically abroad. The state must act strategically to promote the social and political infrastructure that allows market society to emerge and prosper. In this tradition, the state is not merely a referee, but an important player with unique resources.

The Hamiltonian view emphasizes that countries are in competition with each other. States must seek to promote – and if necessary protect – the national economy from the economic exploitation and domination of other countries. Whereas liberals emphasize absolute gains, economic nationalists worry about relative gains, or the idea that even if both sides gain from economic relations, one side might gain disproportionately more and use its gains to dominate the other side. Economic nationalists believe that prosperity and even national security might be compromised if international markets are left to themselves. This view has inspired many countries – particularly less developed countries – to intervene in the economy to protect and promote industries. In Asia, for example, beginning in the 1960s, the governments of Japan, South Korea, and Taiwan protected their domestic industries in sectors such as consumer electronics and automobiles, allowing them to grow strong and become successful export-oriented businesses (Kohli 2009). Recall our

Photo 10.2 High-Tech Industry in Japan
Japan emerged in the 1970s and 1980s as a leading economy in advanced technology, pursuing export-oriented economic development through close partnerships between government and business.

Source: iStock.com/gorodenkoff.

discussion of 'infant-industry' protection in Chapter 9; economic nationalists worry that more advanced economies can be at a competitive advantage, threatening to outperform and displace infant industries in developing economies. The state becomes vital as a shield, creating protected space and support as the industrial economy grows stronger.

Within the world economy, states become important as strategic players seeking to develop congenial political relationships that support national advancement. States are not obstacles to the functioning of national economic systems or the global economy; rather, they are architects and champions of commercial societies that seek to advance in a competitive and potentially threatening international environment. Considering its focus on the need to protect national interests and autonomy in a dangerous world, we may consider this Hamiltonian perspective as the economic component of realist international relations theory.

Marxism

A third tradition of thinking about states and markets is inspired by the ideas of Karl Marx. Recall from Chapter 3 that, in this view, the rise of market economies brings new divisions between the owners of businesses, or the capitalist class which possesses the productive assets of society, and the workers. Marxism argues that economic relations tend to shape political relations, but the main economic actors are classes, rather than individuals or the state.

For Marxists, the state within a capitalist society is neither a neutral referee nor a facilitator of economic development for the nation-state as a whole. Instead, the state has a special mission – to protect and advance the interests of the capitalist class. The state, in Marx's terms, is the 'executive committee of the bourgeoisie,' and its role is to shape the economic game to the advantage of the capitalist class, at the expense of the working class.

Even though capitalists held all the economic and political advantages, Marx was confident the underdog would ultimately win. The underlying conflict of interests between capitalists and workers would lead to a series of political struggles and the ultimate triumph of the working class, ushering in a new post-capitalist society in which all people were the owners and beneficiaries of economic activity.

While liberals argue that there is a deep harmony of interests between different groups and classes in society, and among societies, and realists expect competition among nation-states, Marxists see a zero-sum struggle across classes in which one side's gain is the other's loss. Capitalists seek to protect their advantages and workers seek to gain a greater share of wealth and power. Until the economic system is overturned in a political revolution, ushering in a classless society organized to benefit all workers, the capitalist class will retain their power advantages within society. Workers will work and capitalists will prosper until workers so outnumber capitalists that an effective leader can mobilize them into a meaningful political movement.

Within the wider international system, Marxist thinkers see the state operating in the service of national capitalist interests. As we discussed in Chapter 1, to the Russian revolutionary and Soviet leader Vladimir Lenin this meant that states would be driven by capitalist competition into geopolitical struggle and even war. Indeed, this was the Soviet leader's explanation for World War I. It was a conflict between states seeking to advance their national capitalist interests, particularly the giant banking and manufacturing conglomerates that held sway over these antagonistic states.

In the later decades of the twentieth century, Marxist thinkers acknowledged the remarkable spread of trade and investment, noting the rise of global business firms. National capitalists had become international capitalists, and their states followed, providing international support – including global rules and institutions – for their expanding commercial and financial interests. In this way, Marxists see international economic relations as a continuing drama in which capitalists in rich countries – backed by their states – dominate those in weaker and less developed countries. Today's international economic institutions, in particular the International Monetary Fund and the World Bank, are, they believe, instruments of the rich countries, protecting their interests even as they offer aid and assistance to less developed states. The struggle between workers and the capitalist class within societies is matched by the struggle between the advanced capitalist states and the struggling societies in the poor and less developed parts of the world. Marxist analyses flourish in eras of capitalist crisis, so it is not surprising that many books and articles from this perspective have appeared in the wake of the 2008 financial crisis (Ticktin 2011; Harmon 2009).

Despite their differences, however, most economic liberals, nationalists, and Marxists would acknowledge that states exist within a competitive state system, and this helps shape the way they act within the world economy. We now examine state behavior in the international economic arena, focusing on how governments use markets to strengthen their economies, protect their political autonomy, and compete militarily with other states.

Simulations: What would you do? If you were a Finance Minister tasked with setting up a new economic system, which theoretical tradition would you follow? Visit the companion website to see what would happen!

Levels of Analysis *The Great Traditions of Thought on State and Market*	
👤 **Individual**	🏃 **State**
Individual thinkers such as Adam Smith, Alexander Hamilton, and Karl Marx articulated influential ideologies of state–market relations.	Both economic nationalists and Marxists argue that the state – represented by centralized governmental officials – plays a critical role in shaping markets and capitalist economic development.
	Liberals argue that the state has a more limited role.

STATES AND MARKETS IN A WORLD OF ANARCHY

States are politically sovereign and economically interdependent. The world of commerce and trade must coexist with sovereign-territorial states that compete and cooperate with each other. These two systems – the capitalist world economy and the international state system – emerged together on the world historical stage in the seventeenth century. It has been an uneasy relationship ever since.

Each system has its own ways of operating. Capitalism tends to be transnational; nation-states are inherently territorial. Each has, at various moments, been threatened and destabilized by the other. Market booms and busts and rapid economic change have undermined the political standing of ruling regimes and fueled political conflict within and between states. The Great Depression of the 1930s is probably the most dramatic instance when growth and trade in the world economy plummeted – unemployment climbed to unprecedented levels – and governments were thrown into chaos. The economic crisis led to the collapse of some democracies in Europe and provided the conditions that brought to office such fascist leaders as Germany's Hitler and Italy's Mussolini. The financial crisis that began in 2008 thankfully has not brought war, but has led to political turbulence and conflict, most prominently in the European Union and in particular in Greece. Likewise, interstate competition – and at the extreme, war – has disrupted international flows of trade and investment and set limits on the integration of world markets. As we showed in Box 10.1, the era of world wars in the first half of the twentieth century brought with it a retreat from global economic integration and growth. But the two systems have also worked together: states have taken steps to establish property rights and construct international rules and institutions that support trade and investment between countries (as we discussed in Chapter 9); and capitalism has grown into a global system of production and exchange that provides states with taxes and other resources to cooperate and compete internationally.

If these are the circumstances in which states find themselves, what are the implications for the goals of states in the world economy? Generally, the competitive structure of interstate relations creates incentives for states to intervene in their national economies to promote economic growth and advancement, protect national autonomy, and be responsive to the relative power consequences of international economic relationships. But states also realize the potential benefits of an open system of trade and investment; they find themselves making trade-offs between concerns for security and independence, on the one hand, and opportunities to promote economic growth through trade and exchange, on the other. States, in other words, seek both power and wealth, the ability to protect themselves in a world of competing states and to prosper in the world economy. Generally, the two goals go hand in hand: the more prosperous states economically tend to be the most powerful ones politically. As the Soviet Union eventually found out, it is difficult for a state to be a dominant military power in the long run if it lacks a prosperous economy.

The Two-Sided Government: Managing Domestic and International Relations

The world economy is embedded within the broader system of states. Each individual state, however, must manage its national economy, and to do so requires that it operate simultaneously within domestic and global markets. Regardless of whether one is primarily a liberal, nationalist, or Marxist, it is useful to think of governments as facing both directions, inward to their own societies and economies, and outward to the world system.

From a historical perspective, the relationships of governments to the outside world and to their domestic societies have developed hand in hand. The rise of the modern state in Europe prior to the twentieth century involved the simultaneous process of fighting off foreign rivals while also strengthening the government's relationship with its own society and economy. The more intense the interstate competition, the more governments needed to mobilize and extract resources from their societies. States won wars if they had a strong military, and this depended on the ability of governments to tax and spend. This, in turn, provided incentives to encourage a productive economy and a legitimate role for the state within the society. The more the state needed to make demands on the society and economy, the more incentives it had to make its rule agreeable to domestic individuals and groups, including businesspeople, banks, and workers. This dynamic of war making and state building is perhaps best seen over the two centuries of armed conflict between Britain and France, from the 1660s to the end of the Napoleonic War in 1815. These struggles led each government to seek new ways to bolster and extract taxes and resources from their economies – and from the economies of conquered territories (Liberman 1996). Each developed more elaborate national financial systems to tax and borrow and thereby strengthen the ability of state leaders to pursue war and peace (Kennedy 1987).

As states interact with their own societies, institutions and traditions impose some limits and constraints on what state leaders can do. States differ in their relations with society; this will shape how states can operate at home and within the world system. These differences can be understood as variations in the capacities of states. Some states are more centralized and insulated from society than other states, and as a result they are better able to act in an independent and strategic manner. Other states are more decentralized and less autonomous, and as a result their policies will tend to more directly reflect the class or group interests within society. Among the advanced Western countries, France is often seen as a particularly centralized state in which the government has considerable capacity to shape and direct the economy. The United States is often seen as a decentralized state, with power divided between branches of government and between the national government and state and local governments. Some states can formulate policies and strategies that are independent of society and implement them effectively. Other states are less capable – unable to act coherently and lacking the policy tools with which to pursue independent goals (Krasner 1978; Mastanduno, Lake, and Ikenberry 1989).

Some observers see China and the United States as examples of these two types. China is governed by a single party – the Communist Party – and it commands all the levers of government. It has the authority to intervene in the society and economy to pursue its goals. This ability to 'get things done' was on display during the 2008 Olympics, when the Chinese government acted quickly to build huge athletic facilities and public transportation. When the Olympic Games were being held, the Chinese government was also able to shut down factories to reduce pollution emissions. More generally, working with state-owned firms, the Chinese government has been able to promote trade, investment, and infrastructure development projects with countries in Southeast Asia, South America, and Africa – doing so in the service of Chinese foreign policy goals.

The more purposeful Chinese government is often contrasted today with America's more divided government. The leaders of the US government pursue objectives in a multiparty system where frequent elections and political bickering between the two major political parties make it more difficult to pursue goals in the way China appears to be able to do. However, when faced with a national challenge, the United States has historically set goals and mobilized resources with

Photo 10.3 The Space Race
During the Cold War, the United States and the Soviet Union competed for prestige as leaders in science and space exploration. This picture shows Neil Armstrong, Michael Collins, and Buzz Aldrin, three astronauts from the Apollo 11 Mission.

Source: Corbis/VCG via Getty Images\Corbis.

great effectiveness. During the Cold War, the United States competed with the Soviet Union to show its abilities to 'do great things.' The space program – and the mission to put a man on the moon – was a showcase of the American effort to engage in a great feat of science, technology, and human imagination. On the other hand, many observers today question whether China's more rigid political system will enable the kind of creativity and innovation needed for its economy to become a true global leader.

A variety of factors will shape the capacities of states; the most basic is the sovereign integrity of the state and military and administrative control of its territory. Most developed states around the world have stable governments and territorial borders. The government taxes and regulates the economy. The national borders are protected. But, as we discuss fully in Chapter 12, other states are less fully in control of their borders and territory. In countries such as Sudan or Afghanistan, the central government is weak and its authority does not reach outward to all the regions of the country. Tribal leaders and warlords compete with the state for rule over outlying parties and territorial borders are left unguarded. In these weak or failed states, the basic capacities of government are not yet established (see Chapter 12).

In some cases, governments of what we think of as more developed countries may exhibit limited capacity. In the 1990s, after the Cold War ended, the government of Russia lost control over its society – the rule of law broke down, businesses and households evaded taxes, and organized crime plundered major parts of the economy (Taylor 2001). During the 2000s, it became apparent that the government of Greece was bankrupt because it had spent lavishly but had a limited ability to collect taxes from its population. Greece's financial problems affected all members of the European Union and created resentment in Germany since the more financially disciplined German people felt they should not have to provide the money to bail out the less disciplined Greeks. Germany offered in 2012 to send experts to Greece to assist in the craft of tax collection – an offer many Greeks saw as an insult and an intrusion on their sovereignty (*The Guardian* 2012).

Promoting National Economic Growth

Economic growth enables governments to provide welfare and prosperity at home and is a vital component of state power abroad. In a competitive system, governments are likely to care a great deal about the wealth and prosperity of their respective societies. In the short run, it might be possible for ambitious governments to extract resources from their society forcefully and build up their military capabilities, taking capital and other assets away from more productive uses. Stalin used this technique in the 1930s to modernize the Soviet Union and ensure its place as a great power. But in the long run, as Soviet leaders ultimately learned when they could no longer sustain the Cold War, the power of the state will depend on the wealth of the society it commands. As a result, we should expect states to encourage economic growth and the accumulation of wealth. There may be other reasons why state leaders would want to promote economic growth and wealth creation at home, such as responding to interest group pressures or creating a prosperous electorate that will re-elect the leaders in office. But the competitive international system itself provides a powerful incentive for states to care about the prosperity of the national economy.

If a government wants its country to gain economic strength, to what extent should it participate in the world economy? As we saw in Chapter 9, liberal economic theory would answer that trade openness promotes specialization and maximizes economic gains. South Korea and Taiwan, for example, have over the last 40 years grown rapidly and fostered the development of more advanced and high-technology industries by gradually opening up to foreign investment and joint ventures with leading international businesses. Along the way, they have acquired knowledge and experience that has allowed them to develop their own world-class businesses in many areas.

But states interested in promoting long-term economic growth and advancement have also found reasons to protect domestic industries at their initial stage of development and shelter critical industries and technologies from foreign competition. South Korea and Taiwan were careful not to open their economies too quickly or fully to outside investment. They regulated foreign investment, allowing time and space for their domestic businesses to grow and develop. But they were not completely protectionist. They opened their economies to outside investment gradually to create competition and gain knowledge and experience. As we shall see in Chapter 11, developing countries have experimented with both open, liberal strategies and more insulated, nationalist strategies in their efforts to promote growth and develop strong national economies (Haggard 1990).

Protecting Autonomy

Governments operating in a competitive state system will generally have a second important goal – to protect their country's autonomy. They will not want their economy to be too dependent on others and put the country's security at risk. An open system of world markets may stimulate the growth of the national economy, but too much exposure can create dangerous vulnerabilities and dependencies. States will try to prevent themselves from becoming too dependent on other states, particularly if the other states could eventually become adversaries. But states might also try to make other states dependent on them by providing favorable terms of trade, drawing other states into a dependent relationship that allows the one state more advantages and power. The American government's active encouragement of Japanese imports after World War II, for example, was aimed at stimulating economic revival in East Asia – warding off communist-led political instability – and drawing Japan into America's emerging Cold War alliance system as a reliable junior partner. In these circumstances, states must make difficult choices and trade-offs between interdependence and autonomy.

The problem of dependence on other countries for resources and trade has become an important issue as the world economy has become more interdependent. For example, Ukraine is heavily dependent on neighboring Russia for its energy supplies, particularly oil and gas. In recent years, the government of Ukraine has attempted to strengthen its ties to NATO and the West, a move resisted by Russia, which prefers that Ukraine have a more 'Russia-friendly' than 'West-friendly' orientation. Russia has directly intervened in Ukraine with military forces and aided rebels in the eastern part of the country. In addition, Russia has used its economic leverage over Ukraine by making Ukraine's access to Russian energy supplies dependent on the maintenance of close political ties between the two countries. When Ukraine strays too far from Russia, Russia restricts the flow of natural gas. Ukraine's energy dependence on Russia potentially constrains the freedom and ability of the government of Ukraine to reorient its foreign policy (Olearchyk and Buckley 2010). For their part, Western countries, upset by Russia's intervention in Ukraine, have sought to exploit Russia's renewed connections to the world economy: the United States and Europe are now using economic tools – trade and financial sanctions – to punish Russia for its actions in Ukraine.

Map 10.2 East China Sea

In the ongoing conflict at sea between China and Japan, each side claims an Exclusive Economic Zone (EEZ) in the East China Sea and the two zones overlap. Each side claims the right to control and patrol the area of overlap. The Senkaku Islands (the Chinese call them the Diaoyu), a roughly 4-squaremile area of uninhabited islets, fall within the area of overlap. The disputed area holds great potential for oil and gas exploration, fishing, and the mining of sea-bed metals.

As China's economy has become more powerful, it has exploited the economic dependence of its Asian neighbors for political gain. In September 2010, the Japanese coastguard arrested and detained the captain of a Chinese fishing vessel after it rammed a Japanese coastguard ship in waters off a disputed island in the East China Sea (see Map 10.2). After Japan refused to immediately release the captain, China announced an 'informal embargo' on export of rare earth materials to Japan. China mines and sells over 95 percent of the world's market in rare and expensive minerals used in advanced technologies, such as solar collectors, computers, and mobile phones. China used the dependence of Japanese companies on these resources from China to pressure Tokyo to back down. The Chinese sailor was eventually released, and the crisis was defused. Not surprisingly (see Box 10.3), Japan and other countries took note of China's use of its near monopoly on rare earth resources; these governments responded by taking steps to reduce their dependence on China (Bradsher 2010). In 2017, the Chinese government showed its displeasure with South Korea's decision to deploy an American anti-missile system – a response to North Korean nuclear and missile developments – by reducing auto imports and restricting tour travel to South Korea. China is South Korea's largest trading partner, and although it resisted a complete abandonment of the missile system, Seoul did modify its plans to appease Beijing (Taylor 2017).

A state that opens itself up to dependence on another state must make a series of calculations. First, the threat that energy supplies or other critical resources might be cut off is not as straightforward as it seems. It is useful to make a distinction between **sensitivity** and **vulnerability** to resource cut-offs (Keohane and Nye 1977). If Ukraine can shift the source of its energy imports from Russia to Saudi Arabia (which is eager to sell the same resources to Ukraine), the security implications of dependence on Russia are not that serious. In that case, Ukraine is merely 'sensitive' to disruptions. Alternatively, Ukraine might be able to undertake domestic efforts to substitute the discontinued flow of energy with the building of nuclear energy facilities that serve the same purpose. Again, the implications of disruption are not that severe; Ukraine will pay some cost for the loss of Russian supplies but it will be inconvenienced more than significantly harmed.

Sensitivity
A state is sensitive to another state's actions if those actions can temporarily hamper a state until it finds a replacement for the good or service from another location.

Vulnerability
A state is vulnerable to another state's actions if it is unable to compensate effectively for losses caused by the other state's actions.

But what if Ukraine was not able to make up for the disruption of energy flows from Russia and could not find a domestic substitute? In this situation, Ukraine's dependence on Russia is more severe. Ukraine then is not just sensitive to a Russian cut-off, it is vulnerable to it. This vulnerability has more serious implications in that Ukraine is putting its security at risk by allowing itself to become dependent on one energy source. In cases of extreme dependence, we should expect the dependent state to try to broaden and diversify its imports and trade relationships to limit the power of the single exporting state. The importing state may also try to find domestic substitutes for the resources (see Map 10.3).

Dependence and vulnerability may apply as much to financial relations as trade relations. As Figure 10.2 shows, the United States has found itself increasingly dependent on China as a source of capital. By 2010, China was holding almost

Map 10.3 European Gas Pipelines

The majority of Europe's gas pipelines emanate from Russia, a major global supplier of natural gas. Russia has used its energy dominance as a political tool, most notably in attempts to constrain Ukrainian economic and foreign policy.

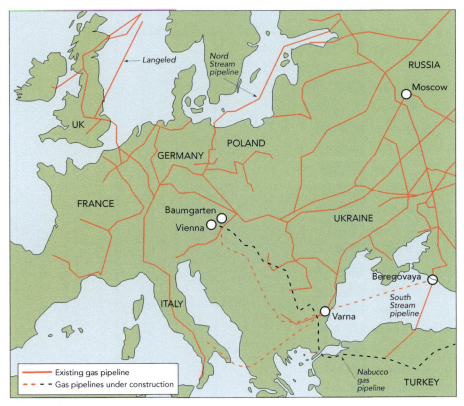

Source: Petroleum Economist.

$1 trillion of bonds issued by the US Treasury. By borrowing this way, the US government has been able to engage in massive spending, including wars in Iraq and Afghanistan, without imposing the immediate costs on American taxpayers. For its part, China has had its own reasons to be such a generous lender. As we discussed in Chapter 9, it has bought American Treasury bonds to take pressure off its own currency, reinforcing an exchange rate that favors Chinese exports.

This situation in which China has been America's de facto banker has led some in Washington to worry if the United States has become indebted to China politically as well as financially. Has the United States developed a dependency on China's financing of budget deficits that gives Beijing leverage over American foreign policy? If China sold its holding of American Treasury notes, the value of the dollar might plummet, and the United States government would be forced to raise interest rates, choking off economic growth and creating a political crisis. Many experts do note that China would also suffer if it did sell off its debt holdings. Their value would also plummet, and the very act could destabilize the world economy on which China depends so heavily. In this sense China and the United States may be symmetrically interdependent – depending so much on each other that neither can afford to disrupt the economic relationship for relative political gain (Drezner 2009).

China and the United States may be mutually constrained because both are large economic powers. But interdependence between larger and smaller economies is usually more one-sided. As we saw in Russia's relations with Ukraine, a large state seeking to expand its political power and enhance its own autonomy might want to

Figure 10.2 Major Foreign Holders of US Treasury Securities, December 2017
China is the single largest foreign holder of US Treasury bonds, followed closely by
America's important Pacific security ally, Japan.

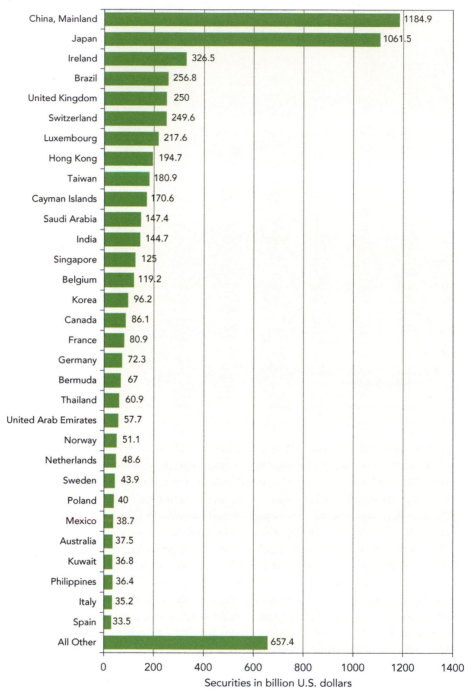

Source: Data from the Federal Reserve, US Department of the Treasury.

promote the dependence of its smaller neighbors (Hirschman 1980). In the classic
study of this strategy, the famous political economist Albert Hirschman looked at
Germany's interwar trade relations with the small countries in Southeast Europe
during the 1930s. To enhance its own autonomy, Germany drew these states into trade
relations that made them dependent on Germany over the longer term by securing

access to raw materials and increasing its leverage in the region. Germany offered very favorable terms to these small states to reorient and deepen these trade relations. As these small states became more dependent on trade with Germany, their 'exit' options became costly. But because these same trade relations played a smaller role in the much larger German economy, the potential costs of disruption were asymmetrical, and the dependent trade relationship also created political dependence. Germany used its own internal market as a tool of state power, enhancing its political autonomy by using trade and economic dependence to develop asymmetrical power relations. During the 1970s and 1980s, South Africa, the dominant regional economic power, pursued a similar strategy against its neighbors (including Zambia, Mozambique, Botswana, and Malawi), creating economic dependencies that made it difficult for those 'frontline' states to implement economic sanctions against South Africa's *apartheid* regime.

Today we should consider the extent to which China is pursuing a 'Hirschman-like' strategy toward its smaller neighbors in East Asia. The Chinese economy has grown so rapidly that it has become a magnet for the imports and exports of the Philippines, Thailand, and South Korea, among others. These countries have become increasingly dependent on China economically while continuing to maintain long-standing political and security ties to the United States. The Chinese establishment of the Asian Infrastructure Investment Bank in 2015, which is a Chinese-led multilateral investment bank supporting development projects across Asia, reflects China's efforts to foster closer economic – and political – ties with its neighbors. China has also unveiled a One Belt, One Road Initiative, which is an ambitious plan to expand trade and investment ties with countries across Eurasia, building a China-centered trading system. The natural concern of American policy makers is that over time, 'the flag will follow trade,' and these American allies will see fit to reorient their foreign policies in the direction preferred by China.

In summary, an open system of trade, money, and finance creates efficiency gains that leave all states better off than if they simply remained national economies. But, a state contemplating expanding its exposure to the world economy must calculate the trade-off between the absolute economic gains from trade and the possible loss of political autonomy that might accompany greater economic dependence. A state that cares about its security in a world of anarchy will be attentive to this trade-off: it will want to achieve all the economic gains it can, because this is part of what creates the national basis of its power position, but it also may be willing to forego some of those economic gains if they create dependence and vulnerability. As Box 10.3 shows, in an era of globalization governments find it increasingly difficult to forego the economic benefits of specialization and trade, even though it may mean extreme dependence on other countries as sources of supply.

Pursuing Relative and Absolute Gains

Finally, states operating within a competitive international environment will care about both absolute gains and their *relative standing* with other states (Baldwin 1993). Liberal economic theory tells us why states should care about absolute gains. Countries will trade freely based on specialization and comparative advantage. In doing so, these countries experience more economic gains than they would if they did not engage in free trade. Each country is economically better off. But in some circumstances, it is the *relative* economic gains that governments worry more about. This will be particularly true if the other country is a rival or a potential enemy in war. The more secure a state feels, the more content it will be to think in terms of absolute gains.

Map 10.4 China and East Asia

China is the world's second largest economy and it has developed rapidly by relying on trade both with the developed world of the United States and Europe and with its smaller neighbors in East Asia. Not surprisingly, economic relations with China figure prominently in the calculations of surrounding countries including Thailand, Vietnam, Malaysia, and even Australia. In 2007, China overtook the United States and Japan to become Australia's largest trading partner.

As we have shown above, the United States and China today appear relatively content to trade and exchange with each other without regard to considerations of relative gains. Both are gaining in absolute terms. The United States has found China to be a source of cheap imports, reducing costs for US consumers. Trade is a large part of Chinese economic growth, and economic growth is vital to economic and political stability within China. But it is possible that a moment might arrive when the United States and China start to worry more about relative gains. The United States, for example, might come to eye China increasingly as a rival and potential enemy. If China comes to look more like a threat than a trading partner, the United States will worry about China profiting more than it is. Relative gains will become more significant.

10.3   MAKING CONNECTIONS
Theory and Practice

The Trade Dispute over China's 'Rare Earth' Mineral Exports

Theory

Countries will seek to minimize extreme levels of dependence on their trading partners for items vital to their economies. This is especially true when the trading partner in question is a potential geopolitical competitor.

Practice

Governments find it difficult to forego the economic benefits of specialization, even when it leaves their economies vulnerable to calculations made by their trading partners.

In 2012, the United States, the European Union, and Japan filed complaints at the World Trade Organization against China over China's restrictions on the export of 17 'rare earth' minerals. The rare earth minerals, with exotic names such as Dysprosium, Neodynium, Yttrium, and Europium, are essential to the production of many technology-intensive products such as tablet computers, hybrid car batteries, mobile phones, and photovoltaic films. The more developed countries making the complaint are heavily dependent on China for the supply of rare earths. In 1995, China produced 40 percent of the world's supply of rare earth minerals; by 2012, it produced an astonishing 95 percent.

The problem emerged because China decided to impose restrictions on its exports of rare earths, allowing in 2012 only about one-half the exports of rare earths that it had allowed in 2005. China's reasons seemed sensible; it cited environmental concerns and a desire to sustain its supply of these minerals over the longer term. But China's trading partners cried foul, contending that Chinese firms were happy to sell their product to other countries, but that the Chinese government was using unfair trading practices to hoard the vital materials for its own domestic use. China has the largest proven reserve of rare earths (about 55 million metric tons as of 2011). But other countries have sizable reserves as well: Russia has 19 million metric tons, and the United States has 13 million. So why then does China provide 95 percent of the world's supply? Rare earths are expensive to mine, and China has large amounts of inexpensive labor. Rare earth production is also environmentally costly, in some cases producing radioactive waste that most countries would prefer not to have on their territories. China has been more willing to absorb these environmental costs. Its trading partners have been happy to avoid these costs and simply buy the minerals from China.

By restricting the supply of rare earths, China will force their prices to go higher. At some point, the higher prices will attract new suppliers into the market from other countries. In recent years, in response to the Chinese restrictions and higher prices, companies in Australia, Canada, the United States, and South Africa have reopened mines to produce rare earths. Production of rare earth minerals outside China increased significantly from 18,000 to 74,000 metric tons between 2013 and 2018, while China's production only increased from 94,000 to 100,000 metric tons (Statista 2018).

Photo 10.4 Japanese Dependence on Chinese Rare Earth Materials

A bulldozer scoops soil containing various rare earth metals, to be loaded onto a ship at a port in Lianyungang, China on September 5, 2010, for export to Japan.

Source: STR/AFP/Getty Images.

We can look more closely at the logic of relative gains, introduced earlier in the chapter. In making choices about economic relations, states can think about the payoffs in one of two ways. One way is to simply make choices that give the state the most economic gains in absolute terms. This is the logic of the neo-classical theory of trade. If policy X leads to 20 units of economic gain for my state, and policy Y leads to 10 units of gain for my state, the choice is obvious: in maximizing my state's absolute economic gains, I will choose policy X. But, in an insecure and dangerous world, conditions may exist that prompt a state to calculate its interests in terms of relative gains. If policy X gives my state 20 units and the other state receives 40 units of economic gains, we both gain but the other state gains more. If policy Y gives me only 10 units of gain, but it gives the other state 5 units of gain, my state's absolute gains are less but its relative gains are greater in comparison to the other state. If my state's goal is to protect its relative power position, the incentive to pursue relative gains over absolute gains may exist.

The ultimate reason a state would worry about the distribution of gains within an economic relationship is the risk of war. The possibility that a state's trading partner might someday be a grave and dangerous adversary will create incentives for that state to calculate in terms of relative gains. But, if the costs of war are huge and the possibilities of war are tiny, then that state will likely calculate that the absolute gains from trade are worth pursuing.

Consider two examples. In trade between the United States and Canada, neither side pays much attention to relative gains. The two neighbors are long-standing allies and the militarily weaker country, Canada, does not fear invasion or conquest from its superpower neighbor. Alternatively, consider that during the Cold War, the United States and Soviet Union were potential military adversaries, each of which thought seriously about the relative gains implications of economic exchange. The Soviets sought to buy or steal Western technology to 'catch up,' or close the relative gap in economic and military capabilities between the two sides. The United States and its NATO allies organized a system of export restrictions, preventing their companies from trading certain technologies to the Soviet Union to maintain the West's relative advantage (Mastanduno 1992). NATO governments believed that free trade with the Soviet Union would benefit both sides but would benefit their potential adversary relatively more. Today, as China grows more powerful, the United States has also increasingly scrutinized and taken steps to block the transfer of advanced technologies – particularly those with military applications – to China.

State Building, War, and Markets

By now it should be clear that most governments have a conflicted view about world markets. They are both attracted to economic openness and in some ways threatened by it. An open world economy can stimulate trade and investment that fuel economic growth, raise living standards, and create a wealth base from which the state can extract resources to pursue its geopolitical goals. But it can also undermine domestic industry, destabilize employment, and leave the society dependent on an external world it cannot control. Governments must continually choose between these dangers and opportunities. For most governments, as the world economy has become more integrated, the balance between interdependence and autonomy has clearly shifted in favor of interdependence. Many governments today claim a commitment to open markets and free trade. Yet, as Box 10.4 shows, the reality does not always match the rhetoric.

10.4   MAKING CONNECTIONS
Aspiration versus Reality

Free Trade in Principle, Not Practice

Aspiration: George W. Bush, Speaking in a Republican Primary Debate, January 7, 2000

> I would be a free trading President, a President that will work tirelessly to open up markets for agriculture products all over the world. I believe our American farmers can compete as long as the playing field is level. That's why I am such a strong advocate of free trade and that's why I reject protectionism and isolation because I think it hurts our American farmers.
>
> Source: Issues 2000; accessed at www.ontheissues.org/
> George_W__Bush_Free_Trade_&_Immigration.htm.

Presidential candidate Bush was simply reiterating a long-standing aspiration in American foreign economic policy: free trade benefits all, as long as the playing field is 'level.' In other words, the United States supports open markets and expects other states to do so as well.

Reality

The reality is quite different, particularly in agriculture. From the early years of the General Agreement on Tariffs and Trade, the United States insisted on special treatment for its agricultural products. US officials have long provided protection for American dairy, sugar, and peanuts. The government provides price supports for domestic producers to ensure that they receive high prices for their crops even if the supply is greater than the demand. In 1986, for example, the US domestic price for sugar was about four times the world price. Consumers, left on their own, would substitute cheaper sugar from Central America for the more expensive US production. But, the US government does not allow free trade in sugar; instead, it negotiates a set of quotas with foreign producers to limit the amount of sugar coming into the US market. In this case, the rhetoric of free trade does not match the reality of a controlled market that benefits less efficient US producers.

Among developed countries, the United States is not alone in practicing agricultural protectionism. The European Union protects its farmers in similar ways and, for decades (as we explored in Chapter 9), Japanese policy makers vowed not to allow a single grain of foreign rice in the Japanese market. As we shall see in Chapter 11, agricultural protectionism is a key issue of contention in relations between developed and developing countries, because many countries in Africa, Latin America, and Asia are producers and exporters of agricultural products. Their economic growth depends, in part, on access to the consumer markets of the United States and Europe.

The dilemma governments face between economic interdependence and political autonomy goes all the way back to early modern European history when capitalism and state formation were both beginning to take shape (Tilly 1985). Political leaders at that early moment were attempting to build themselves up and engage in 'state making,' which also involved protracted wars with neighboring would-be state builders. It is true that the state, or government, makes war; it is also true that war made the state, in the sense that the need to fight wars created incentives for political leaders to assert great control over their territories and populations to mobilize the resources needed to fight wars effectively. Wealth and power were inextricably linked at the dawn of the state system and they still are today.

In the years between 1400 and 1700, rulers mostly contracted with mercenary troops – private individuals hired by the state – to fight their wars and relied heavily on private capitalists within their region for loans and the collection of taxes. After 1700 and into the present era, states created mass armies and navies, with soldiers drawn increasingly from their own populations. The military establishments became a formal part of the state, and the administrative organs of the state became directly responsible for the fiscal management of the national territory.

Over time it became easier for governments to extract resources from their populations. In traditional, non-monetized societies, leaders had to rely mainly on coercion – their representatives had to go out and extract tribute from private actors within its territorial reach. As societies became more commercial and monetized, the ease with which the government could monitor and extract funds increased. In more commercial societies, taxation could shift from tribute, rents, and tolls at strategic ports to trade tariffs and, ultimately, income taxes. States with societies at higher levels of commercialization and capital intensiveness could extract resources more efficiently; those at lower levels of commercialization were at a competitive disadvantage and required a larger and more coercive state apparatus.

The trick for successful governments has always been twofold: to encourage a rising economy and find efficient ways to extract resources from that economy without stifling growth. Put differently, governments want the economy to lay golden eggs, so they can take a few of those eggs for their own purposes. But they need to play the game right: to encourage egg production and pursue egg extraction, without threatening the goose's ability to lay the eggs.

Today, most (but not all) people accept as legitimate that their government has the right to collect taxes and use the proceeds for the collective good of the country as they see it. Companies withhold part of the pay of their employees and send it to the government, and citizens participate in the annual ritual of preparing their individual tax returns for the government. The government uses these resources to build roads and bridges, provide services to those in need, and to redistribute income from the wealthier to the less wealthy. It also uses some part of those resources to conduct foreign policy, including at times the resort to war. Crises such as the Cold War or the attacks of September 11, 2001 tend to expand the size and powers of government, as political leaders react to what they and their populations perceive as a more threatening international environment. Even today, the state makes war and war makes the state.

After laying the foundation for how states balance territorial concerns with economic growth, we now turn to the examination of great national powers, or superpowers, who use open markets to pursue security policy and international order.

Levels of Analysis *State versus Market in a World of Anarchy*

👥 State	🌐 International
States differ in their capacities to intervene in the domestic economy to stimulate and direct economic development.	The anarchic environment in which states operate creates incentives for governments to intervene in the national economy, promoting economic growth and protecting the country's sovereignty and vital industries.

GREAT POWERS AND THE WORLD ECONOMY

All states must manage the trade-off between economic interdependence and political autonomy. But the most powerful states, with the most dynamic economies, have additional opportunities. They can use their disproportionate political and economic power to shape the world economy in which they participate.

More so than 'ordinary' countries, great powers may use markets and the expansion of economic openness and integration as a tool of security policy and international order building. Britain after the Napoleonic Wars of the nineteenth century and the United States after World War II are the most dramatic examples of major states that have had the power and opportunity to build and manage the world economy. The economic goals pursued by these leading states have been closely tied to general political and security goals and ambitions in the creation of an international political order.

There are a variety of ways the expansion of world market relations and increased economic interdependence might serve the political and strategic interests of a leading state. Here we highlight three key political goals states may pursue through economic means: increasing national wealth, influencing the economic and political orientation of other states, and shaping the overall political direction of the international system.

First, a powerful state may take special advantage of the fact that an open world economy increases the nation's access to markets, technology, and resources, fostering greater domestic economic growth and increasing national wealth. This basic logic informed Great Britain's turn from mercantilism to free trade during the first half of the nineteenth century, and the American proposals for rebuilding the world economy after 1945. Britain by the 1820s was the 'workshop of the world,' producing far more than it could consume. The United States emerged from the war as the most advanced and productive economy in the world. Its leading industries were well positioned for global competition. An open world economy, organized around non-discriminatory multilateral rules, was an obvious national interest. American policy makers concerned with national economic advancement were drawn to a postwar agenda of trade barrier reduction and global multilateral economic openness (Gilpin 1987).

The construction of an open world economic order in the aftermath of World War II remains one of the more remarkable accomplishments of the twentieth century. As discussed in Chapter 9, agreements reached by the United States and Britain during the war and ratified at Bretton Woods in 1944 marked a decisive move toward openness. This was a surprising feat given the ravages and dislocations of war and competing national interests. It came only because the United States had formidable political and economic power and was willing to use it to push the world economy in its preferred direction of openness and non-discrimination. For example, America offered recovery assistance to European countries, but only on the condition that they open their economies to multilateral trade and make their currencies convertible on international currency markets.

A second political-strategic interest that might prompt a leading state to pursue market openness and integration is the opportunity to influence the political and economic orientation of other states and regions. Specifically, a world economy divided into closed and rival regional blocs may be contrary to the economic and security interests of the leading state. During World War II, American postwar planners concluded that the United States could not remain a viable great power and be isolated within the Western hemisphere. The American economy would need to integrate itself into a wider pan-regional world economy. The war itself was in part a struggle over precisely this matter. German and Japanese military aggression was aimed at the creation of exclusive regional blocs in Europe and Asia. The American economy would thrive best in a world without blocs; its status as a leading great power depended on economic openness. Except for the Soviet bloc, it succeeded in fostering economic openness. And, in the context of the Cold War, American security depended on having reliable anti-communist allies. US leaders used American economic power to drive Western Europe and Japan into economic interdependence and military alliance with the United States.

In the decade after World War II, the United States took the lead in helping Japan find new commercial relations and raw material sources in Southeast Asia to substitute for the loss of Chinese and Korean markets. The United States also helped foster integration within Europe. To encourage economic growth and stable political relations with former enemies, the western zones of occupied Germany were economically integrated into the wider Western European economy. The celebrated European Coal and Steel Community, which created joint French and German ownership of basic war industries, embodied this strategic goal. Economic integration can create mutual dependencies that make autonomous and destabilizing security competition more difficult. The same logic reappeared more recently during the process of German unification when Germany agreed to tie itself even more fully to Europe through monetary union.

Finally, a leading state may use economic openness and integration to *shape the overall political orientation* of the international system. American officials who embrace liberal beliefs about politics and economics had long anticipated that expanding world trade and investment would indirectly promote and reward movement by states toward liberal democracy. A world of democratic states would reduce security threats and allow the United States to more fully realize its international goals. Trade and investment strengthen the private sectors of countries, empowering civil society as a counterweight to strong states. Economic openness would create vested interests within countries in favor of pluralistic political order and stable and continuous relations between states.

Over the decades, it has been a staple of American foreign policy thinking that the spread of trade and investment into the non-democratic world would stimulate and reinforce the economic and political forces pushing for political change. An expanding market society acts as a counterweight to autocratic states and encourages the rise of a middle class that favors democratic institutions. This concept has been at the center of American thinking about the rise of China, and a US foreign policy that advocates integration of China into the world economy. In the wake of the deal between the two countries in 2001 over Chinese entry into the World Trade Organization, a reporter captured this logic:

> For a president who talks constantly these days about harnessing the forces of economic globalization, the agreement to integrate China into the global trading system marked the culmination of Mr. Clinton's single biggest imprint on American foreign policy: the use of American economic power for strategic ends. That is what this agreement is all about, locking in China's commitment to economic reforms and with it, he is betting, a further opening of Chinese society. (Sanger 1999)

As of 2018, many observers argued that Chinese integration into the world economy had not created the anticipated incentives for Beijing to reform and liberalize its domestic system. In fact, under President Xi Jinping, while China became more interconnected with the world capitalist system, at home the government became more autocratic and less liberal.

Nonetheless, many foreign policy thinkers hold to the conviction that an open and interdependent world order, over the long run, creates dynamics and forces of economic change that move countries around the world in the direction of liberal democracy – and this serves the interests of the United States and the established democracies. Other countries, of course, have their own reasons for pursuing interdependence and engaging with international institutions. In Box 10.5, we review liberal, constructivist, and realist arguments on why China has become more willing to embrace international institutions.

Leadership and the Liberal World Economy

The experience of the United States after World War II led political scientists and economists to theorize more generally about the role of leadership in promoting a liberal or open world economy. The link between openness and leadership was first stressed by Charles Kindleberger in his study of the Great Depression in the

10.5   DIFFERING THEORETICAL APPROACHES

Why Has China Embraced International Institutions?

During the Cold War, the Chinese government was skeptical of international institutions, viewing them as a tool used by Western states to constrain Chinese foreign policy and force China to comply with Western norms and values. Since the mid-1990s, however, China's leaders have embraced international institutions, for example, joining the WTO, CTBT, and leading the Six-Party Talks on North Korea. What explains this shift in policy?

Constructivism

Western states have engaged China, encouraging it to be a responsible player to gain status as a great power. As China has participated in these institutions, it has become socialized into embracing their role and utility. This socialization process occurs when Chinese officials participate in these institutions, slowly acquiring their norms and orientations. Moreover, as China becomes more powerful, it has the opportunity to shape those institutions to reflect better its own values and interests.

Realism

China's embrace is tactical and instrumental. It needs to reassure its neighbors that its rise is non-threatening. Embracing international institutions is one way to do that. As China becomes more powerful, we should expect it to be more selective in its willingness to abide by the rules and norms of international institutions.

Liberalism

China's interest is functional. Its key goal is economic development, and its key strategy is global integration. Joining the WTO is a direct way to integrate into the global trading system. Cooperation in security institutions reinforces the image of China as a responsible rising power providing a stable environment for long-term investment in its economy.

1930s. In his view, Britain was unable and the United States unwilling to provide measures to ensure openness and stability in the world economy during this interwar moment of crisis. By the late 1920s, Britain was no longer the leading world power and the United States, while newly powerful, had not fully recognized its increasing leadership importance and responsibilities. According to Kindleberger, the leading state can exercise leadership during a crisis by keeping its domestic market open to trade in goods from other countries, providing international financing and liquidity, and pursuing expansionary macroeconomic policy measures (Kindleberger 1973). In 1929, the United States failed to recognize its special leadership role and pursued narrow, short-term interests. It followed, along with other major countries, protectionist interests and competitive devaluation of currencies. Rather than attempt to counteract the collapse of world markets, the United States made the situation worse by enacting the infamous Smoot-Hawley tariff, one of the most protectionist bills in American history.

Leadership is more than the exercise of power. The leading state must have some recognition of its special responsibilities for management of the world economy. In the 1930s, the United States did not yet understand this role. The leading state must be able to use its domestic market to stabilize the larger international economy, and it must be able to resist domestic pressures. Leadership requires reforming the leading state's understanding of interests and capacities. Policy makers must grasp the state's larger role and conceive interests in a far-sighted and dynamic way. The state may forego some short-term gains by resisting protection and restrictive policies, but better serve the country's long-term interests.

This focus on leadership of the world economy directs us to questions about the future. The United States has played a leadership role for many decades, using its economic, military, technological, and political capabilities to open and manage the postwar world economy. On balance, the United States used its dominant position to encourage open trade, rules, and institutions that would facilitate economic stability. But, while the United States is still the largest economy in the world and possesses unrivaled military and technological capabilities, other countries are growing bigger and richer. China has become a key player in the world economy and is likely to become more important. So are countries such as India and Brazil. Equally important, the United States – under President Trump – has abruptly ended support for a multitude of trade agreements, including the North American Free Trade Agreement, and seemed deeply skeptical of trade cooperation in general. Trump reflects the sentiment of many ordinary Americans who question whether, after decades of stagnant real wages, deep integration into the world economy still serves their economic interests. Although that domestic pressure had been building gradually, Trump's decisive embrace of it represents a sharp turn in American policy and the consequences for the stability and openness of the world trade system are still uncertain. How far will the United States go to roll back and undermine existing multilateral trade agreements? Will other countries, such as China, step forward to provide more collective leadership? Alternatively, in the wake of declining American leadership, will China seek to pursue a less liberal-oriented organization of the world economy? Will it engage in more mercantilist and state-to-state trading relationships that undercut the openness of the world economy?

The United States provided leadership of the world economy during and after the Cold War, relying on economic partnerships with Japan and European countries, particularly Germany. These countries shared a great deal. They were all liberal democracies and they were alliance partners. But, increasingly, it is now China that the United States must work with over the management of the world economy, at least to the extent that the United States wants to play a leadership role. China is neither a liberal democracy nor an alliance partner. It is, however, seen by many observers as a potential geopolitical rival. How will this new and dynamic situation play itself out? Can China and the United States work together to provide leadership, or will these countries find themselves in competition with each other, reluctant to cooperate to keep the world economy open and stable? This is a key question for the future of the liberal world economy.

Levels of Analysis *Great Powers in the World Economy*	
State	🌐 International
Great powers have special incentives and opportunities to use trade and market relations to influence the orientation of other states and, over time, alter the basic organization of the world economy.	The distribution of power within the global system creates limits and opportunities for major states to lead and manage the world economy.

THE CONTEMPORARY WORLD ECONOMY: GLOBALIZATION AND ITS CHALLENGES

The world economy today is truly a global system of markets and exchange; trade has been steadily expanding across the regions of the world. People buy, sell, and invest across vast reaches of the earth. European consumers buy goods made in China, Malaysia, and Vietnam. Chinese companies invest in mining operations in Africa, and Japanese companies build cars in America and Europe. Global multinational enterprises operate in dozens of countries. Indian firms provide accounting and legal services for offices in New York. Buildings in Beijing are designed in London and built with supplies from all parts of the world. Markets in stocks and bonds link traders and investors in Europe, Asia, and North America. In this integrated global financial system, money speeds across borders in increasing volumes and velocity. In the background, the American dollar provides a 'key currency' for the world economy, facilitating the exchange of currencies and the stability of trade and investment. We live in an era of economic globalization.

But will globalization move forward or retreat? The world economy has become increasingly integrated, but it has also encountered many challenges. To some, globalization is a wonderful development which has united the world and brought people together in new and positive ways. To others, globalization is a process controlled by wealthy states and corporations that has created global winners and losers and generated threats to stability and security.

During the 1990s, globalization was widely viewed as positive, inevitable, and irreversible. To be sure, some critics worried that the homogeneity of products (like McDonald's hamburgers) or social trends would have a detrimental effect on the distinctive character of cultures around the world, or that the poor, without access to the technologies of the information revolution, would be left behind in the new world economy. But most analysts emphasized the positive side of globalization: free trade and open markets would lead to higher global growth, and growth would make everyone better off, even if not to the same extent. China was touted as a success story of globalization, with hundreds of millions of people pulled out of poverty after China integrated into the global economy. Thomas Friedman, the *New York*

Times editorialist, advocated for globalization in a widely discussed book, *The Lexus and the Olive Tree* (1999). Friedman saw globalization transforming the lives of individuals around the world, offering them access to knowledge and the chance to shape their own destinies. Governments, in his view, were subjected to the 'Golden Straitjacket' – to flourish in the new world economy required them to emphasize the private over the government sector, and to keep inflation low, currencies stable, and markets open.

By 2018, the picture looks very different. Globalization is now subject to serious challenge in the United States and in many parts of the world. The financial crisis of 2008 was a great shock not only to the world economy but to the ideology of globalization. Before the shock the 'Washington Consensus' held that the road to prosperity involved privatizing markets and opening economies to trade, finance, and investment. The financial crisis showed the risks of globalization, as unregulated and integrated economies nearly collapsed.

10.6   RESEARCH INSIGHT

Globalization and Inequality

The Problem

What is the relationship between globalization and inequality? Economists have long noted the positive effects of open trade on economies, showing how specialization and comparative advantage facilitate economic growth for all countries. But in the aftermath of the 2008 global financial crisis, scholars began to look more closely at the downside of globalization, including fostering greater inequality within open trading countries.

The Research Insight

Scholars do observe that for the world as a whole – seen as a single world economy – economic globalization over the last several decades has actually helped reduce inequality between countries. Global inequality has declined markedly since 2000, a trend that is largely due to the rapid economic growth of China and India. As these developing countries continue to grow and converge with the developed economies, global inequality will continue to decline.

At the same time, inequality within individual countries has increased. In the advanced industrial countries, the rich are getting richer and the working and middle classes are losing ground or, at best, holding their own. Economists debate the extent of rising inequality and its various causes. But there is wide agreement that globalization is part of the problem. As China and India opened their economies in the 1990s to trade and investment, Western firms began to move their production facilities overseas. The profits of corporations increased but the real wages of workers – particularly unskilled labor – fell. This growth in inequality has been exacerbated by government policies, including reductions in income tax rates, cuts in welfare benefits, and financial deregulation. The growth in the mobility of firms, wealth, and skilled workers has made it harder for governments to combat inequality, as corporations and wealth holders shift their assets to low tax havens. Technological developments, such as automation, have also put downward pressure on unskilled wages, while increasing corporate profits.

One of the most famous portraits of this shifting pattern of economic winners and losers is Branko Milanovic's *Global Inequality* (2016). He presents what he calls the 'elephant curve,' showing the distribution of gains from globalization over the last two decades. The big hump of the elephant, in the middle of the

Equally important, rather than a sharp decline and similarly sharp recovery, the world economy continues to experience slow or stagnant growth some eight years after the beginning of the crisis and recession that followed it. Governments have tried the usual monetary and fiscal tools but have not managed to jumpstart economic growth. Particularly for those in the less educated working class, stagnant economic conditions decrease optimism about the future and increase suspicion of outsiders seeking to take jobs either through exporting goods or by crossing borders.

Slow growth is compounded by growing inequality in income and wealth (see Box 10.6). One of the hard truths of globalization is that the rich get richer – those with the requisite yet relatively scarce skills and education to succeed in a knowledge economy have the added benefit of competing for high-paying jobs on a global scale. Those without such assets compete against an abundant global labor pool for jobs with more stagnant wages – wages depressed further by labor-saving technological innovations (such as robots or automated check-out counters in retail stores). It is

chart (point A), are the workers in China, India, and other emerging economies, who have seen their real wages rise – albeit from a small base – rapidly. The upward thrust of the elephant's trunk (point C) is the richest 1 percent, whose wealth has dramatically increased. Between these groups are the beleaguered workers and middle class of the Western developed world, who are in the bottom of the elephant's curved trunk (point B). Dani Rodrik (2012) has also provided important insights into the connections between trade and financial globalization and inequality. His message is that national governments remain vital actors in managing globalization and protecting citizens from the insecurities that are inevitably produced by global economic integration and change.

Figure 10.3 The Elephant Curve, 1988–2008
This chart shows that people in the emerging economies, particularly China and India, realized strong growth in their income, as did the very richest segment across the world, while middle class incomes in the advanced industrial societies were largely stagnant.

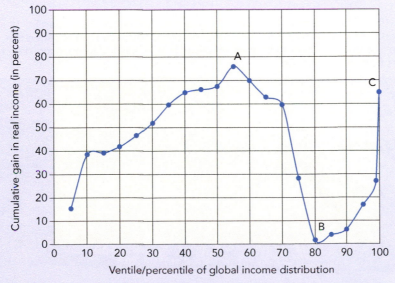

Source: *Global Inequality: A New Approach for the Age of Globalization* by Branko Milanovic, Cambridge, Mass.: Harvard University Press, Copyright © 2016 by the President and Fellows of Harvard College.

perhaps not surprising that many view a system in which benefits seem to concentrate in the hands of the few rather than the many as 'rigged,' rather than as the natural and harmonious consequence of Adam Smith's invisible hand.

Under these new circumstances, many view open borders as a threat rather than as an opportunity or inevitability. In the wake of the Syrian civil war, member states of the European Union agonized over whether and to what extent to allow Muslim refugees into their countries. In late 2015, when the government of Poland, for example, agreed with the European Union to take in 7,000 refugees from the Middle East, the ruling party was thrown out of office and replaced by a 'Law and Justice' party that promised to ban further refugee flows. In the fall of 2016, the United States elected Trump as president under the banner of America First, who vowed to build a wall along the southern border of the country to keep Mexicans and central Americans from crossing illegally, and to prohibit Muslim immigrants until the United States 'figured out' how to manage its terrorism problem.

In many countries, especially in the United States and Europe, politicians are following nationalist and populist public sentiment, and in some cases are encouraging it. In Europe as of 2015 roughly 20 percent of voters backed populist parties of the far right or far left, about double the number that supported such parties during the 1990s. In France, the National Front party headed by Marine Le Pen, which centers its campaign on anti-immigration policies, is no longer a fringe political movement and has become increasingly popular to the point of being a plausible contender in presidential elections. The Law and Justice party that now governs Poland is both anti-immigrant and opposed to foreign banks and corporations. In Greece, Syriza is a left-wing populist party that has gained popularity by resisting the economic austerity measures (i.e., the Golden Straitjacket) that the European Union has sought to impose on Greece as a condition for bailing Greece out of its debt predicament.

As discussed in earlier chapters, the most shocking victory for populist, anti-globalization sentiment came in 2016, when voters in Great Britain voted for Britain's departure from the EU. The British establishment, including bankers, business

Photo 10.5 Refugees and Immigrant Groups Put Pressure on European Societies
This aerial view taken on August 16, 2016, in Calais, northern France shows the 'jungle' camp where over 9,000 migrants lived in a makeshift camp, according to reports from several NGOs.

Source: PHILIPPE HUGUEN/AFP/Getty Images.

leaders, and the majority of policy and academic experts, advocated that Britain remain integrated into the Union. But that long-standing consensus was overturned by a combination of left-wing populists, who viewed the EU as a tool of global capitalism exploiting British workers, and right-wing populists, who viewed the EU as an oppressive, unelected super-state running the lives of ordinary British citizens from Brussels. To the claim that Britain would pay a high price economically and in foreign policy for abandoning its 40-year commitment to European integration, the populists retorted that the opinions of 'the experts' should be ignored for they had neither superior knowledge nor the best interests of Britain in mind.

In Europe and the United States, the major political divide seems to be less about right versus left, and more about, as *The Economist* put it, 'drawbridges up vs. drawbridges down.' The world has become divided into those, on the one hand, who embrace free trade and open markets, embrace immigrants as a source of national renewal, view cultural change as an opportunity, respect the authority of elites, and view governments as potential problem-solvers. The 'drawbridges up' contingent, on the other hand, prefers to protect jobs at home, block immigrants, and resist multiculturalism to 'take their country back.' They also view experts with suspicion and view governments more as a potential threat to individual freedom and initiative than a potential engine of progress. The outcome of this struggle is yet to be determined, but its existence suggests the breakdown of the 1990s consensus on both the desirability and inevitability of globalization.

In the meantime, the non-Western developing countries are engaged in their own rethinking of globalization, focused primarily on the organization and governance of the world economy. During the Great Recession of 2008–09, new forms of global economic governance began to emerge. Countries such as China, India, Brazil, Mexico, and South Africa became more important participants in the world economy and sought and attained greater voice in managing global economic rules and decisions. In the fall of 2008, the then US President Bush hosted a meeting of the G-20, an expanded grouping of states that includes developing countries such as India and China and oil producers such as Saudi Arabia. In the years ahead, the G-20 and other state groups will likely grow in importance as world leaders seek to manage the crises and instabilities of a globalized world economy.

The emergence of the G-20 at the height of the Great Recession of 2008–09, and the increasing importance of fast-growing developing countries such as China, Brazil, and India to global recovery and expansion are signals of great change; a 'changing of the guard' among states that lead and direct the world economy. It remains to be seen whether these rising countries from the Global South can lead the world to a new – and different – era of globalization.

Levels of Analysis *Globalization and Its Challenges*

 State

As China grows more wealthy and powerful, it joins the United States as a leading world economic power, and this raises questions about how the two countries will cooperate or compete in managing stability and openness of the world economy.

🌐 **International**

The globalization of the world economy – in which most of the countries of the world are increasingly interconnected – raises fundamental questions about world politics: political stability, economic fairness, and the future of global leadership. Today, the benefits and dangers of globalization are increasingly debated around the world.

REVISITING THE ENDURING QUESTION AND LOOKING AHEAD

International politics and economics go hand in hand, and this chapter has continued our exploration of how a world of states and a world of markets interact. We have focused at the level of individual governments and explored the challenges and opportunities they face in simultaneously managing domestic politics – relations with their own citizens – and foreign policy – relations with other governments, peoples, and organizations around the world. We have examined the many ways that states rely on their domestic economy for taxes and resources to support their international ambitions. We have seen the complex calculations that states must make to foster open trade but also protect domestic industries from foreign competition. We have analyzed how great powers often seek to use policies of trade and economic integration to promote friendly and stable relations with other great powers. And we have seen the complex ways that a globalized world economy shapes and constrains modern international relations.

In the next chapter, we look in more detail at the challenges faced by developing countries in the world economy. We know that powerful states and corporations have the resources to make the world economy serve their interests. What about poorer or weaker states – what strategies are available to them, and why do some weaker states develop more fully and quickly than others? We will explore the characteristics and problems of development generally and will pay particular attention to some development states that are rising rapidly both politically and economically, including India, China, and Brazil.

STUDY QUESTIONS

1. What major assumptions distinguish the three major schools of thought in international political economy: economic liberalism, nationalism, and Marxism? Which worldview do you find most compelling, and why?
2. Governments are territorial; they control pieces of land and the populations upon them. Economic actors are mobile; traders and investors cross borders and potentially operate anywhere in the world. In what ways can this tension between the logic of states and the logic of markets be resolved?
3. Do international economic relations promote peace? Why or why not?
4. Is it possible in the international system to be a great military power without being a great economic power? Is it possible to be a great economic power without being a great military power?
5. If you were a government leader, how would you resolve the conflict between the proponents and critics of globalization?

FURTHER READING

Kennedy, Paul (1987) *The Rise and Fall of Great Powers: Economic Change and Military Conflict from 1500 to 2000* (New York: Random House). A masterful history of the cycles of rise and decline of the great powers in five centuries of the modern era, tracing the implications of the advancing and receding economic fortunes of states on their geopolitical ambitions and accomplishments.

Kindleberger, Charles (2013) *The World in Depression, 1929–1939*, 40th anniversary edition (Berkeley: University of California Press). Kindleberger seeks to explain the Great Depression and the collapse of the world economy in the 1930s, emphasizing the failure of British and American leadership.

Polanyi, Karl (2001) *The Great Transformation: The Political and Economic Origins of Our Time*, 2nd edn (Boston: Beacon Press). In this classic work of economic history, originally published in 1944, Polanyi offers an account of the rise of market societies in the Western world beginning with the industrial revolution. He argues that the idea of the 'self-regulating market' is a myth. Markets emerged through deliberate government actions as state building and geopolitics gave birth to a modern world economy.

Rosecrance, Richard (1987) *The Rise of the Trading State: Commerce and Conquest in the Modern World* (New York: Basic Books). Rosecrance argues that the nature of capitalism and the world economy has changed, allowing states to trade and grow rich without engaging in old-style imperialism and territorial conquest.

Rodrik, Dani (2012) *The Globalization Paradox: Democracy and the Future of the World Economy* (New York: Norton). Rodrik challenges the widespread view that ongoing increases in globalization – manifest in open and increasing levels of trade and capital integration – is overwhelmingly good for peoples and societies.

Smith, Adam (2013) *The Wealth of Nations* (New York: Simon and Brown, originally published in 1776). The classic statement of the origins and working of markets and commercial society, making the case for the virtues of free trade and enlightened self-interest.

 Visit **www.macmillanihe.com/Grieco-IntroIR-2e** to access extra resources for this chapter, including:

- Chapter summaries to help you review the material
- Multiple choice quizzes to test your understanding
- Flashcards to test your knowledge of the key terms in this chapter
- An interactive simulation that invites you to go through the decision-making process of a world leader at a crucial political juncture
- Pivotal decisions in which you weigh up the pros and cons of complicated decisions with grave consequences
- Outside resources, including links to contemporary articles and videos, that add to what you have learned in this chapter

11 Dilemmas of Development

Enduring question

Does participation in the world economy help or hinder the economic development of poorer countries?

Chapter Contents

Learning Objectives

By the end of this chapter, you will be able to:

→ Recognize the defining characteristics of a developing country and appreciate the recent economic growth experiences of different groups of developing countries.

→ Consider the challenges developing countries face in achieving economic goals that result from past and current linkages to the global economy.

→ Analyze opportunities and problems that the globalization of trade presents to developing countries.

→ Evaluate opportunities and problems that the globalization of finance presents to developing countries.

→ Compare the economic development strategies of countries that may emerge or re-emerge as great powers, such as China, India, Brazil, Russia, and South Africa.

Mariusz Kluzniak

393

South Korea today is wealthy: it has a bustling, modern economy, and its citizens are among the best educated and healthiest in the world. This progress is especially striking since, in 1980, the total output of goods and services that Argentina produced per person, at about $2,700, was approximately 60 percent greater than that of South Korea, at about $1,700. Starting from behind Argentina, and many other developing countries, South Korea surged ahead. By 2016, South Korea and Argentina had reversed their relative economic standing: while South Korea that year produced goods and services worth about $27,500 per person, Argentina's output was about $12,500 per person. Although surpassed by South Korea, Argentina over these 36 years at least experienced an economy with reasonable growth. The Central African Republic, in contrast, made little progress during this period on the economic front: in 1980 its income per person was about $350; in 2016 that figure was about $380 per person.

Why do developing countries differ so much in attaining higher standards of living for their people? This question is clearly important: whether countries develop economically determines in large measure their populations' quality of life, whether they enjoy a full life or suffer an early death, and whether they have growing hope or persistent despair. It is also important from a practical viewpoint: as we will see in later chapters, countries that fail at development are often prone to internal war which brings terrible consequences both for the people living in those countries as well as for neighbors and the larger international community.

Much of the explanation of why countries experience different levels of economic growth concerns what happens within them. However, every national economy is also embedded, to a greater or lesser degree, in the global economy. Then the question becomes: does participation in the world economy help or hinder the economic development of poorer countries? This external side of the development question is the focus of this chapter. We will see below that there are many answers to this question, and debates about the international economy and development form a core element of the field of international political economy.

We will in the first section describe what we mean when we use terms such as economic development and developing country, and show that different groups of countries have had radically different degrees of success in attaining economic development. In the second section, we examine the challenges that developing countries face that arise from their historical as well as their contemporary linkages with the global economy. We then investigate whether commercial and financial linkages between developing countries and the world might present important opportunities for these countries to move ahead economically. Finally, we will look at a group of large and increasingly important developing countries, the so-called BRICS states of Brazil, Russia, India, China, and South Africa.

WHAT AND WHERE ARE THE DEVELOPING COUNTRIES?

Developing country
As noted in Chapter 1, these are poor countries with small economies whose residents have not, on average, attained the living standards typically enjoyed by residents of wealthy countries.

A **developing country** is one whose residents have not yet, on average, attained the living standards typically enjoyed by residents of wealthy nations, such as the United States, Canada, Japan, and the countries of Western Europe. At present, developing countries are mainly located in Latin America, Northern and sub-Saharan Africa, the Middle East (except for Israel), and East, South, and Southeast Asia. China is an interesting case. It was until recently a developing country, but it is now bursting with growth and possesses the world's second largest national economy. However, its population is so large that its *average* living standard is not yet on a par with countries we typically consider developed. As you will recall from Chapter 9, a country's annual total GDP is the final monetary value of the goods and services that are produced in that country in each year, and a country's GDP per capita is a country's total GDP divided by its total population. Developing countries have lower levels of average gross domestic product (GDP) per capita than wealthy nations and may or may not be on a growth trajectory that produces convergence with more developed countries.

One important analysis (Collier 2007) suggests that countries around the world with residents totaling around four billion people have seen improvement in their standard of living, but about one billion people live in countries that have made little or no economic progress. These individuals live, for the most part, in sub-Saharan Africa, but also in such countries as Afghanistan in Central Asia, Laos and Cambodia in Southeast Asia, and Haiti and Bolivia in the western hemisphere. These very poor countries face high barriers to growth, including corrupt governments, poor transportation links to the outside world, and high dependence on exports of natural resources.

What Is Economic Development?

GDP per capita is often employed by economists, governments, and international institutions such as the World Bank and the IMF as a rough measure of the quality of life that individuals can attain through their consumption of goods and services, including basic items like food, education, and medical care. However, we should be very clear: GDP per person is an imperfect measure of the economic wellbeing for each person in a country. Because it reports only the average level of income that individuals have attained, GDP per capita may mask large inequalities in the distribution of income within a country, and, therefore, life opportunities of different residents within that country. Moreover, as the UN Development Program (UNDP) emphasizes, **human development** is a process of enlarging people's choices and giving them a means to lead lives that they value. The UNDP thus has created the Human Development Index (HDI), which consists of average life expectancy, literacy and educational attainment, and per capita income. The UNDP presents a report each year on changes in HDI around the world, and while the index has yet to attain widespread acceptance or use, it deserves examination by students of international development.

Human development
A process of enlarging people's choices and giving them a means to lead lives that they value. Measurements of human development include such factors as life expectancy, income, and education.

Photo 11.1 Human Development: Education
A key element of human development is wider access to education, as illuminated by this photo of a school in Antigua.

Source: Macmillan Education\Rob Judges.

GDP per capita and the HDI index are highly correlated with one another, so the former seems to capture much of what is measured by the latter, but there are exceptions which are what make the HDI index so useful. For example, in 2011, Qatar, a small oil-rich country in the Gulf, had the world's largest per capita GDP at $107,700, more than double that of the United States. But the Human Development Index ranked Qatar 37th when life expectancy and literacy and other educational features were considered.

More generally, when comparing the pair of maps (Map 11.1), we can see there is a close relationship across countries between their GDP per capita in 2015 and their

Map 11.1 A World of Different Life Opportunities
This pair of maps shows that countries with higher levels of income tend to also have higher life expectancies. This suggests that, in general, countries that have achieved a higher level of economic development in terms of per capita income enable residents to live longer.

a) GDP Per Capita around the World, 2015

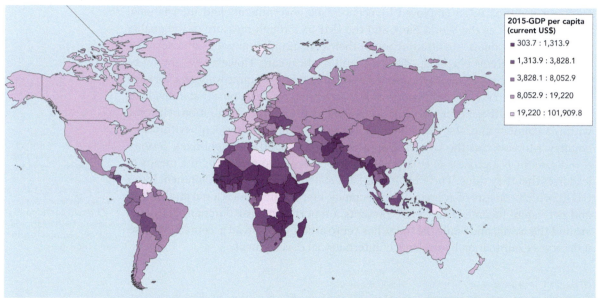

b) Life Expectancy around the World, 2015

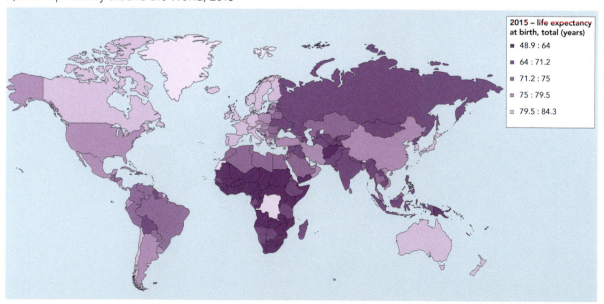

Source: World Bank, Databank, World Development Indicators, available at http://databank.worldbank.org/data/home.aspx.

average life expectancy at birth. Some of the differences around the world on both dimensions are shocking. In 2015, for example, Norway's GDP per capita was about $74,500, and Norwegian babies born that year had an average life expectancy of 82 years; in 2016, GDP per capita in the Central African Republic, as noted above, was only about $380, and babies born in that country had an average life expectancy of only 51 years.

Given the connection between GDP per capita and a basic measure of human wellbeing such as life expectancy, most developing countries seek progressively higher levels of GDP per capita. By consequence, **economic development** is usually taken to mean the attainment by a poorer country of an increase in its rate of growth of GDP per capita.

Economic development
The attainment by a poorer country of an increase in its rate of growth of GDP per capita.

Growth Experiences of Different Groups of Developing Countries

Despite most developing countries aiming to increase their rate of growth of GDP per capita, different regions of the world, as we can observe in Figure 11.1, have had very different experiences. The greatest difference can be observed if we compare the remarkably high and consistent pattern of average growth in the developing countries of East Asia and the Pacific with those in sub-Saharan Africa, which have had much more mixed success, and indeed experienced negative average annual growth rates during the 1980s and 1990s. The countries in sub-Saharan Africa, it should be noted, had a promising first decade of this century in terms of growth in per capita GDP, and growth has in fact accelerated during the current decade. Development scholars were concerned during the first years of the 2000s that sub-Saharan African success may have been due to short-term circumstances (Collier 2007: 9–10) such as increases in prices for the natural resources they exported. However, the fact that sub-Saharan African countries have grown even during the difficult years surrounding the Great Recession of 2008–09 allows for cautious optimism that growth in that region may have firm foundations.

Figure 11.1   Average Annual Rates of Growth in Per Capita GDP, by Region and Decade, 1980–2016
This figure shows how different groups of developing countries have attained different rates of growth in per capita income between 1980 and 2016 or, in the case of the newly free countries that emerged from the Cold War, from the 1990s up to 2016.

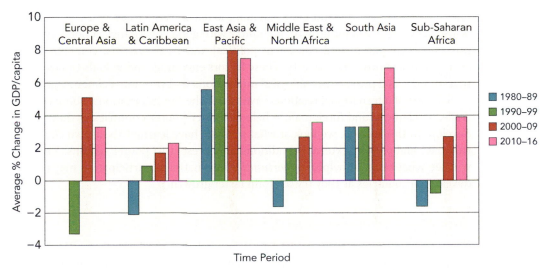

Source: World Bank, World Databank, World Development Indicators, available at http://databank.worldbank.org/data/reports.aspx?source=world-development-indicators.

An important story of recent success can be observed in South Asia. Since the turn of this century that region has experienced accelerating growth in GDP per capita: it reached an average rate of growth of 4.7 percent during 2000–09, and an even more impressive 6.9 percent on average between 2010 and 2016. Given these trends, it is possible that South Asian countries may be moving to a long-term high-growth trajectory that could converge with the massively successful experience of the East Asian countries. Indeed, during the years between 2010 and 2016, India's average annual growth rate in GDP per capita (about 6.4 percent per year) came quite close to that of China's (about 7.1 percent per year). India, in other words, is on the move economically.

Different groups of developing countries have fared differently in terms of growth in recent decades. How might international relations have affected economic development in these countries, and shaped their prospects for development in the future? To address this question we next analyze the effects of history and current global trends on economic development.

Levels of Analysis *Characteristics of Developing Countries*

 Individual

Per capita GDP is an important overall measure of a country's prosperity, but individual citizens also are greatly affected by 'quality of life' measures such as literacy and life expectancy.

 International

Just as there is great inequality among states in international security affairs, there is great inequality among states in the world economy.

INTERNATIONAL RELATIONS AND CHALLENGES TO DEVELOPING COUNTRIES

Why are countries like Germany, Japan, and now South Korea relatively wealthy and prosperous, while countries like Venezuela, Uganda, and Bangladesh are relatively poor and are still in the process of achieving development? Economists have not settled on a single theory of development, but they have learned there are many factors that account for variation in the economic fates of poorer nations, including geography; reliable, extensive access to foreign markets; and the availability of growth-producing national endowments of land, labor, capital, and natural resources. **Good governance** is also very important for growth. A country with good governance at home typically possesses transparent and consistent political and legal systems, combats official corruption, and protects property. These factors encourage individuals to save, make investments, and pursue technological innovations that promote economic growth.

Scholars of international relations have asked whether international connections – trade, investment, and foreign aid – help or hinder poorer countries as they seek to develop. In this section, we look at what scholars have learned about two *challenges* that past and present external conditions may present to poorer nations. Then, we will see what kinds of helpful *opportunities* international participation may provide developing countries as they try to attain faster growth.

Good governance
A country with good governance at home typically possesses transparent and consistent political and legal systems, combats official corruption, and protects property. These factors encourage individuals to save, make investments, and pursue technological innovations that promote economic growth.

Failure to Develop: A Legacy of Colonialism?

Many scholars in the 1960s and 1970s suggested that the lack of growth plaguing many developing countries was due to their colonial heritage. They suggested that former colonies or countries that were highly dominated by European countries or the United States in Latin America, Asia, and Africa might be formally independent, but their economies were still oriented to serving the dominant states at the cost of achieving their own economic wellbeing. These scholars, often informed by some of the Marxist ideas we discussed in Chapter 3, constituted the **dependency** school of underdevelopment (Frank 1966; Dos Santos 1970; Cardoso and Faletto 1979). In response to our enduring question of whether international economic linkages help or hinder development, the dependency school offered the fullest and most consistent answer in the negative.

Dependency
A school of thought that argues that international economic linkages hinder development in developing countries.

Dependency scholars argued that developing countries' elites were controlled by the governments and large corporations in the advanced countries. The local elites directed their national economies toward the needs of the rich nations, serving as a source of raw materials and a market for goods from the rich countries that would be sold to the elite. The result was that a small segment of the population in developing countries prospered, but the country failed to develop indigenous manufacturing and a vibrant working and middle class. World Systems Theory, as put forward most notably by Wallerstein (1974, 1979), argued in a somewhat parallel direction to that of dependency theory that the advanced industrial countries at the 'core' of the world economy dictated how developing countries in the 'periphery' would evolve, and might put constraints on their developmental trajectory. China's attainment during the past quarter-century of a core position in the world economy, and India's progress towards a comparable status, raises questions about the permanence of core-periphery relations as stipulated by World Systems Theory.

Dependency theory commanded progressively less attention from students of development and international relations by around the late 1980s. Perhaps the central reason the approach became less salient and persuasive is that several developing countries, including South Korea, Taiwan, Chile, Mexico, and Brazil, moved toward economic liberalization and integration with the global economy, and all began to achieve economic growth, in some cases dramatically so, even though they were former colonies or were otherwise tightly linked to rich countries through trade and investment. As we will see below, the most prominent dependency writer, Fernando Henrique Cardoso, reversed course and came to favor global economic integration as a pathway to development.

Still, there are good reasons to believe that the impact of colonialism on development has been mixed at best. In some instances, colonial powers created economic infrastructure – roads, railways, ports, and telecommunications systems – that laid the foundation for future growth. In many other instances, colonial powers did little to promote long-term growth. They dictated that their colonies trade exclusively or preferentially with the mother country, instead of having broad access to the markets and products of many other countries. Colonial powers also used coercion to extract economic value. Portugal, for example, used forced or conscripted labor in its African colonies of Angola and Mozambique, often compelling women and children to work without pay to build and pave roads (Anderson 1962). Farmers in Mozambique who traditionally grew subsistence crops for their local communities were forced to cultivate and pick cotton, a cash crop, that is, a crop raised by farmers that is sold in a market for cash rather than consumed by the farmer's household for subsistence, for which Portuguese companies held monopoly rights and reaped the profits.

The development prospects of some former colonies were stunted by the repressive and exploitative practices of their colonial masters. Yet, some former colonies – think for example of the United States, Canada, and South Korea – grew and prospered over time. Moreover, some countries that have faced development challenges are not former colonies (for example, Iran), while others, such as Latin American states that achieved independence in the 1820s and 1830s, broke free of colonial ties long ago. As we noted earlier, what happens within countries over time is, alongside external relations, an important factor in accounting for the development of that country or its lack thereof.

Finally, there is evidence that a colonial legacy *of a certain type* unambiguously imparted harmful dynamics to numerous developing countries (Acemoglu *et al.* 2002; Acemoglu and Robinson 2012). In North America and Australia, where many of the indigenous inhabitants were killed by disease, large numbers of Europeans settled and created laws and political institutions that protected private property and set the stage for long-term economic growth. In Latin America, the Caribbean, and sub-Saharan Africa, where smaller numbers of colonialists settled, the Westerners who did arrive employed highly exploitative legal arrangements to maximize their own short-term profits. The result was a legacy of laws, courts, and regulatory bodies that afforded an inhospitable environment for long-term growth. Hence, in response to our enduring question, there is good reason to say that colonialism kept many countries from achieving long-term growth even after they became independent.

Difficulties in Development: The Division of Labor

In the years immediately after World War II, many developing countries exported agricultural products and raw materials to advanced countries and, in return, imported manufactured goods they needed, such as automobiles, aircraft, or pharmaceuticals. This arrangement would seem to be in everyone's best interest, if we think back to the trade theory presented in Chapter 9. However, as Box 11.1 shows, and reflecting realist concerns that we discussed in Chapters 3 and 9, leaders and policy makers of new countries, from Secretary of the Treasury Alexander Hamilton in the United States in the 1790s to Prime Minister Jawaharlal Nehru of India in the early 1960s, have balked at dependency on other countries for manufactured goods, especially if these goods have an impact on national security.

Reliance on agriculture and raw materials may be a path to development, to the extent that countries use the economic gains created by those activities to generate investments in new areas of manufacturing and services. However, from the 1950s to the present, economists and political scientists have raised concerns about the vulnerability of developing countries that rely too heavily on agriculture and raw materials.

For example, wealthy industrial countries – including the United States, Japan, the member countries of the European Union, and other European countries such as Switzerland – extensively protect their farmers from foreign agricultural competition. Developing countries specializing in agriculture therefore cannot count on full access to those markets. In addition, technological innovations – for example, the use of robotics and computers in the manufacturing of automobiles – improve worker productivity, that is, they enable increases in the amount of output any worker can produce in a fixed period. These technological innovations have been more pervasive in manufacturing than in agriculture or raw materials. These productivity gains promote higher GDP per capita, increasing the economic gap between producers of manufactures and producers of raw materials.

Some raw materials, such as oil, are in high demand and can bring significant profits to their producers. But developing countries blessed with energy reserves must be wary of the '**resource curse**' – the possibility that the possession by developing countries of natural resources, in particular petroleum, is more likely to hinder

Resource curse
The possibility that the possession by developing countries of natural resources, in particular petroleum, is more likely to hinder rather than to advance the development prospects of those countries.

11.1   MAKING CONNECTIONS
Then and Now

State Leaders Describe the Importance of National Economic Self-Sufficiency

Then: Treasury Secretary Alexander Hamilton on Promoting American Industry, 1791

At the outset of its history, the United States had an overwhelmingly agricultural economy, and important American leaders such as Thomas Jefferson believed that America would safeguard its republican institutions most effectively if it remained rooted in agriculture. However, in a major report to Congress in December 1791, Secretary of the Treasury Alexander Hamilton argued that the new nation should possess an agriculture base but also encourage manufacturing. He suggested:

> From these circumstances collectively two important inferences are to be drawn: One, that there is always a higher probability of a favorable balance of trade, in regard to countries in which manufactures, founded on the basis of a thriving agriculture, flourish, than in regard to those which are confined wholly, or almost wholly, to agriculture; the other (which is also a consequence of the first) that countries of the former description are likely to possess more pecuniary wealth or money than those of the latter … Not only the wealth, but the independence and security of a country appear to be materially connected with the prosperity of manufactures. Every nation, with a view to those great objects, ought to endeavor to possess within itself all the essentials of national supply.

> Source: U.S. National Archives. Undated. Founders Online: Alexander Hamilton's Final Version of the Report on the Subject of Manufactures, 5 December 1791. Available at https://founders.archives.gov/documents/Hamilton/01-10-02-0001-0007.

Now: Prime Minister Jawaharlal Nehru on Building MIGs in India, 1962

In June 1962, Prime Minister Nehru announced to the Indian Parliament that India would purchase several Soviet MIG-21 fighter jets rather than seek to buy relatively more advanced fighters from the United States or the United Kingdom. Nehru acknowledged that the MIG-21s India would buy and later build were less advanced technologically than the F-104s that Pakistan had recently purchased from the United States. However, Nehru told the members of parliament that he had selected the MIG-21 option because the Soviets had agreed they would license and assist in Indian domestic manufacture of that model of jet fighters. For Nehru, even though the MIG-21 was not the most advanced fighter aircraft available, the licensing agreement with the Soviets, which would eventually see the production of several such aircraft built in India, was critically important: It was more practical to have the capacity to manufacture second-rate equipment in one's own country than to be tied into an arrangement to buy first-rate equipment from outside. While separated in time by almost two centuries, both America's Alexander Hamilton and India's Jawaharlal Nehru argued that national self-sufficiency in manufacturing is an important and valid economic policy goal for a new country.

Source: Graham (1964): 826.

rather than to advance the development prospects of those countries. Developing countries with large endowments of natural resources, including those for which, like petroleum, there is strong external demand, tend to grow more slowly than do countries without such resources. Think, for example, of the difference in the growth experiences of Nigeria, a major oil exporter, and Singapore, which imports petroleum: while the former's GDP per capita tripled from about $900 in 1980 to about $2,700 in 2015, that of Singapore during the same period grew by a factor of more than ten, from $4,900 to almost $54,000. There are likely to be multiple causes of this observed link between natural resources and sub-par economic performance by developing countries. Most notably, a developing country that exports oil will experience a 'wealth shock,' that is, managers and workers in the oil sector will find that there is a high demand for their services and a corresponding increase in their incomes. That increase in income of participants in the oil sector translates into higher wages throughout the economy; this translates into a decrease in the international competitiveness of domestic producers in manufacturing industries. In addition, external demand for the natural resources of the countries will translate into heightened demand for and price of the country's currency, and this will further depress the competitiveness of non-oil domestic industries. The slackening demand for the output of those domestic industries dampens the overall growth of the country (Sachs and Warner 2001: 833–5).

As we discuss in Box 11.2, there is also growing scholarship by political scientists that suggests another deleterious consequence of the 'resource curse' for many developing countries is that many of them experience disproportionately poor governance, high levels of domestic unrest and civil wars, and even a heightened propensity to launch military conflicts against other countries.

In summary, a colonial past and a lack of national manufacturing in the present, especially if the country possesses natural resources to the extent it experiences the natural resource curse, may combine to inhibit economic growth in the global economy for developing countries. But to what extent can international trade and the resulting globalization serve as a tool for economic development?

11.2 RESEARCH INSIGHT

Natural Resources and Political Dysfunctionality at Home and Abroad

The Problem

Economists have recently identified what is called the 'resource curse' – the possibility that the possession by developing countries of natural resources such as petroleum is more likely to hinder rather than advance their development prospects. Oil production may bring great wealth. However, when we look around the world, it seems that the possession of oil has other deleterious consequences for many developing countries. Consider, for example, the extraordinary civil unrest in recent years in Venezuela and the domestic violence in Nigeria perpetrated by the jihadist militant group, Boko Haram. Some oil-rich developing countries also seem to have a habit of starting military disputes with neighbors, as evidenced by Iraq's aggression against first Iran in 1988 and then Kuwait in 1990. Does the possession of oil not just impair economic development directly, by way for example of a wealth-shock, but indirectly, by instigating growth-retarding domestic strife and international aggression?

Photo 11.2 Evidence of the Resource Curse in Nigeria
Oil from illegal refineries is ferried to the market in Bayelsa, Nigeria in 2013. Over the past decade, militants claiming to be fighting for a fairer distribution of oil revenue attacked oil facilities, carried out widespread kidnappings, and clashed with police in this impoverished Niger Delta region.

Source: PIUS UTOMI EKPEI/AFP/Getty Images.

The Research Insight

In a wide-ranging review of the domestic political-economy literature on this subject, including his own important work (2001, 2004, 2012), Michael Ross shows that the ability of despots to use oil revenues to buy off supporters, purchase weapons and other instruments of state repression, and attract foreign support fortifies authoritarian regimes and makes them resistant to democracy (Ross 2015: 243–8). He also shows that the possession of oil exacerbates government corruption and thus hinders the creation of growth-enabling legal and regulatory institutions (2015: 248–50). Finally, he explains that oil and other natural resources such as diamonds can become both highly prized stakes and revenue-generators that can be used to recruit both rebels and government forces, and by consequence can be spurs to civil wars (250–2).

Similarly, Jeff Colgan (2010, 2012) observes that what he terms 'petrostates,' (countries whose annual oil-export revenues constitute 10 percent or more of that country's annual GDP), have been more than twice as likely since 1970 as non-petrostates to initiate militarized interstate disputes (MIDs, as we discussed in Chapter 6). Colgan shows that not all petrostates are equally bellicose toward other countries. Rather, weaving together insights from security studies and international political economy, Colgan argues that the combination of national oil resources and a government led by a revolutionary regime (that is, a government that has come to power by way of an overthrow, almost always violent, of an incumbent regime) may cause the resulting revolutionary petrostate to be especially prone to launching MIDs. Why this combination? Colgan suggests that, in the first place, oil revenues allow the revolutionary leader to buy support and the means of repression, thus reducing the chances of being deposed if a foreign military operation is unsuccessful. In addition, and in accord with arguments about interstate conflict initiation we examined in Chapter 6, revolutionary leaders may have an especially high tolerance for the risk associated with such operations, and the revolutionary process by which they came to power may have eviscerated domestic institutions and processes that otherwise would have inhibited the launching of MIDs against other countries.

Levels of Analysis *International Challenges to Developing Countries*

🦅 State	🌐 International
National laws and institutions, inherited from a colonial past, can sometimes promote, yet often inhibit, economic growth.	Reliance on agriculture and raw material production can spark economic growth but may also trap countries in an international division of labor in which it becomes difficult to develop more diversified economies.
The resource curse can propel a country's political system and economy in the direction of distorted economic and foreign policies and even its international conflict behavior.	

IS INTERNATIONAL TRADE A PATH TO DEVELOPMENT?

Since World War II, poorer countries have pursued different strategies to overcome the challenges we have previously described and to create opportunities for development. From roughly the 1950s into the 1970s, many developing countries, including such major countries as China, India, Mexico, Brazil, and Turkey, sought to restrict or at least control their trading linkages with developed countries. By the late 1970s and into the 1990s, when it became clear that those market-controlling strategies had failed to deliver sustained growth, these and other developing countries increasingly turned to more outward-looking strategies.

Market-Controlling Trade Strategies

Developing countries have pursued three basic market-controlling strategies to improve their economic position: infant-industry oriented policies to promote national industries, international commodity cartels, and international commodity agreements.

Import-Substituting Industrialization

Import-substituting industrialization (ISI)
A national development strategy that seeks to avoid international economic linkages in favor of focusing on domestic production.

In the two decades after World War II, many developing countries, notably Brazil, India, Mexico, and Turkey, acted in line with the infant-industry logic we discussed in Chapter 9 and pursued **import-substituting industrialization (ISI)**. The intellectual inspiration behind ISI came from an Argentine economist, Raúl Prebisch, who directed the UN's first Economic Commission for Latin America. The roots of ISI also take us once more to the Great Depression of the 1930s, when international markets for raw materials and agricultural products collapsed, and thereby forced developing countries that relied on those markets to search for alternative ways to generate growth. Anti-colonial sentiment also contributed to ISI's appeal. Prebisch and others were critical of the international division of labor that seemed to lock developing states into selling primary goods and buying finished goods from their former colonial masters.

The strategy of ISI was premised on answering our enduring question partially in the negative: under then-existing conditions most developing countries could not benefit greatly from international economic integration if that integration unfolded strictly under the terms of the logic of traditional trade theory. A different approach was needed. In adopting ISI, governmental leaders wanted their consumers to substitute imports of manufactured goods, such as automobiles, with comparable domestically produced goods. Governments pursued ISI with high tariffs on imports of goods targeted for substitution, and subsidies (such as cash grants and low-cost loans) to pre-selected local manufacturers. These **national champions** were firms the government believed could do the best job of producing the substituted industrial goods. Ultimately, the expectation was that these national champions could compete at home without protection, and even become leaders in foreign markets.

ISI registered some success in the initial postwar decades. India, for example, experienced rapid economic growth pursuing ISI, with industrial output doubling during the 1950s and growing by 9 percent annually between 1960 and 1965 (Krueger 1975). India decreased its imports of manufactured goods and created domestic capacity, particularly in the types of machinery and equipment needed to produce final goods. Similarly, Brazil, Mexico, and Argentina enjoyed rapid growth during the 1950s and 1960s and established indigenous capacity in automobiles, steel, and machinery production.

The weaknesses of ISI became apparent by the 1970s. National champions and other domestic firms were safely behind high tariff walls. They did not face international competition and had little incentive to charge low prices at home or make internationally competitive products. The results were current-account deficits and domestic price inflation. Inflation and resulting periodic economic slowdowns sometimes led to political upheaval and military coups, such as in Brazil, Chile, and Argentina during the 1960s. By the 1970s, larger developing countries abandoned the 'go it alone' spirit of ISI and tried to attract foreign direct investment from advanced economies, while smaller developing states engaged the world economy through export strategies, both of which we discuss below.

International Commodity Cartels

Rather than seeking to diversify away from raw material production, some developing countries instead have banded together and tried to gain greater economic benefits from selling their natural resources. These countries have formed state-sponsored **international commodity cartels**, which are groupings of developing-country governments that try to control the supply of a raw material or agricultural product on world markets to drive up prices and maximize their revenues. In recent decades, there have been international commodity cartels in bauxite, rubber, diamonds, and, most notably, oil. For a variety of reasons, such as the entry of new suppliers or the availability of substitutes, these cartels do not appear to have been very successful in maximizing cartel-member revenues.

A partial exception is the Organization of the Petroleum Exporting Countries (OPEC), which was founded in 1960, has 12 members (including Saudi Arabia, Iran, Iraq, Kuwait, Nigeria, and Venezuela), and is headquartered in Vienna, Austria. Representatives of OPEC nations meet periodically to set an overall oil production level for the cartel and allocate production quotas for individual members.

OPEC has had some success in limiting oil supplies on global markets; less supply typically does lead to higher prices. Yet, OPEC's success has been constrained by the fact that cartel members often cheat and produce more than their quotas. Moreover, such oil-producing countries as Russia, Canada, and Mexico are not members of the cartel, and when prices go up these producers have an incentive to increase production. Finally, the United States, making use of new oil-extraction technologies captured by the term 'fracking,' is becoming a major oil producer both for the its home market and global energy markets.

Still, OPEC countries, and especially Saudi Arabia, will be important to the future of the oil industry. As can be observed in Figure 11.2, in 2016 OPEC countries produced

National champion
In a state pursuing a strategy of ISI, the government nominates firms it believes could do the best job of producing the substituted industrial goods.

International commodity cartels
Groupings of developing-country governments that try to control the supply of a raw material or agricultural product on world markets in order to drive up prices and maximize revenues.

405

Figure 11.2 Global Oil Production and Proven Reserves, 2016
These two figures underscore the importance of OPEC, and particularly OPEC member Saudi Arabia, in world production of oil and especially in terms of proven reserves of oil.

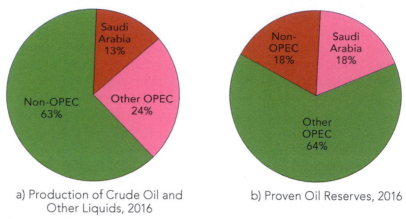

a) Production of Crude Oil and
Other Liquids, 2016

b) Proven Oil Reserves, 2016

Source: For production, see U.S. Energy Information Agency, available at https://www.eia.gov/; for proven reserves, see OPEC, "OPEC Share of World Crude Oil Reserves, 2016" available at http://www.opec.org/opec_web/en/data_graphs/330.htm.

about 37 percent of the world's oil and other energy-related liquids, and that year OPEC countries possessed about 82 percent of the world's proven reserves of crude oil.

International Commodity Agreements

Cartels such as OPEC consist of agreements among suppliers of a good or commodity that seek to limit production to maximize prices and revenues. An alternative approach used by some developing countries has been to press consumer countries (mainly advanced nations) to establish an **international commodity agreement**, or ICA, which would include both supplier and consumer countries, and would seek agreements on the supply and prices for a particular commodity. In these cases, the developing countries have not sought agreements that lead to maximum prices for their commodity exports, but a reduction in price fluctuations for their exports. The objective for developing countries is to attain reasonably good prices and some sense of certainty about what their countries will be earning from their exports. Five ICAs were established from the 1950s to the 1970s for sugar, coffee, tin, cocoa, and rubber.

However, these agreements often did not include all suppliers of the commodity in question (as in the case of cocoa). New suppliers could also enter an industry (the countries that now make up the European Union in regard to sugar) and existing members could exit an agreement (Thailand, Sri Lanka, and Malaysia in connection with the rubber agreement). As a result of these factors, all five ICAs were abandoned between the early 1980s and late 1990s (Gilbert 2004).

Market-Accepting Trade Strategies

Countries that pursued ISI believed, in line with the basic thrust of dependency theory, that participating in world markets created the risk of stunted economic development. However, countries that turned to ISI often experienced high government debts and very low rates of national growth. As an alternative, a few developing countries with smaller domestic markets in the late 1950s and into the 1960s sought renewed growth

International commodity agreement An agreement, generally sought by developing countries' exporters, on the supply and price of that commodity. The goal is not to maximize prices but rather to establish an acceptable, consistent price that the developing country can rely on.

through a strategy of **export-led growth (ELG)**. This strategy basically answers our enduring question in the affirmative: it is premised on the view that the international economy presents important opportunities for development. The strategy typically includes two basic components. First, national producers of goods for the local market are no longer offered preferential access to government credit or foreign exchange. Second, firms producing for export markets are now granted preferential access to credit and foreign currency.

ELG was adopted by Japan after World War II, along with domestic protectionism, and was the basis of the 'economic miracle' that catapulted it from the ruins of war to the world's second largest national economy by the early 1980s. By the 1960s, the four **Asian Tigers** that had been early in choosing or switching to ELG – Taiwan, South Korea, Singapore, and Hong Kong – were achieving fast rates of growth in GDP per capita, and served as models for other East Asian countries that turned to ELG in the 1970s, such as Thailand, Malaysia, and mainland China.

Soon, even countries with large internal markets moved from ISI toward an export-oriented strategy of development. Turkey, Brazil, and Mexico made this shift during the 1980s, and India did so in the early 1990s. Many academics and policy makers shifted from skepticism to optimism about the possibilities of such integration. Indeed, as Box 11.3 shows, the most distinguished dependency writer, Fernando Henrique Cardoso of Brazil, shifted his perspective on the benefits of economic integration, and took on a markedly strong pro-market and pro-integration orientation when he became Finance Minister and then President of Brazil. Using terms we discussed in Chapter 10, Cardoso shifted from a Marxist perspective (underdevelopment was a function of the capitalist world economy) and economic nationalist perspective (the solution was greater national self-sufficiency) to a more liberal perspective (development comes from embracing, not resisting, the liberal world economy).

By the 1990s, many developing countries were not just turning to exports as the path to growth. They were also implementing packages of other policies reflecting what, as we noted in Chapter 9, came to be known as the Washington Consensus. In the present era, in the wake of the global economic crisis and the continuing rise of China, a potential new model of development has come into view, sometimes called the **Beijing Consensus**. This term is meant to suggest that, for some poorer countries, the necessary answer to our enduring question is more nuanced than might be expected from a move from ISI or full autarky to unbridled ELG based on the Washington Consensus. Rather, according to the Beijing Consensus, global economic integration presents important opportunities for development, but in a world of economic turbulence developing countries should use government controls to manage the pace of trade integration, capital inflows and outflows, the movement of labor within the country, and the external value of the national currency. Moreover, while the United States and other wealthy countries have argued that democratic political institutions are most likely to provide the best long-term environment for growth in poorer countries, the Beijing Consensus holds that authoritarianism may enable growth to occur most rapidly in a developing nation. Only time will tell if the Beijing Consensus will gain traction and give state capitalism and authoritarianism new legitimacy in the years ahead.

Recall that Chapter 10 focused on the relationship between states and markets, and on the trade-offs governments face between economic efficiency and political autonomy. Now we see another dimension of the state–market relationship. Countries seeking economic development at times have relied more heavily on government

Export-led growth (ELG)
A strategy that argues developing countries should rely on price-competitive exports to stimulate national economic development.

Asian Tigers
Originally Taiwan, South Korea, Singapore, and Hong Kong, who achieved rapid growth rates using a strategy of export-led growth. Now many rapidly growing Asian countries are considered 'tigers.'

Beijing Consensus
The idea that, for some poor countries, development can be best attained by government controls, trade integration, capital inflows and outflows, the movement of labor, and the external value of the currency.

11.3   DIFFERING PERSPECTIVES

Fernando Henrique Cardoso on the Benefits of International Economic Integration

Cardoso Writing as Academic Critic, 1971/1979:

Of course, imperialist penetration is a result of external social forces (multinational enterprises, foreign technology, international financial systems, embassies, foreign states and armies, etc.). What we affirm simply means that the system of domination reappears as an 'internal' force, through the social practices of local groups and classes which try to enforce foreign interests, not precisely because they are foreign, but because they may coincide with values and interests that these groups pretend are their own. It has been assumed that the peripheral countries would have to repeat the evolution of the economies of the central countries in order to achieve development. But it is clear that from its beginning the capitalist process implied an unequal relation between the central and the peripheral economies. Many 'underdeveloped' economies – as is the case of the Latin American – were incorporated into the capitalist system as colonies and later as national states, and they have stayed in the capitalist system throughout their history. They remain, however, peripheral economies with particular historical paths when compared with central capitalist economies.

Source: Cardoso and Faletto (1979).

Cardoso as Presidential Candidate and then President of Brazil, 1994, 2002:

The international system is a field of opportunities, of resources, that must be sought naturally. We are a great country, with a clear vocation for an active and responsible participation in world affairs. The process of liberalization of the economy and opening toward the outside world will continue, not an objective in and of itself, but as a strategic element in the modernization of our economy

Source: 'Let's Work, Brazil,' the main campaign statement of the then Finance Minister Cardoso as he ran successfully for the first of two terms as President of Brazil, quoted in Brown (1994).

Question: Mr. Cardoso, you are a sociologist and have studied, analyzed and written about the Brazilian society. As President and sociologist what is your advice to foreign investors when they come to invest in Brazil?

Response: My advice is probably superfluous, because the strength of the Brazilian economy speaks for itself. But I will say this: those who bet on Brazil's future stand to gain a lot, because the country has all it takes to continue in the path of social and economic development. For too long has Brazil suffered in stagnation and backwardness. This chapter is now closed. With democracy, economic stability and greater social justice, there is nothing that can stop Brazil in its progress. Our economic environment is business-friendly. Our people [are] hard-working, creative and eager to learn more. The country is not affected by any sort of ethnic rivalries or civil strife. We have world-class universities and world-class scientists. Investors who come to Brazil will be partners in our development and they will get the very significant returns of operating in a market of over 160 million people, or even more if you consider the integration with our neighbors in Mercosul.

Source: interview by World Investment News (WINNE) with President Cardoso, World Investment News (2002).

intervention (the era of ISI) and at times on market forces (the era of the Washington Consensus). If the Beijing Consensus spreads, the pendulum may swing back to a renewed emphasis on the importance of the state in economic development.

 Simulations: What would you do? Visit the companion website to step into the shoes of an Economic Development Secretary in South Asia. Would you follow the Beijing Consensus? See what happens as you pursue different courses of action.

Strategies to Reshape the Rules of International Trade

Many developing countries have accepted and benefited from economic integration and globalization, but this does not mean they have simply removed barriers to trade and allowed global market forces to dictate their trading patterns. Since the end of World War II developing countries have sought, with limited success, to shape the rules of the global economy more in their favor. In the 1960s, as we saw in Chapter 2, developing countries used their power in numbers in the UN to form the Group of 77 and lobby collectively for development-friendly reforms in trade and finance. Their appeals, for the most part, were ignored by the stronger developed countries. Perhaps the most promising negotiating attempt took place in the 1970s, as many countries in the developing world sought to ally with OPEC and use its prominence to demand a New International Economic Order (NIEO). The NIEO demanded preferential trade arrangements, larger aid grants to less developed countries, and controls on multinational enterprises (MNEs) operating within their borders. OPEC countries eventually made their own deals with the United States and Europe, leaving the larger group of developing countries with little leverage to generate change in international trade rules. The NIEO quietly faded away.

In recent years, influential developing nations, such as Brazil and India, have sought to forge a coalition of developing countries to press for better deals in the World Trade Organization (WTO). For example, these two countries, together with China and South Africa, brought together a coalition of developing countries that helped block completion of the Doha Round of WTO multilateral trade negotiations, which as noted in Chapter 9 had been launched in 2001 in Doha, Qatar. If multilateral trade liberalization via the WTO is to have a future, it will require greater accommodation of the demands of these influential developing countries.

Fair trade negotiations may offer potential growth, but what role does international finance play in economic development? The next section will explore types of international financial flows and their impact on economic development.

Levels of Analysis *Trade as an Opportunity for Developing Countries*	
State	International
Developing countries adopt different individual and collective strategies in their efforts to get a better deal from their interaction with the world economy, and in some cases this means their withdrawal from that stage.	Most collective negotiating efforts by developing countries to change the rules of international trade have not been successful, reflecting the lack of developing-country power in international politics and economics.
	Today the situation is changing, as developing countries, led by China, Brazil, and India, have become more influential.

IS INTERNATIONAL FINANCE A PATH TO DEVELOPMENT?

Developing countries often rely on foreign capital, but there is sharp controversy as to whether such capital is helpful to them. Below we define international financial flows, examine the different types, and explore the opportunities and problems they pose for developing countries.

International Financial Flows: Meaning, Types, and Magnitudes

International financial flows
The movement of capital from private or governmental individuals or organizations inside one country to private or governmental individuals or organizations inside another country. These flows consist of both private and official financial flows.

Private financial flows
International financial flows that originate with nongovernmental entities, such as individuals, private charities, or private firms such as banks or multinational enterprises.

Official financial flows
International financial flows that originate with governmental entities.

By an **international financial flow**, we mean the movement of capital – sometimes in the form of actual cash, but usually as a result of electronic transfers – from private or governmental individuals or organizations inside one country to private or governmental individuals or organizations inside another country. There are two basic forms of financial flows to developing countries: private and official. **Private financial flows** are flows that originate with nongovernmental entities, such as individuals, private charities, or private firms such as banks or multinational enterprises. **Official financial flows** are flows that originate with governmental entities. These entities may be individual governments or intergovernmental organizations formed by governments, such as the World Bank, the International Monetary Fund, the European Union, the Asian Development Bank, and the Inter-American Development Bank.

As Figure 11.3 indicates, total financial flows to developing countries have increased steadily since the 1980s, exceeding $1.0 trillion in 2016. Moreover, while in 1980 and 1990 official sources of financial flows to developing countries equaled or exceeded those from private sources, by the 2000s the vast majority of financial flows to developing countries came from private sources (with the exception of sub-Saharan Africa, as we discuss further below). For example, private sources provided about 80 percent of the total external financial resources that went to developing countries in 2016.

As with international investments in general, as we discussed in Chapter 9, there are four basic kinds of private capital flows to developing countries. First,

Figure 11.3 Total Private and Official Financial Flows to Developing Countries, 1980–2016
This figure underscores how private financial flows to developing countries have grown compared to financial flows from official sources.

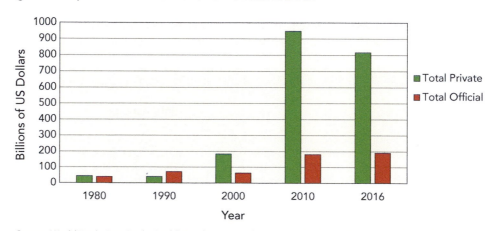

Source: World Bank, DataBank, World Development Indicators, available at http://databank.worldbank.org/data/reports.aspx?source=world-development-indicators.

foreign direct investment (FDI) occurs when an enterprise in one country moves capital to another country with the intention of establishing an ongoing business presence. The investing firm is usually a multinational enterprise. So, for example, when the technology firm IBM establishes a wholly owned subsidiary in Mexico, this constitutes a US FDI in Mexico. Another major type of private capital flow consists of international bank loans, whereby a bank in one country extends a loan to residents (which might be private individuals, firms, or a government) in another country. For example, if Deutsche Bank makes a loan to a private Mexican cement firm, that represents a bank-loan capital flow from Germany to Mexico. A third type of private financial flow to developing countries consists of international portfolio investments. If, for example, a Canadian-based mutual fund buys shares in the hypothetical Mexican cement firm noted above, *but not enough to have any management say in what that cement firm does*, then this is an instance in which there has been Canadian portfolio investment in Mexico. Finally, there are international bonds. For example, if a Mexican cement firm issues bonds in euros that are purchased by French pension funds, then this represents a bond-based capital flow from France to Mexico.

Figure 11.4 illustrates changes in the relative importance of these four kinds of private capital flows to developing countries. As it indicates, foreign direct investment has become by far the biggest single type of private financial flow into developing countries. For example, FDI flows to developing countries in 2016 totaled about $570 billion, representing about 70 percent of total private capital flows to developing countries that year.

There are two basic kinds of official financial flows to developing countries. First, there is bilateral **official development assistance (ODA)**, the provision by a donor government to a developing country of grants or loans with highly favorable repayment terms (for example, 50 years to repay, at 1 percent interest). Second, multilateral institutions such as the IMF and the World Bank, as well as regional financial institutions such as the Asian Development Bank, and the European Bank for Reconstruction and Development (EBRD), make loans to developing countries

Official development assistance (ODA) The provision by a donor government to a developing country of grants or loans with highly favorable repayment terms (for example, 50 years to repay, at 1 percent interest).

Figure 11.4 Composition of Private Financial Flows to Developing Countries, 1980–2016
This figure underscores two key points: first, private flows of capital to developing countries have grown substantially; and second, foreign direct investment has become by far the largest type of private financial flow to developing countries.

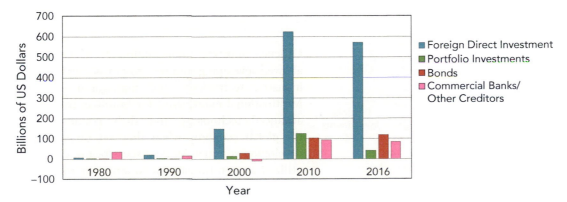

Source: World Bank, World Databank, Development Indicators, available at http://databank.worldbank.org/ ddp/home. do?Step= 12&id=4&CNO=2.

Figure 11.5 Official Financial Flows to Developing Countries, by Type, 1980–2016
Bilateral ODA has been and remains the most important type of official financial flows to developing countries, although loans from multilateral official creditors like the World Bank are important.

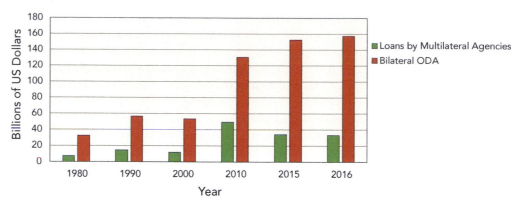

Source: World Bank, World Databank, Development Indicators, available at http://databank.worldbank.org/ddp/home.do?Step= 12&id=4&CNO=2.

Figure 11.6 Private and Official Financial Flows to Countries in Sub-Saharan Africa, 2016
Financial flows to sub-Saharan Africa in 2016 totaled about $100 billion. Funds from official sources (bilateral ODA plus loans from multilateral institutions like the World Bank) represented about 52% of that total. Foreign direct investment also constituted an important source of external flows into the region.

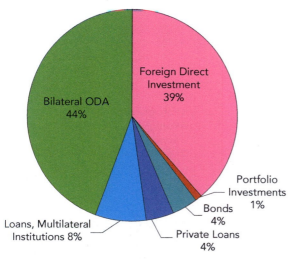

Source: World Bank, World DataBank, World Development Indicators, available at http://databank.worldbank.org/data/reports.aspx?source=world-development-indicators.

with near-market interest rates and repayment periods, to help those countries meet short-term cash needs or pursue big projects like dams and ports. These are termed financial flows from *official creditors*. With this background in mind, we can see in Figure 11.5 that, as of 2016, annual total official flows to developing countries have been in the range of about $190 billion, with about 83 percent of that consisting of ODA.

Official flows remain important for sub-Saharan Africa. As Figure 11.6 indicates, financial flows of all types to developing countries in sub-Saharan Africa totaled about $100 billion in 2016. Of that total, about one-half consisted of ODA and loans from multilateral institutions. Sub-Saharan Africa, then, while making substantial economic progress, still requires official economic assistance to meet its financial needs and attract resources from private investors and creditors.

Opportunities and Challenges for Developing Countries

Official and private financial flows from abroad have allowed developing countries to gain access to foreign industry, technology, and managerial expertise. Multinational enterprises, for example, bring more advanced technology and their connections to the global economy when they set up shop in a developing country. As we discuss below, China has utilized foreign investment to attain its remarkable growth over the past three decades. Yet, although the potential benefits are significant, foreign capital can also create challenges for developing countries.

Bank Loans, Portfolio Investments, and Risk of Financial Crises

Many developing countries have learned that private capital flows from abroad, especially international bank loans and portfolio investments, can be quite volatile. Foreign investors seem to follow a pattern of becoming enthralled with prospects in developing countries, and then, at any warning sign of balance-of-payment or currency difficulties, fear overtakes greed and investors head for the exits. For example, a cycle of strong financial inflows followed by extremely rapid exits of capital contributed to a painful economic crisis during 1994–95 in Mexico. An even more dramatic financial crisis hit the developing world during 1997–98. At that time, a collapse in the stock market and currency in Thailand soon led foreign investors to pull their money out of the Philippines, Indonesia, and Malaysia, and even from seemingly strong countries like Taiwan and South Korea (Haggard 2000). Investors, afraid of having exposure to any developing or emerging market, soon pulled funds out of Russia and Brazil. The Russian government effectively defaulted on the country's debts, and Brazil radically increased the interest rates it paid to its creditors, to make the country attractive once more to foreign investors.

Multinational Enterprises: Opportunities and Concerns

Mainstream economic theory suggests that MNEs that undertake foreign direct investment in a host country, either developed or developing, contribute to the latter's stock of capital, technology, and managerial expertise, and thereby augment the growth of the industries in which the foreign investments occur and the overall economic growth of the country. Engaging with MNEs helps, rather than hinders, economic development. On the other hand, as we discussed in Chapter 9, critics of globalization have suggested that multinational enterprises that move to developing countries exploit workers, especially women and children, and avoid the stronger legal and governmental regulatory standards that protect workers and the natural environment in the advanced industrial countries (Graham 2000; Evans 2000; Neumayer and De Soysa 2006).

One way multinational enterprises have responded to these charges has been to establish codes of conduct (Locke, Amengual, and Mangla 2009). For many years, for example, Pakistani suppliers of soccer balls for such firms as Nike, Adidas, and Puma used child labor. When this practice was made public in a June 1996 story in *Life* magazine, nongovernmental organizations (NGOs) vigorously protested Nike and other multinational sports firms. As a result, the firms entered negotiations with the United Nations International Children's Emergency Fund (UNICEF), the International Labor Organization (ILO), and several NGOs. In early 1997, the international firms and their Pakistani suppliers agreed to a code of conduct, the Atlanta Agreement, named for the city in which it was signed, that committed the international firms, as well as their

Photo 11.3 Child Labor in Developing Countries
A concern about the operations of multinational enterprises in developing countries is that some foreign firms might rely on local contractors that employ child labor.

Source: iStock.com/Tapshanov.

413

Pakistani contractors, to stop using child labor. The trade association that represented the multinational sports firms later reported (Gorgemans 2008) that at least 6,000 children were taken out of soccer-ball workshops in the Pakistani city of Sialkot, where most of the largest suppliers were located.

The debate about FDI, multinational enterprises, and economic development has abated in recent years, in part because it appears that there is no single correct answer to the question of whether MNEs promote economic development. In Asia, for example, foreign investment in manufacturing sectors has had a strongly positive impact on economic development (Wang 2009). More generally, FDI is especially likely to foster growth in both developed and developing host countries, but its effects to date have been more positive in the former than in the latter (Li and Liu 2005). One key reason for this difference appears to be the capacity of the different types of host countries to absorb the technology associated with MNE investments. Among developed countries MNE investments seem to spur technological innovation, and while this sometimes happens in developing countries the positive impact brought about by the technology transfer associated with MNE investments tends not to be as large or certain.

Official Aid Flows: Help or Hindrance to Developing Countries?

For many years there have been serious controversies regarding the benefits or dangers of official aid to developing countries. Indeed, it is regarding foreign aid that we observe the most divergent answers to the enduring question about whether international linkages are a good or bad idea for developing countries. For example, critics suggest that the practice of **tied aid** reduces the beneficial impact of bilateral aid. In tied aid, donor governments often require that the funds they give to a recipient country must be used to purchase goods and services provided by firms from the donor country. The tying of aid suppresses international competition among firms who supply goods and services for the project being funded, which in turn reduces the efficiency of the aid for the developing country. According to the World Bank (1998), the loss in efficiency may reduce the effective value of the aid by about 25 percent.

In recent years, there has also been a serious debate about whether foreign aid promotes growth in developing countries. In theory, as illustrated in Box 11.4, foreign aid is supposed to act as a stepping stone to economic progress for developing countries. In Africa, no such positive association seems to be evident from the 1970s to the end of the 1990s.

Economist William Easterly (2002b, 2006, 2007) has argued that the foreign aid strategies of wealthy donor countries (and the multilateral institutions they control, the World Bank and the IMF) have done little systematic good in the developing world. In addition to the data summarized in Box 11.4, Easterly emphasizes that if we look back over the past five decades, the rich industrial countries have provided $2.3 trillion in aid to developing countries. At the end of that period, three billion people were still living on $2 or less per day, 840 million were suffering from hunger, and 10 million children were dying each year from preventable diseases.

Easterly offers several reasons why aid has not promoted growth in the developing world. First, economists and aid bureaucrats simply do not understand the dynamics of economic growth sufficiently well to design large-scale aid programs that consistently promote growth throughout the developing world. Moreover, providing aid to often highly corrupt developing-country governments greatly reduces the effectiveness of aid. We have, for example, the case of Zaire under the notoriously

Tied aid
A practice in which donor governments require that the funds they give to a recipient country must be used to purchase goods and services provided by firms from the donor country.

11.4   MAKING CONNECTIONS
Theory and Practice

Foreign Aid and Economic Development in Africa
Theory: Foreign Aid as a Spur to Development

Foreign assistance from official sources is supposed to catalyze economic development in poorer countries through a number of pathways. Most important, such financial assistance is supposed to make up for shortfalls in domestic capital formation. Moreover, if foreign official donors provide funds for important infrastructure projects, such as shipping port facilities, roads, or airports, private investors from abroad will be more likely to invest in the country, since it will have stronger foundations for economic activity. Finally, foreign official assistance usually comes with foreign expertise and advice on how to implement economic development projects, providing greater chances of efficient utilization of the resources.

Practice: Apparent Negative Relationship between Aid and Growth in Africa, 1970s–90s

The economist William Easterly constructed the figure below. It reports both the receipt of foreign aid (as a percent of GDP) received by African countries, and the growth in per capita GDP of those countries, from the early 1970s to the late 1990s. While aid increased as a percentage of GDP in the region during this period, growth in GDP per capita went down. Many causes may have acted individually and jointly to eviscerate the effectiveness of the aid: civil wars in numerous African countries may have hampered aid programs, the programs themselves may have been poorly designed or implemented by donor governments, and corruption on the part of recipient governments may have prevented the aid from going to households and firms that would have made efficient use of the aid resources.

Figure 11.7 Foreign Assistance and Economic Growth in Africa, 1970–99*
While foreign official assistance is supposed to serve as a motor of economic development of poorer countries, this positive impact of aid did not occur in Africa over a period of three decades.

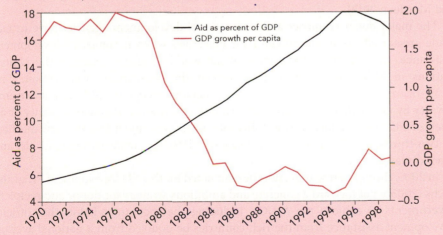

* The data for each year represents the average per capita GDP growth rate and the average rate of aid [as a percenatge of GDP] over the previous 10 years.

Source: William Easterly, 'The Cartel of Good Intentions,' *Foreign Policy* 131 (July-August 2002a), p. 45. Used by permission.

corrupt government headed by Mobutu Sese Seko: between the late 1970s and 1990, the IMF provided the Mobutu government no fewer than 11 loans, none of which materially helped Zaire make progress in attaining economic development.

Easterly does not say that international aid should be altogether ended. Instead, he argues that donor governments should give up on the idea that there is a single 'grand strategy' to institute development in all poor countries. Donor governments should instead design more tailored aid programs that ensure feedback is generated on whether the aid is working, require accountability for national and international officials if the projects they put into place fail to produce results, find ways to bypass corrupt developing-country governments, and provide more targeted assistance to individual entrepreneurs or social activists in recipient countries.

In contrast, economist Jeffrey Sachs (2005a) has suggested that a new grand design for foreign aid by the rich countries could make a major contribution to ending poverty in the developing world. Sachs acknowledges that if a developing country has a deeply corrupt (what he terms a 'predatory') government, economic development is unlikely to occur. However, even a well-governed developing country is unlikely to achieve economic growth, Sachs argues, without outside assistance if that country is caught in a **poverty trap**: when it is so poor that most of its national resources must be used to satisfy the immediate day-to-day needs of the population, with insufficient resources left for savings or investment, such as better irrigation systems for farmers or better railways and roads for commerce, to propel the country toward higher incomes tomorrow. According to Sachs, many of the especially poor countries in sub-Saharan Africa are in precisely this situation.

Poverty trap
When a country is so poor that most of its national resources must be used to satisfy the immediate day-to-day needs of the population, with insufficient resources left for savings or investment.

The solution is to find an alternative source of investment resources. Sachs suggests that a massive injection of outside aid could serve that function for countries in sub-Saharan Africa that commit themselves to good governance. Well-designed aid programs, Sachs suggests, that involve close coordination among the donors and international aid institutions like the World Bank could effectively end poverty if donor countries doubled their ODA flows. In this respect one might add that official aid directed in the form of micro-finance, which is the provision of small loans to individual farmers and businesspeople, and in particular women, might have a positive effect on economic prospects in the developing world (Cull and Morduch 2017).

The major donor countries and international development agencies have in fact made greater efforts to coordinate their objectives when it comes to development assistance. In September 2000, most of the world's leaders agreed at the United Nations in New York to what they termed the Millennium Declaration. The **Millennium Development Goals (MDGs)** included pledges by 2015 to cut extreme poverty by one-half, achieve universal primary education and gender equality at all levels of education, reduce the mortality rate of children under five and new mothers by two-thirds, and decrease the incidence of AIDs/HIV, malaria, tuberculosis, and other diseases.

Millennium Development Goals (MDGs)
A series of goals related to health, education, and poverty, agreed upon by world leaders at the UN in September 2000.

In 2005, through a research effort he conducted for the UN Development Program, Sachs (2005b) put forward a concrete and ambitious strategy for donor and recipient governments to achieve the MDGs, including the recommendation that official development assistance from the rich countries be doubled from a national average of about 0.24 percent to 0.54 percent of GDP. That would still be less than the target of 0.7 percent that rich countries had pledged to achieve as far back as 1970 and as recently as 2002. It is possible that the new aid has helped, since many African countries have had more favorable development experiences, as we highlight below. However, the problem, as explored in Box 11.5, is the continuing failure of many

11.5   MAKING CONNECTIONS
Aspiration versus Reality

Developed Countries' Pledges and Performance on Official Development Assistance 1970 and 2002

Aspiration: Original International Pledge on Official Development Assistance, 1970

In recognition of the special importance of the role which can be fulfilled only by official development assistance, a major part of financial resource transfers to the developing countries should be provided in the form of official development assistance. Each economically advanced country will progressively increase its official development assistance to the developing countries and *will exert its best efforts to reach a minimum net amount of 0.7 percent of its gross national product at market prices by the middle of the Decade.*

Source: United Nations General Assembly, Resolution 2626, October 24, 1970, available at http://www.un.org/documents/ga/res/25/ares25.htm, emphasis added.

Reality: Affirmation of the Pledge, 2002

We urge developed countries that have not done so to make concrete efforts towards the target of 0.7 per cent of gross national product (GNP) as ODA to developing countries.

Source: United Nations (2002): 14.

Figure 11.8 Official Development Assistance as Percent of Gross National Income, Advanced-Country Donors, Five-Year Average, 2012–16
In 1970 and in 2002, the major donor countries pledged to provide official development assistance (ODA) equal to 0.7 percent of their respective national incomes. However, even in recent years only six donors have met or exceeded that target.

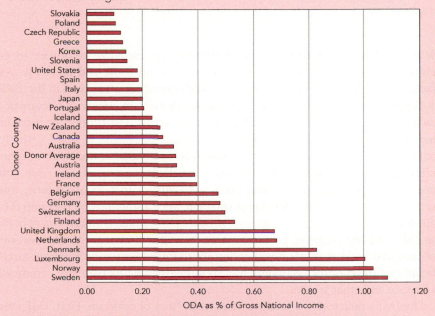

Source: Data from Organization for Economic Cooperation and Development, 'Official Development Assistance as a Percentage of Gross National Income (GNI),' in *OECD International Development Statistics* Volume 2017, available at http://www.oecd-ilibrary.org/development/oecd-international-development-statistics_24142689.

donor countries to increase ODA as a percentage of their respective national incomes to reach the 0.7 percent committed level.

Despite shortfalls in ODA from the developed countries, the UN Millennium Project achieved substantial success by its end-year of 2015. For example, compared to what would have occurred had trends in reducing mortality rates during the 1990s remained in effect during 2000–15, between 21 and 29 million more people were saved by its efforts. Approximately 470 million more people escaped from extreme poverty during 2000–13 than would have occurred if poverty-reduction rates between 1990 and 2002 remained in effect. The majority of lives saved due to the accelerated reduction in mortality rates during 2000–15 were in sub-Saharan Africa, and the biggest decrease in extreme poverty occurred in India (McArthur and Rasmussen 2017).

At a UN Summit in September 2015, world leaders agreed to build on the success of the UN Millennium Project and to pursue a new set of 17 development goals for the period, 2016–30 (United Nations 2017). These benchmarks, called the **Sustainable Development Goals (SDGs)**, constitute what the leaders termed a new Agenda for Sustainable Development. The goals that the governments established, together with the identification of possible strategies in support of meeting the goals (for example, including women more comprehensively in all aspects of the development process), include the eradication of poverty and hunger throughout the world by 2030. The goals also aim to promote more inclusive economic growth, including through the achievement of gender equality and the promotion of above-average income growth of the world's poorer families. Finally, the new goals include commitments by all nations to achieve development while also protecting the natural environment. Important discussions and debates about ODA and other mechanisms by which developed and developing countries can productively work together to promote sustained, just development in poorer countries will likely center on whether these new goals are reached in the years ahead.

IMF Lending to Developing Countries

Many developing countries lack sufficient foreign exchange resources to cover debt obligations and even critical imports, such as oil, food, and medicine. As we discussed in Chapter 9, in those instances such countries often turn to the IMF for short-term loans. To receive those loans, a country must, in almost all circumstances, reach agreements with the Fund regarding the terms and timing for repayment. One element of an agreement is almost always a **stabilization program**, which is a contract between the IMF and the recipient country stipulating what macroeconomic policy changes the country will undertake – usually increasing interest rates, cutting government spending, and raising taxes – to ensure that its short-term foreign exchange shortfall does not become permanent. Such a stabilization program is often paired with a **structural adjustment program (SAP)**, which is an agreement between the IMF and the recipient government on how it will change its microeconomic policies, that is, what efforts it will undertake to introduce stronger market forces by liberalizing the country's economy, and by strengthening its regulatory frameworks in finance and other sectors.

The IMF's policies have produced two main lines of criticism. First, IMF lending may stunt the growth opportunities of developing countries that agree to take on IMF loans and their attendant harsh conditions. This is because cuts in government spending, often at the heart of stabilization programs, may lead to a contraction in overall national demand and thus output of goods and services within the country.

Sustainable Development Goals (SDGs)
World leaders in 2015 agreed to a new Agenda for Sustainable Development, with goals regarding poverty, gender equality, and environmental protection.

Stabilization program
A contract between the IMF and a loan-recipient country stipulating what macroeconomic policy changes the country will undertake to ensure that its short-term foreign exchange shortfall does not become permanent.

Structural adjustment program (SAP)
Agreement between the IMF and the recipient government on how it will change its microeconomic policies, that is, what efforts it will undertake to introduce stronger market forces by liberalizing the country's economy, and by strengthening its regulatory frameworks in finance and other sectors.

Second, it is possible that the IMF contributes to the risk that countries will behave in ways that bring about financial panics. The IMF, by acting as a lender of last resort, may produce **moral hazard** (Meltzer 2000) on the part of both developing-country governments and private lenders. Moral hazard occurs when an individual or some other actor believes they can take very great risks because, if things go badly, someone else will pay for the consequences of the risky behavior. It is possible that developing-country governments and foreign lenders believe that if they engage in what turns out to be overly risky economic behavior (overspending by the governments and overlending to those governments by outside banks and other financial actors), the IMF will bail them out. Those governments and lenders might, by consequence, be more likely to make choices that lead to financial crises and the need for IMF bailouts.

In sum, when we seek to answer the enduring question about international linkages and development, official aid and IMF lending produce extremely divergent views.

As we noted above, developing countries have had very different growth experiences. The next section highlights different paths to economic development that have been taken by a small number of emerging states that are particularly important both for the growth they have achieved and their potential for affecting in turn the growth of the world economy.

Moral hazard
When an individual or some other actor believes they can take very great risks because, if things go badly, someone else will pay for the consequences of the risky behavior. Some accuse the IMF of encouraging moral hazard.

Levels of Analysis *International Finance as an Opportunity for Developing Countries*	
👥 **State**	🌐 **International**
Developing countries that accept international investment might grow more rapidly than they otherwise would, but in so doing they take on risks as domestic and international investment conditions change.	There is disagreement over the extent to which foreign aid and direct and portfolio investment have beneficial impacts on development.

DEVELOPMENT STRATEGIES AND EMERGING POWERS – THE BRICS

The discussion so far highlights that there are different pathways to the achievement of development. Some countries have clearly done better than others. This final section considers a group of developing countries that are singled out for special attention because each has potential to emerge as a major economic power.

In 2001, an analyst working for the financial giant Goldman Sachs coined the term BRIC to refer to a small cluster of emerging states – Brazil, Russia, India, and China (BRIC) – with the collective potential, within several decades, to overtake the combined economic weight of the industrial world. In 2001 this BRIC group already contained 40 percent of the world's population, accounted for 15 percent of global GDP, and held 40 percent of global currency reserves. BRIC countries also shared high future economic potential: China was growing faster than any other country, India was not far behind, Brazil was re-emerging as the dominant economy of South America, and Russia was recovering from its economic collapse at the end of the Cold War. The name stuck, and by the mid-2000s representatives of BRIC countries began meeting as a group. In 2010, South Africa requested that it be included in the group, and it was formally invited to do so in December of that year, and so we now use the term **BRICS** in recognition of South Africa's membership in this informal arrangement.

The four original members and later the five-member BRICS association have made some efforts at crafting joint positions on international economic issues

BRICS
Brazil, Russia, India, China, and South Africa. These five rapidly developing countries have the collective potential, within several decades, to overtake the combined economic weight of the industrial world.

and have taken initial steps to create a new international institution. In June 2009, what were then the four BRIC countries held their first summit in the Russian city of Yekaterinburg. The four agreed on the need for a more stable and diversified international monetary system (translation: less reliance on the US dollar) and reform of international financial institutions to reflect changes in the world economy (translation: more influence for BRIC countries, and less for the United States and Europe, in the World Bank and IMF). In 2014, BRICS members created a New Development Bank (NDB) and pledged to fund it with a reserve currency pool of $100 billion. The NDB is headquartered in Shanghai, China, and signed its first loan agreement in December 2016.

It remains to be seen if the BRICS grouping will become a lasting, influential political force in world economic matters. Scholars working from the realist, liberal, and constructivist perspectives would probably all be cautious in their assessments of the prospects for the BRICS as a political grouping. We highlight in Box 11.6 how those theoretical perspectives would differ in trying to estimate the likely durability and salience of the BRICS group in the future.

Regardless of the prospects of the BRICS as a collective, as individual countries China, India, Brazil, Russia, and South Africa will likely be major actors in the world economy in the years ahead. Below, we briefly describe their development strategies and impending challenges.

China

China is by far the largest and most successful of the BRICS. During its first 30 years under communist rule (1945–75), China possessed a Soviet-type economy with most resource allocation decisions made by central planning authorities rather than market

Photo 11.4 Export Production in Chinese Special Economic Zone, 2004
China made very good use of special economic zones in its early years of export-oriented industrialization, including, as can be seen in this photo from 2004, to produce Christmas products for the US market.

Source: AFP/AFP/Getty Images.

11.6 DIFFERING THEORETICAL APPROACHES

The Future of the BRICS

Background

Brazil, Russia, India, China, and South Africa are working to create a new informal political-economic grouping in the world economy, the BRICS. Their goal is to craft and press common positions on international economic matters, and as such to wield more influence as members of a group of important economies than they might as individual countries, aided by creation of a new development bank. What are the prospects for the BRICS as a political-economic grouping? Scholars working in the realist, liberal, and constructivist traditions might share doubts about the future of the BRICS, but they differ in the kinds of questions they would ask about the grouping in reaching their views as to its likely future health and vitality.

Realism

A realist would ask whether the BRICS countries are subject to threats in common – political, military, and economic – and if they are, then this would augur well for the grouping. A realist would also ask if the BRICS countries have serious conflicts of interest between or among group members, for if they do this would yield pessimism about the prospects for robust cooperation and development. For example, India and China have been locked in a long-standing disagreement about the exact demarcation of their common border, a disagreement that caused a war between them in 1962. This split at the heart of the BRICS, a realist would suggest, might impose limits on the future of the grouping. All the BRICS countries might oppose US pre-eminence in international relations, but while US–China and US–Russia relations have deteriorated in recent years, US–India relations have improved, and this too might again constrain BRICS political and institutional cooperation.

Liberalism

A liberal would argue that, if they were all democracies, the prospects for the BRICS countries to expand and deepen their cooperation would be reasonably good. As it is, the BRICS grouping is composed of countries with highly diverse domestic political regimes: Brazil, India, and South Africa are democracies, and China and Russia have authoritarian regimes. A liberal is likely to look at the differences among the BRICS in terms of domestic regimes and conclude that that variation is likely to hamper development of the group.

Constructivism

A constructivist would suggest that the prospects for the BRICS grouping depends upon the degree to which the political leaders, business elites, and other active members of the societies of the different BRICS countries share common ideas about such matters as the proper role of government in the national economy, the value of working with other countries in international arrangements, and, in line with realist views, whether they were confronting common threats and opportunities in the international domain.

forces. A new communist leadership took over in the mid-1970s and, in 1978, initiated economic reforms that have resulted in China's gradual transition to a market-based economy. These measures included allowing farmers to lease land from the state, the steady privatization of **state-owned enterprises (SOEs)**, and an export-led growth

State-owned enterprises (SOEs) Companies owned directly by the government of a state.

strategy that established special economic zones for Chinese and foreign companies to produce goods for final markets in the West.

China's economic strategy has been remarkably successful. Its export revenues jumped from about $10 billion in 1978 to about $500 billion in 2003, and to $1.2 trillion by 2009. Between 1985 and 2010, the economy grew at an astounding rate of almost 10 percent per year. By 2005, China's total GDP grew to $2 trillion using current exchange rate and $5 trillion in **purchasing power parity (PPP)** terms (PPP is a measure used to compare the value of a similar basket of goods across countries with different living standards and exchange rates). Economists predicted in 2012 that China would have a markedly larger economy in terms of PPP than the United States by 2030 (see Figure 11.9). At the end of 2016, both the IMF and World Bank calculated that China's economy was bigger than that of the United States in PPP terms.

We could therefore be witnessing a transition in global economic hegemony like the one that took place between Great Britain and the United States during the first half of the twentieth century. We might see financial power shift from New York to Shanghai and Beijing. China might become decisive in determining world trade rules and take on the leadership of the IMF and World Bank. Chinese leaders have already extended their diplomacy across Asia, Latin America, and Africa, using their formidable financial and commercial resources to extract political benefits and necessary raw materials on favorable terms. With an additional 20 years of sustained growth, China would be able to challenge American political dominance around the world.

But will China continue to grow at a rapid pace? We should not assume that its future will simply look like its recent past. In fact, China's growth has slowed significantly, and between 2012 and 2016 average annual per capita GDP dropped

Purchasing power parity (PPP)
A measure economists use to compare the value of a similar basket of goods across countries with different living standards and exchange rates.

Figure 11.9 Shares of World GDP 2011 and Projection for 2030
In the foreseeable future China might have the world's largest economy. By the end of the next decade it might be the site of 28% of global economic activity, while in 2011 it was the location of about 17% of world economic output. By comparison, the United States, which in 2011 generated about one-fourth of world output, might be the source of 18% of such activity in 2030.

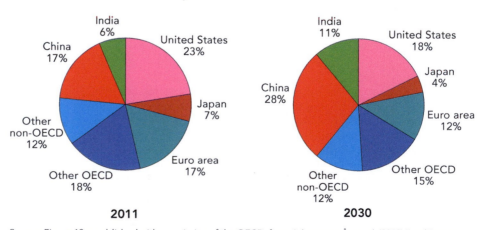

Source: Figure 10 republished with permission of the OECD, from Johansson, Å., *et al.* (2012) 'Looking to 2060: Long-Term Global Growth Prospects: A Going for Growth Report,' OECD Economic Policy Papers, No. 3, OECD Publishing, .23.doi: 10.1787/5k8zxpjsggf0-en. Permission conveyed through Copyright Clearance Center, Inc. See also, Johansson, Å., *et al.* (2013) 'Long-Term Growth Scenarios,' OECD Economics Department Working Papers, No. 1000, OECD Publishing. http://dx.doi.org/10.1787/5k4ddxpr2fmr-en.

from the 10 percent range to roughly 6 to 7 percent (see Figure 11.10). China faces a series of difficult economic and political challenges that could derail its rise to the top. Most importantly, as the world economy has slowed down, so too have China's exports. China thus is attempting to shift its growth strategy from an ELG model to one based on domestic investment and consumption. As it makes this gradual transition, it will also face, by 2030, an aging population and a smaller workforce.

For China's communist leaders, economic performance and regime legitimacy are inextricably linked. So far, China has managed to sustain what the Soviet Union could not – a thriving, quasi-capitalist economy governed by an authoritarian one-party state. The legitimacy of the communist regime is no longer based on revolutionary fervor or the inherent political appeal of communist ideology. Instead, it is based on economic performance, or the ability of the regime to ensure that the economy delivers goods, services, and jobs to its growing population. Significantly slower growth would inevitably lead parts of the population to question the political monopoly of the Communist Party. The greater the questioning, the more tempted the regime would be to exercise repression, which would lead the population to question regime legitimacy even further. It is perhaps not surprising that as China's growth has slowed, President Xi Jinping has sought to crack down on corruption and in the process has increased the control of the Communist Party over China's economy and society.

The communist regime must also deal with the social and economic inequalities that result from successful economic growth. Growing gaps have appeared between rich and poor, urban and rural populations, and residents on the economically vibrant coastline and those in less well-off inland parts of the country. Large gaps in income and life opportunities generate resentment among those at the bottom, who, during the communist era, could at least count on the '**iron rice bowl**,' a guarantee from the state of job security and access to necessities. But there is even discontent among

Iron rice bowl
A guarantee from the government of Communist China of job security and access to basic necessities for Chinese citizens.

Figure 11.10 Chinese Annual GDP Growth, 2008–18
China has experienced stunning growth in GDP per capita in recent years, reaching 10% per year in the first decade of the current century. However, more recently China has experienced a relative abatement (albeit still very high by global standards) in its growth in income per person.

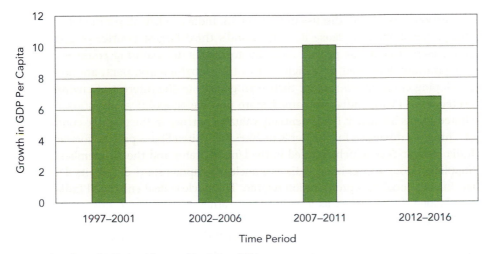

Source: Data from the National Bueau of Statistics of China.

the rising middle class who, as they become well off, have increasing expectations for a higher quality of life and demand a greater say in the political decisions affecting their lives.

In sum, China's prospects for *future* rapid growth are far less predictable than any linear projection of past trends would indicate. China may continue to enjoy sustained growth and may even catch and overtake the United States. But it is also plausible that China will grow more slowly and, at the extreme, face a series of economic, social, and political dislocations.

India

India has long been an exceptionally large, but exceptionally poor, developing country. Why has it gained so much attention in the past decade, to the point of being included in the BRICS? One reason is economic; the other is geopolitical.

During much of the Cold War, the Indian economy was shackled by government intervention and regulation. Modest liberalizing reforms undertaken in the 1980s helped the country attain an annual growth rate of about 5 percent. A currency crisis in 1991 led to more far-reaching reforms: tariff cuts, business tax reductions, and the deregulation of industry. India grew at 6 percent annually between 1992 and 2002, a period that included a major economic disruption in its region, the Asian financial crisis of 1997–98. Between 2002 and 2008, India grew even more rapidly, at 8.8 percent annually, and it maintained 6.4 percent growth annually between 2010 and 2016. As we noted at the beginning of the chapter, India is on the move economically and has achieved recent growth rates close to those of China. With one billion people – about half under the age of 25 – and a rapidly growing economy, India caught and has sustained the attention of the global community. It has experienced especially rapid growth in the service sector, particularly computing and information technology. Its computer services leaders – Wipro and Infosys – have become well known. The same may be said of its leading auto manufacturer, Tata Motors; in 2009, Tata introduced what it claimed to be the world's least expensive car, measuring 10 feet by 5 feet and selling at a base price of $2,200.

India has gained geopolitical attention as well. It has taken on a self-appointed role as leader of developing states seeking a better deal in the world economy in negotiations with the more established industrial states. India helped to derail the Doha Round because it felt the United States and Europe did not make sufficient concessions. As we will discuss in Chapter 13, India is a key player in global climate change negotiations because it is the world's third largest emitter of greenhouse gases. Here, too, it has proved reluctant to cooperate, claiming countries already economically developed, at a high cost to the global environment, are now urging developing countries to restrict their own growth in the interest of environmental protection. Finally, India has gained more positive geopolitical attention from the United States because it is a potentially valuable partner in the possible containment of China. As discussed in Chapter 8, in 2005 the United States pressed forward a US–India nuclear deal, which resulted in the United States and the 45-member Nuclear Suppliers Group recognizing India as a nuclear weapons state, despite its defiance of the international non-proliferation regime. The nuclear deal enhanced India's status and helped distinguish it as a great power rather than just one side of the India–Pakistan regional conflict.

Its recent success and prominence as a BRICS country should not blind us to the formidable development challenges that India continues to face. As of 2005 a remarkable 40 percent of the Indian population – over 450 million people – lived

Photo 11.5 BRICS Leaders
Indian and Chinese officials mark the launch of the BRICS' New Development Bank (NDB) in 2017 during the NDB's second annual meeting in New Delhi, India.

Source: VCG/VCG via Getty Images.

below the poverty line. According to the World Bank, India made significant progress by 2016, but still 22 percent, or 270 million people, lived in poverty. Roughly 30 percent of Indian children suffer from malnutrition, and literacy rates are only at about 70 percent (compared to roughly 95 percent in China). Despite its ability to produce world-class information technology services and globally competitive cinema, India's basic infrastructure remains underdeveloped. Hundreds of millions of people live without electrical power and, in many parts of the country, sanitary conditions are poor, exacerbating disease, malnutrition, and infant mortality.

India's economic progress requires a continuation of economic reforms, along with sustained attention to its deficient infrastructure. Its democratic government is aware of the problems but is not always able to address them effectively. Recall from early in this chapter the importance of good governance as a facilitator of economic development. Corruption plagues the Indian Parliament; as of 2010, some 25 percent of sitting members were facing criminal charges. The ruling coalition government has at times contained more than one dozen parties, making it difficult to sustain itself in power, much less take decisive action to address pressing social and economic problems.

Brazil

Brazil was hit hard by the Great Depression of the 1930s. As Western markets for its coffee and other raw materials collapsed, Brazil's policy makers learned that the country should not excessively rely on the global economy. As a result, they adopted an ISI strategy. The government regulated trade and used tariff barriers and other incentives to encourage local Brazilian firms, sometimes in collaboration with foreign multinational enterprises, to produce goods for the large Brazilian market. ISI produced some growth over the years but, by the 1980s, Brazil was afflicted with high inflation, large external debts, and inefficient industry. By the early 1990s,

Brazil joined many other developing countries in shifting development strategy in a more liberal direction, emphasizing freer trade and privatization of many state-owned firms.

As many developing countries have embraced the world economy since the 1990s, why single out Brazil for special attention? The simple reason is that, like India and China, Brazil is no ordinary emerging economy; it has the potential to be a great power, economically and geopolitically. Brazil's land mass is similar in size to the United States. Its population is about 210 million, or two-thirds that of the United States. Its GDP of roughly $2.1 trillion in 2016 placed it among the top ten countries in the world. Unlike many developing countries, Brazil already possesses a sophisticated and diversified economy. It is a major agricultural producer and exporter of coffee, soybeans, cotton, tropical fruits, and biofuels such as ethanol. It is emerging as a global player in oil and gas. Within the past decade, the state-owned firm Petrobras has made huge new oil discoveries in Brazilian territorial waters, and industry experts estimate that Brazil's reserves have now tripled to about 40 billion barrels, among the top ten globally and equivalent to the reserve positions of long-time OPEC members Nigeria and Venezuela. With over 2,500 miles of coastline, further discoveries are likely. It is ironic that Brazil spent decades developing its manufacturing sector, and now finds raw materials and food to be just as much an engine of its current and future growth. Its large size and economic diversity increase its chances of avoiding the resource curse and other problems that plague developing economies.

Brazil's central government has become stronger and more stable. Brazil returned to democracy in 1985 after two decades of military rule. Its extensive multiparty system ensures that governing coalitions have numerous participants. Yet, only two of the parties, the leftist Worker's Party and the center-left Social Democratic Party, have been able to produce viable presidential candidates, and they have alternated in power over the past 20 years. When in power, each party has managed to form governments capable of getting things done, even with seemingly unwieldy coalitions. Brazilian politics has become more stable and predictable in absolute terms, compared to other countries in the region, such as Venezuela, where populist leaders have sought to manipulate democratic rules to remain in power indefinitely.

The Brazilian state has become more competent in some of the good governance tasks those in the developed world often take for granted – the collection of taxes and implementation of government programs. Between 2003 and 2013 President Luiz Inacio Lula da Silva of the Worker's Party targeted resources to the large numbers of Brazilian poor, emphasizing health care, education, and housing. He maintained the pragmatic and growth-oriented economic policies that enhanced Brazil's ability to compete internationally.

Brazil continues to face major challenges. Its average annual growth rate has been slower than China's (hovering in the 2 percent range between 2008 and 2016), while the government's share of its economy is larger (20 percent versus 14 percent). Large gaps in income and wealth across the population remain. Brazil's emerging dependence on raw material and agricultural exports make it vulnerable to global economic slowdowns. Its Amazon region has become something of a 'wild west,' with loggers, miners, and farmers grabbing what they can at the expense of the local and global (Brazil is a leading emitter of greenhouse gases) environment. Brazilian business and political elites have been caught up in recent corruption scandals; the very popular former President, mentioned above, known as Lula, was convicted and sentenced to 12 years in prison for accepting gifts in exchange for contracts offered to construction firms, and Lula's successor, President Dilma Rousseff, was impeached in

2016 for mishandling Brazil's national finances. There is still much work to be done, but Brazil remains a plausible candidate to join the ranks of the major powers in the decades ahead.

Russia

Under communist rule as the core of the Soviet Union (1917–90), Russia undertook a 70-year experiment in central planning of the economy. The state controlled virtually every aspect of economic interaction; it set prices for goods and services and determined what would be produced, how it would be produced, and in what quantities. The system produced some successes in aggregate economic terms. Stalin's *revolution from above* during the 1930s marshaled economic resources to achieve, at the expense of the peasantry, rapid industrialization and militarization. After World War II, the Soviet-style economic system was put forward as an alternative to liberal capitalism. During the 1950s, it compared relatively well, when the Soviet Union recovered from war and achieved high levels of growth by devoting more land, labor, and capital to the production process. By the 1960s, however, it became apparent that the Soviet system was 'all thumbs and no fingers' – it was good at mass-producing basic commodities, but much less effective at producing a wide range of goods and services of appeal to ordinary consumers. The Soviet economy was a bit like the army; it could produce enough 'standard-issue' shoes or shirts for everyone but could not compete with the variety and quality of goods produced in market economies around the world.

The Soviet Union was a global leader in the production of oil, natural gas, nickel, and other primary commodities, and the boom in commodity prices during the 1970s made the Soviet economy look stronger than it was. When commodity prices fell during the early 1980s, the Soviet economic weakness was exposed, and, as we discussed in Chapter 2, Mikhail Gorbachev took power with a bold plan to reform the Soviet economy while maintaining centralized political control. His experiment ultimately failed, as the Soviet economy was thrown into chaos; the subsequent demands for political liberalization led to the demise of the Soviet empire, the Soviet Union itself, and the Cold War. During the 1990s, Western governments hoped that Russia could be reformed into a liberal democracy and market economy. But economic reform meant that a small segment of powerful elites and their associates became very rich, while most ordinary people faced economic insecurity. The safety net of communism was ripped away but a fully functioning market economy was not put into place. By 2000, Vladimir Putin took advantage of this situation by centralizing power in Moscow and promising the Russian people a return to the tradition of stability and order provided by a strong central government.

In the interim period of the 1990s, the Russian economy faced severe hardship: GDP contracted at the beginning of the decade by 10 to 15 percent annually. Investment slipped, and unemployment and poverty levels rose significantly. Russia was hit hard by an international financial crisis during 1997–98: the ruble collapsed in value and the government defaulted on billions of dollars of its international and domestic debts.

Why, then, has Russia been singled out as a BRICS country? The simple reason is that Russia's economy staged a strong recovery after 1998. Between 2000 and 2008, annual growth averaged almost 7 percent. The government eliminated or repaid its debt and, by 2009, had piled up more than $400 billion in foreign currency reserves, more than any other country other than China and Japan. The benefits spread broadly as jobs were created, poverty levels dropped significantly, and personal incomes and consumer spending rose. The crisis of 1998 forced the government to rein in spending, and the cheaper ruble stimulated Russia's exports.

The key to Russia's success has been energy. Oil and gas prices shot up after 2003, with oil approaching and even breaking through the $100 per barrel mark. It is the world's second largest oil producer and exporter (after Saudi Arabia), and the world's largest natural gas producer and exporter.

Under Putin, Russia's economic revival has been accompanied by a more assertive foreign policy, particularly around the former Soviet Union. Russia has used the threatened or actual cut-off of energy supplies to influence politics in Ukraine, Belarus, and Georgia. In 2008, Russia invaded Georgia to bolster the independence of the Russia-friendly regions of Abkhazia and South Ossetia. The fact that the rest of the world seemed incapable of deterring or stopping Russia from attacking its smaller neighbor (on the eve of the attack, US President Bush and Russian Prime Minister Putin were seen together attending the opening ceremonies of the Beijing Olympics) made Russia look even more formidable. As discussed in Chapter 2, in 2014 Russia annexed the Ukrainian territory of Crimea.

Russia's revival, coupled with China's economic success, led some observers to celebrate the authoritarian capitalist model as an alternative to the liberal capitalist model of the West. In Russia's version of authoritarian capitalism, Putin's government stifled democracy and freedom of the press and expanded the power of the central government in the name of stability, law, and order. By 2008, the government had taken over all major television networks and controlled all major newspapers except one Moscow weekly. In exchange, the Russian people received a share of the economic benefits generated by oil and gas sales. The fact that Putin's approval rating as President approached 80 percent in 2007 seemed to suggest that the authoritarian model was not only effective, but popular. When Putin was replaced as President in 2008 by Dmitry Medvedev, he stayed on as Prime Minister and then again as President in 2012.

Russia's authoritarian capitalist model and economic revival face major challenges and hide significant social and economic problems (McFaul and Stoner-Weiss 2008). Russia's population has been shrinking for at least 20 years, in part due to serious health afflictions. Heart disease, the leading cause of death, occurs at three times the rate of that in the United States. Alcoholism is rampant among young and middle-aged men. Russia has the highest HIV infection rate of any country outside Africa. 'Law and order' is a supposed benefit of rule under Putin but during his tenure the murder rate has increased, and Russia experienced the two worst terrorist attacks in its history, at a Moscow theater in 2002 and in an elementary school in Beslan in 2004. Russia ranks very high in international rankings for corruption and has one of the least friendly business environments in the industrial world. The protection of property rights is weak, Russian authorities regularly harass foreign businesspeople, and the government has used its political clout to redistribute Russia's vast energy and other resources into the hands of a small elite.

Russia's development model may be over-reliant on oil and gas. Energy profits, in fact, have facilitated authoritarianism by giving Russia's central leaders the resources to reward friends, crack down on enemies, and placate the general population. But such circumstances may not last because Russia, like several Middle Eastern oil countries, is susceptible to the resource curse; it has got richer, but it has not developed. The danger for Russia, considering its other problems, is that the next energy downturn will lead to economic and social crisis. Finally, Russia's confrontation with Ukraine in 2014 led Western countries to impose economic sanctions which have only exacerbated the economic challenges Russia already faces. By 2018, those sanctions were strengthened in response to Russia's meddling in Western elections and support for the Syrian regime that has used chemical weapons repeatedly in its brutal civil war.

South Africa

Because of a multi-decade struggle led by Nelson Mandela and the African National Congress, South Africa achieved during the early 1990s a stunning transformation from a deeply racist and authoritarian regime – one that was based on *apartheid*, or separation of the races and subjugation of blacks by whites – to one that is democratic and multiracial. South Africa's initial post-*apartheid* economic performance was reasonably strong. Especially notable was the progress made by South Africa in reducing poverty: the national poverty dropped from about 34 percent in 1996 to about 17 percent in 2011, as the new black majority government spread economic benefits more broadly across the population. However, in recent years, domestic political turmoil and apparent widespread governmental corruption have combined to take a serious toll on South African economic development: at 16 percent, the national poverty rate in 2016 remained almost unchanged from what it had been five years earlier; GDP per capita contracted during the years 2014, 2015, and 2016; and the national unemployment rate in 2016 reached an 11-year high at 28 percent, with youth unemployment at close to 50 percent. In April 2017, an important credit ratings agency, Standard and Poor, downgraded to 'junk status' South African debt that is denominated in foreign currencies (World Bank 2017).

Going forward, South Africa faces both opportunities and challenges. It is a country that has substantial mineral resources including the world's largest reserves of manganese and platinum group metals and among the world's largest of gold and diamonds. It has a skilled workforce characterized by a high degree of gender equity. According to the World Economic Forum, South Africa has the 17th (out of 136 countries) narrowest gender gap in the world, measured in terms of participation in the economy, education, political opportunities, and health (World Economic Forum 2013). Its democratic institutions are robust. Its political system as of 2017 was coded by the prominent NGO Freedom House as free, the highest category employed by that organization in assessing political and civic rights in countries around the world, although Freedom House characterized the South African press as operating in only partly free circumstances (Freedom House 2017b).

At the same time, the country faces serious residual problems from the *apartheid* period: South Africa is still characterized by a high degree of income inequality, and according to the World Bank it has one of the most unequal distributions of land ownership in the world. National health problems and inequalities, including a high incidence of HIV/AIDS infections, constitute a serious barrier to economic development. Recent government corruption, including allegations leveled against former President Jacob Zuma, who was forced to step down in February 2018, is acting as a serious drag on economic growth. South Africa is clearly an important state in Africa, enjoys global influence and respect due to its transition to multiracial democracy, and could be poised to enjoy sustained economic development. However, the degree to which it prospers economically and retains global diplomatic importance will depend upon its capacity to resolve deep-seated social and political problems. Just as many developing countries must address the legacy and lingering effects of colonialism, South Africa must confront the legacy of *apartheid*.

Levels of Analysis *The BRICS*

 State

BRICS countries have pursued different development strategies, reinforcing the idea that there is no single pathway to national economic prosperity.

The challenge of good governance plagues each BRICS country to a greater or lesser degree.

 International

The rise of the BRICS, especially China, demonstrates the connection between economic power and geopolitical influence in the international system.

REVISITING THE ENDURING QUESTION AND LOOKING AHEAD

Economic development is one of the great challenges of our time. In this chapter, we have asked whether economic globalization helps or hinders poorer countries as they seek to attain such development. Globalization seems to be helping many once poor countries, such as South Korea and China, achieve a stunning level of economic development. Most developing countries are likely in the future to pursue at least limited integration with the global economy, through trade, foreign investment by multinational enterprises, and the receipt of financial assistance either from donor countries like the United States or by international institutions like the World Bank. Yet, in doing so, developing countries are likely to be concerned as to whether they are attaining the maximum possible gains from integration, and this concern is likely to translate into bargaining with the wealthier and more powerful countries in the global economy.

Developing countries will become increasingly important for international economics. The BRICS may become a significant force in world politics. Individual BRICS countries, and especially China but also Brazil to a considerable degree and possibly India in the foreseeable future, are central actors in world trade, finance, and economic diplomacy. South Korea has already become an important member of the community of advanced industrial countries.

Still, it remains an open question whether all developing countries, especially the very poorest, can escape from poverty traps and propel themselves onto a trajectory of sustained growth. There is still no strong consensus among academics or policy makers on whether trade, investment, and foreign aid can help in promoting or fortifying change in the poorest countries. Good governance and domestic civil peace are needed to bring about sustained growth and poverty reduction in those countries. The questions of whether, and under what conditions, external engagement promotes internal economic improvement in poorer countries will remain at the center of global politics in the decades ahead.

In many developing countries, economic progress is being challenged or undermined by serious civil conflicts, often driven or accompanied by ethnic political divisions. In addition, high levels of lawlessness in many developing countries contribute to the emergence of powerful drug lords, whose violence and corruption undermine possibilities for improved governance in these countries. The circumstances sometimes become so dire that they threaten the stability and security for the people living in them, neighbors, and even outside states, to such a degree that the international community has forcibly intervened to avert humanitarian disasters and create a minimum of order. In the next chapter, we turn to these countries, their tragedies, and the outside interventions that sometimes occur in reaction to those tragedies.

STUDY QUESTIONS

1. Recall the three key perspectives – liberalism, Marxism, and economic nationalism – discussed in Chapter 10. What do you consider the most important insight from each regarding the dilemmas of development?
2. What are the most important causes of failed efforts by many countries to achieve economic development? Are they more likely to be domestic or international? Are they more likely to be political, economic, or geographic?
3. Evaluate the costs and benefits of international trade, foreign direct investment, and official development aid as engines of development.
4. Imagine you are the foreign minister of Brazil. What strategies would you adopt toward other BRICS countries, the United States, and your immediate neighbors to enhance your country's development prospects?
5. How might developing countries be affected if the price of oil tripled over the next decade?
6. Is the term BRICS a useful analytical construct? Why or why not?

FURTHER READING

Acemoglu, Daron and James Robinson (2012) *Why Nations Fail: The Origins of Power, Prosperity, and Poverty* (New York: Crown Business). This widely read book provides a good argument about how geography and domestic political institutions, as well as the legacies of colonialism, have affected the prospects for growth of development of countries around the world.

Easterly, William (2006) *The White Man's Burden: Why the West's Efforts to Aid the Rest Have Done so Much Ill and So Little Good* (New York: Penguin Press). This is perhaps the most thoughtful and persuasive book on the possible pitfalls and even counter-productive effects of foreign aid from developed to developing countries. It should be contrasted with Sachs' *End of Poverty*, noted below.

Rodrik, Dani (2007) *One Economics, Many Recipes: Globalization, Institutions, and Economic Growth* (Princeton: Princeton University Press). Rodrik offers a balanced analysis of the role of international economic integration in the process of economic development. He argues that countries that have benefited from economic integration did so by first building strong domestic institutions and industries, and he is skeptical of the Washington Consensus.

Ross, Michael (2012) *The Oil Curse: How Petroleum Wealth Shapes the Development of Nations* (Princeton: Princeton University Press). Ross shows how the possession of oil can place serious obstacles before developing countries as they seek to attain good governance and economic development.

Sachs, Jeffrey (2005a) *The End of Poverty: Economic Possibilities for Our Time* (New York: Penguin Press). Sachs puts forward a case for the efficacy and moral necessity of foreign aid from developed to developing countries. It should be read in conjunction with Easterly's *The White Man's Burden*, noted above.

 Visit **www.macmillanihe.com/Grieco-IntroIR-2e** to access extra resources for this chapter, including:

- Chapter summaries to help you review the material
- Multiple choice quizzes to test your understanding
- Flashcards to test your knowledge of the key terms in this chapter
- An interactive simulation that invites you to go through the decision-making process of a world leader at a crucial political juncture
- Pivotal decisions in which you weigh up the pros and cons of complicated decisions with grave consequences
- Outside resources, including links to contemporary articles and videos, that add to what you have learned in this chapter

Part IV

Contemporary Challenges and the Future of International Relations

Author Debates

 Visit **www.macmillanihe.com/Grieco-IntroIR-2e** to watch the authors debating the issues discussed in this Part.

Video 1: What are the main global challenges facing the international community?

Video 2: What might the future hold for international relations?

12 Non-State Actors and Challenges to Sovereignty

Enduring question
Can the state continue to overcome challenges to its authority?

Chapter Contents

- States, Sovereignty, and the Westphalian System
- Challenges to Sovereign States
- International Responses to Weak and Failed States
- Whither the State?
- Revisiting the Enduring Question and Looking Ahead
- Study Questions
- Further Reading

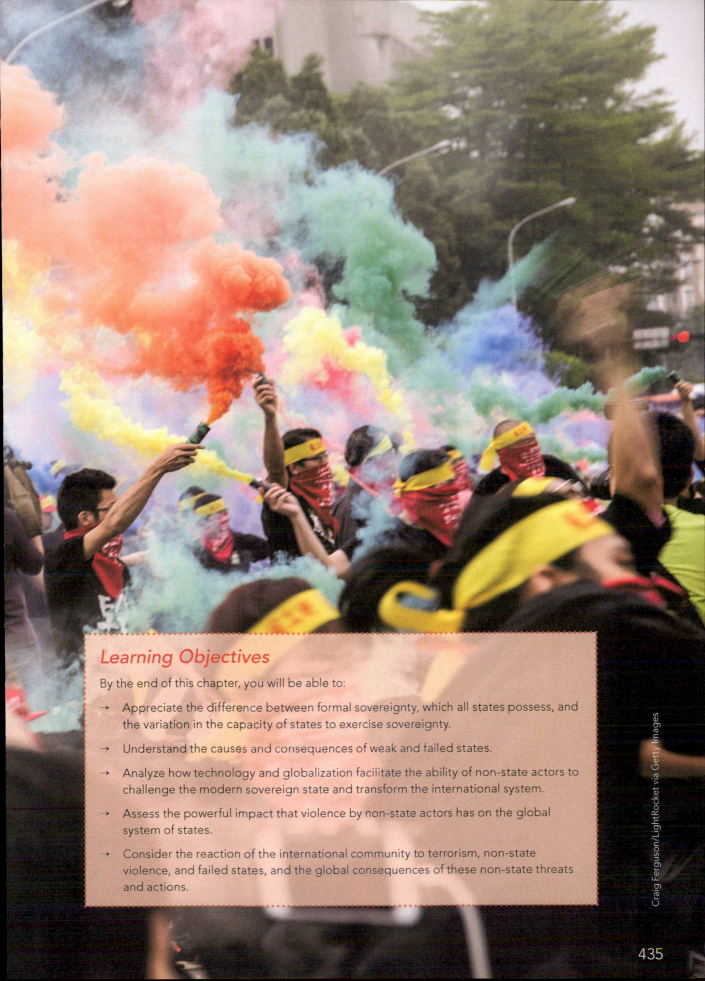

Learning Objectives

By the end of this chapter, you will be able to:

→ Appreciate the difference between formal sovereignty, which all states possess, and the variation in the capacity of states to exercise sovereignty.

→ Understand the causes and consequences of weak and failed states.

→ Analyze how technology and globalization facilitate the ability of non-state actors to challenge the modern sovereign state and transform the international system.

→ Assess the powerful impact that violence by non-state actors has on the global system of states.

→ Consider the reaction of the international community to terrorism, non-state violence, and failed states, and the global consequences of these non-state threats and actions.

Craig Ferguson/LightRocket via Getty Images

435

Many people think that states have always dominated world politics – and always will. But in fact, states have long been challenged in various ways. The ancient and early modern world was dominated by empires, and the nation-state only gained dominance in Europe in 1648. In earlier chapters, we explored moments when single states have tried to take over all or part of the system, such as Napoleonic France and Nazi Germany. The rise of nuclear weapons also led some people to argue that since states could no longer protect their populations, the state would wither away. In the 1970s, multinational corporations grew to be major players in the world economy, challenging the sovereign authority of national governments. In the 1990s, the international financial system – and large global banks – encroached on the ability of national governments to manage the world economy, and the 2008 financial crisis again showed governments at the mercy of financial markets.

In recent decades, the state has appeared to be challenged both from above – by supranational bodies such as the European Union – and from below – by localism, tribalism, and subnational ethnic groups. In addition, nongovernmental organizations (NGOs) – transnational private groupings of citizens and activists – also increasingly populate the international landscape. These transnational groupings range widely in their goals – from promoting global cooperation and social advancement to criminal and violent activities. In the meantime, the growing prominence of failed states in many parts of today's world raises questions about the viability of nation-states, at least in some troubled underdeveloped areas. The growth of NGOs also shows how modern technologies and globalization can challenge and possibly undermine the state's ability to protect its borders and pursue its goals.

In other words, the sovereign state has been continually challenged, both internally and externally, and these challenges have taken different forms in different eras and settings. In this chapter, we look at some of the contemporary challenges to the state, while recalling the enduring nature of the problem.

The combination of violent non-state actors and weak or failed states raises several far-reaching questions. Are these non-state actors gaining a sufficient foothold in the global system to challenge the primacy of the state as the dominant actor in the system and one that monopolizes the effective use of force? To what extent are the forces of globalization, technological change, and political fragmentation eroding the power and authority of states as the central actors in world politics? What are the implications of weak and failed states for the international system?

We first look back at the Westphalian system of sovereign states. Then we examine the challenge posed by weak and failing states, using Afghanistan, Sudan, and Colombia as illustrations. Weak and failing states enable non-state challenges, including by pirates on the high seas, and by warlords, drug gangs, and terror groups who take advantage of a weak state's inability to control its sovereign territory. We also look at the international responses to terrorism, non-state violence, and failed states. When countries fall apart, governments do not function, and private actors are free to pursue crime and violence within and across a state's ungoverned borders, what can the rest of the world do?

STATES, SOVEREIGNTY, AND THE WESTPHALIAN SYSTEM

Our starting point is the observation that states are not the only actors in international relations. There are a multitude of other agents or actors in world affairs, non-state actors who are not beholden to national governments but pursue their agendas privately and transnationally across international borders. Most non-state actors are peaceful in their interests and actions. Human rights groups, such as Amnesty

International, and environmental groups, such as the World Wide Fund for Nature, are well-known examples. We have encountered these groups in earlier chapters: human rights groups in Chapter 5, peace groups in Chapter 7, and multinational corporations in Chapter 9. But there are also non-state actors that behave more like criminal gangs – groups such as pirates, warlords, and terrorists. These non-state actors typically prey on their victims in parts of the world where states are weak or use these weak states as bases of operation to attack more advanced countries. Indeed, in some parts of the world states are so weak that they are often called **failed states**. Failed states are states that lack the basic institutions and capacities of government – taxing, policing, upholding the rule of law, protecting property, providing public roads and services, and maintaining control over territory.

To appreciate the significance of these non-state actors, recall the historic rise and spread of the nation-state system. The rise of the nation-state is one of the great dramas of the modern world. You will recall from Chapter 2 that scholars often date the birth of the state system to the Peace of Westphalia in 1648. This is when the monarchs and other state leaders of Europe agreed that national territorial states were sovereign, independent, and the dominant actors in the international system. Over the centuries that followed, beginning in Europe, the nation-state grew more capable as a political entity and spread to all corners of the world. States developed capabilities as national governments to organize the economy and society. They developed laws and political institutions, systems of taxation and regulation, judicial bodies and agencies of law enforcement, and expansive military organizations. Along the way, the modern territorial state became the dominant political entity in the world.

Two features are most important in characterizing the Westphalian state system, and they operate at different levels of analysis. First, domestically, states are territorial sovereign entities. As the German sociologist Max Weber famously observed, states in a Westphalian system have 'a monopoly on the legitimate use of physical force within a given territory' (Weber 1970). This is the classic understanding of the modern sovereign state. The state, embodied in the national government, has the exclusive right and ability to exercise violence (physical force) within its own territorial boundaries. Groups in society have no rights to act as private armies or police. The state controls violence and force within the society. Second, at the international level, national governments recognize and respect the supreme authority of states as sovereign political entities. Outside actors have no legitimate rights to act inside the territory of a sovereign state. Together, these features capture the essence of the Westphalian system. As the political theorist Chris Brown observes, '[t]he actors in the Westphalian System are sovereign states – territorial polities whose rulers acknowledge no equal at home, no superior abroad' (Brown 2002).

It is important to distinguish the ideal norms of the Westphalian system and the actual capacities of states to live up to these norms. Throughout the modern era, many states claimed status as sovereign entities but were not able to fully enforce their monopoly on the use of violence within their societies. **Warlords** – private authority figures who control their own local armies or militias – and criminal gangs have plagued nation-states across the centuries in both the West and the rest of the world. Certain national governments and their law-enforcement capabilities have often proved incapable of preventing substate groups from wielding violence. Organized criminal gangs are notorious in the United States and other countries. Among the most infamous of these groups is the American Mafia, an Italian-American criminal society that emerged in the late nineteenth century in New York City and spread to other major cities on the East Coast and elsewhere. In Italy, the Mafia has challenged the central state for more than a century. In Mexico, drug gangs have grown into cross-border

Failed states
States that lack the basic institutions and capacities of government – taxing, policing, upholding the rule of law, protecting property, providing public roads and services, and maintaining control over territory.

Warlords
Private authority figures who control their own local armies or militias.

businesses, with private armies that smuggle contraband across the United States border, intimidating and killing politicians and law-enforcement officials. Mexican authorities have struggled to rein in both the drug gangs and the vigilante groups of private Mexican citizens that have emerged to combat them (see Photo 12.1). In Japan, the Yakuza are an infamous organized crime syndicate, operating in many sectors of the economy. In China, warlords and violent gangs operated along territorial borders and in waters off the coast for centuries.

Governments have running battles with these gangs as they terrorize towns and cities and use the threat of violence to extract payments from frightened businesses. States may claim the legitimate monopoly of violence, but they often struggle to make good on this claim.

Recall as well that sovereign states, in a legal sense, are equal as members of the Westphalian system. In practice, however, they differ vastly in their capabilities. In this sense, the norms of equality within the Westphalian system coexist with a system of power inequality and political hierarchy. Some powerful states have more ability to get their way than weak states. Similarly, the norm of sovereign non-intervention exists as an ideal but is often violated. States can claim a supreme authority within their national borders but outside actors, such as strong states or non-state transnational actors, may be able to intervene inside states. States may be unable to enforce border controls, and find their sovereign territorial boundaries transgressed by foreign actors. At the extreme, such transgressions would be the military intervention of a foreign power, as we discussed in Chapter 5 in the case of NATO military intervention in Libya in 2011. A weak state can find itself unable

Photo 12.1 Mexican Drug War

Within the last decade, tens of thousands have been killed in Mexico as rival gangs have fought for control over territory and drug distribution routes. They extort local businesses and rely on kidnappings to finance their rivalry. The Mexican state has tried to re-establish its authority over both the gangs and the vigilantes. In this photo, Mexico's most wanted drug lord, Joaquin Guzman Loera, known as 'El Chapo', is transported to the Maximum Security Prison of El Altiplano in Mexico City, Mexico on January 8, 2016.

Source: Daniel Cardenas/Anadolu Agency/Getty Images.

to resist or defend against a more powerful invading state. But sovereign control by a state can fail in many less spectacular ways. Criminal groups, such as drug lords and gangs, can operate across borders without the national government being able to enforce laws or territorial boundaries.

Challenges to the sovereign authority of states by criminal groups are not new. Pirates, organized crime, and drug cartels have operated for centuries in various parts of the world. States have always been under challenge by non-state groups. As a result, states must constantly find new ways to build and reinforce state control. Below we examine non-state challenges in more detail, and then consider the international responses to these challenges.

Levels of Analysis *Formal Sovereignty and the Varying Ability of States to Exercise It*		
👤 Individual	👥 State	🌐 International
Private individuals and groups, including drug gangs and vigilantes, can sometimes challenge state authority.	States formally claim sovereign authority internally and externally but are not always able to enforce that claim.	The sovereign state system is a defining feature of world politics and has continually adapted to challenges from non-state actors.

CHALLENGES TO SOVEREIGN STATES

The traditional Westphalian idea of the international system – and the modern sovereign state itself – has been challenged in recent decades by a cluster of interrelated developments: failed states, non-state actors empowered by technological change, and the changing norms and expectations of the international community.

First, as the discussion above showed, the capacity of states to retain sovereign control over their national territories varies considerably. In the developing world, there are many nation-states that are sovereign more in name than reality. Afghanistan, South Sudan, and Somalia are just some examples of states so weak that the central government has no effective control over major regions within the formal territorial borders. These unruled territories provide attractive havens for non-state criminal and terrorist groups to operate, offering training sites and launching pads for transnational operations. More established states with capable law-enforcement institutions and courts that uphold the rule of law provide less welcoming conditions for these private wielders of violence, though, as we have noted, even these advanced countries still struggle with organized crime and other violent groups.

Second, advancements in technologies have made it easier for private groups, such as criminal gangs and terrorist groups, to operate and inflict harm across national borders and at longer distances. The internet makes it easier to communicate and transfer funds across the world. These groups can build extended transnational organizational networks. As discussed in Chapter 8, technologies of violence – nuclear, chemical, and biological – potentially provide capabilities that allow non-state actors to wield destructive force that, previously, only states could possess. The world of the internet and cyber connections is putting capabilities in the hands of private groups as well as states. Modern technologies, such as monitoring and surveillance, also give states new tools with which to seek out transnational criminal and terrorist groups. It remains an open question whether these modern technologies give the advantage to non-state groups or the states which seek to detect and prevent their violent activities.

Third, countries around the world have become increasingly concerned with the activities of non-state actors, particularly the violent ambitions of terrorist groups with increasing global reach. The Westphalian system is under threat, and established sovereign states are searching for ways to respond. One response is to target criminal and terrorist groups with intelligence, special operations, covert actions, and counter-insurgent war. For example, in recent years, the United States has expanded its use of unmanned drones in Pakistan, Afghanistan, and Yemen to strike terrorist havens (Harnden 2011). Another strategy of response is to seek to strengthen the weak and failing states that provide havens for outlaw groups.

At the same time, the norms of state sovereignty are evolving, reflected most clearly in the idea of the Responsibility to Protect (R2P). As discussed in Chapter 5, R2P suggests that if a state is inflicting harm or violence on its own citizens or if it is unable to protect its own citizens from harm or violence, the international community has the right – indeed the obligation – to act. The emergence of this proposed responsibility reflects an evolution of thinking within the international community about state sovereignty. Failed states, terrorism, and violations of human rights are driving the international community to rethink the old Westphalian state system and the rules and norms of intervention.

The international system will be transformed by these challenges, struggles, and changing norms. States will either find ways to adapt and strengthen the capacity of their sovereign authority or the world will enter a new epoch of transnational violence and disorder. Technologies and the forces of globalization have brought the world together in new ways but, in the hands of violent and criminal non-state actors, they also threaten to tear the world apart. We can look at three 'faces' of this non-state world: pirates, warlords, and terrorists with global reach. First, we examine the breeding ground for these challenges: weak and failed states.

Weak and Failed States

We have already observed that a modern sovereign state has several key characteristics: it has a functioning central government, can control its borders, and effectively claims a monopoly on the legitimate use of force over its territory. Most observers would agree that a stable, capable state has a defined territory, a distinct population, an effective government, and the capacity to enter formal relations with other states.

Weak states
States with functioning central governments but only weak control over their territory and borders.

Many states in the developing world are only a shadow of this ideal. Some states might be best seen as **weak states**. They have functioning central governments, but they have only weak control over their territory and borders. They are unable to fully tax the population, establish police and military services, and provide other public services. There are multiple causes of state weakness. In some cases, for example contemporary Lebanon and Iraq (after the collapse of the Ba'athist regime), there are deep ethnic or religious divisions and no history or tradition of strong centralized rule. In others, corrupt or otherwise less competent governments can neither eliminate challengers to their authority (for example, gangs or drug cartels) nor provide basic services and thereby earn the allegiance of parts of their population. As noted above, Mexico is an example.

Failed states are states where the government itself no longer functions; the state has essentially collapsed. As I. William Zartman suggests in his widely accepted definition, a failed state is a state where 'the basic functions of the state are no longer performed' (Zartman 1995). Some observers see failed states primarily manifest in the inability of the state to enforce order. This absence of an established capable state will be seen most dramatically when insurgents attack the government and the country is torn by civil war. Map 12.1 shows that failed and fragile states are found in many parts of today's world.

Map 12.1 The Fragile State Index 2018

Each year the Fund for Peace releases its index of fragile states around the world. This is a graphical representation of that index for 2018, along with the scores used to derive the index and rankings for the 20 most vulnerable countries. Notice how those states that are categorized as in critical or dangerous condition tend to cluster together in geographic regions. The international community has tried to respond to the trouble created by the worst of these states, but international organizations are fighting an uphill battle.

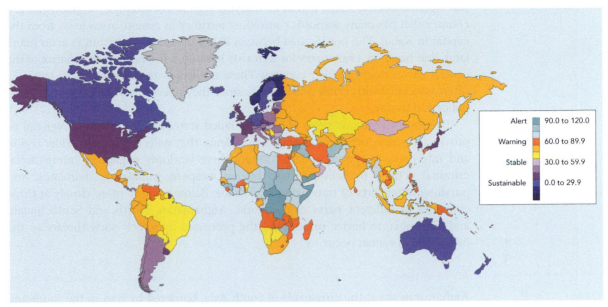

Alert	90.0 to 120.0
Warning	60.0 to 89.9
Stable	30.0 to 59.9
Sustainable	0.0 to 29.9

Source: Reproduced with permission of the Fund for Peace.

As one expert on weak and failed states notes: 'In most failed states, government troops battle armed revolts led by one or more rivals. Occasionally, the official authorities in a failed state face two or more insurgencies, varieties of civil unrest, different degrees of communal discontent, and a plethora of dissent directed at the state and at groups within the state' (Rotberg 2003). Contemporary Pakistan, Iraq, Afghanistan, Syria, and even Mexico and Peru are countries with violent internal rivals – or warlords – challenging the authority of the central government.

Rival groups and warlords within seemingly sovereign states have long played a role in the history of the Westphalian state system. The first states that emerged in early modern Europe in the seventeenth century did not simply emerge whole and sovereign. They had to be created. Central government rulers had to build institutions and establish their supreme authority within an internationally recognized territorial boundary. The first states in Europe were composite states, built through the combining of several political entities. As Daniel Nexon notes:

> Whether confederate or imperial, ruled by hereditary or elected princes, or operating as autonomous republics, most early modern European states were composed of numerous subordinate political communities linked to central authorities through distinctive contracts specifying rights and obligations. These subordinate political communities often had their own social organizations, identities, languages, and institutions. (Nexon 2009)

In Europe during this era, and around the world, the rulers of the central state had to struggle to establish their authority and maintain control over outlying areas.

In some cases, central governments fail to establish rule and order within a sovereign state because outlying provinces and regions want independence. In Europe today, there are active independence movements in northern Spain, the United Kingdom, and elsewhere. Along the Chinese border, provinces such as Tibet are attempting to gain autonomy or independence. Russia has also struggled with secession movements in Chechnya along its southern border. In other cases, it is not an independence movement that threatens state sovereignty and control but criminal gangs and warlords that operate as mini-states within an outlying region. For example, Afghanistan is a country that has many warlords controlling territory in remote areas away from the capital in Kabul. The border area between Pakistan and Afghanistan is a 'no man's land' that has been a sanctuary for terrorists because it lies beyond the control of the central government of either country. These challenges to the centralized state are often associated with crime and violence since they operate beyond the reach of the police and the law.

The most dangerous cases of weak or failed states are those where regional or provincial leaders, or warlords, engage in violence that spills out into the wider region and international system at large. Often, these warlords engage in international criminal activity by selling drugs, buying weapons, smuggling diamonds, and pursuing other sorts of transnational violence. Below we look more closely at three countries in different parts of the world, Afghanistan, North and South Sudan, and Colombia, to better understand the processes by which such threats to the international system occur.

Afghanistan

Afghanistan sits at the crossroads of South Asia, bordered by Iran in the south and west, and Pakistan in the east. It is a landlocked and mountainous country situated over the centuries amidst great empires and trade and migration routes. Afghanistan, with a population of 35 million, is one of the poorest countries in the world, and its largest export is poppies, which are used in making heroin. Afghanistan is the largest provider of poppies in the world, and the international heroin trade depends on its exports (Naím 2005). Afghanistan is also a country with a weak central government and a patchwork of tribal and ethnic groups that control provincial areas and compete with the national government in Kabul for the allegiance of the Afghan people.

Since the late 1970s, Afghanistan has been plagued by civil war. When its pro-Soviet government was threatened by internal tribal uprisings, the Soviet Union intervened with military force. This was followed by a long struggle between Soviet military forces, tied to a Soviet-backed regime in Kabul, and tribal groups resisting foreign domination. As many as 2 million Afghans died in the war with the Soviets. Rebel groups were led by the Afghan Mujahideen, US-supported resistance fighters that struggled against the Soviet invasion of their homeland. American involvement in Afghanistan was primarily motivated by its Cold War competition with the Soviet Union, so after the withdrawal of Soviet troops in 1989, the United States lost interest in Afghanistan. During the 1990s, in the void left by the departure of Soviet and United States troops, a civil war ensued among different tribal and provincial groups vying for control over the country. Out of this struggle the Taliban, a radical Islamic group, developed into a politico-religious organization and seized power in the capital of Kabul, eventually capturing as much as 95 percent of the country by 2000. The Taliban instituted a radical political and religious order, restricting rights and freedoms, particularly of women and girls. Most importantly, under the Taliban, the Al Qaeda terrorist organization was able to set up training camps in the countryside and establish a safe haven from which it could launch the 2001 terrorist attacks on the United States.

Photo 12.2 Poppy Fields in Afghanistan

Nearly 90% of all poppies are grown in rural Afghanistan, says a drug survey released Nov. 13, 2013 by the UN's drug control agency. The area is beyond the control of the central government, and largely controlled by the Taliban. In 2017, Afghanistan opium production reached a record high.

Source: Noorullah Shirzada/AFP/Getty Images.

America's new enemy now had its 'home address,' and it was in Afghanistan. Nonetheless, the Taliban refused to hand over Al Qaeda's leader, Osama bin Laden, and other prominent terrorist leaders. In late 2001, the United States launched an attack on Taliban and Al Qaeda targets in Afghanistan, working with anti-Taliban groups across the country. These assaults on the Taliban culminated with the capture of Kabul by the Northern Alliance, a militia still recognized by the United Nations as the legitimate Afghan government. Along the way, many regional warlords switched their allegiance from the Taliban to the Northern Alliance. For a while, the new government made inroads in rebuilding and establishing rule across the country. But the Taliban slowly began to return to prominence, gathering forces in various outlying regions. The result was a new phase of insurgent civil war. The beleaguered central government struggled to maintain order in the face of rebel acts within regional strongholds. Beginning in 2007, the United States expanded its military operations in the country; to this day, a violent insurgency continues to pull the country apart. Entire parts of the country remain outside the control – and law enforcement – of the government in Kabul (see Box 12.1). Tens of thousands of Afghan civilians have been killed since 2001, and even in Kabul, violent attacks and suicide bombings by Taliban insurgents are a regular occurrence.

 Simulations: What would you do? Imagine you were President George W. Bush on September 12, 2001. How would you handle the aftermath of the Al Qaeda attacks? Go to the companion website and assess your options.

12.1   MAKING CONNECTIONS
Aspiration versus Reality

Building the Afghanistan State

Aspiration

The United States intervened militarily in Afghanistan soon after the September 11, 2001 terrorist attacks, overthrowing the Taliban government. In the aftermath of this intervention, American and NATO forces have spent the last 15 years trying to defeat an insurgency by Taliban forces and other tribal groups. The most ambitious goal that the United States and others have articulated for Afghanistan is to turn it into a functioning democratic state. The goal is to build a strong, legitimate, and accountable central government with all the elements of modern government. Consider the following statement by President George W. Bush:

> With the steady leadership of President Karzai, the people of Afghanistan are building a modern and peaceful government. Next month, 500 delegates will convene a national assembly in Kabul to approve a new Afghan constitution. The proposed draft would establish a bicameral parliament, set national elections next year, and recognize Afghanistan's Muslim identity, while protecting the rights of all citizens. Afghanistan faces continuing economic and security challenges – it will face those challenges as a free and stable democracy. (Remarks by President George W. Bush at the 20th Anniversary of the National Endowment for Democracy, November 6, 2003)

Reality

After many years of military struggle, the Afghan government remained weak. Its powers and authority did not reach much further than the city limits of the capital. The possibility of building a Western-style democratic state was remote. Although voting took place for a national assembly and the leader of the country, the authority of the central government remains limited. Power-sharing schemes that leave tribal areas under separate rule became a more realistic option. Stability, rather than the lofty ideals of nation building and democracy, became the watchword for Afghan politics. Consider the statement by President Barack Obama:

> The goal that we seek is achievable, and can be expressed simply: No safe haven from which Al Qaeda or its affiliates can launch attacks against our homeland or our allies. We won't try to make Afghanistan a perfect place. We will not police its streets or patrol its mountains indefinitely. That is the responsibility of the Afghan government, which must step up its ability to protect its people, and move from an economy shaped by war to one that can sustain a lasting peace. What we can do, and will do, is build a partnership with the Afghan people that endures – one that ensures that we will be able to continue targeting terrorists and supporting a sovereign Afghan government. (Remarks by the President on the Way Forward in Afghanistan, June 22, 2011)

North and South Sudan

Sudan, before South Sudan gained independence in 2011, was the largest country in Africa, with an ancient history, but one that has long suffered from civil war and has been labeled a failed state. It is also a country with rich oil deposits. Over the centuries Sudan has been encroached upon by neighbors such as Egypt. In the late nineteenth century, Sudan was under British control even as other European powers, such as France and Belgium, also pursued claims on parts of its territory. Eventually, the United Kingdom granted the country independence in 1956, but Sudan remained divided between the North, which maintained close ties with Egypt and was predominantly Arab and Muslim, and the South, which was mostly populated by Christians and members of other religious sects. The fact that the United Kingdom divided the country between the North and the South for purposes of administrative rule also reinforced these divisions. In the decades to follow, civil war was rife between the two factions. Military governments were formed in the North and rebel armies organized resistance in the South. The southern 'liberation army' formed in the 1980s and was a Marxist-inspired organization with support from the Soviet Union and Ethiopia. It gradually shed this identity and reached out for Western support by portraying the struggle as one between a Christian South and an Arab Islamic North seeking to dominate the nation.

After two decades of brutal war, peace talks in 2003 did lead to a truce and the granting of autonomy for the South for a period of years to be followed by a referendum on independence. The agreement also mandated joint leadership of the government and the sharing of oil revenues. A United Nations mission to Sudan was established to help implement the agreement. But by 2005, the southern rebel army withdrew from the accord that ended the civil war, protesting its slow implementation. In the meantime, a bloody civil war was also occurring in the western region of Sudan, known as Darfur. Sudanese rebels were seeking autonomy from the central government, which they saw as neglecting the region. Government and rebel groups were both accused of violent atrocities, but the Arab militias operating on behalf of the national government were singled out by outside observers for engaging in acts of genocide. In 2004, American Secretary of State Colin Powell described the conflict in Darfur as genocide, suggesting that it was the worst humanitarian crisis of the new century. Eventually, the Sudanese government and rebel groups signed an agreement, bringing an end to the conflict and establishing a temporary government in the region that would include rebel participation. Ultimately, the agreement did not stop the violence, and civil war continues to pit religious and ethnic tribal groups, both regionally and nationally, against each other (Natsios and Abramowitz 2011).

The decades-long civil war between North and South Sudan culminated in the creation of an independent South Sudan in 2011. A reported 2 million Sudanese lost their lives in this war and resulting famine, and many more have been displaced. Despite its independence, the government of the oil-rich South Sudan has been unable to establish its authority and the country remains in a civil war, spending millions of dollars on arms as the country has experienced famine and economic crisis.

Colombia

Colombia is a country in South America with a constitutional government and a large economy. It gained independence from Spain in 1819 and established the Republic of Colombia in 1886. After several decades of political stability in the early twentieth century, the country found itself in new episodes of political violence and civil war beginning in the 1940s, when armed militias of the Liberal and Conservative parties descended into a vicious circle of violence and retaliation that persisted for decades. By the 1960s, violence between the political parties declined; leading political figures established a united front of shared power and pursued an agenda of economic and social reform.

Despite efforts at building a modern government, political violence and instability were never far from the forefront. Beginning in the 1970s, various guerrilla groups, some dominated by Marxist ideology, emerged to fight the government. Amidst this turmoil, beginning in the late 1970s, violent drug cartels took hold of territory, increasing their power and control of outlying regions. The most famous of these were the Medellin Cartel, led by Pablo Escobar, and the Cali Cartel who, along with various associated groups, exerted increasing political and economic influence in Colombia over the decades. These cartels helped finance an array of illegal armed groups, both right-wing paramilitary groups and left-wing insurgents, and have undermined the authority of the central government. Guerrilla groups emerged first, operating in the countryside under the influence of Marxist revolutionary ideas. Paramilitary groups have also been a prominent part of the Colombian political landscape, often employed by landowners seeking protection against guerrilla groups when the central government could not do so. In the 1980s, these paramilitary groups who, in the past, had worked with agricultural landowners producing legal crops, began to come under the sway of drug lords, using their lands for the growing of coca. Soon, the drug cartels began supporting paramilitary squads (Kline 2003).

Drug groups used their money and firearms to build private security protection arrangements for towns and people, further weakening the state. The central government tried to re-establish its authority and the reach of law enforcement but was largely helpless as the cartels and private security warlords continued to dominate large parts of the country. Harvey F. Kline summarized the downward spiral of Columbia's central governmental power:

> Hence the weak state that existed in Colombia made it possible for drugs to become rooted in the countryside. This, in turn, made the Colombian state even weaker, as drug dealers established private governments in parts of the country. As their illicit wealth increased, they armed themselves and collaborated with both paramilitary groups and guerrilla groups, which made the state weaker yet. (Kline 2003)

Along the way, Colombia became the leading drug-producing country in the world. In recent years, the country continues to be plagued by drug cartels, insurgent movements, and paramilitary groups. Smaller drug trading groups have emerged, employing sophisticated financial and communication technologies to escape the law and operate across international borders. Colombian drug traffickers have found sophisticated ways to 'clean' their money, entrusting their dollars to intermediaries who use the funds to make legal purchases in the United States on behalf of Colombian customers. The customers pay the brokers in local currency that is passed on to the drug dealers (Naím 2005).

In the last decade, the Colombian government has pursued counterterrorism campaigns, economic infrastructure programs, and peace negotiations, seeking to rebuild the fractured country. In 2016, President Juan Manuel Santos announced a deal with the leading rebel group – the Revolutionary Armed Forces of Colombia (FARC) – to end the conflict, for which he was awarded the Nobel Peace Prize (see Photo 12.3).

What Afghanistan, North and South Sudan, and Colombia – until recently – have in common is that the central state has failed to establish its authority and sovereign control over the national territory. These countries have struggled to build what sovereign states must possess – namely, a monopoly over the legitimate use of violence within the territorial borders of the country. Non-state groups such as ethnic militias, separatist forces, guerrilla groups, and warlord armies

Photo 12.3 Colombia's President and the UN Secretary General
Colombian President Juan Manuel Santos was awarded the Nobel Peace Prize in 2016 for his efforts to bring the country's decades-long civil war to an end. The conflict, which has been raging for 52 years, has cost the lives of at least 220,000 people and displaced almost 6 million. In the photo, Santos offers UN Secretary General Ban Ki-moon a copy of the Colombian peace agreement.

Source: Corazon Aguirre/Pacific Press/LightRocket via Getty Images.

usurp authority and violence capacities that are normally reserved for the state. Weak or failing states allow private groups to take control of regions or provinces. This breakdown of political order becomes a vicious cycle; the groups take hold because the state is weak, which weakens the state further, which allows the groups to grow stronger, further weakening the state. Pierre Hassner has described this breakdown of state authority as a 'return to the Middle Ages,' in which the modern state is undermined by a proliferation of competing substate power blocs (Hassner 1993). Through this process, these weak and fragmenting states become theaters for transnational crime and violence. As a result, other countries with established functioning states, and the international system itself, become threatened. If lawlessness emerges in one state or region of the world, it provides a platform for criminal groups to threaten other countries and regions. Weak and failed states are susceptible to three challenges discussed next: piracy, terrorist groups, and the privatization of war.

Piracy

Pirates have been among the most persistent challengers to the authority of states, threatening freedom on the world's oceans over the centuries. **Pirates** are non-state gangs who commit robbery or criminal violence on the high seas. The 1982 United Nations Convention on the Law of the Sea defines piracy as acts of 'violence, detention, or depredation' committed for private ends against the crew or passengers on board ships on international waterways. States care about piracy because the criminal activity itself can be costly, in human and economic terms, and these

Pirates
Non-state gangs who commit robbery or criminal violence on the high seas.

12.2   MAKING CONNECTIONS
Then and Now

Pirates in the Seventeenth and Twenty-First Centuries

Then: Seventeenth-Century Pirates

The Golden Age of pirates, 1650–1720, included famous figures such as Blackbeard (Edward Teach), Henry Morgan, William 'Captain' Kidd, and Bartholomew Roberts. Many of these pirates operated in the Caribbean Sea, seeking to board Spanish ships transporting gold and silver back to Europe. Pirate ships were heavily loaded with canons and sailors, making it easy for them to attack and overwhelm merchant ships. Pirating became so widespread and successful in the eighteenth century that European governments were forced to patrol the waters with heavily armed naval warships. Many famous pirates were killed or captured after these government-sponsored patrols began, and pirating in the New World declined.

Now: Twenty-First-Century Pirates

Beginning in the early 1990s, pirates operating off the coast of Somalia began to attack shipping vessels, kidnapping crews for ransom. The collapse of the Somali government and ensuing civil war provided the setting. The decline of the fishing industry off the coast of East Africa has intensified desperate economic circumstances; some pirates were originally fishermen whose livelihoods were undercut by illegal fishing by foreign crews off Somali waters. Today, Somali pirates armed primarily with machine guns board cargo ships and hold the crew for ransom. Warlords along the coast have organized the pirate networks and split the profits from their operations. Hundreds of attacks occur each year. Recently, warships from various countries, including the United States, the United Kingdom, China, and Japan, have patrolled the waters to deter attacks. These patrols do provide deterrence, but pirates still operate in these waters.

non-state groups amount to a direct challenge to states and their monopoly of control over the use of force in and between states. Pirates operate outside the law, and outside the Westphalian system of states. As Box 12.2 shows, pirates have challenged state sovereignty for centuries. The upsurge of piracy in the contemporary world, most prominently off the coast of East Africa, presents disturbing evidence that at least some states have lost control over the seas today.

With the rise of modern naval power in the late nineteenth and early twentieth centuries, piracy receded around the world. But it was not fully extinguished and has reappeared in recent years. Many of the coastal waters around the globe, such as the coasts of North America, Western Europe, and Northeast Asia, are relatively safe. In these waters, established naval powers safeguard sea lanes and deter pirate gangs. In other regions, however, piracy is a fact of maritime life. As Map 12.2 shows, piracy remains a significant problem in the waters extending from the Red Sea and the Indian Ocean, off the East African coast, and in the Straits of Malacca and Singapore; these waterways are used by as many as 50,000 commercial ships a year. One study indicates that worldwide losses from piracy amount to as much as $13 to $16 billion annually (Hahn 2012).

Map 12.2 Global Pirate Activity in 2016
As the map indicates, the problem of piracy is significant off the coasts of Africa, but also in southeast Asia and in parts of South America.

Source: Data from the International Maritime Bureau.

The most famous instances of modern piracy occur off the coast of Somalia. Major shipping routes take a large flow of cargo ships through narrow water passages, making it easy for pirates to overtake and board them with small motor boats. This is also a region dominated by developing countries with small navies. Somalia itself is a failed state, with ongoing clashes between various factional warlords and criminal gangs. The pirates are typically protected by these factional groups on shore, and the absence of centralized government authority makes effective law enforcement impossible. The major naval powers in the region – which include India and the United States – are unable or unwilling to project consistent naval protection into the area, except in instances where commercial interests are particularly significant. As a result, piracy proliferates. The Somalia pirates are clever enough not to harm crews or vessels. They capture and hold the ships, and demand ransom. With few options, the commercial shipping companies tend to pay the pirates what they demand, and business continues. The US navy has intervened in some instances to rescue hostages taken by pirates (Gettleman 2012). The 2013 Hollywood thriller, *Captain Phillips*, captured the high drama of one such episode.

Modern piracy shows the limits of state capacity to enforce order and provide security on open waters. Piracy comes to life when a leading power, such as the United Kingdom or the United States, is not positioned to offer protection. When great powers are struggling among themselves or if their presence recedes from regions with active commercial maritime traffic, the 'rule of the sea' declines or disappears. Most importantly, piracy is aided by the weakness of states in the region. It is the failure of Somalia to establish the rule of law and a capable central government that allows piracy to prosper. The pirates can be attacked by navies dispatched to the area, but the problem will only be solved when weak or failed states in the area are able to achieve sufficient capabilities to resist the activities of pirates in their harbors and shores. Pirates conduct dangerous business on water but require safe havens on land. The problem of piracy is felt off shore but the solutions, in part, are to be found on shore. The governments of the countries need to be strengthened so that they can establish stable order and defend their territorial waters.

Terrorism

As we discussed in Chapter 2, international terrorism, an enduring problem in the international system, burst onto the global stage in the opening decade of the twenty-first century. The violent Sunni Islamist transnational group, Al Qaeda, carried out attacks in Madrid and London, as well as in Bali, Morocco, and other parts of the developing world. For the United States, the terrorist attacks of September 11, 2001, were a frightening introduction to the potential for non-state violence in the twenty-first century. The attacks were quite simple in their design. A group of 20 hijackers boarded four commercial airlines, took over the controls, and smashed them into buildings. The only weapons they brought with them were box cutting knives. What made the attacks shocking is that the hijacked airplanes became weapons used to inflict great violence on New York City and the Pentagon, the headquarters of the United States Department of Defense. Prior to 9/11, the security of the American homeland had only been attacked in the modern era when Japanese bombers destroyed Pearl Harbor at the beginning of World War II. But September 11, 2001 seemed to shatter the view of America as relatively invulnerable. Violence could come from any direction and hit any place on earth. No people are secure. Small groups of armed gangs, made up of people who hate and are prepared to die, can lash out at established societies and leave their cities burning.

Terrorists employ violence against civilians to achieve a political purpose. Used as a tool of war and political struggle, terrorism may be employed by a group seeking to intimidate, coerce, or manipulate the sentiments of another people by inflicting violence on innocent civilians. This violence may simply be an expression of hatred and anger, but, as shown in Chapter 2, it can also be a calculated step aimed at altering the behavior of an enemy. The immediate victims may be innocent civilians, but the ultimate target is the foreign policy of a state.

In this sense, terrorism, like piracy, is very old. In the nineteenth and early twentieth centuries, terrorism primarily took the form of violence committed by nationalist movements resisting occupation and seeking independence from imperial or colonial domination. In late nineteenth-century Russia, opponents of the Tsarist state, or anarchists, used bombs to kill state officials with the hope of inciting popular revolt. Anarchist figures were responsible for the assassination of Russian Czar Alexander II in 1881 and American President William McKinley in 1901. In the late nineteenth century, Armenian nationalist groups seeking independence from the Ottoman Empire used violence against public officials. Irish nationalists carried out attacks in England, foreshadowing the later activities of the Irish Republican Army, a group that, for decades, carried out assassinations and political violence in their protests against the British armed forces' presence in Northern Ireland. In the early twentieth century, Zionist groups fought the British in their efforts to establish a Jewish state in Palestine. At the same time, the Muslim Brotherhood, which recently won control of the Egyptian government, and then lost it in a military coup, was formed in Egypt as a nationalist group resisting British control. As mentioned in Chapter 2, a terrorist act by a Serbian nationalist was the proximate cause of World War I.

By far the most notorious international terrorist group in the contemporary era is Al Qaeda. Founded in 1988 by Osama bin Laden, this Sunni Islamist extremist movement has carried out acts of violence with the aim of ending foreign influence in Muslim countries and establishing a new Islamic caliphate (transnational Islamic state). In October 2000, Al Qaeda carried out a bombing of the US Navy destroyer USS Cole in the port of Aden in Yemen. But it was the September 11, 2001 attack that brought the threat of international terrorism into a new era.

The terrorist acts of September 11 share the basic characteristics of terrorism as it has appeared over the centuries. It is an act of violence by non-state actors directed at civilians and seeking to send a message. The violence is directed at the enemy, but it is not aimed at defeating an enemy in war. It is an act of violence that seeks to make a political point and alter how others see a political struggle. By reacting to an attack, people will force their government to change its policies. An Al Qaeda spokesman commented on the violence unleashed in the United States in September 2001: 'It rang the bells of restoring Arab and Islamic glory' (Richardson 2007). The symbolic aspect of the September 11 attacks was clear: it was an attack on icons of American power. The World Trade Center's Twin Towers served as a symbol of American global capitalism and the Pentagon as a symbol of American global military power.

More recently, as we discussed in Chapter 2, by 2014 another violent Islamist group – the Islamic State or ISIS – emerged as an offshoot of Al Qaeda and seized large areas of territory in Iraq, which had fragmented into warring factions following the US-led intervention of 2003, and Syria, which had descended into a violent civil war between insurgents and the repressive regime of Bashar al-Assad. ISIS took advantage of these two fragile states and at its peak controlled a land mass equivalent in size to the United Kingdom. Unlike most terrorist groups, ISIS sought to transform itself from a non-state actor to a state with control over territory and population by establishing a caliphate, or state governed in accordance with Islamic law. That effort failed, as ISIS was driven back by the military forces of both the Iraqi and Syrian governments. But its campaign of far-flung violence has continued. Between 2014 and 2018, ISIS carried out 149 attacks in 29 countries (not including Iraq and Syria), resulting in over 2,000 deaths (Lister *et al.* 2018).

So why do terrorists do what they do? What leads people to kill innocent civilians? There are many reasons why angry militants engage in terrorism (Richardson 2007), and as we showed in Chapter 2, the motivations are primarily political and strategic rather than religious. As in its early nineteenth-century manifestations, one motivation for terrorism still appears to be the quest for an independent homeland. The Basques in Spain, the Tamils in Sri Lanka, the Chechens in southern Russia, separatists in Northern Ireland, and many other groups have, over the last century, resorted to terrorist violence as they seek independence. Other groups have had more far-reaching political objectives. Revolutionaries in nineteenth-century Europe sought to overturn capitalism and usher in a new social order. Al Qaeda has sought to force the United States and its military forces out of the Middle East (in particular, Saudi Arabia as the home to Muslim holy sites). Since the days of Muhammad, some Islamist groups, with ISIS as the latest example, have sought to transform the states in the Middle East into a trans-state caliphate. As Box 12.3 suggests, the appropriate response to international terrorism depends at least in part on the assumptions one makes as to the motives of terrorists and the causes of terrorism.

12.3   DIFFERING PERSPECTIVES

How to Cope with the Threat of International Terrorism

George W. Bush Administration

The growing threat of 'terrorism with global reach' is caused by extremists who have resorted to violence because 'they hate who we are.' Al Qaeda and other Islamic extremists are the most prominent and dangerous terrorists operating today. As the Bush administration argued after September 11, the terrorists are threatened by our freedom and liberty. They will not stop until we find them and kill them. We must go directly to their hideouts and build functioning states that are based on representative government and the rule of law. We need to go get them before they come to our shores and get us.

Other Voices

Robert Pape, scholar from the University of Chicago: Terrorists are provoked primarily by the occupation of their lands by foreigners, or at least by their beliefs about such occupation. In this view, the September 11 terrorists were motivated primarily because of the American military presence in Saudi Arabia – the land most holy to Islam – and American support for the conservative Arab regimes in the region and the state of Israel. To reduce the religious and political motivation of terrorism, the United States needs to reduce its presence in the Middle East.

Robert Wright, journalist: Wright was the author of a series of essays in *Slate* online magazine after September 11, where he argued that American force in the region was catalyzing Islamic terrorism rather than undercutting it. The focus needs to be on reducing the grievances and ideological motivations that propel radicals to engage in violence.

Weak and failed states make it possible for terrorists, pirates, warlords, and drug gangs to operate and challenge state sovereignty within and across nation-states. But what tools help these non-state actors transform their global power and reach?

Technology and the Privatization of War

Pirates, warlords, and terrorists are not just citizens committing crimes. They are non-state actors using violence capabilities ordinarily reserved for states to pursue economic or political gains by directly challenging the Westphalian state system. They have always existed at the edges of the state system. What has made these groups increasingly dangerous in the contemporary world is their potential global reach and the growing lethality of their violence. New communication technologies, which have enabled globalization and commerce to flourish, have simultaneously allowed more nefarious non-state actors to become transnational and organize at a great distance. They can operate far afield, sending messages, money, and agents around the world. At the same time, they are also able to gain access to ever more lethal violence capacities. These developments make non-state actors increasingly dangerous. They threaten not just particular cities or states, but global civilization and potentially the Westphalian system itself.

These new developments might be called the **privatization of war**. In the past, only states (primarily powerful states) were able to gain access to violence capabilities that could threaten other societies. As discussed in Chapter 8, it is still a remote possibility, but we can look to the future and foresee the day when small groups or transnational gangs of individuals might be able to acquire weapons of mass destruction (WMD). These technologies and knowledge will almost inevitably diffuse outward. Determined groups of extremists will increasingly be able to obtain WMD. The journalist Robert Wright has called this the 'growing lethality of hatred' (Wright 2006). The actual number of individuals in the world willing to inflict harm on others may not be growing, but their capabilities are. In the past, groups that were willing to use violence to express their hatred were limited in the damage they could inflict. In the future, this limitation may well drop away.

> **Privatization of war**
> The idea that, as technology advances, private groups have greater capacities to wage violence usually reserved for states.

It is possible to imagine a small group of determined individuals camped out in a weak or war-torn country planning a massively destructive event. It would take money, knowledge, and logistical capabilities. The group might find common cause with a few scientists or engineers who work for a government military agency with chemical, biological, or nuclear materials. Secretly, the government experts could find a way to transfer the materials to the non-state group. This could be possible because the state itself is weak or failing, has splintered into competing factions, or has lost the capacity to enforce safety and security for its WMD stockpiles. Organized crime groups or warlords from another state could act as an intermediary between government experts and terrorists. Once in the hands of a terrorist group, it is only a matter of logistics and determination to get the weapon to its target. The target might be a harbor city in Europe or the United States. An exploded nuclear device would kill hundreds of thousands of people, perhaps even a million or more, depending on its explosive capacities. A chemical or biological weapon would kill people more slowly, contaminating and poisoning people on a large scale across a metropolitan area. This is what terrorism could look like with global reach. It is a future spectacle in which the forces of technology and anger threaten the world in new and ominous ways.

In its famous National Security Strategy Report, issued a year after the 9/11 terrorist attacks, the US administration of President Bush proclaimed the danger:

> The gravest danger our Nation faces lies at the crossroads of radicalism and technology. Our enemies have openly declared that they are seeking weapons of mass destruction, and evidence indicates that they are doing so with determination. The United States will not allow these efforts to succeed … America is now threatened less by conquering states than we are by failing ones. We are menaced less by fleets and armies than by catastrophic technologies in the hands of the embittered few. We must defeat these threats to our Nation, allies, and friends. (White House 2002)

In this vision, the most worrisome peril to the United States and other countries of the world was terrorist groups that gained access to WMD from hostile or rogue states and used this violence capability to kill massive numbers of civilians. The immediate threat was from Al Qaeda, but the threat was much more profound and troubling than one terrorist organization. It was the deeper shift in the global system – a shift away from states able to monopolize violence – toward a future in which small gangs of dangerous people could destroy everyone's way of life.

These developments constitute a transformation in the ways and means of collective violence in international politics that is driven by technology and the political structure of the Westphalian system itself. This transformation causes problems for the old norms of sovereignty and the use of force. It raises troubling new questions about the relationship between domestic politics and international relations; regions of the world previously ignored must now be closely scrutinized. It also creates new functional challenges that will, inevitably, influence patterns of security cooperation. A global consensus does not exist on how to deal with this new type of diffuse non-state threat, which plays havoc with old notions of deterrence, alliance, self-defense, and Article 51 of the United Nations Charter (which defines the rights of states for collective self-defense).

Non-state actors engaging in crime and violence have coexisted with states and the states system throughout history. But technological advances and globalization have made them more dangerous and consequential for the global system. These non-state actors are triggering new efforts by states and international organizations, such as the United Nations, to work together to find ways to diminish their activity and impact. Ultimately, this has meant trying to eliminate the political conditions that allow these transnational groups to engage in violence and crime.

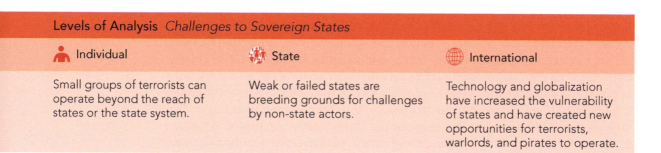

Levels of Analysis *Challenges to Sovereign States*		
👤 Individual	👥 State	🌐 International
Small groups of terrorists can operate beyond the reach of states or the state system.	Weak or failed states are breeding grounds for challenges by non-state actors.	Technology and globalization have increased the vulnerability of states and have created new opportunities for terrorists, warlords, and pirates to operate.

INTERNATIONAL RESPONSES TO WEAK AND FAILED STATES

How the international community, and particularly the United Nations, should respond to the problem of weak and failed states has become a defining issue for world politics in the twenty-first century. Officially speaking, all internationally recognized states are sovereign entities. The United Nations Charter observes in Article 2(7) that the United Nations shall not intervene in 'matters, which are essentially within the domestic jurisdiction of any state.' Chapter VII of the Charter does indicate that exceptions to this general principle of non-interference exist when a country poses a threat to international peace and security. In earlier decades, most of the major powers did not consider weak or failed states to be major threats to international peace and security, so the UN was not seen to have responsibilities in this area. More recently, the UN Security Council has been willing to define dangers to international peace and security more broadly, in recognition, as Box 12.4 suggests, that governments in some states cannot live up to the ideals of state sovereignty. Beginning in the 1990s, the Security Council invoked Chapter VII to authorize various interventions: Somalia in 1992–93, facing a major humanitarian disaster; Haiti in 1994, when a military coup deposed the democratically elected President Aristide; and Albania in 1997, when the state collapsed into chaos. There has been a growing sense around the world that the international community, represented by the United Nations and leading states, needs to prepare to intervene in failed states to prevent or ameliorate humanitarian crises, including mass starvation and genocide, and to prevent failed states from becoming sanctuaries for terrorist groups and other violent non-state actors.

12.4   MAKING CONNECTIONS
Theory and Practice

State Sovereignty

Theory

State sovereignty is one of the most basic ideas about how the international system is organized. It emerged in Europe in the seventeenth century as a set of norms about the primacy and legal pre-eminence of the nation-state. The nation-state is sovereign. There is both an external and internal dimension to sovereignty. Externally, no other foreign government has the legal right to rule or intervene within the internal politics of the nation-state. The national government has the supreme authority and last word on what goes on within the nation-state's borders. Internally, the state – or central government – has an exclusive right to rule within the country, unhindered by private police or armies.

Sovereignty: A government which exercises de facto administrative control over a country and is not subordinate to any other government in that country is a sovereign state (*The Arantzazu Mendi*, [1939] AC 256 referenced in *Stroud's Judicial Dictionary*).

Practice

Many countries have weak governments that simply cannot live up to the ideals of state sovereignty. Externally, the state cannot protect its borders against the illegal movement of private criminal groups or terrorists. Foreign groups or the agents of foreign governments operate within the country without resistance from the central government. Internally, militias and private armies control territory and operate as sort of 'private governments' within regions of the country. The central government is too weak to enforce order within the country or protect its borders.

Yemen – a small country on the southern coast of the Arabian Peninsula – is a prominent example. The countryside is ruled by tribal warlords while government institutions are weak and failing. The President of Yemen has ruled for over three decades and maintains power through co-opting and balancing off the warlord leaders in the provinces. As one Yemeni analyst notes: 'The government is a façade: the real power lies in the hands of the president, the house of the president and his network of patronage' (quoted in the *Financial Times*, January 3, 2010). There are more weapons in the hands of tribal groups than are controlled by the central security ministry. Terrorist groups have established affiliations with local radical Islamic groups and operate in safe havens within the country.

As discussed in Chapter 5, in the current era many national governments believe the international community has a right – even a moral obligation – to intervene in troubled states to prevent genocide and mass killing. NATO intervention in the Balkans and the war against Serbia were defining actions. As diplomatic negotiations at the United Nations Security Council over the crisis in Kosovo unfolded in 1998, Russia refused to agree to authorization of military action in what was an internal conflict. In the absence of UN approval, an American-led NATO operation did intervene (see Photo 12.4). In framing this action, UN Secretary General Kofi Annan articulated a view of the contingent nature of norms of sovereignty and

Photo 12.4 NATO Bombing of Belgrade, 1999

In 1998, a crisis broke out in Kosovo after Slobodan Milošević sent Serbian troops to reclaim areas of Kosovo from the Albanians. In the absence of UN approval to intervene in the crisis, a NATO operation was undertaken in Kosovo, beginning with an air campaign in 1999. This photo shows the destroyed Belgrade residence of Yugoslav President Slobodan Milošević. The NATO strike on April 22, 1999 on Milošević's Belgrade residence did not seek to kill the Yugoslav president but was aimed at putting pressure on his regime, the Pentagon said. Yugoslavia's Tanjug news agency said neither Milošević nor his family were at home when the house in the exclusive Dedinje residential area was hit.

Source: AFP/AFP/Getty Images.

non-intervention, as enshrined in the UN Charter. Strobe Talbott, an American foreign policy analyst, recounts Annan's views:

> If the behavior of a regime toward its own people is egregious, it is not just outsiders' business to object but their responsibility to step in, stop the offenses, and even change the regime. 'State frontiers,' Annan said, 'should no longer be seen as a watertight protection for war criminals or mass murderers. The fact that a conflict is "internal" does not give the parties any right to disregard the most basic rules of human conduct.' He acknowledged that 'the Charter protects the sovereignty of peoples,' and that it prohibits the UN from intervening 'in matters which are essentially within the domestic jurisdiction of any State.' However, he added that the principle 'was never meant as a license for governments to trample on human rights and human dignity. Sovereignty implies responsibility, not just power.' (Talbott 2008)

A year later, Annan observed that 'state sovereignty, in its most basic sense, is being redefined.' Modern states, he argued, are 'now widely understood to be instruments at the service of their people, and not vice-versa … When we read the Charter today, we are more than ever conscious that its aim is to protect individual human rights not to protect those who abuse them' (Talbott 2008).

This new notion that sovereignty entailed responsibilities, as well as rights and protections, reflects a gradual and evolving redefinition of the meaning of national sovereignty. The idea was further developed in one of the most important new global norms to emerge in the decades since the end of the Cold War – the norm of the Responsibility to Protect (R2P). As discussed in Chapter 5 and earlier in this chapter, this norm seeks to qualify and elaborate the older norm of state sovereignty. The norm indicates that states – or the governments of states – have a responsibility to protect their citizens from violence, manifest as genocide, war crimes, crimes against humanity, and ethnic cleansing. States are obligated to act to halt or prevent these mass atrocities. If a state is unable to do so – either because it is the perpetrator of the violence or it is too weak to stop the violence – the international community has an obligation to act.

The Responsibility to Protect norm is spelled out in the 2005 World Summit Outcome Document, which was ratified by the UN General Assembly:

Responsibility to protect populations from genocide, war crimes, ethnic cleansing and crimes against humanity

138. Each individual State has the responsibility to protect its populations from genocide, war crimes, ethnic cleansing and crimes against humanity. This responsibility entails the prevention of such crimes, including their incitement, through appropriate and necessary means. We accept that responsibility and will act in accordance with it. The international community should, as appropriate, encourage and help States to exercise this responsibility and support the United Nations in establishing an early warning capability.

139. The international community, through the United Nations, also has a responsibility to use appropriate diplomatic, humanitarian and other peaceful means, in accordance with Chapters VI and VIII of the Charter, to help to protect populations from genocide, war crimes, ethnic cleansing and crimes against humanity. In this context, we are prepared to take collective action, in a timely and decisive manner, through the Security Council, in accordance with the Charter, including Chapter VII, on a case-by-case basis and in cooperation with relevant regional organizations as appropriate, should peaceful means be inadequate and national authorities are manifestly failing to protect their populations from genocide, war crimes, ethnic cleansing and crimes against humanity ...

The norm of Responsibility to Protect emerged slowly beginning in the late 1990s. The 1994 genocide in Rwanda provided a trigger for global debate about the role and responsibility of the international community in the face of mass violence in a failed state. The United Nations Secretary General, Kofi Annan, pressed global leaders to come to some agreement about when and how member states might respond to such horrific violence. In the meantime, the Canadian government established an International Commission on Intervention and State Sovereignty in 2000 to develop ideas and ultimately came forward with the norm of the Responsibility to Protect (2001). The R2P norm announces that the international community has new obligations to see that basic human rights are protected within countries, particularly when faced with mass atrocities and other acts of organized violence (Evans 2009). The international community, in effect, has positioned itself as a non-state actor challenging the sovereignty of at least some states in the international system.

A further step in the erosion of norms of state sovereignty occurred in the aftermath of September 11. The American-led intervention in Afghanistan – where outside military force was used to topple a regime that actively protected terrorist attackers – was widely seen as a legitimate act of self-defense. The outside world has a legitimate claim to what goes on within a sovereign state if that state provides a launching pad, breeding ground, or protected area for transnational violence. The Bush administration pushed the limits of this principle in its invasion of Iraq. Now, it was the anticipatory threat of a state itself, and its ambitions to gain weapons of mass destruction, that provided the justification for intervention.

This new thinking was captured at the time by an American official at the State Department, Richard Haass:

> [There is] an emerging global consensus that sovereignty is not a blank check. Rather, sovereign status is contingent on the fulfilment by each state of certain fundamental obligations, both to its own citizens and to the international community. When a regime fails to live up to these responsibilities or abuses its prerogatives, it risks forfeiting its sovereign privileges including, in the extreme, its immunity from armed intervention. (Haass 2003)

Haass argued that there are three circumstances when exceptions to the norms of non-intervention are warranted: when a state commits or fails to prevent genocide or crimes against humanity; when a state abets, supports, or harbors international terrorists or is not capable of controlling terrorists operating within its borders; and when a state, particularly one with a history of aggression and support for terrorism, takes steps, such as an attempt to acquire weapons of mass destruction, that are a clear threat to global security.

The international community is still struggling to find ways to respond to weak and failed states. As discussed in Chapter 11, weak states have been recipients of foreign aid and other forms of assistance. When states are fully collapsed and enveloped in civil war, the United Nations has occasionally authorized peacekeeping interventions. On rare occasions, such as Afghanistan, where the state is collapsed, or terrorists are based within its territory, more forceful interventions have occurred.

While the international community has begun to accept these infringements on sovereignty, including large-scale military interventions, the ability of these actions to reverse the collapse and failure of states is more problematic. Two scholars of development have posed questions that the international community must confront:

> How does the international community face up to the realities that the system is only as strong as its weakest link and that as many as sixty states are either on their way to ruin or have already collapsed? What can be done that has not already been tried, unsuccessfully, to rescue and rebuild failing states in Haiti, East Timor, Bosnia, Somalia, Afghanistan, Iraq, Sudan, Nepal, and so many other struggling nations? Empirical studies are depressing: Nearly 50 percent of countries that emerge from conflict revert to hostilities within ten years. Nevertheless, the international system has failed to devise mechanisms to arrest these reversions successfully. In the past twenty years, for example, $300 billion has been spent in Africa alone, yet the continent is still rife with weak and collapsed regimes – two million people a year are dying of AIDS, three thousand children die every day of malaria, and forty million receive no schooling at all. How do we redefine a sovereign state in such a way that we can objectively measure its functionality and success? By what practicable and empirical successful method can we help struggling states get back on their feet on a sustainable basis? (Ghani and Lockhart 2008)

There are no easy solutions to the persistent inability of some countries to develop capable and stable governments that can enforce order and the rule of law.

In struggling with this problem, the international community has also been debating deeper issues about the status of state sovereignty itself. If terrorists can use weak or failed states as platforms to attack other countries, the international community needs to be able to intervene in these countries to deter or eliminate their terrorist threats. The international community also needs to be able to intervene to protect the citizens of these countries from violence, violence that is sometimes committed by a despotic ruler or as an outgrowth of civil war. But the international community has not yet found consensus on when and where the norms and institutions of state sovereignty can be violated in response to internal and transnational violence and human rights abuses.

Levels of Analysis *International Responses*		
Individual	State	⊕ International
Today, the international community is claiming the right and obligation to protect individuals from governments that assert sovereign control over them.	The changing norms of state sovereignty have altered the rights and obligations of nation-states.	Many countries agree in principle, but not always in practice, on the need for international cooperation to strengthen weak states and protect individuals from mass violence.

WHITHER THE STATE?

The sovereign state has always existed in an uneasy relationship with wider global historical forces. Most of the people on earth today live within sovereign nation-states.

A century ago, this was not true. At the turn of the nineteenth century, most of the world's people lived in territories that were not sovereign, such as empires or colonial territories. Through the great dramas of the last hundred years, the Westphalian state system rose up to dominate how and where people live. So, it is a great paradox that the forces of globalization, nationalism, and self-determination have also unleashed non-state actors that threaten the sovereign control of the state. The sovereign territorial state has never been so universal as a form of politics and rule, but today it also faces challenges. And, as Box 12.5 reminds us, while some challenges to sovereignty are violent and destructive, others are potentially more benign.

As we have seen, non-state actors wielding violence and arms have always been an aspect of world politics. States have never been able to completely gain a monopoly on the legitimate use of violence within their own territory. Pirates, warlords, and terrorists have long been part

Photo 12.5 MSF (*Médecins Sans Frontières*, or Doctors Without Borders) at Work
A health worker injects a man with a meningitis vaccine at a field post February 14, 2007 in Arua, Uganda. MSF conducted a massive vaccination campaign and was able to vaccinate over 300,000 people in the district in three weeks. Sovereign states typically resist destructive non-state actors such as terrorists or drug lords, but they welcome what they consider to be helpful ones such as MSF.

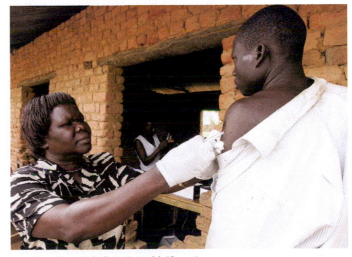

Source: Andrew Caballero-Reynolds/Getty Images.

12.5   RESEARCH INSIGHT

What Is Global Civil Society?

This chapter looks at non-state actors that threaten or undermine sovereign states. But there are also 'good' non-state actors, such as nongovernmental organizations (NGOs), that increasingly play an active role in international relations. In recent years, scholars have tried to explore the activities and impact of these transnational groups on states and the wider global system.

Some scholars find it useful to situate NGOs within what might be called 'global civil society.' In earlier chapters we have looked at the history and theory of states and the Westphalian state system. But this system of states exists within an even wider global system of peoples, nations, and communities. Within countries, the state is often seen in the formal governmental organization that exists alongside 'civil society.' Civil society is the realm of private relationships – clubs, associations, churches, volunteer organizations, and so forth. It is only a small step to see these separate national civil societies as part of a larger global civil society, with a rich array of private-sector groupings and associations. As John Keane (2010) argues in *Global Civil Society?*, there exists a vast assemblage of groups operating across borders and beyond the reach of the state. Whether such organizations constitute a new, increasingly autonomous realm or merely artifacts of Western liberal society is widely debated. Keane argues that a global civil society is taking shape but that its character and implications for the older state system remain unclear. The sheer heterogeneity of groups, activities, and networks that make up global civil society, including non-profits, businesses, social movements, tourists, academics, artists, cultural performers, ethnic and linguistic groups, makes it hard to pin down its overall impact. Keane nonetheless insists that this sprawling rumble does function as a society – or a 'society of societies' – with rules and norms of conduct. He admits, however, that global civil society is still an evolving, open-ended civic sphere whose importance will depend on its ability to become more democratic, better integrated into governance institutions, and invested with universal values.

of the world scene. But forces of globalization, nationalism, and self-determination have also unleashed powerful non-state actors, such as terrorist organizations with global reach, who threaten the stability and order as it is secured by states.

The forces of globalization have made it easier for non-state actors to travel, communicate, and operate on a worldwide basis. Technological innovations in weapons – nuclear, biological, and chemical – allow these actors to potentially gain weapons of such destructive power that it is possible to imagine whole cities suffering at their violent hands. Nationalism and the search by groups for political independence are not new. Certainly, terrorism is partly driven by aspirations for religious, political, and social freedom as peoples in various parts of the world struggle to define independence in a modernizing world. Globalization and the great economic transformations of the modern world have put pressure on people to define their aspirations. The international system also puts pressure on states, including weak and failing ones, to adjust to change and cope with uncertainties. All of these 'moving parts' have created openings for non-state wielders of force and violence to make a dramatic appearance.

What is the future of the state in the face of non-state actors? As Box 12.6 shows, scholars from different theoretical traditions would provide different answers to that question. Although the future remains uncertain, it does appear that non-state actors will be increasingly able to inflict harm on people. Evolving weapons and delivery technologies seem to be giving private groups this opportunity. But, these non-state actors do not seem to have the capacity to replace the state or the state system. They do not have the ability to do what territorial states can do – build political communities

12.6   DIFFERING THEORETICAL APPROACHES

The Future of the Nation-State

Background

Will the nation-state remain the dominant type of political actor in world politics in the coming decades? The theoretical perspectives that we have explored do not give definitive predictions. But they do identify specific challenges and struggles that nation-states face and they offer different expectations of what is to come.

Realism

Realists expect that states will remain the dominant actors in world politics. States have struggled and overcome challenges in the past, and they will in the future. Realists emphasize that sovereign states have many advantages over non-state actors. They can tax and mobilize resources in pursuit of their goals. States are tied to nations, and so they can rely on nationalism as a source of support. States are also widely seen as the most effective organization for the protection of peoples – after all, they have the army and police.

Liberalism

Liberals expect that trade and interdependence between states will grow. States will increasingly find themselves in a world where they need to cooperate with other states to achieve their goals of security and prosperity. In a world that is increasingly interdependent, states will need to make room for other types of actors – transnational groups, multinational corporations, and international institutions. States probably will not disappear, but they will increasingly need to cooperate with each other and other types of actors.

Marxism

Marxism emphasizes the role – often hidden – of the capitalist class in shaping global economics and politics. In looking into the future, Marxists will focus on the expanding power and role of international capitalism. Whether in trade or finance, these international capitalist elites will grow in influence and directly or indirectly continue to limit and constrain the ability of states to control events and challenge capitalist interests.

Constructivism

Constructivism will keep an eye on how people in societies around the world think about states. They will look for evidence of shifts in the identity and loyalty of people to the nation-state or away from it. Will other sorts of identities – to the European Union, for example – grow in salience for people within Europe? Or, as recent developments including Brexit and the rise of populism suggest, will people embrace the sovereign state even more forcefully? What about transnational religious identity? Constructivists will look for how people and societies construct their ideas about the state and other groupings of people.

with institutions that tax, provide services, and offer security. Five hundred years after the rise of the modern state, no other type of political system really can compete with it. Non-state actors can do damage, but they cannot offer an alternative way of organizing society and politics. So, the real question is: how effectively can states work together to protect their borders and strengthen their neighbors? In a sense, all states are vulnerable to the weakest among them. A failed state that cannot enforce rules and order within its society is a seedbed or haven for terrorists. Increasingly, the entire world has a stake in how these weak and failing states respond. The international community will need to find ways to build and strengthen states.

Levels of Analysis *Future of the Nation-State*

Individual	International
The relationship between individuals and nation-states has changed over the last century because of new technologies of communication, transport, and violence.	The sovereign state system today is both more universal and more challenged than in earlier historical eras.

REVISITING THE ENDURING QUESTION AND LOOKING AHEAD

In this chapter, we have explored the ways in which non-state actors have harnessed violence capabilities and challenged the Westphalian system. We have seen that these dramas are not new. But, we have also seen that globalization and technological changes are making the actions of non-state wielders of violence potentially deadlier and more threatening. The international community is challenged to find ways to strengthen states and police the activities of pirates, warlords, and terrorists.

In the next chapter we examine an equally important dilemma that states face as they seek to shape the world of the twenty-first century. The management of the global commons, and the relationship between international politics and the natural environment, are looming large. What strategies are available to states and non-state actors to address key global environmental and resource issues involving the atmosphere, the oceans, and the land?

STUDY QUESTIONS

1. What do you think are the best solutions to the problem of weak and failed states?
2. What sort of political and geographic settings provide congenial settings for piracy and what are the 'solutions' to the problem of piracy?
3. What are some of the technological and global political developments that make terrorism increasingly dangerous?
4. Are states and the Westphalian state system 'winning' or 'losing' in the struggle with non-state transnational groups such as pirates and terrorists?
5. How does the international community reconcile the tensions between a state's sovereignty within its territory and the growing notion of Responsibility to Protect?

FURTHER READING

Law, Richard (2017) *Terrorism: A History* (Cambridge: Polity). A portrait of terrorism across historical eras.

Naím, Moisés (2005) *Illicit: How Smugglers, Traffickers, and Copycats are Hijacking the Global Economy* (New York: Anchor Books). A lively survey of the ways in which criminal commercial groups are operating at the edges of the global economy, outside the law and the reach of the state.

Naudé, Wim, Amelia U. Santos-Paulino, and Mark McGillivray (2011) *Fragile States: Causes, Costs, and Responses* (Oxford: Oxford University Press). A thoughtful inquiry into the causes and consequences of weak and failed states, and a survey of the various ways in which the international community has responded and can respond to these trouble spots.

Nordstrom, Carolyn (2007) *Global Outlaws: Crime, Money, and Power in the Contemporary World* (Berkeley: University of California Press). The author travels through Africa, Europe, Asia, and the United States to document the operation of illegal trade in goods, such as blood diamonds, pharmaceuticals, food, and oil.

Patrick, Stewart (2011) *Weak Links: Fragile States, Global Threats, and International Security* (Oxford: Oxford University Press). Patrick explores the relationships between weak and failing states and various transnational threats and challenges – terrorism, transnational crime, weapons of mass destruction, pandemic diseases, and energy insecurity. He shows that most frequently it is the weak and poor countries that suffer the most, even while also demonstrating that often the origins of the criminal transnational activity lie in the wealthy and more stable societies.

Richardson, Louise (2007) *What Terrorists Want: Understanding the Enemy, Containing the Threat* (New York: Random House). A comprehensive survey of expert knowledge about the sources of terrorism and how to respond to it. A sensible and balanced look at various angles of this complex topic.

Wallace, William and Daphne Josselin (eds) (2002) *Non-State Actors in World Politics* (New York: Palgrave Macmillan). An excellent survey of the diverse sorts of non-state actors that are rising up within the global system. The chapters also offer reflections on how these non-state actors matter.

 Visit **www.macmillanihe.com/Grieco-IntroIR-2e** to access extra resources for this chapter, including:

- Chapter summaries to help you review the material
- Multiple choice quizzes to test your understanding
- Flashcards to test your knowledge of the key terms in this chapter
- An interactive simulation that invites you to go through the decision-making process of a world leader at a crucial political juncture
- Pivotal decisions in which you weigh up the pros and cons of complicated decisions with grave consequences
- Outside resources, including links to contemporary articles and videos, that add to what you have learned in this chapter

13 The Environment and International Relations

Enduring question

How does the natural environment influence international relations?

Chapter Contents

- Sources of Problems for the Global Environment and Natural Resources
- Challenges for the World's Environment and Natural Resources
- Management of International Environmental Problems
- Revisiting the Enduring Question and Looking Ahead
- Study Questions
- Further Reading

Learning Objectives

By the end of this chapter, you will be able to:

→   Explain how environmental problems often include an international dimension.

→   Describe key global environmental and resource issues involving the atmosphere, the oceans, and the land.

→   Explore how governments try to address international environmental and resource problems, with a focus on unilateral, bilateral, and multilateral strategies.

→   Identify the conditions that help or hinder those efforts, including the role of the wealthy developed countries, rising powers such as China and India, and nongovernmental organizations.

There is almost no question we are spewing out enough CO_2 from our automobiles, homes, and factories to warm the earth's atmosphere. There is growing evidence that this process of global warming may cause the Arctic ice sheets to melt and the oceans to rise and possibly overrun parts of South Asia where millions of people live. Government leaders have repeatedly said that they recognize that climate change may be a real problem, but as we will see in this chapter, the first major international climate-change agreement they crafted, the Kyoto Protocol of 1997, has had very little impact on the problem, and the second major effort, the Paris Agreement of 2015, has uncertain prospects and especially so in the wake of the decision of US President Donald Trump in early 2017 to withdraw support. Hence, even though there seems to be a growing international consensus that climate change is a real and pressing threat, governments seem unable to take strong, concerted action to resolve or at least manage that problem.

If we want to understand the past, the present, or especially the future of international relations, we must understand global environmental issues. We therefore devote this chapter to answering this enduring question: How does the natural environment influence international relations?

We begin by equipping you with two analytical tools that scholars have constructed to understand problems involving the quality of the natural environment and the sustainability of the world's natural resources. These tools center on the concepts of negative externalities and the tragedy of the commons. Negative externalities, which have to do with costs of goods not reflected in their prices, and the tragedy of the commons, which is a logic that illuminates how rational action by individuals in the face of scarcity leads to over-usage of resources, drive many of the world's environmental issues. We then discuss a range of environmental and natural-resource problems within and between countries that involve the atmosphere, the oceans, and the land, including such specific problems as climate change and ozone depletion, fresh-water contamination, pollution of the oceans, overexploitation of the world's fish stocks, and deforestation. Next, we look at strategies that states have developed to deal with the international aspects of environmental and natural-resource problems. These strategies include national laws, bilateral agreements, and multilateral treaties. We will see below that each of these strategies has advantages and disadvantages and produce differing levels of success in coping with international environmental and natural-resource challenges.

SOURCES OF PROBLEMS FOR THE GLOBAL ENVIRONMENT AND NATURAL RESOURCES

What are the causal factors that contribute to environmental and natural-resource problems within and between countries? Scholars have identified two such factors: negative externalities and the tragedy of the commons.

Negative Externalities

Externalities
The benefits and costs not reflected in a good's price, such as ideas on how to improve a product in the future (positive externality) or pollution (negative externality).

One concept that helps us identify the sources of environmental problems within and between countries is taken from the discipline of economics. That concept is termed **externalities**, which economists define as the benefits and costs not reflected in a good's price. These externalities can be positive or negative, and their effect may be felt by the consumer, the producer, or a third party.

For example, consider a laptop computer. The price you pay for a laptop *largely* reflects two separate dynamics: the costs a manufacturer must absorb to make the laptop, and the value you assign to the laptop, measured as the goods and services you are willing to forego to buy it. However, prices never *perfectly* reflect the costs of manufacture and the benefits of owning most goods and services. When making your laptop, the manufacturer may learn how to make an even better laptop in the future or a different product, such as a tablet computer; that valuable learning is not reflected in the price for your laptop. The laptop then has a *positive* externality for the producer, or the knowledge of how to make better products. In contrast, imagine if, when making your laptop, the manufacturer releases pollutants into streams and rivers that harm people who, not knowing the source of the pollution, are not compensated by the manufacturer. In that case, your laptop is generating *negative* externalities. The costs incurred by the injured parties are borne neither by the laptop manufacturer nor by you, the laptop consumer.

There are two serious issues that arise from negative externalities. First, it is unfair, in the example above, that people who gained nothing from the laptop you bought incur a harm – that is, experience water pollution – but are not compensated for that harm. Second, without some way to make the laptop manufacturer incorporate the costs of compensating individuals harmed by pollution or prevent pollution in the first place, the manufacturer has no incentive to stop polluting streams and rivers.

Externalities are common in any economy. They have the potential to become international issues when the negative forms of such externalities generate harmful effects that are felt by people across borders and create a need for countries to try to mitigate those effects through international action. Thus, negative externalities are central to answering our enduring question about human-produced environmental problems and international relations.

The example of acid rain in North America illustrates how international negative externalities come into being and how they may elicit an international response. Many electrical utilities and industrial firms use coal or natural gas to fuel their plants. These facilities release chemical compounds (sulfur dioxide and nitrogen oxides) into the atmosphere that can be carried great distances by the winds. These compounds become acidic when they combine with rainfall or land on the earth and come into contact with water. The resulting acids can damage rivers, lakes, and forests.

Canada's own industrial and power plants represent one source of the acid rain that is causing damage to its eastern provinces. However, Canada's acid rain problems have been compounded by transborder pollution originating in the United States. Emissions of sulfur dioxide and nitrogen oxides by US factories and power-generating plants are carried by winds to eastern Canada and cause acid rain. The consequence, the Canadian government has found, is that more than one-half of the acid deposits in the eastern part of Canada are due to emissions from the United States. However, because the costs of reducing or reversing harm were for many years not reflected in the costs that US electricity producers incurred in generating electricity, producers had no incentive on their own to stop acid rain. This is an international negative externality.

Fortunately, in 1991 the United States and Canadian governments reached an agreement which required Canadian and US manufacturers and electrical utilities to make investments to curtail acid rain-producing emissions. The firms and utilities, in turn, have passed on those costs to consumers. Cooperation between the governments of Canada and the United States caused producers and consumers to face up to the true costs of their choices. As a result, there has been some success in changing those choices and reducing acid rain.

The Tragedy of the Commons

Tragedy of the commons
A situation in which individual actors acting in their own rational self-interest combine to create a situation catastrophic to all of the individuals.

Another key dynamic that causes many international environmental and natural-resource problems is the **tragedy of the commons**, which is a process by which agents (which could be persons, households, firms, or countries) that rationally pursue their self-interest in exploiting a limited natural resource in an uncoordinated manner might eventually, through no actor's fault, overuse and exhaust the resource. This term was introduced in 1968 by American ecologist Garrett Hardin in an influential article on the human dynamics that can result in environmental decay or the depletion of important natural resources (Hardin 1968).

To see how humans can create such problems, Hardin invited readers to consider a hypothetical case of multiple cattle herders and a piece of pastureland they hold in common. If the local human population supplied by the herders remains low and stable, the demand for meat remains limited, and the pastureland remains sufficient to maintain the different herds of cattle. If the local population grows, so does the demand for meat. Each herder is tempted to add one more head of cattle to their herd. In doing so, the herder would enjoy all the additional profit from selling that extra head of cattle, while not incurring the full cost of doing so, in terms of stressing the common pastureland. Those costs would be shared, knowingly or not, with the other herders. In these circumstances, Hardin pointed out, all the herders would be tempted to continue adding additional heads of cattle. Doing so would soon cause the common pastureland to be depleted and destroyed, and the herders and the community that depended on them for food would face dire consequences.

Hardin emphasized that this process is a tragedy in the sense that the bad outcome, the destruction of the commons and the resulting harm to the community, does not come about because people are stupid or evil or in any way intend or want the outcome to occur. Instead, in a manner like what we saw in Chapter 5 when we discussed the Prisoner's Dilemma and international law, so too a tragedy of the commons results from the interaction of rational individuals pursuing their own interests and the circumstances in which they find themselves. Those circumstances in the case of a tragedy of the commons consist of a growing population (which creates an incentive for the herders to do things that place stress on resources), finite resources used in common (the pastureland is only so big and has a fixed 'carrying capacity' in terms of cattle it can support), and, perhaps most important, the absence of a governing authority (that can regulate how the common pastureland is employed).

The tragedy-of-the-commons dynamic identified by Hardin drives several problems relating to the international environment and global resources (Barkin and Shambaugh 1999), and is another main mechanism, in response to our enduring question, that links the natural environment to international relations. For example, fishing enterprises and their home countries still treat the oceans as an ungoverned common with unlimited supplies of fish. Yet, as demand for fish has surged in recent decades – in part as a function of world population growth, growing personal incomes, and an increased awareness of the health benefits of eating fish – fishing enterprises have overharvested fish to the degree that many species face collapse.

Deforestation
The clearing or overharvesting of forests, an especially acute problem in the tropics.

Global **deforestation** represents another example of the operation of the tragedy of the commons. Around the world, as we explore in Box 13.1, the extensive, widespread clearing of tropical forests is resulting in the depletion of this world resource, even

Photo 13.1 Deforestation in Haiti

Tree stumps in southeastern Haiti show evidence of deforestation. Haiti has one of the highest rates of deforestation anywhere in the world – only about 2% of its original forests remain. Rural Haitians clear forests to create new farmland, to use firewood for cooking, and to produce charcoal for sale.

Source: tropical pix.

13.1   MAKING CONNECTIONS
Theory and Practice

The Tragedy of the Commons and Deforestation of Tropical Forests

Theory: The Tragedy of the Commons

According to American ecologist Garrett Hardin (1968), rational users of natural resources, in the face of growing demand for those resources or goods derived from them, and in the absence of some governmental authority that regulates their behavior, may over-utilize those resources to the point of exhaustion.

Practice: Global Deforestation

Deforestation has become a serious problem in the tropical regions of the world. Forest land decreased in Africa during the 1990s and early 2000s at such a pace that, as the Food and Agriculture Organization (FAO) has reported, 'Africa lost more than 9 percent of its forest area.' Meanwhile, forests in South America, particularly in the Amazon River Basin, were lost at an annual rate of about 0.46 percent per year during the decade of the 1990s; that loss-rate accelerated to about 0.51 percent per year between 2000 and 2005. Such deforestation has many causes, and among those reasons, as anticipated by Hardin, is the increase in global demand for timber products and local demand for land that can be used for grazing or farming.

Source: United Nations Food and Agriculture Organization (2007): viii–ix.

though no person, logging firm, or government of a forest-rich country wants such harmful levels of deforestation. Instead, just as with Hardin's theoretical example of herders and common grazing lands, and the real-world problem of overfishing, it is the combination of economic self-interests of the individuals and firms clearing the land, and under-regulation by national governments, that drives overharvesting, especially in tropical regions of the world.

Knowledge of the ideas surrounding negative externalities and tragedies of the commons will often help you answer our enduring question about the environment and international relations. Negative externalities and tragedies of the commons are behind many of the world's most pressing international environmental challenges. We now turn our attention to an identification and exploration of some of them.

Levels of Analysis *Negative Externalities and the Tragedy of the Commons*		
Individual	**State**	**International**
Individuals making rational decisions about productive activities that utilize scarce natural resources can bring about tragedies of the commons.	Firms often benefit from positive externalities and, unless constrained by governmental interventions, are sometimes able to avoid incorporating into the prices for their goods the emanation of negative externalities.	Transborder pollution is sometimes characterized by international negative externalities.

CHALLENGES FOR THE WORLD'S ENVIRONMENT AND NATURAL RESOURCES

By virtue of the actions of individual humans, households, firms, and governments, the world faces a host of environmental challenges regarding the atmosphere, water and water-based resources, and the use of the land. Given their intrinsic importance and their capacity to illuminate the relationship between politics and the environment at the international level, we will in this section examine five especially important global environmental problems. We begin with an examination of two particularly urgent environmental problems relating to the atmosphere: climate change and ozone depletion. We will then explore two especially serious environmental challenges relating to the oceans: fresh-water contamination within countries and the possible mismanagement of global marine-life resources. Finally, we will examine the land-based problem of tropical deforestation. This list is not meant to be exhaustive; one might also examine, for example, environmental problems associated with the exploration of natural resources in Antarctica, threats to migratory birds, or the Texas-sized soup of plastic floating in the Pacific Ocean.

Problems with the Atmosphere

Climate change and ozone depletion can each have deleterious consequences for human life, and climate change might even affect the risk of future conflicts within and between countries. They are both important to understand because, as we will see in a subsequent section, while governments around the world have devised what appears to be a strong multilateral agreement to contain the problem of ozone depletion, they have not succeeded in putting into place an efficacious global approach to the problem of climate change.

Climate Change

The world is becoming warmer. There are vivid signs around us, such as the dramatic reduction in sea ice in the Arctic (see Map 13.1). Moreover, it seems likely that average daily temperatures around the earth by the end of this century may increase by no less than 2.0 degrees Celsius (3.6 degrees Fahrenheit) and perhaps a good deal more.

Emissions of carbon dioxide (CO_2), nitrous oxide, methane, and a variety of fluorinated gases contribute to global warming. As we can see in Figure 13.1, there has been a steady, seemingly inexorable yearly increase in CO_2 emissions observed in the atmosphere. These materials are called greenhouse gases because, just as the window panes of a greenhouse trap the sun's heat, these gases trap some of the infrared heat produced by the sun's warming of the earth that would otherwise escape back into outer space, thus producing global warming. Humans produce greenhouse emissions mostly by their use of petroleum-based products and natural gas for cars, trucks, trains, and jet aircraft, and their use of oil, gas, and coal for electricity generating plants and other industrial facilities. Hence, global warming is an international negative externality arising from the economic activities of human beings.

Figure 13.1 Increasing Concentration of CO_2 in the Atmosphere, 1958–2018
Since 1958, the Mauna Loa Observatory in Hawaii has undertaken the longest continuous measurement of carbon dioxide concentrations in the atmosphere. As can be observed in the figure, there has been a remarkably steady annual increase in atmospheric carbon dioxide concentrations.

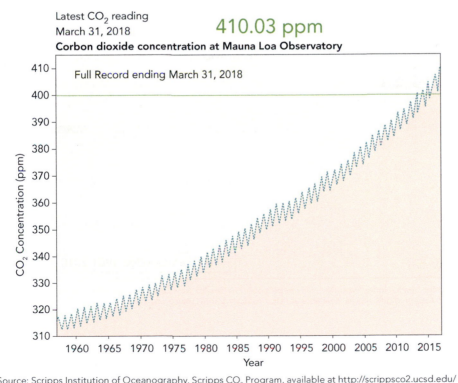

Source: Scripps Institution of Oceanography, Scripps CO_2 Program, available at http://scrippsco2.ucsd.edu/data/atmospheric_co2/mlo

Map 13.1 Possible Sign of Global Warming: Retreat of Arctic Summer Ice, 2017
This map indicates that the extent of the area of the Arctic Ocean that was covered by ice in July 2017 was substantially less than the area covered by summer ice on average between 1981 and 2010. The white section represents the area that was ice-covered in July 2017 compared to the average area that was covered in ice between 1981 and 2010, outlined in orange.

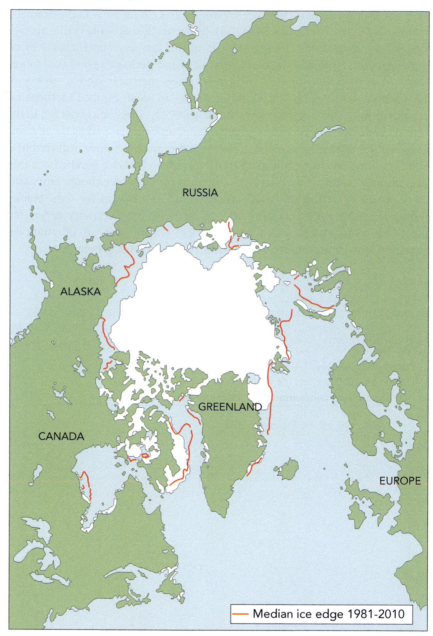

Source: 'Sea Ice Index,' updated daily as part of Arctic Sea Ice News and Analysis, National Snow and Ice Data Center, digital media, available at http://nsidc.org/arcticseaicenews/.

If left unchecked, climate change will change the earth and harm a large portion of the world's population. Some nations in relatively northern latitudes might benefit from global warming: for example, more Canadian lands will become agriculturally productive. Yet, snowpack levels in the US western mountain ranges may decline, and this could have 'adverse impacts on fish populations, hydropower, water recreation, and water availability for agricultural, industrial, and residential use' (National Academies of Science 2008: 17).

The most devastating consequences of climate change will probably take place in the developing world. For example, as illustrated in Map 13.2, the already flood-prone country of Bangladesh might lose a part of its land mass, causing the displacement of millions of people. Moreover, the **Intergovernmental Panel on Climate Change (IPCC)**, established in 1988 by the United Nations, has estimated that if climate change continues unabated, large parts of Africa will experience severe droughts more frequently. Consequently, warns the IPCC (2007: 50), 'agricultural production, including access to food, in many African countries is projected to be severely compromised.'

These hard-hit areas in Bangladesh and Africa may experience in turn large refugee flows, resource disputes, and civil disorder with international implications. However, it is *not* the residents of Bangladesh or Africa who burn fossil fuels to such a degree that the earth's temperatures have been escalating. Instead, residents in the United States, the nations of Western Europe, and China are the major emitters. Hence, while the industrial and industrializing countries are the source of the problem, many of the most harmful effects are being externalized to people in other parts of the world.

Moreover, global warming is a clear instance of the relevance of our enduring question, that is, it shows vividly how an environmental problem consisting of negative externalities is an international problem. This is because there is basically nothing that the government of Bangladesh and those of the countries in Africa can do by themselves to reverse global warming. Unless the United States and the countries of Western Europe, as well as rising powers such as China, India, and Brazil, control their greenhouse emissions, the residents of other (usually very poor) nations are going to suffer serious costs from global warming.

Important political and ethical issues are raised by climate change. Developed and developing countries, we will see in the next main section, have sought through the Paris Agreement to provide a pathway whereby countries will undertake voluntarily and in a legally non-binding manner to reduce their CO_2 emissions. Leaders have had to turn to non-binding undertakings because they fundamentally disagree as to which countries have been and are now most responsible for CO_2 emissions and, therefore, should do the most to curtail them. That is, on the matter of CO_2 emissions produced as a by-product of numerous economic activities, they disagree on which countries should act in a way to pursue sustainable development, a concept we discussed in Chapter 11.

This conflict of interest is crystallized by the information presented in Figure 13.2, which provides data on emissions from the wealthy industrialized countries, that is, the state members of the Organisation for Economic Co-operation and Development (OECD); the developing countries, that is, the non-OECD countries; the particular cases of the United States and Japan which are taken as representatives of the OECD group; and three key developing countries, China, India, and Brazil.

Intergovernmental Panel on Climate Change (IPCC)
A panel established by the UN in 1988 that studies climate change and informs the world of its effects.

Map 13.2 Exposure of Bangladesh to Risk of Rising Seas
A great deal of the landmass of the South Asian country of Bangladesh is close to sea level. If global warming led to rising sea levels, many Bengalis would be forced from their homes, and significant portions of farm land would be lost, causing severe hardship in an already poor country.

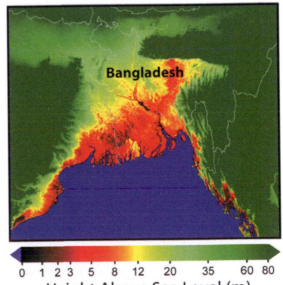

Figure 13.2 Responsibility for Addressing the Problem of Global Warming: Developed and Developing Countries and CO_2 Emissions

The data in Panels A and B suggest that developing countries are projected to be the source of most of the growth in total global CO_2 emissions during the next two decades. The growing importance of India, Brazil, and especially China as developing-country CO_2 emitters during that period is illuminated in Panel B. However, the data in Panel C suggest that, during the next two decades, the United States will remain the world's largest CO_2 emitter on a per capita basis, and the United States and Japan will be more responsible for CO_2 emissions than China, Brazil, and India.

Panel A: Sources of Total CO_2 Emissions, 1990–2035

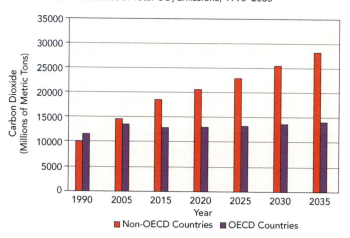

Panel B: Projected Sources of Growth in CO_2 Emissions, 2007–35

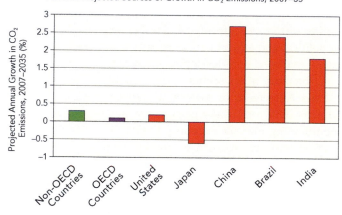

Panel C: Recent and Projected CO_2 Emissions Per Capita, 1990–2035

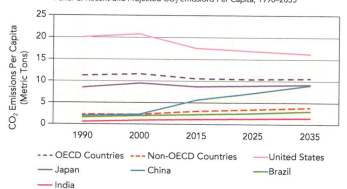

Source: Data from US Energy Information Administration (EIA).

Developed countries such as the United States want to begin with current CO_2 levels and prevent future increases in emissions that might tip the balance toward serious global problems as described above. In framing the question this way, developed countries can focus on trends that are captured in Panels A and B of Figure 13.2, which suggest that developed-country annual CO_2 emissions are likely to level off or decrease, while those of developing countries, including China, Brazil, and India, are projected to increase and in the case of China to do so dramatically. Looking at these projections, developed-country governments believe that developing countries must curtail the growth in their CO_2 emissions.

Developing-country governments prefer to think about CO_2 emissions in terms of the information presented in Panel C of Figure 13.2, which reports on the countries that are the biggest current and future emitters of CO_2 per capita. Using the per capita standard, it does appear that China will catch up to Japan and most of the developed world (but not the United States) as a source of CO_2 emissions. With the exception of China, however, India, Brazil, and the developing world as a whole have not been, and for the foreseeable future are not going to be, significant contributors to global CO_2 when we employ the per capita standard. Thus, most developing-country governments, focusing on current and projected per capita CO_2 emissions, believe that it is the responsibility of the developed countries to do more to curtail those emissions. Developing countries also believe that since most of the buildup in CO_2 up to this point in history has been caused by wealthy nations, those countries now have a responsibility to reduce their emissions and, beyond that, to give developing countries the technology and financial resources needed to switch to a low-carbon future.

Finally, in Chapter 6 we discussed the ways in which competition between individuals, groups, or countries over scarce resources – for example, water, arable land, and diamonds – can contribute to the onset of interstate or civil wars. There has been informed speculation (Homer-Dixon 2007; Podesta and Ogden 2008) that international climate change, by way of its capacity to reduce arable lands, for example, might become a new and powerful animator of civil wars in developing countries, with an associated increase in the risk that such civil wars might spill over into neighboring countries or attract international military interventions. To the extent that there is a link between climate change, greater scarcity of resources, and war, this link highlights how environmental conditions can powerfully affect international relations.

There may be other ways global warming could spur societal unrest and civil violence. For example, global warming could cause international migrations of refugees that originate in drought-stricken parts of sub-Saharan and eastern Africa, or from flooded parts of Bangladesh. Such migrations could induce severe economic, social, and political stress in neighboring countries that receive these refugees, causing an increased risk of civil conflict.

While recognizing that climate change and other environmental conditions *might* raise the risk of civil and international conflicts, scholars have cautioned that we should avoid **environmental determinism**, that is, the view that stresses in the environment like climate change *necessarily* and *automatically* will cause human beings and human communities to react in a particular manner (Salehyan 2008; Buhaug and Gleditsch 2008). According to this line of thinking, global warming is likely to cause environmental stress for massive numbers of people in the years ahead. However, whether that stress translates into civil conflict will depend on the answers to a host of additional questions. Will the governments of the affected peoples be able to respond with policies that mitigate some of the economic and social dislocations

Environmental determinism
The view that changes in the environment like climate change *necessarily* and *automatically* will cause human beings and human communities to react in a particular manner.

arising from climate change? Even more important, will the richer countries of the world provide poorer governments with assistance to deal with the consequences of global warming?

Domestic and international politics, as well as nature, will determine whether climate change becomes a more serious problem. At present it does not appear that climate change by itself is a spur to domestic or interstate conflict, but this risk is something worthy of continuing attention.

Ozone Depletion

Between the mid-1970s and the mid-1980s, scientists determined that the ozone layer in the earth's upper stratosphere was diminishing and had reached such low concentrations over Antarctica that an 'ozone hole' was developing. Scientists also determined that human pollution of the atmosphere or emissions of chemicals, particularly **chlorofluorocarbons (CFCs)**, a chemical used in propellants in aerosol cans and fire extinguishers, and in refrigerants in air conditioners were the cause of ozone depletion. Finally, scientists ascertained that depletion of the ozone layer represented a serious environmental problem. The ozone layer shields the earth from the sun's ultraviolet radiation. As the ozone layer diminishes, ultraviolet radiation hitting the earth's surface greatly increases, contributing to health problems such as skin cancer, eye cataracts, and impairment of human immune systems; harming crops on land; and potentially damaging ocean-based plant life important to the maintenance of fish stocks.

Chlorofluorocarbons (CFCs)
A chemical formerly used in aerosol cans, fire extinguishers, and air conditioners, a cause of ozone depletion, and now outlawed by international agreements.

The ozone layer is a type of global common whose presence protects all humans and other forms of life on earth. The degradation of that layer was an instance of a tragedy of the commons: no one consumer, business enterprise, or national government wanted ozone depletion, but the rational commercial and policy decisions of all these actors regarding air conditioning and other products were leading inexorably to the depletion of the ozone layer. Fortunately, as we will discuss in the next main section, while governments have made only limited progress to date in managing the problem of climate change, the international community reached and has implemented a multilateral agreement that may in time reverse the depletion of the ozone layer.

Damage to the World's Water Resources

Global economic development and population increases have put increasing pressure on fresh-water resources, the health of our oceans, and the bounty of marine life. Oil spills, dangerous run-offs of chemicals and fertilizers, climate change, and overharvesting by the fishing industry all constitute threats to the world's water resources.

Contamination of the World's Fresh-Water Resources

As more countries develop economically, they increasingly utilize fresh water for industrial processes, commercial purposes, and residential uses. At present, about one-third of the world's renewable fresh-water supplies are now being utilized by human beings (Schwarzenbach *et al.* 2010). This intensive use of fresh-water resources is creating the risk of a contraction in drinking water, especially in developing countries.

For example, in many parts of China and India, heavy usage of fresh-water aquifers, underground formations that are permeable and in which water is contained, is leading to increased salt concentrations in fresh-water supplies, which leads to impaired drinking water levels and reduced crop yields. Gold-mining operations that employ mercury and produce cyanide as a waste material are making their way into the water supplies, and may be creating health problems, in such countries as Brazil, Indonesia, Tanzania, and Vietnam. Around the world, pesticides are used to protect commercial agricultural crops and residential gardens; eventually, some of these pesticides reach fresh-water streams, rivers, fresh-water fishing areas, and even the drinking supplies of large human populations.

International trade may create risks to fresh-water supplies. Toxic waste materials are often exported; if not disposed of properly in receiving countries they can ultimately contaminate the latter's fresh-water supplies. One concern often expressed in the 1990s was that, as richer countries imposed more stringent governmental regulations on companies regarding the disposal of dangerous industrial waste, more would show up in poorer countries that needed export revenues and often had less stringent disposal policies. However, richer countries import more hazardous waste products than they export. This finding suggests that all countries are facing the resulting risks to their fresh-water supplies (Baggs 2009).

Oil Pollution in the Oceans

In April 2010, a catastrophic explosion destroyed the Deepwater Horizon drilling rig off the coast of Louisiana in the Gulf of Mexico, which was being operated on behalf of the British oil giant BP. The explosion killed 11 oil-rig workers and produced a rupture in the oil wellhead on the sea floor. Before the wellhead was capped in mid-July, some 5 million barrels of oil were released into the Gulf. The damage caused by this environmental disaster to fish stocks, coastal wildlife, marshlands, and beaches along the coasts of Louisiana, Mississippi, Alabama, and Florida will not be fully understood or calculated for years to come.

Another source of ocean pollution stems from accidents by oil tankers. Overall, there were more than 1,700 such accidents between 1970 and 2008. These oil spills resulted in the release of about 5.7 million tons of oil into the oceans, with some reaching adjacent coastal shorelines. Most accidents involve the discharge of relatively small amounts of oil, but some have produced huge oil spills. Scholars have not been able to estimate the damage these oil spills have done to the environment, wildlife, and fish stocks. However, we do know that enormous resources are often required to clean beaches and adjacent wetlands after an oil spill. For example, the cost of the clean-up for the Exxon Valdez oil spill of 1989 was about $250 million; for the BP oil spill of 2010, the cost will likely be in the tens of billions of dollars.

Threats to Marine Life

In 2011, according to the United Nations Food and Agriculture Organization (UNFAO 2012: 3), humans harvested approximately 154 million tons of fish. About 85 percent of the harvested fish was used directly as food for humans, with the remainder used as feed for livestock and for aquaculture, which is the harvesting of fish reared in ponds or other contained areas. While aquaculture itself generates a great deal of the fish – roughly 40 percent of the total in 2011 – traditional fishing still accounts for the majority of marine life harvesting.

The problem is that, as we discussed in the first main section, a severe tragedy of the commons may be unfolding regarding commercial fishing on the high seas. Humans,

Photo 13.2 The Problem of Overfishing

Overfishing is a good example of the tragedy of the commons. Fishing methods have become more sophisticated, and modern ships rely on advanced sonar to locate shoals of fish with great precision. Bottom trawling – dragging huge nets across the sea floor – results in large catches but also damages marine life at the bottom of the ocean.

Source: Getty Images/Cultura RF\Monty Rakusen.

not out of malice or irrationality, are overharvesting many marine species. As we discuss in Box 13.2, scientific studies suggest that, in the past, humans overharvested in a sporadic manner, but more recent overharvesting may be sufficiently engrained and widespread that we are simultaneously putting at risk a large number of the world's marine species that are important for human consumption.

The dire projection discussed in Box 13.2 is based on the premise that the global community will do nothing to reverse current trends toward the exhaustion of marine species. The projection may well prove to be overly pessimistic, especially if, as in the case of the ozone layer, governments take positive action to reverse the tragedy of the commons we see developing at present in world fisheries.

Still, as we can see in Figure 13.3, trends in global fish utilization, as reported by the FAO, have not been promising. We see in that figure that about 10 percent of the world's most important varieties of fish were being overexploited in 1979 – that is, actual catches were less than what would be the case were overfishing not depleting those types of fish. By 2013 some 30 percent of the key fish stocks were being overexploited. In addition, by 2013 approximately 60 percent of the world's fish stocks were being exploited at maximum sustainable levels, that is, catches could not grow without depleting stocks and future catches. There is then not much room for additional growth in annual harvesting of important global fish stocks as we move into the future, without risking future harvests. Other dynamics may be reducing commercial fish stocks, including accidental and intentional oil pollution, run-offs of dangerous substances such as chemicals and fertilizers, and climate change. However, the main problem is a tragedy of the commons: the world is overharvesting fish.

13.2   MAKING CONNECTIONS
Then and Now

From Sporadic Overfishing to Possible Collapse of Vital Marine Life

Then: Overharvesting

According to recent scholarship conducted by the History of Marine Populations at the University of New Hampshire, humans may have started to harvest ocean-based marine life to a significant degree approximately 1,000 years ago, in part because they had by that time begun to overharvest fresh-water fish. Major innovations in sixteenth- and seventeenth-century ship design and fishing techniques, including the employment of nets cast by pairs of ships, led to major increases in fish hauls and problems of overharvesting specific fish species. For example, while fishing fleets harvested roughly 70,000 tons of cod annually from the Gulf of Maine in the 1860s, today, even with more advanced fishing technologies, they can harvest cod in the range of 3,000 tons per year.

Now: Possible Crisis Point

Growing demand for fish and the absence of effective international regulation are driving overharvesting of many fish species. It is possible that once a marine species reaches about 10 percent of its historical levels, it has only a small chance of rebounding. As Figure 13.3 shows, approximately 30 percent of marine-life species *have already reached* the 10 percent crisis point. If current trends continue, by the middle of the current century it is possible that essentially all species of marine life important to human sustenance will hit the 10 percent crisis point.

Sources: Doyle (2009); Worm *et al.* (2006): 788. For a good overview of the findings of this study, see Dean (2006).

Figure 13.3 Utilization of World Marine Fish Stocks, 1974–2013

We can see from the figure that the percentage of overexploited fish varieties around the world has steadily increased during the past 35 years, and almost 60% of the varieties of fish are already being harvested at the maximum level possible without jeopardizing future harvests of those types of fish.

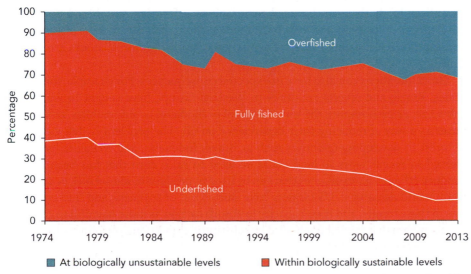

Source: Figure 13 from Food and Agriculture Organization of the United Nations, 2016, *The State of World Fisheries and Aquaculture: Contributing to Food Security and Nutrition for All*. Rome: available at http://www.fao.org/3/a-i5555e.pdf. Reproduced with permission.

Two additional issues relating to marine life have been important international problems for many years. First, there is the continuing issue of the commercial hunting of whales for consumption of whale meat (Andresen 2002). Humans have brought many species of whales to the point of extinction. Governments, working through the International Whaling Commission (IWC), agreed in 1982 to ban commercial whale harvesting. However, utilizing provisions of the whaling moratorium agreement that envisioned very limited whale harvesting for non-commercial purposes, such as scientific studies, fishing enterprises from Norway, Iceland, and Japan have continued to kill a significant number of whales each year. Norwegian whalers, for example, kill approximately 1,000 minke whales per year. Norway and Japan have both also been criticized for the methods they employ in killing whales, namely grenade-tipped harpoons and rifles.

The second international marine life issue concerns dolphins. For many years, dolphins were being killed in the Eastern Tropical Pacific region, off the coasts of California, western Mexico, and western Central America, not because they are valued as food, but as collateral damage arising from fishing techniques aimed at tuna. For unknown reasons, tuna and dolphins in the Eastern Pacific congregate together, and fishing crews can sight dolphins from great distances. In these circumstances, unless constrained, fishing crews would sight dolphins, deploy large nets that surround both the tuna and the dolphins, and kill and dump the dolphins while retaining the tuna catch. Fortunately, as we will see below, because of US governmental actions, American consumer activism, and international accords, fishing fleets now largely use 'dolphin-safe' harvesting techniques for tuna, and the killing of dolphins has decreased significantly.

Damage to the Land

Deforestation is the clearing or overharvesting of forests. This problem is particularly acute in the tropics, where some of the world's most important forest resources are located, as seen in Map 13.3.

Deforestation, as we discussed at the outset of this chapter, is a stark instance of the tragedy of the commons. No person, firm, or government wants to overharvest the world's forests. However, strong commercial demand for timber products as well as lands that can be used for grazing or farming, combined with weak government conservation efforts by individual countries as well as the international community, have resulted in overharvesting of important forest stocks around the world.

Good intentions can also have unexpected consequences. For example, the United States, Brazil, and several countries in Western Europe have sought to encourage, subsidize, or even require the use of ethanol or biodiesel in automobiles, trucks, and buses as a way of reducing their dependence on oil. The problem is that vast tracts of forest in developing countries such as Brazil, Indonesia, and Malaysia have been cleared in recent years so land could be used to raise corn that has been used to produce ethanol, palm oil trees that can be used to produce biodiesel fuel, or soybeans to fill world demand as US farmers have shifted out of soybeans and into corn. The loss of these forests, and their capacity to absorb carbon, is more harmful to the earth than any gain that might be achieved by substituting traditional gasoline with ethanol or biodiesel (Borrell 2009).

Map 13.3 Worldwide Distribution of Tropical Forests
This map shows the location of tropical forests around the world. Notice the particularly heavy concentrations in the Amazon region of South America, central sub-Saharan Africa, and the Indonesian Archipelago.

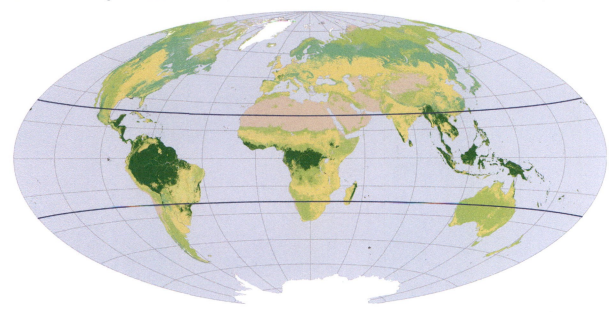

Source: NASA Earth Observatory Image by Robert Simmon, based on Moderate Resolution Imaging Spectroradiometer Land Cover Classification data.

Tropical deforestation poses two serious risks to the global environment. First, fire is often used to clear forests; this clearing technique contributes to global warming. During the 1990s, tropical deforestation accounted for roughly 20 percent of all greenhouse emissions released by humans into the atmosphere. If current rates of deforestation continue until the year 2100, the amount of carbon released into the atmosphere would be equal to the total carbon released since the beginning of the utilization of fossil fuels.

The second problem arising from deforestation relates to **biodiversity**. Biodiversity refers both to the variety of forms of life on earth, including different species of plants, animals, marine life, insects, and microorganisms (such as bacteria), and to variability within species, such as different types of corn, cattle, or bees. The maintenance of a diverse biological world ensures that humans will have many different sources of building supplies, clothing, food, and medicine.

Governments recognize the importance of biodiversity, and have sought to preserve it by way of an international agreement, the **Convention on Biological Diversity** of 1992. Deforestation may be an especially serious challenge to biodiversity. As a report from the international secretariat responsible for implementation of the convention has noted, 'forests are home to much of the known terrestrial biodiversity' (United Nations 2000: 5). So, as we lose the world's forests, we also lose a major repository of the world's biodiversity. As a result, we may be putting our food supplies and ability to identify new medicines at risk.

Biodiversity
Variety of forms of life on earth, including plants, animals, marine life, insects, and microorganisms, and variability within species, such as different types of corn, cattle, or bees.

Convention on Biological Diversity
An international agreement aiming to protect and preserve biodiversity, passed in 1992.

Photo 13.3 Destruction of a Rain Forest in Guyana
The destruction of rain forests, as depicted in this photo of forest-clearing at a gold mining site in Guyana, can have serious detrimental effects on global biodiversity.

Source: Getty Images/Robert Harding World Imagery\Mick Baines & Maren Reichelt.

We see from the discussion above that, in response to our enduring question, there are many specific international challenges regarding natural resources and the environment. How, then, do governments try to address these challenges? How, in other words, do international environmental issues prompt national and international action? We address that question in the next section.

Individual	State	International
Preferences of individuals for commercial products, such as gasoline, timber, or fish, can contribute to negative externalities or tragedies of the commons that end in international environmental problems.	Unless constrained by governments, firms can often generate international environmental problems such as overharvesting of fisheries or timber resources.	Many global resources, such as the earth's ozone layer and a great deal of the world's fisheries, are controlled by no single government, and this complicates the process of addressing threats to those resources.

Levels of Analysis *Environmental and Resource Challenges*

MANAGEMENT OF INTERNATIONAL ENVIRONMENTAL PROBLEMS

Governments have pursued three basic strategies to address international environment problems: unilateral policies, bilateral agreements, and multilateral accords through international organizations. In response to our enduring question, these strategies illuminate how international environmental problems spark national and international actions.

Whether these efforts succeed or not depends on the interplay of five factors. First, in accord with constructivist theories, we will see that NGOs, discussed in greater detail in Chapter 5, play a vital role in the international environmental domain (Betsill and Corell 2001). NGOs often help raise awareness of international environmental issues, press for national and international policy responses, and put a public spotlight on governments that are not carrying out their commitments to improve the world's environment. Another important ingredient for successful international cooperation on the environment, one that is also emphasized in constructivist theory, is the creation of a consensus among policy leaders that the existence of an environmental problem is underpinned by solid scientific data (Haas 2004). Third, efforts by developed nations to consider the special needs of developing countries are essential in obtaining the support of these key actors on the environment. In accord with liberal theories, international institutions have played a positive role in helping developing countries grapple with international environmental issues and the possibilities for mutually beneficial cooperation to address those problems. Fourth, there is the issue of cost: the greater the economic sacrifice that governments and societies need to incur to solve an international environmental problem, the less likely they will be to pursue that solution. Finally, and in accord with expectations of realist theory, international environmental cooperation, we will see below, requires the active support of major countries, and especially the United States.

In the discussion below we will focus on how governments interact with one another in bilateral and multilateral settings. However, political conditions *within* countries are likely to be highly important in influencing how environmental problems are addressed through government action. For example, as we discuss more fully in Box 13.3, countries that are in transition from authoritarianism to democracy may experience increases in deforestation. Thus, stronger efforts by major democratic states to help accelerate and fortify the process of democratization of countries undergoing such transitions may have environmental benefits, since those efforts might help move those countries to levels of democracy where heightened efforts to address the problem of deforestation may be expected.

Unilateral Responses

An important example of a purely national effort to remedy an international resource problem involved the United States and the above-noted problem of the killing of dolphins by tuna fishing fleets operating in the Eastern Pacific Ocean. In 1972, the US Congress passed the Marine Mammal Preservation Act (MMPA), which limits the number of dolphins that US tuna fleets could kill annually because of harvesting tuna. However, by the early 1980s, it was clear that foreign fleets not covered by MMPA were not using dolphin-safe fishing techniques. A wide range of NGOs, including Greenpeace, the Environmental Defense Fund, and the Earth Island Institute, launched a national campaign to raise public awareness of the issue, including a boycott of canned tuna and demonstrations at corporate stockholders' meetings. In addition, NGOs launched a federal lawsuit to force the US government to implement the Marine Act more vigorously, pressed the government to exclude foreign-harvested tuna not caught with dolphin-safe techniques from the US

13.3   RESEARCH INSIGHT

Does Democratization Help the Environment?

The Problem

Since the end of the Cold War many countries have experienced democratization and have attained different points along the spectrum from full autocracy to consolidated democracy. Scholars have investigated the ramifications of this differential success in attaining democracy. For example, there is work that suggests that democratizing states, especially those that become bogged down and fail to attain full democratic status, may be inclined to become embroiled in interstate wars (Mansfield and Snyder 2007). Does variation in the degrees of success in democratization also affect the institutional capacity and political commitment of countries to address national and global environmental problems?

The Research Insight

Significant scholarship on democratization and the environment has focused on the problem of deforestation. That scholarship seems to be converging on the identification of an interesting pattern (Buitenzorgy and Mol 2011; Obydenkova, Nazarov, and Salahodjaev 2016). That is, compared to countries that have either a highly autocratic or a fully democratic political regime, countries that are in the middle range, which are often seeking to become democratic, display higher rates of deforestation. Why do we see this pattern? It is possible that the democratizing states lack the capacity of authoritarian counterparts to impose restrictions on societal groups that may be inclined toward overexploitation of forest resources and to turn forests into farmland. At the same time, democratizing states may lack the institutional pathways that are present in mature democracies through which citizens can press for forest conservation, and especially to work toward that end through NGOs (Shandra, Esparza, and London 2012). Finally, it is possible that new political regimes, whether they are democratic or autocratic, permit greater deforestation because they are seeking to buttress domestic support and because they lack administrative strength needed to prevent it (Kuusela and Amacher 2016). One possible inference from this line of work is that major democratic states that are seeking to promote democratization abroad need to be resolute in their efforts and help democratizing states to escape that intermediate position and to press ahead to full democratic status.

market, and pressured the Heinz Corporation, parent company of the largest tuna canner StarKist, to only sell tuna it could certify had been harvested in dolphin-safe nets.

Eventually, the activists were successful. In 1990, the major tuna canners promised to market only tuna harvested with dolphin-safe nets, and the US government embargoed the importation of Mexican tuna since their fishing fleets were not meeting that standard. Mexico challenged the United States on this embargo in the General Agreement on Tariffs and Trade (GATT), received a ruling in its favor and against the United States, but elected not to press the matter (Wapner 1995).

This effort by a variety of globally minded NGOs to prod the US government to take actions to protect dolphins resulted in a decrease in dolphin kills from perhaps 500,000 per year at the beginning of the 1970s to less than 20,000 by the end of that decade, and, in the wake of an international agreement in 1999 to limit dolphin kills, a subsequent decrease to about 3,000 per year (US National Oceanic and Atmospheric Administration undated).

Simulations: What would you do? Imagine that you are the President of the United States and want to pursue unilateral policies to begin to tackle climate change. Go to the companion website to work through different options and their resultant effects.

Bilateral Efforts

Faced with clear evidence that acid rain constituted a threat to the United States and Canada, in 1990 the US Congress amended the Clean Air Act of 1963, and mandated limits on emissions by American power plants of sulfur dioxide and nitrous oxides. The following year the United States and Canada signed the US–Canada Air Quality Agreement. This bilateral agreement has been important in bringing the problem of acid rain under greater control. Under the terms of the agreement, the two countries committed to reduce acid rain precursors, pursue joint projects to address the problem, and meet annually to assess progress. Between 1990 and 2010, total US emissions of nitrogen oxides dropped by about one-half, and between 1990 and 2005 (the last year of documented data), emissions of sulfur dioxide fell by about one-third (US Environmental Protection Agency 2012; US Environmental Protection Agency undated a).

Multilateral Approaches

Governments have pursued several multilateral approaches to the management of environmental problems, with mixed success. As we noted above, a major example of successful multilateral cooperation on the environment concerned ozone depletion. This success was directly related to the negotiation, widespread acceptance, and high level of compliance with the 1987 **Montreal Protocol on Substances that Deplete the Ozone Layer** (Haas 1992; Sunstein 2007). The Protocol, named for the Canadian city in which the last negotiations occurred, and where the Protocol was signed, now has more than 180 members, and effectively bans the use of chlorofluorocarbons. In accord with the requirements of the Protocol, worldwide CFC use has declined by 95 percent and ozone levels are expected to return to normal by 2050.

Montreal Protocol on Substances that Deplete the Ozone Layer
An international agreement passed in 1987 that has successfully combated the depletion of the ozone layer by banning CFCs. Ozone layers are expected to return to normal by 2050.

The Montreal Protocol came into being, in part, because there was a significant community of scientists around the world who agreed there were grounds for concern that the ozone layer was being depleted due to the introduction of CFCs and other chemicals into the atmosphere. These scientists helped create an international consensus that something had to be done about CFCs. In addition, the government negotiators who worked to forge an agreement in this area recognized that developing countries would struggle to make the transition away from CFCs. They agreed that the developing countries would have a grace period before reducing their use and allocated $400 million to facilitate the transition.

Finally, reflecting ideas in realist theory, the United States used its economic power to facilitate the bringing of CFCs under international control. The American public became concerned about ozone depletion during the first half of the 1970s, and the US Environmental Protection Agency (EPA) banned most uses of CFCs as aerosol-can propellants in 1978. When, in 1986 and 1987, it appeared that international negotiations to ban CFCs were stalled, the Reagan administration advised its international negotiating partners that if they did not reach an agreement on a CFC ban, the United States would unilaterally ban such products from entering the US market. This threat of unilateral action prompted the completion of the Montreal Protocol in 1987.

It should be emphasized that international institutions have played an important role in providing assistance to developing countries to meet international environmental obligations, and therefore, in accord with liberal expectations, these institutions have made it more likely that developing countries are willing to accept such obligations and comply with them. Developed countries provide this assistance through the **Global Environmental Facility (GEF)**. The GEF began as a World Bank pilot project in 1991 and was formally established in 1994. It is located at the World Bank in Washington, DC, and is jointly managed by the World Bank, the United Nations Development Programme (UNDP), and the United Nations Environment Programme (UNEP). The GEF provides grants to developing countries to help them meet international legal obligations in four areas: climate change, desertification, international water pollution, and biodiversity. Since 1991, the GEF has directly provided about $15 billion in grants to developing countries. This funding has had moderate success in the areas of biodiversity and water pollution, but been less effective in helping developing countries with climate change (Clemencon 2006).

The World Bank also provides its own funding for environmental projects in developing countries. However, there has been controversy as to whether bank loans have had, on balance, a positive or a negative impact on the environment in developing countries. During the 1980s, NGOs were especially outraged by a $450 million World Bank loan for the Polonoroeste project, a network of roads and rural development in the Brazilian state of Rondonia. Instead of helping local inhabitants, the project led to large-scale deforestation and serious health problems for the people living in the region. There is also concern whether recent efforts to integrate environmental concerns into loan-making decisions have been sufficient to make the bank more responsive to ecological issues in its lending operations (Gutner 2005).

Governments have used a variety of strategies, with some success, to confront the international dimensions of acid rain, ozone depletion, and intentional oil discharge. In marked contrast, they have been less successful with issues such as whaling, forest depletion, and, especially, climate change. The **Kyoto Protocol** serves as an example of a particularly unsuccessful multilateral effort in the environmental area.

The Kyoto Protocol was negotiated in 1997, in large measure due to the leadership of the countries of the European Union as well as the European Commission. The Protocol came into effect in 2005, and by 2013 had more than 191 signatories.

Global Environmental Facility (GEF)
A program managed by the World Bank and the UN that provides grants to developing countries to help them meet international environment obligations regarding climate change, desertification, international water pollution, and biodiversity.

Kyoto Protocol
A multilateral agreement negotiated in 1997 to reduce the total emissions of signing states. The Protocol came into effect in 2005 but was ultimately unsuccessful in curbing emissions.

It was built on the Framework Convention on Climate Change of 1992, which had only committed countries to the general goal of reducing greenhouse emissions. The Kyoto Protocol established specific targets: total worldwide emissions by 2012 were to be reduced by 5 percent compared to levels observed in 1990, and most developed-country participants who signed the Protocol were to meet specific percentage targets for the reduction of their greenhouse emission by 2012.

The Kyoto Protocol has not had a great deal of success in reducing global greenhouse emissions, which as noted above continue to grow at an alarming rate. There are several reasons why the Protocol has had only a modest impact. First, developing countries are exempted from the Protocol's requirement that greenhouse emissions be cut by specific amounts by specific dates, but, as we discussed in the previous main section, India, Brazil, and, especially, China are major sources of emissions. Second, as we can see in Box 13.4, there has been a great deal of variability among developed-country signatories to the Protocol in meeting their commitments to cut emissions. The United Kingdom, Germany, France, and especially Sweden had made great strides by 2010 toward meeting their Kyoto targets; other countries, including Canada, Australia, and Spain, had not fared so well. Finally, the United States, which until recently has been the world's largest source of greenhouse gases (it has been surpassed by China), signed but did not ratify the Kyoto Protocol.

For many years governments sought to negotiate an accord that would replace the Kyoto Protocol and accelerate international efforts to address the problem of climate change. This effort commenced formally in the Danish capital of Copenhagen in December 2009. The initial negotiations were nearly a complete failure, with key countries such as India and China working hard to stop efforts by rich countries to move toward binding targets on all major countries to cap national emissions of carbon gases. Subsequent multilateral talks in 2010 in Cancun, Mexico, and in 2011 in Durban, South Africa, witnessed sharp disagreements between the United States and China. Talks in 2012 in Doha, Qatar, and then in Warsaw in 2013, were less acrimonious but also produced little headway.

Finally, governments in late 2015 reached an agreement in Paris, which by 2018 had 195 signatories. The agreement represented both progress in the sense of attracting the support of more countries, especially China and India, as well as, temporarily, the United States. However, the agreement also made manifest the difficulty in establishing a common international program for the limitation and reduction of carbon emissions and associated climate change (Christoff 2016; Young 2016). According to the **Paris Agreement**, governments committed on a non-binding basis that they individually and collectively should strive to prevent global warming due to human activities from exceeding 2 degrees Celsius (3.6 degrees Fahrenheit), and indeed laid down an even more ambitious, but also non-binding, goal of limiting global warming to no more than 1.5 degrees Celsius (2.7 degrees Fahrenheit). However, by the Paris Agreement governments are not legally obliged to undertake common and binding commitments to reduce carbon emissions so as to prevent global warming. Instead, they are obliged by virtue of the agreement to announce individual, voluntary – that is, legally non-binding – 'nationally determined contributions' (NDC) as to their respective efforts to reduce emissions. For example, in a Sino-American joint announcement at the end of 2014 that helped press forward

Paris Agreement
An international environment agreement reached in 2015 in which parties committed on a non-binding basis to act individually and collectively to prevent global warming.

13.4   MAKING CONNECTIONS
Aspiration versus Reality

Compliance with the Kyoto Protocol

Aspiration

The Kyoto Protocol committed countries to cut their emissions of greenhouse gases. Different countries had different targets assigned to them in terms of percentage cuts in emissions compared to their respective emission levels in 1990, but they averaged about 5 percent.

Reality

Figure 13.4 depicts the extent to which countries met or failed to meet their respective Kyoto targets as of 2010. Countries highlighted in red failed to meet their commitments; countries highlighted in blue exceeded their commitments. The score for each country is the absolute value of the difference between its 2012 Kyoto goal and its performance as of 2010 in cutting emissions relative to the base year of 1990. If a country was supposed to cut its emissions between 1990 and 2012 by 5 percent, but by 2010 had increased its emissions by 5 percent, then its score in terms of falling short in cutting emissions relative to1990 levels was 10 percentage points. If a country was supposed to reduce its emissions by 5 percent by 2012, but by 2010 had cut its emissions by 15 percent, then its score in terms of exceeding its Kyoto commitment was 10 percentage points. As can be seen in the figure, by 2010 it was clear that countries such as Canada and Australia were not meeting their Kyoto goals, and Canada withdrew from the Protocol in December 2012. In contrast, by 2010 the United Kingdom, Germany, France, and especially Sweden had already met and exceeded their 2012 targets. Notice that the countries that exceeded their Kyoto targets the most are Russia and several former Soviet bloc countries; the reason is that the economies of these countries collapsed during the 1990s, and those economies, and thus their emissions of greenhouse gases, have taken years to recover.

Figure 13.4 Meeting Kyoto Protocol Commitments to Cut Greenhouse Gases

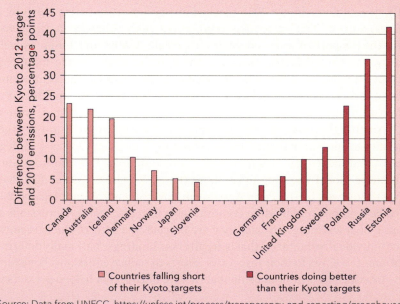

Source: Data from UNFCC. https://unfccc.int/process/transparency-and-reporting/greenhouse-gas-data/greenhouse-gas-data-unfccc/kyoto-protocol-base-year-data and https://unfccc.int/process/transparency-and-reporting/greenhouse-gas-data/greenhouse-gas-data-unfccc.

the final multilateral negotiations in Paris the following year, China announced that its first NDC would consist of a commitment to take policy steps whereby total annual Chinese CO_2 emissions would peak in 2030 (that is, not go down but stop going up after that year), and the United States offered as its non-binding commitment a promise that US total annual carbon emissions by 2025 would decrease from its level in 2005 by somewhere between 26 percent and 28 percent. The signatories have agreed that they will meet every five years to assess their individual progress in meeting their voluntary carbon-reduction targets, and to try to make, on a voluntary basis, more ambitious commitments to further reduce emissions. However, in early June 2017, as noted in Chapter 4, the Trump administration announced that the United States would not be bound even by its voluntary NDC commitment to reduce US carbon emissions. It is not clear if this will impair efforts by the remaining participants to meet their respective emission-reduction goals, let alone serve as a basis for attracting from them more ambitious emission-reduction commitments in the future.

It is possible to look to the future and see what an agreement on climate change would need to include if it is to be more effective than previous attempts. It seems likely that it will need specific emission-reduction targets for all developed countries, including the United States. Important developing countries such as India, China, and Brazil will also need to accept emission-reduction goals, although these might not be binding. There remain sharp differences in perspectives between developed and developing countries on this matter, which we highlight in Box 13.5.

Photo 13.4 Air Pollution and the Shanghai Skyline
Shanghai, China is one the world's fastest developing cities. A significant portion (by some estimates, up to 30%) of its industrial pollution comes from factories that manufacture products for export to the United States. Some of the pollution is exported as well, carried by winds to the US west coast.

Source: iStock.com/lukyeee1976.

13.5   DIFFERING PERSPECTIVES

The United States, India, and Greenhouse Gas Emissions

Background

During a visit to India in July 2009, Secretary of State Hillary Clinton and US special negotiator on climate change Todd Stern met with Indian Environment Minister Shri Jairam Ramesh at a new energy-efficient Indian office building outside New Delhi. The event was supposed to highlight Indian-American mutual interests in dealing with global warming, but the Secretary and the Minister aired sharp differences on what commitments India and other major developing countries should make in a post-Kyoto greenhouse emissions agreement. The Minister distributed a note to the media that summarized his opening comments at a meeting with the Secretary, and a US news reporter who attended the meeting took notes on the discussion between the Minister and the Secretary.

At the Meeting

Indian Environment Minister Ramesh

> …India's position on the ongoing climate change agreement negotiations is clear, credible and consistent … Even with 8–9 percent GDP growth every year for the next decade or two, our per capita emissions will be well below that of developed-country averages … There is simply no case for the pressure that we, who have among the lowest emissions per capita, face to actually reduce emissions … if this pressure was not enough, we also face the threat of carbon tariffs on our exports to countries such as yours … Apart from vastly greater financial flows from the developed world, we see a critical role for international technology cooperation in enabling countries like India to adapt to climate change.
>
> Source: Summary provided by Government of India, Press Information Bureau (2009).

Secretary of State Clinton

Clinton responded that she 'completely' understood India's argument about per capita emissions, according to the notes of a US reporter permitted to observe the discussion. 'On one level, it's a fair argument,' she said, but she argued that the per capita argument 'loses force' as developing countries rapidly become the biggest emitters.

Indian Environment Minister Ramesh

Ramesh replied that India's position on per capita emissions is 'not a debating strategy' because it is enshrined in international agreements. 'We look upon you suspiciously because you have not fulfilled what [developed countries] pledged to fulfill,' he said, calling it a 'crisis of credibility.'

Source: Kessler (2009).

At the News Conference

Secretary of State Clinton

> I want to make two points as clearly as I can. First, the United States does not and will not do anything that would limit India's economic progress … But we

also believe that there is a way to eradicate poverty and develop sustainably that will lower significantly the carbon footprint of the energy that is produced and consumed to fuel that growth.

And secondly, we in the United States, under the Obama administration, are recognizing our responsibility and taking action …

But it is essential for major developing countries like India to also lead, because over 80 percent of the growth in future emissions will be from developing countries.

Now, China is, by far, the largest emitter in the world right now, and certainly the largest among developing countries. But India's own greenhouse gas pollution is projected to grow by about 50 percent between now and 2030. So, climate change would not be solved even if developed countries stopped emitting greenhouse gas emissions today, unless action is taken across the world. So we have to work together. And I was very heartened, and I agree with the minister's comment that we must achieve an agreement in Copenhagen that is equal to the task.

Indian Environment Minister Ramesh

All I can say is that India already has a national action plan of climate change which was unveiled last year. And that action plan is overwhelmingly oriented towards programs and projects that will enable India to adapt to the effects of climate change. But it also has very specific and very pointed policies oriented towards mitigating emissions.

India has been saying that its primary focus will be adaptation. But there are specific areas where we are already in a policy framework [inaudible] mitigation, which means actual reduction of emissions.

So, whether that will convert into legally binding emission [inaudible] is the real question. And India's position is – I would like to make it clear that India's position is that we are simply not in a position to take on legally binding emission-reduction targets … Now, this does not mean that we are oblivious of our responsibilities for ensuring that [inaudible] the incremental addition to greenhouse gases that both special envoy Stern, and Madame Secretary of State spoke about. We are fully conscious of that. Energy efficiency is a very fundamental driver of our economic strategy.

Sources: Still4Hill (2009); Gollus (2009).

It is difficult to estimate the likelihood that the major developed and developing countries will reach a comprehensive climate-change agreement in time to avert serious global environmental damage. The Paris Agreement of 2015 suggests that there could be a pathway to international action on this matter, although as noted above the agreement itself did not lay down explicit and binding CO_2 reduction targets, and the US at present appears to be unwilling to help move forward the international climate-change agenda. We can consider how different theoretical perspectives in the field of international relations might try to assess the chances of success in the negotiations: we do this in Box 13.6.

In sum, states employ unilateral, bilateral, and multilateral strategies to address the harm that humans cause to natural resources and the environment. Those strategies as well as their interaction and success or failure are becoming an important substantive feature of international relations, and they rightly command the interest of students and scholars of international affairs.

13.6   DIFFERING THEORETICAL APPROACHES

Factors Affecting the Likelihood of a Comprehensive Climate-Change Agreement

Developed and developing countries have been unable to reach a comprehensive agreement to reduce greenhouse emissions and thus avert a host of national and transborder environmental problems that would be due to (and may already be resulting from) climate change. What are the chances that countries will reach such an accord?

Realism

A realist would suggest that the chances a climate change agreement will be reached will depend on at least three factors: first, the chances of success depend on the degree to which countries would suffer from not reaching an agreement; second, countries will need to be assured that some countries do not benefit more from the agreement than do others, and therefore there will need to be in the agreement a balanced sharing both of gains and costs; and third, success will in all likelihood require the leadership of the most powerful developed and developing countries, such as the United States and the EU countries on the one hand and India and especially China on the other.

Constructivism

A constructivist would largely agree with the points made by the realist, and especially about the need for state leaders and policy officials to believe that they have a national interest in attaining a climate change agreement. However, a constructivist would suggest that more is needed. Leaders and officials of different countries must share common understandings about what causes climate change, namely, greenhouse gas emissions, and they must share common ideas about what are effective ways to reduce such emissions, namely, jointly agreed limits by governments, rather than, for example, allowing market forces to induce firms and households to reduce emissions. Perhaps most important, leaders and officials in developed countries must share with counterparts in developing countries the view that the wealthy countries have a responsibility to help developing nations bear the costs that they will need to incur to reduce their emissions.

Liberalism

A liberal would mostly agree with the points made by the realist and constructivist colleagues. However, the liberal would argue that there is a higher likelihood that leaders and officials from developed and developing countries would understand their common interest in addressing the problem of climate change, and the special responsibilities that developed countries have toward developing countries in dealing with this problem, if the main countries on both sides were robust, deeply rooted democracies. This would increase the chances that governments in the talks would trust each other's intentions to reach an accord as well as to comply with it, and to avoid seeking relative gains from the agreement. Truly democratic developing countries, the liberal would also suggest, would be more likely to make effective use of externally provided resources to make the necessary changes to their economies to comply with a climate change agreement, and this would enhance the chances that the developed countries would be willing to provide such resources.

Photo 13.5 Scientists Tracking Climate Change
Earth scientists drill holes and remove ice cores in the world's polar regions to monitor the vulnerability of the ice shelf to climate change.

Source: MACMILLAN AUSTRALIA.

Levels of Analysis *Management of International Environmental Problems*

Individual	State	International
Individuals, such as NGO activists and scientists, have played important roles in pressing governments to recognize and address international environmental problems.	The important role of the US Congress and courts in advancing US environmental policy has spurred the US government on occasion to be more active in seeking international solutions to global environmental and natural-resource problems.	The United States, governments of EU countries, and to some extent international organizations like the GEF have been central to the success or failure of international efforts to address such environmental problems as North American acid rain, ozone depletion, and climate change.
	The willingness of India and China in the Paris Agreement increases the chances that climate change problems are addressed.	Future progress on addressing the problem of climate change has been hampered to date by a conflict of interest between already industrialized countries on the one hand, and still-industrializing countries.
	NGOs are especially able to exercise influence in raising consciousness about international environmental problems in democratic countries such as Japan, the United States, and in Western Europe.	

REVISITING THE ENDURING QUESTION AND LOOKING AHEAD

We began this chapter with a question: how do international environmental problems influence international relations? We have seen, in response to that question, how international environmental and natural-resource problems for many years have been an important element of world affairs. If we think about the issues of water pollution or fisheries management or deforestation or especially climate change, we can see how the natural environment will continue to influence global affairs in the years ahead.

Environmental issues highlight how difficult it is for states to be successful in pursuing their international interests exclusively through their own efforts. Instead, states must work together to address mutual environmental challenges. In some instances, such as in the case of ozone depletion, governments have achieved substantial success in crafting an international arrangement aimed at alleviating global environmental problems. However, in other areas, including deforestation, global fisheries, and most notably climate change, governments have yet to construct effective international responses to pressing problems relating to the environment and natural resources. Will citizens and their governments have the foresight to realize that they are facing global environmental tragedies of the commons? Can governments of developing countries accept limits on emissions of greenhouse gases even if this means an abatement of national economic growth? Above all, can governments of wealthy countries make or encourage the domestic investments needed to create new, more efficient transportation and power-generating technologies and provide the financial and technological resources that developing-country partners will need to bring global warming under control? How these questions are addressed will have a large, lasting impact on the fate of the earth and the future of international relations for many decades to come.

What else will be important for the future of international relations? In the next and final chapter, we examine five possible models of the future international system in the context of both theoretical traditions and enduring questions.

STUDY QUESTIONS

1. In the text we discussed overharvesting of fish and deforestation as important international examples of the tragedy of the commons; can you think of another example?
2. What is the role of the United States in the contemporary world both as a perpetrator of international environmental problems and as a motivator of international action to address those problems?
3. What do you think is the likelihood that climate change will be managed at the international level during the next 25 years?
4. There has been stalemate between major wealthy states like the US and developing countries like China and India on forging a new international agreement on CO_2 and other greenhouse gas emissions that might be related to climate change. What proposal would you make to break the deadlock, given their positions on this matter?
5. What are the benefits and costs of using different strategies – unilateral, bilateral, or multilateral – to address an environmental problem of interest to you?

FURTHER READING

Haas, Peter (1990) *Saving the Mediterranean: The Politics of International Environmental Cooperation* (New York: Columbia University Press). In this pathbreaking work, Haas deployed constructivist theory to help explain variation in international cooperation on environmental issues, and in so doing also contributed to that theoretical perspective.

Hardin, Garrett (1968) 'Tragedy of the Commons,' *Science* 162 (3589): 1243–8. This essay, which showed how many environmental problems are tragedies of the commons, has had enormous influence in political science, economics, and legal studies, and is essential reading for students of international environmental problems.

Homer-Dixon, Thomas (1999) *Environment, Scarcity, and Violence* (Princeton: Princeton University Press). This book provides the most persuasive argument that environmental problems that ultimately produce scarcities of important resources, such as forests, water, and arable land, can generate serious social stresses within countries and thereby contribute to the onset of violence, even civil wars, in those countries.

Miles, Edward L., Arild Underdal, Steinar Andresen, Jorgen Wettestad, Jon Skjaerseth, and Elaine Carlin (eds) (2002) *Environmental Regime Effectiveness: Confronting Theory with Evidence* (Cambridge: MIT Press). This edited volume addresses two fundamentally important questions: how do we measure variation in the effectiveness of different international agreements on the environment, and what accounts for that variation?

 Visit **www.macmillanihe.com/Grieco-IntroIR-2e** to access extra resources for this chapter, including:

- Chapter summaries to help you review the material
- Multiple choice quizzes to test your understanding
- Flashcards to test your knowledge of the key terms in this chapter
- An interactive simulation that invites you to go through the decision-making process of a world leader at a crucial political juncture
- Pivotal decisions in which you weigh up the pros and cons of complicated decisions with grave consequences
- Outside resources, including links to contemporary articles and videos, that add to what you have learned in this chapter

14 Facing the Future: Six Visions of an Emerging International Order

Enduring question
Will the international system undergo fundamental change in the future?

Chapter Contents

Learning Objectives

By the end of this chapter, you will be able to:

→   Evaluate critical influences on international politics in the years ahead.

→   Recognize the reasons why some scholars believe economic power will become more important than military power.

→   Identify trends that indicate whether the international system will swing to a multipolar or bipolar political structure.

→   Compare world political theories that transcend the concept of the traditional nation-state, such as democratic peace and clash of civilizations models.

→   Understand why some scholars believe the nation-state will be of declining significance in the years ahead.

→   Analyze the importance of enduring questions in predicting future influences on international relations.

As we look ahead to the next decade, will the international system undergo some type of fundamental change? Although the future is impossible to predict, the different assumptions scholars make about state behavior and the dynamics of international relations lead them to very different expectations about how world politics will turn out in the years ahead.

The durability and character of the Westphalian international system is an enduring question for students of international relations. In this text, we have provided a broad perspective by looking at the history of international relations and how it has been understood by liberal, realist, constructivist, Marxist, and feminist thinkers. We have also focused on contemporary international issues and challenges. This final chapter builds on earlier chapters and prompts you to examine the future of international relations through six possible models of the emerging international system. No one can know for certain which of these models, if any, is most likely to characterize international relations in the years ahead. Nevertheless, we believe that defining and evaluating alternative visions of the future can be a valuable analytical exercise. The six models are based on different assumptions about what matters in international politics. In some models, the nation-state remains a key actor; international relations revolve around militarized great-power dynamics. In other models, economic power is far more valuable than military, or the nation-state is no longer the central focal point. Some models anticipate a world of greater cooperation; others see enhanced conflict. A critical examination of different models of the future forces us to examine our own assumptions about what is fundamental and what transitory in world politics. This concluding chapter provides an exercise to reinforce the central theme of the book – the effort to focus on and understand the enduring questions and features of international relations across time and space.

The six competing models are: a world of geo-economic competition; a return to multipolarity; a return to bipolarity; the emergence of a democratic peace; the clash of civilizations; and the global fracture of the international system. We examine the logic, core assumptions, and key features of each model and defend its plausibility. We also provide a critical assessment of each, pointing to trends or evidence that reinforce the likelihood of the model and raising a set of critical questions that any proponent of each model must address. No model is completely right or wrong, but each may prove to be useful as an analytical device to enhance our understanding of what matters most in international relations and whether the international system is undergoing fundamental change.

MODEL 1: A WORLD OF GEO-ECONOMIC COMPETITION

Any student with an appreciation of the history of international relations should be deeply impressed by how the Cold War ended. The US–Soviet competition not only ended abruptly in 1989–91, it ended *peacefully*.

This fact is remarkable in historical context. Struggles between rising and declining great powers have usually ended in great wars, such as the Peloponnesian War of the fifth century BCE, the Napoleonic Wars of the early nineteenth century, and the two world wars of the first half of the twentieth century. But the collapse of the Soviet Union turned out differently. In a remarkably short time, the Soviets lost control of their key satellite states in Eastern Europe and the Soviet Union itself broke apart into more than a dozen new sovereign states. The complete collapse of the power, influence, and prestige of a superpower took place without inciting a

Map 14.1 The Soviet Union and Eastern Europe during the Cold War
During the Cold War, the Soviet Union was a vast multinational state that included diverse nations including Russians, Estonians, Latvians, Ukrainians, Georgians, and Armenians among others. The Soviet Union dominated the Warsaw Pact alliance that included European countries east of the Iron Curtain depicted here.

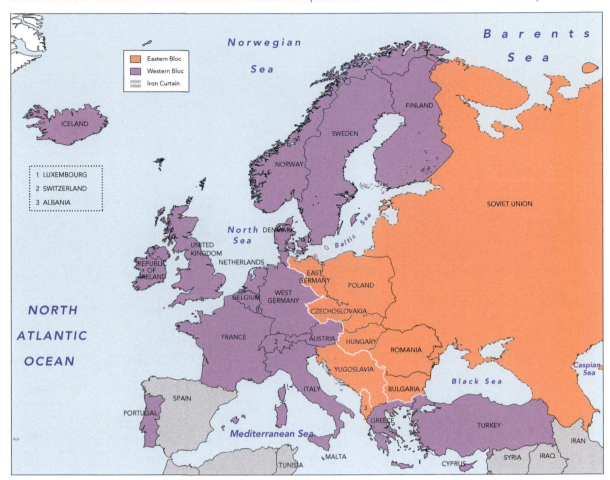

larger systemic war. Indeed, the Soviet empire collapsed without a single shot being fired across the highly militarized East–West front that characterized world politics for decades.

There are multiple explanations for this remarkable outcome. We review, in Box 14.1, how constructivists, liberals, and realists might explain the end of the Cold War. The model we focus on in this section, however, draws insights from several theoretical traditions. In accounting for the peaceful end of the Cold War, proponents of the geo-economic model would point to what liberal theorists view as an increasingly powerful trend in the international system – the *declining utility of military force* in relations among great powers. The United States and Soviet Union were formidable nuclear powers; any war between them carried the risk of escalation that would result in the all-out destruction of both societies and, most likely, the international system itself. As discussed in Chapter 8, nuclear weapons are so powerful that even a modest arsenal carries great destructive potential. In a nuclear age, great powers can no longer initiate wars against their rivals to overpower,

Map 14.2 Russia and the Eastward Expansion of NATO
The former Eastern European members of the Warsaw Pact – Poland, Hungary, Czechoslovakia, Bulgaria, Romania, and East Germany – are now all part of NATO, along with Latvia, Lithuania and Estonia, countries that were formerly part of the Soviet Union itself.

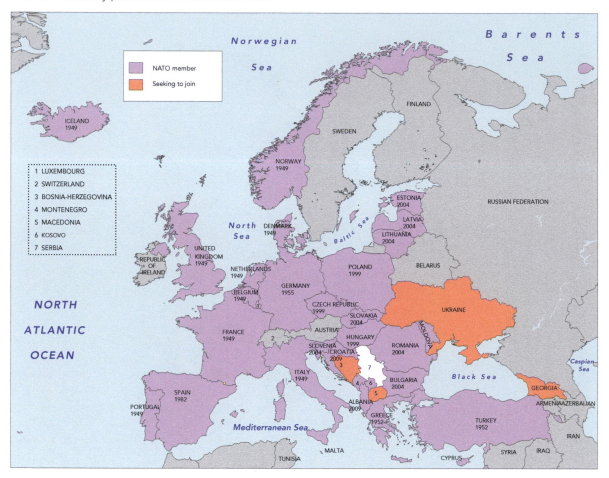

conquer, or dominate (Mueller 1989). From this perspective, the total wars of the twentieth century, requiring societal mobilization and protracted fighting among great powers over many years, are a thing of the past. The Soviet Union, unlike the great powers that preceded it, simply did not have a viable global military option to shore up the shaky foundations of its empire and arrest its decline. The United States and NATO, in turn, had no incentive to conquer, occupy, and administer the vast territories of its collapsing enemy.

Characteristics of Geo-Economic Competition

The geo-economic model presumes that great-power war is a thing of the past. But does the end of great-power war necessarily mean the end of great-power competition? For proponents of the geo-economic model, the answer is no. In the emerging international system, great-power competition simply changes form. Traditional military competition is replaced by economic competition – a 'struggle

14.1   DIFFERING THEORETICAL APPROACHES

Explaining the End of the Cold War

The end of the Cold War was one of the most important international events of the twentieth century. Not surprisingly, scholars working within different theoretical traditions are compelled to provide explanations for this key unanticipated outcome. These different explanations showcase key variables, or what matters most to each tradition, both in explaining international change in the past and in anticipating likely changes in international relations in the future.

Constructivism

Constructivists might offer a two-part argument for why the Cold War ended. First, ideas matter. Once the Cold War became entrenched, many scholars and political leaders came to treat the US–Soviet conflict as a necessary and enduring feature of the international landscape. They believed that the future would resemble the past. For constructivists that view is an example of how decision makers and analysts can become trapped by their own self-reinforcing assumptions. What if, instead, policy makers and scholars envisioned a different international reality, one in which East and West were not locked in immutable conflict? Second, constructivists would point to leaders as carriers of new ideas, that is, as people with the willingness and ability to bring about significant international change. Mikhail Gorbachev was one such leader; he explicitly referred to new ideas and new thinking as he positioned the Soviet Union to make an historic accommodation with the West, one that involved reconsidering whether the Soviet Union needed to maintain an empire in Eastern Europe and the developing world to be secure. Leaders in Germany and the United States proved receptive to this radical rethinking of the international context and joined Gorbachev as partners in the remaking of international order.

Liberalism

Liberal theorists focus on the role of social forces that gradually eroded the seemingly secure foundation of the Cold War. Global interdependence involved the movement of goods, people, and ideas across borders. This process eventually influenced the Soviet elite, a significant fraction of which came to believe, alongside Gorbachev, that the economic costs of sitting outside of the liberal world economy no longer justified the Soviet Union's traditional emphasis on military competition in preparation for military conflict with the West. At the same time, transnational coalitions formed across East and West to draw attention to the dangers of nuclear war. Scientists, doctors, clergy, and ordinary citizens pressured governments on either side of the East–West divide to scale back risky military competition. In short, the mechanism for change consisted of societal pressures that gained a receptive hearing among government leaders in the Soviet Union, Europe, and the United States.

Realism

Realists view the end of the Cold War as a function of the shifting balance of power between East and West in general and between the Soviet Union and United States in particular. The centrally planned economies of the East simply could not keep pace with the more dynamic, productive, and technologically innovative economies of the West. Economic power is the foundation of military power, and Gorbachev recognized what other Soviet leaders had refused to accept, namely that over the long run the Soviet Union would not be able to keep up its side of the East–West military competition. Gorbachev's Soviet Union faced a painful set of choices. It could try to keep racing with the West and bankrupt its economy, it could initiate a military conflict that risked the destruction of the planet, or it could try to scale back its international commitments and reach an accommodation with the West that would allow breathing space to reform its struggling economy. Gorbachev chose the latter course and could not control the consequences it unleashed. For realists, the end of the Cold War is a story of how a power balance became a power asymmetry – two sides were racing, and one realized it could no longer keep up.

for the world product,' in the words of former German Chancellor Helmut Schmidt. States that used to see territorial acquisition or protection from conquest by other great powers as the primary concern of security policy now focus on a struggle to capture export markets, raw materials, and the highest value-added jobs for their people (Helleiner and Pickel 2005). In this new world, **economic security,** or the ability to maintain prosperity in a world of scarcity, replaces military security as the key nation-state objective. Governments that primarily mobilized resources for military competition will emphasize economic competition. Recall our discussion of economic nationalism in Chapter 10; the geo-economic model elaborates that perspective as the central feature of international relations. In theoretical terms we might describe this model as 'economic realism' in that the basic dynamic is state competition, but the competition is in the economic arena. Geo-economic competition is also consistent with the Marxist tradition; recall Lenin's argument, from Chapter 1, that anticipated capitalist states and their respective corporations competing along national lines.

Economic security
The ability to maintain prosperity in a world of scarcity.

What are the central features of world geo-economic competition? The most prominent would include the development of **competing economic blocs,** with groups of states organized around the economies and currencies of major economic powers. In a fully formed geo-economic world, we should anticipate the consolidation of a North American bloc organized around the United States economy and use of the dollar as a reserve and exchange currency. A European bloc would center on core members of the European Union and increased reliance on the euro as a key currency. The American economist Lester Thurow, whose 1992 book *Head to Head* helped articulate the geo-economic model, pointed to the natural competitive advantages enjoyed by a European bloc with a well-educated work force, German standards of productivity, French and Italian design contributions, and British and Swiss banking experience (Thurow 1992). In East Asia, there might be one bloc or two, depending on the willingness and capacity of Japan to organize its economic relations to either compete with, or depend on, a rising China.

Competing economic blocs
Groups of states in economic competition organized around the economies and currencies of major economic powers.

According to the geo-economic model, each bloc would look to spread its influence into nearby regions. Because of geography and history, the United States would want to make sure Latin America was incorporated into its sphere of economic influence. European Union members would take a similar approach to central European countries and, perhaps, former colonies in North Africa. States in Southeast Asia would be the logical zone of dependence for a bloc organized by China or Japan. Other regions, particularly those with rich resources, would be 'up for grabs.' For example, the energy resources of the Middle East and mineral resources of sub-Saharan Africa would naturally attract the attention of each of the competing blocs.

Leading governments in each of the competing blocs would look to form close working relationships with key firms in leading sectors, such as banking, communications, information technology, and transportation, perhaps by cultivating national champions, which, as we discussed in Chapter 10, are companies explicitly supported by their governments to compete in key areas of the world economy. A good example of a national champion is Airbus, a European consortium that has worked closely with European governments to mobilize resources and develop the scale of operations necessary to compete on a global scale with the American firm Boeing (a beneficiary of American defense contracts) in the production of civilian aircraft. Close relations with governments serve the profit and market share interests of national champion firms, and their success helps governments serve national economic interests as well.

International Trends

It is not difficult to point to trends or evidence in support of the emergence of a geo-economic model. Over the past 25 years, there has been a steady rise of economic integration within the three major regions of international economic activity. The United States, Canada, and Mexico forged the North American Free Trade Agreement (NAFTA) to oversee and regulate the continued integration of their neighboring economies. The United States also sought to spread regional integration southward, initiating free trade agreements (FTAs) with Chile in 2003, Peru in 2006, and six Central American nations (the Dominican Republic, Costa Rica, El Salvador, Honduras, Guatemala, and Nicaragua) in 2004. In 2012, the United States concluded free trade agreements with Colombia and Panama.

European integration proceeded even more rapidly and deeply. The core states of the European Union not only consolidated a single integrated market for goods and services but surrendered national currencies in favor of the euro. Economic integration in East Asia was strengthened with the creation of APEC (Asia-Pacific Economic Cooperation) in 1989 and the development of ASEAN plus Three (the ten members of the Association of Southeast Asian Nations plus Japan, China, and South Korea) during the late 1990s. In line with the expectations of the geo-economic

Map 14.3 Regional Economic Blocs: NAFTA, European Union, and APEC
Regionalism characterizes, in different ways, economic relations in North America, Europe, and East Asia. The North American Free Trade Agreement (NAFTA) governs trade relations among the United States, Canada, and Mexico. The European Union has created a single integrated market among 28 European states, with 19 of them sharing a common currency, the euro. APEC (Asia-Pacific Economic Cooperation) is a looser grouping of states bordering the Pacific Ocean, with its 21 members seeking to reduce barriers to trade and promote economic cooperation.

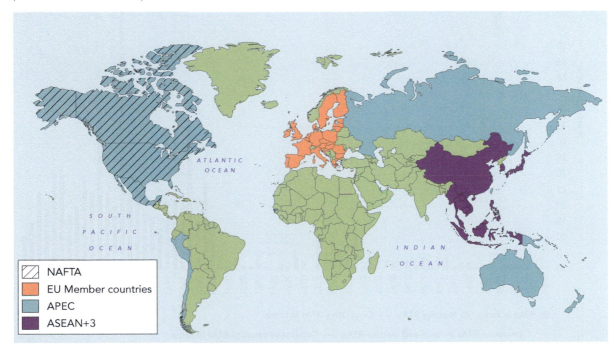

model, regional economic agreements rose sharply after the end of the Cold War (see Figure 14.1). At the same time, a backlash against globalization occurred and trade negotiations at the global level almost slowed to a standstill. The Uruguay Round of multilateral negotiations, which created the WTO in 1995, took nearly ten years to complete. The Doha Development Round began in 2001, but by the end of 2015, negotiations concluded without any comprehensive agreement.

Competition for natural resources among leading states has been intensifying as well. One could plausibly view the post-Cold War wars in Iraq in 1990–91 and 2002–03 as efforts by the United States to ensure that the Gulf oil reserves remain in friendly hands (Clark 2005). As its economy has grown rapidly, China has stepped up efforts to consolidate political relations with important suppliers of energy and other raw materials in Central Asia and Africa. As Table 14.1 shows, Chinese foreign direct investment (FDI) in Asian and African countries has increased significantly since 2003.

Relations between business and government in both Europe and Japan have typically been marked by close cooperation in pursuit of national development goals. As we saw in Chapter 11, a similar model has characterized China's export-led growth strategy since 1978. The global financial and economic crises that began in 2008 only reinforced these trends, creating incentives for governments to step into their

Figure 14.1 Evolution of Regional Trade Agreements (RTAs), 1948–2014
The figure shows all Regional Trade Agreements notified to the GATT/WTO since 1948. Note that the trend line moves sharply upward beginning in the early 1990s. This reflects the spread of regional agreements as it became increasingly difficult for states to conclude comprehensive global trade negotiations.

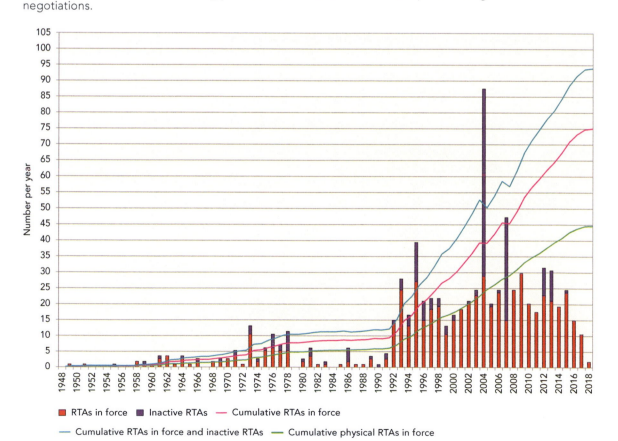

Source: Data from WTO RTA Database [http://rtais.wto.org/]. WTO Secretariat – June 27, 2018. © World Trade Organization 2018.

Table 14.1 Chinese FDI Flows to Asia and Africa (Millions of Dollars), 2003–12
According to secret memos published on WikiLeaks, US diplomats expressed concerns about China's growing role in Africa. The cables between Washington and the US Embassy in Nigeria describe China as 'aggressive and pernicious,' and 'in Africa primarily for China.' American officials noted that if China were to begin military cooperation with African countries, train armies, or sign military base agreements, American uneasiness with Chinese activities in Africa would grow exponentially.

	2003	2004	2005	2006	2007	2008	2009	2010	2011	2012
Asia	1,491	2,985	4,351	7,541	16,174	42,834	39,978	43,962	44,800	61,182
Africa	75	317	392	520	1,574	5,591	1,439	2,112	3,173	2,517

Source: UNCTAD FDI/TNC database, based on data from the Ministry of Commerce (MOFCOM).

national economies to rescue ailing firms and save jobs for their populations. Even the government of the United States, the rhetorical champion of the free market, made major investments in the financial and automotive sectors, including costly rescues of the insurance firm American International Group (AIG) and the automotive giant General Motors.

Recent developments involving the world's two largest national economies lend further credence to the geo-economic model. China has sought to organize under its control economic relations across east and central Asia. It opened in 2016 the Asian Infrastructure Investment Bank (AIIB) as a regional financing alternative to the IMF, it has promoted a regional trade initiative, the Regional Comprehensive Economic Partnership (RCEP) that excludes the United States, and it has launched an ambitious project, the Belt and Road Initiative, to use Chinese financing and materials to develop economic infrastructure across Eurasia. For its part, the United States under President Donald Trump has proclaimed that economic security is the key to national security. Trump, reflecting the zero-sum logic of the geo-economic model, has emphasized bilateral negotiations with US trading partners designed to increase American exports and eliminate trade deficits, and promised that in future trade deals America will be the winner rather than the loser.

Contrary Evidence and Questions

The geo-economic model is certainly plausible. But what contrary evidence might its proponents have overlooked? First, this model, which depicts businesses in different regions working with their respective governments to conquer world markets, must come to terms with the operations of modern transnational corporations. Liberal theorists point out that companies such as US-based Nike and General Electric, Europe-based Philips and Siemens, and Asia-based Sony and Toyota have cross-regional identities and interests. They have established operations and are players in all major regions of the world, not just their home countries or regions. As global players with global interests, most big firms do not simply 'line up' politically with their primary home governments to do economic battle with other business/government clusters. How could the Japanese electronics giant Fujitsu view the US or European governments as adversaries when it has merged its European operations with the German electronics national champion Siemens, has its European headquarters in Amsterdam, and operates facilities in 20 US states with a North American headquarters in Sunnyvale, California? Regional economic conflicts work against the economic interests of transnational firms that have set up global production and supply networks (Brooks 2005).

This leads to a second important observation. International economic relations are more 'positive sum,' in which economic cooperation can create increasing prosperity for all regions or countries, than 'zero sum,' in which one region or country gains at the expense of others. If everyone can win from increasing the overall size of the economic pie, then the incentives for geo-economic mobilization and competition diminish for governments as well as firms.

Third, it is important to ask whether regional economic blocs are more open or closed. The more open regional economic arrangements are, the more difficult it is to depict them as self-contained competitive units. To date, contemporary regionalism is more open than closed. For example, Malaysia led an effort as the Cold War ended to create an East Asian economic bloc that would exclude the United States and other non-Asian players. US and Japanese policy makers resisted this vision, and the entity that eventually emerged, APEC, was trans-Pacific rather than exclusively East Asian and included not only the United States but Mexico and Canada as well. Although the United States is not a member of the EU, it has supported European economic integration on the condition that the EU remains open to global trade and investment. For the most part it has. NAFTA hardly constitutes an exclusionary bloc, as numerous European and Asia-based firms operate in one NAFTA country, thereby gaining access to the others. Regionalism has progressed and stands alongside globalism as a key feature of the international economic landscape. But, as Box 14.2 shows, today's regions are considerably different from the more exclusionary competitive blocs of the 1930s.

14.2   MAKING CONNECTIONS
Then and Now

Regional Economic Blocs

Then: Regional Blocs during the 1930s

During the Great Depression of the 1930s, the global multilateral trading system was essentially replaced by a set of regional economic blocs. As world economic activity retracted, great powers responded by turning inward or strengthening regional economic arrangements that gave them special access to the resources and markets of associated countries. Japan, for example, proclaimed the Greater East Asian Co-Prosperity Sphere, comprising Japan, China, and parts of Southeast Asia, with the intention of creating a self-sufficient political and economic bloc of Asian nations free from Western influence. Similarly, Nazi Germany organized regional trade and financial arrangements with its eastern and central European neighbors, and used those arrangements to help finance its rearmament strategy free of the constraints imposed by Western powers after World War I. The United Kingdom created a currency area, based on its pound sterling, that included its colonies and protectorates. It forced those weaker countries to grant the UK preferential trade relations, while the UK raised its tariffs in trade with countries outside of the sterling area. The Soviet Union, under the leadership of Stalin, turned almost completely away from the world economy and relied on internal resources for economic development. The United States, because of the Smoot-Hawley tariff of the 1930s, sharply curtailed its participation in world trade. In general, the regional economic blocs of the 1930s were insulated from each other and were used by great powers to mobilize the resources they felt would be needed as the world moved from one world war to the next.

Now: Regional Blocs after the Cold War

Today, regional blocs are once again a prominent feature of the world economy. The United States, Canada, and Mexico have formed a regional economic bloc called NAFTA. European countries have deepened their economic integration through the European Union and share a common currency. In East Asia, a regional grouping called APEC serves as an umbrella for organizing the trade and financial relations of countries in Asia and the Pacific region.

This time, however, regional blocs are far less insulated and exclusionary. The United States has a regional arrangement with its immediate neighbors, but also trades and invests extensively with the rest of the world. APEC is designed according to the idea of *open regionalism*; instead of trying to exclude, for example, the United States, it is a member of APEC. Today, transnational companies based in one country or region operate simultaneously across multiple regions. Economic regions sit alongside the multilateral trading system, rather than serving as an alternative to it.

Table 14.2 shows that between 1962 and 1994, intraregional trade increased as a percentage of total trade for the European Union, NAFTA, the countries of Mercosur, and the countries of East Asia. Yet, it also suggests that *intra*regional trade did not replace *inter*regional trade. Trade among the three NAFTA countries, for example, accounted for less than half of their total trade in 1994. Africa, interestingly, has very little intraregional trade, and its portion of intraregional trade did not change significantly from 1962 to 1994.

The trend of increasing intraregional trade has continued since 1994. According to the WTO, for the EU, between 1995 and 2014, intraregional trade on average accounted for 70 percent (.70) of total trade. For North America, the comparable figure was .50 and for East Asia, .52. Africa showed the most significant increase, to .18.

Source: WTO (2015): 27.

Table 14.2 Intraregional Trade as a Share of Total Trade of Each Region, 1962–94

NAFTA countries are United States, Canada, and Mexico. European Union includes Belgium, Luxembourg, Denmark, France, Germany, Greece, Ireland, Italy, Netherlands, Portugal, Spain, United Kingdom, Austria, Finland, and Sweden. Mercosur includes Argentina, Brazil, Paraguay, and Uruguay. East Asia includes China, Hong Kong, Japan, South Korea, Taiwan, Brunei, Indonesia, Malaysia, Philippines, Singapore, and Thailand.

Region	1962	1975	1985	1994
East Asia	0.33	0.31	0.38	0.50
EU-15	0.56	0.54	0.60	0.64
NAFTA	0.36	0.38	0.40	0.43
Mercosur	0.06	0.07	0.07	0.19
Africa	0.04	0.03	0.04	0.03

Source: Jeffrey A. Frankel (1997) *Regional Trading Blocs in the World Economic System* (Washington, DC: Institute for International Economics), p. 22.

Finally, critics of the geo-economic model might question whether the political foundation of regionalism is eroding in Europe and the United States. In Europe, Brexit represents perhaps the first significant step backward for the postwar European integration project. In the United States, the Trump administration has demanded that NAFTA be renegotiated, putting at risk the durability of that 25-year arrangement.

To sum up, the geo-economic model points to key future possibilities including the intensification of international economic competition and the primacy of regionalism over multilateralism. However, proponents of the model must grapple with the idea of economic relations as mutually beneficial, with the global presence of multinational enterprises, and with the relative openness of today's regions.

Levels of Analysis *The Geo-Economic Model*	
State	**International**
In the geo-economic model, states and their national firms work together and share a common understanding of the national interest.	Although competition among nation-states remains the central feature of international relations in this model, the form it takes changes from military to economic.

MODEL 2: A RETURN TO A MULTIPOLAR BALANCE-OF-POWER SYSTEM

Instead of geo-economic competition, some scholars believe that international relations will return to a more traditional international order, one that entails a multipolar distribution of international power with military capabilities as the key source of international influence. This view is prominent among scholars who work within the realist school of thought (Layne 2006; Mearsheimer 2003). Many realists believe that while the United States was a disproportionately powerful and influential state for a decade or so after the Soviet Union collapsed, the world has now moved to a multipolar international structure.

Proponents of this view presume that military competition among nation-states will continue to matter significantly as the defining feature of international politics. Even if great powers are not prone to fight all-out wars with each other, they must still be prepared to fight more limited conflicts and use military force as a coercive instrument to advance their interests. From this perspective, a nation-state can only acquire great power by developing and mobilizing formidable military as well as economic capabilities.

Realists who believe we live in multipolarity view the balance of power as the central dynamic in international relations. The natural state of international affairs features multiple great powers engaged in an ongoing balancing game. The long era of international relations dominated by Europe, from 1648 to 1945, was the *normal* state of the world in international affairs, in which multiple great powers competed for primacy and security. The world of 1945 to 1990, with only two superpowers balancing each other, was an exceptional era; the era since 1990, with only one apparent superpower, has been even more exceptional. However, the proponents of multipolarity believe that the world will revert to its more natural state of multiple great powers that engage in balancing through both internal efforts, such as fortifying their military and technological capabilities, and traditional balance-of-power external strategies that rely on diplomacy and alliances.

Characteristics of Multipolarity

What would be the key features of a twenty-first-century multipolar system? World politics would be dominated by three or more great powers that would engage in complex combinations of peace and hostility, or cooperation and competition. These countries would include the United States, China, probably Russia, possibly India, and Germany and Japan on regional security and economic matters, as well as some global issues (Kupchan 2012). These are the countries that possess the lion's share of global material capabilities (military, economic, and scientific), and are able, in differing degrees, to project military power beyond their respective territories. Each of these great powers also has the societal capacity and administrative machinery to conduct foreign policy. Influence in international organizations would reflect the new geopolitical reality rather than, as for example in the case of the Permanent 5 in the UN Security Council, the geopolitical reality present after World War II.

Flexible alliances, in which countries form temporary pacts and shift from one partner to the other depending on the circumstances, are a hallmark of international politics in the context of multipolarity. A premium is placed on diplomacy, and alliances take on greater importance when there are a handful of competing great powers. During the bipolar years **fixed alliances**, in which countries remained allied with the same partners over long periods of time, took shape in NATO and the Warsaw Pact. In a new multipolar world, the famous assertion of Lord Palmerston, a nineteenth-century British Prime Minister, that the United Kingdom had 'no permanent friends and no permanent enemies, only permanent interests' would more likely apply to the foreign policies of the great powers. In a multipolar world, China and Russia might ally to contain the United States in some circumstances, but Japan and Russia might form an alliance against China. In some instances, such as combating global terrorism, Germany would work closely with the United States, but resist US admonishments to get tougher on Russia, a key energy supplier for Germany. Great powers might fight limited wars against each other to defend smaller allies, maintain access to resources, or establish dominance in a region. An all-out great-power war might be considered unlikely, not because of polarity dynamics, but because of nuclear weapons.

Flexible alliances
Temporary alliances in which states form pacts but shift from one partner to the other depending on the circumstances.

Fixed alliances
Alliances in which countries remain allied with the same partners over long periods of time.

International Trends

There is mounting evidence for the re-emergence of multipolarity. Not long after the Cold War ended, many states, including allies of the United States, expressed anxiety about life in a unipolar world. Government officials from Russia, France, India, and China expressed the fear that, even if the United States fully intended to act in a benign manner, it might be tempted by its extraordinary power advantage to remake the world to suit its preferences and, in the process, threaten the interests or security of others (Jervis 2009). After the terrorist attacks of September 11, 2001, when the United States under President George W. Bush singled out Iran, Iraq, and North Korea as an 'axis of evil,' challenged the world to be 'for or against' the United States, and undertook what many viewed as an aggressive and discretionary war in Iraq, these fears seemed confirmed.

Governments alarmed by the great disparity in power between the United States and everyone else initially had limited options. They came to rely on what political scientists now call **soft balancing** – steps to constrain or hobble the United States that fall well short of the significant mobilization of military power in opposition to the United States or the formation of anti-US security alliances.

Soft balancing
Steps to constrain or hobble a great power (such as the United States today) that fall well short of the significant mobilization of military power in opposition to that power or the formation of security alliances united against the power.

Photo 14.1 Leaders Pose at an SCO Foreign Ministers' Meeting, April 2017
The Foreign Ministers of China, Russia, and four Central Asian nations (Uzbekistan, Tajikistan, Kazakhstan, and Kyrgyzstan) pose for photos in April 2017 prior to a meeting of the Shanghai Cooperation Organization. The Foreign Ministers of India and Pakistan are included; both countries joined the SCO in 2017.

Source: Aliia Raimbekova/Anadolu Agency/Getty Images.

Shanghai Cooperation Organization (SCO)
An agreement among Russia, China, and the central Asian states of Uzbekistan, Tajikistan, Kazakhstan, and Kyrgyzstan formed in 2001 to enhance the security of member states against threats of terrorism and ethnic conflict.

Examples of soft balancing include opposing US initiatives in the UN Security Council, refusing to go along with US sanctions against what it considers to be rogue states, seeking alternatives to the dollar as a reserve or exchange currency, and mobilizing diplomatic opposition to US intervention abroad. Another form of soft balancing is the formation of international agreements that are not explicitly anti-American but might be useful in countering US initiatives. The **Shanghai Cooperation Organization (SCO)**, an agreement among Russia, China, and the central Asian states of Uzbekistan, Tajikistan, Kazakhstan, and Kyrgyzstan, was formed in 2001 to enhance the security of member states against threats of terrorism and ethnic conflict. Although the SCO proclaims that it is not an alliance directed against any state, member states and observers have used it as a platform to criticize the United States and US policies. The United States applied for SCO observer status in 2005, but its application was politely rejected. In the late 2000s, after discussions at SCO summits, the governments of Kyrgyzstan and Uzbekistan evicted the United States from military bases in their territory used to pursue the war on terrorism.

The argument for multipolarity progressed further during the second decade of the twenty-first century. Russia reasserted its regional authority in armed conflicts against neighboring Georgia and Ukraine in 2014 and intervened against US interests in the civil war in Syria in 2016. China claimed control of the South China Sea in defiance of US interests and sought to advance its Belt and Road Initiative to develop infrastructure and cultivate influence with states across Eurasia. In 2017, the Trump administration's first national security strategy downplayed US primacy and depicted world politics as an arena for renewed great-power competition, singling out China and Russia as geopolitical competitors rather than as potential partners in a US-centered international order.

Contrary Evidence and Questions

Is a return to the classic multipolarity of the nineteenth and early twentieth centuries just around the corner? First, it depends on the extent to which multiple nation-states have the capability and determination to achieve great-power status. In terms of cumulative economic and military capabilities, the world remains rather lopsided, despite the foreign policy and economic difficulties experienced by the United States in the latter 2000s. Other candidates have some distance to travel before joining the great-power club as full members. Japan is a formidable economic power with technologically advanced, though limited, military capabilities. But, because of domestic politics, Japan lacks nuclear weapons capabilities and, more importantly, the political will to distance itself from dependence on the United States. Russia can exercise influence against weaker neighbors, but the ability to project power and influence beyond its neighborhood is questionable. Its economy, as seen in Chapter 11, has more of the dependent, raw-material-producing character of a developing country than the more diversified and technologically advanced character of a contemporary great power. China and India have great potential but are essentially great power 'works in progress,' with large populations, developing economies, and an array of challenges to political stability. China, having begun to translate its economic success into greater military and diplomatic clout, is further along the great-power road than India. Germany is a powerful state in Europe, and the central leader of the European Union. However, the EU, relative to its overall capability, is a weak actor in world affairs; German leadership of that organization does not readily translate into global influence. Achieving great-power status is not impossible for these states, but remains a challenge, regardless of whether the United States seems on the verge of empire, as in 2000, trapped by its own mistakes, as in 2008, or seemingly in retreat, as in 2017.

Let us assume that multiple great powers do arise within the next decade. There is still the question of whether twenty-first-century multipolarity would operate in the same fashion as it did in the nineteenth century. First, to what extent would alliances truly be flexible? The United States has long-standing alliance ties to the states of Europe and Japan. These countries are not just allies, but democratic allies. How strong are those binding ties? How likely is it that the United States and Europe or Japan might find they are on opposite sides of a serious political or military conflict in a multipolar world? That question forces us to directly examine our assumptions about what is of primary analytic importance in international relations – the anarchy of the international system as emphasized by realists, or the importance of common political systems as emphasized by liberal thinkers. It is possible, as we discuss in Model 4, A Democratic Peace, to conceive of a cooperative or harmonious multipolarity populated by democratic great powers. In Box 14.3, we review the different assumptions liberals and realists make about the durability of the NATO alliance.

Second, in what ways might nuclear weapons complicate the workings of multipolarity? In the classic nineteenth-century version, great powers fought frequent small wars against each other to maintain the balance of power and prevent any single state from achieving dominant status. But the Cold War demonstrated that nuclear great powers are cautious about fighting any kind of direct war with each other, for fear that conventional conflict might escalate to the nuclear level. Perhaps nuclear-armed, multipolar great powers would fight by proxy, as the Soviet Union and United States did in Korea and Vietnam during the Cold War. Or perhaps they wouldn't fight at all, lending credence to the geo-economic model discussed in Model 1, or the democratic peace model to be discussed in Model 4.

14.3   MAKING CONNECTIONS
Theory and Practice

The Future of NATO under Multipolarity

Theory: Realists versus Liberals on the Purpose of Alliances

Realists believe that alliances are instruments of convenience that are adopted and maintained by states when it is in their security interests to do so. Alliances come and go; states have permanent interests, but no permanent friends in an anarchic international system.

Liberals generally agree that states form alliances for multiple strategic purposes. But liberals also strongly believe in the importance of regime type and the distinctive relations among nation-states that are democracies.

Practice: Realists versus Liberals on Why the NATO Alliance Persists

From the realist perspective, there is nothing special or extraordinary about the NATO alliance among the United States, Canada, and the countries of Europe. NATO was formed to contain the Soviet Union. It has outlived the Soviet Union because the United States, the dominant player in the alliance, continues to find NATO useful as an instrument to project power in post-Cold War Europe. But, if one or more European states emerged as peer competitors in a multipolar system, most realists assume NATO would wither away. One of the most prominent realists in international relations, Kenneth Waltz, predicted in 1993 that the world would quickly revert to multipolarity, and argued that, in a multipolar world, even if we could not predict NATO's precise demise, its years would be numbered (Waltz 1993).

For liberals, the ties that bind democracies are stronger than mere strategic convenience. The democracies of the United States and Europe are especially closely linked because they share a common heritage and civilization, political tradition, and beliefs in the rule of law and the rights of the individual. From this perspective, NATO is truly a special alliance. Liberals expect that even if Europe collectively, or individual European states, emerged as peer competitors to the United States, some form of the transatlantic alliance would remain intact. Multipolarity would not mean the end of the security community of democratic nations, even if it brought other key changes to international politics. Liberals are not surprised by the persistence of NATO after the Cold War because they believe it rests on shared political characteristics rather than the temporary convergence of strategic interests.

Levels of Analysis   *A Return to Multipolarity*

State	International
Countries with the potential to emerge as great powers in a multipolar world would need to develop both economic and military capabilities.	Because they make different assumptions about what matters in international relations, realists and liberals differ over the extent to which a future multipolar world would be conflict-prone or peaceful.

MODEL 3: A RETURN TO BIPOLARITY

Rather than multiple great powers arising, it is possible that only one will emerge to challenge the dominant position of the United States. In this view, the era of 1945 to 1990 has become the *normal* state of international affairs. Great powers need to be superpowers; they need to be of continental size, with large populations and global reach. Very few nation-states can attain superpower status. In the coming years, the most likely candidate to join the United States in that exclusive club is China. Proponents of a new bipolarity expect the rise of China to eventually cause the United States and China to clash geopolitically similar to the struggle of the Cold War (Friedberg 2011).

It is not difficult to imagine a new bipolar struggle. The postwar United States organized its foreign policy around a central threat. During the Cold War the focus was the Soviet Union. During the 2000s, the United States was sufficiently powerful not to face a peer competitor, and instead focused its attention on the periphery of the international system and the war on terrorism. But by 2015, American policy makers perceived China as a possible regional and eventual global challenger. China combines many typical great-power attributes – large size, rapid economic growth, modernizing military capabilities, and foreign policy ambitions. It has a long history of being the dominant power in East Asia, and Chinese leaders carry the historical baggage of resentment against Western powers for frustrating China's global great-power ambitions. Now that China has emerged intact from the tumultuous early decades of its communist revolution and sustained rapid economic growth and development over three decades, it is ready to reassume the mantle of great-power status (Goldstein 2005). In 2012, China's new leader, Xi Jinping, played into this view by proclaiming that the Chinese dream was the 'great revival of the Chinese nation' (*The Economist* 2013).

US–China relations have been generally positive since the two countries opened diplomatic engagement in 1971. But it is not hard to imagine a downward, action–reaction spiral. The more China grows, the more anxiety it creates among US officials, and the more Chinese leaders become emboldened to seek status and influence commensurate with their capabilities. China and the United States have different social and political systems and define human rights differently. Many Americans are critical of Chinese labor policies, environmental policies, and repression of religious freedom. Many Chinese view US criticisms as arrogant, hypocritical, and an unwelcome intrusion upon their sovereignty. One obvious flashpoint that could spark a downward spiral is Taiwan. China considers the small island adjacent to its mainland a renegade province that is rightfully part of China. For the United States, the nationalist regime governing Taiwan is a long-standing ally that stood side by side with America in the long struggle against global communism. America's diplomatic approach to Taiwan is a pragmatic one; it seeks to deter China from attacking Taiwan, while deterring Taiwan from provoking China by asserting its independence. This delicate strategy of double deterrence has worked but is no guarantee against China or Taiwan initiating a conflict with the potential to draw in the United States. A similar potential exists in the East China Sea, where China and America's ally, Japan, contest for control over islands that each claim as their own territory. In the South China Sea, China's territorial claims conflict with those of five other states, including American allies, and with the principle of freedom of navigation defended by the United States.

Characteristics of a New Bipolarity

What might be the central features of a new bipolarity? China and the United States would face off in a replay of the Cold War. Each would be the central focus of the other's foreign policy. At both the government and societal levels, the United States would view China as its principal geopolitical competitor and potential adversary. China would view the United States in a similar fashion. As the rising challenger, Beijing would also try to offer some type of ideological alternative to an international system dominated politically, economically, and in terms of values by the United States.

The United States and China would try to enlist the support of other states, either informally or in formal alliances. The precise coalitions would depend on how political and economic relationships played out over time. America's long-standing alliances with the European Union and Japan might remain intact, forcing China to cultivate new partners in Russia, Southeast Asia, and Africa. South Korea (or perhaps a unified Korea?) might be caught between its modern, postwar allegiance to the United States and its historical role as a dependent client state in a Chinese sphere of influence. Regardless of the diplomatic and alliance configurations, the main feature of the new bipolarity would be US–China suspicion and hostility organized around competing coalitions. The competition would likely begin in East Asia, with China struggling to assert its regional hegemony, and the United States seeking to maintain its postwar status as the dominant regional power. Competition would likely take place globally as well.

International Trends

The emergence of a full-blown bipolar competition is not yet apparent. During the decade of the 2000s, US–China relations were mostly cooperative. The United States sought a partnership with China and enlisted its support in the US-initiated war on terrorism, nuclear non-proliferation, and environmental efforts, and after the great financial crisis of 2008–10 to help stabilize and grow the global economy. China, for its part, acted as a patient challenger. It characterized its foreign policy strategy as peaceful rise, meaning that it sought to develop economic capability and political influence without threatening or provoking regional neighbors or the broader global community.

Beneath the surface of cooperation, however, were signs that each side was quietly preparing for the possibility of future geopolitical competition. During the years the United States focused on shooting wars in the Gulf and Southwest Asia, it also put the elements of a future China containment strategy into place. It reinvigorated and expanded its Cold War security alliances in East Asia, particularly with Japan, Australia, and selected Southeast Asian countries. It cultivated ties with India and Vietnam, two states with a history of conflicts with China. During the 2000s, the Pentagon began publicizing an annual report on Chinese military capabilities, highlighting new and potentially disturbing developments. This was a direct echo of the Cold War – the 1980s annual publication *Soviet Military Power* was replaced 20 years later by a very similar annual publication titled *Chinese Military Power* (US Department of Defense 2012).

For its part, China coupled its patient challenger approach with subtle yet clear signs that it expected to exert greater influence regionally and globally to support its interests and acknowledge the higher international status to which it had become entitled. Chinese leaders directed a combination of military intimidation and economic cooperation at Taiwan, suggesting its willingness to use sticks and carrots to ensure that the renegade province was eventually brought back into the fold. China expanded its naval power and asserted control over the South China Sea. It accused its main regional rival, Japan, of failing to make amends for its aggressive imperial history, and Chinese ships confronted their Japanese counterparts in several scuffles in waters patrolled by the two navies. China sent diplomatic missions and economic aid to countries in the Middle East and Africa that could supply raw materials and

Photo 14.2 Chinese Administrative Facility, Paracel Islands, 2012
In July 2012 China reinforced its claim over the South China Sea by establishing a military garrison at its administrative post in Yongxing Island (known in Vietnam as Phu Lam Island). Notice in this photo that China has already constructed an air facility that takes up a good proportion of the island.

Source: © Zha Chunming/Xinhua Press/Corbis.

offer secure sources of oil and natural gas. The 2008–10 financial crisis also provided the opportunity for China to display the advantages of its own economic model of state capitalism which, as discussed in Chapter 11, combines centralized political control with a decentralized economic system.

Contrary Evidence and Questions

It is certainly plausible to imagine a new bipolar era, but how likely is it? Two important caveats are worth considering. First, China is growing rapidly but is not necessarily on a linear path to superpower status. The challenges facing China that could jeopardize its steady rise are formidable. These include the need to maintain extraordinarily high levels of growth, not just for economic reasons, but to ensure social stability. A growth slowdown would also call into question the legitimacy, or right to rule, of the one-party state. The legitimacy of the Communist Party depends less on ideological appeal and more on its ability to 'deliver the goods' to a growing Chinese population with higher and higher expectations. The growing disparity between China's rich and poor adds to social and political tensions. China's environmental problems – one consequence of rapid, coal-based economic growth – are increasingly severe (Economy 2007). In several decades it must also confront the demographic challenge of a large, aging population for which the state must provide. In short, we should neither presume China's rise will be uncomplicated nor treat it as a foregone conclusion.

Second, assuming China does continue to rise and emerge as a peer competitor to the United States, will the resulting bipolar structure necessarily generate the hostility of the Cold War? The Soviet Union and the United States were not only politically hostile to each other, but largely *independent* of each other economically. China and the United States are economically interdependent in finance, trade, and investment. Economic interdependence makes it difficult for the two sides to isolate each other politically. Would American business, for example, support economic warfare against China? Would any American government jeopardize an arrangement in which China's central bank finances American fiscal and budget deficits by holding roughly $1 trillion in US financial assets? Economic interdependence also complicates the formation of rival political blocs. Would Japan, Thailand, or South Korea, with strong security ties to the United States and strong economic ties to China, be eager to choose sides and line up on one side or the other of the bipolar divide? A future US–China bipolarity would be more complicated than the Cold War when economic, political, and ideological differences reinforced each other across the great geopolitical divide.

Levels of Analysis *A New Bipolarity*	
State	International
China's continued rise to great-power status depends vitally on domestic economic and political developments.	Liberal thinkers believe that China and the United States may coexist peacefully in a multipolar world, especially if China becomes a democracy.
	Economic interdependence makes the emerging US–China great-power relationship very different from that between the Soviet Union and United States during the Cold War.

MODEL 4: A DEMOCRATIC PEACE

The multipolar and bipolar models essentially take a realist view of international politics. They see the international arena as one of competition and conflict and view nation-states, especially great powers, as the central players in world politics. However, the democratic peace model reflects liberal and constructivist approaches to international relations. It focuses inside nation-states and the attributes of their domestic political systems as the key drivers of international behavior and outcomes. Proponents of a democratic peace are more optimistic than their realist counterparts. Instead of viewing international politics as an endless cycle of conflict and competition, they emphasize the potential for progress. Relations among states can improve over time and become more peaceful as states become more democratic (Russett 1993).

Characteristics of Democratic Peace

The democratic peace model rests on two key premises. The first is that the democratic form of government will continue to spread. This spread is inevitable because advocates see democracy as the wave of the future; it defeated its most formidable twentieth-century competitors, including fascism and communism, and displays resilience for the long haul not shared by other political forms (Fukuyama 1992). Sir Winston Churchill once famously remarked that 'democracy is the worst form of government except for all the others that have been tried.' The collapse of the Soviet empire provided additional impetus to the theory of inevitability for democracy. The lesson of those revolutionary events seemed to be that ordinary people could only be held down for so long; given a taste of freedom, they will embrace it wholeheartedly and make the democratic project their own.

The second critical premise, as discussed in Chapters 6 and 7, is that democracies do not fight wars *with each other*. Democratic states may be as war-prone as any other type of state. Since 1900, for example, both the democratic United Kingdom and non-democratic Russia have each engaged frequently in interstate wars. However, proponents of democratic peace hold that in relations with each other, democracies will be more restrained and pacific. Democracies do not fight each other because of political structure and political norms.

The argument that democratic political structures have a constraining effect on war goes back as far as German philosopher Immanuel Kant's famous 1795 essay, 'Perpetual Peace.' Kant reasoned that ordinary citizens had little interest in war because they had to fight it, pay for it, and 'painfully repair the devastation war leaves behind' (Kant [1795] 2009). This basic idea has been carried forward by contemporary democratic peace proponents, including Bruce Russett and Michael Doyle, who suggest that war might be in the material or prestige interest of dictators or unelected elites, but in democratic political systems the natural pacific interests of the people serve as a constraint on the realization of those aspirations (Doyle 2011). Democratic peace proponents expect democracies to go to war when attacked or provoked by other states. But, in general, for democracies to fight requires the broad mobilization of public support, rather than simply the capricious desire of a leader. In relations among democracies, this structural inhibition is mutually reinforcing. Political scientists also argue that because democracies are open political systems, their intentions are more transparent and their commitments to abide by agreements are more credible. Therefore, it is easier for democracies to reach deals with each other as alternatives to war and stick with them.

Recall from our discussion in Chapters 6 and 7 that the war-inhibiting effects of democratic political structures are reinforced by the effects of democratic norms. Some theorists argue that a democratic culture within a nation-state creates habits of negotiation, compromise, and consensus building. Democratic states carry these habits into foreign policy and are more inclined than authoritarian states to search for solutions to disagreements short of war. Democracy also encourages a tolerance for individual differences, rather than an expectation of conformity to the beliefs of a group. The experience of democracy leads individuals to appreciate the point of view of others and be less inclined to perceive irreconcilable differences. Democratic peoples might perceive an authoritarian government as an enemy, yet have a harder time thinking in those terms about a government selected by its own population.

If we combine these two central claims – the inevitable spread of democracy, and the scarcity of war among democracies – we are left with an optimistic vision of future world order. As more and more countries become democratic, military conflict among states should become less prevalent. An expanding world of democratic states would enable the international system to approximate a security community – a grouping of political actors within which the resort to war as an instrument of statecraft has become highly unlikely, if not impossible. Political scientists frequently refer to the member states of the contemporary European Union as a security community. War between Germany and France, possible throughout most of European history, has become virtually unthinkable today as these two stable democracies find their political and economic decision-making increasingly intertwined.

The pacific effects of democracy are reinforced by other structures and relationships. As noted in Chapter 5, democratic countries are typically eager to embed their political relationships within international institutions that establish common norms and expectations for nation-state behavior. The rule of law in politics within democratic nation-states is thereby reinforced and reflected by the rule of law among democratic nation-states acting in the international arena. Also, most democratic nation-states are simultaneously capitalist nation-states and, liberal theorists believe, free trade among them further reinforces the democratic peace. The *New York Times* columnist and best-selling author Thomas Friedman popularized this argument with the much-celebrated McDonald's (or Golden Arches) theory of war (Friedman 1999). He observed that no two countries, each of which had a McDonald's restaurant on its territory, ever went to war with each other. The underlying logic was that if a country reached the point at which its middle class was sufficiently large and well developed to attract the McDonald's chain, that country probably also had the other social, political, and economic attributes that make war among capitalist democracies unlikely. Skeptics search for the Golden Arches in warring capitals and are quick to point to the relatively small number of disconfirming examples, such as the India–Pakistan war of 1999 or the war between Russia and Georgia in 2008.

International Trends

The democratic peace model is certainly plausible in theory – is there sufficient supportive evidence to make it viable as a future global order? We can take each of the two central arguments in turn. As we saw in Chapters 6 and 7, the empirical evidence for the proposition that 'democracies do not fight wars with each other' is robust. Numerous statistical analyses have demonstrated strong correlations between democratic political systems and peaceful relations. This correlation, according to political scientist Jack Levy, is 'as close as anything we have to an empirical law in international relations' (Levy 1988). There is no major exception, no obvious war between democracies to which we can point. Critics of the robust correlation between democracy and peace typically comb through history for a possible exception here or there, and the ensuing debates usually hinge on differing definitions of 'democracy.' For example, was the Spanish–American War of 1898 a war between democracies, or was Spain not technically a democracy because its competing parties alternated in power not by election but by prior political arrangement? Was the 2006 war between Israel and Lebanon a democratic war, or should it be coded differently because Lebanon, despite having what the international community judged a fair election in 2005, could hardly be considered a stable democracy over time? It is important to recognize that, from a statistical perspective, even a handful of exceptions would not necessarily invalidate the empirical regularity of the correlation between democracy and the absence of war.

What of the other premise – democracy's inevitable spread around the world? This proposition has appeared increasingly plausible over the past several decades as the democratic form of government has spread among nation-states in different regions of the world. In Latin America during the 1980s, military rule gave way to elections and the restoration of civilian rule in Peru, Argentina, Brazil, and Uruguay. In central Europe, the monopoly of the Communist Party collapsed at the end of the 1980s and opposition parties were legalized in Poland, Bulgaria, Czechoslovakia, Hungary, Romania, and in the Soviet Union. Authoritarian capitalism gave way to democratic capitalism in the Philippines in 1986 and the Republic of Korea in 1987. South Africa threw off the *apartheid* regime and held multiracial elections in 1994. A Freedom House survey in 1987 found that 66 out of 167 countries could reasonably be characterized as electoral democracies. Some 20 years later, in 2008, they found 121 electoral democracies out of 193 countries. Of those 193 countries, 90 were considered 'free,' 60 considered 'partly free,' and 43 'not free' (Freedom House 2008). In its 2017 survey of 195 countries, Freedom House coded 87 as 'free,' 59 as 'partly free,' and 49 as 'not free' (Freedom House 2017a).

Contrary Evidence and Questions

Advocates of the democratic peace model must address three challenges. The first concerns democracy's ability to continue to spread. Today, Russia and China represent prominent examples of major powers bucking the democratic trend. These large players are not simply authoritarian by default; their rulers believe that authoritarian regimes hold significant advantages over democracy, and they have managed to persuade or coerce sufficient portions of their populations to accept (or at least tolerate) that view. During the 1990s, it appeared that Russia and China might conform to democracy, but by 2017 that outcome appeared much less certain as authoritarian leaders, Vladimir Putin and Xi Jinping, centralized their control over Russia and China respectively.

Revolutionary upheaval against authoritarian regimes does not necessarily imply that democracy will result. In 2011, most of the world welcomed what became known as 'the Arab Spring,' which began in Tunisia in December 2010, when a young man without a job burned himself to death in protest when police prevented him from selling vegetables on the street. Protests against authoritarian governments spread like wildfire across the region in 2011. The Tunisian leader was toppled and mass demonstrations in Egypt led to the resignation of President Hosni Mubarak after 30 years in power. Violent protest spread to Yemen, Bahrain, Libya, and Syria. With the assistance of NATO countries, Libyan rebels brought down the regime of long-standing dictator Muammar Gaddafi.

The Arab Spring held great hope for democracy in a region where dictators have long repressed their populations politically and economically, often with the support of the United States. As Box 14.4 explains, however, the Arab Spring represents a complicated set of political developments that guarantees neither democracy nor stability in a key region of the world. As of 2016, just three years beyond the Arab Spring, Freedom House reported that countries in the Middle East and North Africa had the worst freedom ratings in the world (Freedom House 2017b).

We should also bear in mind that the democratic process is not irreversible. Zimbabwe held multiracial elections upon gaining independence in 1980, but by 1987 had reverted to authoritarianism. Pakistan held elections in 1988 but found its nascent democracy replaced by military rule a decade later. In Venezuela, Hugo Chavez was initially elected in 1998 yet, over the next ten years, found ways to side track his country's two-party system and concentrate power in his own hands. In 2009, Venezuelans approved a referendum lifting presidential term limits, making it possible for Chavez to maintain power indefinitely. Chavez died in March 2013, and six weeks later his handpicked successor won a six-year term in a close and controversial election. Poland and Hungary, democracies created by the end of the Cold War, have gradually slid in the direction of authoritarianism. Hungary's Prime Minister, Viktor Orban, has touted the virtues of 'illiberal democracy' and singled out Russia, China, and Turkey as international 'stars.' Illiberal democracy seems to imply that leaders elected by popular mandate have only modest limits on their power, including the authority to roll back individual freedoms (Rohac 2018).

The Venezuelan, Polish, and Hungarian examples remind us that not all democracies are the same. The Freedom House survey of 2008, for example, qualified 121 countries as electoral democracies, but also found that 32 of them did not provide

14.4   MAKING CONNECTIONS
Aspiration versus Reality

Revolutionary Upheaval in the Middle East

Aspiration

On June 20, 2005, US Secretary of State Condoleezza Rice gave a provocative speech in Egypt, at the American University of Cairo. She stated:

> We should all look to a future when every government respects the will of its citizens – because the ideal of democracy is universal. For 60 years, my country, the United States, pursued stability at the expense of democracy in this region here in the Middle East – and we achieved neither. Now, we are taking a different course. We are supporting the democratic aspirations of all people … Throughout the Middle East, the fear of free choices can no longer justify the denial of liberty. It is time to abandon the excuses that are made to avoid the hard work of democracy … Liberty is the universal longing of every soul, and democracy is the ideal path for every nation.

The Bush administration hoped that by invading Iraq and overthrowing Saddam Hussein in 2003, they would spread democracy not only to Iraq but elsewhere in the Middle East. Secretary of State Rice made clear that the United States intended to help that process along by promoting democracy whenever possible. In 2011, President Barack Obama welcomed the Arab Spring and called for a genuine transition to democracy in Egypt, meaningful reform in Bahrain, and a more representative government in Iran.

Source: Rice (2006).

Reality

Reality is more complicated. A popular uprising against authoritarianism may or may not lead to democracy. Iran's revolution in 1979 has led, over three decades, to the consolidation of an Islamist regime hostile both to democracy and to the United States. Although post-Mubarak Egypt does not seem headed in that direction, its democratic future is clouded by a likely power struggle among various groups including the traditionally powerful military and an emerging Islamist group, the Muslim Brotherhood. By 2014, the military was back in full control. In Syria, the uprising associated with the Arab Spring led not to democracy but to increased bloodshed as radical elements in the government and opposition strengthened and clashed in a brutal civil war.

The United States has also learned to be careful about what it wishes. In the Palestinian territories, the Islamist group Hamas, whose charter proclaims the goal of eliminating Israel, won parliamentary elections in 2006 that were held at the insistence of Secretary Rice. In Lebanon, Hezbollah, which the United States has designated as a terrorist organization, has gained considerable influence through democratic processes beginning in 2009.

To the extent democracy emerges in the Middle East, it may result at least in the short term in a loss of US influence. American behavior in the region has been unpopular since the United States has long been associated with the repressive regimes that popular protesters are determined to unseat. It is unlikely that new democracies in the Middle East will be immediately friendly to the United States and its allies. Over time, however, and to the extent the logic of the democratic peace holds, these new democracies and the world's most powerful one may come to find common ground.

minimal or systematic protection for basic civil liberties. Ten years later, Freedom House reported that democracy scores for most countries had declined for the 12th consecutive year.

Second, even though mature democracies may not fight each other, the *transition* to democracy may be a rocky and dangerous one. Ed Mansfield and Jack Snyder show that countries in the transition phase from non-democracy to democracy become more war-prone and do fight democratic states (Mansfield and Snyder 1995). Their research suggests that countries making the biggest leap, from total autocracy to mass democracy, were about twice as likely as states that remained autocratic to fight wars in the decade after democratization. This argument has important policy implications. To the extent it is correct, global efforts to make the world safer – for example, by coaxing China, Russia, and Middle Eastern states into democratic transitions – could prove counter-productive and lead to a more dangerous world of international conflict.

Third, some critics argue that the true test of democratic peace is yet to come. In historical terms, the prevalence of democracy is a relatively recent development. Much of the statistical data in support of the democratic peace hypothesis reflects conditions under which most states were not democracies, or democratic states were allied in conflicts against non-democratic adversaries, such as the decades the democratic states of NATO banded together against the non-democratic Soviet Union. A much harder but more meaningful test of the democratic peace model will take place if more democratic states displace non-democratic ones.

To appreciate this logic, consider two thought experiments. Let's say that China emerges as a peer competitor to the United States in a bipolar system and, in the process, transforms itself into a mass democracy. Will relations between a democratic great-power China and United States be more cooperative or conflictual? Liberal theorists would predict cooperation based on compatible regime types. Realists would expect that the United States and even a democratic China with equivalent capabilities would have plenty of grounds for conflict.

Another thought experiment would take this model's logic to its extreme and imagine a world composed exclusively of mature democratic states. Would war be eliminated in such a world? The logic of the democratic peace suggests the answer is yes; to accept that answer requires you to believe that regime type outweighs all other causes of war discussed in Chapter 6. Realists are skeptical that a world of democracies would be a peaceful one; liberals and constructivists are more hopeful.

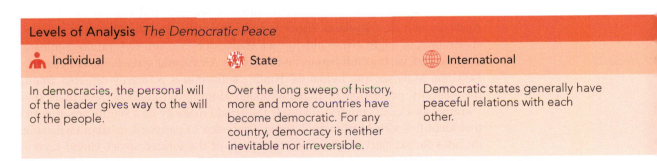

Levels of Analysis *The Democratic Peace*

👤 Individual	👬 State	🌐 International
In democracies, the personal will of the leader gives way to the will of the people.	Over the long sweep of history, more and more countries have become democratic. For any country, democracy is neither inevitable nor irreversible.	Democratic states generally have peaceful relations with each other.

MODEL 5: A CLASH OF CIVILIZATIONS

Our fifth model is similar to democratic peace in that it focuses our attention on features of world politics that transcend the traditional nation-state. But it paints a very different and far more pessimistic picture. The idea of a clash of civilizations was first popularized in a 1993 article by the American political scientist Samuel Huntington (Huntington 1993, 1996). Writing shortly after the end of the Cold War, Huntington was reacting to what he perceived as the misplaced euphoria of Western triumph, particularly the expectation that the defeat of the Soviet Union meant the end of the great battles over ideas in world politics. Rather than the **end of history**, or the end of ideological conflict and the victory of liberal values, Huntington prophesied the continuation of history, though not necessarily in the same political form. Although Huntington would not typically be viewed as a constructivist, his argument focuses on cultural identity, a key variable in the constructivist tradition.

End of history
The end of ideological conflict and the victory of liberal values.

Characteristics of a Clash of Civilizations

The **clash of civilizations** model begins with the premise that modern world politics has always been, and will continue to be, characterized by some form of inter-group conflict. From the founding of the Westphalian system in 1648 until the outbreak of the Napoleonic Wars in 1799, that conflict was centered in Europe and took place among the monarchs and princes who controlled European territory and populations. From 1800 until the end of the Cold War in 1990, the main combatants were modern nation-states, which first appeared in Europe and spread globally. After 1990, nation-states are still relevant, but the battle has shifted to *civilizations*. According to Huntington, civilization is a loose term that incorporates religious, cultural, ethnic, and, to some extent, linguistic similarity. A civilization might share the same territory with a particular nation-state but is often spread across multiple nation-states. It is also possible for one nation-state to be divided among different civilizations. In Ukraine, for example, Orthodox Slavic culture dominates the eastern part of the country and European-oriented Catholics dominate the western part. Huntington asserted that 'the fault lines between civilizations will be the battle lines of the future.' For Huntington, nation-states may still be the agents of conflict, but the driving forces of conflict and, thus, world politics are civilizations.

Clash of civilizations
The idea that international conflict in the future will be characterized not by interstate conflict but rather by conflict between civilizations, a term that incorporates religious, cultural, ethnic, and, to some extent, linguistic similarity.

Which major civilizations are in possible conflict? As Map 14.4 shows, Huntington identified nine civilizations, including Sino-centric, Western, Muslim, Hindu, Orthodox Christian, and sub-Saharan African. The Sino-centric civilization includes China, present-day North and South Korea, Vietnam, Singapore, Taiwan, and the Chinese diaspora found in various Southeast Asian countries. Western civilization spreads geographically across North America, western and central Europe, and Australia and New Zealand. Latin America might be considered part of Western civilization, or might evolve into its own civilization. Muslim civilization dominates the Middle East, the Gulf region, and Northern Africa, and spreads further east into Pakistan, Malaysia, and Indonesia. Hindu civilization is primarily centered among the majority population in India, although Huntington characterizes India (like Ukraine) as a 'cleft' country; alongside the Hindu majority lie a significant minority that identifies with Muslim civilization. Orthodox or eastern Christian civilization includes Russia, part of Ukraine, other parts of the former Soviet Union such as Moldova and Belarus, Bulgaria, Greece, and, after the breakup of Yugoslavia, Serbia. Sub-Saharan African civilization includes most nation-states in the eastern, central, and southern parts of the continent.

The reasons that Huntington and his supporters might expect civilizations to clash rather than cooperate with each other are not hard to fathom. Different

Map 14.4 The Clash of Civilizations

Samuel Huntington divided the world into nine civilizations and argued that differences across them could become a major source of conflict in the post-Cold War world.

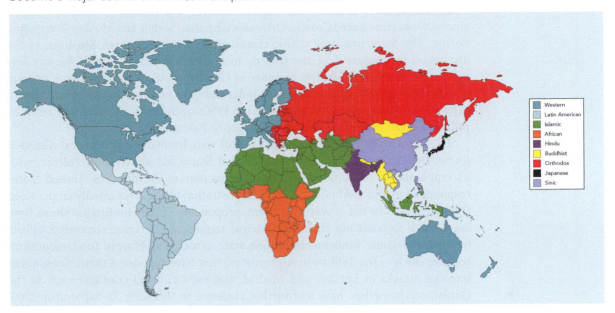

civilizations have different, deeply held values. Western civilization embraces individualism and social equality, while Sino-centric civilization focuses on the importance of the group and social hierarchy. Western and Muslim civilizations differ on the role and education of woman and the desirability or threat of modernity.

Conflict is likely because civilizations believe not only in their values, but in the universality of their values. The Western insistence that liberal democracy and human rights are universal values that must be embraced by all often infuriates members of other civilizations. In both Muslim and Western worlds, missionary religions send forth adherents seeking to convert others to their cause. Huntington points out that Islam and Christianity are 'all or nothing' religions that encourage their faithful to believe theirs is the one true faith.

Clash, rather than cooperation, is also predicted in the Marxist idea of the law of uneven development. The Sino-centric world is enjoying rapid economic growth and an increase in international political influence and prestige. China's increase in power will tempt it to reassert its traditional cultural role as leader of a hierarchical political order in East Asia. Its desire for cultural and political leadership in that region could easily lead to conflict with the United States, which has strong economic and security interests there, and is determined to remain a resident great power in East Asia. In the Islamic world, there is uneven development of a different sort. The explosion of population in the Middle East and elsewhere, coupled with slower economic growth, fuels instability within that civilization and brings it into conflict with others. Huntington speculates on a possible alliance between Islamic and Sino-centric civilizations since both have grievances against the populations in dominant Western civilization that have written the rules of the contemporary global system and enjoy much of its benefits.

International Trends

Conflicts over the past 25 years lend a degree of plausibility to Huntington's gloomy vision. The breakup of the former Yugoslavia during the 1990s led to bloody struggle among Western-oriented Croatia, Orthodox Christian Serbia, and Muslim-dominated Bosnia. The Serbs practiced ethnic cleansing against the Bosnian Muslims, as the discussion in Chapter 1 of the tragedy in Srebrenica demonstrated. Russia's war against the breakaway Muslim province of Chechnya was especially brutal, as were Chechnya's reprisals against Russians. India and Pakistan, now both nuclear-armed, came close to war several times during the 1990s over Kashmir, a territory ruled by India but populated by Muslims sympathetic to Pakistan.

The terrorist attacks of September 11, 2001 were framed in cultural or civilization terms; the target was not simply the United States but all Western culture, with its emphasis on consumer capitalism and secular modernity. The United States responded forcefully. Although Bush administration officials repeatedly emphasized that the West was not at war with Islam, proponents of the Huntington thesis have been quick to point out that the principal targets of US counterterrorism efforts have been Islamic fundamentalist non-state actors and Islamic fundamentalism regimes (such as the Taliban in Afghanistan) that have supported them. Subsequent terrorist attacks in London and Madrid, and even cultural conflicts such as the Danish cartoon crisis, have lent further credence to this view. In September 2005, a Danish newspaper published 12 editorial cartoons depicting the Islamic prophet Muhammad in disrespectful attire or situations (wearing devil horns or shown with a bomb in his turban). Protests across the Muslim world escalated into violence, including the burning of Danish embassies in Syria and Iran and death threats against the cartoonist and others. Over 100 people died in various countries as security forces tried to restore order. Supporters of the cartoons defended them as legitimate exercises of free speech in a free country and pointed out that the newspapers in question often published satirical material about other religions. Critics viewed the cartoons as racist, anti-Islamic, and an echo of past Western imperialism.

The rise of ISIS in 2014 provides further support for the clash of civilizations model. The group came to global attention not simply due to its battlefield successes in Iraq and Syria but also by the brutality of its behavior. Members of ISIS captured and beheaded Western and Japanese journalists, drove Christians and Turks out of its controlled territory, sought to exterminate a religious minority group of Yazidis in northern Iraq, destroyed valuable antiquities as they moved through Syria and Iraq, and forced women into sexual slavery. ISIS tried to establish a 'caliphate,' an Islamic government led by a caliph (a person considered a political and religious successor to the prophet Muhammad), across the Muslim world. By 2017, a coalition of local and Western forces retook control of most territory in Iraq and Syria that ISIS had seized. The caliphate project was defeated, but we should expect ISIS to live on as an insurgent non-state actor, and as of 2018 it continued to carry out terrorist attacks in Europe and elsewhere.

Contrary Evidence and Questions

Proponents of the clash of civilizations model must address some critical questions about the plausibility of their future vision. First, to what extent do cultures or civilizations form coherent or functional political units? One might reasonably point to the long-standing political, economic, and security links in the West between the European Union and United States as an example of a politically functional

Photo 14.3 The Destruction of Historical Monuments
The remains of Triumph's Arch, in the ancient Syrian city of Palmyra, after it was destroyed by Islamic State jihadists in October 2015. IS jihadists destroyed ancient ruins for shock value and because they view ancient cultural heritage as a challenge to their political and religious authority.

Source: JOSEPH EID/AFP/Getty Images.

civilization across nation-state lines. But in other presumed civilizations, political relations are ambiguous at best. The Sino-centric world includes China and Vietnam, countries that are long historical adversaries who fought a war as recently as 1979. It is difficult to conceive of China (including US ally Taiwan), the Koreas (North and South), and Vietnam as somehow forming a viable political unit under the rubric of a common civilization.

The same might be said of the eastern Orthodox world. Cultural and religious similarities do not translate easily into significant political cohesion. Greece, Bulgaria, and Romania are eastern in Huntington's civilization typology but are politically and economically allied with the West through NATO and the European Union. In the Middle East, despite centuries of perceived oppression at the hands of the West, no charismatic leader or leaders have emerged to craft a pan-Islamic movement that transcends the interests of nation-states. ISIS certainly did not attract widespread appeal. Countries of the Middle East and the Gulf region share Islam as a religion but are ethnically fragmented, with Arabs, Turks, Palestinians, and others having competing political orientations. Being part of the same civilization did not prevent Iran and Iraq from fighting a brutal and bloody war between 1980 and 1988. Some countries and non-state actors within the Muslim civilization regard Israel as a mortal enemy and refuse to acknowledge its right to exist. Others, such as Egypt, have made peace with Israel. Saddam Hussein's quest to unify the Arab civilization against the West was met by resistance from fellow Arab states such as Saudi Arabia. The United States may be fighting some Muslims in the war on terrorism, but it has defended others – the Bosnian Muslims under attack from Serbia and Croatia, and Albanians in Kosovo under attack from Serbia – in prior conflicts. Civilizations do not necessarily form political units and cultural affinities do not always dictate political behavior among nation-states.

Second, even if we accept the utility of 'civilization' as an organizing concept, must relations among civilizations be characterized by conflict? There are numerous examples of cross-civilization cooperation in world politics. Furthermore, some extreme groups resist modernization precisely because one of the consequences is the transmission of different values, integration of various cultures, and the softening of stark distinctions across civilizations. Seventy years ago, the United States and Japan were mortal adversaries and culturally alien to each other. Today they are long-standing allies whose cultures and foreign policies have become increasingly intertwined. Americans can experience baseball in Tokyo just as Japanese can enjoy sushi in almost every American city.

The clash of civilizations is a provocative vision that has generated widespread criticism in the scholarly community. Some argue that economic opportunities and environmental challenges create more cohesion, rather than conflicts, across civilizational divides. Others point to global trends in favor of secularism, and still others observe that most conflicts in the world today occur between members, either within or across nation-states, of the same civilization (Gurr 1994). Finally, as noted in Box 14.5, some analysts have worried that Huntington's thesis could create a self-fulfilling prophecy. To stipulate a clash of civilizations as the defining feature of international relations reinforces the views of the most anti-Western extremists in the Middle East and the most xenophobic nationalists in Western Europe and the United States. By stressing differences among cultures, rather than interactions and reciprocal influences, Huntington's thesis risks generating the very conflicts he is analyzing.

Photo 14.4 The Tokyo 'Big Egg'
Baseball is highly popular in Japan. In Tokyo, over 50,000 people can watch the home team Yomiuri Giants play in the Tokyo Dome, commonly called the 'Big Egg' due to its white dome-shaped roof.

Source: iStock.com/TkKurikawa.

14.5   DIFFERING PERSPECTIVES

The Clash of Civilizations

Below, Samuel Huntington makes the analytical point that future conflict is likely to develop along cultural or 'civilizational' lines. Edward Said finds that argument overly simplified and likely to confuse more than clarify. Barack Obama emphasizes that different cultures must look for common interests rather than emphasizing their differences.

Samuel Huntington, Harvard Professor of Political Science

It is my hypothesis that the fundamental source of conflict in this new world will not be primarily ideological or primarily economic. The great divisions among humankind and the dominating source of conflict will be cultural. Nation-states will remain the most powerful actors in world affairs, but the principal conflicts of global politics will occur between nations and groups of different civilizations. The fault lines between civilizations will be the battle lines of the future.

Source: Huntington (1993).

Edward W. Said, Columbia University Professor of English and Comparative Literature

This is the problem with unedifying labels like Islam and the West: They mislead and confuse the mind, which is trying to make sense of a disorderly reality that won't be pigeonholed or strapped down as easily as all that … These are tense times, but it is better to think in terms of powerful and powerless communities, the secular politics of reason and ignorance, and universal principles of justice and injustice, than to wander off in search of vast abstractions that may give momentary satisfaction but little self-knowledge or informed analysis. The 'Clash of Civilizations' thesis is a gimmick like 'The War of the Worlds,' better for reinforcing defensive self-pride than for critical understanding of the bewildering interdependence of our time.

Source: Said (2001).

President Barack Obama

I have come here to seek a new beginning between the United States and Muslims around the world; one based upon mutual interest and mutual respect; and one based upon the truth that America and Islam are not exclusive and need not be in competition. Instead, they overlap, and share common principles – principles of justice and progress; tolerance and the dignity of all human beings.

I do so recognizing that change cannot happen overnight. No single speech can eradicate years of mistrust, nor can I answer in the time that I have all the complex questions that brought us to this point … There must be a sustained effort to listen to each other; to learn from each other; to respect one another; and to seek common ground … I know there are many – Muslim and non-Muslim – who question whether we can forge this new beginning. Some are eager to stoke the flames of division, and to stand in the way of progress. Some suggest that it isn't worth the effort – that we are fated to disagree, and civilizations are doomed to clash. Many more are simply skeptical that real change can occur. There is so much fear, so much mistrust. But if we choose to be bound by the past, we will never move forward.

Source: White House (2009) 'A New Beginning,' Remarks in Cairo, Egypt, June 4.

Levels of Analysis *The Clash of Civilizations*	
State	🌐 International
The clash of civilizations model posits that allegiance to the nation-state will be less powerful in the future than allegiance to cross-national cultures or civilizations.	Conflict among cultures, rather than interaction among nation-states, are the key drivers of world politics in this model.

MODEL 6: GLOBAL FRACTURE: PRE-MODERN, MODERN, AND POST-MODERN ZONES

Global fracture
A model of the future international system in which sovereign states give way to various 'zones' with differing characteristics.

Our final model questions whether it still makes analytical sense to posit a single, coherent international system of sovereign nation-states. Proponents of the **global fracture** model view the sovereign nation-state as under attack from above and below. Supranational institutions, such as the European Union, have gained political authority as states pool their sovereignty or cede it to transnational authorities. At the same time, as discussed in Chapter 12, local actors including tribes, drug cartels, and terrorist groups have challenged the authority of central governments and have even established control over territories, populations, and the provision of services. In some parts of the world, the nation-state is alive and well. But in others it no longer dominates other political forms.

State success, as well as state failure, might help to account for the demise of the traditional nation-state. In some parts of the world, such as Western Europe, sovereign states have been so successful in providing security and prosperity to their people, or in resolving differences with their neighbors, that they are no longer needed to take on the functions they have traditionally performed. But in other parts of the world, such as parts of central Africa, sovereign states have failed. Their inability to provide people with security and a functioning economy, or even basic life necessities, have led other actors to take matters into their own hands. Significant variation in the role, capacity, and necessity of the modern nation-state means that we live in a fractured world, no longer usefully characterized in terms of a single integrated state system.

Characteristics of Global Fracture

Versions of the global fracture thesis have been put forth by various authors. In 1993, Max Singer and Aaron Wildavsky argued that the traditional ways of understanding international politics needed to be replaced by new thinking:

> The key to understanding the new world order is to separate the world into two parts. One part is zones of peace, wealth, and democracy. The other part is zones of turmoil, war, and development. There are useful things to say about the zones of peace; and there are useful things to say about the zones of turmoil; but if you try to talk about the world as a whole all you can get is falsehoods or platitudes. (Singer and Wildavsky 1993: 3)

Along similar lines, in 2003 Robert Cooper, a former foreign policy advisor to British Prime Minister Tony Blair, published *The Breaking of Nations* (Cooper 2003). Cooper also sees the new world order as transcending the traditional Westphalian system of interacting, sovereign nation-states. He criticizes realists for assuming all states objectively pursue determined interests and seek to accumulate power. Cooper suggests instead that some states can radically change their interests and identities, while others are simply incapable of purposive action because they lack organizational capacity or legitimacy. Cooper's model is representative of the global fracture vision of the emerging world order.

Cooper argues that three different political forms coexist uneasily in what used to be an integrated international system. He describes pre-modern, modern, and post-modern worlds. The **pre-modern world** is a haven of lawlessness where states have either failed completely or cannot wield authority over subnational actors who control territory, command the allegiance of parts of the population, and may even control their own private or local armies. Much of our discussion in Chapter 12 relates to what Cooper would term the pre-modern world. One example is Somalia, which has struggled for two decades to establish some degree of political centralization and stability in the face of resistance from autonomous tribal warlords. In 2000, the United Nations recognized a Transitional Federal Government as the ruling body for the entire nation-state. But that government proved unable to control even the capital city, Mogadishu, much less outlying regions. A new president was chosen by the Somali parliament in 2004, but the election and legislative session had to be held in neighboring Kenya because Mogadishu was under siege. Over two dozen militia groups run by tribal warlords have set up semi-functional governments in different parts of the country and engage in military conflicts with each other. Since 1991, there have been over a dozen efforts, none ultimately successful, at national reconciliation. Other examples of the pre-modern world would include the parts of Syria and Iraq that could not be controlled by central governments and were taken over in 2014 by ISIS (which also proved unable to control them).

Cooper's **modern world** reflects the familiar system of Westphalian nation-states. Sovereign governments control their countries internally and mobilize resources to

Pre-modern world
A haven of lawlessness where states cannot wield authority over subnational actors who control territory, command the allegiance of parts of the population, and may even control private armies.

Modern world
The traditional system of Westphalian nation-states in which sovereign governments control their countries internally and mobilize resources to pursue national interests.

Map 14.5 Israel and Its Neighbors
Israel has long been a quintessential 'modern' state in Cooper's terms.

Photo 14.5 A Eurofighter Typhoon (L) and a Dassault Rafale, Germany, 2018
Showcasing German defense expertise at the ILA Berlin International Aerospace Exhibition at Schoenefeld Airport near Berlin in April 2018. German military technology is sophisticated, but its defense spending remains below what one might expect of a major international power.

Source: Getty Images.

Post-modern world
States that have given up their sovereignty in favor of larger, civilian-led cooperative unions (such as the EU).

pursue national interests. They engage in diplomacy, play balance-of-power politics, form alliances, and threaten or reassure their neighbors as part of efforts to enhance their influence, extract resources, or secure borders. Postwar Israel is an exemplar of Cooper's modern world. Over 50 years it has fought wars with Egypt and Syria, made peace with and granted territorial concessions to Egypt, and occupied and retreated from Lebanon. Israel was attacked by Iraq during the 1990–91 Persian Gulf War but was convinced by the United States not to escalate. Today it uses various tools of statecraft to prevent the emergence of an autonomous Palestinian state and mobilizes for regional conflict with its nemesis, Iran.

According to Cooper, much of Europe itself is no longer part of the modern world that European states created back in 1648. The core states of the European Union constitute a **post-modern world**. They have willingly relinquished some of the key attributes of the traditional, sovereign nation-state. Contemporary Germany, for example, does not look much like the country that unified in 1870, enhanced its power through a careful balance-of-power strategy, and mobilized its resources to fight two world wars to dominate the politics of its continent. Germany today has merged much of its economic and foreign policies with those of its traditional adversary, France, and other neighboring countries. It has ceded much of its sovereign authority to the collective EU enterprise. It gave up its national currency, the Deutschmark, in favor of a common European currency. Even after reunification in 1990–91, Germany has proved more interested in enhancing the prosperity and welfare of its citizens than mobilizing resources to enhance its influence, prestige, and grandeur on the world stage. As of 2017, for example, German defense spending was about 1.2 percent of its GDP, well below the 2 percent goal NATO members targeted in 2014. Germany is a 'civilian' great power, bound tightly to its neighbors and enmeshed in complicated layers of supranational decision-making.

International Trends

The global fracture model clearly illustrates the divergent political units of the current and emerging international system. We can point to ample evidence for the existence of pre-modern, modern, and post-modern politics that cut across traditional nation-state boundaries. Parts of South America are pre-modern as governments struggle to harness drug cartels that control their own military forces and administer large areas of cocaine-producing territory, simultaneously protecting and exploiting the peasants who work the land. The arc of instability stretching across the Middle East, North Africa, and Southwest Asia contains failed states such as Yemen, weakly centralized states such as Lebanon and Afghanistan, and states unable to control large and remote parts of their own territory, such as Pakistan and, as of 2014, Iraq and Syria. Much of the war against Al Qaeda has taken place in the 'no man's land' on the mountainous Afghanistan–Pakistan border, under no real control by either central government.

Examples of modern nation-states abound. One could point to Iran, Israel, and Saudi Arabia in the Middle East, emerging great powers China, India, and Brazil, and former great powers seeking to recover their status such as Russia. The European Union, comprising the area that used to be the core of the sovereign nation-state system, is the most prominent example of post-modernism. It is a highly developed, institutionalized, and legitimate system for nation-states to interfere at all levels in the affairs of their neighbors, from foreign and financial policy all the way down to the ingredients that are acceptable in the production of cheese and beer.

Contrary Evidence and Questions

Global fracture offers a plausible snapshot of the contemporary world. Yet does it capture the essence of international politics more effectively than the other models? One key challenge for its proponents is to establish the nature of interaction – or lack of interaction – among the three different political forms. The model of a fractured international system would be especially powerful if the pre-modern, modern, and post-modern worlds formed self-contained subsystems of limited interaction with each other. In that circumstance the global fracture model would resemble, as discussed in Chapter 2, a pre-Westphalian world in which the key units were isolated from each other rather than integrated into a single system.

The recent backlash against globalization, and the rise of populism in Europe and the United States, offer support to the global fracture model's expectation of limited interaction. As we noted in Chapter 2, the major political divide in America and Europe appears to be less about right vs. left, and more about 'drawbridges up vs. drawbridges down.' Within Western countries there exists division between those who welcome immigrants as a source of national renewal, embrace free trade and open markets, and view cultural change as an opportunity, and those (the drawbridges up contingent) who prefer to block immigrants, protect jobs at home, and resist multi-culturalism in order to 'take their country back.' If the forces of populism, nationalism, and anti-globalization continue to strengthen, we would likely see a diminution in the interaction across Cooper's three zones.

At present, however, and notwithstanding these recent challenges, Cooper's three worlds seem drawn together in many ways. The chaos and instability of the pre-modern world spills over into the modern and post-modern worlds (Kaplan 2012). Refugees from pre-modern war zones in Africa and the Middle East cross borders and make their way to Europe and North America. Genocide and famine in the pre-modern world are often too horrible in humanitarian terms for governments and people in the post-modern world to ignore; recall from Chapters 5 and 12 the discussion of how the international community has taken on a 'responsibility to protect' civilians in crisis around the (usually pre-modern) world. Aggrieved groups in the pre-modern world threatened by 'post-modernity' can lash out using weapons of the weak – terrorism and weapons of mass destruction. There is also a strong historical connection. It is arguable that the modern world helped to create the instability of the pre-modern; as discussed in Chapter 11, the legacy of colonialism hampers economic development in the southern part of the globe, and great powers drew arbitrary colonial borders that created conflicts across ethnic and tribal lines that remain unresolved.

Other connections across worlds may be less obvious, yet no less important. To what extent is the security of the post-modern world a function of protection by modern states using very modern means? The post-modern, civilian power zones enjoyed by the European Union and Japan developed under the security umbrella provided during the Cold War by the United States. Particularly in Japan, that security umbrella remains in place. In the absence of a secure environment provided by others, it is possible that today's post-modern world might be forced to return to the modern one. Absent a US security guarantee, and facing nuclear-armed neighbors, Japan might be forced to reconsider its identity as a civilian great power. European states, facing a resurgent Russia not balanced by the United States, might have to rethink their long-standing preference for consumer, rather than military spending. In other words, the 'post-modernity' of Japan and the European countries may be a reflection, not necessarily guaranteed over time, of American power and protection.

Levels of Analysis *Global Fracture*	
State	**International**
The global fracture model reminds us that both failed states such as Somalia and supranational institutions such as the EU pose challenges to the primacy of the Westphalian nation-state.	Global fracture takes us back to a pre-Westphalian world characterized by the lack of an integrated international system.

LOOKING BACK: A REMINDER TO FOCUS ON ENDURING QUESTIONS

Our survey of six different visions of the emerging international order should make one thing clear – there is no obvious winner. No doubt, some students will be uncomfortable with the gloomy pessimism of the clash of civilizations, the seemingly naive optimism of the democratic peace, or the frustrating historical cycle of multipolar or bipolar balance-of-power politics. Nonetheless, the debate is a useful one because it helps us map the overall terrain and contemplate what types of changes are plausible in world politics. It also forces us to reflect on our assumptions about what matters most in international relations. The six models, taken together, also illuminate two central questions about the future.

First, will the sovereign nation-state remain the central actor in world politics? No model predicts the disappearance of the nation-state, but they do divide on the question of whether it will continue to be the key driver of cooperation and conflict. The first three models place their bets in different ways on the continued primacy of the nation-state. The latter three give more weight to either political units or processes that cross nation-state boundaries, or features of certain nation-states (for example, democracy) in answering the question of what will likely matter most in future world politics.

Second, how much will military power continue to matter? No model believes the military factor will be eliminated from global politics but, again, a clear divide is evident. The bipolar, multipolar, and clash-of-civilizations models expect that political actors will prepare for and, likely, engage in military competition and conflict as a key feature in their international relationships. For different reasons, the geo-economic and democratic peace models downplay the importance of military power and point instead to fundamental changes in how future states will interact.

These two questions take us back to where we began, with a focus on the enduring questions of international relations. Our approach in this book has tried to encourage students to step away from the immediate politics of the moment and appreciate the knotty problems that have long engaged scholars and practitioners of world politics. On the hardest questions of our discipline, there are no easy answers. That makes it even more essential to identify and struggle with these questions, understand how and why they have been answered in the past, develop your own answers, and learn to defend them logically through evidence drawn from the rich past and fascinating present of the international system.

STUDY QUESTIONS

1. Which vision of a future international order do you find most compelling, and why? Which do you find least compelling, and why?
2. What features are most important in distinguishing the multipolar balance-of-power model from the democratic peace model?
3. Is the clash of civilizations a realist model? Why or why not?
4. Do you believe a world of democratic states would be a more peaceful world than the current international order? Why or why not?
5. Which models do you believe might usefully be combined into a 'hybrid' model of the future international system, and why?
6. Consider an unrealistic thought experiment: If the United States disappeared from the international system tomorrow, which model of international order would likely emerge as the dominant one, and why?
7. From the perspective of China, is a bipolar world in which they are one of two dominant powers preferable to a multipolar world in which they are one of five major powers? What about from the perspective of a non-major power, for example, Vietnam?
8. What are the implications of Brexit for the global fracture model?

FURTHER READING

Cooper, Robert (2003) *The Breaking of Nations* (New York: Grove/Atlantic). This is a provocative book by a British and European Union diplomat and former advisor to British Prime Minister Tony Blair. Cooper lays out a vision of a fractured world consisting of modern, pre-modern, and post-modern zones coexisting uneasily with each other.

Kupchan, Charles (2012) *No One's World: The West, the Rising Rest, and the Coming Global Turn* (New York: Oxford University Press). Kupchan emphasizes that Western values are not universal, and the 'Western' international order is giving way to one in which no set of values will dominate.

Mueller, John (1989) *Retreat from Doomsday: The Obsolescence of Major War* (New York: Basic Books). Mueller's argument, partly constructivist and partly liberal, is that in modern times war has fallen out of fashion – following in the footsteps of previously robust social practices such as slavery or settling personal differences by dueling.

Ohmae, Kenichi (1996) *The End of the Nation-State: The Rise of Regional Economies* (New York: Free Press). A Japanese commentator argues that the forces of economic globalization have undermined the role and effectiveness of the nation-state. Economic power in this new world is held in regions rather than by governments.

Rifkin, Jeremy (2009) *The Empathetic Civilization: The Race to Global Consciousness in a World of Crisis* (New York: Penguin). Rifkin takes a 'first-level' approach to future world order. He draws on biology and cognitive neuroscience to suggest human beings are fundamentally empathetic rather than aggressive, and re-interprets history from this perspective.

Zakaria, Fareed (2009) *The Post-American World* (New York: Norton). Zakaria is the host of CNN's *Fareed Zakaria GPS* and a well-known international commentator. His book focuses on the diffusion of international power and the 'rise of the rest' including China, India, South Africa, and Brazil.

 Visit **www.macmillanihe.com/Grieco-IntroIR-2e** to access extra resources for this chapter, including:
- Chapter summaries to help you review the material
- Multiple choice quizzes to test your understanding
- Flashcards to test your knowledge of the key terms in this chapter
- Outside resources, including links to contemporary articles and videos, that add to what you have learned in this chapter

Glossary

Absolute advantage A situation in which one state has a productive advantage over another in two (or more) goods, but trade can still be mutually beneficial due to the principle of comparative advantage.

Absolute gains An important element of economic liberalism, absolute gains is the idea that economic interactions create only winners, even if some gain more than others. Contrasts with relative gains.

Alliances Coalitions of states formed for mutual protection.

Anarchy The fact that in international relations there is no centralized authority, no government of the whole world to adjudicate disputes among states and protect weak ones from strong ones.

Appeasement An effort by one state to reduce conflict with another by accommodating the demands of the latter.

Asian Tigers Originally Taiwan, South Korea, Singapore, and Hong Kong, who achieved rapid growth rates using a strategy of export-led growth. Now many rapidly growing Asian countries are considered 'tigers.'

Austerity A policy by which governments raise interest rates or reduce government spending in an effort to discourage consumption and investment at home and, in so doing, reduce inflation and inflationary pressures.

Autarky The separation of a country from the world economy in an effort to protect its economy from the effects of the global market.

Balance of payments A summary of the international transactions of a state's residents, including individuals, households, private enterprises, and the government, with residents in the rest of the world during some fixed period, usually a quarter (three months) or a year.

Balance of power Process by which a state or coalition of states increases its capabilities to prevent the dominance of an opposing state or group of states.

Bandwagoning When smaller, weaker states ally with a larger, powerful state for protection. Contrasts with balance of power.

Battle of Stalingrad A battle between September 1942 and February 1943 in which Soviet forces destroyed a massive German army. It was a major turning point of World War II's European Theater.

Beggar-thy-neighbor policies Policies designed to shift the negative consequences of the global economic downturn onto a state's neighbors, pursued by many countries during the Great Depression.

Beijing Consensus The idea that, for some poor countries, development can be best attained by government controls, trade integration, capital inflows and outflows, the movement of labor, and the external value of the currency.

Berlin Wall The wall that divided Soviet East Berlin from American, French, and British West Berlin during the Cold War, until its fall in 1989.

Biodiversity Variety of forms of life on earth, including plants, animals, marine life, insects, and microorganisms, and variability within species, such as different types of corn, cattle, or bees.

Biological weapons A category of WMD that kills people by spreading bacteria or viruses.

Bipolarity In an international system, the characteristic of being driven by the existence of and competition between two especially powerful states.

Blast effect The immediate explosive effect of a nuclear weapon. Can be powerful enough to level all buildings in a several-mile radius and to produce destructive winds of between 100 and 200 miles per hour.

Bretton Woods system The international system created in 1944 to encourage progressive trade liberalization and stable monetary relations between all the countries of the world. Although initial membership was fairly low due to Cold War tensions, membership in the resulting organizations steadily increased to include the vast majority of the world's countries. The ITO, GATT, WTO, IMF, and World Bank were all created as a result of the Bretton Woods system.

Brexit The 'British exit,' or decision made by British citizens in a popular referendum to have the United Kingdom leave the European Union.

BRICS Brazil, Russia, India, China, and South Africa. These five rapidly developing countries have the collective potential, within several decades, to overtake the combined economic weight of the industrial world.

Bureaucratic politics A possible influence on a country's strategy characterized by national leaders and their subordinates engaging in foreign policy debates, building coalitions, and generally seeking to influence each other.

Caliphate A state governed in accordance with Islamic law.

Chemical weapons A category of WMD that uses manufactured chemicals to kill people.

Chlorofluorocarbons (CFCs) A chemical formerly used in aerosol cans, fire extinguishers, and air conditioners, a cause of ozone depletion, and now outlawed by international agreements.

Civil defense Defenses, such as fallout shelters, designed to protect civilians in case of a nuclear strike from an adversary.

Civil society Collections of non-state actors that operate outside the sphere of government or business control.

Civil war A sustained clash between forces that are controlled by the national government and forces that are controlled by an organized opposition group within the country.

Clash of civilizations The idea that international conflict in the future will be characterized not by interstate conflict but rather by conflict between civilizations, a term that incorporates religious, cultural, ethnic, and, to some extent, linguistic similarity.

Class conflict Conflict between the capitalist owners of wealth and industrial production and the workers they employ.

Coercive diplomacy Aggressive actions short of the immediate large-scale use of military force (such as moving an aircraft carrier closer to the shores of another country) designed to convince a country to rethink some behavior.

Cold War Period from the mid-1940s to the late 1980s in which there was high tension and risk of war between the United States and the Soviet Union.

Collective security Security provided by the members of an international cooperative institution in which, if any state threatened or actually used military force illegally against a member state, the other members pledged to form an overwhelming coalition to defeat the aggressor.

Colonies Areas and people conquered and exploited by a colonizing power over which the colonizer has political and economic control.

Commercial liberalism The idea that market society and economic interdependence tend to have a pacifying impact on relations among states. As the economic relations between two states increase, the interests of these states in stable and continuous relations grow.

Commitment problem A state's fear that an agreement with an adversary that is reached today will be violated at some point in the future when that adversary is stronger.

Comparative advantage One country has a comparative advantage over another in the production of a good if, in order to make one more unit of that good, it has to forego less of another good.

Competing economic blocs Groups of states in economic competition organized around the economies and currencies of major economic powers.

Concert of Europe An agreement among the great powers, beginning in the early nineteenth century, to maintain order collectively within Europe.

Conditional cooperation A strategy (also called tit-for-tat) in game theory capable of resolving the Prisoner's Dilemma wherein each player cooperates so long as the partner cooperates; each retaliates immediately against cheating with cheating; and each returns to cooperation if the partner does so.

Contagion The spread of an internal war in one country to another, often caused by rebels seeking shelter in a neighboring country and beginning conflict there.

Containment A strategy by which one state employs diplomacy, economic assistance, and military power to counter and check what it believes are efforts by an adversary state to extend its global sphere of influence.

Convention on Biological Diversity An international agreement aiming to protect and preserve biodiversity, passed in 1992.

Convertible currency A currency that can be exchanged at market price for the currency of another country.

Cosmopolitanism The tendency of peoples in different countries to embrace each other as fellow global citizens. Cosmopolitanism can be contrasted with nationalism.

Covert operations Activities that a government directs against the interests of another government or non-state actor in such a way that the foreign targets and others are kept from knowing that the initiating government is responsible for the activities.

Cruise missile Missile, capable of being launched from land, air, or sea, that can travel below radar detection and guide itself around obstacles to deliver the warhead it carries.

Currency market intervention The purchase or sale of currency by a state government in international markets to maintain a constant exchange rate between that government's currency and another currency.

Current account The current account consists of the country's balance of trade in goods and services (the value of exports minus the value of imports), plus its income receipts such as the receipt of earnings from past investments abroad or the payment of such earnings to foreigners, and other transfers such as remittances that workers send out of the country or local residents receive from abroad.

Customary international law Legal norms that, while not written down as formal law, have come to be seen by states as having some capacity to control their behavior.

Cyber operations The use or manipulation of information on the internet to advance foreign policy interests.

Cyber-warfare The use of the internet and related technologies by governments to damage or disrupt the activities or systems of an adversary or a private entity of value to an adversary.

Decolonization The process by which imperial powers relinquished their overseas holdings leading to an increase in the number of independent nations around the world.

Deforestation The clearing or overharvesting of forests, an especially acute problem in the tropics.

Demand curve A demand curve specifies the quantity of a good that consumers wish to purchase at different prices. Along with supply curves, demand curves can show the likely price of goods, including currencies, in international markets.

Democratic peace theory The theory that democracies are unusually peaceful toward each other. Democracies, or republics, are understood as states that have elected governments, a free press, private property, and the rule of law.

Dependency A school of thought that argues that international economic linkages hinder development in developing countries.

Détente A relaxing of tension in the middle of the Cold War in which economic interdependence began to develop between East and West.

Deterrence The use of power resources to discourage a state from acting aggressively.

Developed countries Wealthy countries with advanced economies.

Developing country Poor countries with small economies whose residents have not, on average, attained the living standards typically enjoyed on average by residents of wealthy countries.

Diplomacy The process by which representatives of two or more governments meet and discuss matters of common concern.

Diplomatic immunity The privileges and immunities granted by a host country to foreign ambassadors and embassy staff, exempting them from the full force of local laws.

'Dirty bomb' A device that, without the profound power of a nuclear explosion (and its attendant heat and blast effects), disperses some type of radioactive material.

Dissatisfied states States who feel that their influence, status, and material benefits should be higher than what they are actually achieving.

Dynastic states States ruled by 'imperial dynasties' or 'dynastic families,' in which members of a given extended family, over a number of generations, maintain power within a state or empire.

Economic development The attainment by a poorer country of an increase in its rate of growth of GDP per capita.

Economic incentive An instrument of persuasion in foreign policy. Economic incentives are basically carrots: country A promises some economic gain to B, and delivers it if B does what A wants it to do.

Economic sanctions The restriction of customary trade and investment relations with a target state. An instrument of coercion in foreign policy. Economic sanctions are basically sticks: A threatens B with some form of economic loss if B does something A does not want it to do, or fails to do something A wants it to do.

Economic security The ability to maintain prosperity in a world of scarcity.

Economic warfare Aggressive actions by a state intended to damage another state economically.

Empires Political entities that contain a substantial geographical space, often over many different peoples, and over which a single powerful ruler governs.

End of history The end of ideological conflict and the victory of liberal values.

Enduring questions Questions which have engaged and challenged generations of international relations scholars and students – large, challenging questions that have stood the test of time. This book is organized around these questions.

Environmental determinism The view that changes in the environment like climate change *necessarily* and *automatically* will cause human beings and human communities to react in a particular manner.

Ethnic cleansing Sustained, organized violence perpetrated against a particular ethnic group with the goal of eradication of that group.

Euro The common currency of the eurozone.

European Union A group of 28 European countries that abide by common laws and practices.

Eurozone The world's most prominent currency union, consisting of 18 countries in Europe all using the euro as a national currency.

Exchange rate The amount of one currency that must be offered to purchase one unit of a foreign currency.

Exclusive Economic Zone (EEZ) According to the LOS treaty, the area up to 200 nautical miles from a state's shoreline, within which, according the LOS treaty, that state's national government has the right to control all sea-related commercial activities by national and foreign agents, for example, fishing or drilling and extracting oil and gas from the seabed below the waters of the EEZ.

Export-led growth (ELG) A strategy that argues developing countries should rely on price-competitive exports to stimulate national economic development.

Extended deterrence The threat by one country to use its nuclear forces to protect other countries.

External balancing The process by which states enter into security alliances with other states to balance the power of a particularly strong state or coalition of states.

Externalities The benefits and costs not reflected in a good's price, such as ideas on how to improve a product in the future (positive externality) or pollution (negative externality).

Extra-state war A violent clash between the national government of a recognized state and an entity that is not an internationally recognized state, or a non-state actor located in a foreign state.

Failed states States that lack the basic institutions and capacities of government – taxing, policing, upholding the rule of law, protecting property, providing public roads and services, and maintaining control over territory.

Fallout effect The tertiary effect of a nuclear explosion. Because nuclear weapons cause dirt and air particles to become radioactive, an explosion can expose people hundreds of miles from the blast site to fatal cancers over time. This exposure to radiation is the fallout effect, and affects a much wider range than the blast or thermal effects.

Feudalism A system in which individuals act as 'vassals' and receive land in exchange for swearing loyalty to specific high-ranking leaders (e.g., counts, dukes) and, at the apex of the system, the king.

First-strike capability The negation of another country's second-strike capability. A state has first-strike capability if, and only if, it has sufficient nuclear capability to entirely eliminate an adversary's capacity to respond to a preliminary strike.

Fission An atom-splitting chain reaction that is central to the working of a nuclear weapon.

Fixed (or pegged) exchange-rate system A system in which a currency trades at a government-specified rate against a particular currency or a group of currencies, and the government intervenes in the foreign exchange market or takes monetary or fiscal policy measures to keep those rates in place.

Fixed alliances Alliances in which countries remain allied with the same partners over long periods of time.

Fixed capital The value of assets a company utilizes in an ongoing way in the production of a good or service.

Flexible (or floating) exchange-rate system A system in which a government allows supply and demand in foreign exchange markets to determine the exchange rate of its national currency.

Flexible alliances Temporary alliances in which states form pacts but shift from one partner to the other depending on the circumstances.

Foreign affairs media Those individuals and organizations who report or comment on foreign developments in print, on television, over radio, and through the internet.

Foreign exchange market The marketplace in which individuals, firms, and even governments sell and buy foreign currencies.

Framing The process by which media participants select or present particular elements of a news story in such a way as to influence the opinions of recipients of the story.

Functionalism The liberal idea that institutions are tools that allow states to develop more efficient and durable forms of cooperation.

Garrison state A highly militarized state in which the government controls economic, social, and political life in order to maximize military power.

General Agreement on Tariffs and Trade (GATT) When the ambitious ITO fell through, GATT represented an initial, less ambitious attempt by the United States and other Western countries to lower their respective tariff rates on a wide variety of goods and to establish a first set of rules to resolve trade disputes among nations (finalized in 1947).

General war A war that involves many or all of the most powerful states in a particular historical era. Synonymous with major war.

Genocide Violent crimes committed against a particular national, racial, religious, or ethnic group with the intent of destroying the existence of that group.

Global civil society The realm of private activity that lies outside the political system, where religious, ethnic, and civic groups flourish. Global civil society refers to these transnational groups and activities across borders.

Global Environmental Facility (GEF) A program managed by the World Bank and the UN that provides grants to developing countries to help them meet international environment obligations regarding climate change, desertification, international water pollution, and biodiversity.

Global fracture A model of the future international system in which sovereign states give way to various 'zones' with differing characteristics.

Globalization The ongoing process of international economic and technological integration, made possible by advances in transportation and communication.

Good governance A country with good governance at home typically possesses transparent and consistent political and legal systems, combats official corruption, and protects property. These factors encourage individuals to save, make investments, and pursue technological innovations that promote economic growth.

Great Depression An international economic disaster precipitated by the 1929 crash of the US stock market. The disaster promptly blocked Europe's path to economic recovery and political reconciliation.

Greed A person's intense desire to possess goods or money. On the individual level of analysis, a primary mechanism that increases the likelihood of internal war.

Grievance A person's belief that he or she is being victimized by or excluded from important institutions in a country; a primary mechanism that increases the likelihood of internal war.

Gross domestic product (GDP) The world's GDP is the total monetary value of all goods and services produced by all countries of the world in a year. A country's gross domestic product is the monetary value of goods and services produced within its borders in a year.

Gross fixed capital formation The total increase in fixed capital that occurs in a country or in the world during a given period of time, usually a year.

Group of 20 (G-20) The G-7, newly rising economic powers like China and India, oil producers like Saudi Arabia and Russia, and middle powers such as Australia, Turkey, and Argentina, which has replaced the G-7 in international economic decision-making.

Group of 7 (G-7) Seven countries (United States, United Kingdom, France, Germany, Japan, Italy, and Canada) that sought to govern international economic relations after the collapse of the Bretton Woods system by coordinating their exchange rates and their domestic monetary and fiscal policies.

Group of 8 (G-8) The Group of 7 (G-7) plus Russia. In the aftermath of the Cold War, Russia was added as a symbolic move. Russia was suspended from the G-8 in 2014 in response to its annexation of Crimea.

Groupthink Psychological need on the part of individuals to be accepted by colleagues that can cause national leaders and advisors to make serious errors during a foreign policy crisis.

Hegemonic leader A particularly powerful state whose presence, according to realist theory, may be necessary to help facilitate cooperation between and among less powerful partner-states.

Hegemonic war A war the outcome of which determines which states will have predominant influence in the international system in the coming years or even decades.

Hegemony The dominance of one state over other states. Many scholars believe that a hegemonic international system is most prone to peace.

High seas According to the LOS treaty, the area of the seas beyond 200 nautical miles, over which no individual state has exclusive jurisdiction.

Human development A process of enlarging people's choices and giving them a means to lead lives that they value. Measurements of human development include such factors as life expectancy, income, and education.

Hybrid warfare The blending of conventional warfare with informational warfare, including the spreading of fake news and the disruption of normal political functions (for example, elections) in target countries.

Idealism The notion that ideas matter in international relations.

Immediate cause of a military conflict Disagreement, or the conflict of interest, that causes one state or another to escalate to the threat or actual use of military force.

Imperialism A state strategy in which one country conquers foreign lands to turn them into colonies.

Import-substituting industrialization (ISI) A national development strategy that seeks to avoid international economic linkages in favor of focusing on domestic production.

Incentives Rewards of some form offered by one state to another designed to influence the foreign policy of the recipient. Incentives are a form of persuasion.

Infant-industry protection A policy in which imports of a certain type of good are restricted (in theory temporarily) to allow for the development of the capacity to produce that good domestically.

Innocent passage Concept originally in customary international law and now stipulated in the LOS treaty according to which vessels from a seafaring state may move through a coastal state's territorial waters so long as they do so in an expeditious, non-threatening manner.

Institutional constraints The constitutional or customary checks within a country that impede, slow, or limit the capacity of a leader unilaterally to undertake some action.

Inter-communal wars A war in which members of different religious communities in a country become embroiled in large-scale organized violence.

Intercontinental ballistic missile (ICBM) Missile that in under an hour can travel thousands of miles through outer space and release multiple nuclear warheads, each carrying a payload of several hundred kilotons and independently guided to explode within several hundred feet of a separate target.

Interest groups Individuals or organizations that share a common set of political concerns and band together in an association to persuade leaders and the public to pursue, support, or accept policies that are in accord with the preferences of the association.

Interest Some condition of the world sufficiently important that a state is willing to pay meaningful costs to attain or maintain it.

Intergovernmental Panel on Climate Change (IPCC) A panel established by the UN in 1988 that studies climate change and informs the world of its effects.

Internal balancing The process by which states muster their own power to balance rival states by mobilizing their economy and increasing their defense capabilities.

Internal war Any war within a state, contrasted with war between two or more states.

International commodity agreement An agreement, generally sought by developing countries' exporters, on the supply and price of that commodity. The goal is not to maximize prices but rather to establish an acceptable, consistent price that the developing country can rely on.

International commodity cartels Groupings of developing-country governments that try to control the supply of a raw material or agricultural product on world markets in order to drive up prices and maximize revenues.

International Criminal Court (ICC) Permanent body to prosecute individuals suspected of international war crimes or genocide.

International financial flows The movement of capital from private or governmental individuals or organizations inside one country to private or governmental individuals or organizations inside another country. These flows consist of both private and official financial flows.

International governmental organizations (IGOs) Organizations that states join to further their political or economic interests.

International institutions Sets of rules, principles, and expectations that govern interstate interaction.

International law Explicit rules that stipulate the rights and the obligations that states have with respect to other states or other actors covered by the law; the rules stipulate rights and obligations and usually take the form of *prescriptions for* or *prohibitions against* specified states' action.

International Monetary Fund (IMF) An international institution created in 1946 to facilitate and reinforce the exchange-rate system created in the aftermath of World War II. The IMF remains one of the world's most important international economic institutions.

International organization A body or association established by two or more states, usually formed to help states implement their obligations under a relevant international law.

International system States and non-state actors, taken collectively, coexisting and interacting at some point in history.

International Trade Organization (ITO) An ambitious scheme for global trade management proposed in 1947. The ITO eventually failed because the United States refused to support it and was largely replaced by the less ambitious GATT.

International tribunals Ad hoc legal proceedings that are less formal than court proceedings and are applied to specific international situations, such as genocide in Rwanda during the 1990s.

Internationalism A strategy in which a state is fully engaged with other states through institutionalized arrangements directed at maintaining world security and promoting global economic prosperity.

Internationalization of civil war During a civil war, one or more foreign states intervenes and supports one or another of the warring sides with equipment or troops.

Interstate war When two or more national governments direct military forces against each other in organized, sustained, and oftentimes deadly clashes.

Intra-firm trade The cross-country movement of different components that are put together at one or more final assembly plants in one or more countries.

Invisible hand A term coined by Adam Smith to describe the uncoordinated behavior of individuals and firms acting in their own selfish interest in the marketplace.

Iron Curtain A term coined by British leader Winston Churchill to capture the profound political and human divisions separating the Western and Eastern parts of Europe.

Iron rice bowl A guarantee from the government of Communist China of job security and access to basic necessities for Chinese citizens.

Isolationism The practice by the United States, before World War II, of avoiding alliances and engaging only sporadically in European balance-of-power politics and the management of global affairs.

Jus ad bellum The international law that stipulates the legitimate grounds under which a state may go to war. In today's world that law is found in Chapter VII of the UN Charter.

Kellogg-Briand Pact A 1928 international pact outlawing war, authored by US Secretary of State Frank Kellogg and French Foreign Minister Aristide Briand.

Kyoto Protocol A multilateral agreement negotiated in 1997 to reduce the total emissions of signing states. The Protocol came into effect in 2005 but was ultimately unsuccessful in curbing emissions.

League of Nations An international body established by the Treaty of Versailles at the end of World War I and designed to provide states with an ongoing international legal and institutional framework to solve their disputes and avoid war.

Levels of analysis Different ways of looking for answers to questions in international relations, generally grouped into the individual, state, and international levels.

Limited war Smaller war in which major powers avoid fighting each other directly, contrasted with general or major war.

Lobbying Meeting and speaking with members of legislatures and officials in executive departments in an attempt to influence policy. Interest groups often engage in lobbying.

Locarno Accords An agreement in which Germany accepted its borders with France and Belgium, and promised to resolve border disputes with Poland and Czechoslovakia via arbitration rather than force.

Lootable wealth Natural resources that can be readily acquired, transported, and sold for cash. In some countries, greed and lootable wealth combine to make internal conflict more likely.

Manhattan Project The secret project that brought together expert scientists to build a super-weapon, culminating in the creation of the first atomic bomb. The Manhattan Project was begun by the United States around the time it entered World War II.

Marshall Plan A US plan to counteract Soviet influence in Europe by providing economic aid to help European nations rebuild after World War II.

Meiji Restoration Beginning with the rise of Emperor Meiji in 1868, leaders who set Japan on a course of selective adaptation of Western science, education, and industrial technology for the purposes of strengthening Japan economically and militarily.

Mercantilism A doctrine that states that military power is the central goal of states; such power rests on financial wealth, and the financial wealth of the world is a fixed quantity.

Militarized interstate dispute (MID) An instance in which a state threatens or uses force against another state.

Military-industrial complex A large military bureaucracy and a powerful network of defense firms, united to exercise influence over national security policy (generally applied to the United States).

Millennium Development Goals (MDGs) A series of goals related to health, education, and poverty, agreed upon by world leaders at the UN in September 2000.

Mixed interests In game theory, a situation in which two players may each benefit from some form of cooperation, but each can do even better by successfully cheating on the other, and each is made materially worse off (compared to not cooperating at all) if it is successfully cheated upon by its erstwhile partner.

Mode of production The basic organization of the economy – the way in which people relate to one another and to the material world.

Modern world The traditional system of Westphalian nation-states in which sovereign governments control their countries internally and mobilize resources to pursue national interests.

Modernization The idea that mankind is constantly inventing, innovating, improving, and creating.

Montreal Protocol on Substances that Deplete the Ozone Layer An international agreement passed in 1987 that has successfully combated the depletion of the ozone layer by banning CFCs. Ozone layers are expected to return to normal by 2050.

Moral hazard When an individual or some other actor believes they can take very great risks because, if things go badly, someone else will pay for the consequences of the risky behavior. Some accuse the IMF of encouraging moral hazard.

Multinational enterprise (MNE) A firm that has its headquarters in one country and ongoing business operations in one or (more typically) several other countries.

Munich Analogy A reference, sometimes invoked by political leaders, to the 1938 transfer of a part of Czechoslovakia to Nazi Germany by Western European democratic leaders. It is generally invoked as a criticism of policy or strategy that resembles appeasement.

Mutual Assured Destruction (MAD) A situation in which two adversaries each possess assured destruction capability, meaning that a nuclear conflict would likely inflict unacceptable damage on both countries.

Naming and shaming Strategy of national but especially global NGOs to highlight publicly the possible non-compliance of states with their obligations under international humanitarian and human rights laws, with the goal of compelling those states to react to the unfavorable depictions by bringing their behavior more in line with international legal norms.

Nation Collections of people who share a common culture, history, or language.

National champion In a state pursuing a strategy of ISI, the government nominates firms it believes could do the best job of producing the substituted industrial goods.

National leaders Individuals who hold executive offices as a result of which they are entitled to make foreign policy and military decisions on behalf of their countries.

National treatment A clause in the EEC (non EU), negotiated by the United States, that allows for American firms to be treated as though they are European firms.

Nationalism A term that describes an intense political identity a people share, or a sense of collective fate as a political community.

Nationalism *Relative* value that an individual assigns to that person's state; a person is nationalistic if that person thinks his or her country is superior to other countries.

Nation-state A political unit inhabited by people sharing common culture, history, or language.

Nazi–Soviet Non-Aggression Pact A pact signed between Nazi Germany and Soviet Russia in 1939 in which the two countries agreed not to attack each other and to jointly attack Poland, dividing the country between them.

Non-Aligned Movement A movement founded in 1955 to create a pathway by which member states could remain aloof from the confrontations of the Cold War. The NAM now includes over 100 countries, representing over one-half of the world's population.

Non-state actors Actors others than states that operate within or across state borders with important consequences for international relations.

Non-tariff barrier (NTB) Policies, such as anti-dumping duties, import quotas, or controlled government procurement, by which a state can control imports and import prices without imposing tariffs.

Normative change The idea that as global learning and international socialization occur, ideas about what is or is not acceptable or 'normal' change. As normative change occurs, it can impact international relations.

Normative constraints The beliefs, values, and attitudes that inform and shape the behavior of a leader.

North Atlantic Treaty Organization (NATO) A defense pact formed in 1949 between the US, the UK, and several other western European states. It has since expanded and is still very active today.

Nuclear club The group of states believed to possess nuclear weapons.

Nuclear deterrence Using the threat of retaliation to protect oneself from an attack. Nuclear states use the threat of nuclear retaliation to deter other states from attacking them.

Nuclear freeze A plan that would stop an arms race in its place by simply preventing two adversaries from developing or deploying any new warheads or delivery systems.

Nuclear Utilization Theory (NUTS) Contrary to MAD proponents, many Cold War policy makers followed this strategy, which argues that the United States should do everything it can to be prepared to fight a nuclear war.

Nuclear winter A situation, feared by many scientists in the 1980s, in which the smoke and soot resulting from numerous nuclear explosions blocked out the sunlight from the earth's surface for extended periods of time.

Objective A state's goal in international relations, generally the attainment or maintenance of some interest.

Official development assistance (ODA) The provision by a donor government to a developing country of grants or loans with highly favorable repayment terms (for example, 50 years to repay, at 1 percent interest).

Official financial flows International financial flows that originate with governmental entities.

Opportunity cost The cost of producing more of a certain good in foregone production of another good. Opportunity costs are crucial in considering comparative advantage and the possibility for mutual gains from trade.

Paris Agreement An international environment agreement reached in 2015 in which parties committed on a non-binding basis to act individually and collectively to prevent global warming.

Patriotism *Absolute* value an individual assigns to that person's state, including its history, culture, and political system, independent of how that person feels about other states.

Peace of Westphalia Treaties that ended the Thirty Years War and divided Europe into sovereign states independent of higher authorities.

Peaceful change The problem of how the international system copes with the transition of order based on the domination of one state over other states.

Peacekeeping UN operations in which UN-sponsored troops are deployed in countries in the aftermath of war or civil violence to keep the warring groups apart and enforce the peace settlement.

Peacemaking UN action before war breaks out designed to prevent two states from going to war with each other by brokering peaceful settlements. Contrasts with peacekeeping, which occurs in the aftermath of war.

Pirates Non-state gangs who commit robbery or criminal violence on the high seas.

Plutonium Along with uranium, one of the two materials that can be used to create a nuclear weapon. Rarely found in nature, plutonium is found as a by-product when energy is generated by a nuclear power plant and must then be extracted and reprocessed to become weapons grade.

Policy instrument A tool used by a state's government to attain its interests. Policy instruments come in many forms, divided into persuasive and coercive forms.

Pollution haven Countries that have low standards or lax enforcement of their environmental rules and regulations, which may attract foreign companies.

Populism A political idea or movement that proposes to support the interests of common people rather than those of a privileged elite.

Positive illusions The idea that what we think we can accomplish is often greater than what we would expect to achieve if we had a truly accurate picture of our capabilities.

Post-modern world States that have given up their sovereignty in favor of larger, civilian-led cooperative unions (such as the EU).

Poverty trap When a country is so poor that most of its national resources must be used to satisfy the immediate day-to-day needs of the population, with insufficient resources left for savings or investment.

Power balancing Efforts by states to protect themselves in a dangerous world by arraying power against power, consisting of both internal balancing and external balancing.

Power transitions When the relative power of two (or more) states changes, often due to technological innovations and uneven economic growth.

Pre-modern world A haven of lawlessness where states cannot wield authority over subnational actors who control territory, command the allegiance of parts of the population, and may even control private armies.

Price inflation A situation in which too much money is chasing too few goods, pushing up prices of goods and services.

Prisoner's Dilemma Analytical device that illustrates both the value of cooperation and the difficulty of obtaining it.

Private financial flows International financial flows that originate with nongovernmental entities, such as individuals, private charities, or private firms such as banks or multinational enterprises.

Private information problem Conflict-exacerbating tendency of states to overstate their resolve and capabilities during a crisis because no international authority forces them to reveal truthful information.

Privatization of war The idea that, as technology advances, private groups have greater capacities to wage violence usually reserved for states.

Production possibilities frontier (PPF) A graphical representation of the different combinations of goods that a country may produce during some period of time with the resources it has in its possession.

Propaganda The selective use of information, and at times misinformation, in order to advance a state's interests.

Protectionism Any of a number of policies in which a country puts restrictions on incoming goods in an effort to protect the domestic economy.

Proxy wars Military conflicts of the Cold War in which the US and USSR never directly engaged each other, but instead backed opposing sides of smaller conflicts to gain influence throughout the world.

Purchasing power parity (PPP) A measure economists use to compare the value of a similar basket of goods across countries with different living standards and exchange rates.

'Race to the bottom' A situation in which two or more countries put into place progressively lower policy rules and standards regarding the environment and worker rights out of a fear of losing, and perhaps out of greed for attracting, foreign investments from multinational enterprises.

Rally 'round the flag effect A commonly observed boost in the popularity of a leader due to external conflicts or war.

Regulatory chill The possible strategy by MNEs to use trade and investment agreements to cause governments with strong safety and health regulations to incur such high legal costs in defending those regulations that they will be deterred from new and more ambitious regulations in the future.

Relations of production The system by which the people in a productive system are related, or the relations between those people. According to Marxism, the relations of production will be characterized by class conflict.

Relative gains As opposed to absolute gains, which are simply the total materials gains made by a state, relative gains focus on the gains one state makes compared to a rival. Realists emphasize the importance of relative gains.

Resource curse The possibility that the possession by developing countries of natural resources, in particular petroleum, is more likely to hinder rather than to advance the development prospects of those countries.

Responsibility to protect (R2P) Doctrine that in the event of massive humanitarian crises, when host governments are unable or unwilling to respond, other states have an obligation to intervene to relieve the suffering.

Revolution According to Marxism, in any instance of class conflict a breakpoint is eventually reached when the workers take control from the capitalist owners. Revolution is the dominant mode of political change in the Marxist school.

Rhineland Crisis In March 1936, in clear violation of the Versailles settlement, Hitler ordered troops to reoccupy the Rhineland. The United Kingdom and France did not respond forcefully, allowing Hitler to continue to bully Europe.

Ruhr Crisis When Germany failed to meet its reparations payments in 1923, France occupied Germany's Ruhr valley. The Germans replied with work stoppages; the German government paid its workers simply by printing more paper money, and hyperinflation ensued.

Rum Triangle A transatlantic trading triangle active in the seventeenth and eighteenth centuries between Europe, West Africa, and the Americas.

Schlieffen Plan A German military plan believed by the Germans to be foolproof in which German forces undertake a massive sweep through Belgium and France and, after outflanking and destroying French forces, then turn east and destroy the Russian army.

Scramble for Africa The carving up of Africa by colonial powers after 1870.

Secessionist civil war A civil war in which the rebel group seeks to bring about the breaking away of a part of the territory of a country to form a new, separate state.

Second-strike capability The ability and will to inflict unacceptable damage on an adversary – even after the adversary hits first with its best nuclear attack. Also known as **assured destruction**.

Security dilemma A situation in which a state takes actions to become more secure yet ends up becoming less secure due to the reaction it provokes in other states.

Self-determination The idea that every people should determine and manage their own political systems. Self-determination was a popular idea among colonized people fighting for independence and decolonization.

Sensitivity A state is sensitive to another state's actions if those actions can temporarily hamper a state until it finds a replacement for the good or service from another location.

Shanghai Cooperation Organization (SCO) An agreement among Russia, China, and the central Asian states of Uzbekistan, Tajikistan, Kazakhstan, and Kyrgyzstan formed in 2001 to enhance the security of member states against threats of terrorism and ethnic conflict.

Smoot-Hawley Tariff A 1930 US law that raised tariffs to high levels to protect the US economy. The act had disastrous consequences and contributed to the Great Depression in the United States.

Socioeconomic classes Groupings of peoples based on their relationship to the economy.

Soft balancing Steps to constrain or hobble a great power (such as the United States today) that fall well short of the significant mobilization of military power in opposition to that power or the formation of security alliances united against the power.

Sovereignty The effective and recognized capacity to govern residents within a given territory and an ability to establish relationships with governments that control other states.

Sphere of influence A geographic-political space, consisting of one or more countries, whose foreign and domestic policies and political institutions are greatly influenced by an external power.

Stabilization program A contract between the IMF and a loan-recipient country stipulating what macroeconomic policy changes the country will undertake to ensure that its short-term foreign exchange shortfall does not become permanent.

State A political entity with two key features a piece of territory with reasonably well-defined borders, and political authorities who enjoy sovereignty.

Statecraft The use of policy instruments, including military force, economic sanctions or incentives, or diplomacy to achieve foreign policy objectives.

State-owned enterprises (SOEs) Companies owned directly by the government of a state.

Statutory international law Written laws that are agreed upon and codified by participating states.

Strategic culture Refers to assumptions about the nature of the global system – for example, which states are friends and enemies – and strategies of action that are shared by government elites.

Strategy The overarching connection of means to an end for a state. A strategy aims at a policy objective, and outlines what policy instruments will be used to attain that objective.

Structural adjustment program (SAP) Agreement between the IMF and the recipient government on how it will change its microeconomic policies, that is, what efforts it will undertake to introduce stronger market forces by liberalizing the country's economy, and by strengthening its regulatory frameworks in finance and other sectors.

Submarine-launched ballistic missile (SLBM) Missile that can produce much the same effect as an intercontinental ballistic missile (ICBM) from a platform deep beneath the ocean's surface.

Supply curve A curve specifying how much producers are willing to offer of a good at different prices. Along with demand curves, supply curves can show the likely price of goods, including currencies, in international markets.

Sustainable Development Goals (SDGs) World leaders in 2015 agreed to a new Agenda for Sustainable Development, with goals regarding poverty, gender equality, and environmental protection.

Taboo A strong and widely held normative condemnation against some form of behavior; in constructivist international relations theory.

Tariff A tax collected by the government on goods coming into the country.

Terms of trade The rate at which goods will be exchanged between two states.

Territorial Sea From customary international law, codified now in the LOS treaty, the area that extends 12 nautical miles from a state's shoreline, and within which the coastal state, with only a few exceptions, has nearly complete sovereignty.

Theory A group of ideas intended to explain some empirical phenomenon.

Thermal effect The secondary effect of a nuclear explosion, in which the heat waves from the explosion can cause third-degree burns up to five miles from the detonation site.

Thermonuclear bomb A type of nuclear weapon, even more powerful than a conventional nuclear weapon, that relies on the power of a contained fission explosion to trigger the fusing of hydrogen particles, a process that yields even greater amounts of destructive energy than a fission reaction alone. Also known as a **fusion** bomb.

Tied aid A practice in which donor governments require that the funds they give to a recipient country must be used to purchase goods and services provided by firms from the donor country.

Total war War in which belligerent states mobilize all resources and target civilians as part of their war strategy.

Tragedy of the commons A situation in which individual actors acting in their own rational self-interest combine to create a situation catastrophic to all of the individuals.

Transit passage Concept originally in customary international law and now stipulated in the LOS treaty according to which vessels from a sea-faring state may move through a strait that connects two bodies of the high seas or two EEZs even if such transit requires movement through the territorial seas of a coastal state.

Transnational business Businesses that operate across state lines.

Transnationalism The tendency of groups within countries to build cooperative associations with groups in other countries.

Treaty A formal agreement between two or more states designed to settle a dispute or set down guidelines for future action.

Triple Alliance A military alliance finalized in 1882 between Germany, Austria-Hungary, and Italy sought and signed by Germany to isolate France.

Triple Entente A military alliance finalized in 1907 between France, the United Kingdom, and Russia, forming the other pole (countering the Triple Alliance) that divided early twentieth-century Europe.

Truman Doctrine The declaration by Harry Truman that US assistance would be given to 'free peoples everywhere facing external aggression or internal subversion.' Truman declared this pledge in response to perceived Soviet designs on Greece and Turkey.

Truth and Reconciliation Commissions Public hearings about humanitarian crimes, such as in South Africa after *apartheid*.

Unacceptable damage The level of damage that a state is absolutely unwilling to sustain.

Underlying cause of a military conflict The set of circumstances that made escalation to the threat or use of military force possible or even inevitable.

United Nations An international organization, that today includes virtually all countries, founded in 1945 to increase political and economic cooperation among its members.

Unmanned Aerial Vehicles (UAVs) More commonly drones, are pilotless vehicles that can be operated and targeted by remote control.

Uranium Along with plutonium, one of two materials that can be used to create a nuclear weapon. Unlike plutonium, uranium can be found in nature, but is not suitable in that form (U-238) for nuclear weapon use. It needs to be highly enriched in a sophisticated technical facility to produce the concentrated uranium (U-235) that can sustain a chain reaction.

Veto player A person or organization within a political system whose consent is required for some policy to be accepted and implemented. There are typically more veto players in democracies than in non-democracies.

Vulnerability A state is vulnerable to another state's actions if it is unable to compensate effectively for losses caused by the other state's actions.

Warlords Private authority figures who control their own local armies or militias.

Warsaw Pact An alliance between the Soviet Union and several mid-level powers in Europe. The Warsaw Pact formed a Soviet sphere of influence in much the same way that NATO formed an American one.

Washington Consensus Controversial US-backed free-market policies set forth by the IMF as the necessary path to prosperity from the 1980s until the Great Recession of 2008–10, when the Consensus began to be widely questioned.

Weak states States with functioning central governments but only weak control over their territory and borders.

Weimar Republic Republic formed by democratically elected German delegates in the aftermath of World War I to replace the old imperial system.

Westphalian state system The modern state system in which each state is sovereign, with no higher authority (such as a church or empire).

World Bank The International Bank for Reconstruction and Development, initially created to provide loans to countries to help them with economic recovery from World War II, today finances and manages projects to foster the economic growth of developing countries.

World Trade Organization (WTO) Since 1995 the successor body to the GATT, with more explicit rules and guidelines than the GATT and a more highly developed mechanism for resolving trade disputes.

Zone of peace The number of democratic countries and the geographic space they possess within which states do not want to use military force or believe it will be used against them, in keeping with the democratic peace theory.

References

Acemoglu, Daron and James Robinson (2012) *Why Nations Fail: The Origins of Power, Prosperity, and Poverty*. New York: Crown Business.

Acemoglu, Daron, Simon Johnson, and James Robinson (2002) 'Reversal of Fortune: Geography and Institutions in the Making of the Modern World Income Distribution,' *Quarterly Journal of Economics* 117 (4): 1231–94.

Acheson, Dean (1945) 'Bretton Woods: A Monetary Basis for Trade,' Address before Economic Club of New York, April 16.

Albrecht-Carrie, Rene (1968) *The Concert of Europe: 1815–1914*. New York: Harper and Row.

Allison, Graham (1971) *Essence of Decision*. Boston: Little, Brown.

Allison, Graham (2004) *Nuclear Terrorism: The Ultimate Preventable Catastrophe*. New York: Times Books.

Allison, Graham and Philip Zelikow (1999) *Essence of Decision: Explaining the Cuban Missile Crisis*, second edition. New York: Longman.

Amery, Hussein (1997) 'Water Security as a Factor in Arab-Israeli Wars and Emerging Peace,' *Studies in Conflict & Terrorism* 20 (1): 95–104.

Anderson, Perry (1962) 'Portugal and the End of Ultra-Colonialism 2,' *New Left Review* 1 (12): 88–123.

Andresen, Steinar (2002) 'The International Whaling Commission (IWC): More Failure than Success,' in Edward L. Miles, Arild Underdal, Steinar Andresen, Jorgen Wettestad, Jon Skjaerseth, and Elaine Carlin (eds), *Environmental Regime Effectiveness: Confronting Theory with Evidence*. Cambridge: MIT Press: 379–403.

Art, Robert J. and Patrick Cronin (eds) (2003) *The United States and Coercive Diplomacy*. Washington, DC: United States Institute of Peace.

Asal, Victor and Kyle Beardsley (2009) 'Winning with the Bomb: The Advantages of Being a Nuclear Power,' *Journal of Conflict Resolution* 53 (2): 278–301.

Auboin, Marc and Floriana Borino (2017) 'The Falling Elasticity of Global Trade to Economic Activity: Testing the Demand Channel,' World Trade Organization Working Paper ERSD-2017-09, accessed at https://www.econstor.eu/bitstream/10419/157264/1/884588238.pdf.

Baggs, Jen (2009) 'International Trade in Hazardous Waste,' *Review of International Economics* 17 (1): 1–16.

Baker III, James A. (1995) *The Politics of Diplomacy: Revolution, War, & Peace, 1989–1992*. New York: Putnam.

Baldwin, David (ed.) (1993) *Neorealism and Neoliberalism: The Contemporary Debate*. New York: Columbia University Press.

Barkin, J. Samuel and George E. Shambaugh (1999) 'Hypotheses on the International Politics of Common Pool Resources,' in Barkin and Shambaugh (eds) *Anarchy and the Environment: The International Relations of Common Pool Resources*. Albany: SUNY Press: 1–21.

BBC News (2013) 'Timeline: Siege of Srebrenica,' accessed at http://www.bbc.co.uk/news/have_your_say/.

Bell, P.M.H. (2007) *The Origins of the Second World War in Europe*, third edition. Harlow: Pearson.

Berinsky, Adam J. and Donald R. Kinder (2006) 'Making Sense of Issues Through Media Frames: Understanding the Kosovo Crisis,' *Journal of Politics* 68: 640–56.

Betsill, Michele and Elisabeth Corell (2001) 'NGO Influence in International Environmental Negotiations: A Framework for Analysis,' *Global Environmental Politics* 1 (4): 65–85.

Bevin, Ernest (1948) Speech before House of Commons, col. 407–8, January 22.

Black, Jeremy (2010) *A History of Diplomacy.* London: Reaktion Books.

Blainey, Geoffrey (1988) *The Causes of War*, third edition. New York: Free Press.

Blanchard, Jean Marc F. and Norrin M. Ripsman (1996/97), 'Commercial Liberalism Under Fire: Evidence from 1914 and 1936,' *Security Studies* 6 (2): 4–50.

Bloom, Mia (2005) *Dying to Kill: The Allure of Suicide Terror.* New York: Columbia University Press.

Borrell, Brendan (2009) 'Biofuel Showdown: Should Domestic Ethanol Producers Pay for Deforestation Abroad?' *Scientific American.com*, accessed at http://www.scientificamerican.com/article.cfm?id=biofuel-showdown.

Bosco, David (2017) *Rough Justice: The International Criminal Court in a World of Power Politics.* New York: Oxford University Press.

Bradsher, Keith (2010) 'Amid Tension, China Blocks Vital Exports to Japan,' *New York Times*, September 23.

Braithwaite, Alex (2010) 'Resisting Infection: How State Capacity Conditions Conflict Contagion,' *Journal of Peace Research* 47 (3): 311–19.

Brodie, Bernard (1946) *The Absolute Weapon.* New York: Harcourt Brace.

Brooks, Stephen G. (2005) *Producing Security: Multinational Corporations, Globalization, and the Changing Calculus of Conflict.* Princeton: Princeton University Press.

Brown, Chris (2002) *Sovereignty, Rights and Justice: International Political Theory Today.* Cambridge: Polity Press.

Brown, Ken (1994) 'Word for Word: Fernando Henrique Cardoso: Having Left Campus for the Arena, Winner in Brazil Shifts to Right,' *New York Times*, November 20.

Brzezinski, Zbigniew (1986) *Game Plan: A Geostrategic Framework for the Conduct of the US-Soviet Contest.* Boston: Atlantic Monthly Press.

Buckley, Chris (2017) 'These Seven Men Now Run China,' *New York Times*, October 25.

Bueno de Mesquita, Bruce, Alastair Smith, Randolph Siverson, and James Morrow (2003) *The Logic of Political Survival.* Cambridge: MIT Press.

Buhaug, Halvard and Kristian Gleditsch (2008) 'Contagion or Confusion? Why Conflicts Cluster in Space,' *International Studies Quarterly* 52 (2): 215–33.

Buhaug, Halvard, Nils Gleditsch and Ole Theisen (2008) 'Implications of Climate Change for Armed Conflict,' prepared for the World Bank Group, accessed at http://siteresources.worldbank.org/INTRANETSOCIALDEVELOPMENT/Resources/SDCCWorking Paper_Conflict.pdf.

Buitenzorgy, Meilanie and Arthur Mol (2011) 'Does Democracy Lead to a Better Environment? Deforestation and the Democratic Transition Peak,' *Environmental and Resource Economics* 48 (1): 59–70.

Bull, Hedley (1977) *The Anarchical Society: A Study of Order in World Politics.* New York: Columbia University Press.

Bull, Hedley and Adam Watson (eds) (1985) *The Expansion of International Society.* Oxford: Oxford University Press.

Burr, William (ed.) (2007) *The Atomic Bomb and the End of World War II: A Collection of Primary Sources.* National Security Archive Electronic Briefing Book No. 162, April 27, accessed at www.gwu.edu/nsarchive.

Bush, George W. (1991) Address to the 46th Session of the United Nations General Assembly in New York City, September 23, accessed at http://www.presidency.ucsb.edu/ws/index.php?pid=20012.

Bush, George W. (2003) 'Bush: Leave Iraq within 48 Hours,' March 17, accessed at http://www.cnn.com/2003/WORLD/meast/03/17/sprj.irq.bush.transcript/.

Bush, George W. (2003) Address before the United Nations General Assembly, September 23, accessed at http://www.whitehouse.gov/news/releases/2003/09/20030923-4.html.

Bush, President George W. (2005) Second Inaugural Address, January 20, accessed at https://www.npr.org/templates/story/story.php?storyId=4460172.

Bussmann, Margrit (2010) 'Foreign Direct Investment and Militarized International Conflict,' *Journal of Peace Research* 47 (2): 143–53.

Buzan, Barry (2004) *From International to World Society?* Cambridge: Cambridge University Press.

Caldwell, Leigh Ann (2013) 'Obama may have won now, but next three years could be tough,' CNN, October 18.

Canadian Broadcasting Company (1969) 'Trudeau's Washington Press Club Speech,' CBC Digital Archives, March 29.

Caprioli, Mary and Mark Boyer (2001) 'Gender, Violence, and International Crisis,' *Journal of Conflict Resolution* 45 (4): 503–18.

Cardoso, Fernando and Enzo Faletto (1979) *Dependency and Development in Latin America.* Berkeley: University of California Press.

Carr, Edward Hallett [1939] (1964) *The Twenty Years' Crisis, 1919–1939: An Introduction to the Study of International Relations.* Reprint, New York: Harper and Row.

Cederman, Lars-Erik, Andreas Wimmer, and Brian Min (2010) 'Why Do Ethnic Groups Rebel? New Data and Analysis,' *World Politics* 62 (1): 87–119.

Chapman, Terrence and Dan Reiter (2004) 'The United Nations Security Council and the Rally 'Round the Flag Effect,' *Journal of Conflict Resolution* 48 (December): 886–909.

Cheney, Dick (2002) 'Vice President Cheney's Speech to the Veterans of Foreign Wars,' August 26, accessed at http://www.newamericancentury.org/iraq-082602.htm.

Chimni, B.S. (1993) *International Law and World Order: A Critique of Contemporary Approaches.* New York: Sage Publications.

Chiozza, Giacomo and Hein Goemans (2011) *Leaders and International Conflict.* Cambridge: Cambridge University Press.

Christoff, Peter (2016) 'The Promissory Note: COP 21 and the Paris Climate Agreement,' *Environmental Politics* 25 (5): 765–87.

Clark, Christopher (2012) *The Sleepwalkers: How Europe Went to War in 1914.* New York: Harper Collins.

Clark, Duncan (2012) 'Has the Kyoto Protocol Made Any Difference to Carbon Emissions?' *The Guardian*, November 26.

Clark, William (2005) *Petrodollar Warfare: Oil, Iraq, and the Future of the Dollar.* Gabriola Island, Canada: New Society Publishers.

Clarke, Harold, Matthew Goodwin, and Paul Whiteley (2017) *Brexit: Why Britain Voted to Leave the European Union.* Cambridge: Cambridge University Press.

Claude Jr, Inis L. (1956) *From Swords into Ploughshares: The Problems and Process of International Organization.* New York: Random House.

Clemencon, Raymond (2006) 'What Future for the Global Environmental Facility,' *Journal of Environment and Development* 15 (1): 50–74.

Clinton, Hillary (2009) 'Remarks on the Human Rights Agenda for the 21st Century,' address at Georgetown University, December 14.

Clinton, President Bill (1994) State of the Union Address, January 25, accessed at http://www.let.rug.nl/usa/presidents/william-jefferson-clinton/state-of-the-union-1994-(prepared-version).php.

Colgan, Jeff (2010) 'Oil and Revolutionary Governments: Fuel for International Conflict,' *International Organization* 64 (4): 661–94.

Colgan, Jeff (2012) *Petro-Aggression: When Oil Causes War.* Cambridge: Cambridge University Press.

Colgan, Jeffrey (2013) *Petro-Aggression: When Oil Causes War.* Cambridge: Cambridge University Press.

Collier, Paul (2007) *The Bottom Billion: Why the Poorest Countries are Failing and What Can be Done About It.* Oxford: Oxford University Press.

Collier, Paul, Anke Hoeffler, and Dominic Rohner (2009) 'Beyond Greed and Grievance: Feasibility and Civil War,' *Oxford Economic Papers* 61 (1):1–27.

Commager, Henry Steele (ed.) (1949) *Documents of American History*, fifth edition. New York: Appleton-Century-Crofts.

Constantinescu, Cristina, Aaditya Mattoo, and Michele Ruta (2014) 'Slow Trade,' *Finance and Development*, accessed at http://www.imf.org/external/pubs/ft/fandd/2014/12/pdf/constant.pdf.

Cooley, John (1984) 'The War Over Water,' *Foreign Policy* 54 (Spring): 3–26.

Cooper, Robert (2003) *The Breaking of Nations: Order and Chaos in the 21st Century.* New York: Atlantic Monthly Press.

Costello, Sam (2017) 'Where is the iPhone Made?' *Lifewire*, March 13, accessed at https://www.lifewire.com/where-is-the-iphone-made-1999503.

Council of the European Union (2012) *Human Rights and Democracy: EU Strategic Framework and EU Action Plan*. Brussels, Belgium, June 25, accessed at http://data.consilium.europa.eu/doc/document/ST-11855-2012-INIT/en/pdf.

Cox, Robert (1981) 'Social Forces, States and World Order: Beyond International Relations Theory', *Millennium: Journal of International Studies* 10 (2): 126–55.

Cox, Robert and Timothy J. Sinclair (1996) *Approaches to World Order*. Cambridge: Cambridge University Press.

Cox, Robert W. (1987) *Production Power and World Order: Social Forces in the Making of History*. New York: Columbia University Press.

Crowley, Roger (2005) *1453: The Holy War for Constantinople and the Clash of Islam and the West*. New York: Hyperion.

Crowley, Roger (2008) *Empire of the Sea: The Siege of Malta, the Battle of Lepanto, and the Contest for the Center of the World*. New York: Random House.

Cull, Robert and Jonathan Morduch (2017). 'Microfinance and Economic Development', Washington: *World Bank Policy Research Working Paper No. 8252*, accessed at https://papers.ssrn.com/sol3/papers.cfm?abstract_id=3076231.

Dao, James and Dalia Sussman (2011) 'For Obama, Big Rise in Poll Numbers after Bin Laden Raid', *New York Times*, May 4.

de Carvalho, Benjamin, Halvard Leira, and John Hobson (2011) 'The Big Bangs of IR: The Myths That Your Teachers Still Tell You about 1648 and 1919', *Millennium: Journal of International Studies* 39 (3): 735–58.

Dean, Cornelia (2006) 'Study Sees "Global Collapse" of Fish Species', *New York Times*, November 3.

Dehio, Ludwig (1962) *The Precarious Balance: Four Centuries of the European Power Struggle*. New York: Knopf.

Diamond, Jared (1999) *Guns, Germs, and Steel: The Fates of Human Societies*. New York: W.W. Norton.

Dos Santos, Theotonio (1970) 'The Structure of Dependence', *American Economic Review* 60 (2): 231–6.

Downes, Alexander (2008) *Targeting Civilians in War*. Ithaca: Cornell University Press.

Downs, George, David Rocke, and Peter Barsoom (1996) 'Is the Good News about Compliance Good News about Cooperation', *International Organization* 50 (3): 379–406.

Doyle, Alexander (2009) 'Europeans Over-Fishing Began 1000 Years Ago: Report', Reuters, May 24, accessed at https://uk.reuters.com/article/uk-oceans/european-over-fishing-began-1000-years-ago-idUKTRE54N1Q520090524.

Doyle, Michael (1983a) 'Kant, Liberal Legacies, and Foreign Affairs, Part 1', *Philosophy and Public Affairs* 12 (3): 205–35.

Doyle, Michael (1983b) 'Kant, Liberal Legacies, and Foreign Affairs, Part 2', *Philosophy and Public Affairs* 12 (4): 323–53.

Doyle, Michael (1997) *Ways of War, Ways of Peace: Realism, Liberalism, Socialism*. New York: Norton.

Doyle, Michael (2011) *Liberal Peace: Selected Essays*. New York: Routledge.

Drezner, Daniel (2009) 'Bad Debts: Assessing China's Financial Influence in Great Power Politics', *International Security* 34 (2): 7–45.

Dunbabin, John (2008) *The Cold War: The Great Powers and their Allies*, second edition. Harlow: Pearson.

Dunne, Timothy (1998) *Inventing International Society: A History of the English School*. New York: Palgrave Macmillan.

Dyson, Freeman (1985) 'On Russians and their Views of Nuclear Strategy', in Charles Kegley and Eugene Wittkopf (eds), *The Nuclear Reader*. New York: St. Martin's Press.

Earle, Edward Mead (1971) 'Adam Smith, Alexander Hamilton, Friedrich List: The Economic Foundations of Military Power', in Edward Mead Earle, *Makers of Modern Strategy*. Princeton: Princeton University Press: 117–54.

Easterly, William (2002a) 'The Cartel of Good Intentions', *Foreign Policy* 131 (July–August): 40–9

Easterly, William (2002b) *The Elusive Quest for Growth: Economists' Adventures and Misadventures in the Tropics*. Cambridge: MIT Press.

Easterly, William (2006) *The White Man's Burden: Why the West's Efforts to Aid the Rest Have Done So Much Ill and So Little Good*. New York: Penguin.

Easterly, William (2007) 'The Ideology of Development,' *Foreign Policy* 161: 30–5.

Economist, The (2013) 'Chasing the Chinese Dream,' May 4.

Economy, Elizabeth (2007) 'The Great Leap Backward?' *Foreign Affairs* (September–October): 98–113.

Eichengreen, Barry and David Leblang (2008) 'Democracy and Globalization,' *Economics and Politics* 20 (3): 289–334.

Eisenhower, Dwight (1961) 'Military-Industrial Complex Speech,' accessed at http://coursesa. matrix.msu.edu/~hst306/documents/indust.html.

Elshtain, Jean Bethke (1987) *Women and War.* New York: Basic Books.

Enemark, Christian (2006) 'Biological Attacks and the Non-State Actor,' *Intelligence and National Security* 21 (6): 911–30.

England, Andrew (2010) 'Al-Qaeda exploits failures of weak state,' *Financial Times,* January 3, accessed at https://www.ft.com/content/7f0db11c-f895-11de-beb8-00144feab49a.

Englebert, Pierre, Stacy Tarango, and Matthew Carter (2002) 'Dismemberment and Suffocation. A Contribution to the Debate on African Boundaries,' *Comparative Political Studies* 35 (10): 1093–118.

English, Robert (2005) 'The Sociology of New Thinking: Elites, Identity Change and the End of the Cold War,' *Journal of Cold War Studies* 7: 43–80.

Enloe, Cynthia (2014) *Bananas, Beaches, Bases: Making Feminist Sense of International Politics.* Berkeley: University of California Press, updated edition.

Entman, Robert (2004) *Projections of Power: Framing News, Public Opinion, and US Foreign Policy.* Chicago: University of Chicago Press.

Equitymaster (2017) 'Deglobalisation: The Answer to Inequality?', January 18, accessed at https://www.equitymaster.com/outsideview/detail.asp?date=01/18/2017&story=2&title=Deglobalisation-The-Answer-to-Inequality-Nitin-Gregory.

Eric Neumayer, (2005) 'Do International Human Rights Treaties Improve Respect for Human Rights?' *Journal of Conflict Resolution* 49 (6/December): 926–53.

Eskeland, Gunnar and Ann Harrison (2003) 'Moving to Greener Pastures? Multinationals and the Pollution Haven Hypothesis,' *Journal of Development Economics* 70 (1): 1–23.

Evans, Gareth (2009) *The Responsibility to Protect: Ending Mass Atrocity Crimes Once and For All.* Washington: The Brookings Institution Press.

Evans, Peter (2000) 'Fighting Marginalization with Transnational Networks: Counter-Hegemonic Globalization,' *Contemporary Sociology* 29 (1): 230–41.

E-World (1997) 'Albert Einstein's Letters to Franklin Delano Roosevelt,' accessed at www.hypertext-book.com/eworld.

Fairbanks, John K. (1992) *China: A New History,* with Merle Goldman, enlarged edition. Cambridge: Harvard University Press.

Fearon, James (1995) 'Rationalist Explanations for War,' *International Organization* 49 (3): 379–414.

Fearon, James and David Laitin (2003) 'Ethnicity, Insurgency, and Civil War,' *American Political Science Review* 97 (1): 75–90.

Feis, Herbert (1970) *From Trust to Terror: The Onset of the Cold War.* New York: W.W. Norton.

Ferguson, Niall (2004) *Empire: The Rise and Demise of the British World Order and the Lessons for Global Power.* New York: Basic Books.

Ferguson, Niall (2006) *The War of the World: Twentieth Century Conflict and the Descent of the West.* New York: Penguin.

Finnemore, Martha (2003) *The Purpose of Intervention: Changing Beliefs about the Use of Force.* Ithaca: Cornell University Press.

Finnemore, Martha (2008) 'Paradoxes in Humanitarian Intervention,' in Richard Price (ed.), *Moral Limit and Possibility in World Politics.* Cambridge: Cambridge University Press: 197–224.

Finnemore, Martha and Kathryn Sikkink (1998) 'International Norm Dynamics and Political Change,' *International Organization* 52 (4): 887–917.

Fisher, Max (2012) 'The Dividing of a Continent: Africa's Separatist Problem,' *The Atlantic,* September 10.

Fiske, Susan and Shelley Taylor (1984) *Social Cognition.* Reading, MA: Addison-Wesley.

Fitzmaurice, Malgosia (2014) 'The Practical Working of the Law of Treaties,' in Malcolm Evans (ed.), *International Law,* fourth edition. Oxford: Oxford University Press: 166–97.

Fortna, Virginia Page (2008) *Does Peacekeeping Work? Shaping Belligerents' Choices after Civil War.* Princeton: Princeton University Press.

Frank, Andre (1966) 'The Development of Underdevelopment,' *Monthly Review* 18: 17–31.

Frankel, Jeffrey (2016) *Globalization and Chinese Growth: Ends of Trends?* HKS Faculty Research Working Paper Series Number RWP16-029 (July), accessed at https://research.hks.harvard.edu/publications/workingpapers/citation.aspx?PubId=11326&type=WPN.

Frankel, Jeffrey A. (1997) *Regional Trading Blocs in the World Economic System.* Washington, DC: Institute for International Economics.

Freedman, Lawrence (2004) *Deterrence.* New York: Polity Press.

Freedom House (2008) *Freedom in the World 2008*, accessed at https://freedomhouse.org/report/freedom-world/freedom-world-2008.

Freedom House (2017a) 'Populists and Autocrats: The Dual Threat to Global Democracy,' Freedom in the World 2017, accessed at https://freedomhouse.org/report/freedom-world/freedom-world-2017.

Freedom House (2017b) *Freedom in the World 2017: South Africa Profile*, accessed at https://freedomhouse.org/report/freedom-world/2017/south-africa.

Friedberg, Aaron (2000) *In the Shadow of the Garrison State: America's Anti-Statism and its Cold War Grand Strategy.* Princeton: Princeton University Press.

Friedberg, Aaron (2011) *A Contest for Supremacy: China, America, and the Struggle for Mastery in Asia.* New York: Norton.

Frieden, Jeffry (2006) *Global Capitalism: Its Fall and Rise in the Twentieth Century.* New York: W.W. Norton.

Friedman, Thomas (1999) *The Lexus and the Olive Tree.* New York: Anchor Books.

Friedman, Thomas (2005) *The World is Flat: A Brief History of the Twenty-First Century.* New York: Farrar, Straus, Giroux.

Fukuyama, Francis (1992) *The End of History and the Last Man.* New York: Free Press.

Fukuyama, Francis (1998) 'Women and the Evolution of World Politics,' *Foreign Affairs* 77 (5): 24–40.

Gaddis, John Lewis (2006) *The Cold War: A New History.* New York: Penguin.

Galbraith, Jean (2003) 'The Bush Administration's Response to the International Criminal Court,' *Berkeley Journal of International Law* 683 (2003): 683–702, accessed at: http://scholarship.law.berkeley.edu/bjil/vol21/iss3/10.

Gallagher, Mary (2002) ' "Reform and Openness": Why China's Economic Reforms Have Delayed Democracy,' *World Politics* 54 (3): 338–72.

Gartzke, Erik (2007) 'The Capitalist Peace,' *American Journal of Political Science* 51 (1): 166–91.

Gartzke, Eric and Matthew Kroenig (2016) 'Nukes with Numbers: Empirical Research on the Consequences of Nuclear Weapons for International Conflict,' *Annual Review of Political Science* 19: 397–412.

Gartzke, Erik and Quan Li (2003) 'War, Peace, and the Invisible Hand: Positive Political Externalities of Economic Globalization,' *International Studies Quarterly* 47 (4): 561–86.

Gause, Gregory (2001) 'Iraq and the Gulf War: Decision-Making in Baghdad,' *Columbia International Affairs Online* October 1.

Geddes, Barbara (2003) *Paradigms and Sand Castles: Theory Building and Research Design in Comparative Politics.* Ann Arbor: University of Michigan Press.

Gelpi, Christopher, Peter Feaver, and Jason Reifler (2009) *Paying the Human Costs of War: American Public Opinion and Casualties in Military Conflicts.* Princeton: Princeton University Press.

George, Alexander and Robert Keohane (1980) 'The Concept of National Interest: Uses and Limitations,' in Alexander George (ed.), *Presidential Decision-Making in Foreign Policy: The Effective Use of Information and Advice.* Boulder: Westview Press.

German Marshall Fund of the United States (2013) *Transatlantic Trends: Key Findings 2013*, accessed at http://www.gmfus.org/publications/transatlantic-trends-2013.

Gettleman, Jeffrey (2012) 'US Swoops in to Free 2 from Pirates in Somali Raid,' *New York Times*, January 25.

Ghani, Ashraf and Clare Lockhart (2008) *Fixing Failed States: A Framework for Rebuilding a Fractured World.* New York: Oxford University Press.

Ghosn, Faten, Glenn Palmer, and Stuart Bremer (2004) 'The MID3 Data Set, 1993–2001: Procedures, Coding Rules, and Description,' *Conflict Management and Peace Science* 21 (2): 133–54.

Gibbon, Edward (1996) *The History of the Decline and Fall of the Roman Empire.* London: Penguin.

Gilbert, Christopher (2004) 'International Commodity Agreements as Internationally Sanctioned Cartels,' in Peter Grossman (ed.), *How Cartels Endure and How They Fail: Studies in Industrial Collusion*. Cheltenham: Edward Elgar: 224–52.

Gill, Stephen (1992) *American Hegemony and the Trilateral Commission*. Cambridge: Cambridge University Press.

Gilpin, Robert (1975) *US Power and the Multinational Corporation: The Political Economy of Foreign Direct Investment*. New York: Basic Books.

Gilpin, Robert (1981) *War and Change in World Politics*. Cambridge: Cambridge University Press.

Gilpin, Robert (1987) *The Political Economy of International Relations*. Princeton: Princeton University Press.

Gilpin, Robert (2000) *The Challenge of Global Capitalism* (Princeton: Princeton University Press).

Gleditsch, Nils Petter, Kathryn Furlong, Havard Hegre, Bethany Lacina, and Taylor Owen (2006) 'Conflicts over Shared Rivers: Resource Scarcity or Fuzzy Boundaries?' *Political Geography* 25 (4): 361–82.

Glendon, Mary Ann (2001) *A World Made New: Eleanor Roosevelt and the Universal Declaration of Human Rights*. New York: Random House.

GlobalSecurity.org (undated) 'US Casualties in Iraq,' accessed at http://www.globalsecurity.org/military/ops/iraq_casualties.html.

Globe and Mail (2018) 'Forex – Major Rates,' May 30, accessed at https://www.theglobeandmail.com/investing/markets/currencies/.

Goldstein, Avery (2005) *Rising to the Challenge: China's Grand Strategy and International Security*. Stanford: Stanford University Press.

Goldstein, Joshua S. (2001) *War and Gender: How Gender Shapes the War System and Vice Versa*. New York: Cambridge University Press.

Goldstein, Judith, Miles Kahler, Robert Keohane, and Anne-Marie Slaughter (2000) *Legalization and World Politics: Special Issue of International Organization*. Boston: MIT Press.

Gollus, David (2009) 'US, India Clash Over Climate Change Remedies,' VOA News.com, July 19.

Gorgemans, Andre (2008) 'Addressing Child Labor: An Industry Approach,' posted August 1 on America.gov and accessed at http://www.america.gov/st/hr-english/2008/August/20080818091032SrenoD0.390423.html.

Government of India, Press Information Bureau (2009) 'India Seeks Cooperation from America in Research Projects, Environment Planning, and Building Institutional Capacities,' July 19, Release ID 50585, accessed through search of Press Bureau online depository at http://pib.nic.in/newsite/erelease.aspx?relid.

Graham, Edward (2000) *Fighting the Wrong Enemy: Antiglobal Activists and Multinational Enterprises*. Washington: Institute for International Economics.

Graham, Ian C.C. (1964) 'The Indo-Soviet MIG Deal and Its International Repercussions,' *Asian Survey* 4 (May): 826.

Gray, Christine (2008) *International Law and the Use of Force*, third edition. Oxford: Oxford University Press.

Gray, Christine (2014) 'The Use of Force and the International Legal Order,' in Malcolm Evans (ed.), *International Law*, fourth edition. Oxford: Oxford University Press: 618–48.

Gray, Colin (1979) 'Nuclear Strategy: The Case for a Theory of Victory,' *International Security* 4 (Summer): 54–87.

Grieco, Joseph, Christopher Gelpi, Jason Reifler, and Peter Feaver (2011) 'Let's Get a Second Opinion,' *International Studies Quarterly* 55 (June): 563–83.

Guardian, The (2012) 'German tax collectors volunteer for Greek Duty,' February 26.

Guardian, The (2013) 'Syria Crisis: David Cameron Still Wants "Robust" Response,' August 30.

Guicherd, Catherine (1999) 'International Law and the War in Kosovo,' *Survival* 41 (2): 19–34.

Gurowitz, Amy (2004) 'International Law, Politics, and Migrant Rights,' in Christian Reus-Smit (ed.), *The Politics of International Law*. Cambridge: Cambridge University Press: 131–50.

Gurr, Ted Robert (1994) 'Peoples Against the State: Ethnopolitical Conflict and the Changing World System,' *International Studies Quarterly* 38: 347–7.

Gutner, Tamar (2005) 'World Bank Environmental Reform: Revisiting Lessons from Agency Theory,' *International Organization* 59 (3): 773–83.

Haas, Peter (1992) 'Banning Chlorofluorocarbons: Epistemic Community Efforts to Protect Stratospheric Ozone,' *International Organization* 46 (1): 187–224.

Haas, Peter (2004) 'When Does Power Listen to Truth? A Constructivist Approach to the Policy Process,' *Journal of European Public Policy* 11 (4): 569–92.

Haass, Richard (2003) 'Sovereignty: Existing Rights, Evolving Responsibilities,' lecture at Georgetown University, January 14.

Haggard, Stephan (1990) *Pathways From the Periphery: The Politics of Growth in the Newly-Industrializing Countries.* Ithaca, NY: Cornell University Press.

Haggard, Stephan (2000) *The Political Economy of the Asian Financial Crisis.* Washington, DC: Institute for International Economics.

Hahn, Juergen (2012) 'Ship Piracy Evolve in East, West Africa,' *Breakbulk Magazine,* May 14, accessed at http://www.breakbulk.com/commentary/ship-piracy-evolves-east-west-africa

Halle, Louis (1991) *The Cold War as History.* New York: Harper Perennial.

Hampton, Mary N. (1995) 'NATO at the Creation: US Foreign Policy, West Germany, and the Wilsonian Impulse,' *Security Studies* 4 (3): 610–56.

Hampton, Mary N. (1996) *The Wilsonian Impulse: US Foreign Policy, the Alliance, and the Reunification of Germany.* New York: Praeger Publishers.

Hardin, Garrett (1968) 'The Tragedy of the Commons,' *Science* 162 (3589): 1243–8.

Harmon, Chris (2009) *Zombie Capitalism: Global Crisis and the Return of Marx.* London: Bookmarks.

Harnden, Toby (2011) 'US Secretly Shifts Armed Drones to Fight Terrorists in Pakistan,' *The Telegraph,* July 7.

Hassner, Pierre (1993) 'Beyond Nationalism and Internationalism: Ethnicity and World Order,' in Michael Brown (ed.), *Ethnic Conflict and International Security.* Princeton, Princeton University Press: 125–41.

Helleiner, Eric and Andreas Pickel (eds) (2005) *Economic Nationalism in a Globalizing World.* Ithaca: Cornell University Press.

Visato.com (2012) 'Henley Visa Restriction Index for Top 100 Countries in 2012,' accessed at http://news.visato.com/visit-visa-2/henley-visa-restriction-index-for-top-100-countries-in-2012/20120905.

Herz, John (1950) 'Idealist Internationalism and the Security Dilemma,' *World Politics* 2 (2): 157–80.

Hirschman, Albert (1980) *National Power and the Structure of Foreign Trade.* Berkeley: University of California Press.

Holmes, Kim (2014) 'The Weakness of the Responsibility to Protect as an International Norm,' *Heritage Foundation*, January 7, accessed at http://www.heritage.org/defense/commentary/the-weakness-the-responsibility-protect-international-norm.

Holsti, Kalevi J. (1991) *Peace and War: Armed Conflicts and International Order, 1648–1989.* New York: Cambridge University Press.

Holsti, Ole (1972) *Crisis, Escalation, War.* Montreal: McGill-Queen's.

Holsti, Ole (2004) *Public Opinion and American Foreign Policy.* Ann Arbor: University of Michigan Press.

Homer-Dixon, Thomas (2007) 'Terror in the Forecast,' *New York Times*, April 24, accessed at http://www.nytimes.com/2007/04/24/opinion/24homer-dixon.html.

Hsu, Spencer (2006) 'Katrina Report Spreads Blame,' *Washington Post*, February 12.

Hudson, Valerie M., Donna Lee Bowen, and Perpetua Lynne Nielsen (2015) 'Clan Governance and State Stability: The Relationship between Female Subordination and Political Order,' *American Political Science Review* 109 (3/August): 535–55.

Hudson, Valerie M., Bonnie Ballif-Spanvill, Mary Caprioli, and Chad F. Emmett (2014) *Sex and World Peace*, revised edition. New York: Columbia University Press.

Hudson, Valerie, Mary Caprioli, Bonnie Ballif-Spanvill, Rose McDermott, and Chad Emmett (2008/2009) 'The Heart of the Matter: the Security of Women and the Security of States,' *International Security* 33 (3): 7–40.

Hufbauer, Gary Clyde, Jeffrey J. Schott, Kimberly Ann Elliott, and Barbara Oegg (2009) *Economic Sanctions Reconsidered*, third edition. Washington: Peterson Institute for International Economics.

Hull, Cordell (1938) 'The Outlook for the Trade Agreements Program,' speech delivered before the 25th National Foreign Trade Convention, New York City, November 1.

Huntington, Samuel (1993) 'The Clash of Civilizations?' *Foreign Affairs* 72 (3/Summer): 22–49.

Huntington, Samuel (1996) *The Clash of Civilizations and the Remaking of World Order.* New York: Touchstone.

Hurwitz, Jon and Mark Peffley (1987) 'The Means and Ends of Foreign Policy as Determinants of Presidential Support,' *American Journal of Political Science* 31: 236–58.

Ikenberry, G. John (2001) *After Victory: Institutions, Strategic Restraint, and the Rebuilding of Order after Major Wars.* Princeton: Princeton University Press.

Ikenberry, G. John (2011) *Liberal Leviathan: The Origins, Crisis, and Transformation of the American World Order.* Princeton University Press.

Ikenberry, G. John, Michael Mastanduno, and William Wohlforth (eds) (2011) *International Relations Theory and the Consequences of Unipolarity.* Cambridge: Cambridge University Press.

Intergovernmental Panel on Climate Change (2007) *Climate Change 2007: Synthesis Report,* accessed at http://www.ipcc.ch/pdf/assessment-report/ar4/syr/ar4_syr.pdf.

International Monetary Fund (1976) 'International Monetary Fund, Annual Report, 1976,' accessed at https://www.imf.org/external/pubs/ft/ar/archive/pdf/ar1976.pdf: 43-46.

International Monetary Fund (2008) *World Economic Outlook* database for real GDP, April 2008, accessed at https://www.imf.org/external/pubs/ft/weo/2008/01/weodata/index.aspx.

International Monetary Fund (2018) 'IMF Members' Quotas and Voting Power, and IMF Board of Governors,' March 18, accessed at http://www.imf.org/external/np/sec/memdir/members.aspx.

Iriye, Akira (1987) *The Origins of the Second World War in Asia and the Pacific.* Harlow: Pearson.

Irwin, Douglas (2011) *Peddling Protectionism: Smoot-Hawley and the Great Depression.* Princeton: Princeton University Press.

Jackson, Patrick Thaddeus (2003) 'Defending the West: Occidentalism and the Formation of NATO,' *Journal of Political Philosophy* 11 (3): 241.

Jackson, Patrick Thaddeus (2006) *Civilizing the Enemy: German Reconstruction and the Invention of the West.* Ann Arbor: University of Michigan Press.

Janis, Irving (1982) *Groupthink: Psychological Studies of Policy Decisions and Fiascoes.* Boston: Houghton Mifflin Company.

Jentleson, Bruce W. (2010) *American Foreign Policy: The Dynamics of Choice in the 21st Century,* fourth edition. New York: Norton.

Jervis, Robert (1978) 'Cooperation Under the Security Dilemma,' *World Politics* 30: 167–214.

Jervis, Robert (1984) *The Illogic of American Nuclear Strategy.* Ithaca: Cornell University Press.

Jervis, Robert (1985) 'The Madness beyond MAD,' in Charles Kegley and Eugene Wittkopf (eds), *The Nuclear Reader.* New York: St. Martin's Press.

Jervis, Robert (1988) 'War and Misperception,' *Journal of Interdisciplinary History* 18 (4): 675–700.

Jervis, Robert (1989a) *Pyschology and Deterrence.* Baltimore: Johns Hopkins University Press.

Jervis, Robert (1989b) *The Meaning of the Nuclear Revolution.* Ithaca: Cornell University Press.

Jervis, Robert (2001) 'Was the Cold War a Security Dilemma?' *Journal of Cold War Studies,* 3 (1): 36–60.

Jervis, Robert (2006) 'Understanding Beliefs,' *Political Psychology* 27: 641–63.

Jervis, Robert (2009) 'Unipolarity: A Structural Perspective,' *World Politics* 61 (1):188–213.

Johansson, Å. *et al.* (2012) 'Looking to 2060: Long-Term Global Growth Prospects: A Going for Growth Report,' OECD Economic Policy Papers, No. 3, OECD Publishing, accessed at doi: 10.1787/5k8zxpjsggf0-en.

Johansson, Å. *et al.* (2013) 'Long-Term Growth Scenarios,' OECD Economics Department Working Papers, No. 1000, OECD Publishing, accessed at http://dx.doi.org/10.1787/5k4ddxpr2fmr-en

Johnson, Dominic (2004) *Overconfidence and War: The Havoc and Glory of Positive Illusions.* Cambridge: Harvard University Press.

Johnson, Dominic D.P. (2006) 'Overconfidence in Wargames: Experimental Evidence on Expectations, Aggression, Gender and Testosterone,' *Proceedings of the Royal Society* 273: 2512–20.

Johnson, Dominic, Rose McDermott, Emily Barrett, Jonathan Cowden, Richard Wrangham, Matthew McIntyre, and Stephen Rosen (2006) 'Overconfidence in Wargames: Experimental Evidence on Expectations, Aggression, Gender and Testosterone,' *Proceedings of the Royal Society* 273 (1600): 2513–20.

Johnson, Lyndon Baines (1965) 'Statement by President Johnson at White House News Conference on July 28, 1965: We Will Stand in Viet-Nam,' *Department of State Bulletin*, August 16, accessed at http://www.mtholyoke.edu/acad/intrel/pentagon4/ps2.htm.

Johnson, Simon and James Kwak (2010) *13 Bankers: The Wall Street Takeover and the Next Financial Crisis*. New York: Pantheon Books.

Johnston, Alastair I. (1995) *Cultural Realism: Strategic Culture and Grand Strategy in Chinese History*. Princeton: Princeton University Press.

Johnston, Alistair Iain (2008) *Social States: China in International Institutions, 1980–2000*. Princeton: Princeton University Press.

Joll, James and Gordon Martel (2007) *The Origins of the First World War*, third edition. Harlow: Pearson.

Jones, Eric (2003) *The European Miracle: Environments, Economics, and Geopolitics in the History of Europe and Asia*, third edition. Cambridge: Cambridge University Press.

Junhao, Hong (2005) 'The Internet and China's Foreign Policy Making: The Impact of Online Public Opinions as a New Societal Force,' in Yufan, Hao and Su Lin (eds), *Chinese Foreign Policy Making: Societal Forces and Chinese Foreign Policy*. Aldershot: Ashgate Press: 93–109.

Kaiser, David (2000) *Politics and War: European Conflict from Philip II to Hitler*. Cambridge: Harvard University Press.

Kalyvas, Stathis and Laia Balcells (2010) 'International System and Technologies of Rebellion: How the End of the Cold War Shaped Internal Conflict,' *American Political Science Review* 104 (3): 415–29.

Kalyvas, Stathis and Matthew Kocher (2009) 'The Dynamics of Violence in Vietnam: An Analysis of the Hamlet Evaluation System,' *Journal of Peace Research* 46 (3): 335–55.

Kamen, Henry (2004) *Empire: How Spain Became a World Power, 1492–1763*. New York: Perennial.

Kan, Shirley (2007) *China/Taiwan: Evolution of the 'One China' Policy – Key Statements from Washington, Beijing, and Taipei* (CRS Report for Congress), accessed at http://www.fas.org/sgp/crs/row/RL30341.pdf.

Kang, David (2010) *East Asia Before the West: Five Centuries of Trade and Tribute*. New York: Columbia University Press.

Kant, Immanuel ([1795] 2009) *Perpetual Peace*. Rockville, MD: Wildside Press.

Kaplan, Robert (2012) *The Revenge of Geography: What the Map Tells Us about Coming Conflicts and the Battle Against Fate*. New York: Random House.

Katzman, Kenneth (2018) *Iran Sanctions*. Washington, DC: Congressional Research Service, January 10.

Kaufman, Chaim (1994) 'Out of the Lab and into the Archives: A Method for Testing Psychological Explanations of Political Decision Making,' *International Studies Quarterly* 38 (4): 557–86.

Keane, John (2010) *Global Civil Society?* Cambridge University Press.

Keck, Margaret and Kathryn Sikkink (1998) *Activists Beyond Borders: Advocacy Networks in International Politics*. Ithaca, NY: Cornell University Press.

Keeny, Spurgeon and Wolfgang Panofsky (1981–82) 'Nuclear Weapons in the 1980s: MAD vs. NUTS,' *Foreign Affairs* 60 (2/Winter): 287–304.

Kellenberg, Derek (2009) 'An Empirical Investigation of the Pollution Haven Effect with Strategic Environment and Trade Policy,' *Journal of International Economics* 78 (2): 242–55.

Kemp, R. Scott (2012) 'Cyberweapons: Bold Steps in a Digital Darkness?' *Bulletin of the Atomic Scientists*, June 7, accessed at http:/thebulletin.org/web-edition.

Kennedy, Paul (1987) *The Rise and Fall of the Great Powers*. New York: Random House.

Keohane, Robert (1984) *After Hegemony: Cooperation and Discord in the World Political Economy*. Princeton: Princeton University Press.

Keohane, Robert (1989) 'International Relations Theory: Contributions of a Feminist Standpoint,' *Millennium – Journal of International Studies*: 245–53.

Keohane, Robert and Joseph Nye (1977) *Power and Interdependence*. Boston: Little, Brown.

Keohane, Robert O. and Lisa L. Martin (1995) 'The Promise of Institutionalist Theory,' *International Security* 20 (1/Summer): 39–51.

Kessler, Glenn (2009) 'Clinton, Indian Minister Clash Over Emissions Reduction Pact,' *Washington Post*, July 20.

Keylor, William (2011) *The Twentieth Century World and Beyond: An International History Since 1900*, sixth edition. Oxford: Oxford University Press.

Kindleberger, Charles (1973/1986) *The World in Depression: 1929–1939*, revised and enlarged edition. Berkeley: University of California Press.

Kirshner, Jon (2007) *Appeasing the Bankers: Financial Caution of the Road to War.* Princeton: Princeton University Press.

Kirshner, Jonathan (2014) *American Power after the Financial Crisis.* Ithaca: Cornell University Press.

Kline, Harvey R. (2003) 'Colombia: Lawlessness, Drug Trafficking, and Carving Up the State,' in Robert I. Rotberg (ed.), *State Failure and State Weakness in a Time of Terror.* Washington: Brookings Institution Press: 167–9.

Klotz, Audie (1995) *Norms in International Relations: The Struggle Against Apartheid.* Ithaca: Cornell University Press.

Knock, Thomas (1995) *To End all Wars: Woodrow Wilson and the Quest for a New World Order.* Princeton: Princeton University Press.

Knox, Robert (2016) 'Marxist Approaches to International Law,' in Anne Orford and Florian Hoffmann (eds), *Oxford Handbook of the Theory of International Law.* Oxford: Oxford University Press: 306–25.

Kohli, Atul (2009) 'Nationalist versus Dependent Capitalist Development: Alternative Pathways of Asia and Latin America in a Globalized World,' *Studies of Comparative International Development* 44 (4): 386–410.

Kramer, Roderick (1998) 'Revisiting the Bay of Pigs and Vietnam Decisions 25 Years Later: How Well Has the Groupthink Hypothesis Stood the Test of Time?' *Organizational Behavior and Human Decision Processes* 73 (2/3): 236–71.

Krasner, Stephen (1982) 'Structural Causes and Regime Consequences: Regimes as Intervening Variables,' *International Organization* 36 (2): 185–205.

Krasner, Stephen (1995) 'Sovereignty and Intervention,' in Gene Lyons and Michael Mastanduno (eds), *Beyond Westphalia? State Sovereignty and International Intervention.* Baltimore: Johns Hopkins University Press: 228–49.

Krasner, Stephen D. (1978) *Defending the National Interest: Raw Materials Investments and US Foreign Policy.* Princeton: Princeton University Press.

Kreps, Sarah (2016) *Drones: What Everyone Needs to Know.* New York: Oxford University Press.

Kroenig, Matthew (2013) 'Nuclear Superiority and the Balance of Resolve: Explaining Nuclear Crisis Outcomes,' *International Organization* 67 (1): 141–71.

Krueger, Anne (1975) *The Benefits and Costs of Import Substitution in India: A Microeconomic Study.* Minneapolis: University of Minnesota Press.

Krueger, Anne O. (1997) 'Trade Policy and Economic Development: How We Learn,' *American Economic Review* 87 (March): 11–12.

Kupchan, Charles (2012). *No One's World: The West, the Rising Rest, and the Coming Global Turn.* Oxford: Oxford University Press.

Kuusela, Olli-Pekka and Gregory Amacher (2016) 'Changing Political Regimes and Tropical Deforestation,' *Environmental and Resource Economics* 64 (3): 445–63.

LaFeber, Walter (2006) *America, Russia and the Cold War 1945–2006*, tenth edition. New York: McGraw-Hill.

Lascurettes, Kyle (2017) *The Concert of Europe and Great-Power Governance Today.* RAND Corporation.

Lasswell, Harold (1941) 'The Garrison State,' *American Journal of Sociology* 46 (4): 455–68.

Layne, Christopher (2006) *The Peace of Illusions: American Grand Strategy from 1940 to the Present.* Ithaca: Cornell University Press.

Leahy, William (1950) *I was There: The Personal Story of the Chief of Staff to Presidents Roosevelt and Truman.* New York: McGraw-Hill.

Lebow, Richard Ned and Thomas Risse-Kappen (eds) (1995) *International Relations Theory and the End of the Cold War.* New York: Columbia University Press.

Lee, Hoon and Sara McLaughlin Mitchell (2012) 'Foreign Direct Investment and Territorial Disputes,' *Journal of Conflict Resolution* 56 (4): 675–703.

Legatum Institute (2016) *2016 Africa Prosperity Report*, accessed at http://www.li.com/activities/publications/2016-africa-prosperity-report.

Legro, Jeffrey W. (2000) 'Whence American Internationalism,' *International Organization* 54: 253–89.

Lemkin, Raphael (1944) *Axis Rule in Occupied Europe: Laws of Occupation, Analysis of Government, Proposals for Redress.* Washington, DC: Carnegie Endowment for International Peace.

Leng, Russell (2004) 'Escalation: Competing Perspectives and Empirical Evidence,' *International Studies Review* 6 (4): 51–64.

Leng, Russell (2005) 'Realpolitik and Learning in the India-Pakistan Rivalry,' in T.V. Paul (ed.), *The India-Pakistan Conflict: An Enduring Rivalry.* Cambridge: Cambridge University Press: 103–28.

Lenin, Vladimir I. (1916) *Imperialism: The Highest Stage of Capitalism.* New York: International Publishers.

Levy, Jack (1988) 'Domestic Politics and War,' *Journal of Interdisciplinary History* 18 (4): 653–73.

Levy, Jack (1994) 'Learning and Foreign Policy: Sweeping a Conceptual Minefield,' *International Organization* 48: 279–312.

Levy, Jack and William Thompson (2011) *The Arc of War: Origins, Escalation, and Transformation.* Chicago: University of Chicago Press.

Lewis, Michael (2010) *The Big Short: Inside the Doomsday Machine.* New York: Norton.

Li, Cheng (2012) 'Opportunity Lost? Inside China's Leadership Transition,' *Foreign Policy*, November 16.

Li, Xiaoying and Xiaming Liu (2005) 'Foreign Direct Investment and Economic Growth: An Increasingly Endogenous Relationship,' *World Development* 33 (3): 393–407.

Liberman, Peter (1996) *Does Conquest Pay? The Exploitation of Occupied Societies.* Princeton: Princeton University Press.

Lieber, Keir A. (2007) 'The New History of World War I and What It Means for International Relations Theory,' *International Security* 32 (2): 155–91.

Lipson, Charles (2003) *Reliable Partners: How Democracies Have Made a Separate Peace.* Princeton: Princeton University Press.

Lister, Tim, Ray Sanchez, Mark Bixler, Sean O'Key, Michael Hogenmiller, and Mohammed Tawfeeq (2018) 'ISIS Goes Global,' CNN, February 12, accessed at https://edition.cnn.com/2015/12/17/world/mapping-isis-attacks-around-the-world/index.html

Lobell, Steven (2007) 'The Second Face of Security: Britain's "Smart" Appeasement Policy Towards Japan and Germany,' *International Relations of the Asia-Pacific* 7 (1): 73–98.

Locke, Richard, Matthew Amengual, and Akshay Mangla (2009) 'Virtue out of Necessity? Compliance, Commitment, and the Improvement of Labor Conditions in Global Supply Chains,' *Politics & Society* 37 (3): 319–51.

Machida, Satoshi (2017) 'National Sentiments and Citizens' Attitudes in Japan Toward the Use of Force Against China,' *Asian Journal of Comparative Politics* 2 (1/March): 87–103.

Maddison, Angus (2001) *The World Economy: A Millennial Perspective.* Paris: Organisation for Economic Co-operation and Development.

Malinak, Daniel (2008) 'Women in International Relations,' *Politics & Gender* 4 (1): 122.

Mansfield, Edward (1994) *Power, Trade and War.* Princeton: Princeton University Press.

Mansfield, Edward and Jack Snyder (1995) 'Democratization and War,' *Foreign Affairs* 74 (3/May–June): 79–97.

Mansfield, Edward and Jack Snyder (2007) *Electing to Fight: Why Emerging Democracies Go to War.* Cambridge: MIT Press.

Maoz, Zeev (1989) 'Joining the Club of Nations: Political Development and International Conflict, 1816–1976,' *International Studies Quarterly* 33 (2): 199–231.

Marshall, George (1948) 'Congressional Testimony on the European Recovery Program,' *Department of State Bulletin* 71.

Martin, Lisa (1992) *Coercive Cooperation: Explaining Multilateral Economic Sanctions.* Princeton: Princeton University Press.

Mastanduno, Michael (1992) *Economic Containment: CoCom and the Politics of East-West Trade.* Ithaca: Cornell University Press.

Mastanduno, Michael (1999) 'Economic Statecraft, Interdependence, and National Security: Agendas for Research,' *Security Studies* 9 (1–2): 218–316.

Mastanduno, Michael (2011) 'Economic Statecraft,' in Steve Smith, Amelia Hadfield, and Tim Dunne (eds), *Foreign Policy: Theory, Actors, Cases.* Oxford: Oxford University Press: 204–22.

Mastanduno, Michael, David Lake, and G. John Ikenberry (1989) 'Toward a Realist Theory of State Action,' *International Studies Quarterly* 33: 457–74.

Mattingly, Garrett (1988) *Renaissance Diplomacy*. New York: Dover Publications, Inc.

Maxfield, Sylvia (1998) 'Understanding the Political Implications of Financial Internationalization in Emerging Market Countries,' *World Development* 26 (7): 1201–19.

Maxfield, Sylvia (2000) 'Comparing East Asia and Latin America: Capital Mobility and Democratic Stability,' *Journal of Democracy* 11(4): 95–106.

Mazower, Mark (1998) *Dark Continent: Europe's Twentieth Century*. New York: Vintage Books.

McArthur, John W. and Krista Rasmussen (2017) *Change of Pace: Accelerations and Advances During the Millennium Development Goal Era*. Brookings Economy and Development Working Paper 97. Washington: Brookings.

McDermott, Rose, Dustin Tingley, Jonathan Cowden, Giovanni Frazzetto, and Dominic Johnson (2009) 'Monoamine Oxidase A Gene (MAOA) Predicts Behavioral Aggression Following Provocation,' *Proceedings of the National Academy of Sciences* 106 (7): 2118–23.

McDonald, Mark (2011) 'North Korea Suggests Libya Should Have Kept Nuclear Weapons Program,' *New York Times*, March 24.

McFaul, Michael and Kathryn Stoner-Weiss (2008) 'The Myth of the Authoritarian Model,' *Foreign Affairs* 87 (1): 68–84.

McMillan, Susan M. (1997) 'Interdependence and Conflict,' *Mershon International Studies Review* 41 (1): 33–58.

McNeill, William (1965) *The Rise of the West: A History of the Human Community*. Chicago: University of Chicago Press.

Mearsheimer, John (1994) 'The False Promise of International Institutions,' *International Security* 19: 5–49.

Mearsheimer, John (2001) *The Tragedy of Great Power Politics*. New York: Norton.

Mearsheimer, John (2003) *The Tragedy of Great Power Politics*. W.W. Norton, updated edition.

Mearsheimer, John and Stephen Walt (2007) *The Israel Lobby and US Foreign Policy*. New York: Farrar, Straus & Giroux.

Meltzer, Allan (2000) 'Statement of Allan H. Meltzer on the Report of the International Financial Institution Advisory Commission,' Senate Committee on Banking, Housing, and Urban Affairs, accessed at http://www.gsia.cmu.edu/afs/andrew/gsia/meltzer/.

Milanovic, Branko (2016) *Global Inequality: A New Approach for the Age of Globalization*. Cambridge: Harvard University Press.

Milbank, Dana (2005) 'Intelligence Design and the Architecture of War,' *Washington Post*, December 8, accessed at http://www.washingtonpost.com/wp-dyn/content/article/2005/12/07/AR2005120702224.html.

Miller, Steven, Sean Lynn-Jones, and Stephen Van Evera (eds) (1991) *Military Strategy and the Origins of the First World War*, revised and expanded edition. Princeton: Princeton University Press.

Milner, Helen (1997) *Interests, Institutions, and Information*. Princeton: Princeton University Press.

Ministry of Foreign Affairs, People's Republic of China (2014) 'Position Paper of the Government of the People's Republic of China on the Matter of Jurisdiction in the South China Sea Arbitration Initiated by the Republic of the Philippines,' December 7, accessed at http://www.fmprc.gov.cn/mfa_eng/zxxx_662805/t1217147.shtml.

Montiero, Nuno (2014) *Theory of Unipolar Politics*. Cambridge: Cambridge University Press.

Morgenthau, Hans (1985) *Politics Among Nations: The Struggle for Power and Peace*, sixth edition. New York: Knopf.

Morgenthau, Hans J. (1967) *Politics Among Nations*, fourth edition. New York: Knopf.

Mosley, Layna, and Saika Uno (2007) 'Globalization and Collective Labor: Racing to the Bottom or Climbing to the Top? Economic Globalization and Collective Labor Rights,' *Comparative Political Studies* 40 (8): 923–48.

Mueller, John (1973) *War, Presidents, and Public Opinion*. New York: Wiley.

Mueller, John (1989) *The Obsolescence of Major War*. New York: Basic Books.

Mueller, John (2009) 'War Has Almost Ceased to Exist: An Assessment,' *Political Science Quarterly* 124: 297–321.

Mueller, John and Karl Mueller (1999) 'Sanctions of Mass Destruction,' *Foreign Affairs* 78 (May/June).

Naím, Moisés (2005) *Illicit: How Smugglers, Traffickers, and Copycats are Hijacking the Global Economy*. New York: Anchor Books.

National Academies of Science (2008) *Understanding and Responding to Climate Change: Highlights of National Academies Reports*, accessed at http://dels.nas.edu/dels/rpt_briefs/climate_change_2008_final.pdf.

National Resources Defense Council (2002) 'The Consequences of a Nuclear War between India and Pakistan', June 4, accessed at www.ndrc.org/nuclear/southasia.asp.

Natsios, Andrew and Michael Abramowitz (2011) 'Sudan's Secession Crisis', *Foreign Affairs*, 90 (1): 19–26.

NBC (2003) *Meet the Press*, 'Interview with Vice-President Dick Cheney', Transcript for March 16, accessed at https://www.mtholyoke.edu/acad/intrel/bush/cheneymeetthepress.html.

Neff, Stephen (1990) *Friends but No Allies: Economic Liberalism and the Law of Nations.* New York: Columbia University Press.

Neier, Aryeh (2013) *The International Human Rights Movement: A History.* Princeton: Princeton University Press.

Neumayer, Eric and Indra De Soysa (2006) 'Globalization and the Right to Free Association and Collective Bargaining: An Empirical Analysis', *World Development* 34 (1): 31–49.

Neustadt, Richard (1976) *Presidential Power: The Politics of Leadership, with Reflections on Johnson and Nixon.* New York: John Wiley.

New York Times (2009) 'Clinton Softens Her Tone on China', February 20, accessed at https://www.nytimes.com/2009/02/20/world/asia/20iht-clinton.4.20337969.html

Newnham, Randall (2002) *Deutsche-Mark Diplomacy: Positive Economic Sanctions in German-Russian Relations.* University Park: Penn State University Press.

Nexon, Daniel H. (2009) *The Struggle for Power in Early Modern Europe.* Princeton: Princeton University Press.

Nicolson, Harold (1963) *Diplomacy.* Oxford: Oxford University Press.

Nye, Joseph (2004) *Soft Power: The Means to Success in World Politics.* Cambridge.MA: Public Affairs.

Obydenkova, Anastassia, Zafar Nazarov, and Raufhon Salahodjaev (2016). 'The Process of Deforestation in Weak Democracies and the Role of Intelligence', *Environmental Research* 148: 484–90.

Obydenkova, Anastassia, Zafar Nazarov, and Raufhon Salahodjaev (2016) 'The Process of Deforestation in Weak Democracies and the Role of Intelligence', *Environmental Research* 148: 484–90.

Office of Technology Assessment, US Congress (1979) *The Effects of Nuclear War.* Washington, DC: Government Printing Office.

Olearchyk, Roman and Neil Buckley (2010) 'Russia–Ukraine Gas Peace Threatens to Unravel', *Financial Times*, September 23.

Oneal, John R. and Bruce Russett (1997) 'The Classic Liberals Were Right: Democracy, Interdependence, and Conflict, 1950–1985', *International Studies Quarterly* 41 (2): 267–94.

Organisation for Economic Co-operation and Development (2017) 'Official Development Assistance as a Percentage of Gross National Income (GNI)', in *OECD International Development Statistics, Volume 2017*, accessed at http://www.oecd-ilibrary.org/development/oecd-international-development-statistics_24142689

Osgood, Robert (1983) 'The Expansion of Force', in Robert Art and Kenneth Waltz (eds), *The Use of Force*, second edition, Lanham, MD: University Press of America: 75–100.

Overy, R.J. (2008) *The Origins of the Second World War*, third edition. London: Longman Press.

Owen, John (1994) 'How Liberalism Produces Democratic Peace', *International Security* 19 (2): 87–125.

Palmer, Glenn, Vito D'Orazio, Michael Kenwick, and Matthew Lane (2015) 'The MID4 Dataset, 2002–2010: Procedures, Coding Rules and Description', *Conflict Management and Peace Science* 32 (2): 222–42.

Pape, Robert (2006) *Dying to Win: The Strategic Logic of Suicide Terrorism.* New York: Random House.

Paterson, Thomas G., J. Garry Clifford, Shane J. Maddock, Deborah Kisatsky, and Kenneth J. Hagan (2006) *American Foreign Relations, Volume I: to 1920.* Boston: Houghton Mifflin.

Pelc, Krzysztof (2017) 'What Explains the Low Success Rate of Investor-State Disputes?' *International Organization* 71 (3): 559–83.

Permanent Court of Arbitration (2016) 'Press Release: South China Sea Arbitration', July 12, accessed at https://pca-cpa.org/wp-content/uploads/sites/175/2016/07/PH-CN-20160712-Press-Release-No-11-English.pdf.

Petersen, Marie Juul (2016) 'Islam and Human Rights: Clash or Compatibility?' *Religion and Global Society*, London School of Economics, October 26, accessed at http://blogs.lse.ac.uk/religionglobalsociety/2016/10/islam-and-human-rights-clash-or-compatibility/.

Phythian, Mark (2006) 'The Perfect Intelligence Failure? US Pre-War Intelligence on Iraqi Weapons of Mass Destruction,' *Politics & Policy* 34 (2): 400–24.

Pilling, David (2016) 'Kofi Annan Defends International Criminal Court despite African Row,' *Financial Times,* June 16.

Podesta, John and Peter Ogden (2008) 'The Security Implications of Climate Change,' *Washington Quarterly* 31 (1): 115–38.

Power, Samantha (2002) *A Problem from Hell: America and the Age of Genocide.* New York: Basic Books.

Price, Richard (1998) 'Reversing the Gun Sights: Transnational Civil Society Targets Land Mines,' *International Organization* 52: 613–44.

Price, Richard (2004) 'Emerging Customary Norms and Anti-Personnel Landmines,' in Christian Reus-Smit (ed.), *The Politics of International Law*. Cambridge: Cambridge University Press: 106–30.

Recchia, Stefano (2015) 'Soldiers, Civilians, and Multilateral Humanitarian Intervention,' *Security Studies* 24: 251–83.

Record, Jeffrey (2002) *Making War, Thinking History: Munich, Vietnam, and Presidential Uses of Force from Korea to Kosovo.* Annapolis: US Naval Institute Press.

Reus-Smit, Christian (2004) *The Politics of International Law.* Cambridge: Cambridge University Press.

Rhodes, Richard (1986) *The Making of the Atomic Bomb.* New York: Simon & Schuster.

Rice, Condoleezza (2006) '*Transformational Diplomacy,*' speech at Georgetown University, January 18.

Richardson, Louise (2007) *What Terrorists Want: Understanding the Enemy, Containing the Threat.* New York: Random House.

Ripsman, Norrin and Jack Levy (2008) 'Wishful Thinking or Buying Time? The Logic of British Appeasement in the 1930s,' *International Security* 33 (2): 148–81.

Ristic, Marija (2017) 'Hague Tribunal Prepares for Shutdown in 2017,' *Balkan Investigative Reporting Network*, June 4, accessed at http://www.balkaninsight.com/en/article/the-last-year-for-the-icty-01-02-2017-1.

Roberts, J.M. and O.A. Westad (2013) *The Penguin History of the World*, sixth edition. Harmondsworth: Penguin.

Rodrik, Dani (2006) 'Goodbye Washington Consensus, Hello Washington Confusion? A Review of the World Bank's Economic Growth in the 1990s: Learning from a Decade of Reform,' *Journal of Economic Literature*, XLIV (December): 973–87

Rodrik, Dani (2012) *The Globalization Paradox: Democracy and the Future of the World Economy.* New York: Norton.

Rohac, Dalibor (2018) 'Hungary and Poland Aren't Democratic. They're Authoritarian,' *Foreign Policy* February 5.

Rohde, David (1997) *Endgame: The Betrayal and Fall of Srebrenica, Europe's Worst Massacre Since World War II.* New York: Farrar, Straus, & Giroux.

Roider, Karl A. (1987) *Baron Thugut and Austria's Response to the French Revolution.* Princeton: Princeton University Press.

Rosecrance, Richard (1999) *Rise of the Virtual State: Wealth and Power in the Coming Century.* New York: Basic Books.

Rosen, Stephen (2005) *War and Human Nature.* Princeton: Princeton University Press.

Rosenau, James (1995) 'Sovereignty in a Turbulent World,' in Gene Lyons and Michael Mastanduno (eds), *Beyond Westphalia? State Sovereignty and International Intervention.* Baltimore: Johns Hopkins University Press: 191–227.

Ross, Michael (2001) 'Does Oil Hinder Democracy?' *World Politics* 53 (3): 325–61.

Ross, Michael (2004) 'What Do We Know about Natural Resources and Civil War?' *Journal of Peace Research* 41 (3): 337–56.

Ross, Michael (2012) *The Oil Curse: How Petroleum Wealth Shapes the Development of Nations.* Princeton, Princeton University Press.

Ross, Michael (2015) 'What Have We Learned about the Resource Curse?' Annual Review of Political Science 18: 239–59.

Rotberg, Robert I. (2003) 'Failed States, Collapsed States, Weak States: Causes and Indicators,' in Rotberg (ed.), *State Failure and State Weakness in a Time of Terror*. Washington, DC: The Brookings Institution: 1–25.

Roy, Olivier (2017) *Jihad and Death: The Global Appeal of Islamic State*. London: Hurst.

Rudra, Nita (2005) 'Globalization and the Strengthening of Democracy in the Developing World,' *American Journal of Political Science* 49 (4): 704–30.

Ruggie, John (1982) 'International Regimes, Transactions, and Change: Embedded Liberalism in the Postwar Economic Order,' *International Organization* 36 (2): 379–415.

Russett, Bruce (1993) *Grasping the Democratic Peace: Principles for a Post-Cold War World*. Princeton: Princeton University Press.

Rutland, Peter (2006) 'Russia's Economic Role in Asia: Toward Deeper Integration,' in Ashley Tellis and Michael Wills (eds), *Strategic Asia 2006–07: Trade, Interdependence and Security*. Seattle: National Bureau of Asian Research: 173–202.

Sachs, Jeffrey (2005a) *The End of Poverty: Economic Possibilities for Our Time*. New York: Penguin.

Sachs, Jeffrey (2005b) *Investing in Development: A Practical Plan to Achieve the Millennium Development Goals*. New York: UN Development Program, accessed at http://www.unmillenniumproject.org/reports/fullreport.htm.

Sachs, Jeffrey, and Andrew Warner (2001) 'The Curse of Natural Resources,' *European Economic Review* 45 (4–6): 827–38.

Sagan, Scott (1988) 'The Origins of the Pacific War,' *Journal of Interdisciplinary History*, 18 (4): 893–922.

Sagan, Scott (1994) 'From Deterrence to Coercion: The Road to Pearl Harbor,' in Alexander George and William Simons (eds), *Limits of Coercive Diplomacy*, second edition. Boulder: Westview Press: 57–90.

Sagan, Scott (2017) 'The Korean Missile Crisis: Why Deterrence is Still the Best Option,' *Foreign Affairs*, 96 (6/November–December).

Sagan, Scott and Kenneth Waltz (2002) *The Spread of Nuclear Weapons: A Debate Renewed*, second edition. New York: Norton.

Sagan, Scott, Kenneth Waltz, and Richard Betts (2007) 'A Nuclear Iran: Promoting Stability or Courting Disaster,' *Journal of International Affairs* 60 (2): 135–50.

Said, Edward W. (2001) 'The Clash of Ignorance,' *The Nation* October 4, accessed at https://www.thenation.com/article/clash-ignorance/

Salehyan, Idean (2008) 'From Climate Change to Conflict? No Consensus Yet,' *Journal of Peace Research* 45 (3): 315–26.

Sanger, David (1999) 'A Deal That America Just Can't Refuse,' *New York Times*, November 16.

Sanger, David (2012) *Confront and Conceal: Obama's Secret Wars and the Surprising Use of American Power*. New York: Random House.

Sarkees, Meredith Reid, and Frank Wayman (2010) *Resort to War: A Data Guide to Inter-State, Extra-State, Intra-state, and Non-State Wars, 1816–2007*. Washington: CQ Press.

Saunders, Elizabeth (2009) 'Transformative Choices: Leaders and the Origins of Intervention Strategy,' *International Security* 34: 119–61.

Schlesinger, Arthur (1967) 'Origins of the Cold War,' *Foreign Affairs* 46 (1): 22–52.

Schmitt, Eric and Mark Mazzetti (2011) 'Pakistan Arrests CIA Informants in Bin Laden Raid,' *New York Times*, June 14.

Schrock-Jacobson, Gretchen (2012) 'The Violent Consequences of the Nation: Nationalism and the Initiation of Interstate War,' *Journal of Conflict Resolution* 56 (5/April): 825–52.

Schwartz, Stephen (1998) *Atomic Audit: The Costs and Consequences of US Nuclear Weapons Since 1940*. Washington: The Brookings Institution.

Schwarzenbach, Rene, Thomas Egli, Thomas B. Hofstetter, Urs von Gunten, and Bernhard Wehrli (2010) 'Global Water Pollution and Human Health,' *Annual Review of Environment and Resources* 35: 109–36.

Scott, Joan W. (2018) *Gender and the Politics of History*. New York: Columbia University Press.

Sechser, Todd and Matthew Furmann (2013) 'Crisis Bargaining and Nuclear Blackmail,' *International Organization*, 67 (1): 173–95.

Sechser, Todd and Matthew Furmann (2017) *Nuclear Weapons and Coercive Diplomacy*. Cambridge: Cambridge University Press.

Senese, Paul and John Vasquez (2005) 'Assessing the Steps to War,' *British Journal of Political Science* 35 (4): 607–34.

Shandra, John, Louis Esparza, and Bruce London (2012) 'Nongovernmental Organizations, Democracy, and Deforestation: A Cross-National Analysis,' *Society & Natural Resources* 25: 251–69.

Shandra, John, Louis Esparza, and Bruce London (2012) 'Nongovernmental Organizations, Democracy, and Deforestation: A Cross-National Analysis,' *Society & Natural Resources* 25: 251–69.

Shapiro, Robert Y. and Lawrence R. Jacobs (2002) 'Public Opinion, Foreign Policy, and Democracy: How Presidents Use Public Opinion,' in Jeff Manza, Fay Lomax Cook, and Benjamin I. Page (eds), *Navigating Public Opinion: Polls, Policy, and the Future of American Democracy*. New York: Oxford University Press: 184–99.

Sharma, Dinesh (2011) *Barack Obama in Hawaii and Indonesia: The Making of a Global President*. Santa Barbara: Praeger Publishers.

Shih, Victor (2008) *Factions and Finance in China: Elite Conflict and Inflation*. Cambridge: Cambridge University Press.

Shultz, George, William J. Perry, Henry A. Kissinger, and Sam Nunn (2007) 'A World Free of Nuclear Weapons,' *Wall Street Journal*, January 4.

Simmons, Beth and Lisa Martin (2001) "International Organizations and Institutions,' in Walter Carlnaes, Thomas Risse and Beth Simmons (eds), *Handbook of International Relations*. Sage: 192–211.

Singer, J. David (1961) 'The Levels-of-Analysis Problem in International Relations,' *World Politics* 14 (October): 77–92.

Singer, Max and Aaron Wildavsky (1993) *The Real World Order: Zones of Peace, Zones of Conflict*. London: Chatham House.

Sjoberg, Laura (2012) 'Gender, Structure, and War: What Waltz Couldn't See,' *International Theory* 4 (1/March): 1–38.

Skocpol, Theda (1974) *States and Social Revolutions: A Comparative Analysis of France, Russia, and China*. Cambridge: Cambridge University Press.

Slater, Dan (2003) 'Iron Cage in an Iron Fist: Authoritarian Institutions and the Personalization of Power in Malaysia,' *Comparative Politics* 36 (1): 81–101.

Slaughter, Anne-Marie (1995) 'International Law in a World of Liberal States,' *European Journal of International Law* 6: 503–38.

Smith, Adam ([1776] 1937) *The Wealth of Nations*, edited by Edwin Cannan. New York: The Modern Library.

Snyder, Jack (1991) *Myths of Empire: Domestic Politics and International Ambition*. Ithaca: Cornell University Press.

Snyder, Jack (2000) *From Voting to Violence: Democratization and Nationalist Conflict*. New York: W.W. Norton.

Snyder, Timothy (2010) *Bloodlands: Europe Between Hitler and Stalin*. New York: Basic Books.

Sobel, Richard (2001) *The Impact of Public Opinion on US Foreign Policy Since Vietnam: Constraining the Colossus*. New York: Oxford University Press.

Spiegel Online (2016) 'Interview with Ugandan President Museveni,' accessed at http://www.spiegel.de/international/world/interview-with-ugandan-president-yoweri-museveni-a-1096932.html

Spruyt, Hendrik (2005) *Ending Empire: Contested Sovereignty and Territorial Partition*. Ithaca: Cornell University Press.

Statista (2018) 'Projected Rare Earth Production for China and the Rest of World from 2013 to 2018 (in Metric Tons REO),' accessed at https://www.statista.com/statistics/279953/rare-earth-production-in-china-and-outside/.

Statista (2018a) 'Major Foreign Holders of US Treasury Securities, as of March 2018 (in Billion US Dollars),' accessed at https://www.statista.com/statistics/246420/major-foreign-holders-of-us-treasury-debt.

Stein, Janice Gross (1994) 'Political Learning by Doing: Gorbachev as Uncommitted Thinker and Motivated Learner,' *International Organization* 48: 155–83.

Steiner, Zara (2005) *The Lights That Failed: European International History 1919–1933*. Oxford: Oxford University Press.

Stephen C. Roach (ed.) (2007) *Critical Theory and International Relations: A Reader*. Routledge.

Stiglitz, Joseph E. (2002) *Globalization and Its Discontents*. New York: Norton.

Still4Hill (2009) 'Remarks Following ITC Green Building Tour and Discussion,' July 19, accessed at https://still4hill.com/2009/07/19/hillary-clinton-on-tour-of-itc-green-building-in-new-delhi/.

Stimson, Henry (1947) 'The Decision to Use the Atomic Bomb,' *Harper's Magazine* February: 97–107.

Strack, Columb (2017) 'The Evolution of the Islamic State's Chemical Weapons Efforts,' *CTC Sentinel* 10 (9/October): 19–23.

Straus, Scott (2005) 'Darfur and the Genocide Debate,' *Foreign Affairs* 84 (1): 123–33.

Stroud, Frederick (2017) *Stroud's Judicial Dictionary of Words and Phrases*. Sweet & Maxwell

Sunstein, Cass (2007) 'Of Montreal and Kyoto: A Tale of Two Protocols,' *Harvard Environmental Law Review* 31 (1): 1–65.

Swire, Nathan (2008) 'Mearsheimer Explores Threat of China,' *The Dartmouth*, November 14.

Tadec, Boris (2010) 'An Apology for Srebrenica,' *Wall Street Journal,* April 16, p. A17.

Talbot, Strobe (2008) *The Great Experiment: The Story of Ancient Empires, Modern States, and the Quest for a Global Nation*. New York: Simon & Schuster.

Tannenwald, Nina (1999) 'The Nuclear Taboo: The United States and the Normative Basis of Nuclear Non-Use,' *International Organization* 53 (3): 433–68.

Tannenwald, Nina (2008) *The Nuclear Taboo: The United States and the Non-Use of Nuclear Weapons since 1945*. Cambridge: Cambridge University Press.

Taylor, A.J.P. (1996/2005) *The Origins of the Second World War*. New York: Athenium.

Taylor, Adam (2017) 'South Korea and China Move to Normalize Relations after THAAD Dispute,' *Washington Post*, October 31.

Taylor, Jeffrey (2001) 'Russia is Finished,' *Atlantic Monthly*, 287 (5): 35–49.

Thompson, Alexander (2006) 'Coercion Through IOs: The Security Council and the Logic of Information Transmission,' *International Organization* 60, (Winter 2006): 1–34.

Thucydides (1954, translated by Rex Warner) *The Peloponnesian War*. Harmondsworth: Penguin.

Thurow, Lester (1992) *Head to Head: The Coming Battle Among Japan, Europe, and America*. New York: Warner Books.

Tickner, Ann (1988) 'Hans Morgenthau's Principles of Political Realism: A Feminist Reformulation,' *Millennium: Journal of International Studies* 17 (3/December): 429–40.

Tickner, J. Ann (1997) 'You Just Don't Understand: Troubled Engagements Between Feminists and IR Theorists,' *International Studies Quarterly* 41: 621.

Tickner, J. Ann (1999) 'Why Women Can't Rule the World: International Politics According to Francis Fukuyama,' *International Studies Review* 1 (3): 3–11.

Ticktin, Hillel (2011) *Marxism and the Global Financial Crisis.* New York: Routledge.

Tilly, Charles (1985) 'War Making and State Making as Organized Crime,' in Peter B. Evans, Dietrich Rueschemeyer, and Theda Skocpol (eds), *Bringing the State Back In*. New York: Cambridge University Press: 169–191.

Tilly, Charles (1990) *Coercion, Capital, and European States, AD 900–1900*. Cambridge: Blackwell.

Tilly, Charles, (ed.) (1975) *The Formation of National States in Western Europe*. Princeton: Princeton University Press.

Tow, William, (ed.) (2009) *Security Politics in the Asia Pacific: A Regional-Global Nexus?* Cambridge: Cambridge University Press.

Tsebelis, George (2002) *Veto Players: How Political Institutions Work*. Princeton: Princeton University Press.

United Nations (1982) *United Nations Convention on the Law of the Sea*, accessed at http://www.un.org/Depts/los/convention_agreements/texts/unclos/closindx.htm.

United Nations (2000) *Sustaining Life: How the Convention on Biological Diversity Promotes Nature and Human Well-Being*, accessed at http://www.cbd.int/doc/publications/cbd-sustain-en.pdf.

United Nations (2001) 'Report of the High-level Panel on Financing for Development,' June 21, p. 41, accessed at: http://www.un.org/en/events/pastevents/financing_for_development_report.shtml.

United Nations (2002) 'Monterrey Consensus of the International Conference on Financing for Development,' in *Report of the International Conference on Financing for Development*, accessed at http://www.un.org/esa/ffd/monterrey/MonterreyConsensus.pdf,

United Nations (2017) *The Sustainable Development Goals Report 2017*. New York: United Nations, accessed at https://unstats.un.org/sdgs/report/2017/.

United Nations Conference on Trade and Development (UNCTAD) (2017) *World Investment Report 2017: Investment and the Digital Economy*, accessed at http://unctad.org/en/PublicationsLibrary/wir2017_en.pdf

United Nations Food and Agriculture Organization (2007) *State of the World's Forests 2007* Rome: FAO.

United Nations Food and Agriculture Organization (2012) *The State of World Fisheries and Aquaculture: 2012*, accessed at http://www.fao.org/docrep/016/i2727e/i2727e00.htm.

United Nations Food and Agriculture Organization (2016) *The State of World Fisheries and Aquaculture: Contributing to Food Security and Nutrition for All*. Rome: FAO, accessed at http://www.fao.org/3/a-i5555e.pdf.

US Department of Defense (1977) *Protection in the Nuclear Age*. Defense Civil Preparedness Agency, H-20, February.

US Department of Defense (2012) *Military and Security Developments Involving the People's Republic of China, 2012*. Annual Report to Congress, Washington.

US Department of Energy, Energy Information Administration (2009) *International Energy Outlook 2009*, accessed at http://www.eia.doe.gov/oiaf/ieo/emissions.html.

US Environmental Protection Agency (2012) 'Nitrogen Dioxide: National Trends in Nitrogen Dioxide Levels,' accessed at http://www.epa.gov/airtrends/nitrogen.html.

US Environmental Protection Agency (undated a) 'Sulfur Dioxide Emissions' accessed at http://cfpub.epa.gov/eroe/index.cfm?fuseaction=detail.viewInd&lv=list.listByAlpha&r=219694&subtop=341.

US Environmental Protection Agency (undated b) Future of Climate Change, accessed at https://19january2017snapshot.epa.gov/climate-change-science/future-climate-change_.html.

US National Archives. Undated. Founders Online: Alexander Hamilton's Final Version of the Report on the Subject of Manufactures, 5 December 1791. Available at https://founders.archives.gov/documents/Hamilton/01-10-02-0001-0007.

US National Oceanic and Atmospheric Administration, Fisheries Service (undated) 'The Tuna-Dolphin Issue,' accessed at http://swfsc.noaa.gov/textblock.aspx?Division=PRD&Parent-MenuId=228&id=1408.

Valentino, Benjamin, Paul Huth, and Dylan Balch-Lindsay (2004) ' "Draining the Sea": Mass Killing and Guerrilla Warfare,' *International Organization* 58 (2): 375–407.

Van Evera, Stephen (1984) 'The Cult of the Offensive and the Origins of the First World War,' *International Security* 9 (1): 58–107.

Voeten, Erik (2005) 'The Political Origins of the UN Security Council's Ability to Legitimize the Use of Force,' *International Organization* 59: 527–57.

Von Stein, Jana (2005) 'Do Treaties Constrain or Screen? Selection Bias and Treaty Compliance,' *American Political Science Review* 99 (4/November): 611–22.

Wallerstein, Immanuel (1974) *The Modern World System: Capitalist Agriculture and the Origins of the European World-Economy in the Sixteenth Century*. New York: Academic Press.

Wallerstein, Immanuel (1979) *The Capitalist World-Economy*. Cambridge: Cambridge University Press.

Walt, Stephen (1984) *The Origins of Alliances*. Ithaca, NY: Cornell University Press.

Walt, Stephen (1996) *Revolution and War*. Ithaca: Cornell University Press.

Walt, Stephen (2000) 'Rush to Failure: The Flawed Politics and Policies of Missile Defense,' *Harvard Magazine* (May–June 2000).

Waltz, Kenneth N. (1959) *Man, the State, and War: A Theoretical Analysis*. New York: Columbia University Press.

Waltz, Kenneth (1979) *Theory of International Politics*. Reading: Addison-Wesley.

Waltz, Kenneth (1993) 'The Emerging Structure of International Politics,' *International Security* 18 (2): 44–79.

Wang, Miao (2009) 'Manufacturing FDI and Economic Growth: Evidence from Asian Economies,' *Applied Economics* 41 (8): 991–1002.

Wapner, Paul (1995) 'Politics Beyond the State: Environmental Activism and World Civic Politics,' *World Politics* 47 (3): 311–40.

Weber, Max (1970) 'Politics as a Vocation,' in H.H. Gerth and C. Wright Mills (eds), *From Max Weber: Essays in Sociology.* London: Routledge: 77–128.

Weeks, Jessica (2012) 'Strongmen and Straw Men: Authoritarian Regimes and the Initiation of International Conflict,' *American Political Science Review* 106 (2): 326–47.

Weinstein, Jeremy (2005) 'Resources and the Information Problem in Rebel Recruitment,' *Journal of Conflict Resolution* 49 (4): 598–624.

Weiss, Jessica Chen (2013) 'Authoritarian Signaling, Mass Audiences, and Nationalist Protest in China,' *International Organization* 67 (1/January): 1–35.

Wendt, Alexander (1999) *Social Theory of International Politics.* New York: Cambridge University Press.

Westad, Odd Arne (2005) *The Global Cold War.* Cambridge: Cambridge University Press.

Wheeler, Nicholas (2004) 'The Kosovo Bombing Campaign,' in Christian Reus-Smit (ed.), *The Politics of International Law.* Cambridge: Cambridge University Press: 189–216.

White House (2002) *The National Security Strategy of the United States of America.*

White House (2009) 'A New Beginning,' Remarks in Cairo, Egypt, June 4.

White House (2015) 'Statement by the President on the Paris Climate Agreement,' December 12, accessed at https://obamawhitehouse. archives.gov/the-press-office/2015/12/12/ statement-president-paris-climate-agreement.

White House (2017) 'Statement by President Trump on the Paris Climate Accord,' June 1, accessed at https://www.whitehouse. gov/the-press-office/2017/06/01/statement-president-trump-paris-climate-accord

Wilson, Woodrow (1917), Address to the Senate, January 22.

Wohlforth, William (1999) 'The Stability of a Unipolar World,' *International Security* 24 (1): 5–41.

Woloch, Isser (1986) 'Napoleonic Conscription: State Power and Civil Society,' *Past and Present* 111 (May): 101–29.

World Bank (1998) *Assessing Aid: What Works, What Doesn't, and Why*, accessed at http://www. worldbank.org/research/aid/.

World Bank (2013a) *South Africa Overview*, accessed at http://www.worldbank.org/en/ country/southafrica/overview.

World Bank (2013b) *World Databank: World Development Indicators*, accessed at http:// databank.worldbank.org/ddp/home. do?Step=12&id=4&CNO=2.

World Bank (2017) *The World Bank in South Africa: Overview.* Updated May 3, accessed at http://www.worldbank.org/en/country/ southafrica/overview.

World Economic Forum (2013) *Global Gender Gap Report 2013*, accessed at www.weforum.org/ issues/global-gender-gap.

World Investment News (2002) 'Interview with H. E. Fernando Henrique Cardoso,' July 2002, accessed at http://www.winne.com/topinter-views/cardoso.htm.

World Trade Organization (2015) International Trade Statistics 2015, accessed at https://www. wto.org/english/res_e/statis_e/its2015_e/ its2015_e.pdf.

World Trade Organization (2016) 'Report on G20 Trade Measures,' accessed at https://www.wto.org/ english/news_e/news16_e/trdev_09nov16_e.htm.

World Trade Organization (2017) *World Trade Statistical Review 2017*, accessed at https:// www.wto.org/english/res_e/statis_e/wts2017_e/ WTO_Chapter_03_e.pdf.

Worm, Boris *et al.* (2006) 'Impacts of Biodiversity Loss on Ocean Ecosystem Services,' *Science* 314 (November): 787–90.

Wright, Robert (2006) 'Will Globalization Make Hatred More Lethal?' *The Wilson Quarterly*: 35–6.

Xin-An, Lu (2005) 'Ministry of Foreign Affairs in the Age of the Internet,' in Yufan, Hao and Su Lin (eds), *Chinese Foreign Policy Making: Societal Forces and Chinese Foreign Policy.* Aldershot: Ashgate Press: 111–22.

Xing, Y. and N. Detert (2010) 'How the iPhone Widens the United States Trade Deficit with the People's Republic of China,' *ADBI Working Paper No. 257.* Tokyo: Asian Development Bank Institute.

Young, Oran (2016) 'The Paris Agreement: Destined to Succeed or Doomed to Fail?' *Politics and Governance* 4 (3): 124–32.

Zartman, William (1995) 'Introduction: Posing the Problem of State Collapse,' in William Zartman (ed.), *Collapsed States: The Disintegration and Restoration of Legitimate Authority.* Boulder: Lynne Rienner: 1–11.

Index

Page numbers in *italic* indicate figures, maps and photos, and in **bold** indicate tables.